PRACTICAL CASE ANALYSIS

PRACTICAL CASE ANALYSIS

LINDA L. EDWARDS, J.D.

Phoenix College

WEST PUBLISHING COMPANY

Minneapolis/St. Paul

New York

Los Angeles

San Francisco

Cover Image: Artist, Charlotte Segal
  Represented by Carol Jones Gallery,
  300 W. Superior St., Chicago.
  Original painting, titled "Firebird No. 2,"
  oil on canvas, 1992.

Text Design: Jeanne Lee
Copyediting: Rosemary Root
Composition: Parkwood Composition, Inc.

WEST'S COMMITMENT TO THE ENVIRONMENT

In 1906, West Publishing Company began recycling materials left over from the production of books. This began a tradition of efficient and responsible use of resources. Today, 100% of our legal bound volumes are printed on acid-free, recycled paper consisting of 50% new paper pulp and 50% paper that has undergone a de-inking process. We also use vegetable-based inks to print all of our books. West recycles nearly 27,700,000 pounds of scrap paper annually—the equivalent of 229,300 trees. Since the 1960s, West has devised ways to capture and recycle waste inks, solvents, oils, and vapors created in the printing process. We also recycle plastics of all kinds, wood, glass, corrugated cardboard, and batteries, and have eliminated the use of polystyrene book packaging. We at West are proud of the longevity and the scope of our commitment to the environment.

West pocket parts and advance sheets are printed on recyclable paper and can be collected and recycled with newspapers. Staples do not have to be removed. Bound volumes can be recycled after removing the cover.

Production, Prepress, Printing and Binding by West Publishing Company.

 TEXT IS PRINTED ON 10% POST CONSUMER RECYCLED PAPER ∞

British Library Cataloguing-in-Publication Data. A catalogue record for this book is available from the British Library.

Copyright © 1996   By WEST PUBLISHING COMPANY
    610 Opperman Drive
    P.O. Box 64526
    St. Paul, MN 55164-0526

All rights reserved

Printed in the United States of America

03 02 01 00 99 98   8 7 6 5 4 3 2

Library of Congress Cataloging-in-Publication Data

Edwards, Linda L.
    Practical case analysis / Linda L. Edwards.
      p. cm.
    Includes index.
    ISBN 0-314-06434-6 (soft : alk. paper)
    1. Law—Study and teaching—United States. 2. Case method.
I. Title.
KF280.E38   1996
340'.071'173—dc20

95-26178
CIP

TABLE OF CONTENTS

PREFACE

PURPOSE OF TEXT

Dedicated to the art of legal analysis, this text can either stand alone in a course on reading and analyzing case law or be used as a supplementary text in courses on legal research and/or writing. It is designed to take students systematically through cases, showing them how to identify procedural history, critical facts, issues, holdings, rationale, and dicta and then assimilate these components into a brief. It touches on some basic principles of logic and implements these principles by comparing cases and statutes. The mystery of legal analysis is unraveled via the infamous IRAC method, enabling students to understand how lawyers and courts like to receive and present legal arguments. An overview of the elements of a legal memorandum is offered, and some basic organizational schemes are explored. Although this text is not intended to delve deeply into the subject of legal writing, some of the most important attributes of concise, clear writing are discussed.

FEATURES OF TEXT

The "Cognitive Calisthenics" exercises contain cases from a variety of legal disciplines (contract law, constitutional law, probate, and criminal procedure), so instructors can select areas of interest to them or their students. The cases present varying degrees of reading and comprehension difficulty, so instructors can also choose the appropriate level of difficulty. Case law is, for the most part, unedited so that students are exposed to cases as they actually appear in reporters. Any editing merely eliminated sections that were irrelevant to the issues being discussed in the exercises.

Suggested responses to some of the "Cognitive Calisthenics" exercises are provided in Appendix B and allow students to receive feedback. (The responses to the remaining exercises are included in the instructor's manual.)

"Putting It into Practice" exercises that are interspersed throughout the chapters allow students to practice concepts as they are presented and receive immediate feedback. (Responses to these are also found in Appendix B.)

"Practice Pointers" offer practical application that students will find helpful in the classroom and in the field.

SUPPLEMENTS AND TEACHING AIDS PROVIDED BY WEST PUBLISHING

The **instructor's manual** not only provides suggested answers to some of the exercises but also includes copies of a few cases not included in the text and teaching suggestions where appropriate. A unique feature of this manual is a diagnostic grammar and punctuation test as well as a follow-up test that keys students into applicable rules of grammar and punctuation when they incorrectly answer a question. This self-help tool allows students to discover which rules they have not yet mastered, acquaints them with these rules, and then gives them an opportunity to assess whether they have learned to correctly apply the rules in question.

West's Law Finder

West's Law Finder is a brief (seventy-seven-page) pamphlet that describes various legal-research sources and how they can be used. Classroom quantities are available.

Sample Pages, Third Edition

This 225-page, soft-cover pamphlet introduces all of West's legal-research materials. The accompanying *Instructor's Manual* gives ideas for effectively using the material in the classroom. Classroom quantities are available.

Citation-at-a-Glance

This handy reference card provides a quick, portable reference to the basic rules of citation for the most commonly cited legal sources, including judicial opinions, statutes, and secondary sources, such as legal encyclopedias and legal periodicals. *Citation-at-a-Glance* uses the rules set forth in *A Uniform System of Citation*, Fifteenth Edition (1991). A free copy of this valuable supplement is included with every student text.

Guide to *Shepard's Citations*

How to Shepardize: Your Guide to Complete Legal Research through Shepard's Citations—1993 WESTLAW Edition is a sixty-four-page pamphlet that helps students understand the research technique of Shepardizing case citations. The pamphlet is available in classroom quantities (one copy for each student who purchases a new text).

Strategies for Paralegal Educators

Strategies and Tips for Paralegal Educators, a pamphlet by Anita Tebbe of Johnson County Community College, provides teaching strategies specifically designed for paralegal educators. It concentrates on how to teach and is organized in three parts: the WHO of paralegal education—students and teachers; the WHAT of paralegal education—goals and objectives; and the HOW of paralegal education—methods of instruction, methods of evaluation, and other aspects of teaching. A copy of this pamphlet is available to each adopter. Quantities for distribution to their adjunct instructors are available for purchase at a minimal price. A coupon in the pamphlet provides ordering information.

WESTLAW

West's on-line computerized legal-research system offers students "hands-on" experience with a system commonly used in law offices. Qualified adopters can receive ten free hours of WESTLAW. WESTLAW can be accessed with Macintosh and IBM PCs and compatibles. A modem is required.

WESTMATE Tutorial

This interactive tutorial guides students through the process of accessing legal resources on WESTLAW by using WESTMATE, the special software that West has created for that purpose. There are two versions of the tutorial, one for DOS and one for Windows.

ACKNOWLEDGEMENTS

Although only the author is credited with the publication of a text, the commitment and perseverance of many people are reflected in the final product. I would like to first thank my husband, Stan Edwards, for his patience and encouragement. As coauthor of another legal text (*Tort Law for Legal Assistants*), he was well aware of the tremendous amount of energy required to "birth" a book. Undaunted, he enthusiastically supported my desire to create again and offered his suggestions as well as technical assistance.

Second, I would like to thank the many students who conscientiously reviewed the chapters as they evolved and who bravely offered their recommendations after repeated assurance that their adverse comments would bear no negative repercussions from the "keeper of the grades." Because of their insights and questions, this is a "student-friendly" text that anticipates many of the questions students commonly ask and the concepts they typically puzzle over.

Third, the excellent production team at West deserves many accolades. Not only do they excel in their craft, but they carry out their responsibilities graciously and with compassion. Having worked most closely with Patty Bryant, Developmental Editor, on this project, I would like to especially thank her for her professionalism and unshakable congeniality. She could not have carried out her tasks, however, without the outstanding assistance of Kara ZumBahlen, Associate Production Editor; Carrie Kish, Promotion Manager; and Elizabeth Hannan, Acquisitions Editor.

Fourth, I owe thanks to my family and friends. Their unflinching support and earnest desire to see this endeavor through to fruition made the process much easier. Some, such as my mother, Audrey Dixon, and my friend, June Knack, agreed to test the "readability" quotient of the text and stalwartly plowed through pages of legal concepts in which I know they had little or no interest.

Final thanks go to the reviewers who took their tasks to heart and conscientiously and laboriously wrote their suggestions and observations. Their candid reflections greatly enhanced the quality of this text, and I hope they find the final outcome to be worthy of their efforts.

Anneta A. Buster
Johnson County Community College

Wendy Edson
Hilbert College

Ellen Erzen
Cuyahoga Community College

Barry S. Grossman
Nebraska College of Business

Margaret A. Nelson
Phillips Business College

Peggy Nickerson
William Woods University

Vitonio F. San Juan
University of La Verne

Martha Wright Sartoris
North Hennepin Community College

Laurel A. Vietzen
Elgin Community College

Pamela Poole Weber
Seminole Community College

Francisco R. Wong
City College of San Francisco

Norma K. Wooten
Johnson County Community College

Christine A. Yared
Grand Valley State University

DEDICATION

To BLISS EDWARDS, my devoted and trusted companion of twenty-five years, who died during the production of this work, but whose spirit lives on forever in my heart.

CHAPTER ONE

PROLOGUE TO CASE ANALYSIS

Chapter Objectives

In this chapter you will learn:

- Why the law cannot be easily defined and compartmentalized.

- The primary sources of the law.

- Why facts and reasoning are so important in the law.

- How cases are reported.

- Where cases are published.

- How court opinions are formatted.

- The difference between primary and secondary authority and between binding and persuasive authority.

- The limits under which appellate courts must function.

- The elements of a case brief.

- Why reading court opinions can be challenging and how to effectively cope with that challenge.

- Why analyzing case law is an art that cannot be reduced to a simple formula.

WHY DO YOU WANT TO READ CASES? Court Opinions

Before we begin reading case law, let us ponder why reading cases is important. What is the purpose of legal research? Perhaps the most obvious answer is that we want to know "what the law is." Consider the phrase "what the law is." Does it imply that the law is static? That the law is a body of rules that can be memorized and applied in a mechanical, methodical manner? If that were true, we probably would not have so many disputes. Someone would simply drag out the "rule book" (the law), and everyone would immediately know the answer.

If your perception of legal research is looking for and finding a definitive answer to every problem you are assigned, you might want to consider a profession more given to clear-cut rules and regulations. Otherwise you will surely find yourself becoming disenchanted with the law. The law, as you will discover, is not always absolute. Like anything shaped by humans, it has many dimensions. Although grounded in solid principles and well-defined precepts, the law is not always easily captured by language and is subject to the predispositions and motivations of those who interpret it. A brief consideration of the sources of the law will help you understand its somewhat mercurial nature.

Sources of the Law

The law can be traced to three basic sources—the legislative, executive, and judicial branches of government.

Legislative Branch

Legislatures at both the state and federal levels create statutes, while city councils and county boards of supervisors create ordinances. Both statutes and ordinances are designed to define and regulate appropriate and inappropriate behaviors. They cannot, however, conflict with either U.S. or state constitutions. (Constitutions are another source of the law. Their language is necessarily so broad that their meaning is subject to ongoing debate.)

Arguably, statutes and ordinances should be clear-cut and above dispute, but, as you will find in Chapter Eight, such clarity and definitiveness has been attained by few lawmakers. Much litigation is devoted to the unraveling of ambiguous legislation.

Executive Branch

Administrative agencies fall within the executive branch of government. They are responsible for both carrying out duties delegated to them by the legislative branch and creating rules to govern the process by which they carry out those duties. The Social Security Administration, for example, must allocate Social Security benefits according to the guidelines established by Congress and must also create procedures by which those allocations can be distributed as well as challenged.

Administrative regulations are fraught with the same ambiguities that plague statutes and ordinances. These ambiguities contribute to the uncertainty that some-times exists in the law.

Judicial Branch

Courts also create law by virtue of their decisions (referred to as **case law**) and their rule-making powers (their authority to create procedural rules). Legal disputes are

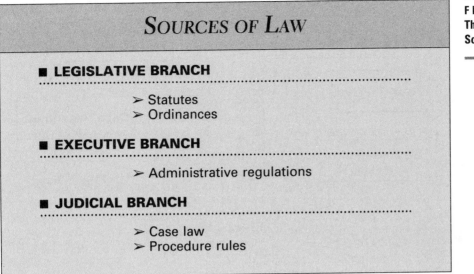

FIGURE 1.1
The Three
Sources of Law

usually resolved at the trial court level (the first level of the court system), but when litigants are unhappy with that resolution they have the option of appealing to an appellate court (the court at the next level in the judicial hierarchy). Appellate courts frequently (but not always) publish their discussion of the legal issues at stake in **court reporters.** A reporter is a compilation of court opinions. The court opinions found in these reporters comprise the essence of case law.

Lower courts within the jurisdiction of an appellate court are obligated to follow the **precedents** set by the appellate court's decisions. Under the principle of *stare decisis* (which literally means "let the decision stand"), courts are obligated to adhere to their previous decisions as well as the decisions of those courts that review their opinions. The Arizona Court of Appeals, for example, must render decisions that are consistent not only with its own previous decisions but also with the decisions of the Arizona Supreme Court (which is the reviewing court for the Court of Appeals). *Stare decisis* is an integral feature of the American legal system and is revered because of the desire to retain stability and predictability in the law.

If courts are confined to the parameters of case precedent, why isn't the law more absolute and concrete? The answer lies within the courts' right to **distinguish** (differentiate) cases that are factually different. In other words, *stare decisis* applies only to factually similar cases. If the facts vary significantly, a court is justified in altering its conclusion and possibly even its analysis. A court that finds a legal right to an abortion for an adult, for example, may come to a very different conclusion when faced with a juvenile seeking an abortion, even if all of the other facts are the same. Similarly, the law in reference to abortion is dependent on the stage of pregnancy, the funding source of the abortion, and the immediacy of the abortion (whether a waiting period is required), among other things. In short, the law is usually contingent on a number of factors.

Nature of the Law

Rather than being an answer to a specific question, case law is more accurately described as the resolution of fact-specific disputes. In other words, case law tells a

FIGURE 1.2
What Is the Law?

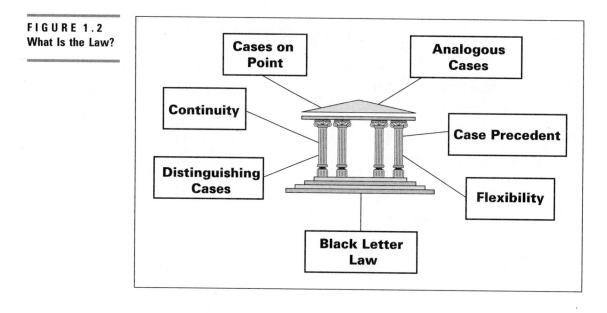

story—a story of the problems brought before a court and how that court resolved them. This definition implies that the answer will change as the factual context of the problem changes. It also implies that the answer may change depending on the time period and who is resolving the problem. If nothing else, this definition suggests that the law is malleable and flexible, supplying answers that cannot be restricted to the sterile (albeit comforting) confines of a formula. Scales, not slide rules, are used to measure justice, for in the law we seek balance more than mere duplication.

Case law, statutes, ordinances, administrative regulations—all strive for consistency and continuity. But they are subject to the philosophies and attitudes of the times in which they are interpreted. The law generated during the horse-and-buggy and Pony Express era is not easily translated into a time of supersonic jets and Internet. New technologies and changing social conditions challenge the legal community and result in changes and additions to the law. Community norms also have an effect; the law is interpreted somewhat differently in rural America than in metropolitan areas. Therefore, the law cannot be reduced to a single rule book. Law libraries filled with volumes dedicated to an understanding of the law attest to its complexity and flexibility. Learning the law means knowing the historical, social, and factual context in which the law was created and appreciating the economic, political, and humanistic concerns the law was intended to address.

SO HOW DO WE MAKE SENSE OUT OF CASE LAW?

Facts drive the law. These facts may pertain to the particular circumstances of the litigants or the social conditions and times in which the legal dispute arises. Nevertheless, as the facts change, so too do the answers to the problems presented to the courts. Obviously, then, you cannot master the law by simply memorizing rules, because the rules are contingent on the facts. But if you are seeking continuity and the rules cannot be reduced to simple algebraic formulae, how do you find consistency in the myriad of cases rendered every year in our court system?

Black Letter Law

First, let me assure you that some rules do indeed exist. Some law is so standard and so unequivocal that it is referred to as **black letter law.** The basic elements of a contract or tort, for example, are defined by black letter law, as are the elements of defenses, such as self-defense. All contracts require a showing of an offer, acceptance, and consideration. All torts require proof of a duty of care, that the defendant breached that duty, that the breach was the cause of the plaintiff's injury, and that the plaintiff suffered damages. Claims of self-defense require that the defendant use reasonable force that she or he reasonably believes is necessary to prevent imminent harm to self or another. These basic definitions do not change, regardless of the facts.

Reasoning of the Courts

If our inquiry moves from general principles to a specific situation, however, we move from black letter law into a realm of greater ambiguity. For example, if we ask whether a landowner used excessive force when he allowed his dog to attack a burglar who was assessing the accessibility of the landowner's home (i.e., "casing" the place), we are dealing with law that is more dependent on specific facts and, therefore, less uniform. In other words, all courts follow black letter law that requires that any force people use to protect themselves and others be reasonable, but courts vary in terms of how they assess reasonableness. To determine what is reasonable in a particular jurisdiction, we would have to consult the case law in that state. We could not find the answer by simply reading a legal textbook, which usually focuses on black letter law.

When we shift from black letter law to law that is less homogenous, we must look to the reasoning of the courts to find consistency. A court's reasoning will help us predict how future cases will be resolved. If we can dissect the reasoning process for one case, we can then apply that same reasoning process to factually **analogous cases.** Analogous cases are those in which the facts and legal issues are sufficiently similar to the facts and legal issues of your client's case so that the same principles of law can be applied.

The law, for example, requires a homeowner to disclose the presence of termites to a buyer, because termites are considered "latent defects" that a reasonable buyer could not discover on his or her own. Using that reasoning, is a seller required to disclose that someone was murdered in the house being sold? In other words, is the existence of a murder analogous to the existence of termites? Are they both "latent defects" that impose the same kind of legal obligation? The key to this question lies in the validity of the analogy being made. If a termite and an undisclosed murder are not analogous, in that termites present a potential for structural damage while a previous murder does not, then a seller may be obligated to disclose the presence of termites but not the murder. Since reasoning by analogy provides the basis for most legal arguments, we will examine this type of reasoning (also known as inductive reasoning) in more detail in Chapter Five.

For the time being, however, remember that what you will be focusing on as you read case law will not be the decisions (holdings) of courts but their reasoning in the context of the facts they were given. If you will remember this, you will not make the mistake of looking only for cases in which the facts are identical to yours. Cases that are **on point** (also known as being "on all fours") in that their facts

<table>
<tr><td>

**Practice
Pointer**

</td><td>

If cases "on point" are rarely found, how do you know when to
terminate a research project? Most research could conceivably go
on indefinitely (since more cases and commentaries can usually be
found given sufficient time). A good time to stop, however, is when
you have updated your cases and other resources and you
continue to be led back to the same cases.

</td></tr>
</table>

are virtually identical to your client's fact pattern are almost never found. If your
focus is on the reasoning process, you will not be so driven to search for factual
similarities. Rather, you will be content to seek cases in which the reasoning process
is applicable to your situation.

How Do Cases Get Appealed?

By virtue of having grown up in the twentieth century, you probably have some
awareness of the litigation process in this country. Having been weaned on "Perry
Mason" or "L.A. Law" (depending on your generation), you are no doubt aware
that disputes progress from the complaint stage through the discovery phase and
culminate in a trial if they cannot be resolved along the way.

State Courts

A party may decide to appeal any rulings rendered by or judgment entered by the
trial court. The party who initiates the appeal (the **appellant**) and the party responding to the appeal (the **appellee**) must file briefs with the appellate court articulating
their positions. The court will then allow oral arguments, and, based on those
arguments as well as its review of the trial transcripts, the pleadings (documents
filed at the beginning of the lawsuit, including the complaint and the answer), and
motions made by the parties, the court will render its decision. The appellate court
may decide to affirm, modify, or reverse the lower court's decision; to affirm, modify, or reverse a particular ruling; and/or to remand (send) the case back to the trial
court to cure the error.

     Since most states have a three-tiered system, consisting of a court of original
jurisdiction (in which the trial takes place), an intermediate appellate court, and a
supreme court, the parties may also decide to appeal from the decision of the
intermediate appellate court. After reading the briefs submitted by the attorneys,
the supreme court listens to oral arguments. Once it has reviewed the arguments
made by the parties and the decisions of the trial court and appellate court, the
supreme court has the same options as the intermediate appellate court.

     The decisions of the appellate courts (both intermediate and supreme) are
usually published in a state court reporter.

Federal Courts

At the federal level, disputes are tried in the district courts (as well as other courts
of original jurisdiction) and appealed to the circuit courts (of which there are thirteen) and then to the U.S. Supreme Court. The federal court system is divided into

FIGURE 1.3
The Thirteen Federal Circuits

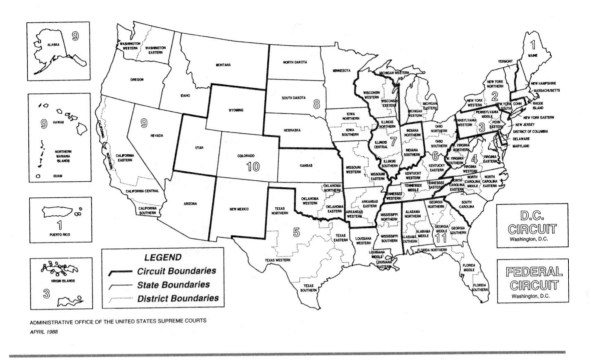

ADMINISTRATIVE OFFICE OF THE UNITED STATES SUPREME COURTS
APRIL 1988

twelve geographic circuits, each of which has its own circuit court. As you can see from the map in Figure 1.3, Arizona is in the Ninth Circuit while Texas is in the Fifth Circuit. The Federal Circuit Court of Appeals (which is the Thirteenth Circuit) has authority to hear disputes initiated in the U.S. Claims Court or U.S. Court of International Trade as well as appeals generated by the federal district courts involving patents, copyrights, or trademarks.

WHERE ARE CASES REPORTED?

Cases are published in sets of books called reports or reporters. **Official reporters** are published by governmental authorities; **unofficial reporters** are published by private companies, such as West Publishing Company or Lawyers' Co-operative Company.

State Courts

State court cases (at the intermediate appellate court and supreme court levels) can be found in seven regional reporters.

Pacific Reporter	Northwest Reporter
Atlantic Reporter	Southern Reporter
Northeast Reporter	Southeast Reporter
	Southwest Reporter

FIGURE 1.4
Regional Reporter System Map

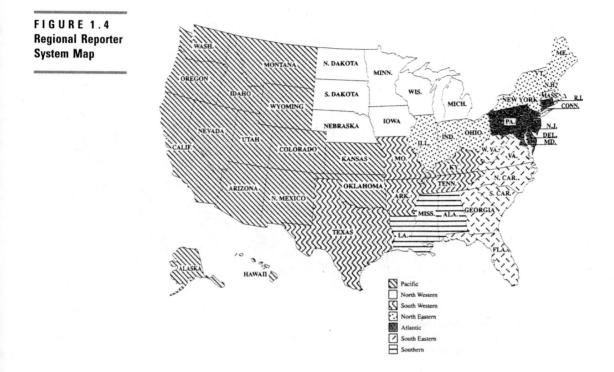

These are all unofficial reporters, published by West, that cover designated geographic areas (see Figure 1.4). Each of these regional reporters has a first and second (and, in some cases, third) series. After a designated number of volumes is published, West begins a new series. You might understandably assume that the number in parentheses following the name of the reporter would refer to an edition; however, the number actually refers to the series. Therefore, Pacific Reporter (second) refers to the second series of Pacific Reporters and not to a second (or revised) edition.

About two-thirds of the states also publish an official state reporter; for some states, West publishes a separate unofficial reporter. In essence, most state court opinions can be found in two places—in the regional West reporter system and in the state court reporter (if one exists).

Selected cases are also published in *American Law Reports* (published by Lawyers' Co-operative Publishing Company). Unlike the reporters, this specialized research tool contains only a limited number of cases. These cases are, however, extensively annotated (referenced to other cases and legal sources). Such annotations are invaluable to the researcher because they quickly identify related resources.

Federal Courts

U.S. Supreme Court decisions are published in the following reporters.

U.S. Reports (official reporter)

Supreme Court Reporter (unofficial reporter, published by West)

United States Reports, Lawyers' Edition (unofficial reporter, published by Lawyers' Co-operative)

U.S. Law Week (weekly update, published by Bureau of National Affairs)

U.S. Supreme Court Bulletin (weekly update, published by Commerce Clearing House)

U.S. Court of Appeals opinions are published in these reporters.

Federal Reporter (published by West)

Federal Reporter, Second Series (published by West)

A.L.R. Fed. (published by Lawyers' Co-operative selected cases only)

U.S. district court opinions are published in these reporters.

Federal Supplement (published by West)

A.L.R. Fed. (published by Lawyers' Co-operative selected cases only)

Availability of Cases

Not all appeals are published. The highest courts in the states generally publish all of their opinions, but the intermediate courts usually select only certain opinions to be published. In some states, important trial court decisions are also published, but this is the exception rather than the rule. At the federal level, only those decisions dealing with new principles of law are published by the district and circuit courts, while all decisions rendered by the U.S. Supreme Court are published. All court decisions are considered public records and can be obtained from the court clerk's office even if they are not published.

CASE REPORTERS

■ STATE

➤ Atlantic Reporter
➤ Pacific Reporter
➤ Northeast Reporter
➤ Northwest Reporter
➤ Southern Reporter
➤ Southeast Reporter
➤ Southwest Reporter

■ FEDERAL

➤ U.S. Reports *Federal*
➤ Supreme Court Reporter *West Publishing*
➤ United States Reports, Lawyers' Edition
➤ U.S. Law Week
➤ U.S. Supreme Court Bulletin
➤ Federal Reporter
➤ A.L.R. Fed.
➤ Federal Supplement

FIGURE 1.5
Case Reporters

Electronic Research

In this computer age, it should come as no surprise that cases are also available by computer. Westlaw and Lexis are two of the most common computer research programs. Although neither has eliminated the need for hard-copy research, they are becoming increasingly accessible to lawyers, law students, and paralegals. The competent legal researcher should have a working knowledge of Westlaw and/or Lexis.

WHAT IS THE FORMAT OF A TYPICAL COURT OPINION?

If a variety of resources exists, how do you know which one to select a case from? Scanning a typical court opinion will allow you to see very quickly why unofficial reporters are usually easier to work with than official reporters.

Advantages of Unofficial Reporters

The key factor that differentiates reporters is that unofficial reporters contain research aids while official reporters do not. Notice that the unofficial reporter (a sample of which is reproduced in Figure 1.7) contains short numbered paragraphs that precede the court opinion. These paragraphs, referred to as **headnotes,** identify the point of law being discussed using the West **key numbering system.** Headnotes, which are written by West editors, summarize specific principles of law discussed by the Court. In the West key numbering system, legal issues are organized alphabetically by topic and numerically by subtopic. Each key contains a topic name (key name) and section number (key number). In *Olson v. Walker,* for example, headnote 1 has the key name and number "Damages Key 87(1)." This means that

FIGURE 1.6
Sample WESTLAW Screen

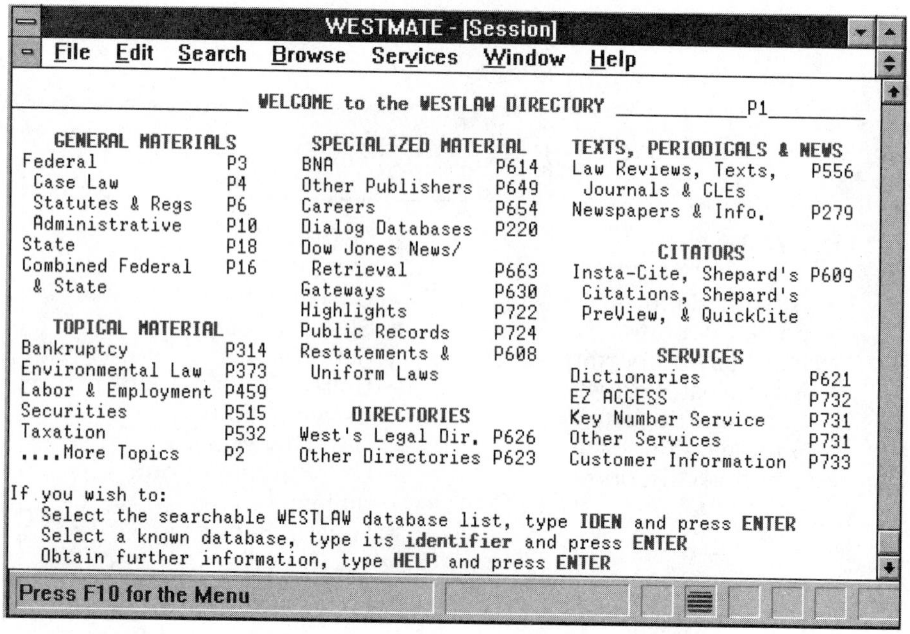

```
 ┌─────────────────────────────────────────────────────────────────────┐
 │                      WESTMATE - [Session]                        ▼  ▲ │
 │  File   Edit   Search   Browse   Services   Window   Help          ↕ │
 │ ─────────────────────────────────────────────────────────────────  ↑ │
 │ _____ WELCOME to the WESTLAW DIRECTORY _____ P1 _____   │
 │                                                                       │
 │  GENERAL MATERIALS        SPECIALIZED MATERIAL    TEXTS, PERIODICALS & NEWS │
 │ Federal          P3      BNA              P614   Law Reviews, Texts,  P556 │
 │  Case Law        P4      Other Publishers P649    Journals & CLEs          │
 │  Statutes & Regs P6      Careers          P654   Newspapers & Info.   P279 │
 │  Administrative  P10     Dialog Databases P220                        │
 │ State            P18     Dow Jones News/           CITATORS           │
 │ Combined Federal P16      Retrieval       P663   Insta-Cite, Shepard's P609 │
 │  & State                 Gateways         P630    Citations, Shepard's │
 │                          Highlights       P722    PreView, & QuickCite │
 │  TOPICAL MATERIAL        Public Records   P724                        │
 │ Bankruptcy       P314    Restatements &   P608          SERVICES      │
 │ Environmental Law P373    Uniform Laws            Dictionaries        P621 │
 │ Labor & Employment P459                          EZ ACCESS           P732 │
 │ Securities       P515        DIRECTORIES         Key Number Service  P731 │
 │ Taxation         P532    West's Legal Dir. P626  Other Services      P731 │
 │ ....More Topics  P2      Other Directories P623  Customer Information P733 │
 │                                                                       │
 │ If you wish to:                                                       │
 │   Select the searchable WESTLAW database list, type IDEN and press ENTER │
 │   Select a known database, type its identifier and press ENTER        │
 │   Obtain further information, type HELP and press ENTER             ▼ │
 │ ─────────────────────────────────────────────────────────────────── │
 │ Press F10 for the Menu                              ▤                 │
 └─────────────────────────────────────────────────────────────────────┘
```

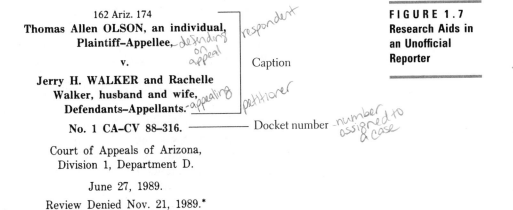

162 Ariz. 174

**Thomas Allen OLSON, an individual,
Plaintiff–Appellee,** *descending on appeal* *respondent*

v. Caption

**Jerry H. WALKER and Rachelle
Walker, husband and wife,
Defendants–Appellants.** *appealing* *petitioner*

No. 1 CA–CV 88–316. ———— Docket number *number assigned to a case*

Court of Appeals of Arizona,
Division 1, Department D.

June 27, 1989.

Review Denied Nov. 21, 1989.*

Defendant appealed from an order of
the Superior Court of Maricopa County,
Cause No. C–600994, Cheryl K. Hendrix, J.,
which rendered judgment for plaintiff in
personal injury action and awarded punitive damages. The Court of Appeals,
Grant, C.J., held that: (1) evidence was
sufficient to warrant punitive damages; (2)
punitive damage award was not excessive;
(3) punitive damage award did not violate
due process, prohibition against excessive
fines or double jeopardy; and (4) trial court
did not abuse discretion in refusing to instruct jury to disregard expert testimony
regarding arthritic changes in plaintiff's
back.

Affirmed. *Reverse Remand*

Gerber, J., dissented and filed opinion.

Syllabus *Synopsis*

Never quote or base case on this - only use as research tool. Need to read actual case

Key name
and number

1. Damages ⬅87(1)

Punitive damages are awarded primarily to punish wrongdoer and deter others
from similar conduct and thus, award of
punitive damages is limited to situations
where these objectives can be furthered.

Headnotes

Important rules of laws

2. Damages ⬅184

Award of punitive damages against intoxicated driver may only be had upon
clear and convincing evidence of driver's
evil mind.

*Court of Appeals:
- no witnesses evidence
- based on transcripts briefs oral arguments*

FIGURE 1.7
**Research Aids in
an Unofficial
Reporter**

if you look in any of the digests published by West under "Damages" (key name), section 87(1) (key number), you will find a discussion about damages being used to punish wrongdoers and deter others. By going to any digest and looking under this key number, you can find other state and federal cases dealing with the same subject.

By the same token, you can use headnotes to read cases more efficiently. If you are interested only in certain issues, you may read only the sections dealing with those issues by looking for the applicable headnotes. In *Olson v. Walker*, for example, if you were interested in reading only about the relationship between punitive damages and double jeopardy, you could refer to headnote 12 "Double Jeopardy Key 23" and focus your attention on that specific area of the opinion. Beware, however, of relying too heavily on headnotes. Reading headnotes is no substitute for reading the actual case. Analyzing a case requires that you read the court's actual words, not an editor's interpretation of those words.

In unofficial reporters, you will also find a **syllabus** written by an editor. A syllabus is a brief synopsis of the pertinent facts, issues, and holdings in the opinion. Official reporters also contain a syllabus, prepared by a designee of the court. Never rely on a syllabus or a headnote in preparing a memorandum, as they do not necessarily accurately reflect what the court actually said.

Practice Pointer	Case citations (commonly referred to as cites) identify the name, volume, and page of the reporter in which the case is located. The date the case was decided is also included.

Pastorini v. Hobbs,   101   U.S.   437   (1992).
Case Name   Volume   Reporter Page   Decision Date
101—Volume number   U.S.—U.S. Reports   437—Page number

Conveniently, all citations for cases follow the same basic format (volume number, name of reporter, page number). Some also give the name of the court that rendered the decision if the decisions of more than one court are found in the same reporter.

Wallace v. Ladmo, 156 Ariz. 99 (Ct. App. 1993).

The "Ct. App." in parentheses identifies the Court of Appeals as the court that delivered the opinion. Such identification is necessary because opinions for both the Arizona Court of Appeals and the Arizona Supreme Court are published in the Arizona Reports.

A parallel cite includes both the official and unofficial reporters.

Wallace v. Ladmo, 156 Ariz. 99, 201 P.2d 234 (Ct. App. 1993).
                    Official   Unofficial

The "P.2d" refers to the Pacific Reporter, which is the regional (unofficial) reporter that publishes Arizona cases. The "2d" indicates that this case is found in the second series of the Pacific Reporter. Remember that most reporters have two or three series (not editions).

Commonalities between Official and Unofficial Reporters

Other features of court opinions are found in both official and unofficial reporters. The names of the parties and the nature of their relationship are found in the **caption** at the beginning of a case. Directly above the caption, you will find the **citation** for the case (information that identifies where a case can be found; see the Practice Pointer below for an example). Directly beneath the caption, you will see the **docket number** (the number assigned by the court clerk). Beneath the docket number is the identity of the court that rendered the opinion and the date it was rendered. Also included are the names of counsel for each side as well as the identities of the judges who heard the case and wrote the opinion.

WHAT IS THE DIFFERENCE BETWEEN PRIMARY AND SECONDARY AUTHORITY?

Primary Authority

Court opinions are considered one source of **primary authority.** Primary authority is the law which is generated by the judiciary (in the form of cases), by legislatures (in the form of statutes), or by administrative agencies (in the form of administrative rules and regulations) or which emanates from a U.S. or state constitution. Such law may be **binding** on a court in that the court is obligated to follow it, or it may be merely **persuasive** in that the court has the option of either following it or disregarding it. Sound confusing? It all depends on what jurisdiction and what lawmaking entity generated the law. For example, if a decision is rendered by the Alaska Supreme Court, the lower courts in that state are obligated to adhere to the decision. In other words, the decision would be considered binding primary authority for the lower courts in Alaska. It would be considered persuasive primary authority, however, for the Oregon courts, since the Alaska and Oregon courts belong to different jurisdictions. Statutes and administrative regulations are also binding on parties in the jurisdiction that promulgated such statutes or regulations.

Secondary Authority

In contrast, **secondary authority** encompasses informational sources outside of primary authority upon which a court may rely. Treatises, dictionaries, periodicals,

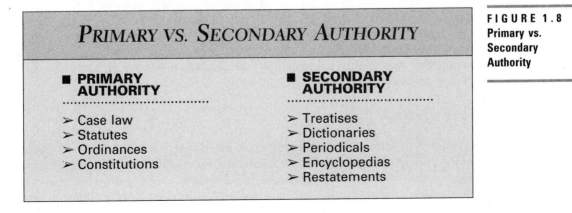

FIGURE 1.8
Primary vs. Secondary Authority

PRIMARY VS. SECONDARY AUTHORITY

■ **PRIMARY AUTHORITY**
- ➢ Case law
- ➢ Statutes
- ➢ Ordinances
- ➢ Constitutions

■ **SECONDARY AUTHORITY**
- ➢ Treatises
- ➢ Dictionaries
- ➢ Periodicals
- ➢ Encyclopedias
- ➢ Restatements

encyclopedias, restatements, and a variety of other resources written by legal scholars, law students, and attorneys fall within the realm of secondary authority. While primary authority serves as a source of the law, secondary authority explains and discusses the law. Both primary and secondary authority can be used by parties in constructing arguments and to justify their position. Secondary authority does not have the persuasive power of primary authority, however, and can be cited only when primary authority is not available.

WHAT CONSTRAINTS ARE PUT ON APPELLATE COURTS?

Questions of Law vs. Questions of Fact

Contrary to the belief of some people, appellate court judges do not have the prerogative of enforcing their own personal agendas in the opinions they write. Rather, they are constrained by judicial parameters that dictate the possible contours of their opinions.

Appellate courts generally focus on **questions of law** rather than **questions of fact.** An appellate court must honor the factual findings of the trial court. Even if the appellate court might question these findings, it cannot interfere with them unless the trial court "clearly abused its discretion." If a trial court, for example, finds that the defendant was present at the crime scene, the appellate court cannot disturb this finding as long as evidence in the record supports it. The question of presence at the scene involves a factual rather than legal issue. The rationale behind this rule is that the trial court is in a better position to evaluate testimony and other evidence than an appellate court, by virtue of being physically present during the presentation of the evidence. (Appellate courts review the record prepared at trial but do not hear any testimony.)

Appellate courts have more discretion when confronted with questions of law. They examine the legal principles and reasoning used by the lower court. For example, let's say that the question before the trial court was whether testimony regarding the defendant's presence at the crime scene was admissible. The question of admissibility is a legal question. Appellate courts are obligated to correct any legal errors committed by the lower tribunal. They cannot, however, address legal issues that are not presented to them. If a party fails to make a timely objection, thereby preserving it in the court record, the appellate court is denied any opportunity to correct errors made by the lower tribunal. By the same token, if a party fails to adhere to any of the multitude of rules governing appellate practice, the appellate court is denied review of any legal errors committed.

Appellate practice is highly structured and bound by rules. Procedural obstacles exist at every turn. Unwary litigants may be unwittingly deprived of access to an appellate court if they fail to comply with any one requirement dictated by the rules of appellate practice.

Stare Decisis

In addition to being confined by procedural rules, appellate courts are constrained by the principle of *stare decisis.* As mentioned earlier, this principle requires appellate courts to follow the precedents established by courts within the relevant jurisdiction. Trial courts and appellate courts, for example, must conform to the decisions of the highest court in their jurisdiction. *Stare decisis* promotes consistency (so that litigants in like situations receive the same treatment) and judicial efficiency (in that the courts do not have to repeatedly explore legal issues that have already been resolved).

Distinguishing Cases

Stare decisis can be somewhat confining if fairness dictates a different outcome in a particular case. Not all people who commit crimes, for example, deserve the same treatment. Someone who steals bread to feed his or her children arguably should be treated differently than someone who steals out of greed. A legal system that mandated strict conformance to precedent in such cases could be stifling. Courts can escape this rigidity if they can distinguish the case before them from legal precedent. The most common way of distinguishing cases is by looking to the factual differences. If the facts differ, the court is justified in coming to a different conclusion.

In the famous case *Miranda v. Arizona*, for example, the U.S. Supreme Court held that officers could not interrogate defendants in their custody until the defendants were advised of their constitutional rights. In a subsequent decision (*U.S. v. Quarles*), however, the Court found that officers were not obligated to advise defendants of their rights before asking them a question that affected the public safety. In *Quarles*, when the officer arrived at the scene of an armed robbery, he was concerned that a child might find the defendant's gun and therefore asked the defendant where the gun was before advising him of his rights. The Court reasoned that the concern about public safety did not exist in *Miranda* and that this distinction was sufficiently important to justify excusing the officer in *Quarles* from giving the litany of *Miranda* rights before asking this one question.

Adherence to Statutes

Appellate courts are also constrained by the legislatures to some extent. They cannot ignore a statute they find distasteful unless they believe it to be unconstitutional. If the legislative intent is clear, the courts must adhere to the statute. Since legislative intent is often unclear, however, appellate courts frequently find leeway in their interpretation of a statute's purpose.

Adherence to Constitutions

Appellate courts are bound to follow the U.S. and state constitutions, but the extent to which they are so bound depends on their judicial philosophy. Judges whom some commentators categorize as **conservative** believe that they are limited to a strict interpretation of statutes and constitutions. So-called **liberal** judges perceive their role as going beyond such literal interpretation and view themselves as protectors of minority groups and the politically disenfranchised.

A relatively conservative court wrote *Plessy v. Ferguson*, which allowed the maintenance of segregation in this country. This opinion did not mean that the judges themselves philosophically agreed with the principles of segregation but rather that they felt obligated to defer to the legislative branch of government. Their more liberal counterparts in *Brown v. Board of Education* found segregated schools to be in violation of the Constitution. The difference between these two panels of

FIGURE 1.9
Constraints on
Courts

CONSTRAINTS ON COURTS

- **Confined to questions of law**
  ....
- **Stare decisis**
  ....
- **Adherence to statutes**
  ....
- **Adherence to constitutions**
  ....

judges lay not in their personal philosophies but in their judicial philosophies. The *Brown* Court perceived its role as a protector of the politically powerless, a protector that intervened when the legislative branch failed to represent all of its constituents. The *Plessy* Court, on the other hand, perceived itself as confined by the will of the legislature.

All of these rules shape appellate court practice and prevent appellate judges from behaving capriciously and frivolously. While personal philosophy no doubt colors the opinions of appellate judges to some degree, the rules of appellate decision-making preclude the appellate process from becoming a forum for personal agendas.

WHAT'S THE BEST WAY TO UNDERSTAND CASE LAW?

We have examined some of the mechanics underlying the development and presentation of case law. But how are you to translate this case law into concepts that you can work with? One of the best ways to transform legal abstractions into workable principles is to **brief** cases. A **case brief** dissects and summarizes a case, and contains the following elements:

Procedural history

Facts

Issues

Holdings - Conclusion of law

Rationale - Reasoning of the court

Briefs are condensed versions (usually one or two pages) of case law and contain only the most pertinent information. Briefing cases allows you to review the essential elements of a case without having to read the entire case again.

Practice Pointer	Briefs come in two forms in the legal world. Case briefs are truly "brief" and are intended to condense the essentials of a case into one or two pages. Legal briefs, on the other hand, are anything but "brief," typically consisting of twenty pages or more. They are aimed at convincing a judge to adopt a particular legal position.
	Case briefs are used to help the reader understand and compare case law. Legal briefs are written by attorneys and are the culmination of considerable research. Most university and state law libraries have such briefs available for your review.
	Although the elements listed above are the typical components of a brief, formats can vary. You will have to look to your attorney or instructor for specific guidance. In this text, we will examine each element of a brief in some depth (Chapters Two through Five), culminating in the preparation of a brief (Chapter Six). Thus, you will have ample opportunity to thoroughly familiarize yourself with the contents of a brief.
	Why base the bulk of a text on the structure of a brief? Case law is built on courts' holdings. These holdings are molded out of courts' rationale. Their rationale is contingent on the facts and issues presented to them. The precedential value of a case is to some degree a reflection of procedural history. Therefore, briefing cases familiarizes you with the crucial aspects of case law, which in turn prepares you to analyze case law and thus to write memoranda comparing case law. Hence, the ability to accurately and succinctly brief cases lies at the heart of legal analysis.

What Makes Reading Cases Challenging?

If you recognize initially that reading cases is a challenging prospect, you are less likely to become discouraged when you discover that understanding case law is a very time-consuming and potentially frustrating experience. What makes reading cases challenging?

First, many of the legal concepts you will be confronted with will be complex. After all, the "easy" cases rarely go up on appeal. Some of the issues that courts must grapple with are very abstract, and others require juggling of existing case law that is inconsistent or highly convoluted.

Second, some judges do not write clearly and simply. Their writing may be obtuse and pretentious. Judges are not required to demonstrate their competency to express themselves clearly and concisely before assuming their judicial duties. Consequently, readers may be forced to wend their way through a language maze that further complicates an already complex thought process.

Third, judges assume that their readers understand basic legal principles and concepts. They do not explain legal processes and terminology that they presume are common knowledge to the lawyers who constitute the bulk of their readership.

FIGURE 1.10
The Challenge of Reading Cases

WHY IS THE LAW CHALLENGING?

■ **Concepts are complex.**
....

■ **Some legal writing is unclear.**
....

■ **Basic legal processes and terminology are not explained.**
....

How to Get Around These Challenges

To make reading case law less frustrating, be patient with yourself. Give yourself time, and realize that you will have to read hundreds of cases before you become reasonably efficient in reading case law. Have a dictionary in hand every time you sit down to read a case, and assume that you are going to have to consult it frequently. Avoid the temptation of guessing what a word means or a process entails. The time you invest when you start reading cases will save you time eventually. As your knowledge base grows, you will have to rely on the dictionary and other references less and less.

Remember that your ability to read and understand cases is a reflection of your experience, not your intelligence. Give yourself the time and opportunity to build your skill level, and never compare your proficiency with that of those who have been reading case law for years. Briefing cases will help you better understand them. By virtue of preparing a case brief, you will immediately recognize your weaknesses in understanding a case and will know where you have to focus your efforts in order to remedy your misunderstanding.

WHAT'S THE FORMULA FOR ANALYZING CASE LAW?

The task of reading and briefing case law is challenging enough, but analyzing case law and committing that analysis to paper (in the form of a memorandum) is even more demanding. Analysis of case law involves the dissecting of courts' reasoning, coming to a conclusion regarding the status of the law, and applying that conclusion to a current dispute. No magic formula will guide you in this process. You will learn that memos can be organized in conformance with a variety of organizational schemes. But you must decide which of these organizational skeletons to use in reference to a specific memo assignment. By the same token, no one can ever tell you with scientific certainty whether a particular case should be used in your analysis. Neither will you discover any precise method for seeing relationships between cases and drawing analogies to your client's case.

HOW TO SUCCESSFULLY READ CASES

- ■ **Have dictionary at your side.**
  ....

- ■ **Brief cases.**
  ....

- ■ **Read lots of cases.**
  ....

- ■ **BE PATIENT WITH YOURSELF.**
  ....

FIGURE 1.11
How to Successfully Read Cases

Although case analysis is governed to some extent by rules, it is by its very nature a creative process. As such, it cannot be reduced to a simple formula. Asking for such a formula makes as much sense as asking an artist for her artistic "recipe." Although she could suggest general rules to teach the mechanics of painting (certain colors enhance one another, certain shapes induce predictable responses in viewers, etc.), she could never capture the essence of creation by using a paint-by-number approach. The creation process defies pure logical explanation.

Seeing connections between cases, drawing inferences from those connections, generating principles from those inferences, applying those principles to specific fact patterns, and explaining this whole process in a clear, concise manner to another is not unlike creating a work of art. You are arranging a set of conclusions (court opinions) in a pattern that makes sense to you and, on the basis of that arrangement, creating a principle that you use to resolve a problem. Others looking at the same set of conclusions will perceive different patterns and create different principles leading to different resolutions of the same problem. How persuasively you can communicate your resolution to others (litigants and triers of fact) determines how viable your creative process is. You can expect to learn the general rules for engaging in this process from reading this book, but please do not expect the uncompromising but fail-safe directions of a how-to book. Such books may build great swing sets, but they do not make for compelling memos.

Practice Pointer

An interoffice memorandum explains how the law applies to a particular fact pattern. Intended to be objective in nature, it is addressed by one member of a firm or organization to another and is designed to educate the attorney about the inherent problems and possible resolutions of specific legal issues. A brief, on the other hand, is submitted by an attorney to a court with the intent of convincing the court how to resolve a legal point of contention. Although a brief may draw on some of the arguments presented in a memorandum, it has a persuasive rather than objective tone.

CHAPTER SUMMARY

The statutes, ordinances, constitutions, administrative regulations, case law, and procedural rules that are derived from the legislative, executive, and judicial branches of government are more than a collection of rules. They are subject to change and interpretation based on the philosophies and attitudes of the times. An understanding of the law requires going beyond merely memorizing black letter law and demands comprehension of the facts and reasoning that form the basis of case law. Legal reasoning frequently centers around comparison of analogous cases.

Cases that are published by appellate courts appear in court reporters. These reporters are organized according to the type of court authoring the opinions (state, regional, or federal) and may be either official or unofficial. Unofficial reporters are often preferred by researchers, because they contain aids such as headnotes and a key numbering system. All reporters identify cases using citations, docket numbers, and captions.

Legal authority in general is categorized as either primary or secondary. Primary authority can be either binding or persuasive; secondary authority is merely persuasive.

Appellate courts are limited in their review of decisions. They must confine their review to questions of law (unless a lower tribunal abused its discretion in regard to a finding of fact), and they cannot review issues that are not properly presented to them. Appellate courts are further constrained by the principle of *stare decisis*, from which they can deviate only if they find grounds upon which to distinguish a case. They must also act within constitutional guidelines and must conform to statutes unless they find them to be unconstitutional. Conservative and liberal judges differ philosophically in terms of how they perceive their role in evaluating constitutional issues.

Briefing cases helps focus you on the key aspects of a case and assists you in preparing a legal memorandum. Although reading cases is challenging, analyzing case law and committing that analysis to paper is even more demanding. Preparing case briefs is one way to facilitate this process. Ultimately, analyzing case law and writing legal memoranda is a creative process that takes time and practice to master.

KEY TERMS

analogous cases	case brief	headnote	primary authority
appellant	case law	key numbering system	question of fact
appellee	citation	liberal judge	question of law
binding authority	conservative judge	official reporter	secondary authority
black letter law	court reporter	on point	*stare decisis*
brief (a case)	distinguish (a case)	persuasive authority	syllabus
caption	docket number	precedent	unofficial reporter

CHAPTER TWO

PARTIES AND PROCEDURAL HISTORY

Chapter Objectives

In this chapter you will learn:

- How to read a caption.

- How to convert a caption into a case name for a citation.

- The value of *A Uniform System of Citation* (the bluebook).

- The typical procedural routes a case can follow.

- How to evaluate the relative status of a case.

- Why it is important to know the procedural history of a case.

- The elements of a procedural history.

- How to summarize a procedural history.

In the classic skit by Abbott and Costello, the comedians struggle to communicate the names of the players on a baseball team. Abbott begins by telling Costello the names of the players on first base, second base, and third base.

> *Abbott:* " 'Who's' on first, 'What's' on second, and 'I Don't Know's' on third."
> *Costello:* "You don't know the fella's name?"
> *Abbott:* "Yes."
> *Costello:* "Well, then, who's playing first?"
> *Abbott:* " 'Who.' "
> *Costello:* "The fella playing first base for St. Louis?"
> *Abbott:* " 'Who.' "
> *Costello:* "The guy on first base."
> *Abbott:* " 'Who' is on first."
> *Costello:* "What are you asking me for?"
> *Abbott:* "I'm not asking you; I'm telling you. 'Who' is on first."

Abbott and Costello continue to wrangle over these names, but Costello never does understand who is playing what position. You may sometimes experience this same confusion when reading case law. Trying to figure out who did what to whom and when can be very exhausting. In the end, you may still wonder who's on first and what's on second.

To fully understand court opinions, you must be able to decode the terminology used by the courts to describe the roles of the parties. You must also be aware of some of the basic procedural paths that parties follow in wending their way to the appellate courts. In this chapter, you will be examining the "who" and "how" of case law, that is, who the relevant parties are and how they arrived at their current positions.

DECODING THE CAPTION

Begin your journey through case law by considering the **caption.** The caption appears at the beginning of an opinion and is akin to a title in that it contains identifying information. The caption includes the names of the parties and their relationships in the appellate process, that is, whether they are **appellants** (the parties who filed the appeal) or **appellees** (the parties responding to the appeal). In some states, an appellee is referred to as a **respondent.**

The caption contains the full names of all of the parties. However, only the last names of the parties who appear first in the caption need to be included in the case name in a brief or citation. Consider the following caption.

Jack LUCAS and Lucy Lucas, his wife; Tom Titus and Tina Titus, his wife; Bruce Cabot; and Michelle Douglas; Appellants,

v.

CITY OF TEMPE, a municipal corporation; Huey Short, Mayor of the City of Tempe; La Borgata, a general partnership; Appellees.

FIGURE 2.1
Sample Caption
(in shaded area)

162 Ariz. 174

Thomas Allen OLSON, an individual, Plaintiff–Appellee,

v.

Jerry H. WALKER and Rachelle Walker, husband and wife, Defendants–Appellants.

No. 1 CA–CV 88–316.

Court of Appeals of Arizona, Division 1, Department D.

June 27, 1989.

Review Denied Nov. 21, 1989.*

This caption would be shortened to the following case name in a brief or citation.

Lucas v. City of Tempe.

Notice that Jack Lucas's last name and the name "City of Tempe" are capitalized in the caption. These are the names that will appear in any citation for this case.

For an example of an actual caption, look on p. 22. This caption informs you that Thomas Allen Olson, an individual, is suing the married couple Jerry H. and Rachelle Walker and that the Walkers (the appellants) filed the appeal to which Olson (the appellee) has responded.

Paying careful attention to the relationships of the parties in a caption will help you more easily follow the facts. For example, a party may be designated as the defendant at the trial court level and as the **petitioner** (one who files a petition for review) at the appellate level. The person who is the plaintiff at the trial court level may be the respondent (one who responds to an appeal or petition for review) at the appellate level.

Steven Brown, Defendant and Petitioner,

v.

Lucy Flynn, Plaintiff and Respondent.

However, captions do not necessarily indicate the positions of the parties at the trial court level. The caption may, for example, indicate only who the appellant and the appellee are.

Steven Brown, Appellant,

v.

Lucy Flynn, Appellee.

In such cases, you must read the facts to determine who initiated the action. Be forewarned that some court opinions are written in such an unclear manner that you may not understand the relationships between the parties even after reading the entire case. Fortunately, such opinions are relatively rare.

Practice Pointer

To facilitate your reading of captions, familiarize yourself with these commonly used phrases.

Et al.—and others.

    May Chang, *et al.,* Defendants and Petitioners,

                      v.

    Linda Miller, *et al.,* Plaintiffs and Respondents.

In re—in the matter of.

    In re Jack Dreyer, Petitioner

Ex rel.—in report to (applies to cases instigated by private parties and then brought by a government agency, such as the state).

    Ex rel. Maria Sanchez

Ex ux.—and wife.

    In re Estate of Roy Finlayson, et ux.

FIGURE 2.2
Anatomy of a Citation

ANATOMY OF A CITATION

Smith v. Jones	101	P.2d	62	(Ariz. Ct. App.	1994)
↓	↓	↓	↓	↓	↓
Case Name	Volume	Reporter	Page	Court Rendering Decision	Date

CITATIONS

Federal Courts! [handwritten]

A better understanding of citations will assist you in translating captions into citations. You may remember from Chapter One that a **citation** (also known as a cite) provides the information necessary to find a case or any other legal resource. In essence, a citation is a key (which is easily deciphered) that unlocks the doors to the kingdom we call the law library.

Look at the following citation.

Supreme Court [handwritten]

Rochester v. Tucker, 488 U.S. 960 (1992).

The citation begins with the case name (*Rochester v. Tucker*). The first number that follows the case name refers to the volume number of the reporter (in this case, volume 488). The reporter is identified by the abbreviation (in this case, U.S., which refers to the United States Reports). The number following the reporter is the page number in the reporter (page 960). The date in parentheses indicates the year the opinion was published.

In opinions written by courts other than the United States Supreme Court, the level of the court is given in parentheses. In the following example, "5th Cir." refers to the Fifth Circuit Court, which rendered the opinion.

Circuit Court [handwritten]

Flynn v. Brown, 106 F.2d 987 (5th Cir. 1972).

The "F.2d" indicates that the opinion appears in the Federal Reporter (second series). If the case had been tried in the district court before being heard in the Fifth Circuit, its citation might appear as follows:

District Court [handwritten]

Flynn v. Brown, 96 F. Supp. 456 (S.D.N.J. 1971).

The "S.D.N.J." indicates that the case was tried in the southern district court of New Jersey. District court opinions are published in the Federal Supplement, as indicated by "F. Supp." in the citation.

State court cases follow the same general format. The volume number precedes the abbreviation for the reporter, and the page number follows that abbreviation. The information in parentheses, in addition to the date, designates the court that rendered the opinion. The following example illustrates this.

Singh v. Thomas, 167 Ariz. 22 (Ct.App. 1989).

The "App." indicates that the Arizona Court of Appeals rendered the decision. If the highest court in the state (in this case, the Arizona Supreme Court) had issued the opinion, only the date would appear in the parentheses.

Singh v. Thomas, 167 Ariz. 22 (1983).

Again, no designation of the court in parentheses indicates that the highest court (in this case the Arizona Supreme Court) heard the case.

THE BLUEBOOK

To find out everything you could possibly want to know about citations, look to *A Uniform System of Citation*, also called the **bluebook** (because it always comes with a blue cover). Designed to maintain a consistent system for citing references, the bluebook is considered the "Bible" by those lawyers who wish to conform their writing to standard citing practices. This reference will enlighten you about the proper format for citing every type of legal and nonlegal reference you could possibly allude to in your research. It will also provide you with proper abbreviations, guide you in the use of underlining, advise you as to the order in which you cite references, and so on.

"Bluebooking" (checking the accuracy of legal citations) is a task often relegated to paralegals. Your familiarization with the rules of the bluebook at the early stages of your education will assist you in conforming to these rules when you begin your active practice. To assist you in adapting to the standards outlined in *A Uniform System of Citation*, the bluebook rules are followed throughout this text.

PUTTING IT INTO PRACTICE

Captions
Read the case on pp. 252–257 in Appendix A. Convert the caption into a case name as it would appear in a citation. See page 352 in Appendix B for a suggested answer.

PROCEDURAL HISTORY

Typical Procedural Routes

The **procedural history** includes the nature and result of all proceedings that occurred previously in regard to the case currently being reviewed as well as the nature

| Practice Pointer | To facilitate your reading of case law, you may want to familiarize yourself with this list of some of the most commonly used abbreviations in citations. |

United States Supreme Court

United States Reports—U.S.

Supreme Court Reporter—S. Ct.

United States Supreme Court Reports, Lawyers' Edition—L.Ed.

United States Courts of Appeal

Federal Reporter—F. (also F.2d [Second Series] and F.3d [third series]

United States District Courts

Federal Supplement—F. Supp.

Regional Reporters (State Courts)

Atlantic Reporter—A. and A.2d
  Connecticut, Delaware, District of Columbia, Maine, Maryland, New Hampshire, New Jersey, Pennsylvania, Rhode Island, Vermont
North Eastern Reporter—N.E. and N.E.2d
  Illinois, Indiana, Massachusetts, New York, Ohio
North Western Reporter—N.W. and N.W.2d
  Iowa, Michigan, Minnesota, Nebraska, North Dakota, South Dakota, Wisconsin
Pacific Reporter—P. and P.2d
  Alaska, Arizona, California, Colorado, Hawaii, Idaho, Kansas, Montana, Nevada, New Mexico, Oklahoma, Oregon, Utah, Washington, Wyoming
South Eastern Reporter—S.E. and S.E.2d
  Georgia, North Carolina, South Carolina, Virginia, West Virginia
South Western Reporter—S.W. and S.W.2d
  Arkansas, Kentucky, Missouri, Tennessee, Texas
Southern Reporter—So. and So.2d
  Alabama, Florida, Louisiana, Mississippi

of the current proceeding. For example, a procedural history may indicate that a case currently being reviewed by a trial court was initiated at an administrative agency and that, unhappy with the decision of the administrative law judge (ALJ), one or more of the parties appealed to a trial judge.

Trial court

↑

ALJ's decision appealed

↑

Administrative agency *or IRS*

Alternatively, a case may have been initiated at the trial court level and one or more of the parties who were disgruntled with the court's **judgment** (resolution of the dispute) may have opted to appeal that judgment to an appellate court. Or they may have appealed a particular ruling of the court if that ruling was critical to the case; such an **interlocutory appeal** takes place during the trial before a judgment is entered.

Appellate court

↑

Appeal of judgment or interlocutory appeal

↑

Trial court

In some cases, the procedural history involves both state and federal systems. In a criminal case, for example, a defendant may have been prosecuted in state court and may have appealed his conviction to both the intermediate and highest courts in that jurisdiction. If the conviction was sustained, the defendant may then have pursued an appeal at the federal level, beginning at the district court level and moving up to the Court of Appeals and finally to the U.S. Supreme Court.

U.S. Supreme Court

↑

Circuit court of appeals   *if constitutional issue*

↑

U.S. district court

↑

State supreme court

↑

State court of appeals

↑

State trial court

Appellate courts are not necessarily required to hear every case that is brought before them. In some cases, parties have a "right" to appeal a case (i.e., the appeal is allowed by statute) but the appeal can be dismissed if the appellate court determines that the issue is not significant. When no right to appeal exists, parties still have the option of filing a petition for **certiorari**. This petition seeks to convince the court that the issue the party wishes it to consider merits the court's attention. At the level of the U.S. Supreme Court, the vast majority of requests for certiorari (cert) are denied. (A citation for a case for which certiorari was denied will indicate this denial using the phrase *cert. denied.*)

Why Is Tracing the Procedural History of a Case So Important?

Knowing the procedural history enables you to better understand the reviewing court's reasoning and actions. Unless you are aware of what the litigants requested at earlier hearings and how the tribunals responded, you will find it difficult to understand the reviewing court's reactions.

Why might a reviewing court, for example, defer to a lower court's findings in one case and not in another? To answer that question, you must know the stage at which the case is being reviewed. If a trial court dismisses a case pursuant to a motion for summary judgment (a motion to dismiss a case on the grounds that no genuine dispute as to material facts exists), the court need not make any findings of fact (because no factual dispute exists according to the court). If an appellate court concludes, to the contrary, that a genuine dispute does exist, the appellate court need not defer to the trial court, since the trial court made no formal findings of fact in rendering its decision. If, however, the appellate court overturns a judgment after the trial court has completed its finding of facts, the appellate court must defer to the trial court's findings (unless no reasonable basis for those findings exists).

Status of Case Law

Although awareness of the procedural lineage of a case is always important, not all cases are "created equal." The status of a case is affected by the level of the court addressing the issue, the degree of attention the court devotes to the issue, the closeness of the vote, and the reaction of reviewing courts to the decision.

Level of Reviewing Court

Before reading the body of an opinion, note the level of the court writing the opinion. Is it an intermediate appellate court, a state court, a federal court, a trial

FIGURE 2.3
The Status of a Case

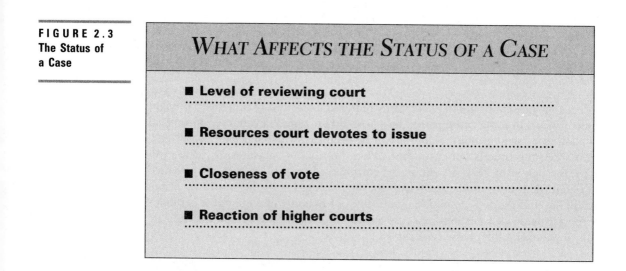

WHAT AFFECTS THE STATUS OF A CASE

■ **Level of reviewing court**

■ **Resources court devotes to issue**

■ **Closeness of vote**

■ **Reaction of higher courts**

court? Knowing this simple fact will assist you in unraveling the procedural history and assessing the relative importance of the case. Obviously, an opinion written by a state's highest court holds more weight than one written by a lower court, just as an opinion by the United States Supreme Court has more precedential value than one written by a lower federal court.

Resources Court Devotes to Case

How much of its resources the court devotes to a case also affects the status of the case. At the court of appeals level, an opinion may be rendered **en banc** (involving all the judges) or by a panel of judges (typically involving only three judges). Appellate courts sit en banc only to hear cases involving critical legal issues that the court feels merit the attention of all the judges. At the other extreme, a **per curiam opinion** (which has no designated author) or a **memorandum decision** (which identifies a court's decision or order but offers no opinion) involves little or no discussion. The court merely offers its disposition of the case and/or considers the legal issues so straightforward that no explanation is warranted. Although such decisions have precedential value, they lack the persuasiveness of more fully developed opinions.

the court as a whole is writing it

Closeness of Vote

Opinions that are supported by a clear majority of the judges tend to carry more weight than those in which the vote is close. An opinion supported by seven out of nine judges is more likely to stand over time than an opinion in which the vote is five to four. With the latter opinion, the majority could shift if one judge were to be replaced or change votes.

not used as a precedent

    Plurality opinions, in which no majority exists because the judges come to the same conclusion but for different reasons, carry less weight than decisions commanding a clear majority. In a plurality opinion, seven justices may reach the same conclusion, but four may decide on the basis of reason A while three decide on the basis of reason B. The plurality opinion is the opinion authored by the four justices who subscribe to reason A. Lower courts have difficulty conforming to such opinions, because the reasoning is not clear. How the higher court will apply its reasoning to slightly different fact patterns is hard for practitioners and judges to predict, and reasonable people may disagree about the outcome of future cases dealing with the same issue.

Reaction of Higher Court

Opinions that are implicitly endorsed by higher courts have greater precedential value than those that are accepted for review. If a petition for certiorari (cert) is denied by the U.S. Supreme Court or by the highest court in the state, the lower court's decision stands, since the higher court has refused to review it. If cert is accepted, on the other hand, the lower court's decision may be overturned. Obviously, greater reliance can be placed on a decision in which appellate remedies have been exhausted than on one in which review is still possible.

Components of a Procedural History

Now that you are aware of the value and general aspects of the procedural history, let us examine its elements. The body of the procedural history is generally found at the beginning of the opinion. In reading this, be alert to who initiated the legal

FIGURE 2.4
Procedural History

PROCEDURAL HISTORY

- **Parties' names**
  ....
- **Parties' relationships**
  ....
- **Claims and defenses**
  ....
- **Tribunals involved**   *Courts*
  ....
- **Results of proceedings**
  ....
- **Parties who appeal and why**
  ....

action, what claims and defenses were raised, what tribunals were involved, and how each tribunal disposed of the case. The **disposition** of a case is the practical effect of the court's decision. An appellate court may dispose of a case, for example, by "reversing" the lower court or by **"remanding"** (returning) the case to the lower court for further proceedings. A trial court, on the other hand, may dispose of a case, for example, by entering an "award for damages" or a "dismissal based on a motion for summary judgment."

A typical procedural history contains the following elements.

Names of parties

Relationships between parties

Claims and defenses

Names of tribunals involved

Results of each proceeding

Names of parties who appealed and why

Notice that the procedural history refers to the events leading up to the current proceedings. In the Procedural History section of your brief, you will also want to mention the nature of the current proceedings, what tribunal is involved, and what the parties are seeking. For clarity, when summarizing the procedural history of a case, distinguish between prior proceedings and current proceedings.

Procedural History in Practice

Nienstedt. v. Wetzel

Look now at an actual procedural history in *Nienstedt v. Wetzel* (pp. 32–35). Read the caption and facts carefully.

Philip R. NIENSTEDT and Barbara
Nienstedt, husband and wife,
Plaintiffs—Appellees,

v.

Manfred R. WETZEL and Nancy Wetzel,
husband and wife,
Defendants—Appellants.

Notice that the Wetzels, who are bringing the appeal, were the defendants at the trial court level, while the Nienstedts, who are responding to the appeal, were the plaintiffs at trial.

It is not until you read the facts, however, that you become aware that two causes of action existed at the trial court level. The first was brought by the Wetzels on the basis of an alleged breach of contract. Then, because of the actions of the Wetzels during this litigation, the Nienstedts filed suit against the Wetzels for abuse of process. Since the actions of the Wetzels during the contract suit are essential to the abuse of process suit and to the issues raised on appeal, the facts regarding the contract dispute should be included in the Facts section of the brief.

The Procedural History section should indicate the two actions at the trial court level and the disposition of those actions as follows.

Prior Proceedings ▪ The Wetzels sued the Nienstedts for alleged breach of contract. The trial court dismissed the Wetzels' complaint as a sanction pursuant to Rule 37 of the Arizona Rules of Civil Procedure. The Nienstedts then filed suit, alleging abuse of process in the prior litigation. A jury awarded them $7,350 in compensatory damages and $50,000 in punitive damages.

Current Proceedings ▪ The Wetzels are appealing the judgment entered on the jury verdict.

Korzep v. Superior Court

A more convoluted procedural history is found in *Korzep v. Superior Court*, 172 Ariz. 534 (1991). This case centers around the interpretation of a self-defense statute (A.R.S. 13—411) that justifies the use of deadly physical force when an individual reasonably believes that such force is necessary to prevent an aggravated assault. The defendant had killed her husband during a fight in which she feared he would strangle her. The question is whether the degree of force she used was reasonable under the circumstances.

> On March 12, 1987, Roberta was indicted on second degree murder. Following the denial of a motion to remand, she petitioned for special action relief. In the first of three already published appellate decisions in her case, the court of appeals ordered a remand because of hearsay statements presented to the grand jury. (cite omitted)
>
> After a new indictment issued on February 5, 1988, for voluntary manslaughter, the trial court denied her second motion to remand based on failure to instruct the grand jury on A.R.S. 13—411. The case proceeded to trial and ended with a manslaughter verdict. At this trial, the court refused a jury instruction on A.R.S. 13—411 and denied a post-verdict motion for a new trial based on this refusal.

FIGURE 2.5
Procedural History
(in shaded areas)
Nienstedt v.
Wetzel

discretion in deciding that its probative value justified its admission.

For the foregoing reasons, the judgment and sentence are affirmed.

CORCORAN, Acting P. J., and HAIRE, J., concur.

Volume   Reporter   Page

133 Ariz. 348

Philip R. NIENSTEDT and Barbara Nienstedt, husband and wife, Plaintiffs-Appellees,

v.

Manfred R. WETZEL and Nancy Wetzel, husband and wife, Defendants-Appellants.

No. 1 CA–CIV 5106.

Court of Appeals of Arizona,
Division 1, Department A.

July 8, 1982.

Rehearing Denied Aug. 25, 1982.

Review Denied Sept. 28, 1982.

Action was brought to recover damages allegedly sustained as result of abuse of process by defendants in prior litigation between the parties. The Superior Court, Maricopa County, Cause No. C–351561, Warren C. Ridge, J., rendered judgment on jury verdict awarding punitive and compensatory damages, and defendants appealed. The Court of Appeals, Haire, J., held that: (1) word "process" as used in the tort abuse of process is not restricted to the narrow sense of that term but encompasses entire range of procedures incident to litigation process and includes such matters as notice of depositions, entry of defaults and motions to compel production, etc.; (2) showing that wrongful use of process has resulted in seizure of plaintiff's person or property is not required; (3) evidence was for

jury; (4) award of attorney fees in prior action was not res judicata of instant claim that purpose of alleged abuse of process was to subject defendants to unreasonable **attorney fees; (5) testimony concerning defendant husband's suspension from practice was relevant; and (6) award of $50,000** punitive damages was not excessive.

Affirmed.

1. Process ☜168

Word "process" as used in the tort of abuse of process is not restricted to the narrow sense of that term but has been interpreted broadly and encompasses the entire range of procedures incident to the litigation process and the tort is not restricted to utilization of process in the nature of attachment, garnishment or warrants of arrest. A.R.S. § 1–215, subd. 26.

See publication Words and Phrases for other judicial constructions and definitions.

2. Process ☜168

For purpose of tort of abuse of process, "process" included noticing of depositions, entry of defaults and utilization of various motions such as motions to compel production, for protective orders, for change of judges, for sanctions and for continuances.

3. Process ☜168

To establish a claim for abuse of process there must be a showing that defendant has used a legal process against plaintiff primarily to accomplish a purpose for which the process was not designed and that harm has been caused to plaintiff by such misuse of process.

4. Process ☜168

Essential elements of tort of abuse of process include a willful act in the use of judicial process for an ulterior purpose not proper in the regular conduct of the proceedings.

5. Process ☜168

Showing that wrongful use of process has resulted in seizure of plaintiff's person or property is not an element of the tort of abuse of process.

FIGURE 2.5
continued

and exhibits listed were identical to those previously filed. 16 A.R.S. Rules Civ.Proc., Rule 26(e)(1).

19. Pretrial Procedure ⊸1

Refusal to dismiss lawsuit or place it on inactive calendar for defendants' failure to file pretrial statement was not abuse of discretion where trial court permitted defendants to join in plaintiffs' pretrial statement and found that no prejudice occurred as a result of the joint statement. 17A A.R.S. Sup.Ct.Rules, Rules 16, 16(c)(4).

20. Witnesses ⊸336

Evidence of abuse of process defendant's suspension from practice was relevant to impeach defendant's credibility in making purportedly authoritative statements on legal ethics and admission of the evidence was not abuse of discretion where inquiry was limited to one question and one answer. 17A A.R.S. Rules of Evid., Rules 401, 403.

21. Damages ⊸94

There is no compensatory-punitive damage ratio limit.

22. Damages ⊸94

Whether punitive damages are excessive is based solely on the circumstances and one of the factors a jury may consider is defendant's wealth, although wealth is not a necessary prerequisite to an award of punitive damages.

23. Appeal and Error ⊸205 .

A defendant attacking a punitive damages award may not complain of absence of evidence of his wealth when he has made no effort to introduce such evidence.

24. Damages ⊸208(8)

Amount of punitive damages is a matter of discretion with the trier of fact.

25. Appeal and Error ⊸1004.1(10)

Punitive damages award will not be disturbed unless it is so unreasonable in light of circumstances as to show influence of passion or prejudice.

26. Appeal and Error ⊸1004.1(10)

Size of punitive damage verdict alone is not sufficient evidence of passion or prejudice to warrant setting aside.

27. Damages ⊸91(1)

Punitive damages are allowed where conduct of the wrongdoer is wanton, reckless or shows spite or ill will.

28. Appeal and Error ⊸1004.3

Where the trial court has refused to interfere with jury's determination of punitive damages the reviewing court cannot interpose its own judgment unless convinced that the verdict is so excessive as to suggest passion or prejudice.

29. Process ⊸171

Award of $50,000 punitive damages for tort of abuse of process was not so excessive as to suggest passion or prejudice as jury could reasonably conclude that defendants' conduct in prior litigation reflected spite, ill will and reckless indifference to the interests of plaintiffs.

Law Offices of Donald Maxwell, P. C. by Donald Maxwell and William G. Poach, Jr., Scottsdale, for plaintiffs-appellees.

Black, Robertshaw, Frederick, Copple & Wright, P. C. by Jon R. Pozgay, Phoenix, for defendants-appellants.

OPINION

HAIRE, Judge.

Appellees, Philip R. and Barbara Nienstedt, husband and wife, commenced this action in Maricopa County Superior Court to recover damages allegedly sustained as a result of abuse of process by appellants Manfred R. and Nancy Wetzel, husband and wife, in prior litigation between the parties. A jury verdict awarded the Nienstedts $7,350 as compensatory damages and $50,000 as punitive damages. The Wetzels have appealed from the judgment entered on that verdict.

Although several issues have been raised on appeal, we will first address appellants' contentions concerning the applicability of abuse of process concepts to the claim involved here, as well as the contention that the evidence was insufficient to justify submission of the claim to the jury.

FIGURE 2.5
continued

ABUSE OF PROCESS

Viewing the evidence in a light most favorable to supporting the judgment, we find that the following facts were established at trial.

In February 1975, Manfred Wetzel, then an attorney licensed to practice law in Arizona, filed a complaint against the Nienstedts in Maricopa County Cause No. C–307988 for breach of an alleged oral contract, fraud and defamation.[1] Appellants and the Nienstedts were neighbors when this complaint was filed and the lawsuit involved an alleged oral contract pursuant to which the parties were to share the cost of building a retaining wall on appellants' property adjacent to the Nienstedts' property. The Nienstedts' liability under the alleged oral contract would have amounted to $780.69. Appellant Manfred Wetzel had purchased the home prior to his marriage to Nancy Wetzel and brought suit solely in his name. The Nienstedts answered the complaint and counterclaimed against both of the appellants on the assumption that Nancy Wetzel, even though not named as a plaintiff in the complaint, might have a legal interest in the home. In his capacity as the Wetzels' attorney, Manfred Wetzel thereafter filed a pleading entitled a "Counter-counterclaim" on behalf of his wife. This pleading was essentially a reiteration of the original complaint naming Nancy Wetzel as the "Counter-counterclaimant."

On May 13, 1975, the Nienstedts filed a motion to dismiss and strike the counter-counterclaim as an improper pleading. On January 29, 1976, the Nienstedts not having filed an answer or a reply, appellants entered their default on the counter-counterclaim. On February 27, 1976, a default hearing before a superior court judge was conducted at which time the default was set aside and the court set April 2, 1976, as the time for hearing the Nienstedts' motion to dismiss and strike, as well as other pending motions. On that date the court, by minute entry order, denied the motion to dismiss

and strike, and stated that following completion of discovery the court would consider realignment of the parties.

On April 27, 1976, appellants entered another default against the Nienstedts on the counter-counterclaim and noticed a default hearing before a court commissioner for May 27, 1976. The Nienstedts filed a motion to quash the default hearing, and at the hearing on this motion the trial court vacated the default hearing and realigned the parties denominating Nancy Wetzel as a plaintiff. The court further joined the counter-counterclaim with the complaint and held that the answer previously filed by the Nienstedts would be considered as an answer to the counter-counterclaim and that the counterclaim previously filed by the Nienstedts would be considered as a counterclaim against both appellants.

Numerous discovery motions were filed by both parties. At one point the trial court imposed sanctions for what it described as obstructionist activities of appellants.

In August 1976, one day prior to the scheduled trial, appellant Manfred Wetzel moved for a continuance. The motion stated that he was committed to represent a client at another trial scheduled on the same day on a matter having a lower cause number. In response, the Nienstedts filed an affidavit stating that appellant Manfred Wetzel did not appear as the counsel of record on that particular case. However, appellant Manfred Wetzel filed an uncontroverted affidavit stating that although his brother's name appeared as the attorney of record, he and his brother had associated on the case and he was in fact trying the case.

In response to one of the Nienstedts' motions to produce, appellants filed a motion for a protective order to prevent disclosure of two tape recordings allegedly containing conversations of the Nienstedts which Manfred Wetzel had filed with the court in a sealed envelope. Manfred Wetzel had indicated to the Nienstedts that these tapes

---

1. The disposition in that action is also on appeal to this court, 1 CA–CIV 5685. It is a separate appeal and is not considered in this opinion.

FIGURE 2.5
continued

proved the existence of an oral contract, and if played at trial, could be used to prove perjury by the Nienstedts. He represented to the court that these tape recordings were to be used for impeachment purposes and also were subject to protection because they constituted his work product as an attorney inasmuch as the questions on the tape "were structured" by him. He further requested that the court review the tapes in chambers and determine whether they were privileged as his work product. At the hearing on appellants' motion for the protective order appellants were represented by counsel other than Manfred Wetzel. Following the court's denial of his motion for a protective order, Manfred Wetzel admitted to the court that the tapes were blank, contrary to his prior express affirmation to the court that the tapes contained questions structured by him. The court then found that appellant Manfred Wetzel had deceived the court, had willfully and intentionally failed to comply with the Nienstedts' motion for production, and had filed motions for enlargement of time and for a protective order which were a sham and unjustified. Consequently, the court dismissed appellants' complaint as a sanction pursuant to Rule 37, Arizona Rules of Civil Procedure, 16 A.R.S. The court further awarded the Nienstedts $500 in attorney's fees incurred on their motion to produce and their response to appellants' motion for protective order, plus their total court costs incurred in that action.

The Nienstedts then commenced this litigation against appellants claiming that abuse of process in the prior litigation had occurred when appellants: sought recovery of punitive damages in a contract action; filed a motion to continue by reason of another pending action in which appellant Manfred Wetzel did not appear as attorney of record; entered default on an improper pleading; entered a second default and scheduled a hearing before a court commissioner when the appellants knew that the trial judge had set aside an identical default

and contemplated realignment of the parties; and failed to act in good faith in discovery proceedings. The Nienstedts contended that in engaging in the aforementioned procedures, the primary goal of the appellants was to utilize processes of the court to harass the Nienstedts by purposely subjecting them to excessive legal fees in defending against appellants' claims. In this connection, there was evidence that during discovery proceedings appellant Manfred Wetzel told the Nienstedts that through this case he was going to make the Nienstedts' attorney a rich man; that he (Wetzel) could break people financially (impliedly through subjecting them to legal fees and expenses); and, that because he was a lawyer representing himself it would not be necessary for him to incur similar fees and expenses.

[1, 2] Against this factual background we now address the legal requirements necessary for the establishment of an abuse of process claim. First, we note that through developing case law the word "process" as used in the tort "abuse of process" is not restricted to the narrow sense of that term.[2] Rather, it has been interpreted broadly, and encompasses the entire range of procedures incident to the litigation process. *Barquis v. Merchants Collection Association of Oakland, Inc.,* 7 Cal.3d 94, 496 P.2d 817, 101 Cal.Rptr. 745 (1972); *Thornton v. Rhoden,* 245 Cal.App.2d 80, 53 Cal.Rptr. 706 (1966); *Younger v. Solomon,* 38 Cal.App.3d 289, 113 Cal.Rptr. 113 (1974); *Foothill Industrial Bank v. Mikkelson,* 623 P.2d 748 (Wyo.1981). Thus it has been held that a request for admissions will, under appropriate circumstances, support a complaint for abuse of process, *Twyford v. Twyford,* 63 Cal.App.3d 916, 134 Cal.Rptr. 145 (1976). *See also Hopper v. Drysdale,* 524 F.Supp. 1039 (D.Mont. 1981) (the noticing of depositions). As applied to this case, we therefore consider as "processes" of the court for abuse of process purposes, the noticing of depositions, the entry of defaults, and the utilization of

2. See A.R.S. § 1–215(26) which, for statutory interpretation purposes, gives a restricted definition of the word "process".

> After the court of appeals affirmed. . . , our supreme court reversed the conviction for failure to instruct the trial jury on A.R.S. 13–411. (cite omitted) After the case returned to the trial court, the trial court denied Roberta's motion to reconsider a remand for failure to instruct the grand jury on A.R.S. 13–411. From the denial Roberta then filed this special action in this court . . .

To simplify a procedural history as lengthy as this one, rewrite it numerically, breaking it down into single steps.

Prior Proceedings

1. Defendant was indicted on second degree murder.

2. Defendant filed motion to remand.

3. Motion was denied.

4. Defendant filed special action.

5. Court of appeals ordered remand because of hearsay statements presented to jury.

6. New indictment was issued for voluntary manslaughter.

7. Defendant filed motion to remand based on failure to instruct grand jury on A.R.S. 13–411.

8. Motion was denied.

9. Trial ended in verdict for manslaughter.

10. Defendant filed motion for new trial based on trial court's refusal to give jury instruction on A.R.S. 13–411.

11. Court of appeals affirmed conviction.

12. Supreme court reversed conviction based on failure of trial court to instruct jury on A.R.S. 13–411.

13. Case was returned to trial court.

14. Defendant filed motion to reconsider remand for failure to instruct grand jury on A.R.S. 13–411.

15. Trial court denied motion.

Current Proceedings

1. Defendant is filing special action in court of appeals based on trial court's denial of motion to reconsider remand.

Translating the court's narrative on procedural history into chronological steps will clarify the process for you. As you write the steps out, each phase of litigation will become more real, especially if you make an effort to visualize what each phase entailed. If you wrote out the procedural history for *Korzep*, for example, you would begin to appreciate the extent of litigation that preceded the court of appeals' consideration of the issue. After you plow your way through cases with complex procedural histories, you will realize that you cannot fully comprehend the substantive issues in a case until you have a firm grasp of its procedural path.

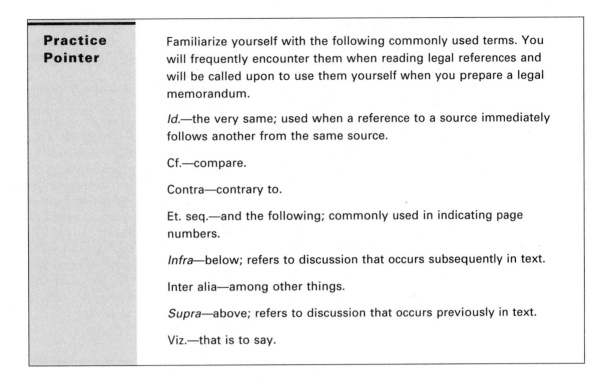

Practice Pointer

Familiarize yourself with the following commonly used terms. You will frequently encounter them when reading legal references and will be called upon to use them yourself when you prepare a legal memorandum.

Id.—the very same; used when a reference to a source immediately follows another from the same source.

Cf.—compare.

Contra—contrary to.

Et. seq.—and the following; commonly used in indicating page numbers.

Infra—below; refers to discussion that occurs subsequently in text.

Inter alia—among other things.

Supra—above; refers to discussion that occurs previously in text.

Viz.—that is to say.

Common Procedural Terms

In the glossary, you will find procedural terms that are commonly used in opinions. Although this is not a complete list, you will discover that acquainting yourself with those terms that are foreign to you will facilitate your reading of cases. For a more comprehensive index of terms, consult a text on procedural law. Always keep a law dictionary handy, however, whenever you are reading case law, so that you can quickly look up unfamiliar terms. Avoid trying to guess the meaning of words from their context, because, particularly in the procedural area, you may lose information that is essential to your clear understanding of the case.

PUTTING IT INTO PRACTICE

Read *Weirum v. RKO General, Inc.,* which is found on pp. 252–257 in Appendix A. Summarize the procedural history, dividing it into prior and current proceedings. See page 352 in Appendix B for a suggested answer.

CHAPTER SUMMARY

A caption identifies the parties involved in a case and the nature of their relationships. Case names are shortened forms of captions and contain only the names of the primary parties. Phrases in captions, such as et al., et ux., *ex rel.*, and *in re* provide the reader with additional information about the nature of the case and the types of parties involved. A citation contains the case name as well as the volume and page number of the reporter in which the case can be found.

The procedural history details the proceedings leading up to the case presently before the court as well as the nature of the current proceedings. Being cognizant of the procedural history helps you understand the reviewing court's reasoning and actions and alerts you to the level of deference the reviewing court must afford the lower tribunal. Awareness of procedural history includes understanding the relative status of a case. This status is influenced by the level of the court addressing the issue, the degree of attention the court commits to the issue, the closeness of the vote, and the reaction of the reviewing courts to the decision. Majority opinions carry more weight than plurality opinions, for example, and opinions rendered by a court sitting en banc carry more weight than per curiam opinions.

Typically found at the beginning of a case, the procedural history usually indicates the names and relationships of the parties, the claims and defenses that were raised, the names of each tribunal and how it disposed of the case, and who appealed and why. The procedural history also includes the nature of the current proceeding, what tribunal is involved, and what the parties are seeking.

KEY TERMS

appellants	citation	judgment	plurality opinions
appellees	disposition	memorandum decision	procedural history
bluebook	en banc	per curiam opinion	remanding
caption	interlocutory appeal	petitioner	respondent
certiorari			

COGNITIVE CALISTHENICS

1. Identify the following terms.
   (a) Et ux.
   (b) *Ex rel.*
   (c) Et al.
   (d) *In re*
   (e) Respondent
   (f) Petitioner
   (g) Disposition
   (h) Per curiam opinion
   (i) Plurality opinion
   (j) Interlocutory appeal
   (k) Petition for certiorari
   (l) *Id.*
   (m) *Supra*
   (n) Cf.
   (o) Inter alia
   (p) Et seq.

2. Write the parties' names as they would appear in the citation in a brief as well as the procedural history for the following cases. Answers to #2 are found in Appendix B on page 352.
   (a) Sandra LINTHICUM, widow, surviving wife and Personal Representative of the Estate of Jerry Linthicum, deceased, Plaintiff-Appellee, v. NATIONWIDE LIFE INSURANCE CO., an Ohio corporation, and Dan R. Wagnon and Associates, Inc., an Arizona corporation, Defendants-Appellants.
   (b) Henry WHITE and Sandra White, his wife, Plaintiffs-Appellees, v. Christopher MITCHELL and Deborah Mitchell, his wife; and D. L. Sitton Motor Lines, Inc.,

a foreign corporation; Defendants-Appellants.

(c) Thomas Allen OLSON, an individual, Plaintiff-Appellee, v. Jerry H. WALKER and Rachelle Walker, husband and wife, Defendants-Appellants.

3. Write the parties' names as they would appear in the citation in a brief as well as the procedural history for the following cases.

(a) Irma C. CUNDICK, Appellant, v. J. R. BROADBENT, Appellee. *p 279*

(b) In the Matter of the Estate of Grace SWENSON, deceased. Jane Troyer and Urinda Laura Lee Russell, Respondents, v. Cora PLACKETT, Personal Represen-

tative of the Estate of Grace Swenson, Appellant.

(c) Miriam BenSHALOM, Plaintiff, v. John O. MARSH, Jr., Secretary of the U.S. Army; Commanding Officer H.Q. 84th Division, U.S. Army Reserve; Commanding Officer 5091st U.S. Army Reception Battalion, Defendants.

(d) MINNESOTA, Petitioner, v. Timothy DICKERSON. *293*

4. Write out the procedural history for *Vo v. Superior Court*, 172 Ariz. 195 (1992) (found on pp. 88–98 in Chapter 5). Since this case has a rather extensive procedural history, write it out chronologically using a numerical format.

CHAPTER THREE

ESSENTIAL AND SIGNIFICANT FACTS

Chapter Objectives

In this chapter you will learn:

- How to identify essential and significant facts.

- How to deal with complicated fact patterns by using time lines, charts, and diagrams.

"ONE MILLION DOLLARS FOR LOSS OF FINGERTIP"

Have you ever read a newspaper headline similar to this in which the plaintiff won a fantastic sum of money for what appeared to be a relatively minor injury? This is the type of case that tort reformers put forth as their primary evidence of a system gone berserk. While the issue of tort reform goes beyond the scope of this text, I would like to use this headline to illustrate the importance that the facts assume in most cases. You see, in the case referred to in this headline, the plaintiff was a world-class pianist who was forced into premature retirement by his injury. He was unable to give concerts after the loss of the fingertip on the ring finger of his right hand. What he was able to earn on the lecture circuit and as a music professor at a university paled in comparison with what he had been able to earn as a concert pianist.

Notice how this one simple fact—that the plaintiff was a concert pianist—changed your entire perspective. While your immediate reaction to the headline may have been one of contempt for a legal system that allows such outrageous recoveries, your reaction after having the additional fact was more likely one of disrespect for a reporter who omitted pertinent information.

WHY ARE FACTS IMPORTANT?

The point of this simple illustration is to impress upon you how important the facts are to case law. Case law is very simply legal principles woven around facts. Without facts to flesh them out, legal principles are hollow recitations. What is the meaning of a doctrine, for example, that prohibits "vague" statutes? How do you know, without specific statutes as a reference, what is meant by the term "vague"? Suppose, however, you were to read a statute that prohibited loitering but failed to describe any specific conduct that constituted loitering. If a court struck down the law as being too vague because of the legislature's failure to clearly define the prohibited conduct, then you would have some measuring stick to evaluate the term "vague." Notice how a few facts convert an abstract principle into something more concrete.

The concepts in this chapter, therefore, are instrumental to your understanding of case law. You will learn how to identify **essential facts** in an opinion, and you will learn how to distinguish essential facts from **significant facts,** which are helpful but not essential, and from **insignificant facts,** which are neither essential nor significant.

Before you expend mental energy learning to recognize and distinguish essential, significant, and insignificant facts, you probably want to know why you are doing this. In the next chapter, you will be asked to write issue statements. Issue statements include essential facts but not significant facts. Therefore, to write a concise but accurate issue statement, you will need to be able to sift out the essential facts from a court opinion. Significant facts are important, however, because they are included in the facts section of a case brief or legal memorandum. Consequently, you need to learn to separate significant from insignificant facts if you want to avoid cluttering your facts section with insignificant details.

FIGURE 3.1
The Three Types of Facts

ESSENTIAL, SIGNIFICANT, AND INSIGNIFICANT FACTS

■ ESSENTIAL FACT

➢ Any fact whose absence or modification would alter the outcome of a case. Essential facts must be included in issue statements.

■ SIGNIFICANT FACT

➢ A background or historical fact that enhances understanding of the nature of a dispute but whose absence or modification would not alter the outcome of the case. Significant facts need not be included in issue statements.

■ INSIGNIFICANT FACT

➢ A detail that is interesting but need not be included in the brief or memorandum.

<table>
<tr><td>

Practice Pointer

</td><td>

Facts sections are found in case briefs, legal briefs, and legal memoranda. Paralegals typically do not prepare legal briefs; lawyers write legal briefs to persuade a judge to adopt a particular course of action or interpretation of law. Paralegals do, however, prepare case briefs and legal memoranda.

In a case brief, the facts section contains a summary of the essential and significant facts of the case being briefed. In a legal memorandum, the facts section contains the facts of the case being litigated. Every fact that is mentioned in the memorandum must be included in the facts section. In the discussion section of the memorandum, pertinent cases are discussed. When a particular case merits extensive discussion (when the case is essentially being briefed by the writer), the essential and significant facts of the case are included.

</td></tr>
</table>

WHAT IS AN ESSENTIAL FACT?

The first question, then, is "What is an essential fact"? Essential facts are those facts whose modification or absence would alter the outcome of the case. In other words, when deciding whether a fact is essential to an opinion, ask yourself whether the court would have altered its decision if this particular fact had been different or had been deleted.

Modification of Fact

Suppose that a court, for example, decides that a transaction between two "backyard" horse breeders does not fall within the scope of the Uniform Commercial Code (U.C.C.) because the breeders are not "merchants" as defined by the U.C.C. Is the fact that these breeders are "backyard" breeders a critical fact? Suppose you discover that if they had been professional breeders whose only business was the raising and showing of horses, the breeders would have been considered "merchants" for purposes of the U.C.C. Knowing that fact, you can then deduce that a breeder's status as professional or nonprofessional is an essential fact when discussing the U.C.C. Notice how a minor modification of a single fact can dramatically alter the outcome of a case.

Deletion of Fact

The deletion of a fact can also be significant to a court's decision. In tort law, the duty of care that landowners owe people who enter their property depends on how the person on the property is classified. Individuals who enter the property for the purpose of conducting business are classified as invitees and are owed a high duty of care. Individuals who enter the property for social reasons are classified as licensees and are owed a lesser duty of care than invitees.

Suppose that two men are officers in a fraternal organization and that they meet one evening to discuss business in the home of one of the men, the organization's president. While there, the other man is assaulted by the president's son, and he ultimately sues the president to recover his damages. Let us now delete the fact that they met to discuss business. Would that deletion affect the outcome of the case? Probably yes. The plaintiff might very well be classified as an invitee if he were conducting business but as a licensee if he were there simply as a friend. Since the standard of care owed to a licensee is substantially less than that owed to an invitee, any facts relating to that classification would be essential. Therefore, in this instance, the purpose of their meeting would be an essential fact.

HOW TO IDENTIFY ESSENTIAL FACTS

You can see that simple and sometimes subtle alterations in fact patterns can radically affect the outcome of cases. The question that naturally arises in your mind at this point is how you determine whether the modification or deletion of a particular fact would alter a court's decision. Although no definitive checklist exists that allows you to objectively categorize facts as essential, you can consider certain factors in deciding how to classify a fact.

Adjectives Used to Describe Facts

A court may use such terminology as "very important," "noteworthy," or "determinative" to describe certain facts. Such adjectives signal the reader that the court believes these facts to be of particular importance.

Repeated References to Facts

By the same token, a court may repeatedly refer to particular facts, thus suggesting the relative importance of those facts. In particular, if a court alludes to a fact in its analysis, that fact is most likely essential, especially if the court discusses how a modification of the fact could affect the outcome of the case.

FIGURE 3.2
What Are Essential Facts?

CLUES FOR SPOTTING ESSENTIAL FACTS

✓ ■ **Adjectives used to describe fact**   *very important crucial*
....

✓ ■ **Repeated reference to fact, especially in analysis**
....

■ **Court's reaction to parties' evaluation of fact**
....

■ **Court's reaction to lower tribunal's characterization of fact**
....

■ **Comparison to differing fact in other cases**
....

Court's Reaction to Parties' Evaluation of Facts

Oftentimes, parties will focus their arguments around certain facts. The court's reaction to a party's evaluation of those facts will clue you into the court's notion of whether those facts are actually essential to the case. For example, if a defendant in a sexual assault case belabors the victim's sexual history in arguments to the court but the court ignores that history in its discussion, you can infer that the victim's past behavior is not essential to the issue.

Court's Reaction to Lower Tribunal's Characterization of Facts

Similarly, a court's commentary regarding a lower court's or agency's characterization of certain facts provides evidence of the court's attitude toward those facts. If an appellate court, for example, points out that the lower court incorrectly focused on a party's statements rather than the party's conduct, the appellate court is clearly indicating that it considers the party's conduct an essential fact.

Comparison to Differing Facts

Perhaps a more subtle indication of the importance attributed by a court to particular facts is the court's comparison of those facts with contrasting fact patterns. Suppose a court is struggling with whether a three-month-old fetus is a "human being" for purposes of a criminal statute. If the court distinguishes (differentiates) the case before it from another case in which a seven-month-old fetus was determined to be a human being, you can safely conclude that the age of the fetus is an essential fact. Therefore, the age of the fetus should be included in an issue statement.

Do not enter into the search for essential facts with a heavy heart; it does not merit that kind of weighty concern. Courts have generally very graciously summarized the significant facts for you. Your task is simply to sift out the nonessential facts and include only the essential facts in the issue statement of your brief. But if you should err by including nonessential facts, you have certainly not committed a mortal sin. The only "punishment" that comes to those who include too many facts in their issue statements is that of committing more words to paper than is absolutely required. Also, since parties often disagree as to what the essential facts of an opinion are (indeed, this type of disagreement lies at the core of legal advocacy), you can generally be assured that someone will agree that the facts you selected are essential.

PUTTING IT INTO PRACTICE
....

Essential Facts
Read the facts of *Weirum v. RKO Industries, Inc.* (found on pp. 252–257 in Appendix A) and identify the essential facts. Compare your list of essential facts with that of others in your class. Be prepared to defend your decision to classify a fact as essential.

....

WHAT IS A SIGNIFICANT FACT?

A fact that is not essential, in that it is not pertinent enough to be included in the issue statement of a brief, may be a significant fact. Significant facts are those background and historical facts that allow the reader to understand the nature of the dispute between the parties. They should be included in the facts section of a case brief so that the reader has a vivid mental picture of what transpired. The content and timing of negotiations leading up to a contractual dispute could be significant facts in a case in which the question is when a contract was formed. Events preceding an accident that help the reader understand why liability is an issue may be significant facts. Basically, a court's reasoning is much easier to track when the context of the case is clear. Significant facts provide this context.

INSIGNIFICANT FACTS

Any facts that a court includes in its opinion that are neither essential nor significant are insignificant facts, and they need not be mentioned in a case brief or legal memorandum. While these facts may provide interesting detail or a more complete background, they are not required for a full understanding of the case. Locations, dates, damages awarded, and exact testimony are insignificant facts if their omission would not affect the reader's comprehension of the case.

Again, you should not spend a large amount of energy debating whether a fact is significant or insignificant. The only consequence of putting arguably insignificant facts in your facts section is that your summary of the facts will be longer than necessary. When in doubt, you are better off including a fact. It is better to tell your reader too much than not enough.

PUTTING IT INTO PRACTICE
....

Significant Facts
Identify the facts in *Weirum v. RKO Industries, Inc.* (found on pp. 252–257 in Appendix A) that you consider significant. Compare your list of significant facts with that of others in your class. Be prepared to defend your decision to classify a fact as significant.

....

GENERAL GUIDELINES FOR DEALING WITH FACTS

Generally, a court will have sifted out most of the extraneous facts in its summary of the facts, but you will probably find that you can pare it down even more. Although you want to be as succinct as possible when briefing a case or summarizing it in a memorandum, never sacrifice understanding for the sake of brevity.

Practice Pointer	Visual aids allow you to perceive related or sequential concepts in a more graphic manner than language by itself permits. They assist you in visualizing relationships and chronology. Remember this when trying to convey information to an attorney, judge, or jury. Although not everyone benefits from visual representations, many people do, and some will not understand a concept until it is portrayed visually. Even though translating narratives into time lines, charts, and diagrams is time-consuming, it can often greatly enhance comprehension.

You should have a clear comprehension of the events leading up to the controversy between the parties and of the relationships among the parties. If the nature of their interrelationships is complicated or if the sequence of events escapes you, prepare time lines, charts, diagrams, or other visual aids that will assist you in grasping relationships and chronology.

To further assist you in understanding and remembering the nature of the dispute in some cases, you may decide to use labels that reflect the legal relationships between the parties rather than the parties' proper names. For example, rather than referring to the parties as Mr. White and Ms. Black (names whose significance will escape you shortly after reading the case), you could refer to them as "Employer" and "Employee," "Landlord" and "Tenant," "Testatrix" and "Beneficiary," or "Buyer" and "Seller." Of course, if the controversy is whether a party is indeed a buyer or a tenant or an employee, then do not use labels that reflect a legal conclusion on your part.

In other cases, the least confusing way to refer to the parties may be by their proper names. Proper names are especially useful when the parties have participated in a series of litigations, taking turns being the defendant and the plaintiff or the appellant and the appellee.

Use your best judgment in assigning labels. The terms that you use should be helpful to you in recalling the essence of the case. If you must refer back to the case when reading your case brief in order to clarify the relationships between the parties, you may need to assign more meaningful labels.

REAL CASE, REAL FACTS

Thus far, our discussion has been fairly abstract. So let us jump into the legal trenches and confront a real fact situation, *Olson v. Walker* (found on pp. 257–262 in Appendix A). Read this case carefully to make sure you understand the basic issue before the court. As you can deduce from reading the opinion, the outcome

FIGURE 3.3
Reviewing the
Facts

OLSON v. WALKER   Ariz. **1015**
Cite as 781 P.2d 1015 (Ariz.App. 1989)

drove by the disabled vehicle. *Scottsdale Jaycees v. Superior Court*, 17 Ariz.App. 571, 499 P.2d 185 (1972).

Under Arizona law, an employee is acting within the scope of his employment while he is doing any reasonable thing which his employment expressly or impliedly authorizes him to do or which may reasonably be said to have been contemplated by that employment as necessarily or probably incidental to the employment.

Ray Korte Chevrolet v. Simmons, 117 Ariz. 202, 207, 571 P.2d 699, 704 (App. 1977).

Lippincott contends there was evidence that whenever a highway patrol officer occupies a highway patrol vehicle, he or she is considered to be "on duty." In his deposition taken in May 1982 in Rebecca Lippincott's lawsuit against the state, Watkins testified as follows: "I don't remember if I went by the truck in my squad car or my patrol car or if I went by it with my wife. I recall that my patrol car was already being repaired. And I believe I was with my wife when we went by the accident in my personal car." Watkins testified that he had driven to Salome prior to the accident to have some repair work done on his patrol car. Both earlier and later in his first deposition, Watkins stated that he was in his personal vehicle that morning. Earlier he testified, "I had gone by it [the disabled truck] with my wife in my own personal car." Later, in response to the following question, "There is no question in your mind but that you weren't in your patrol vehicle that morning; correct?" he stated, "If I recall correctly, I believe I was with my wife in my personal car, because I remember remarking to her about the truck."

At his second deposition, taken in February 1987 in this case, Watkins testified that he drove to Salome that morning to check on his patrol car and that he was certain the vehicle was already in the garage that morning.

We find that Watkins' uncertain testimony with regard to which vehicle he occupied

at the time he drove by the disabled truck raises a material fact issue on the question of whether he was then acting within the course and scope of his employment.

Therefore, the summary judgment entered in favor of the state is reversed, and the case is remanded for trial.

ROLL, P.J., and LACAGNINA, C.J., concur.

162 Ariz. 174
Thomas Allen OLSON, an individual, Plaintiff–Appellee,

v.

Jerry H. WALKER and Rachelle Walker, husband and wife, Defendants–Appellants.

No. 1 CA–CV 88–316.

Court of Appeals of Arizona, Division 1, Department D.

June 27, 1989.

Review Denied Nov. 21, 1989.*

Defendant appealed from an order of the Superior Court of Maricopa County, Cause No. C–600994, Cheryl K. Hendrix, J., which rendered judgment for plaintiff in personal injury action and awarded punitive damages. The Court of Appeals, Grant, C.J., held that: (1) evidence was sufficient to warrant punitive damages; (2) punitive damage award was not excessive; (3) punitive damage award did not violate due process, prohibition against excessive fines or double jeopardy; and (4) trial court did not abuse discretion in refusing to instruct jury to disregard expert testimony regarding arthritic changes in plaintiff's back.

Affirmed.

Gerber, J., dissented and filed opinion.

* Moeller, J., of the Supreme Court, voted to grant   review as to Issues B, C and D.

FIGURE 3.3
continued

ny on current arthritis and defendant was not prejudiced by x-ray testimony.

———

Harrison, Harper, Christian & Dichter, P.C. by Douglas L. Christian and Gregg H. Temple, Phoenix, for defendants-appellants.

Berry & Martori by Frederick C. Berry, Jr., Phoenix, for plaintiff-appellee.

OPINION

GRANT, Chief Judge.

This appeal primarily concerns the award of punitive damages in a personal injury action. A secondary issue concerns the trial court's refusal to strike certain expert testimony. For the reasons explained below, we affirm.

FACTS

We view the facts most favorably to upholding the jury verdict. *Venerias v. Johnson*, 127 Ariz. 496, 622 P.2d 55 (App. 1980). Thomas Allen Olson and Jerry H. Walker were involved in a motor vehicle accident at approximately 6:30 p.m. on October 30, 1985. [1] Immediately prior to the accident, Walker spent approximately two hours at a bar with his accountant and one other acquaintance. During that time, the three men played pool and drank at least two pitchers of beer between approximately 4:30 p.m. and 5:30 p.m. When they left the bar, the accountant drove to a community college where he taught an accounting class. Walker drove east on Bell Road, which has a posted speed limit of 40 miles per hour. [2] A witness testified that Walker was traveling at least 50–55 miles per hour, that he swerved in and out of traffic, that he cut the witness off, and that he lost control of his vehicle.

Meanwhile, Olson was driving his motorcycle to pick up a pizza. He was almost stopped in the left-hand turn lane on Bell Road, waiting for traffic to clear so he could turn left, when Walker's vehicle rear-ended him. Walker did not immediately stop, but when he did get out of his car, he staggered, smelled strongly of alcohol, and

had trouble standing. He had bloodshot eyes and slurred his speech. [3] A witness testified that Walker attempted to leave the scene, but was stopped by two bystanders. Walker was arrested for driving while intoxicated. *See* A.R.S. § 28–692. As a result, he ultimately paid a fine of $372.50 and had his driver's license temporarily suspended.

[4] Based upon his blood-alcohol level approximately one hour after the accident, an expert toxicologist testified that Walker's blood-alcohol level at time of the accident was .155 percent. He also testified that Walker must have consumed ten or more twelve-ounce cans of beer during the one-hour period he was drinking. There was also disputed testimony that Walker took 20 mg. of Valium approximately one-half hour before the accident. The toxicologist testified that the Valium and alcohol would have intensified the effect of each other.

A jury trial resulted in an award of $133,000 compensatory damages and $100,000 punitive damages to Olson. After the trial court denied his motion for a new trial or, in the alternative, remittitur, Walker brought this appeal.

ISSUES

Walker raises the following issues:

(1) Whether the evidence at trial was insufficient to warrant punitive damages;

(2) Whether the $100,000 punitive damages award is excessive and the result of passion and prejudice;

(3) Whether the punitive damages award is unconstitutional because it violates Walker's due process rights, is an excessive fine, or constitutes double jeopardy; and

(4) Whether the trial court erred by refusing to instruct the jury to disregard certain testimony regarding arthritic changes in Olson's lower back.

Additional facts will be added as necessary for the discussion of each issue.

FIGURE 3.3
continued

I. PUNITIVE DAMAGES AWARD

Walker argues that the evidence at trial was insufficient to warrant a punitive damages instruction. Specifically, he argues that there was no evidence that Walker intended to injure Olson or that he knowingly and consciously disregarded a substantial risk of harm to Olson or others.

Although an award of punitive damages should be upheld if there is any reasonable evidence to support it, an award may be reversed when the punitive damages issue has been submitted to the jury on slight and inconclusive evidence. *Filasky v. Preferred Risk Mutual Ins. Co.*, 152 Ariz. 591, 599, 734 P.2d 76, 84 (1987). To properly analyze Walker's argument, we must examine the punitive damages standard that has evolved in recent years and then determine whether there was more than slight or inconclusive evidence to warrant an award.

A. *Punitive Damages Standard*

[1] Punitive damages are awarded primarily to punish the wrongdoer and deter others from similar conduct. *Linthicum v. Nationwide Life Ins. Co.*, 150 Ariz. 326, 330, 723 P.2d 675, 679 (1986). The award of punitive damages is limited to situations where these objectives can be furthered. *Gurule v. Illinois Mutual Life and Casualty Co.*, 152 Ariz. 600, 601, 734 P.2d 85, 86 (1987). Punitive damages are therefore awarded only where the defendant's wrongful conduct is the result of an "evil mind," something more than the mere commission of a tort. *Linthicum*, 150 Ariz. at 330, 723 P.2d at 679. Accordingly, the primary inquiry is based on the wrongdoer's state of mind or attitude. *Id.* An evil mind is found where the defendant intended to injure the plaintiff, or where the defendant, not intending to cause injury, "consciously pursued a course of conduct knowing that it created a substantial risk of significant harm to others." *Rawlings v. Apodaca*, 151 Ariz. 149, 162, 726 P.2d 565, 578 (1986). An evil mind can be inferred when the defendant's conduct is so outrageous or egregious that it can be assumed he intended to injure or that he

consciously disregarded the substantial risk of harm created by his conduct. *Gurule*, 152 Ariz. at 602, 734 P.2d at 87; *Rawlings*, 151 Ariz. at 162–63, 726 P.2d at 578–79.

The Arizona Supreme Court first announced the standard described above in insurance bad-faith cases. *See Rawlings; Linthicum.* The court correspondingly imposed a more stringent standard of proof, thereby allowing the recovery of punitive damages only upon clear and convincing evidence of the defendant's evil mind. *Linthicum*, 150 Ariz. at 332, 723 P.2d at 681; *see also Gurule.* These standards have since been applied to other types of cases, including products liability, *see Volz v. Coleman Co.*, 155 Ariz. 567, 748 P.2d 1191 (1987), and personal injury actions. *See Ranburger v. Southern Pacific Transportation Co.*, 157 Ariz. 551, 760 P.2d 551 (1988).

[2] Previously, the question of punitive damages against intoxicated drivers was allowed to go to the jury upon a showing of gross or wanton negligence. *E.g., Smith v. Chapman*, 115 Ariz. 211, 564 P.2d 900 (1977); *Rustin v. Cook*, 143 Ariz. 486, 694 P.2d 316 (App.1984). The current standard for awarding punitive damages developed by recent case law applies to these types of cases and must be utilized in determining whether punitive damages are recoverable in this case.

B. *Sufficiency of the Evidence*

We must next determine whether the evidence was clear and convincing that Walker acted with an "evil mind," in that he consciously pursued a course of conduct knowing it created a substantial risk of significant harm to others.

In support of the punitive damages award, Olson points to Walker's testimony that he knew that it was dangerous to drive while intoxicated, and that intoxicated drivers create a substantial risk of harm to others. Olson also refers us to the following evidence:

[5]

(1) Walker's intoxilyzer test results were .14 and .15 percent one hour after the

FIGURE 3.3
continued

accident. An expert toxicologist testified that Walker consumed at least ten beers during the hour he admits he was drinking and that his blood alcohol level would have been at least .155 percent at the time of the accident;

(2) There was testimony that Walker took 20 mg. of Valium 25 minutes before the accident. The Valium and alcohol would have enhanced the effects of each other;

[6]   (3) Walker drove recklessly before the accident and caused another driver to take evasive action;

(4) Walker was speeding at the time of the accident;

(5) Walker did not brake or take other evasive action until after he collided with Olson's motorcycle;

(6) Walker attempted to flee the scene and was physically restrained by two bystanders; and

(7) Walker was agitated after he was arrested and stated that he needed more Valium.

Although Olson suggests that a determination of voluntary intoxication is sufficient to warrant a punitive damages instruction, he claims there is abundant additional evidence showing Walker's "evil mind" and the punitive damages award should therefore be affirmed.

Walker, on the other hand, contends that a plaintiff must show more than defendant's voluntary intoxication; he must show that when the defendant got into his car to drive, he either *knew* he was too intoxicated to drive safely, or that he deliberately became intoxicated knowing he would later drive. Walker points to his own testimony that he did not feel that his driving ability was impaired when he left the bar and that he did not *know* he might be creating a substantial risk of significant harm to others by driving. There is no evidence, he claims, that he became intoxicated knowing he would later create a substantial risk of harm to others by driving.

[7]   He points to undisputed testimony that he met with his two companions to discuss business and to relax after work, as op-posed to becoming intoxicated, and that one of his companions taught an accounting class after consuming the same amount of alcohol as Walker.

[3]   We do not agree with Walker's ultimate conclusion that there was no evidence to support a punitive damages jury instruction. Walker ignores the fact that an evil mind can be inferred by egregious or outrageous conduct. We believe there was sufficient evidence that Walker's conduct was so outrageous that an evil mind could be inferred.

Preliminarily, we note that we are looking beyond the undisputed evidence that Walker was negligent, or even grossly negligent, as he candidly admits. Viewing the evidence most favorably to supporting the verdict, Walker's blood-alcohol level indicated that he drank at least ten beers within the one-hour period he admits he was drinking. This large amount of alcohol in a short period of time supports an inference that he intended to become intoxicated or at least knew that would be the result. In addition, he took 20 mg. of Valium. Even assuming Walker did not know he was intoxicated when he sat behind the wheel of his car, he does not claim he did not know he had been drinking. Between the drinking and the Valium, it can be readily inferred that Walker disregarded the fact that his ability to drive safely was impaired, thereby creating a substantial risk of significant harm to others. Walker drove to the bar, and he does not suggest he intended to leave by another method. When he left, he drove recklessly and was speeding in the middle turn lane, instead of driving cautiously in an attempt to minimize the risk to others.   [9]

This evidence amply supports a finding of an evil mind. To hold otherwise based on Walker's testimony that he neither knew of nor consciously disregarded the substantial risk he was creating would be tantamount to determining punitive damages exclusively on a defendant's own testimony of his lack of an evil mind, even when his conduct indicates otherwise. The mental states of intent and knowledge can-

[8]

FIGURE 3.3
continued

not be disproved on a defendant's mere denial of them.

[4] It is sufficient that Walker *should* have known that his conduct was so egregious that it created a substantial risk of harm to others. *See Linthicum,* 150 Ariz. at 330, 723 P.2d at 679 ("It is only when the wrongdoer *should* be consciously aware ... that his conduct is so outrageous, oppressive or intolerable....") (emphasis added). In *White v. Mitchell,* 157 Ariz. 523, 759 P.2d 1327 (App.1988), this court upheld a punitive damages award against a truck driver based upon testimony that an experienced driver *would* have known the brakes were unsafe. We concluded that even though the evidence was circumstantial, the jury could have found that the driver knew the truck was unsafe, giving rise to a substantial risk of serious injury to other drivers and pedestrians. *Id.* at 529, 759 P.2d at 1333. In this case, a person who knows it is unsafe to drink and drive would have known it was unsafe to drive after drinking ten beers in an hour.

Walker's reliance on case law from other jurisdictions is misplaced. For example, he cites *Baker v. Marcus,* 201 Va. 905, 114 S.E.2d 617 (Ct.App.1960) in which a Virginia court refused to sustain a punitive damages award against an intoxicated driver. The reason for the court's holding, however, was that the facts did not indicate the accident was the result of the defendant's intoxication, as opposed to simple negligence when she momentarily took her eyes off the road. *Id.* at 910, 114 S.E.2d at 621. The defendant's degree of intoxication was considered "borderline" and she was only charged with reckless driving. *Id.* at 907, 114 S.E.2d at 619; *see also Miskin v. Carter,* 761 P.2d 1378 (Utah 1988). Similarly, in *Detling v. Chockley,* 70 Ohio St.2d 134, 139, 436 N.E.2d 208, 212 (1982), the court held that punitive damages were not recoverable against a drunk driver where there were *no surrounding circumstances* demonstrating the malice required to impose punitive damages. In *Gesslein v. Britton,* 175 Kan. 661, 266 P.2d 263 (1954), the court refused to allow a claim for punitive damages based on the defendant's intoxication

alone because the plaintiff had failed to allege any facts showing "gross and wanton negligence." The fact that the defendant drove while intoxicated was insufficient standing alone to award punitive damages. *Id.* at 664, 266 P.2d at 265.

By contrast, here there was clear and convincing evidence that Walker's intoxication was well beyond borderline and that the accident occurred solely because he was intoxicated. In addition, Walker had taken Valium and was driving recklessly in excess of the speed limit. Intoxication alone, in the absence of other compelling circumstances, may not warrant punitive damages. *E.g., Biswell v. Duncan,* 742 P.2d 80 (Utah Ct.App.1987). In this case, however, additional circumstances beyond intoxication were clearly shown. The trial court properly allowed the question of punitive damages to go to the jury. [10] [11]

II. AMOUNT OF PUNITIVE DAMAGES

Walker next argues that the $100,000 punitive damages award is excessive and that the jury acted out of passion or prejudice. Such an award, he argues, will destroy him financially. At the time of trial, Walker claimed his business was in bankruptcy, that he supported his wife and two children on an annual income of $38,000, that he had about $4,000 in the bank, and after paying bills had approximately $500 left over every month. He contends that $100,000 is well beyond the average working person's ability to pay. He points out that, even assuming he had $500 to pay at the end of every month, it would take him nearly seventeen years to pay the award, excluding any interest.

Olson responds that although Walker's employer was in bankruptcy, there was no evidence that Walker had ever filed bankruptcy. He also points out that Walker's income the year previous to trial was $44,356 and that Walker owns his own home.

As a general rule, the amount of a punitive damages award is within the fact finder's discretion and will not be disturbed on appeal, unless it is so unreasonable that it is the product of passion or prejudice.

of this case is largely determined by the facts. So let us look at some specific facts and decide whether they are essential to the case.

Blood Alcohol Level

Is the blood alcohol level of the defendant (Walker) an essential fact? The court offers us several clues to indicate that it is. First, in its litany of facts at the beginning of the opinion, the court notes that Walker's blood alcohol level was estimated to be .155 percent at the time of the accident. [4] (The numbers in brackets refer to the numbered sentences in the opinion.) Second, the court includes the defendant's blood alcohol level in its list of the factors that the plaintiff (Olson) relied on in arguing that a punitive damage award was justified. [5] Third, the court uses this blood alcohol level (translated into number of beers consumed) to support its contention that sufficient evidence existed to conclude that the defendant created a substantial risk of significant harm to others and, therefore, acted with the requisite evil mind. [8] We can reasonably infer that had the defendant's blood alcohol level been lower, the court might not have been persuaded that punitive damages were justified. Fourth, the court looks to other case law in which the defendants' intoxication was considered "borderline." [10] The court then distinguishes that case law from the case before it on the grounds that Walker's intoxication was not "borderline." This discussion is yet another indication that the court focused strongly on the extent of the defendant's intoxication in terms of blood alcohol content.

Of course, we do not know the dividing line for the court in terms of blood alcohol content. Would the court have decided differently, for example, if the defendant's blood alcohol level had been below the presumptive level of .100 percent? We do know that the court considered blood alcohol level in conjunction with a number of other factors and that the court considered the totality of the facts in arriving at its conclusion. Therefore, we cannot definitively predict that a lower blood alcohol level by itself would have altered the court's decision. However, the myriad of facts the court examined does not lessen the importance of the blood alcohol level. Even though a different blood alcohol level alone may not necessarily have altered the court's decision, it was certainly a key factor in the court's reasoning. The frequent mention of this fact by the court and its inclusion in the court's reasoning process earns it the status of an essential fact.

Reckless Driving

What about the fact that the defendant was driving recklessly before the accident? Again, the court mentions the defendant's reckless behavior in its original declaration of the facts. [2] It also mentions that the plaintiff included this factor in the evidence that the plaintiff contended justified punitive damages. [6] The court does not focus as intently on the defendant's reckless driving as it does on his intoxication, but it does allude to the defendant's driving in its reasoning. The court's contention that the defendant's reckless driving after leaving the bar reflected outrageous conduct is based on its observation that he had the option of driving more cautiously in his intoxicated state to minimize the risk to others. [9] In its conclusion, the court includes the fact that the defendant had driven recklessly in its evidence that the defendant's intoxication surpassed being "borderline." [11] The court's extensive reliance on the defendant's recklessness in its reasoning strongly supports classifying this as an essential fact.

Attempt to Flee Scene

A fact that the court includes in its recitation of facts, and one that the plaintiff includes in the laundry list of factors supporting a claim of punitive damages, is the defendant's attempt to flee the scene and his restraint by two bystanders. [3] The court does not, however, allude to this fact in its reasoning, and this makes the argument that it is an essential fact a little less compelling. You could certainly argue, however, that this fact corroborates the extreme recklessness of the defendant and further supports the court's conclusion that the defendant acted with an "evil mind." On the other hand, the court probably would not have altered its conclusion had the defendant remained voluntarily at the scene. This fact should not be included in an issue statement. Although the court and the plaintiff mentioned it and it was part of the totality of facts that made the defendant's conduct outrageous, it does not appear to be key to the court's reasoning. This is a significant fact that should be included in the statement of facts of a brief to provide a complete picture of how the defendant behaved.

Drinking with Colleagues

A fact that is certainly not essential to the court's opinion and probably not even significant is that the defendant was drinking with colleagues prior to driving. [1] Although the court mentions this in its original outline of the facts and the defendant uses this fact to argue that he was merely socializing with friends and had no intention of getting drunk [7], the court dismisses this argument summarily and never alludes to this fact in either its reasoning or its conclusion. Without question, this fact would not be included in an issue statement, and many attorneys would not include it in the facts section of a brief, although clearly it would not be "wrong" to do so. The decision to not include it in the facts section is based primarily on the court's rather curt dismissal of this fact in its discussion and its failure to consider it in its reasoning.

COMPLEX FACT PATTERNS

Now let us examine a case with a more complicated factual scenario—*Frigaliment Importing Co. v. B.N.S. International Sales Corp.* Read this case before going on.

FRIGALIMENT IMPORTING CO., Ltd., Plaintiff,
v.
B.N.S. INTERNATIONAL SALES CORP., Defendant.
United States District Court
S. D. New York.
Dec. 27, 1960.

Action by buyer of fresh frozen chicken against seller for breach of warranty. The District Court, Friendly, Circuit Judge, held that buyer failed to sustain its burden of proving that the word "chicken" in contract referred only to chickens suitable for broiling and frying, and did not include stewing chickens.

Complaint dismissed.

1. Sales k441(1)

In action by buyer of fresh frozen chicken against seller for breach of warranty, buyer failed to sustain its burden of proving that the word "chicken" in contract referred only to chickens suitable for broiling and frying, and did not include stewing chickens. Personal Property Law N.Y. § 95.

See publication Words and Phrases, for other judicial constructions and definitions of "Chicken".

2. Contracts k284(1)

Where parties failed to avail themselves of contractual provision whereby any disputes were to be settled by arbitration by produce exchange, the court would treat such failure as an agreement eliminating that clause of the contract.

3. Customs and Usages k12 (1, 2)

Under New York law, in order to establish that a term in a contract has a definite trade meaning, if one of the parties is not a member of the trade, it must either be shown that that party had actual knowledge of the usage, or that usage is so generally known in community that actual individual knowledge of it may be inferred, and to show the latter it must be shown that usage is of such long continuance, so well established, so notorious, so universal and so reasonable in itself, that the presumption is violent that the parties contracted with reference to it and made it part of their agreement. Personal Property Law N.Y. § 95.

4. Customs and Usages k19 (3)

A witness' consistent failure to rely on an alleged trade usage, which his testimony is supposed to establish, deprives his opinion testimony of much of its effect.

Riggs, Ferris & Geer, New York City (John P. Hale, New York City, of counsel), for plaintiff.

Sereni, Herzfeld & Rubin, New York City (Herbert Rubin, Walter Herzfeld, New York City, of counsel), for defendant.

FRIENDLY, Circuit Judge.

[1] The issue is, what is chicken? Plaintiff says "chicken" means a young chicken, suitable for broiling and frying. Defendant says "chicken" means any bird of that genus that meets contract specifications on weight and quality, including what it calls "stewing chicken" and plaintiff perjoratively terms "fowl". Dictionaries give both meanings, as well as some others not relevant here. To support its, plaintiff sends a number of volleys over the net; defendant essays to return them and adds a few serves of its own. Assuming that both parties were acting in good faith, the case nicely illustrates Holmes' remark "that the making of a contract depends not on the agreement of two minds in one intention, but on the agreement of two sets of external signs—not on the parties' having *meant* the same thing but on their having *said* the same thing." The Path of the Law, in Collected Legal Papers, p. 178: I have concluded that plaintiff has not sustained its burden of persuasion that the contract used "chicken" in the narrower sense.

[2] The action is for breach of the warranty that goods sold shall correspond to the description, New York Personal Property Law, McKinney's Consol. Laws, c. 41, § 95. Two contracts are in suit. In the first, dated May 2, 1957, defendant, a New York sales corporation, confirmed the sale to plaintiff, a Swiss corporation, of

> "US Fresh Frozen Chicken, Grade A, Government Inspected, Eviscerated
> 2½–3 lbs. and 1½–2 lbs. each
> all chicken individually wrapped in cryovac, packed in secured fiber cartons or wooden boxes, suitable for export
> 75,000 lbs. 2½–3 lbs ....@$33.00
> 25,000 lbs. 1½–2 lbs ....@$36.50
> per 100 lbs. FAS New York

> scheduled May 10, 1957 pursuant to instructions from Penson & Co., New York."[1]

The second contract, also dated May 2, 1957, was identical save that only 50,000 lbs. of the heavier "chicken" were called for, the price of the smaller birds was $37 per 100 lbs., and shipment was scheduled for May 30. The initial shipment under the first contract was short but the balance was shipped on May 17. When the initial shipment arrived in Switzerland, plaintiff found, on May 28, that the 2½–3 lbs. birds were not young chicken suitable for broiling and frying but stewing chicken or "fowl"; indeed, many of the cartons and bags plainly so indicated. Protests ensued. Nevertheless, shipment under the second contract was made on May 29, the 2½–3 lbs. birds again being stewing chicken. Defendant stopped the transportation of these at Rotterdam.

This action followed. Plaintiff says that, notwithstanding that its acceptance was in Switzerland, New

---

1. The court notes the contract provision whereby any disputes are to be settled by arbitration by the New York Produce Exchange; it treats the parties' failure to avail themselves of this remedy as an agreement eliminating that clause of the contract.

York law controls under the principle of Rubin v. Irving Trust Co., 1953, 305 N.Y. 288, 305, 113 N.E.2d 424, 431; defendant does not dispute this, and relies on New York decisions. I shall follow the apparent agreement of the parties as to the applicable law.

Since the word "chicken" standing alone is ambiguous, I turn first to see whether the contract itself offers any aid to its interpretation. Plaintiff says the 1½–2 lbs. birds necessarily had to be young chicken since the older birds do not come in that size, hence the 2½–3 lbs. birds must likewise be young. This is unpersuasive—a contract for "apples" of two different sizes could be filled with different kinds of apples even though only one species came in both sizes. Defendant notes that the contract called not simply for chicken but for "US Fresh Frozen Chicken, Grade A, Government Inspected." It says the contract thereby incorporated by reference the Department of Agriculture's regulations, which favor its interpretation; I shall return to this after reviewing plaintiff's other contentions.

The first hinges on an exchange of cablegrams which preceded execution of the formal contracts. The negotiations leading up to the contracts were conducted in New York between defendant's secretary, Ernest R. Bauer, and a Mr. Stovicek, who was in New York for the Czechoslovak government at the World Trade Fair. A few days after meeting Bauer at the fair, Stovicek telephoned and inquired whether defendant would be interested in exporting poultry to Switzerland. Bauer then met with Stovicek, who showed him a cable from plaintiff dated April 26, 1957, announcing that they "are buyer" of 25,000 lbs. of chicken 2½–3 lbs. weight, Cryovac packed, grade A Government inspected, at a price up to 33¢ per pound, for shipment on May 10, to be confirmed by the following morning, and were interested in further offerings. After testing the market for price, Bauer accepted, and Stovicek sent a confirmation that evening. Plaintiff stresses that, although these and subsequent cables between plaintiff and defendant, which laid the basis for the additional quantities under the first and for all of the second contract, were predominantly in German, they used the English word "chicken"; it claims this was done because it understood "chicken" meant young chicken whereas the German word, "Huhn," included both "Brathuhn" (broilers) and "Suppenhuhn" (stewing chicken), and that defendant, whose officers were thoroughly conversant with German, should have realized this. Whatever force this argument might otherwise have is largely drained away by Bauer's testimony that he asked Stovicek what kind of chickens were wanted, received the answer "any kind of chickens," and then, in German, asked whether the cable meant "Huhn" and received an affirmative re-

sponse. Plaintiff attacks this as contrary to what Bauer testified on his deposition in March, 1959, and also on the ground that Stovicek had no authority to interpret the meaning of the cable. The first contention would be persuasive if sustained by the record, since Bauer was free at the trial from the threat of contradiction by Stovicek as he was not at the time of the deposition; however, review of the deposition does not convince me of the claimed inconsistency. As to the second contention, it may well be that Stovicek lacked authority to commit plaintiff for prices or delivery dates other than those specified in the cable; but plaintiff cannot at the same time rely on its cable to Stovicek as its dictionary to the meaning of the contract and repudiate the interpretation given the dictionary by the man in whose hands it was put. See Restatement of the Law of Agency, 2d, § 145; 2 Mecham, Agency § 1781 (2d ed. 1914); Park v. Moorman Mfg. Co., 1952, 121 Utah 339, 241 P.2d 914, 919, 40 A.L.R.2d 273; Henderson v. Jimmerson, Tex.Civ.App.1950, 234 S.W.2d 710, 717–718. Plaintiff's reliance on the fact that the contract forms contain the words "through the intermediary of:
", with the blank not filled, as negating agency, is wholly unpersuasive; the purpose of this clause was to permit filling in the name of an intermediary to whom a commission would be payable, not to blot out what had been the fact.

[3] Plaintiff's next contention is that there was a definite trade usage that "chicken" meant "young chicken." Defendant showed that it was only beginning in the poultry trade in 1957, thereby bringing itself within the principle that "when one of the parties is not a member of the trade or other circle, his acceptance of the standard must be made to appear" by proving either that he had actual knowledge of the usage or that the usage is "so generally known in the community that his actual individual knowledge of it may be inferred." 9 Wigmore, Evidence (3d ed. 1940) § 2464. Here there was no proof of actual knowledge of the alleged usage; indeed, it is quite plain that defendant's belief was to the contrary. In order to meet the alternative requirement, the law of New York demands a showing that "the usage is of so long continuance, so well established, so notorious, so universal and so reasonable in itself, as that the presumption is violent that the parties contracted with reference to it, and made it a part of their agreement." Walls v. Bailey, 1872, 49 N.Y. 464, 472–473.

[4] Plaintiff endeavored to establish such a usage by the testimony of three witnesses and certain other evidence. Strasser, resident buyer in New York for a large chain of Swiss cooperatives, testified that "on chicken I would definitely understand a boiler." However, the force of this testimony was considerably

weakened by the fact that in his own transactions the witness, a careful businessman, protected himself by using "broiler" when that was what he wanted and "fowl" when he wished older birds. Indeed, there are some indications, dating back to a remark of Lord Mansfield, Edie v. East India Co., 2 Burr. 1216, 1222 (1761), that no credit should be given "witnesses to usage, who could not adduce instances in verification." 7 Wigmore, Evidence (3d ed. 1940), § 1954; see McDonald v. Acker, Merrall & Condit Co., 2d Dept. 1920, 192 App.Div. 123, 126, 182 N.Y.S. 607. While Wigmore thinks this goes too far, a witness' consistent failure to rely on the alleged usage deprives his opinion testimony of much of its effect. Niesielowski, an officer of one of the companies that had furnished the stewing chicken to defendant, testified that "chicken" meant "the male species of the poultry industry. That could be a broiler, a fryer or a roaster", but not a stewing chicken; however, he also testified that upon receiving defendant's inquiry for "chickens", he asked whether the desire was for "fowl or frying chickens" and, in fact, supplied fowl, although taking the precaution of asking defendant, a day or two after plaintiff's acceptance of the contracts in suit, to change its confirmation of its order from "chickens," as defendant had originally prepared it, to "stewing chickens." Dates, an employee of Urner-Barry Company, which publishes a daily market report on the poultry trade, gave it as his view that the trade meaning of "chicken" was "broilers and fryers." In addition to this opinion testimony, plaintiff relied on the fact that the Urner-Barry service, the Journal of Commerce, and Weinberg Bros. & Co. of Chicago, a large supplier of poultry, published quotations in a manner which, in one way or another, distinguish between "chicken," comprising broilers, fryers and certain other categories, and "fowl," which, Bauer acknowledged, included stewing chickens. This material would be impressive if there were nothing to the contrary. However, there was, as will now be seen.

Defendant's witness Weininger, who operates a chicken eviscerating plant in New Jersey, testified "Chicken is everything except a goose, a duck, and a turkey. Everything is a chicken, but then you have to say, you have to specify which category you want or that you are talking about." Its witness Fox said that in the trade "chicken" would encompass all the various classifications. Sadina, who conducts a food inspection service, testified that he would consider any bird coming within the classes of "chicken" in the Department of Agriculture's regulations to be a chicken. The specifications approved by the General Services Administration include fowl as well as broilers and fryers under the classification "chickens." Statistics of the Institute of American Poultry Industries

use the phrases "Young chickens" and "Mature chickens," under the general heading "Total chickens." and the Department of Agriculture's daily and weekly price reports avoid use of the word "chicken" without specification.

Defendant advances several other points which it claims affirmatively support its construction. Primary among these is the regulation of the Department of Agriculture, 7 C.F.R. § 70.300–70.370, entitled, "Grading and Inspection of Poultry and Edible Products Thereof." and in particular § 70.301 which recited:

> "*Chickens.* The following are the various classes of chickens:
> (a) Broiler or fryer . . .
> (b) Roaster . . .
> (c) Capon . . .
> (d) Stag . . .
> (e) Hen or stewing chicken or fowl . . .
> (f) Cock or old rooster . . .

Defendant argues, as previously noted, that the contract incorporated these regulations by reference. Plaintiff answers that the contract provision related simply to grade and Government inspection and did not incorporate the Government definition of "chicken," and also that the definition in the Regulations is ignored in the trade. However, the latter contention was contradicted by Weininger and Sadina; and there is force in defendant's argument that the contract made the regulations a dictionary, particularly since the reference to Government grading was already in plaintiff's initial cable to Stovicek.

Defendant makes a further argument based on the impossibility of its obtaining broilers and fryers at the 33¢ price offered by plaintiff for the 2½–3 lbs. birds. There is no substantial dispute that, in late April, 1957, the price for 2½–3 lbs. broilers was between 35 and 37¢ per pound, and that when defendant entered into the contracts, it was well aware of this and intended to fill them by supplying fowl in these weights. It claims that plaintiff must likewise have known the market since plaintiff had reserved shipping space on April 23, three days before plaintiff's cable to Stovicek, or, at least, that Stovicek was chargeable with such knowledge. It is scarcely an answer to say, as plaintiff does in its brief, that the 33¢ price offered by the 2½–3 lbs. "chickens" was closer to the prevailing 35¢ price for broilers than to the 30¢ at which defendant procured fowl. Plaintiff must have expected defendant to make some profit—certainly it could not have expected defendant deliberately to incur a loss.

Finally, defendant relies on conduct by the plaintiff after the first shipment had been received. On

May 28 plaintiff sent two cables complaining that the larger birds in the first shipment constituted "fowl." Defendant answered with a cable refusing to recognize plaintiff's objection and announcing "We have today ready for shipment 50,000 lbs. chicken 2½–3 lbs. 25,000 lbs. broilers 1½–2 lbs.," these being the goods procured for shipment under the second contract, and asked immediate answer "whether we are to ship this merchandise to you and whether you will accept the merchandise." After several other cable exchanges, plaintiff replied on May 29 "Confirm again that merchandise is to be shipped since resold by us if not enough pursuant to contract chickens are shipped the missing quantity is to be shipped within ten days stop we resold to our customers pursuant to your contract chickens grade A you have to deliver us said merchandise we again state that we shall make you fully responsible for all resulting costs."[2] Defendant argues that if plaintiff was sincere in thinking it was entitled to young chickens, plaintiff would not have allowed the shipment under the second contract to go forward, since the distinction between broilers and chickens drawn in defendant's cablegram must have made it clear that the larger birds would not be broilers. However, plaintiff answers that the cables show plaintiff was insisting on delivery of young chickens and that defendant shipped old ones at its peril. Defendant's point would be highly relevant on another disputed issue—whether if liability were established, the measure of damages should be the

difference in market value of broilers and stewing chicken in New York or the larger difference in Europe, but I cannot give it weight on the issue of interpretation. Defendant points out also that plaintiff proceeded to deliver some of the larger birds in Europe, describing them as "poulets"; defendant argues that it was only when plaintiff's customers complained about this that plaintiff developed the idea that "chicken" meant "yong chicken." There is little force in this in view of plaintiff's immediate and consistent protests.

When all the evidence is reviewed, it is clear that defendant believed it could comply with the contracts by delivering stewing chicken in the 2½–3 lbs. size. Defendant's subjective intent would not be significant if this did not coincide with an objective meaning of "chicken." Here it did coincide with one of the dictionary meanings, with the definition in the Department of Agriculture Regulations to which the contract made at least oblique reference, with at least some usage in the trade, with the realities of the market, and with what plaintiff's spokesman had said. Plaintiff asserts it to be equally plain that plaintiff's own subjective intent was to obtain broilers and fryers; the only evidence against this is the material as to market prices and this may not have been sufficiently brought home. In any event it is unnecessary to determine that issue. For plaintiff has the burden of showing that "chicken" was used in the narrower rather than in the broader sense, and this it has not sustained.

This opinion constitutes the Court's findings of fact and conclusions of law. Judgment shall be entered dismissing the complaint with costs.

---

2. These cables were in German; "chicken," "broilers," and, on some occasions, "fowl," were in English.

Notice that *Frigaliment* contains a considerably more complex fact pattern than the other cases you have been exposed to. Rather than trying to master the factual intricacies, observe in general how you can deal with convoluted scenarios, especially those that are replete with insignificant details.

First, notice that the facts are strewn throughout the opinion rather than condensed at the beginning of the case, as courts typically do. To fully comprehend what the parties did, you will find it helpful to construct a time line of events. Doing this will not only help you clarify the chronology of events but will assist you in understanding the negotiation process and transactions the parties entered into.

Although the court discusses the provisions of the contract before discussing the parties' negotiations, the time line you construct should indicate the actual sequence of events.

Date	Transaction
April 23	P reserves shipping space; at this time, price of 2½–3-pound chickens is 35 to 37 cents per pound.
April 26	P sends cable indicating intent to buy 2½–3-pound chickens on May 10 at 33 cents per pound.
April ?	D accepts P's offer.
April ?	Supplier of chickens to D asks D to clarify whether "frying chickens" or "fowl" are desired.
May 2	D confirms sale to P for two contracts (one due May 10 and the other due May 30).
May 10	First shipment of chickens is sent.
May 17	Balance of chickens under first contract is sent.
May 28	P protests that chickens are stewing chickens (also called "fowl").
May 28	D fails to respond to P's objections and asks whether P will accept shipment.
May 29	P responds to D's telegram, and D ships chickens.

Notice that the dates and some of the details of the parties' transactions are insignificant facts. Nevertheless, if you are to really grasp the parties' arguments and the court's reasoning, you must understand the sequence of events leading up to the standoff between the parties. The defendant argues, for example, that it was justified in relying on the plaintiff's conduct in interpreting the word "chicken." To appreciate this argument, you must be aware of the plaintiff's conduct after receiving the first shipment of chickens and the defendant's response. By reconstructing their communiques, you can begin to see the source of the parties' confusion and their justification for their interpretations. The court does not discuss the chain of events leading up to the suit sequentially, so a time line assists you in retracing the parties' actions.

Having graphically represented the chronology of events, you can then summarize the essential and significant facts. Even though you will not include all of the details from your time line in your summary, you will find your completion of the time line to be helpful in organizing your summary. Your summary of the facts might look as follows.

> Defendant-seller (a New York sales corporation) entered into negotiations with plaintiff-buyer (a Swiss corporation) regarding the purchase of chickens. When asked by defendant's representative what kind of chickens plaintiff wanted, plaintiff's spokesman replied "any kind of chicken," and when asked to clarify an ambiguous cable, plaintiff's spokesman affirmed that the cable was intended to apply to the purchase of either stewing or broiler chickens. Two contracts were entered into via cablegrams. Plaintiff agreed to buy the chickens, believing them to be broiler chickens, while the defendant believed it was selling stewing chickens (also called "fowl"). Stewing chickens were worth 35 to 37 cents per pound at the time; plaintiff-buyer paid 33 cents per pound for the chickens it purchased. After receiving the first shipment of chickens, which was short, plaintiff-buyer sent two cables, complaining that the chickens were "fowl." Defendant-seller refused to rec-

ognize plaintiff-buyer's complaint and asked whether plaintiff-buyer would accept its shipment. Based on plaintiff-buyer's ambiguous response, defendant-seller shipped stewing chickens to complete first order and fill second order.

You might have included additional facts had you written this case brief. In fact, some attorneys and paralegals might very well disagree with whether individual facts should be included. As mentioned previously in this chapter, disagreements regarding the classification of essential, significant, and insignificant facts are common. As long as you err on the side of including too many facts in your facts section, you will not undermine your case analysis. With experience, you will learn to delete unnecessary facts and to focus on those that are most important.

CHAPTER SUMMARY

Essential facts are facts whose absence or modification could alter the outcome of a case. Significant facts are those background and historical facts that assist the reader in understanding the dispute. Insignificant facts are those facts that are neither essential nor significant. Issue statements contain essential facts; the facts sections of case briefs and legal memoranda contain significant and essential facts.

In deciding whether a fact is essential, consider the terminology the court uses in referring to the fact, whether the court repeatedly refers to the fact, how the court reacts to the parties' evaluation of the fact and the lower tribunal's treatment of the fact, and how the court deals with contrasting facts in other cases. The distinction between essential facts, significant facts, and insignificant facts is not always clear and can certainly be debated.

Complicated fact patterns can be better understood when they are reduced to time lines, charts, symbolic maps, or other aids that visually depict relationships and time sequences.

KEY TERMS

essential fact   insignificant fact   significant fact

COGNITIVE CALISTHENICS

1. Identify each of the following facts in *Olson v. Walker* as either essential or significant. Explain your reasoning.
   (a) Defendant took 20 mg of Valium approximately one-half hour before the accident.
   (b) Defendant was traveling 50 to 55 mph in a 40-mph speed zone before the accident.
   (c) Plaintiff was turning left when Defendant rear-ended him.
   (d) Defendant was agitated after the accident and said he needed more Valium.
   (e) An expert testified that Defendant consumed at least ten beers an hour before the accident.
   (f) The jury awarded Plaintiff $100,000 in punitive damages.

(g) Defendant had an annual income of $38,000.

(h) If Defendant pays $500 per month, he will need 17 years to pay off the punitive damage award of $100,000.

2. Read the following cases in Appendix A and prepare a summary of the essential and significant facts. (Answers are found in Appendix B on page 353.)

(a) *Linthicum v. Nationwide Life Ins. Co.*

(b) *White v. Mitchell*

(c) *Nienstedt v. Wetzel*

3. Read the following cases and prepare a summary of the essential and significant facts.

(a) *Cundick v. Broadbent*

(b) *Matter of Estate of Swenson*

(c) *BenShalom v. Marsh*

(d) *Minnesota v. Dickerson*

CHAPTER FOUR

ISSUES AND HOLDINGS

Chapter Objectives

In this chapter you will learn:

- How to identify issues and holdings.

- How to distinguish between holdings and findings.

- How to distinguish between holdings and dicta.

- How to recognize clues given by courts that assist in the identification of issues.

- How to write an issue statement and a holding.

Have you ever walked up to friends who were engaged in a conversation and tried to figure out from the context of their discussion what they were talking about? Or have you ever sat in class and listened to a professor drone on for what seemed like hours without ever understanding the point? Frustrating experiences, weren't they? The frustration resulted from not knowing the question being addressed. The same frustration can be experienced in reading a case in which you are not clear about the question the court is answering. In legal terms, the question of law the court is answering is referred to as the **issue**.

Before you can begin to comprehend a court's reasoning, you must comprehend the issue. You cannot resolve a legal issue until you are crystal clear on what the question is. You might be surprised at how easy it is to misinterpret a legal issue. If you find that you do not understand a court's conclusion or the thought process that resulted in that conclusion, you need to check first to make sure that your concept of the issue squares with the court's concept of the issue. What appear to be inconsistencies in the court's logic may disappear when you come to grips with the question being answered.

HOLDINGS VS. FINDINGS

Before examining issue statements in more depth, you need to understand the relationship between **holdings** and **findings**. Issue statements involve questions of

FIGURE 4.1
The Relationship
between Holdings
and Findings

HOLDING VS. FINDING

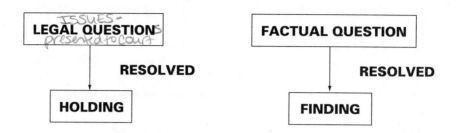

law, such as whether the parties were negligent, whether a contract was formed, or whether a statute was violated. Questions of fact, on the other hand, are usually relegated to trial courts to resolve and are rarely considered by appellate courts. Factual questions revolve around who did what to whom—did the defendant pull out into traffic without looking, did the testatrix sign the will, did the parties discuss the terms of the contract. A court's resolution of a question of law is called a holding. Its resolution of a factual dispute is called a finding.

Holdings and findings are related, however, in that questions of law invariably spring from factual disputes. An appellate court will accept the findings of the trial court and use those findings in creating its holding. In other words, an appellate court will not resolve the factual controversies but will apply the facts as they were identified at the trial level to shape its holding.

Suppose, for example, that a jury finds that a defendant legally entered a store but once in the building stole some valuable documents. Suppose further that the defendant appeals his conviction for burglary based on the argument that he did not commit a burglary because he did not illegally enter the building. The appellate court may use the jury's findings in its holding that defendants can be convicted of burglary even if they enter a building legally so long as they remain there for unlawful purposes.

WRITING ISSUE STATEMENTS

Using Essential Facts

Which facts must be included in issue statements? Issue statements should contain only essential facts. In a sense, issue statements serve as sieves in that they strain out the significant and insignificant facts. As you work on drafting your issue statement, you eliminate more and more facts until you are left with only those that are essential to the case.

Beginners sometimes err by eliminating even the essential facts. Such omission results in issue statements that are so broad that they are not very instructive. Let's use the hypothetical burglary case to illustrate. Someone might write this issue statement.

Did the defendant commit a burglary?

Notice that without some factual information detailing the circumstances under which the defendant was accused of committing a burglary, this statement alone

FIGURE 4.2
Issue Statements

CHARACTERISTICS OF A GOOD ISSUE STATEMENT

- ■ **Contains essential facts**
  ....

- ■ **Detailed enough to be distinguished from other cases**
  ....

- ■ **Able to stand alone and be understood**
  ....

- ■ **Able to be answered yes or no (if possible)**
  ....

is virtually meaningless. You might argue that this statement would be meaningful if read in the context of the statement of facts. While that may be true, issue statements are written with more detail for three reasons.

First, and probably most importantly, spelling out the issue in concrete terms (using the essential facts) forces you to analyze the issue to ensure that you really understand it. As in any field of scholarship, you will gain only a superficial understanding of a case by using general terms and making broad, sweeping statements. True understanding comes with specificity and detail.

Second, an issue statement should be sufficiently detailed so that the case it describes can be distinguished from other case law. If you are to successfully wend your way through the maze of case law you often encounter when researching a particular problem, you must be able to discern even subtle distinctions between cases. Writing fact-specific issue statements will assist you in doing this.

Third, an issue statement should be able to stand alone so that, in your brief, you can ascertain the issue in the context of the essential facts without having to reread the facts section. Being able to do this not only saves time but saves you from having to duplicate your efforts.

In light of this discussion, let us modify the general, vague issue statement offered above. A more helpful issue statement would frame the legal issue around the factual setting.

> Can a defendant who legally enters a building but who remains unlawfully in order to steal documents be convicted of burglary?

This formulation of the issue identifies specifically what the defendant did to be charged with burglary and includes the critical element at stake, i.e., whether burglary can be committed when the defendant enters legally.

Making the Issue Too Broad

A novice reader of our hypothetical opinion dealing with burglary might misinterpret the issue as being "Did the trial court err?" Although, generally speaking, the appellate court is examining whether the trial court committed an error, the legal question the appellate court is analyzing is more narrow. In other words, the issue must be framed more specifically to be of any value in a brief or memorandum. Ask yourself if you would find a case brief helpful in assisting you to recall the precise legal question if the issue statement simply stated "Did the trial court err?" Remember that one of the purposes of a case brief is to facilitate your recall of the key elements of a case. Therefore, the more narrowly and specifically you formulate the issue, the more informative that issue statement will be for you and others who refer to it.

How to Phrase an Issue That Can Be Answered Yes or No

Notice that the issue in the hypothetical burglary case was phrased in the form of a question that could be answered yes or no. By phrasing the issue narrowly, holdings can be simply stated as yes or no. Such simple holdings not only relieve you of some writing but make it easier to remember case law. So, while your issue statements may be rather complex, your holdings will generally be very simple.

Of course, issue statements cannot always be answered yes or no just as not all questions can be answered yes or no. The classic question used to illustrate this point is "Did you stop beating your wife?" Obviously, either a yes or no is undesirable and, hopefully, inaccurate. An accurate answer might very well require the explanation "I have never beaten my wife." By the same token, a holding may require an explanation. If the issue before the court is what standard of care is required of a driver, then the holding must reflect an explanation of that standard of care. A simple yes or no would be inadequate.

IDENTIFYING ISSUES

Court's Wording and Organization

Writing an issue statement for a case brief or legal memorandum necessitates being able to identify the issues as the court perceives them. Will the courts offer you any clues about the whereabouts of issues lurking within opinions? Well-written opinions will do just that. Courts that author such opinions will say such things as "The issue before us . . ." or "The question we are faced with . . ." Alternatively, a court may divide an opinion into various subsections, each of which deals with a different issue. One part of the opinion, for example, may be entitled "Sufficiency

Practice Pointer	While you are usually encouraged to write as simply and concisely as possible, you will discover that issue statements are often very long and sometimes complex. Such length and complexity is necessary if you are to incorporate all of the essential facts into the legal question and if you are to be able to answer the issue statement using a yes or a no. Do not abandon the general rules of good writing in preparing briefs and memoranda, but be aware of this one exception to the rule of brevity.

of Evidence," another "Equal Protection," and yet another "Competency to Testify." These titles alert you to the issue being discussed in a particular subsection and assist you in preparing your issue statements.

Even helpful courts, however, generally write incomplete issue statements. They may pose the question, for example, "Is the defendant competent to testify?" but omit the pertinent facts that inform you why and how the question of competency to testify arose. If you were to simply copy this issue for your brief or memorandum, you would be accused (and rightfully so) of writing an incomplete issue statement. Arguing that your issue statement parroted what the court had written would be an ineffective defense. Remember that a court's purpose in writing an opinion differs from your purpose in briefing a case. The court states an issue in the context of the facts previously given in the opinion, while you are attempting to summarize the issue as succinctly but as completely as possible. You are seeking to sharpen your understanding of the case and to be able to recall the case in adequate detail at a later date. The court is writing in a different context and for a different audience. Therefore, your issue statements will frequently be more detailed (by including the essential facts) than issue statements found in case law.

Court's Holdings

Although you may not be able to model your issue statement after the one written by the court, you may be able to use the court's holding to fashion your issue statement. A court's holding is sometimes a complete statement of the issue before it. A court may, for example, state:

> We, therefore, hold that those who enter a building lawfully but who remain unlawfully to steal documents may be convicted of burglary.

Turn that statement into a question, and you have an issue statement.

> Can those who enter a building lawfully but who remain unlawfully to steal documents be convicted of burglary?

You can often use this simple technique to efficiently and accurately prepare your issue statements.

Parties' Arguments

But how do you contend with courts that fail to provide even a basic road map of the issues they address? What other telltale signs signal the presence of an issue? Courts will often imply issues by stating claims or arguments made by parties. They might say, for example, "The appellant argues that a contract was never formed" or "The defendant claims that she owed no duty to the plaintiff." Although, as noted above, such statements could not be considered complete issue statements, they provide evidence as to the nature of the issue before the court. You can use such evidence in constructing your issue statements.

Sometimes a court will refute a party's statement of the issue and then give what it perceives as a more accurate statement. A court that states that "The defendant incorrectly framed the issue as being a question of duty" will undoubtedly go on to explain that "The issue is more accurately framed as one of causation." Such a statement definitively points you to the issue.

Errors of Lower Tribunals

Another hint offered by courts is the statement that a lower tribunal made an error. The appellate court may observe, for example, that "The administrative law judge incorrectly calculated the compensatory damages due the plaintiff" or that "The trial court erred in admitting evidence of the defendant's prior admissions" or that "The court of appeals overlooked a jurisdictional obstacle to the plaintiff's claim." Such statements draw your attention to the issue before the court but do not provide a complete issue statement.

Generally, the errors involve interpretation or application of statutes, common law, constitutions, ordinances, administrative regulations, or procedural/evidentiary rules. The issue may be obscured by the court's discussion of the legal principles surrounding such interpretation or application. Nevertheless, if you get a sense that the court is critical of how a lower court or administrative agency interpreted or applied the law, then you know you have discovered an issue.

Concurring and Dissenting Opinions

Concurring and dissenting opinions can also clarify issues. Judges write concurring opinions when they agree with the opinion of the majority but reach that opinion using different or additional reasoning. Sometimes judges feel that the majority has not adequately explained or illustrated its reasoning and wish to offer additional examples, supportive case law, and arguments. Concurring opinions are helpful to practitioners, because they offer additional support for a legal rationale and are sometimes easier to read than the majority opinion.

Dissenting opinions are also helpful, even though they represent the "losing" side. The "losing" argument today may become the prevailing argument in the future. In the criminal procedure area, for example, much of the case law of today regulating searches and seizures has its origin in the dissenting opinions of cases written twenty or thirty years ago. Not only may dissenting opinions give you a clue as to the future of case law in a particular area, but they may also assist you in formulating a response to an opponent who cites the majority's argument. If the case law the opposing party is citing is not binding on the court, you can certainly use the dissenting opinion to mount your rebuttal.

More specifically in reference to issues, judges who draft the concurring or dissenting opinions will sometimes disagree with the majority as to exactly what the issue is. Their discussion about this difference can help you in framing the issue more clearly. The concurring or dissenting judges may also state the issue more clearly than the majority. A majority opinion can be so perfunctory that you have trouble gleaning the nature of the controversy, but the concurring or dissenting opinions may contain a more enlightening discussion of the issue.

Multiple Issues

In many cases, multiple issues are at stake. Sometimes, however, the dilemma is whether the court is analyzing multiple issues or a single issue with several subparts or rationales. Suppose a court is asked to determine whether the owner of a wild animal is strictly liable for injuries caused by that animal and what defenses the owner is entitled to raise. The court is being called on to address two issues: (1) the level of liability of an owner of a wild animal and (2) the defenses available to an owner of a wild animal. Each of these issues would be analyzed separately by the court and, therefore, each would be treated separately in a case brief.

In contrast, consider *Weiner v. Ash*. The court clearly identifies the issue (see paragraph 1) as being "whether the Weiners are entitled to damages for their fear that if Ash fails to take the prescribed medication he will again seek to kill them." The court goes on to address three arguments made by defendant Ash. In paragraph 1, the court says, "Ash argues first that the award impermissibly compensates the Weiners for fear of a second, separate tort unrelated to the first." In paragraph 2, "Ash next argues that the event the Weiners fear is too remote and speculative to be compensable," and, in paragraph 4, ". . . Ash argues that any fear the Weiners may have of a future attack results from Ash's condition, not from his tortious conduct." Although addressed by the court in separate paragraphs, each of these arguments relates to the core issue of whether the plaintiffs are entitled to recover for damages. The defendant is offering three reasons why the plaintiffs should not be able to recover; the defendant is not raising three unique issues. Therefore, a brief of *Weiner v. Ash* should contain only one issue statement. The rationale section of this brief should be organized in accordance with the court's responses to the defendant's arguments and should devote a separate paragraph to each argument.

Similarly, a court answering the question of whether a particular class of plaintiff constitutes a "suspect" class for purposes of the Equal Protection Clause would be faced with only one issue. The court would have to consider several characteristics of a "suspect" class (i.e., whether the class possessed certain immutable characteristics, had suffered invidious discrimination, and was politically powerless) and would undoubtedly devote several paragraphs to each of these characteristics. Nevertheless, the court would be dealing with one issue with three subparts and not three issues.

Jeffrey A. WEINER and Barbara S. Weiner, husband and wife; and Merton B. Weiner and Jean Weiner, husband and wife, Plaintiffs/Appellees,
v.
Steven Perry ASH and Christine L. Ash, husband and wife, Defendants/Appellants.
No. 2 CA-CV 88-0326.
Court of Appeals of Arizona,
Division 2, Department A.
April 25, 1989.
Reconsideration Denied June 1, 1989.
Review Denied Nov. 21, 1989.*

Shooting victim and passenger in car at time of shooting brought suit against defendant who had fired shots. The Superior Court, Pima County, Cause No. 222383, Michael Brown, J., awarded damages and ordered that defendant undergo psychiatric treatment.

The Court of Appeals, 157 Ariz. 232, 756 P.2d 329, determined that trial court lacked authority to order treatment and reversed conditional award for future damages. On remand, the Superior Court, awarded passenger and victim $250,000 in damages for future fear, anxiety, and mental distress. Defendant appealed. The Court of Appeals, Livermore, P.J., held that award of $250,000 to shooting victim and passenger in car at time of shooting for fear that, if defendant failed to

---

*Feldman, V.C.J., of the Supreme Court, recused himself and did not participate in the determination of this matter.

take prescribed medicine for paranoid schizophrenia, he would again seek to kill victims was not impermissible compensation for fear of second, separate tort unrelated to first, but was for present fear of possible future attack, and such fear was compensable.

Affirmed.

OPINION

LIVERMORE, Presiding Judge.

This is an appeal from the judgment of the trial court awarding $250,000 in damages for future fear, anxiety, and emotional distress.

The award arises out of an incident in which appellant Steven Ash shot at the appellees, wounding Jeffrey Weiner and causing Merton Weiner to suffer cardiac problems. Ash was tried criminally but was found not guilty by reason of insanity. In the ensuing civil action the court found, among other things, 1) that Ash suffers from paranoid schizophrenia which is currently in remission or controlled by drugs and therapy, 2) that he has a history of schizo-affective mental illness and failure to take prescribed medication to control the illness, and 3) that failure to take the medication is a significant problem in the care, treatment, management, and control of the illness. The Weiners were awarded damages for past and future medical bills, past and future pain, suffering and disability, and past emotional distress and anxiety. They were also awarded $250,000 for future emotional distress and anxiety, but only if Ash failed to comply with the court's orders that he continue to take prescribed medications and undergo psychotherapy and random periodic urinalysis to determine the level of anti-psychotic medication in his bloodstream. In a prior appeal, we reversed the conditional award for future damages, holding:

> There is ample evidence of continuing fear by the plaintiffs that defendant, if he stops taking his medication, will again suffer a paranoid delusion about plaintiffs and will again seek to kill them. But it is also clear from the findings that in the trial judge's view no compensable future damage will occur if defendant does not again deteriorate mentally. The judgment, therefore, cannot be affirmed on the basis that it is an actual award of compensation for probable future damages.

Weiner v. Ash, 157 Ariz. 232, 234–35, 756 P.2d 329, 331–32 (App.1988). The case was remanded for an award of presently proven future damages. On remand judgment was entered in favor of the Weiners in the amount of $250,000 "for future fear, anxiety and emotional distress." This appeal followed.

[1] At issue is whether the Weiners are entitled to damages for their fear that if Ash fails to take the prescribed medication he will again seek to kill them. Ash argues first that the award impermissibly compensates the Weiners for fear of a second, separate tort unrelated to the first. We disagree. The Weiners are not being compensated for a possible future attack by Ash. They are being compensated for the present *fear* of a possible future attack, a fear that clearly arises from the shooting incident and resulting physical injuries. *See Lavelle v. Owens-Corning Fiberglas Corporation*, 30 Ohio Misc.2d 11, 507 N.E.2d 476 (1987).

Although there are no cases directly on point from this jurisdiction, a number of cases from other jurisdictions have held such fears to be compensable. In *Hardin v. Munchies Food Store*, 521 So.2d 1200 (La.App.1988), the court found that the general damages awarded the victim of an assault was inadequate to compensate her for fright and distress emanating from the attack, including a continuing fear of men and phobia of entering crowds of people. In *Reardon v. Department of Mental Health*, 157 Mich.App. 505, 403 N.W.2d 582, (1987) *rev'd on other grounds, Reardon v. Dep't of Mental Health*, 430 Mich. 398, 424 N.W.2d 248 (1988), the court upheld an award of damages to a sexual assault victim whose damages included worry about recurrence of the assault, fear of strangers, and a distrust of men. In *Berry v. City of Monroe*, 439 So.2d 465 (La.App.1983), the plaintiff suffered epileptic seizures after colliding with a support column. Finding that further seizures had been prevented by medication, the court nevertheless permitted an award of damages for the fear of future seizures, noting that "[w]hile mere speculation of such an event cannot provide the basis for an award, the anxiety produced by the possibility of another seizure is one of the compensable items we include in the award." 439 So.2d at 468.

[2] Ash next argues that the event the Weiners fear is too remote and speculative to be compensable. *See Howard v. Mt. Sinai Hospital, Inc.*, 63 Wis.2d 515, 217 N.W.2d 383 (1974). The reason the trial court gave for making the initial award contingent on continued treatment was "to alleviate any reasonable basis for future mental distress." Implicit in the second award, however, is the trial court's belief that given Ash's past history of failing to take prescribed medication and the court's inability to coerce him to do so, the possibility that Ash would again experience paranoid delusions and attack the Weiners was not so remote and speculative that the fear of such an attack was uncompensable. The record supports this conclusion.

[3] Finally, noting that recovery in tort is limited to the results of tortious conduct, Ash argues that any

3) fear the Weiners may have of a future attack results from Ash's condition, not from his tortious conduct. We find this argument unpersuasive. Tortious behavior is always the product of the tortfeasor's character. Fear of future behavior arises both from the past attack and what it demonstrates about that character. To deny recovery for present fear clearly arising from past tortious conduct on the ground that it rests in part on fear of the tortfeasor's character would be to deny a very real element of the harm initially caused.

Affirmed.

HATHAWAY and HOWARD, JJ., concur.

Reading Older Cases

Aids to issue identification are more likely to be found in recent case law than in older cases. Modern courts have generally adopted Plain English, the current writing movement that promotes the use of concise, clear language and discourages the use of "legalisms" that obscure understanding. Their opinions are designed to facilitate reading and comprehension. Older opinions, such as *Broadnax v. Ledbetter*, are often more challenging to read.

BROADNAX v. LEDBETTER
(Supreme Court of Texas. Feb. 27, 1907.)
Reward — Recovery — Prior Knowledge of Offer — Necessity.
Prior knowledge of a reward offered by a sheriff for the arrest and return of an escaped prisoner and performance in accordance therewith are essential to a right to recover.
[Ed. Note.—For cases in point, see Cent. Dig. vol. 42, Rewards, § 7.]

Certified Question from Court of Civil Appeals of Third Supreme Judicial District.

Action by S. H. Broadnax against A. L. Ledbetter. Judgment for defendant, and plaintiff appeals. Questions certified by the Court of Civil Appeals to the Supreme Court. Judgment affirmed.

Jackson & Littleton, for appellant. Kenneth Foree, for appellee.

WILLIAMS, J. This case is sent up by the Court of Civil Appeals for the third district upon the following certificate:

"The Court of Civil Appeals of the Third Supreme Judicial District of the state of Texas certifies that the above-styled and numbered cause is now pending on appeal in this court, and states that the cause of action asserted by the appellant against appellee is set out in plaintiff's original petition, which is as follows:

" 'State of Texas, County of Dallas. In the County Court of Dallas County, Texas. To the Honorable Judge of Said Court: Your petitioner, S. H. Broadnax, who is a resident citizen of Dallas County, Tex., hereinafter called "plaintiff," complaining of A. L. Ledbetter, who resides in Dallas county, Texas,

hereinafter called "defendant," respectfully shows to the court: That defendant is now and was on the dates hereinafter mentioned the duly elected, qualified, and acting sheriff of Dallas county, Tex., that heretofore, to wit, on or about the 21st day of December, 1904, one Holly Vann was, in the criminal district court of Dallas county, Tex., duly convicted of murder in the first degree, and his punishment assessed at death; that from the date of conviction, as aforesaid, until the 25th day of January, 1905, said Vann was a prisoner in the custody of said defendant, as sheriff of Dallas county, Tex., and was confined in the county jail of said county; that on said last-named date, and pending the appeal of said case of said Vann to the Court of Criminal Appeals of the state of Texas, he, the said Vann, by some method and means unknown to plaintiff, effected his escape from said jail, and from the custody of said defendant, and remained at large, a fugitive from justice, until the evening of the 25th day of January, 1905; that after the escape of the said prisoner, Vann, and during the time he was at large, a fugitive from justice, said defendant did make, and cause to be made, publish, and cause to be published, circulate, and cause to be circulated, an offer, to the effect that he, the said defendant, would pay as a reward the sum of $500 to any party or parties who would recapture the said prisoner, Vann, and return him to the Dallas county jail, from which he escaped, or to any other jail or jailer in the state of Texas; that said offer to pay such reward was made to the public generally—that is, to any person or persons who would capture the said prisoner and return him to custody, as aforesaid, and was not made to any special person or officer—that subsequent to the making, publishing, and circulating of said offer to pay such reward, and in conformity therewith and before the revocation thereof, said plaintiff did on, to wit, the 25th day of January, 1905, recapture, restrain, hold, and return the said prisoner, Vann, for whose capture said reward was offered, to the custody of said defendant, and to the county jail of Dallas county, Tex., and there delivered said prisoner to the custody of said defendant, and performed all the conditions contained in said offer to pay such reward; that by reason of the premises and the full performance by plaintiff of the services for which said reward was offered said plaintiff is entitled to said reward, and said defendant became liable to plaintiff, and promised to pay plaintiff the full amount thereof, to wit, $500; that, though often requested, defendant has failed and refused, and still fails an refuses, to pay the same or any part thereof, to plaintiff's damage in the sum of $500. Wherefore your petitioner prays for citation hereon, as required by law, and upon final hearing for judgment for the sum of $500 and for cost of suit, and for general and special relief.'

"In the trial court the appellee interposed demurrers on the ground that the petition stated no cause of action, because it was not alleged that the plaintiff had knowledge or notice of the reward when the escaped prisoner was captured and returned to jail by the plaintiff. These demurrers were by the court sustained, and, plaintiff declining to amend, judgment was entered dismissing plaintiff's case, with a judgment against him for all costs, etc. In view of the above statement, we propound the following question: Was notice or knowledge to plaintiff of the existence of the reward when the recapture was made essential to his right to recover?"

Upon the question stated there is a conflict among the authorities in other states. All that have been cited or found by us have received due consideration, and our conclusion is that those holding the affirmative are correct. The liability for a reward of this kind must be created, if at all, by contract. There is no rule of law which imposes it except that which enforces contracts voluntarily entered into. A mere offer or promise to pay does not give rise to a contract. That requires the assent or meeting of two minds, and therefore is not complete until the offer is accepted. Such an offer as that alleged may be accepted by any one who performs the service called for when the acceptor knows that it has been made and acts in performance of it, but not otherwise. He may do such things as are specified in the offer, but, in so doing, does not act in performance of it, and therefore does not accept it, when he is ignorant of its having been made. There is no such mutual agreement of minds as is essential to a contract. The offer is made to any one who will accept it by performing the specified acts, and it only becomes binding when another mind has embraced and accepted it. The mere doing of the specified things without reference to the offer is not the consideration for which it calls. This is the theory of the authorities which we regard as sound. Pollock on Contracts, 20; Anson on Contracts, 41; Wharton on Contracts, §§ 24, 507; Story on Contracts (5th Ed.) 493; Page on Contracts, § 32; 9 Cyc. Law & Proc. 254; 29 Am. & Eng. Ency. Law, 956. The decisions of the courts upon the question are cited by the authors referred to.

Some of the authorities taking the opposite view seem to think that the principles of contracts do not control the question, and in one of them, at least, it is said that "the sum offered is but a boon, gratuity, or bounty, generally offered in a spirit of liberality, and not as a mere price, or a just equivalent simply for the favor or service requested, to be agreed or assented to by the person performing it, but, when performed by him, as justly and legally entitling him to a fulfillment of the promise, without any regard whatever to the motive or inducement which prompted him to perform it." Eagle v. Smith, 4 Houst. (Del.) 293. But the law does not force persons to bestow boons, gratuities, or bounties merely because they have promised to do so. They must be legally bound before that can be done. It may be true that the motive of the performer in rendering service is not of controlling effect, as is said in some of the authorities above cited in pointing out the misapprehension of the case of Williams v. Carwardine, 6 English Ruling Cases, 133, into which some of the courts have fallen. But this does not reach the question whether or not a contractual obligation is essential.

Other authorities say that it is immaterial to the offerer that the person doing that which the offer calls for did not know of its existence; that the services are as valuable to him when rendered without as when rendered with knowledge. Dawkins v. Sappington, 26 Ind. 199; Auditor v. Ballard, 9 Bush. (Ky.) 572, 15 Am. Rep. 728. But the value to the offerer of the acts done by the other party is not the test. They may in supposable cases be of no value to him, or may be no more valuable to him than to the person doing them. He is responsible, if at all, because, by his promise, he has induced another to do the specified things. Unless so induced, the other is in no worse position than if no reward had been offered. The acting upon this inducement is what supplies, at once, the mutual assent and the contemplated consideration. Without the legal obligation thus arising from contract there is nothing which the law enforces.

Reasons have also been put forward of a supposed public policy, assuming that persons will be stimulated by the enforcement of offers of rewards in such cases to aid in the detection of crime and the arrest and punishment of criminals. But, aside from the fact that the principles of law to be laid down cannot on any sound system of reasoning be restricted to offers made for such purposes, it is difficult to see how the activities of people can be excited by offers of rewards of which they know nothing. If this reason had founda-tion in fact, it would hardly justify the courts in requiring private citizens to minister to the supposed public policy by paying rewards merely because they have made offers to pay upon which no one has acted. Courts can only enforce liabilities which have in some way been fixed by the law. While we have seen no such distinction suggested, it may well be supposed that a person might become legally entitled to a reward for arresting a criminal, although he knew nothing of its having been offered, where it is or was offered in accordance with law by the government. A legal right might in such a case be given by law without the aid of contract. But the liability of the individual citizen must arise from a contract binding him to pay.

The question is answered in the affirmative.

Issues in older cases must often be inferred from the discussion of legal principles, since the issues are often not overtly stated. Be aware that older courts (and some modern courts) sometimes merged their discussions of issues, making it difficult to identify the issues accurately, let alone follow the reasoning behind the court's decision.

We will read modern case law in this text, thus sparing you the pain of plowing through obtuse case law. But be forewarned that such murky writing does exist and that you will at times be forced to struggle your way through a verbal maze to ferret out the issues.

PUTTING IT INTO PRACTICE

Write out the issue in *Weirum v. RKO General, Inc.* (found on pp. 252–257 in Appendix A). (Suggested response is in Appendix B.)

HOLDINGS

If you have phrased the issue statement in the form of a question, then the holding is simply a yes or no response to that question. Some lawyers prefer to offer an explanation in their holdings, but in this text we will reserve explanations for the rationale unless the issue cannot reasonably be answered with a yes or a no. An example of an issue that defies a simple negative or affirmative answer is "What is the standard of care required of a neurosurgeon when performing routine neurosurgery?" The holding might be "A neurosurgeon is held to the standard of care of a reasonable neurosurgeon practicing in that locality." The "reasonable" standard and its application would then be discussed in the rationale.

A court will not typically phrase its holding in the same way that you will in your brief. While courts' issue statements are less complete than we want in a brief, their holdings are more complete than is desired in a brief. In its holding, a court resolves the controversy at issue; the holding in a brief merely provides a short answer to the question posed in the issue statement. A court's holding is generally found in a statement that begins "We hold," "We find," "We conclude," or "In our opinion" or uses similar phraseology that indicates to the reader that the court is rendering its ultimate conclusion. A court's holding often provides evidence as to what the issue is, so you are advised to seek out holdings before trying to formulate issues.

PUTTING IT INTO PRACTICE

Write the holding for *Weirum v. RKO General, Inc.* (found on pp. 252–257 in Appendix A).

DICTA

Once the issue is correctly identified and properly phrased, the holding is relatively straightforward. Possible confusion may arise, however, in distinguishing a holding from a **dictum.** The term dictum is a shorthand version of the Latin phrase *obiter dictum;* dicta is the plural of dictum.

Dicta are remarks made by a court that are unnecessary to the court's decision and, most importantly, pertain to issues that were not raised by the parties. Dicta, therefore, are not binding on other courts and parties and cannot be cited to another court as the law. In fact, presenting dicta to a court as legal precedent is unethical, because doing so would mislead the court. You may suggest that a court follow dicta, and you may offer all the reasons for doing so, but you must clearly identify what you are presenting as dicta.

If you are to avoid citing a dictum as a holding, you must learn to distinguish between the two. The distinction is not always clear, but the language used by the court is the key. If a court says, for example, that it does not have to decide a particular issue but then discusses how it would decide if the issue were before it,

FIGURE 4.3
Holding vs.
Dictum

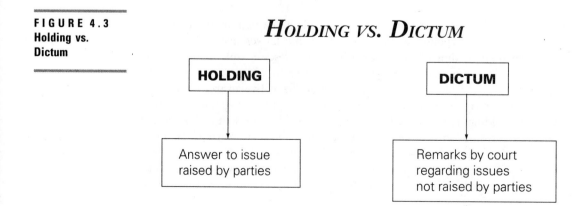

HOLDING VS. DICTUM

HOLDING	DICTUM
Answer to issue raised by parties	Remarks by court regarding issues not raised by parties

that discussion falls into the realm of dicta. The court is merely offering a gratuitous comment that is not essential to its decision.

You may recognize gratuitous comments as those sometimes uttered by instructors when they are asked a question that sparks their imagination or interest and they digress into stories or explanations about subjects the student asking the question had never even considered. Just as you know you are not bound to remember such comments, you should know that unsolicited answers given by a court are not binding on other courts.

Other indicators of dicta are statements such as "Even if the defendant had tried to escape ..." or "We believe the defendant could have been found liable if ..." Such statements imply that if the facts had been different, the court might have decided differently. But given the existing facts, such conjecture by the court is mere hypothesis and cannot be granted the same status as a holding.

Therefore, in distinguishing a dictum from a holding, ask yourself whether the court changed the facts in any way from those presented. Did the court engage in some kind of legal prophesy about issues that might hypothetically occur in the future? In the spirit and words of Sergeant Joe Friday of TV's "Dragnet," holdings concern "the facts and nothing but the facts," while dicta toy with the "maybes" and the "might-have-beens."

PUTTING IT INTO PRACTICE

Identify any dicta in *Weirum v. RKO General, Inc.* (found on pp. 252–257 in Appendix A).

REAL ISSUES

Having now been exposed to the abstract definitions and descriptions, let us examine an actual case and see if we can identify its issues and holdings. Read *White v. Mitchell* (on pp. 268–274 in Appendix A) carefully. Pay particular attention to the rather extensive facts, and make sure that you have a clear picture of the facts leading up to the dispute between the parties.

In Figure 4.4 on the next page, you will notice that immediately preceding paragraphs 1 to 3 the court very helpfully provides a subheading to forewarn you about the issue: "Should the Trial Court Have Instructed the Jury on Punitive Damages?" This subheading is a general description of the issue but not a complete issue statement. The statement provides no factual context and therefore fails to address why punitive damages were even an issue.

Look for the court's holding, and you will have another building block to construct the issue statement. At the end of paragraph 4, the court answers the question it posed in the subheading, saying, "The trial court correctly instructed the jury on the issue of punitive damages as to Mitchell." At the beginning of that same paragraph, the court presents its holding: "In our opinion the evidence presented at trial was sufficient to justify a punitive damages instruction as to Mitchell's conduct." This statement alerts you that the question involving punitive damages revolves around the sufficiency of evidence.

FIGURE 4.4
Case Opinion

though she had authority to do so. Instead, Burkhart "told him we needed to work him back into Joplin." Mitchell was to return to straighten out his license.

White and his wife brought this action against Mitchell and his wife and Sitton on November 27, 1985. It was tried before a nine-person jury, which returned a seven-person majority verdict as follows on January 14, 1987:

> We, the Jury, duly empaneled and sworn in the above entitled action, upon our oaths, do find in favor of the Plaintiff, HENRY WHITE, and find the damages to be $330,000.00 and SANDRA WHITE $10,000.00.
>
> We find the relative degrees of fault to be:
>
> | Defendant Sitton | 70 % |
> | Defendant Mitchell | 30 % |
> | | 100 % |
>
> We assess punitive damages against Defendant Sitton in the amount of $100,-000.00.
>
> We assess punitive damages against Defendant Mitchell in the amount of $30,-000.00.

(Underlined portions filled in by jury.) The trial court entered judgment in accordance with the verdict on January 27, 1987. By formal order entered March 18, 1987, the trial court denied appellants' motion for remittitur and motion for new trial. This timely appeal followed.

Should the Trial Court Have Instructed the Jury on Punitive Damages?

[1–3] We first examine appellants' argument that the trial court's instruction on punitive damages was an inaccurate statement of the law. The trial court instructed:

> Only if you have awarded compensatory damages, you may also consider whether to award plaintiffs White punitive damages against defendants Mitchell and/or D.L. Sitton, Inc. Such damages are awarded in excess of full compensation to the plaintiff in order to punish the defendant and to deter others from emulating his conduct.

Such damages are exemplary or punitive damages. To recover exemplary or punitive damages, plaintiffs White must prove by clear and convincing evidence that said defendants consciously pursued a course of conduct knowing that it created a substantial risk of significant harm to others. They must also prove aggravated and outrageous conduct by the defendants.

Appellants now contend that the wording of this instruction failed to convey the "evil mind" requirement for recovery of punitive damages under *Rawlings v. Apodaca,* 151 Ariz. 149, 726 P.2d 565 (1986) and *Linthicum v. Nationwide Life Insurance Co.,* 150 Ariz. 326, 723 P.2d 675 (1986). In the trial court, however, appellants' counsel objected to the giving of the trial court's instruction based only on the contention that the evidence was insufficient to warrant submitting the issue of punitive damages to the jury. Moreover, appellants' counsel not only failed to challenge the correctness of the proposed instruction's text, but also repeated part of that instruction almost verbatim in stating his understanding of the then current criteria for punitive damages under Arizona law. Rule 51(a), Arizona Rules of Civil Procedure (Rule), provides in part:

> No party may assign as error the giving or the failure to give an instruction unless he objects thereto before the jury retires to consider its verdict, stating distinctly the matter to which he objects and the grounds of his objection.

An appellant's failure to raise a specific ground of objection to an instruction before the trial court precludes him from arguing that ground on appeal. *Long v. Corvo,* 131 Ariz. 216, 639 P.2d 1041 (App.1981); *Watson Construction Co. v. Amfac Mortgage Corp.,* 124 Ariz. 570, 606 P.2d 421 (App. 1979). Further, a party who is dissatisfied with instructions the trial court proposes to give is under a duty to submit other instructions for the trial court's consideration. *See Dubreuil v. Gardner,* 99 Ariz. 312, 409 P.2d 23 (1965). In our opinion appellants failed to preserve on appeal their challenge to the wording of the trial court's punitive damages instruction.

FIGURE 4.4
continued

WHITE v. MITCHELL   Ariz. **1333**
Cite as 759 P.2d 1327 (Ariz.App. 1988)

from which defendant's motives may be inferred. The more outrageous or egregious the conduct, the more compelling will be the inference of "evil mind." Of course, defendant's state of mind may be evidenced by other factors and may be established or inferred even if defendant's conduct was outwardly unexceptional. The inquiry in every punitive damage case focuses on the defendants' state of mind, which may be established by either direct or circumstantial evidence.

152 Ariz. at 602, 734 P.2d at 87. *See also Volz v. The Coleman Company, Inc.*, 155 Ariz. 567, 748 P.2d 1191 (1987); *Bradshaw v. State Farm Mutual Automobile Ins. Co.*, 157 Ariz. 411, 758 P.2d 1313 (May 18, 1988); *Ranburger v. Southern Pacific Transportation Co.*, — Ariz. —, 760 P.2d 551 (1988). In addition, the supreme court has made it clear that a jury will not be permitted to consider an award of punitive damages if the evidence supporting such an award is only slight and inconclusive. *See Filasky v. Preferred Risk Mutual Insurance Co.*, 152 Ariz. 591, 599, 734 P.2d 76, 84 (1987); *Farr v. Transamerica Occidental Life Insurance Co.*, 145 Ariz. 1, 9, 699 P.2d 376, 384 (App.1984) (approved in *Rawlings v. Apodaca*, 151 Ariz. at 161, 163, 726 P.2d at 577, 579).

[4] In our opinion the evidence presented at trial was sufficient to justify a punitive damages instruction as to Mitchell's conduct. Though the evidence was largely circumstantial, the jury could have found that Mitchell was well aware he was driving a tractor-trailer rig that was in such dangerous condition that its continued operation gave rise to a very substantial risk of causing serious personal injury or death to pedestrians or other motorists, and yet deliberately persisted in doing so over a long period of time. The trial court correctly instructed the jury on the issue of punitive damages as to Mitchell.

[5] We reach the opposite conclusion, however, with respect to punitive damages against appellant D.L. Sitton Motor Lines, Inc. The evidence would unquestionably have supported a finding that Sitton's retention of Mitchell as a driver, and its failure to ensure regular and adequate inspection of his truck or exercise due care to prevent him from operating a dangerous vehicle, constituted gross, wantonly negligent conduct. *See Nichols v. Baker*, 101 Ariz. 151, 416 P.2d 584 (1966). There was, however, no sufficient evidence from which any jury could reasonably have found that Sitton, like Mitchell, was *aware of* and *consciously disregarded* a substantial and unjustifiable risk that significant harm would occur, such that it could be characterized as having acted with the requisite "evil mind." *Rawlings v. Apodaca*, 151 Ariz. at 162, 726 P.2d at 578. In contrast to the situation with Mitchell, the case for punitive damages against Sitton was no more than slight and inconclusive. *Farr v. Transamerica Occidental Life Insurance Co.*, 145 Ariz. at 9, 699 P.2d at 384. Further, the supreme court has expressly barred awards of punitive damages based on gross negligence or mere reckless disregard of the circumstances. *Volz v. The Coleman Company, Inc.*, 155 Ariz. at 570, 748 P.2d at 1194. The award of $100,000 punitive damages against Sitton must accordingly be vacated.

[6, 7] We reject Mitchell's argument that White failed to introduce sufficient evidence from which the jury could have determined an appropriate amount of punitive damages to award against him. Contrary to Mitchell's argument, *Hawkins v. Allstate Insurance Co.*, 152 Ariz. 490, 733 P.2d 1073 (1987) does not require specific proof of Mitchell's "wealth, property, income, education, earning capacity, debts, savings, or credit." The plaintiff, in a punitive damages case, need only introduce evidence sufficient to allow the trier of fact to calculate an award that is reasonable under the circumstances. *Hawkins v. Allstate Insurance Co.*, 152 Ariz. at 497, 733 P.2d at 1080. It is true that *Hawkins* listed the defendant's financial position among the elements of relevant proof on this point, but it did not hold that such evidence was always required. Here, though no comprehensive information was introduced con-

The question, then, is "Sufficient to prove what?" If you review the court's discussion, you will see that the court is grappling with what must be shown to prove that a defendant has an "evil mind." The issue appears to be whether the facts in this case support a punitive damage award in that they show that the defendant possessed an "evil mind" as defined in previous Arizona case law.

Based on this discussion, you need to consider what the essential facts are. (See the discussion in Chapter Three.) Incorporate those facts into the question relating to the evidence necessary to prove that the defendant acted with an "evil mind." Ask yourself what Mitchell (the driver) did that the plaintiff alleged was indicative of an "evil mind." Essentially, he knowingly drove a vehicle that had severely defective brakes, which created a substantial risk of causing injury to others. The key facts revolve around what he did (drove with defective brakes), what mental state he had (knowingly), and what danger he created to others (substantial risk of injury). Putting these elements into a question format, you would have the following question.

> Is a driver's awareness that he is driving with defective brakes that create a substantial risk of injury to others sufficient evidence of the "evil mind" required to award punitive damages?

Read on, and you will notice that the same issue is posed in reference to D. L. Sitton Motor Lines, the defendant who employed Mitchell. The court signals the appearance of another issue with its opening statement in paragraph 5: "We reach the opposite conclusion, however, with respect to punitive damages against appellant D. L. Sitton Motor Lines, Inc." The question again is whether Sitton's action were sufficient evidence of an "evil mind." What did Sitton do that arguably led to the plaintiff's injury? Essentially, the company failed to exercise due care in retaining Mitchell as an employee once it was aware of his suspended license. The company also failed to inspect his vehicle and allowed him to drive it in a dangerous condition. With those facts in mind, you might write this issue statement.

> Is an employer's retention of an employee with a suspended license and its failure to prevent him from driving a vehicle with defective brakes sufficient evidence of the "evil mind" required to award punitive damages?

The court continues its discussion of punitive damages in the next paragraph (paragraph 6), previewing the next issue with this holding: "We reject Mitchell's argument that White failed to introduce sufficient evidence from which the jury could have determined an appropriate amount of punitive damages to award against him." Before drafting an issue statement, we need to determine what type of evidence is alleged by the defendant to be missing. The next few sentences inform us that it is evidence of the defendant's financial status. We now have enough information to frame the issue. We might write it as follows.

> Must a jury be provided with evidence of a defendant's wealth to award punitive damages?

ART OR SCIENCE?

Keep in mind that writing briefs and analyzing case law is not like performing a mathematical computation. Legal analysis is not an exact science. It lends itself to creative discussion. Therefore, you or your instructor may wish to include more facts and legal principles in issue statements. The examples given above are suggestions to guide you in crafting your own issue statements. Part of the attraction of the law is its flexibility and its dynamic nature. Do not sacrifice these attributes by trying to become too rigid in what you view as "correct" and "incorrect" issue statements.

Remember, too, that preparing case briefs is a skill that improves with practice and experience. The more cases you read and brief, the easier the process will become and the more accurate and concise your briefs will be.

CHAPTER SUMMARY

The question of law posed by a court is referred to as an issue, and the answer to that question is a holding. A court's resolution of a factual question is referred to as a finding. Appellate courts generally defer to a lower court's findings and use those findings in shaping their holdings.

Issue statements should contain the essential facts in a case. They should spell out the issue in concrete terms, should be sufficiently detailed so that they can be distinguished from the issues in other cases, and should be able to stand alone in a brief without reference to the facts section. Furthermore, they should be drafted as narrowly as possible and in such a manner that they can be answered with a simple yes or no if possible.

To identify issues in a court opinion, observe the wording and organizational headings used by the court. Remember, however, that the court's formulation of the issue will generally be less complete than that desired in a case brief. Arguments made by the parties, reactions of the court to a lower tribunal's actions, and the reasoning used in concurring or dissenting opinions can also be used to identify issues. Courts' holdings can often be converted into questions and used to create issue statements in briefs. Issues with multiple subparts or rationales are single issues, although they may be inaccurately perceived as multiple. Generally, issues are easier to identify in newer cases than in older case law because modern-day judges avoid legalisms that obscure meaning.

If possible, the holding is a yes or not response to the question posed in the issue statement. Some issues defy such a simple answer, however, and require explanation. Finding the holding in a court opinion assists in determining the issue. Any comments that are unnecessary to the opinion and that pertain to issues not raised by the parties are considered dicta. A dictum cannot be presented to a court as legal precedent, because it is not binding.

KEY TERMS

dictum
finding
holding
issue

COGNITIVE CALISTHENICS

1. Identify the issues, holdings, and dicta (if any) in the following cases. (Answers are found in Appendix B.)
   (a) *Nienstedt v. Wetzel*
   (b) *Linthicum v. Nationwide Life Ins. Co.*
   (c) *Olson v. Walker*

2. Identify the issues, holdings, and dicta (if any) in the following cases.
   (a) *Cundick v. Broadbent*
   (b) *Matter of Estate of Swenson*
   (c) *BenShalom v. Marsh*
   (d) *Minnesota v. Dickerson*

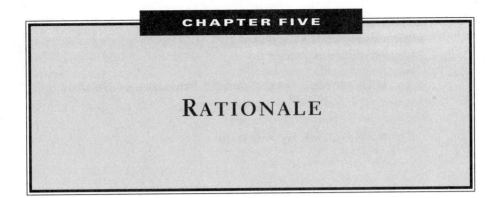

CHAPTER FIVE

RATIONALE

Chapter Objectives

In this chapter you will learn:

- How to identify and apply inductive and deductive reasoning.

- How to identify four basic patterns that courts use to organize their rationale.

- Some of the procedural rules that limit the ability of appellate courts to provide relief to parties.

At least once in your life, you have probably asked "Why?" when commanded not to do something and were told "Because I told you so, that's why!" Do you remember how dissatisfied you were with that answer? As humans, we seem to have an innate need to question, to understand why. For that reason, lawyers and litigants are rarely satisfied with a result (a holding) without reasons to support it. Also for that reason, the **rationale** (reasoning) offered by courts must be mastered by those who practice law. Understanding case law is based on an understanding of rationale, not on a mere knowledge of holdings.

Students of the law sometimes focus their energies on committing holdings to memory but then skim briefly over the rationale. Much to their dismay, they find on exams that their teachers are more interested in the reasoning used by the courts than by the actual black letter law. They ultimately discover that knowledge of black letter law is important but that complete comprehension of courts' reasoning is even more important if black letter law is to be applied to a client's facts. Clients are no more impressed with simply being told that they can or cannot do something than you were with being told that as a child. They want to know "why." The "why" is derived from a court's rationale. Therefore, the rationale of cases must be mastered.

FIGURE 5.1
Inductive
Reasoning

INDUCTIVE REASONING

■ **Reasoning from Specific Premises to General Conclusions**

■ **Reasoning by Analogy**

FIGURE 5.1
Inductive
Reasoning

INDUCTIVE VS. DEDUCTIVE LOGIC

To assist you in following the reasoning process used by courts, we will examine some basic rules of logic. Logic is the glue that holds rationale together. Just as scientists take pride in adhering to the scientific method in reaching their conclusions, judges take pride in adhering to the rules of logic. Having some familiarity with fundamental logic patterns will, therefore, facilitate your understanding of courts' reasoning and will also provide you with some guidance when it comes time for you to construct your own reasoning.

The two basic forms of reasoning are inductive and deductive. Both are used in the law.

Inductive Reasoning

With **inductive reasoning,** one reasons from a series of premises (assumptions) to a general conclusion, or, alternatively, one reaches a conclusion in a specific case using reasoning by analogy (i.e., on the basis of similarities). For example, if one classifies objects A, B, C, and D in group 1 because they all have the same characteristics, then one could reason by analogy that object E also belongs in group 1 if it has the same characteristics as A, B, C, and D. In more concrete terms, imagine that you had never seen dogs before and one day were told that an Airedale, a Boxer, a Chihuahua, and a Dachshund were all members of the canine species. You observe that these animals are very different in appearance but that each has four legs and a tail and barks. Using inductive reasoning, you could conclude that all dogs have four legs and a tail and bark.

Babies are masters of inductive reasoning. They cry when they are hungry, and someone comes to their rescue. They cry when they are lonely, and someone consoles them. They cry when they are wet, and someone relieves their discomfort. Soon they reason that crying, the common denominator in all their experiences, makes big people appear! They are off to a lifetime of using inductive reasoning to learn and adapt.

FIGURE 5.2
Example of Inductive Reasoning

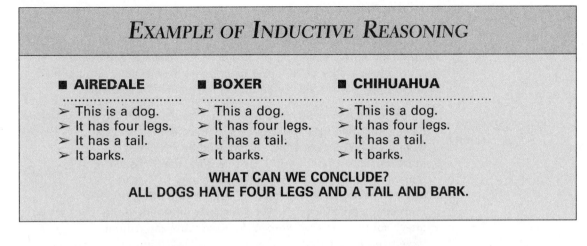

EXAMPLE OF INDUCTIVE REASONING

■ AIREDALE

➢ This is a dog.
➢ It has four legs.
➢ It has a tail.
➢ It barks.

■ BOXER

➢ This a dog.
➢ It has four legs.
➢ It has a tail.
➢ It barks.

■ CHIHUAHUA

➢ This is a dog.
➢ It has four legs.
➢ It has a tail.
➢ It barks.

WHAT CAN WE CONCLUDE?
ALL DOGS HAVE FOUR LEGS AND A TAIL AND BARK.

PUTTING IT INTO PRACTICE

Inductive Reasoning
How might you use inductive reasoning to decide whether you will go to see a particular movie? Assume that you have seen previous movies starring the same actors as in the movie in question.

Under the equal protection clause of the United States Constitution, members of a protected class cannot be discriminated against. Let us look at equal protection to see how inductive reasoning is used in this area of the law. If a class of persons is to successfully argue that they have been denied equal protection of the law, they must first show that they are members of a "suspect class." A "suspect class" is one that suffers invidious discrimination, possesses immutable characteristics, and experiences a sense of political powerlessness. If courts concluded that African-Americans, Hispanics, and Native Americans qualified as "suspect classes," then you might reason by analogy that Chinese-Americans should also be a "suspect class" because they, like African-Americans, Hispanics, and Native Americans, have suffered invidious discrimination, possess immutable characteristics, and have experienced a sense of powerlessness.

Practice Pointer	The study of inductive and deductive reasoning is a course in itself. The purpose of this chapter is to merely introduce you to these concepts. If you really want to become proficient in the rules of logic, you should attend classes or read books in this area. One particularly helpful book designed for lawyers is *Logic for Lawyers: A Guide to Clear Legal Thinking* by Ruggero Aldisert.

PUTTING IT INTO PRACTICE

Inductive Reasoning in a Case

How does the following excerpt from *Kline v. 1500 Massachusetts Av. Apartment Corp.* (printed in full on pp. 111–119 in Chapter 6) illustrate inductive reasoning? In this case, the issue is whether a landlord owes a duty of care to a tenant who is criminally assaulted by a third party when such an attack is reasonably foreseeable.

[I]nnkeepers have been held liable for assaults which have been committed upon their guests by third parties, if they have breached a duty which is imposed by reason of the innkeeper-guest relationship. By this duty, the innkeeper is generally bound to exercise reasonable care to protect the guest from abuse or molestation from third parties, be they innkeeper's employees, fellow guests, or intruders, if the attack could, or in the exercise of reasonable care, should have been anticipated.

Liability in the innkeeper-guest relationship is based as a matter of law either upon the innkeeper's supervision, care, or control of the premises, or by reason of a contract which some courts have implied from the entrustment by the guest of his personal comfort and safety to the innkeeper. In the latter analysis, the contract is held to give the guest the right to expect a standard of treatment at the hands of the innkeeper which includes an obligation on the part of the latter to exercise reasonable care in protecting the guest. Other relationships in which similar duties have been imposed include landowner-invitee, businessman-patron, employer-employee, school district-pupil, hospital-patient, and carrier-passenger. In all, the theory of liability is essentially the same: that since the ability of one of the parties to provide for his own protection has been limited in some way by his submission to the control of the other, a duty should be imposed upon the one possessing control (and thus the power to act) to take reasonable precautions to protect the other one from assaults by third parties which, at least, could reasonably have been anticipated. . .

Upon consideration of all pertinent factors, we find that there is a duty of protection owed by the landlord to the tenant in an urban multiple unit apartment dwelling. . .

[I]f we reach back to seek the precedents of common law, on the question of whether there exists or does not exist a duty on the owner of the premises to provide protection against criminal acts by third parties, the most analogous relationship to that of the modern day urban apartment house dweller is not that of a landlord and tenant, but that of innkeeper and guest.

FIGURE 5.3
Deductive
Reasoning

DEDUCTIVE REASONING

■ **Reasoning from General Principles to Specific Situations**

■ **Reasoning Using Syllogisms**

Deductive Reasoning

Deductive reasoning begins with a general principle that is then applied to a specific situation. The most common form of deductive reasoning used in the law is a **syllogism.** With a syllogism, a conclusion is derived from a major premise and a minor premise. One of the most common syllogisms is:

MAJOR PREMISE:	All men are mortal.
MINOR PREMISE:	Socrates is a man.
CONCLUSION:	Socrates is mortal.

If the conclusion is to be valid, both the major premise and the minor premise must be accurate. The following syllogism is fallacious, for example, because the major premise is false.

MAJOR PREMISE:	All animals in the sea are fish.
MINOR PREMISE:	Whales live in the sea.
CONCLUSION:	Whales are fish.

While the error in this argument is obvious, society often adopts conclusions founded on erroneous premises. The next syllogism was popular in the 1960s, although the error of the major premise is readily recognized today.

MAJOR PREMISE:	Everyone who uses marijuana goes on to use hard drugs.
MINOR PREMISE:	Jill uses marijuana.
CONCLUSION:	Jill will go on to use hard drugs.

Faulty major premises continue to abound today. Just look at some of the arguments commonly made in reference to the criminal justice system.

MAJOR PREMISE:	Anyone who plea-bargains is guilty.
MINOR PREMISE:	David plea-bargained.
CONCLUSION:	David is guilty.

OR

MAJOR PREMISE:	Legal rules that permit guilty people to be released cause the crime rate to increase.

FIGURE 5.4
Syllogisms

EXAMPLE OF A SYLLOGISM

MAJOR PREMISE: All men are mortal
MINOR PRESMISE: Socrates is a man.
CONCLUSION: Socrates is mortal.

MINOR PREMISE: The Exclusionary Rule (which prohibits the admission of illegally obtained evidence) permits guilty people to be released.

CONCLUSION: The Exclusionary Rule has caused the crime rate to increase.

OR

MAJOR PREMISE: Any judge who gives probation to a convicted child molester is soft on crime.

MINOR PREMISE: Judge Green gave probation to a convicted child molester.

CONCLUSION: Judge Green is soft on crime.

The major premises in these three syllogisms are all flawed. Many have found their way into political rhetoric, sometimes creating public policy. Be on guard, therefore, for the accuracy of major premises in others' arguments and your own as well. Scrutinize them for factual errors. Remember that broad generalizations are frequently flawed.

Minor premises, too, may be erroneous and may lead to invalid conclusions. Assume that the major premise that judges who grant probation to convicted child molesters are soft on crime is true. If Judge Green granted probation to a child molester who was a first-time offender only because the law mandated probation and counseling for first-time offenders, then he did not willingly grant probation. Any conclusions regarding his stance on crime based on this one case would be invalid.

Examine the following syllogism.

MAJOR PREMISE: An individual inside his/her home has a high expectation of privacy for purposes of the Fourth Amendment.

MINOR PREMISE: A prison cell is a prisoner's home.

CONCLUSION: A prisoner inside his/her cell has a high expectation of privacy.

Although prisoners have argued the validity of this argument, the U.S. Supreme Court attacked the minor premise, refusing to grant "home" status to a prison cell. The syllogism then crumbled, resulting in the conclusion that prisoners should not have any expectation of privacy in their cells.

> **PUTTING IT INTO PRACTICE**
> ....
>
> **Deductive Reasoning**
> What is the error in this reasoning?
>
> > Gerald is a juvenile who committed a crime. He should be put in jail because all juveniles who commit crimes should be jailed.
>
> What might be the flaw in this reasoning?
>
> > I heard that Mrs. Brown gives really hard exams. Since I want to get good grades, I am not going to take any classes from Mrs. Brown. (suggested responses in Appendix B)
>
> ....

In developing deductive arguments to present to a court, you will build your major premise from the general principles established in the case law you researched. You will construct your minor premise from the facts of your case. If, for example, you establish the elements of fraud using cases that have set forth those elements (major premise) and you then prove that the defendant fulfilled each of these elements (minor premise), you can logically conclude that the defendant in your case committed fraud. Of course, the defendant will put just as much effort into demonstrating that either the elements are lacking or that you have incorrectly interpreted what those elements are.

> **PUTTING IT INTO PRACTICE**
> ....
>
> **Deductive Reasoning in a Case**
> How does the court use deductive reasoning in *In the Matter of Charlotte K.*, 102 Misc.2d 848 (1980) (found on page 302 in Appendix A)?
>
> ....

Combining Inductive and Deductive Reasoning

In many cases, both inductive and deductive reasoning are used to arrive at a conclusion. Phobias, for example, arise from inductive reasoning and are maintained by virtue of deductive reasoning. If, for example, one experiences an anxiety attack in an elevator, some time later experiences similar anxiety in a small room, and then again in another enclosed place, one creates the phobia by inductively reasoning from a series of events to a general conclusion that enclosed places create anxiety. The phobia is then maintained using deductive reasoning. The major premise is that enclosed places cause anxiety, the minor premise is that this place (elevator, airplane, etc.) is an enclosed place, and the conclusion is that being in

FIGURE 5.5
Combining
Inductive and
Deductive
Reasoning

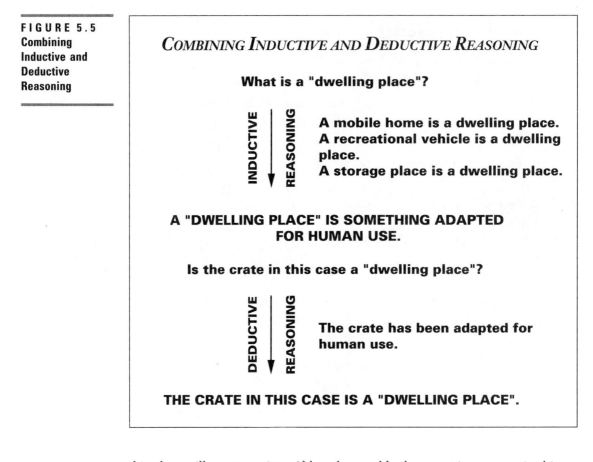

COMBINING INDUCTIVE AND DEDUCTIVE REASONING

What is a "dwelling place"?

INDUCTIVE REASONING

**A mobile home is a dwelling place.
A recreational vehicle is a dwelling place.
A storage place is a dwelling place.**

A "DWELLING PLACE" IS SOMETHING ADAPTED FOR HUMAN USE.

Is the crate in this case a "dwelling place"?

DEDUCTIVE REASONING

The crate has been adapted for human use.

THE CRATE IN THIS CASE IS A "DWELLING PLACE".

this place will create anxiety. Although arguably the reasoning process in this example is flawed in that enclosed places are not inherently dangerous, it is illustrative of how the two types of reasoning can be used in conjunction with one another.

Similarly, courts often combine inductive and deductive reasoning. Suppose, for example, that a court must decide whether a crate resided in by a homeless person can be burglarized. The burglary statute limits the offense to "dwelling places." In trying to determine what a "dwelling place" is, the court considers previous case law. It discovers that a mobile home, a recreational vehicle, and a storage place "adapted for human use" have all been deemed dwelling places. Using inductive reasoning, the court concludes that the common denominator in these cases is the "adaptation for human use" and that any place "adapted for human use" is a dwelling place for the purposes of the burglary statute. Using deductive reasoning, the court reasons that the crate in this case has been adapted for human use and is, therefore, subject to burglary.

PUTTING IT INTO PRACTICE
....

Weirum v. RKO General, Inc.
What type of reasoning does the court use in *Weirum v. RKO General, Inc.* (found in Appendix A on pp. 252–257)?
....

Practice Pointer	The use of logical reasoning does not necessarily mean that all parties will arrive at the same conclusion. If two individuals start with different major premises, they may arrive at equally valid but different conclusions. In *Watkins v. United States Army* (found on pp. 303–322 in Appendix A), for example, the majority bases its conclusion on the principle of equitable estoppel while the concurring judge uses the equal protection doctrine to formulate his conclusion. As a result, they come to different but equally defensible conclusions.

HOW COURTS APPLY THE LAW

Within the context of inductive and deductive reasoning, the courts follow a few basic patterns in organizing their rationale. They may:

- Define an ambiguous term or concept;

- Choose between conflicting provisions of the law;

- Apply legal principles to a fact situation that differs to some degree from the fact patterns in other appellate decisions; or

- Decide how public policy would best be served.

Definition of Ambiguous Terms or Concepts

Courts are called in as "referees" when lawmakers write ambiguous statutes, ordinances, or administrative regulations. Their task is to resolve ambiguities and reconcile any apparent conflicts. One of the ways they do this is by determining **legislative intent,** which is the intent of the legislative body that created the legislation.

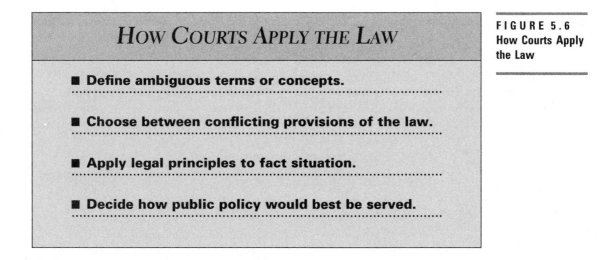

HOW COURTS APPLY THE LAW

- ■ **Define ambiguous terms or concepts.**
- ■ **Choose between conflicting provisions of the law.**
- ■ **Apply legal principles to fact situation.**
- ■ **Decide how public policy would best be served.**

FIGURE 5.6
How Courts Apply the Law

Be aware at the onset that the pursuit of legislative intent is often futile. The greatest obstacle to a clear expression of intent is the great diversity of motivations and agendas that exists in most legislative entities. When a body of legislation is enacted, the people who vote to enact it do so for a multitude of reasons, only some of which have anything to do with what is being voted on. Consider a controversial piece of legislation such as Medicare. How much compromise and bargaining do you think led to the evolution of that legislation? Do you think it represents any single intent on the part of the legislature that drafted it? Certainly, one cannot deny the important role that politics plays in the legislative process. The reality of politics makes it extremely difficult to determine precisely what any group's intent was in using particular words and phrases.

Determining intent is even more difficult when construing an older document, such as a constitution. Clearly, none of us can be sure what the drafters of the United States Constitution had in mind when they used certain phraseology; therefore, it is rather presumptuous to pretend that we can accurately infer their motives from the transcripts of their debates. Undaunted by the magnitude of such a task, nonetheless, the justices of the United States Supreme Court have long vied with one another in debating the intent of our forefathers.

When a court interprets ambiguous language, it looks first to any definitions provided by the enacting body. Because such definitions are often lacking, the court will look to the plain meaning of the language (i.e., the meaning normally accorded such language in everyday life). A court may also consult other opinions in the same jurisdiction to see whether the word or phrase has been defined, albeit in a different context.

If none of these efforts is fruitful, a court's only recourse may be the legislative history of the statute or constitution. In reviewing this history, the court will pay particular attention to changes in language as the bill was amended as well as committee reports or legislative discussion.

Permeating all of a court's efforts to penetrate legislative intent is its desire to determine the public policy reasons behind the passage of legislation. A court will look for any comments that indicate why the bill was introduced, what social ills it was intended to redress, and/or how it fit into a particular legislative scheme.

Vo v. Superior Court nicely illustrates the process used by courts in defining ambiguous terms.

Nghia Hugh VO and Richard Paredez, Petitioners,

v.

SUPERIOR COURT of the State of Arizona, In and For the COUNTY OF MARICOPA, the Honorable David R. Cole, a judge thereof, Respondent Judge, The STATE of Arizona, ex rel., Richard ROMLEY, Maricopa County Attorney, Real Party in Interest.

No. 1 CA–SA 91–327.

Court of Appeals of Arizona,
Division 1, Department B.

Jan. 30, 1992.

Review Denied Sept. 22, 1992.

Codefendants charged by indictment with two counts of first-degree murder for deaths of adult victim and

her unborn fetus brought special action from denial by the Superior Court, Maricopa County, Cause No.

CR 91–03478, David R. Cole, J., of motion to dismiss count alleging first-degree murder of fetus. The Court of Appeals, Jacobson, P.J., held that legislature did not intend to include a fetus in the definition of "person" or "human being" contained in murder statute, and thus killing of a fetus does not constitute first-degree murder.

Jurisdiction accepted, relief granted.

1. **Courts k207.1**   As a general rule, special action is not an appropriate vehicle for review of a denial of a motion to dismiss; however, where an issue is one of first impression, is a purely legal question, is of statewide importance, and is likely to arise again, special action jurisdiction may be warranted.

2. **Statutes k241(1)**   Although rule of strict construction of criminal statutes no longer applies, where meaning of a statute is unclear, the "rule of lenity" requires Court of Appeals to resolve any doubt in defendant's favor.

3. **Constitutional Law k200**   Court of Appeals may not expand scope of a crime by judicial decision to punish a defendant for an action that was not criminal when it was performed.

4. **Statutes k212.6**   Although there are no common-law crimes in Arizona, when a crime such as murder is enacted by its common-law name, Court of Appeals assumes the legislature was aware of the common-law meanings of the words in that statute and intended their use.

5. **Homicide k1**   Legislature did not intend to include a fetus in the definition of "person" or "human being" contained in murder statute; thus, killing of a fetus does not constitute first-degree murder. A.R.S. §§ 13–1101, subd. 3, 13–1105, subd. A, par. 1.

See publication Words and Phrases for other judicial constructions and definitions.

6. **Common Law k11**   Arizona is a "code state," and Court of Appeals is legislatively precluded from creating new crimes by expanding the common-law through judicial decision. A.R.S. § 13–103.

Philip A. Seplow and Morton Rivkind, Phoenix, for petitioner Vo.

Humberto Rosales, Phoenix, for petitioner Paredez.

Richard Romley, Maricopa County Atty. by Alfred M. Fenzel, Deputy County Atty., and Grant Woods, Atty. Gen. by Paul J. McMurdie, Chief Counsel, Crim. Div., Phoenix, for real party in interest.

OPINION

JACOBSON, Judge.

In this special action from the trial court's denial of defendants' motion to dismiss, or in the alternative, to remand to the grand jury for a redetermination of probable cause, we must decide whether the killing of a fetus can constitute first degree murder under A.R.S. § 13–1105.

Facts and Procedural Background

Nghia Hugh Vo and Richard Paredez (petitioners) are co-defendants in superior court, charged by indictment with, among other things, two counts of first degree murder in violation of A.R.S. § 13–1105, for the deaths of an adult victim, a pregnant female, and her unborn fetus. Both died as a result of a gunshot wound to the mother's head, allegedly fired by Vo during a freeway shooting on May 14, 1991.

The evidence presented to the grand jury was that Vo, Paredez, and a third defendant allegedly were riding in a stolen car on May 14, 1991. Paredez was driving and Vo was in the front passenger seat. They entered Interstate 17 at the Peoria entrance, headed south, and accelerated into the fast lane, behind a pickup truck in which the victim and her husband were driving. Following an alleged exchange of gestures between the occupants of the two vehicles, Vo allegedly rolled down the window and fired two shots at the pickup truck. One of the shots struck the victim, who was the passenger in the pickup truck, killing her and her fetus. The investigating police officer testified as follows about the fetus:

> Q. There was also a discussion [with the medical examiner who performed the autopsy] about the baby. What was the cause of death of the baby?
> A. He said the baby died as a direct result of the shooting death of its mother.

The first degree murder statute, A.R.S. § 13–1105(A)(1), was read to the grand jury, along with the definition of "person" as "a human being," which is contained in A.R.S. § 13–1101(3). A grand juror later questioned the prosecutor:

> [GRAND JUROR]: Under definitions, suppose children who are under 14. *Has that been clearly defined to include unborn children?*
> [PROSECUTOR]: We're going to give you a definition of a person and *in part of that definition is that there is a civil case in Arizona that held that a person encompasses a stillborn viable fetus.* There is a civil case on that. There is no criminal case that I am aware of, but there is a civil case that says that.

The parties agree that the civil case referred to is *Summerfield v. Superior Court*, 144 Ariz. 467, 698 P.2d 712 (1985).

On June 4, 1991, the grand jury returned indictments against petitioners for, among other things, two counts of first degree murder in violation of A.R.S. § 13–1103. On July 17, 1991, Vo moved to dismiss, or, in the alternative, to remand for a new finding of probable cause on Count II of the indictment, which alleged first degree murder of the fetus. The motion to dismiss was based on the contention that a fetus is not a "cognizable 'victim'" under Arizona's first degree murder statute. Alternatively, Vo argued that the prosecutor engaged in prosecutorial misconduct by misinforming the jury about that law (1) by not instructing the jury about the manslaughter statute, A.R.S. § 13–1103(A)(5), which includes the death of an unborn child; (2) by giving the jury a definition of "person" from a civil case; and (3) by eliciting misleading testimony about the status of the development of the fetus.

The state responded that the prosecutor's instructions to the grand jury were proper under Arizona law because the Arizona Supreme Court has defined a stillborn, viable fetus as a "person" within the civil context of the wrongful death statute, based on *Summerfield*. The state pointed out that two other jurisdictions have applied the definition of "person" within their wrongful death statutes to a criminal charge involving the death of a fetus. *See Commonwealth v. Cass*, 392 Mass. 799, 467 N.E.2d 1324 (1984), and *State v. Horne*, 282 S.C. 444, 319 S.E.2d 703 (1984). The state also reasoned that the manslaughter statute was inapplicable to Vo in the absence of evidence that he knew the victim was pregnant or that he intended harm to the fetus. *See State v. Amaya-Ruiz*, 166 Ariz. 152, 172–73, 800 P.2d 1260, 1280–81 (1990). In a supplemental response, the state also argued that the manslaughter statute applied only to "non-viable fetuses, while the other homicide statutes may be applied to viable fetuses."[1]

Subsequently, petitioner Paredez joined in both the motion to dismiss and the alternative motion for redetermination of probable cause.

After a hearing on the consolidated motions, the trial court issued its minute entry ruling on November 7, 1991. With regard to the issue of the prosecutor's conduct before the grand jury, the court found "that there was no misconduct that would warrant an order remanding this matter to the grand jury, much less dismissing the charges against defendant [Vo]." The court found that the prosecutor's decision not to read the manslaughter statute to the grand jury was justified by its inability to show defendant's mental state toward the fetus, and that the reference to *Summerfield* "was neither inaccurate nor misleading." Regarding Vo's motion to dismiss, the court ruled:

> Intertwined throughout Defendant's Motion is the argument that he cannot be held criminally responsible for the death of a fetus. Pursuant to A.R.S. §§ 13–1105(A)(1) and 13–1101(3), the State must establish that an unborn child is a "person" before first degree murder liability can attach. The Court concludes that the unborn ... child was a human being, and thus a "person," for purposes of A.R.S. § 13–1105. *See Com. v. Cass*, 392 Mass. 799, 467 N.E.2d 1324 (1984); *Mone v. Greyhound Lines, Inc.* [368 Mass. 354], 331 N.E.2d 916 (Mass.1975). Having reviewed a number of opinions dealing with this question, it is clear to this Court that the law has evolved to the point that one who causes the death of an unborn child can be held criminally liable. To the extent that one can divine legislative intent in Arizona, the Court concludes that, for the reasons stated in *Summerfield, supra*, as well as reasons that are apparent from a review of Chapter 11 of the Arizona Criminal Code, the Arizona Legislature intended that criminal liability attach in cases like the present.

The court also concluded that "prospective-only application is not warranted here," and denied Vo's motions.

On December 20, 1991, Vo and Paredez moved the trial court to stay further proceedings so that they could file this special action, and the court granted a sixty-day stay. Vo filed his petition for special action in this court on December 27, 1991, and Paredez requested permission to join the action on January 2, 1991, which this court granted by order dated January 3, 1991.

Special Action Jurisdiction

Petitioners procedurally framed their arguments in the trial court as a motion to dismiss or an alternative motion to remand for redetermination of prob-

---

1. No evidence was presented to the grand jury in this case that the fetus was viable at the time of the mother's death. Indeed, the record does not indicate the gestational age of the fetus on the date of the incident. Although counsel informed this court at oral argument that the victim was 23 weeks pregnant at the time of her death, that information was not available in the record before either the grand jury or the trial court.

able cause. The nature of the relief they were seeking, however, was a determination that a fetus is not a "person" within the meaning of the first degree murder statute, and that they therefore could not be charged with murder under existing Arizona statutory criminal law. This argument, if successful, would require an order of dismissal, based on a finding that the indictments were insufficient as a matter of law, rather than a remand for a new determination of probable cause for denial of a substantial procedural right. *Compare* Rule 16.5 *with* Rule 12.9, Arizona Rules of Criminal Procedure. We therefore consider their special action petition to seek relief primarily from the denial of a motion to dismiss, regardless of how their arguments were procedurally labeled in the trial court.

[1] As a general rule, special action is not an appropriate vehicle for review of a denial of a motion to dismiss. *See State v. Superior Court*, 123 Ariz. 324, 329–30, 599 P.2d 777, 782–83 (1979). However, where an issue is one of first impression of a purely legal question, is of statewide importance, and is likely to arise again, special action jurisdiction may be warranted. *Id.* We also note that this case raises an issue analogous to the one addressed by special action review in *Summerfield*, where the court accepted special action jurisdiction for the following reasons:

> In the situation at bench, there are several pending cases in the superior courts which present the same issue. Normal appellate procedures will result in unnecessary cost and delay to all litigants. . . . The question presented is a clear issue of law with obvious statewide significance. The congruence of these factors militates in favor of our accepting jurisdiction.

144 Ariz. at 469, 698 P.2d at 714 (citations omitted). Moreover, our special action jurisdiction has been properly invoked to consider the legal issue whether the grand jury was properly instructed on the definition of "person." In deciding this issue we, of necessity, must decide the issue underlying the motion to dismiss. Because of these factors, in the exercise of our discretion, we accepted special action jurisdiction, and issued an order granting relief with an opinion to follow. This is that opinion.

Merits

I. *Legal Background*

In 1977, the Arizona Legislature revised the entire criminal code. *See generally*, Laws 1977, Ch. 142, §§ 1 to 178, effective October 1, 1978. The drafters specifically abolished all common law crimes and provided that "no act or omission constitutes an offense unless it is an offense under this title or under another

statute or ordinance." A.R.S. § 13–103. Because of this enactment, Arizona is a "code state" as far as its criminal law is concerned.

Homicide crimes were codified in Chapter 11 of Title 13. *See* Laws 1977, Ch. 142, § 60. The first degree murder prohibition at issue in this case provides:

> A person commits first degree murder if:
> 1. Knowing that his conduct will cause death, such *person* causes the death of *another* with premeditation. . . .

A.R.S. § 13–1105(A)(1) (emphasis added).[2] The definition of "person" for purposes of Chapter 11 provides:

> In this chapter, unless the context otherwise requires:
> . . . .
> 3. "Person" means a human being.

A.R.S. § 13–1101(3).

The manslaughter statute, also enacted in 1977, similarly provided that that crime was committed by "[r]ecklessly causing the death of another *person*." A.R.S. § 13–1103(A)(1) (emphasis added). However, in 1983, the legislature amended the manslaughter statute to add the following provision:

> A. A person commits manslaughter by:
> . . . .
> 5. Knowingly or recklessly causing the death of *an unborn child* at any stage of its development by any physical injury to the mother of such child which would be murder if the death of the mother had occurred.

A.R.S. § 13–1103(A)(5), amended by Laws 1983, Ch. 268, § 2. This amendment did not affect the provision regarding death of a person in subsection (A)(1), nor did it change the definition of "person" in A.R.S. § 13–1101(3).

Although no Arizona appellate case has ever addressed the issue whether the term "person" within the first degree murder statute includes an unborn fetus, the Arizona Supreme Court has held that a stillborn, viable fetus is a "person" entitled to recover tort damages for its wrongful death under the statutory au-

---

2. Although this statute has been amended since 1977, the words "person" and "another" have remained unchanged. We assume, and the parties agree, that the term "another" refers by implication to "another person." *See, e.g., State v. Larsen*, 578 P.2d 1280, 1282 (Utah 1978) ("another" implies "another person").

thority of A.R.S. § 12–611.[3] *Summerfield*, 144 Ariz. at 479, 698 P.2d at 724. The court suggested that the legislature that enacted Arizona's first wrongful death statute in 1887 did not intend to preclude the judiciary from expanding the remedy under evolving common law principles. *Id.* at 472, 698 P.2d at 717. The court also noted that the legislature had not included a statutory definition of "person" within the wrongful death statute. *Id.* at 475, 698 P.2d at 720.

In recognizing the majority rule in thirty-two other jurisdictions that survivors of a viable fetus may recover for wrongful death, the *Summerfield* court acknowledged that "the common law has evolved to the point that the word 'person' does usually include a fetus capable of extrauterine life." 144 Ariz. at 477, 698 P.2d at 722. Apart from the legislative goal of compensating survivors implicit in the remedial purpose of A.R.S. § 12–611, the court also discerned a "legislative goal of protecting the fetus" by analogy to other areas of the law, including the statutory amendments adding "an unborn child" to the manslaughter statute. *Id.* at 476, 698 P.2d at 721. Although the court speculated that the 1887 legislature probably never considered whether a fetus was a person when it passed the wrongful death act, *id.* at 467, 698 P.2d at 712, the court concluded that the issue has now "come within the province of common law development." *Id.* at 479, 698 P.2d at 724. The court recognized that no prosecution would lie for murder of a fetus at common law, but concluded that "the analogy between civil liability for tort and criminal liability for causing death is not apt." *Id.* at 474, 698 P.2d at 719. The court also recognized that "[t]he word 'person' can mean different things in different contexts," and rejected the argument that it was precluded from recognizing a fetus as a person for purposes of tort recovery by the holding of *Roe v. Wade*, 410 U.S. 113, 93 S.Ct. 705, 35 L.Ed.2d 147 (1973), that a fetus is not a person within the meaning of the fourteenth amendment to the United States Constitution. *Id.* 144 Ariz. at 478, 698 P.2d at 723.

---

3. Arizona's wrongful death statute provides:
When death of a *person* is caused by the wrongful act, neglect or default, and the act, neglect or default is such as would, if death had not ensued, have entitled the party injured to maintain an action to recover damages in respect thereof, then, and in every such case, the person who or the corporation which would have been liable if death had not ensued shall be liable to an action for damages, notwithstanding the death of the person injured, and although the death was caused under such circumstances as amount in law to murder in the first or second degree or manslaughter.
A.R.S. § 12–611 (emphasis added).

The state urges us to now adopt in the criminal area the civil rule articulated in *Summerfield*. This issue requires us to construe the statutory meaning of "person" and "human being" within the limited context of the criminal first degree murder statute. In doing so, we need to emphasize that this court is not embarking upon a resolution of the debate as to "when life begins." Rather our task is specifically to determine the legislative intent in defining first degree murder of a "person."

II. *Rules of Criminal Statutory Construction in Arizona*

[2] The legislature has abolished the common law rule of strict construction of criminal laws, and has provided that criminal laws "must be construed according to the fair meaning of their terms to promote justice and effect the objects of the law, including the purposes stated in A.R.S. § 13–101." A.R.S. § 13–104; *see also State v. Tramble*, 144 Ariz. 48, 695 P.2d 737 (1985). Among the purposes of the criminal law in Arizona, the legislature has included the following:

> It is declared the public policy of this state and the general purposes of the provisions of this title are:
>
> . . . .
>
> 2. To give fair warning of the nature of the conduct proscribed and of the sentences authorized upon conviction. . . .

A.R.S. § 13–101(2). Although the rule of strict construction of criminal statutes no longer applies, where the meaning of a statute is unclear, the "rule of lenity" requires us to resolve any doubt in a defendant's favor. *State v. Pena*, 140 Ariz. 545, 683 P.2d 744 (App.1983), *approved* 140 Ariz. 544, 683 P.2d 743 (1984); *State v. Sirny*, 160 Ariz. 292, 772 P.2d 1145 (App.1989).

[3] We must also consider a criminal defendant's constitutional right to due process: "The first essential of due process is fair warning of the act which is made punishable as a crime." *Keeler v. Superior Court*, 2 Cal.3d 619, 633, 470 P.2d 617, 626, 87 Cal.Rptr. 481, 490 (1970). We may not expand the scope of a crime by judicial decision to punish a defendant for an act that was not criminal when it was performed. *Bouie v. Columbia*, 378 U.S. 347, 353–54, 84 S.Ct. 1697, 1702–03, 12 L.Ed.2d 894 (1964).

III. *Legislative Intent*

With these general principles of statutory construction in mind, we must next determine whether the Arizona legislature intended to include a fetus within the definition of a "person" within the homicide statutes as "a human being." *See* A.R.S. § 13–1101(3).

[4] In determining this intent, we look first to the way in which the words of the statute were understood at the time the legislation was enacted. *Kriz v. Buckeye*

Petroleum Co., 145 Ariz. 374, 701 P.2d 1182 (1985). Although there are no common law crimes in Arizona, when a crime such as murder is enacted by its common law name, we assume the legislature was aware of the common law meanings of the words in that statute and intended their use. *See Engle v. State*, 53 Ariz. 458, 90 P.2d 988 (1939); *State v. Bowling*, 5 Ariz. App. 436, 427 P.2d 928 (1967). *See also Keeler v. Superior Court*, 2 Cal.3d at 628, 470 P.2d at 622, 87 Cal.Rptr. at 486; *People v. Greer*, 79 Ill.2d 103, 106, 37 Ill.Dec. 313, 319, 402 N.E.2d 203, 209 (1980); *State v. Amaro*, 448 A.2d 1257, 1259 (R.I.1982) ("the Legislature would have expressly deviated from the common-law born-alive meaning of 'person' had it meant to do so.").

[5] The common law rule was that only persons "born alive" could be subject to homicide; thus, the commonly accepted meaning of the statutory words "human being" or "person" in 1977, when the legislature enacted the current criminal code, did not include a fetus. *See generally* Forsythe, *Homicide of the Unborn Child: The Born Alive Rule and Other Legal Anachronisms*, 21 Val.U.L.Rev. 563 (1987). The reason for the "born alive rule," according to the case in which it was first enunciated in 1601, was the difficulty of proving whether a stillborn child would have survived its birth absent the act that would have constituted murder after the child were born alive, because of the high rate of fetal mortality at that time.[4] *Id.* at 384, quoting *Sim's Case*, 75 Eng.Rep. 1075 (K.B. 1601) (cited as authority for the "born alive rule" in American common law).

Although legislative history is scarce on this point, one authoritative commentator noted that " '[h]omicide' and 'person' are largely self-explanatory. 'Person' does not include unborn children. *Roe v. Wade*, 410 U.S. 113, 93 S.Ct. 705, 35 L.Ed.2d 147 (1973)." R. Gerber, *Criminal Law of Arizona* (State Bar of Arizona 1978) at 147. These remarks, attributed

to the Arizona Criminal Code Commission,[5] are in accord with the definition of "human being" as a "person who has been born and is alive" in the Model Penal Code at that time. *See* Model Penal Code § 211.0(1), 10 U.L.A. 532 (1974).

Another indication of legislative intent is the way in which the legislature has referred to a fetus in other sections of the criminal code. For example, the manslaughter statute, in two separate subsections, prohibits not only "[r]ecklessly causing the death of another *person*," A.R.S. § 1103(A)(1), but also expressly prohibits "[k]nowingly or recklessly causing the death of an *unborn child* at any stage of its development by any physical injury to the mother of such child which would be murder if the death of the mother had occurred," A.R.S. § 13–1103(A)(5). Thus, the legislature treated a fetus as separate and distinct from a "person" in a criminal context. *See also* A.R.S. § 13–702(D)(10) (the death of an "unborn child" is an aggravating factor for purposes of criminal sentencing). The legislature's inclusion of an "unborn child" in a statute that separately refers to a "person" indicates an intent to exclude a fetus from other statutes in which it is not specifically included. *See Pima County v. Heinfeld*, 134 Ariz. 133, 134, 654 P.2d 281, 282 (1982) (specific inclusion in one class may indicate exclusion from other classes where not mentioned).

In another area of the criminal law, the legislature has not seen fit to treat prohibited abortions as murders. *See* A.R.S. §§ 13–3603 to –3605.[6] In the

---

4. The "born alive rule" has received wide criticism in light of recent advances in medical technology that make determinations of the cause of a fetal death routine today. *See generally* Forsythe, *supra; see also* Note, *State v. Beale and the Killing of a Viable Fetus: An Exercise in Statutory Construction and the Potential for Legislative Reform*, 68 N.C.L.Rev. 1144 (Sept. 1990). However, because we are statutorily restrained from construing our criminal statutes based on evolving common law, we do not address the wisdom of the common law rule. We merely point out its existence at the time our current criminal code was enacted, in an effort to determine the legislature's intent in defining "person" as a "human being" subject to the homicide statutes.

5. These remarks are set forth in a section entitled "Explanation of Statute" referring to A.R.S. § 13–1101(3). "Explanation of Statute" is described as providing a "generally objective exposition of statutory meaning and coverage as these appear on the face of the statute and in the comments of the Code Commission." R. Gerber, *supra*, at vii. Although the conclusion that a fetus is not a person for purposes of homicide is not necessarily compelled by *Roe v. Wade, see* Kader, *infra*, this statement of what the Code Commission believed the law to be in 1977 gives us an indication that its intent may have been to exclude a fetus by defining "person" as "human being" in the context of the murder statute.

6. We note that the abortion statutes, as currently codified, may be unenforceable under the constitutional principles articulated in *Roe v. Wade*, 410 U.S. 113, 93 S.Ct. 705, 35 L.Ed.2d 147 (1973). *See State v. New Times, Inc.*, 20 Ariz. App. 183, 185, 511 P.2d 196, 198 (1973); *State v. Wahlrab*, 19 Ariz.App. 552, 553, 509 P.2d 245, 246 (1973); *Nelson v. Planned Parenthood Center*, 19 Ariz.App. 142, 152, 505 P.2d 580, 590 (1973). However, we cite these provisions for the limited purpose of ascertaining the scope of the protection the legislature intended to afford a fetus in enacting the existing criminal law.

same year that the homicide statutes were enacted into the current criminal code, punishing first degree murder by either life imprisonment or death, the legislature enacted criminal abortion statutes, punishing the abortional death of a fetus by two to five years imprisonment. *Compare* A.R.S. § 13–1101 (1977) (homicide) *with* A.R.S. § 13–3603 (1977) (abortion). Conceivably, by separating the crimes of murder of a person and abortion of a fetus, the legislature intended to retain a distinction between a fetus and a person. *See, e.g., Hollis v. Commonwealth,* 652 S.W.2d 61, 64 (Ky.1983) (because legislature enacted murder and abortion statutes simultaneously, "the legislature intended conduct directed to cause the unlawful abortion of a fetus . . . to be punished under the abortion statute"). We also note that, under the prior Arizona criminal code, an acquittal of murder would not necessarily exonerate a defendant of a charge of abortion because abortion did not require the "killing of a human being." *Hightower v. State,* 62 Ariz. 351, 353, 158 P.2d 156, 157 (1945) (construing former Code 1939, p. 43–301).

An examination of noncriminal areas of Arizona statutory law in which the legislature has protected unborn children also indicates that the legislature did not intend a fetus to constitute a "person" for all purposes. For example, a certificate must be filed for a fetal death, A.R.S. § 36–329, but this is a separate requirement from a death certificate being filed for a "person." A.R.S. § 36–327. The legislature found it necessary to include within the Uniform Anatomical Gift Act a separate definition of "decedent" as including "a stillborn infant or fetus." A.R.S. § 36–841. Indeed, within Title 36, the legislature has specifically defined "viable fetus" not as "a human being" but as "the unborn offspring of human beings which has reached a state of fetal development so that, in the judgment of the attending physician on the particular facts of the case, there is a reasonable probability of the fetus' sustained survival outside the uterus, with or without artificial support." A.R.S. § 36–2301.01(D). This separate treatment of a fetus, apart from other "persons" in noncriminal areas of statutory law, also points to the conclusion that where the legislature intends to protect the unborn, it does so by specific reference to a fetus, separate and apart from the general definition of "person" or "human being."

These observations lead us to conclude, as a matter of statutory construction, that the legislature did not intend to include a fetus in the definition of "person" or "human being" within the murder statute. Although we agree with the commentators that perhaps the time has come to reexamine the protections afforded unborn children under Arizona's criminal law in light of the scientific advances in the areas of ob-

stetrics and forensics,[7] we believe that any expansion of the law in this area is the prerogative of the Arizona legislature, not of the courts.

The policy reasons for deferring to the legislature in this area are strong. First, the legislature has the sole authority to create new crimes by virtue of A.R.S. § 13–103. Second, the legislature is composed of regularly elected members, subject to the electoral will of the population of their respective districts, and thus the legislature is more attuned to the will of the public on public policy than are the courts. Third, the legislature conducts public hearings in a nonadversarial manner, and is more able to explore all prospective aspects of a situation that may factually occur when it creates a crime. This court, however, is limited to ruling solely on the specific issue in the single case before it, and we base our decision on the facts as developed by adversarial parties as applied only to the limited issues preserved for review. *See, e.g., Hollis v. Commonwealth,* 652 S.W.2d at 61 ("Our decision is limited to whether Hollis can be charged with violating this statute. . . . The much larger metaphysical question of WHEN DOES LIFE BEGIN? is *not* the subject of this opinion.") We agree with the conclusion of the Connecticut Supreme Court on this issue:

> For this court to explore new fields of crime is foreign to modern concepts of justice and raises serious questions of separation of powers between it and the legislature. Therefore, any redefining of the word "person" must be left to the legislature, which has the primary authority to define crimes.

State v. Anonymous, 40 Conn.Supp. 498, 516 A.2d 156 at 159 (1986).

IV. *Other Jurisdictions*

The result we reach is in accord with the overwhelming majority of courts in our sister states. Other jurisdictions that have decided this issue have held, nearly unanimously, that a fetus or unborn child is not a "person," a "human being," or "another" within the meaning of their murder, vehicular homicide, or man-

---

7. *See, e.g.,* Note, *supra,* N.C.L.Rev. at 1147. Physicians can now determine the existence and approximate age of a live fetus by fetal heart monitoring, sonography, and other methods. The cause of a fetal death can often be determined to a medical certainty. Additionally, "birth itself is no longer a violent perilous adventure." *Id.* Some authorities estimate the fetal survival rate after twenty weeks of pregnancy at ninety-nine percent. *Id.; see also People v. Guthrie,* 97 Mich.App. 226 at 232, 293 N.W.2d 775 at 778 (1980).

slaughter statutes absent an express direction from the legislature. *See, e.g., Clarke v. State,* 117 Ala. 1, 23 So. 671 (1898) (recognizing "born-alive" rule for homicide); *Meadows v. State,* 291 Ark. 105, 722 S.W.2d 584 (1987) (not a "person"; manslaughter); *Keeler v. Superior Court,* 2 Cal.3d 619, 87 Cal.Rptr. 481, 470 P.2d 617 (1970) (not a "human being"; murder); *State v. Anonymous,* 40 Conn. Supp. 498, 516 A.2d 156 (1986) (not a "human being"; murder); *State v. McCall,* 458 So.2d 875 (Fla.D.Ct.App.1984) (not a "human being"; vehicular homicide and DWI manslaughter); *Billingsley v. State,* 183 Ga.App. 850, 360 S.E.2d 451 (1987) (not a "person"; vehicular homicide); *People v. Greer,* 79 Ill.2d 103, 37 Ill.Dec. 313, 402 N.E.2d 203 (1980) (not a "person"; murder); *State v. Trudell,* 243 Kan. 29, 755 P.2d 511 (1988) (not a "person"; vehicular homicide); *Hollis v. Commonwealth,* 652 S.W.2d 61 (Ky.1983) (not a "person"; criminal homicide); *State v. Gyles,* 313 So.2d 799 (La.1975) (not a "human being"; murder); *People v. Guthrie,* 97 Mich.App. 226, 293 N.W.2d 775 (1980) (not "another"; negligent vehicular homicide); *State v. Soto,* 378 N.W.2d 625 (Minn.1985) (not a "human being"; vehicular homicide); *State v. Doyle,* 205 Neb. 234, 287 N.W.2d 59 (1980) (fetus must be "born alive" for manslaughter); *State v. Beale,* 324 N.C. 87, 376 S.E.2d 1 (1989) (not "murder"); *In re A.W.S.,* 182 N.J.Super. 278, 440 A.2d 1144 (1981) (not a "human being"; criminal homicide); *State v. Willis,* 98 N.M. 771, 652 P.2d 1222 (App.1982) (not "human being"; vehicular homicide); *People v. Joseph,* 130 Misc.2d 377, 496 N.Y.S.2d 328 (1985) (not "death" of a "person"; criminally negligent homicide and vehicular manslaughter); *State v. Dickinson,* 28 Ohio St.2d 65, 275 N.E.2d 599 (1971) (not a "person"; homicide by vehicle); *State v. Harbert,* 758 P.2d 826 (Okla. Crim.App.1988) (not a "person"; homicide by vehicle); *State v. Amaro,* 448 A.2d 1257 (R.I.1982) (not a "person"; vehicular homicide); *State v. Evans,* 745 S.W.2d 880 (Tenn.Crim.App.1987) (not "person" or "human life"; vehicular homicide); *Showery v. State,* 690 S.W.2d 689 (Tx.App.1985) (not "homicide"); *State v. Larsen,* 578 P.2d 1280 (Utah 1978) (not "another"; automobile homicide); *Lane v. Commonwealth,* 219 Va. 509, 248 S.E.2d 781 (1978) (no *corpus delicti*; murder); *State ex rel. Atkinson v. Wilson,* 175 W.Va. 352, 332 S.E.2d 807 (1984) (not "murder"); *Huebner v. State,* 131 Wis. 162, 111 N.W. 63 (1907) (recognizing "born-alive" rule); *Bennett v. State,* 377 P.2d 634 (Wyo.1963) (manslaughter requires that infant was born alive); *see generally* Annotation, *Homicide Based on Killing of Unborn Child,* 40 A.L.R.3d 444 (1971 & Supp. Aug. 1991).

Subsequent to many of these decisions, the legislatures of those states amended the relevant statutes

to unambiguously include a viable fetus or an unborn child at any stage of development.[8]

Only two courts have judicially determined that a fetus was within the protection of homicide statutes based on common law principles.[9] *See Commonwealth v. Cass,* 392 Mass. 799, 467 N.E.2d 1324

---

8. For example, following the decision in *Keeler v. Superior Court,* the California legislature revised its murder statute to provide:

> Section 187. Murder defined; death of a fetus
> (a) Murder is the unlawful killing of a human being, *or a fetus,* with malice aforethought.
> (b) This section shall not apply to any person who commits an act that results in the death of a fetus if any of the following apply:
> (1) The act complied with the [abortion statutes].
> (2) The act was committed by a holder of a physician's and surgeon's certificate . . . in a case where, to a medical certainty, the result of childbirth would be death of the mother of the fetus or where the death from childbirth, although not medically certain, would be substantially certain or more likely than not.
> (3) The act was solicited, aided, abetted, or consented to by the mother of the fetus.
> (4) Subdivision (b) shall not be construed to prohibit the prosecution of any person under any other provision of law.

Cal.Penal Code § 187 (West 1988). In sentencing, California does not distinguish between murder of a "person" and murder of a "fetus." *See* Cal.Penal Code §§ 189–190.6 (West 1988). The term "fetus" within this statute has been judicially limited to a viable fetus. *People v. Smith,* 59 Cal.App.3d 751, 756, 129 Cal.Rptr. 498, 501 (1976).

See also, e.g., Fla.Stat.Ann. § 782.09 (1976); La.Rev. Stat.Ann. § 14:2(7) (West 1986); Ill.Rev.Stat.Ch. 38, §§ 9–1.1, 12–3.1 (1986 Supp.); Minn.Stat.Ann. § 609.266 (West 1988); N.Y.Penal Laws § 125.00 (McKinney 1987); R.I.Gen.Laws 11–23–5 (1981). The Minnesota statute prohibits "murder of an unborn child," while the New York statute approaches "death of an unborn child" as "abortion in the first degree." *Compare* Minn.Stat.Ann. § 609.266 (West 1988) *with* N.Y.Penal Laws § 125.00 (McKinney 1987).

See generally, Forsythe, *Homicide of the Unborn Child: The Born Alive Rule and Other Legal Anachronisms,* 21 Val.U.L.Rev. 563, 619–625 & App. A (1987) (proposing model legislation).

9. We note that one other court has recently held that a fetus is a "person" within the meaning of its involuntary manslaughter statute. *See State v. Knapp,* 1991 WL 254275 (Dec. 3, 1991). This holding was based not on common law principles, however, but on a reading of "legislative intent" from the repeal of a manslaughter statute that included "an unborn quick child," to include a fetus as a "person" within that statute. *Id.* (interpreting Mo.Rev.Code § 565.024). We note that Missouri is a "code state" rather than a "common law" state. *See* Mo.Rev.Code § 556.026 ("No conduct

(continued on next page)

(1984) (8-1/2 month fetus is a "person" within intent of vehicular homicide statute); *State v. Horne*, 282 S.C. 444, 319 S.E.2d 703 (1984) (nine-month fetus is a "person" within meaning of statutory definition of murder).

In both *Cass* and *Horne*, the court expanded the criminal law through principles of common law interpretation that are not available to this court in the present case. For example, in *Horne*, the South Carolina Supreme Court reasoned as follows:

> This court has the right and the duty to develop the common law of South Carolina to better change an everchanging society as a whole. In this regard, the criminal law has been the subject of change. . . . The fact that this particular issue has not been raised or ruled on before does not mean we are prevented from declaring the common law as it should be.

319 S.E.2d at 704. In *Cass*, the court reasoned:

> [W]e reject the notion that we are unable to develop common law rules of criminal law because the Legislature has occupied the entire field of criminal law. While this may be true in code jurisdictions, it is not true in this Commonwealth, where our criminal law is largely common law.

467 N.E.2d at 1327. This distinction, between "code states," which have abolished common law crimes and provide that no crime can be defined other than by the legislature, and "common law states," which recognize common law crimes and allow judicial decisions to fashion expanded definitions of crimes, is critical. *See, e.g., State v. Soto*, 378 N.W.2d at 627–30 (rejecting the reasoning of *Cass* and *Horne* because, although Massachusetts and South Carolina are "common law states," Minnesota is a "code state").

[6] Arizona is a "code state," and this court is legislatively precluded from creating new crimes by expanding the common law through judicial decision. A.R.S. § 13–103. Our function, therefore, is limited to interpreting what the legislature has prohibited in light of its intent, rather than expanding the criminal law based on our own sense of changing societal perceptions of what the law should be. Unlike the courts

in *Cass* and *Horne*,[10] therefore, we cannot expand the scope of the crime of murder based on evolving common law principles. Furthermore, we cannot consider the wisdom or soundness of policy of legislative enactments, because such matters are clearly addressed to the legislature, not to the courts. *See, e.g., Schrey v. Allison Steel Mfg. Co.*, 75 Ariz. 282, 286, 255 P.2d 604, 606 (1953). We do agree, however, with the *Cass* and *Horne* courts that due process problems might arise in this case if we applied the first degree murder statute to a fetal murder in view of the lack of prior authority. This is particularly true given that the manslaughter statute, which is the only homicide statute that specifically prohibits the "death of an unborn child," has been construed to require a separate criminal intent toward the fetus. *See Amaya-Ruiz*, 166 Ariz. at 172–73, 800 P.2d at 1280–81.[11]

V. *Application of Summerfield to the Murder Statute*

Based on our previous discussion, we reject the state's argument and the trial court's conclusion that the *Summerfield* holding that a viable fetus is a "person" within the meaning of our wrongful death statute expands the common law definition of "person" within the penal murder statute. We also do not believe the *Summerfield* decision applies in the criminal context for several other reasons.

First, the *Summerfield* court clearly rejected any analogy between civil tort liability and criminal liabil-

---

9. *(continued)*

constitutes an offense unless made so by this code or by other applicable statute"). We also note that, although the Missouri Court of Appeals did not rely on it in *Knapp*, the Missouri legislature has enacted a statute, effective January 1, 1988, that requires all laws of that state to be interpreted to recognize an unborn child as a person from the moment of conception until birth. *See* Mo.Rev. Code § 1.205. For those distinguishing reasons, we find *Knapp* unpersuasive.

10. Additionally, we note that in both *Cass* and *Horne*, the courts held that their decisions applied prospectively only, and not to the defendant in a case of first impression, because their expanded definition of the crime was "unforeseeable" and would cause due process problems if retroactively applied to their decisions. *Cass*, 467 N.E.2d at 1329 ("Our decision may have been unforeseeable. . . . We find it highly unlikely that the defendant could have relied on prior law in judging his conduct"); *Horne*, 319 S.E.2d at 7904 ("at the time of the stabbing, no South Carolina decision had held that killing of a viable human being *in utero* could constitute a criminal homicide. The criminal law whether declared by the courts or enacted by the legislature cannot be applied retroactively").

11. In *Amaya-Ruiz*, the court noted, although it did not decide, that the statutory language of the manslaughter statute, " '*if* the death of the mother *had occurred*,' might also support an argument that the statute is inapplicable if the woman is murdered, and is only applicable if she survives." 166 Ariz. at 173 n. 1, 800 P.2d at 1281 no. 1 (emphasis in original). We express no opinion regarding the application of the manslaughter statute to the limited facts before us. *But see State v. Brewer*, 170 Ariz. 486, 507–508, 826 P.2d 783, 804–05 (Ariz.1992), (upholding trial court's ruling that state was free to proceed with manslaughter charge for death of a fetus when mother also died).

ity for causing death, noting that the common law probably did not recognize murder of a fetus. 144 Ariz. at 474, 698 P.2d at 719. Second, we point out that the wrongful death statute, unlike the murder statute, is a remedial statute in derogation of the common law that should be liberally construed to "advance the remedy" not provided by the common law that it abrogated. *See Carrow Co. v. Lusby,* 167 Ariz. 18, 804 P.2d 747 (1990); *Terry v. Linscott Hotel Corp.,* 126 Ariz. 548, 617 P.2d 56 (App.1980). The criminal statutes, however, must be interpreted to give "fair warning." A.R.S. § 13–101(2). Third, as the *Summerfield* court pointed out, "The issue of recovery for tort law damage to the fetus has come within the province of common law development." 144 Ariz. at 479, 698 P.2d at 724. As we have already explained, the development of the criminal law through common law principles has been abolished in Arizona. A.R.S. § 13–103. Fourth, the *Summerfield* court noted that the Arizona legislature had not provided a definition of the word "person" as used in A.R.S. § 12–611. 144 Ariz. at 475, 698 P.2d at 720. However, the legislature has defined "person" within the meaning of the homicide statutes as "a human being," A.R.S. § 13–1101(3), and has otherwise included a fetus within the protection of the manslaughter statute as "unborn child." A.R.S. § 13–1105(A)(1).

Finally, we recognize, as did the *Summerfield* court, that "[t]he word 'person' can mean different things in different contexts." 144 Ariz. at 478, 698 P.2d at 723. The court concluded that the holding of *Roe v. Wade,* 410 U.S. 113, 93 S.Ct. 705, 35 L.Ed.2d 147 (1973), that a fetus is not a "person" within the meaning of the fourteenth amendment, "neither prohibits nor compels" the inclusion of a fetus as a "person" in the context of the wrongful death statute. *Summerfield,* 144 Ariz. at 478, 698 P.2d at 723; *see also* D. Kader, *The Law of Tortious Prenatal Death Since Roe v. Wade,* 45 Mo.L.Rev. 639 (1980). Nor do we believe *Roe v. Wade* controls the issue before us for the same reasons as those expressed in *Summerfield.*

Based on these distinctions between the tort issues involved in *Summerfield* and the criminal issue involved here, we agree with other courts that have held that tort decisions are neither binding nor persuasive in deciding whether a fetus is a person under the murder statute. *See, e.g., State v. Soto,* 378 N.W.2d at 630 ("It does not follow that because we held . . . that next of kin might recover damages arising out of the destruction of a viable fetus in a civil action . . ., that a viable fetus is a 'human being' for purposes of the criminal law"); *People v. Greer,* 79 Ill.2d at 155, 37 Ill.Dec. at 319, 402 N.E.2d at 209 ("Differing objectives and considerations in tort and criminal law foster . . . different principles governing the same fac-

tual situation"); *State ex rel. Atkinson v. Wilson,* 332 S.E.2d at 810 ("there exists a distinction between a court's power to evolve common law principles in areas in which it has traditionally functioned, i.e., the tort law, and in those areas in which the legislature has primary or plenary power, i.e., the creation and definition of crimes and penalties.")[12]

We do not question the constitutional power of the state legislature to prohibit conduct that causes the death of a fetus. In the context of *Roe v. Wade,* the state "has a compelling interest in the life of a fetus when it reaches the state of viability sufficient to legislate legal sanctions punishing those who destroy it, subject to the limitations that such sanctions shall not apply where the life or health of the mother is involved." *Hollis,* 652 S.W.2d at 63. However, we believe the state's interest in defining the criminal penalties for those who would harm the unborn can be asserted only by the legislature.

Conclusion

Because we find that the legislature has not evidenced an intent to include a fetus within the meaning of "person" in the first degree murder statute, that crime is not cognizable in Arizona. This court does not have the power to expand the criminal law through evolving common law principles applied in the civil tort context of *Summerfield v. Superior Court;* only the legislature can enact a statute that prohibits death of a fetus as first degree murder.

Because petitioners could not be indicted for first degree murder of a fetus as a matter of law, we hold that the trial court erred in refusing to dismiss this count as to both petitioners. *See* Rule 16.5, Arizona Rules of Criminal Procedure. Because we hold that dismissal is warranted as a matter of law, we need not address the alternative issue of prosecutorial misconduct in instructing the grand jury.

The counts of first degree murder pertaining to the death of the fetus are dismissed as to each petitioner, without prejudice to the state to seek re-

---

12. We also point out that one of the two jurisdictions that applied its civil decision that a fetus can recover for wrongful death to its criminal statute did so on the basis that the vehicular homicide statute at issue was enacted subsequent to its civil decision allowing recovery for the death of a fetus under the wrongful death statute, and presumed that the legislature had knowledge of that development in the common law. *Cass,* 467 N.E.2d at 1325. In Arizona, however, the current murder statute has included the definition of "person" since its adoption in 1977, at which time the current state of the "common law" was that a fetus was not a person within the meaning of the wrongful death statute. *See Kilmer v. Hicks,* 22 Ariz.App. 552, 529 P.2d 706 (1974).

indictment of the petitioners on charges of manslaughter under A.R.S. § 13–1105(A)(5).[13] This matter is remanded for proceedings consistent with this opinion.

Jurisdiction accepted, relief granted.

KLEINSCHMIDT, Vice C.J., and GARBARINO, J., concur.

---

13. We express no opinion on whether the state has shown evidence sufficient on the facts in this limited record to establish the elements of manslaughter as set forth in *State v. Amaya-Ruiz*, 166 Ariz. at 173, 800 P.2d at 1271. We leave that issue for the grand jury, should the state choose to pursue those charges against these petitioners.

In *Vo v. Superior Court*, the issue is whether the killing of a fetus is encompassed by the Arizona first degree murder statute. The statute provides that "A person commits first degree murder if: Knowing that his conduct will cause death, such person causes the death of another with premeditation. . ." Elsewhere, the term "person" is defined as a "human being." The court had in a previous civil case (*Summerfield*) defined "person" as including a fetus but had never defined the term for criminal purposes.

After considering the rules of statutory construction in Arizona, the court sets about determining legislative intent in reference to the definition of "person" for purposes of first degree murder. The court looks first to the "way in which the

FIGURE 5.7
Defining an Ambiguous Term

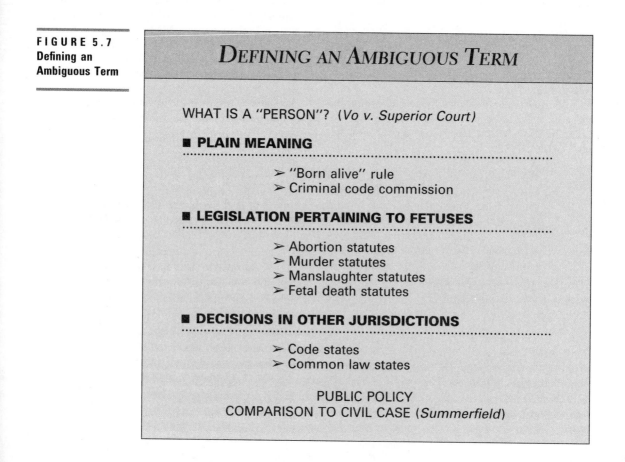

DEFINING AN AMBIGUOUS TERM

WHAT IS A "PERSON"? (*Vo v. Superior Court*)

■ **PLAIN MEANING**
···
     ➤ "Born alive" rule
     ➤ Criminal code commission

■ **LEGISLATION PERTAINING TO FETUSES**
···
     ➤ Abortion statutes
     ➤ Murder statutes
     ➤ Manslaughter statutes
     ➤ Fetal death statutes

■ **DECISIONS IN OTHER JURISDICTIONS**
···
     ➤ Code states
     ➤ Common law states

PUBLIC POLICY
COMPARISON TO CIVIL CASE (*Summerfield*)

words of the statute were understood at the time the legislation was enacted." In its analysis of the plain meaning of the phrase "human being," the court focuses on the common law "born alive" rule and the comments of one of the participants of the Criminal Code Commission (the committee appointed by the legislature to draft the statute) and concludes that both define a "human being" as a "person who has been born and is alive."

The court then reviews legislation in which the legislature specifically alluded to a fetus. It concludes that if the legislature had intended to include fetuses in the first degree murder statute, they would have done so just as they had in other statutes. The court bolsters its conclusion with policy reasons for deferring to the legislature and support from opinions rendered by courts in other jurisdictions. Finally, the court distinguishes the two cases from other jurisdictions that reached the opposite conclusion and also explains why *Summerfield* (the civil decision it had previously rendered) is inapplicable in a criminal case.

PUTTING IT INTO PRACTICE

Defining Ambiguous Terms

How did the *Vo* court answer the following questions?

1. How must criminal laws in Arizona be construed?

2. If the meaning of a statute is unclear, how must any doubts be resolved?

3. What was the "born alive" rule under the common law?

4. According to *Roe v. Wade* and the Arizona Criminal Code Commission, does the term "person" include unborn children?

5. How does the manslaughter statute support the court's position that the legislature intended to treat fetuses separately from persons in the criminal context?

6. Why is it significant that the legislature did not treat prohibited abortions as murder?

7. Are there any other areas of Arizona law that indicate that the Arizona legislature did not intend for a fetus to constitute a person?

8. Why does the court defer to the legislature in regard to the definition of "person"?

9. How does this court's resolution of the issue compare with the decisions of courts in other jurisdictions?

10. What is the relevance of being a "code state"?

11. Why does the court refuse to apply the *Summerfield* decision to a criminal case?

FIGURE 5.8
Conflicts in the Law

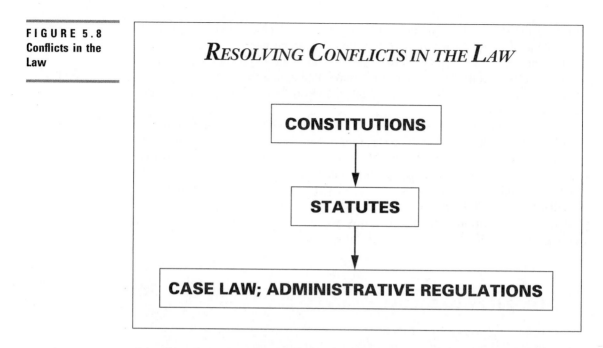

RESOLVING CONFLICTS IN THE LAW

CONSTITUTIONS

STATUTES

CASE LAW; ADMINISTRATIVE REGULATIONS

Conflicts in the Law

Another common task of courts is the resolution of conflicts in the law. Conflicts may exist between case law created by lower appellate courts, between case law and a constitution, between a statute and a constitution, etc. Often such conflict arises in cases in which a legislative body has created legislation or a court has rendered a decision that does not square with a provision in the state or national constitution. In recent times, for example, the courts have become embroiled in the abortion issue because they have been asked to review state legislation restricting abortions. Such legislation has arguably been at odds with the U.S. Supreme Court's interpretation of the right to privacy as expressed in *Roe v. Wade*, 410 U.S. 113 (1973).

In reviewing such legal conflicts, courts are required to conform to these basic principles.

- Statutes must defer to constitutions.

- Administrative regulations must defer to statutes.

- Case law must defer to statutes.

Under these guidelines, states cannot pass legislation that violates the U.S. Constitution or their own constitutions. Similarly, an administrative agency cannot create a regulation that is at odds with legislation in that jurisdiction or its own enabling act (the act by the legislature that enabled the administrative agency to create regulations).

PUTTING IT INTO PRACTICE
....

Conflicts in the Law
Read the following excerpt from *St. Joseph's Hospital and Medical Center v. Maricopa County,* 688 P.2d 986 (Ariz. 1984), the full text of

PUTTING IT INTO PRACTICE *(continued)*

....

which is found on pp. 348–351 in Appendix A, and explain what conflict the court is resolving. What basic principle must the court follow in resolving this conflict?

> At the time of the events at issue A.R.S. Sect. 11–291(A) charged the County Board of Supervisors with the authority "to provide for the hospitalization and medical care of the indigent in the county." Also, at that time, A.R.S. Sec. 11–297.01(B) provided that the county reimburse private hospitals for emergency care given to "qualified" patients, and that this reimbursement be retroactive to the inception of care. . . Those "qualified" for such emergency treatment are described in Sec. 11-297(A), which requires that the patient be indigent and "a resident of the county for the preceding twelve months." Thus, the issue may be characterized as follows: Under Arizona's statutes is the county's duty to reimburse a private hospital for emergency care delivered to indigents who have been a "resident of the county" relieved merely because the indigents, otherwise bona fide residents, are undocumented aliens? . . .
>
> The county draws attention to the Maricopa County Department of Health Services Eligibility Manual, which sets forth certain regulations regarding residency. Specifically, Regulation 4.05–3 states that an undocumented alien is ineligible for county subsidized health care. The county contends that this regulation reflects the intent of the state eligibility statutes. We reject this contention. The county regulation is invalid because it seeks to amend a statute enacted by the legislature and impermissibly limits the reach of the statutory language. . . [R]ules and regulations by an administrative or executive officer or body are always subordinate to the terms of the statute and in aid of the enforcement of its provisions. . .
>
> A county's attempt to limit the statutory definition of eligibility by administrative regulation, modifying the word "resident" by adding the adjective "legal," restricts the county's duty of reimbursement. Instead of reimbursing private hospitals for emergency medical care rendered to indigent "residents," the county, by its own regulation, seeks to limit its duty to reimbursing only for such care to "legal residents." The legislature is obviously aware of the considerable number of undocumented aliens in our state. Had it wished to limit emergency care to legal residents, or attempt to impose on private hospitals a duty to provide such care to "illegals" without reimbursement, it could have supplied the missing adjective itself. We believe the regulation is inconsistent with the legislature's choice not to limit the statutory language. . .

....

Fitting the Facts

Courts are often given a fact situation and must decide whether the facts satisfy recognized principles of the law. Many tort cases, for example, revolve around the question of negligence. A court must examine the facts, lay out elements of a negligence cause of action, and then decide whether the facts conform to the legal elements of negligence. (These elements are duty, breach of duty, causation, and damages.)

If a child is injured while riding a horse at a riding stable, for example, the court will have to decide whether the stable owner breached its duty of care to the child even though the owner required the child's parents to sign a release before allowing the child to ride. If the court decides that the release protected the owner from suit for ordinary negligence, the court will then have to determine if the owner's actions fell within the purview of gross negligence (which involves more outrageous conduct on the part of the defendant than ordinary negligence). To do so, the court would have to examine each fact carefully: what care did the owner use in selecting the horse to be ridden, what precisely caused the child to be hurt, what precautions had the owner taken to prevent such accidents, and so on. The court would then hold up each fact to the appropriate legal principles and look for a "fit." If the facts "fit" gross negligence, the court would hold accordingly.

PUTTING IT INTO PRACTICE
....

Fitting the Facts
Read *In the Matter of Charlotte K.,* 102 Misc.2d 848 (1980) (found in Appendix A on page 302) and explain how this case requires the court to "fit the facts."
....

Public Policy

Public policy is another guideline that courts frequently use in framing their decisions. It centers around concerns of fairness and justice. In trying to resolve a conflict where the legal principles are ambiguous or maybe even absent, a court may be driven by motives to do that which is most equitable for the parties and future litigants. Search and seizure law is largely driven by public policy concerns as courts struggle to balance the need of society for security against the privacy interests of individuals. The United States Supreme Court has bowed to the needs of law enforcement in limiting defendants' right to privacy in the last decade. Thus, the Court is relying on public policy to interpret the Fourth Amendment, which is the source of constitutional protection against unreasonable searches and seizures.

Another public policy argument is the "**slippery slope**." Although this argument is more concerned with efficiency than with justice and fairness, its intent is to protect the courts from an influx of cases. Using this argument, a court reasons that if it were to decide the case before it in a particularly beneficial way for one of the parties, the decision would open a floodgate of litigation that would overwhelm the court system. In other words, if the court were to take that first step down the "slippery slope," social chaos would ensue.

In *New York v. Riss*, 240 N.E.2d 860 (N.Y. 1968), for example, the court refused to allow a young woman to recover from the New York City Police Department after she was badly disfigured by a man who threw acid in her face. The plaintiff had repeatedly conveyed her fears of being assaulted by her eventual assailant to the police department, but they did not respond. The court refused the woman's recovery in part because of a fear that allowing her to do so would result in a barrage of litigation by crime victims who had notified the police of their apprehension of future attacks. Extrapolating the potential costs to the city and contemplating the spectre of bankruptcy, the court used a slippery slope argument to avoid what it perceived as a financial disaster.

Sometimes public policy arguments are more rationalizations for decisions than justifications dictated by the rigors of logic. A court may argue, for example, that the plight of a sympathetic plaintiff requires that relief be granted so that others similarly situated be protected, or it may argue that even though the plaintiff is a sympathetic one, his/her demands cannot be met lest it open the doors for similarly sympathetic future plaintiffs. Arguably, however, such arguments ensure the humanity of the law and protect us from purely mechanical, robotic decision making by judges. Regardless of your attitude toward public policy arguments, they are commonly used by the court and you should be alert to them.

PUTTING IT INTO PRACTICE

Public Policy

In which section of *In the Matter of Charlotte K.*, 102 Misc.2d 848 (1980) (located in Appendix A on page 302) does the court resort to a slippery slope argument?

In *Kline v. 1500 Massachusetts Ave. Apartment Corp.* (the full text of which is found in Chapter Six), the court is asked to determine whether a landlord owes a duty of care to protect his tenants from foreseeable criminal attack. How does the following excerpt from *Kline* illustrate a public policy argument?

> As between tenant and landlord, the landlord is the only one in the position to take the necessary acts of protection required. He is not an insurer, but he is obligated to minimize the risk to his tenants. Not only as between landlord and tenant is the landlord best equipped to guard against the predictable risk of intruders, but even as between landlord and the police power of government, the landlord is in the best position to take the necessary protective measures. Municipal police cannot patrol the entryways and the hallways, the garages and the basements of private multiple unit apartment dwellings. They are neither equipped, manned, nor empowered to do so. In the area of the predictable risk which materialized in this case, only the landlord could have taken measures which might have prevented the injuries suffered by appellant.
>
> We note that in the fight against crime the police are not expected to do it all; every segment of society has obligations

(continued)

Putting It into Practice *(continued)*

to aid in law enforcement and to minimize the opportunities for crime. The average citizen is ceaselessly warned to remove keys from automobiles and, in this jurisdiction, may be liable in tort for any injury caused in the operation of his car by a thief if he fails to do so, notwithstanding the intervening criminal act of the thief, a third party. . . In addition, auto manufacturers are persuaded to install special locking devices and buzzer alarms, and real estate developers, residential communities, and industrial areas are asked to install especially bright lights to deter the criminally inclined. It is only just that the obligations of landlords in their sphere be acknowledged and enforced.

PUTTING IT INTO PRACTICE

Which of the four organizational patterns does the court use in *Weirum v. RKO* to structure its rationale?

PROCEDURAL LIMITATIONS

In addition to *stare decisis*, which requires courts to work within the confines of existing legal principles, appellate courts are restricted as to what they can and cannot decide. Most importantly, they must defer to the decisions of lower courts in reference to factual issues. Findings of fact by a lower court or administrative agency are not to be disturbed unless there is no rational basis for the lower tribunal's decision. The reasoning behind this rule is that since the trial court or agency has the benefit of actually hearing testimony and observing the demeanor

**FIGURE 5.9
Procedural
Limitations**

PROCEDURAL LIMITATIONS

- **Findings of facts are not to be disturbed unless there is no rational basis for findings.**

- **Issues must be properly raised before court.**

 ➢ Objections must be made in timely manner.
 ➢ Objections must be appropriate.
 ➢ Appeals must be filed in timely and proper manner.

of witnesses it is in a far better position than appellate courts, which have only a sterile record for their review, to determine the credibility of evidence.

Because of this procedural rule, appellate judges are bound by factual findings that they may disagree with. This can be frustrating to the judge and misunderstood by those who read the appellate decision and believe that the appellate judge was in accord with the factual findings. Suppose an administrative law judge (ALJ) reviews an individual's application for reinstatement of a real estate license that was revoked because of the individual's commission of fraud. After listening to extensive testimony from character witnesses indicating that the individual is reformed and has led an exemplary life for seven years since the revocation and hearing no adverse testimony, the ALJ decides that none of the character evidence is credible and refuses to reinstate the license. Despite feelings to the contrary, an appellate judge is obliged to defer to the ALJ's findings regarding the credibility of the witnesses unless the appellate judge can find no rational basis for the findings. Such deference reflects nothing about the appellate judge's attitude about the testimony; it simply demonstrates adherence to appellate principles.

Furthermore, a court cannot review an issue that is not raised in accordance with the procedural rules governing the trial and appellate courts. Therefore, if at trial a party fails to object in a timely manner, to use the appropriate objection, or to file an appeal in a timely and proper manner, the appellate court is constrained from providing relief from a lower court's errors no matter how much it may desire to do so. The appellate process has often been compared to an obstacle course that presents hurdles for litigants to surmount if they are to be successful. At every step, parties are seemingly discouraged from pursuing appellate relief, and only those who "play the game" properly are afforded the opportunity to present their claims.

Appellate courts must also adhere to other constitutionally imposed and court-created restrictions that we will not discuss here. These include such doctrines as

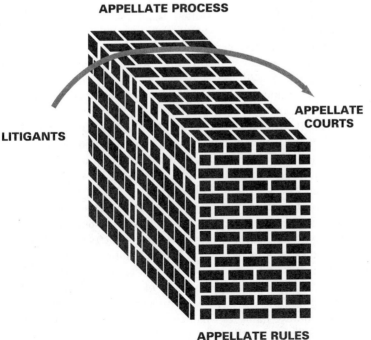

APPELLATE PROCESS

LITIGANTS

APPELLATE COURTS

APPELLATE RULES
Litigants have to jump over obstacles

FIGURE 5.10
Appellate Process

Practice Pointer	What happens at the trial level is extremely important, because appeals are costly and unlikely to change a judgment or verdict. A party wanting to appeal must post a bond and must pay attorneys to prepare the appeal, both of which are beyond the financial reach of many people. Attorneys are then limited in reference to appealable issues they can select because of the restrictions mentioned above. In the criminal area, even if an error is discovered by the appellate court, the error is often considered "harmless" and the conviction is preserved. For all of these reasons, experienced trial attorneys realize that if they are to prevail, they must do so at the trial level, because they are unlikely to find relief at the appellate level.

standing, ripeness, mootness, advisory opinions, and the avoidance of political questions. You will learn about these concepts in other courses. They are mentioned here only to make you aware that appellate decisions are in many respects straitjacketed by the limitations imposed on the courts by legislative enactment or constitutional provisions. These limitations are designed to encourage the finality of litigation at the trial court level. By preventing the endless overturning of cases, a fairer, more efficient system of dispute resolution is created.

ANALYSIS OF A RATIONALE

Read *Linthicum v. Nationwide Life Ins. Co.*, found on pp. 262–268 in Appendix A, carefully, making sure you digest the facts, identify the issues, and then focus on the court's reasoning. The court's task centers around the clarification of an ambiguous term—"evil mind." Notice how the court begins its analysis with a litany of existing legal principles as expressed in Arizona law, the law of other jurisdictions, and legal treatises. Courts commonly lay this groundwork of known principles before delving into the area of law that remains unresolved.

The court then examines the legal patchwork that has been built around the concept of "evil mind." It observes with dismay that this concept has been painted with such broad strokes that the term has become virtually meaningless and susceptible to unprincipled manipulation by attorneys. The court decides it must establish a "less broad standard for punitive damages . . ." Reviewing the conclusions reached by other courts and its own previous decisions, the court uses inductive reasoning to arrive at a general principle. It concludes that punitive damages require conduct that is "outwardly aggravated, outrageous, malicious or fraudulent" with an "intent to injure the plaintiff" or with "deliberate indifference [to] the rights of others, consciously disregarding the unjustifiably substantial risk of significant harm to them." In essence, the court reviews a series of decision and formulates a general principle that captures the common denominator in existing case law and preserves the essence of punitive damages—namely, that they are to be reserved to punish only the most egregious of tortfeasors.

Then, using deductive reasoning, the court applies its definition to the facts at hand. The court looks at specific acts of Nationwide and concludes that while demonstrative of bad faith these acts do not evidence a "desire to ... consciously disregard the Linthicums' rights, as is necessary to warrant punitive damages." The court concludes that although "Nationwide follows a tough claims policy ... it is not "aggravated, outrageous, oppressive or fraudulent." Notice how the court in its conclusion mimics the terminology ("aggravated," "outrageous," and "fraudulent") used in its definition of "evil mind." Keep this technique in mind when you are preparing a memorandum. This transference of language from the "rule" to the "conclusion" is an excellent analytical practice that you will want to emulate.

CHAPTER SUMMARY

Knowing black letter law is not sufficient; the rationale of case law must be mastered. The rationale is based on inductive and deductive reasoning. Inductive reasoning is reasoning by analogy or reasoning from a series of premises to a general conclusion. Deductive reasoning begins with a general principle and results in application to a specific situation. The syllogism, which consists of a major and minor premise and a conclusion, is the most common form of deductive reasoning used in the law. If either of the premises is flawed, the conclusion is necessarily false.

Within the context of inductive and deductive reasoning, courts organize their rationale on the basis of four basic patterns: (1) definition of ambiguous terms or concepts; (2) resolution of conflicting provisions of the law; (3) application of legal principles to a fact situation that differs from fact patterns in other appellate decisions; and (4) discussion of public policy. Appellate courts are constrained by a number of procedural rules that limit their options in terms of providing relief to parties. For that reason, parties who fail to prevail at the trial court level are unlikely to do so at the appellate level.

KEY TERMS

deductive reasoning	legislative intent	rationale	syllogism
inductive reasoning	public policy	slippery slope	

COGNITIVE CALISTHENICS

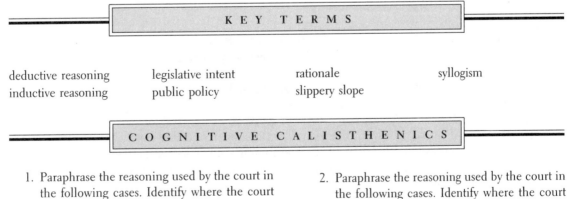

1. Paraphrase the reasoning used by the court in the following cases. Identify where the court used inductive or deductive arguments (suggested responses in Appendix B).
   (a) *Nienstedt v. Wetzel*
   (b) *White v. Mitchell*
   (c) *Olson v. Walker*

2. Paraphrase the reasoning used by the court in the following cases. Identify where the court used inductive or deductive arguments.
   (a) *Cundick v. Broadbent*
   (b) *Matter of Estate of Swenson*
   (c) *BenShalom v. Marsh*
   (d) *Minnesota v. Dickerson*

CHAPTER SIX

BRIEFING CASES

Chapter Objectives

In this chapter you will learn:

- Why briefing cases is important.

- The standard format for a case brief.

- How to prepare a case brief.

- How to synthesize cases.

WHAT IS A CASE BRIEF?

A case brief is a summary of the essential components of a case. By reading a case brief, you can quickly ascertain what the essential facts of the case are, what proceedings led up to the case, what issue was before the court, and what the court decided and why. (See Figure 6.2.)

You will not find universal agreement among law professors and practitioners as to the optimal makeup of a case brief. A suggested format will be offered here, but you may want to modify it to meet your needs or the demands of your employer or professor. In some respects, briefing cases is similar to taking notes. Your style of taking notes should reflect your unique listening and analytical preferences. So, too, should your case briefs reflect your own needs and preferences (unless you are preparing them for someone else).

Remember that a case brief differs from a brief prepared for a court. The purpose of the latter is to persuade a court to render a particular decision or to affirm, reverse, or modify a lower court's decision. Such a brief is anything but brief—being typically in the 15- to 25-page range. A case brief, on the other hand, usually requires only a few pages.

## PURPOSE OF A CASE BRIEF	**FIGURE 6.1** **Purpose of a Case** **Brief**

- ■ **Gain better understanding of cases.**
  ....

- ■ **Actively read cases.**
  ....

- ■ **Facilitate case synthesis.**
  ....

- ■ **Reduce rereading of cases.**
  ....

WHAT IS THE PURPOSE OF A CASE BRIEF?

Typically, you will brief cases for yourself, but you may be called upon to do it for an attorney. In law school, students are strongly encouraged to brief the cases they are reading to enhance their understanding. No matter who the audience, the purpose is to summarize the key elements of the case. Rather than having to reread the entire case, you can read your brief to refresh your memory. Likewise, an attorney can read the brief to understand the legal principles involved and to decide whether the actual case is significant enough to warrant reading it.

When doing legal research, you will find briefing cases to be absolutely essential to gaining an understanding of case law. Simply reading cases fosters passive participation. In other words, you can read a case over and over without gaining any real understanding of the court's reasoning. But if you put pen to paper and translate what you have read into your own words, you become actively engaged. This active engagement dramatically enhances your ability to critically reflect on the case. Writing forces the brain to engage in a creative process. In this process, you begin to see connections and interrelationships, to ask critical questions, and to postulate possible extensions of legal principles. Without engaging in such a critical thinking process, you might never get past a superficial understanding of a case. You might also find that you are confused or do not really understand what the court is saying.

To better understand the difference between active and passive learning, reflect for a moment on the difference between your preparation for a multiple-choice test and your preparation for an essay test. Is it not true that your understanding of a subject need be only fairly superficial for you to pass a typical multiple-choice test? Do you not have to be much better prepared and possess a much higher level of understanding to pass an essay exam on the same material? By the same token, reading a case several times may allow you to pass a superficial multiple-choice examination on it, but writing a case brief better prepares you for an in-depth essay exam. To draft a memorandum, your understanding of the case law you are working with must be of the latter caliber.

Case brief preparation facilitates the **synthesis** (integration) of cases. The difficulty in reading large numbers of cases is seeing the commonality among them or distinguishing them. After a while, all the cases begin to blur together. The fact patterns swim in your head and become entangled with one another. Briefing cases allows you to sort out the cases on an orderly basis. You can glean the essential facts and associate them with the rationale offered by the courts. With the facts, holdings, and rationale clearly filed in your mind, you will more readily see similarities and dissimilarities in fact patterns and will understand why courts arrived at apparently contradictory holdings. As patterns emerge, the logic (or lack of logic) of case law will appear. Where there was once chaos, you will begin to see order. At this point, you can synthesize a number of cases by reducing all of the holdings into some general rules of law.

As the benefit of briefing cases becomes clearer to you, you may wonder why this practice is not second nature to every student of the law. That question might best be answered with another question. Why do people continue to diet even though the evidence is almost irrefutable that diets do not work over the long term? Could it be that losing weight takes time and effort, i.e., eating less and exercising more, and that people are constantly looking for shortcuts? Just as good health requires more than fad diets and capricious exercise, the analysis of case law requires more than cursory reading. Briefing cases takes time and effort. Many people take the shortcut and just passively read cases. But the shortcut does not achieve the same level of clarity or synthesis that briefing does.

You will no doubt find yourself tempted after a while to circumvent briefing, either because of time constraints or because you have rationalized that you are just as proficient whether or not you brief cases. This is a tempting trap, but those who have succumbed to it have inevitably discovered that the shortcut cost them time.

Reading is simply not a viable substitute for writing. Writing requires you to actively interact with the material. Writing requires your mind to seek relationships. Writing requires you to put your understanding in words and phrases that have special significance to you. Writing requires you to be mentally alert (relatively speaking, at least). None of this can be accomplished by merely highlighting key phrases. (Even that bright yellow pen will not grace you with clarity.) I think you will discover that, in the long run, briefing cases saves you time. Issues become clearer sooner, and you are often spared rereading cases unnecessarily.

THE FORMAT OF A BRIEF

Having convinced yourself that briefing is important (reread the section "What Is the Purpose of a Case Brief?" until you are so convinced), consider now the elements of a typical brief. Most briefs contain the following.

1. Case identification
2. Procedural history
3. Facts
4. Issue(s)
5. Holding(s)
6. Rationale
7. Synthesis

Remember that briefing is akin to taking notes. No one method has ever been proclaimed the winner of the "how to correctly brief" contest. (Although many a heady debate has undoubtedly been devoted to the resolution of this question.) Some people favor one order of these elements over another. Some include additional elements, while others delete some of the elements. After you familiarize yourself with the basic process, adapt your briefs to meet your needs in any particular research situation. Just as note taking is intended to facilitate your recollection and integration of key concepts, briefing is intended to facilitate your recollection of key facts and integration of related issues. Use the form of briefing that best promotes the accomplishment of these goals for you.

The case of *Kline v. 1500 Massachusetts Ave. Apartment Corp.* is used here to demonstrate the preparation of a case brief. Having a basic understanding of this case will help you more readily identify the elements included in a brief.

Sarah B. KLINE, Appellant,

v.

1500 MASSACHUSETTS AVENUE APARTMENT CORPORATION et al.
No. 23401.

United States Court of Appeals,
District of Columbia Circuit.

Argued April 10, 1970.

Petition for Rehearing Denied
Sept. 8, 1970.

Action to recover for injuries sustained by tenant when she was criminally assaulted in common hallway of apartment house. The United States District Court for the District of Columbia, Alexander Holtzoff, J., entered judgment for landlord, and tenant appealed. The Court of Appeals, Wilkey, Circuit Judge, held that evidence that landlord had notice, both actual and constructive, that tenants were being subjected to crimes against their persons and their property in and from common hallways and that, for period just prior to time of assault on tenant, apartment building was undergoing a rising wave of crime established that landlord was aware of conditions which created a likelihood that further criminal attacks on tenants would occur and thus, at time of attack, landlord was under a duty of protection; accordingly, where applicable standard of care in providing such protection was that standard which landlord himself was employing at time tenant became a resident on premises, which standard was not maintained, landlord was liable for resulting injuries to tenant.

Reversed and remanded for determination of damages.

MacKinnon, Circuit Judge, dissented and filed opinion.

1. **Landlord and Tenant k162, 167(1)**   Rationale of rule that landlord reserving under his control halls, stairs, or other parts of property for use in common by all tenants has a duty to all those on promises of legal right to use ordinary care and diligence to maintain retained parts in a reasonably safe condition is the same, whether applied to a physical defect in building leading to tenant's injury or predictable criminal acts by third parties.

2. **Landlord and Tenant k162**   Rationale of general rule exonerating a third party from any duty to protect another from a criminal attack has no applicability to landlord-tenant relationship in multiple dwelling houses.

3. **Landlord and Tenant k162**   Where landlord has notice of repeated criminal assaults and robberies, has notice that these crimes occurred in portion of premises exclusively within his control, has every reason to expect like crimes to happen again, and

has exclusive power to take preventive action, duty is on landlord to take those steps which are within his power to minimize predictable risk to tenants.

4. **Landlord and Tenant k162, 167(1)** Duty of taking protective measures guarding entire premises and areas peculiarly under landlord's control against perpetration of criminal acts is on landlord, the party to lease contract having effective capacity to perform necessary acts.

5. **Landlord and Tenant k169(6)** Evidence that landlord had notice, both actual and constructive, that tenants were being subjected to crimes against their persons and their property in and from common hallways and that, for period just prior to time of assault on tenant, apartment building was undergoing a rising wave of crime established that landlord was aware of conditions which created a likelihood that further criminal acts on tenants would occur, and thus, at time of attack, duty of protection was on landlord, breach of which made landlord liable for resulting injuries to tenant.

6. **Landlord and Tenant k162** There is implied in contract between landlord and tenant an obligation on landlord to provide those protective measures which are within his reasonable capacity.

7. **Landlord and Tenant k162** Under facts presented, applicable standard of care in providing protection for tenant against criminal attacks in common hallways by intruders was that standard which landlord himself employed at time tenant became resident on premises and, without regard to whether precise measures for security which were then invoked should have been kept up, same relative degree of security should have been maintained.

Mr. Albert J. Ahern, Jr., Washington, D.C., for appellant.

Mr. Laurence T. Scott, Washington, D.C., for appellee.

Before TAMM, MacKINNON and WILKEY, Circuit Judges.

WILKEY, Circuit Judge:

The appellee apartment corporation states that there is "only one issue presented for review * * * whether a duty should be placed on a landlord to take steps to protect tenants from foreseeable criminal acts committed by third parties". The District Court as a matter of law held that there is no such duty. We find that

there is, and that in the circumstances here the applicable standard of care was breached. We therefore reverse and remand to the District Court for the determination of damages for the appellant.

I

The appellant, Sarah B. Kline, sustained serious injuries when she was criminally assaulted and robbed at approximately 10:15 in the evening by an intruder in the common hallway of an apartment house at 1500 Massachusetts Avenue. This facility, into which the appellant Kline moved in October 1959, is a large apartment building with approximately 585 individual apartment units. It has a main entrance on Massachusetts Avenue, with side entrances on both 15th and 16th Streets. At the time the appellant first signed a lease a doorman was on duty at the main entrance twenty-four hours a day, and at least one employee at all times manned a desk in the lobby from which all persons using the elevators could be observed.[1] The 15th Street door adjoined the entrance to a parking garage used by both the tenants and the public. Two garage attendants were stationed at this dual entranceway; the duties of each being arranged so that one of them always was in position to observe those entering either the apartment building or the garage. The 16th Street entrance was unattended during the day but was locked after 9:00 P.M.

By mid-1966, however, the main entrance had no doorman, the desk in the lobby was left unattended much of the time, the 15th Street entrance was generally unguarded due to a decrease in garage personnel, and the 16th Street entrance was often left unlocked all night. The entrances were allowed to be thus unguarded in the face of an increasing number of assaults, larcenies, and robberies being perpetrated against the tenants in and from the common hallways of the apartment building. These facts were undisputed,[2] and were supported by a detailed chronologi-

---

1. Miss Kline testified that she had initially moved into the building not only because of its central location, but also because she was interested in security, and had been impressed by the precautions taken at the main entrance.

2. At trial, the allegations of paragraph 8 of the Complaint—except as they related to the question of notice to the landlord—were stipulated as true. Paragraph 8 reads as follows:

   8. Plaintiff says unto the Court that prior to this assault upon your plaintiff the defendants had been on notice of a *series of assaults, robberies and other criminal offenses* being perpetrated upon its tenants, and yet said defendants while on notice of this dangerous condition negligently failed to hire a sufficient number of guards to impose any

cal listing of offenses admitted into evidence. The landlord had notice of these crimes and had in fact been urged by appellant Kline herself prior to the events leading to the instant appeal to take steps to secure the building.[3]

Shortly after 10:00 P.M. on November 17, 1966, Miss Kline was assaulted and robbed just outside her apartment on the first floor above the street level of this 585 unit apartment building. This occurred only two months after Leona Sullivan, another female tenant, had been similarly attacked in the same common-way.

---

2. (*continued*) of the normal security requirements that in the exercise of due care they owed to plaintiff in her capacity as a tenant, when said defendants were on actual notice of complaints filed by other tenants prior to the assault on your plaintiff, said complaints occurring on the following dates and involving the following apartments:
(citing 25 individual instances).
(Emphasis added.)
During trial, when plaintiff's counsel attempted to pursue the question of the frequency of assaults or other crimes with his witness, the court cut off his examination, since it felt that the point had already been conceded. Vis, the following:

Q. Now in your talks with Miss Bloom were you aware between January of 1966 and November of 1966 when you were assaulted of any other assaults or crimes within this apartment house other than what you have already testified to about police cars being present?
A. It is hard to pin them down to the specific date but there were so many happening. My girl friend's apartment was broken into, five of them within an hour. I don't know what date that was.
Q. I am not asking for dates. I am asking were you generally aware of offenses and crimes being committed in this apartment complex between January—
The Court: You allege that in Paragraph 8 of your complaint and *that was conceded.* (Emphasis added.)
Mr. Ahern: I stand corrected, Your Honor.
We also note that on brief, and at oral argument, 1500 Massachusetts Avenue never challenged the assertions of the appellant regarding the frequency of assaults and other crimes being perpetrated against the tenants on their premises. With the record in this posture, we can only conclude that what was alleged and stipulated was what actually occurred.

3. Appellant Kline testified that one could hardly fail to notice the police cars about the building after each reported crime. She further testified that in 1966, before her assault, she herself had discussed the crime situation with Miss Bloom, the landlord's agent at the premises, and had asked her "why they didn't do something about securing the building". Moreover, the record contains twenty police reports of crimes occurring in the building in the year 1966, showing that in several instances these crimes were an almost daily occurrence. Such reports in themselves constitute constructive notice to the landlord.

II

At the outset we note that of the crimes of violence, robbery, and assault which had been occurring with mounting frequency on the premises at 1500 Massachusetts Avenue, the assaults on Miss Kline and Miss Sullivan took place in the hallways of the building, which were under the exclusive control of the appellee landlord. Even in those crimes of robbery or assault committed in individual apartments, the intruders of necessity had to gain entrance through the common entry and passageways.[4] These premises fronted on three heavily traveled streets, and had multiple entrances. The risk to be guarded against therefore was the risk of unauthorized entrance into the apartment house by intruders bent upon some crime of violence or theft.

While the apartment lessees themselves could take some steps to guard against this risk by installing extra heavy locks and other security devices on the doors and windows of their respective apartments, yet this risk in the greater part could only be guarded against by the landlord. No individual tenant had it within his power to take measures to guard the garage entranceways, to provide scrutiny at the main entrance of the building, to patrol the common hallways and elevators, to set up any kind of a security alarm system in the building, to provide additional locking devices on the main doors, to provide a system of announcement for authorized visitors only, to close the garage doors at appropriate hours, and to see that the entrance was manned at all times.

The risk of criminal assault and robbery on a tenant in the common hallways of the building was thus entirely predictable; that same risk had been occurring with increasing frequency over a period of several months immediately prior to the incident giving rise to this case; it was a risk whose prevention or minimization was almost entirely within the power of the

---

4. The plaintiff testified that she had returned to her apartment after leaving work at 10:00 PM. We are in agreement with the trial court that her assailant was an intruder. *See* the court's comment in note 24, *infra.*

That such intruders did enter apartments from the hallways is substantiated by the Police reports which appear in the Record. In a number of instances doors are described as having been forced; in another instance, a tenant surprised a man standing in his front hallway; and there are still more instances of female tenants being awakened in the early morning hours to find an intruder entering their front doors. We also take notice of the fact that this apartment building is of the high rise type, with no easily accessible means of entry on the floors above the street level except by the hallways.

landlord; and the risk materialized in the assault and robbery of appellant on November 17, 1966.

III

In this jurisdiction, certain duties have been assigned to the landlord because of his *control* of common hallways, lobbies, stairwells, etc., used by all tenants in multiple dwelling units. This Court in Levine v. Katz, 132 U.S.App.D.C. 173, 174, 407 F.2d 303, 304 (1968), pointed out that:

> It has long been well settled in this jurisdiction that, where a landlord leases separate portions of property and reserves under his own control the halls, stairs, or other parts of the property for use in common by all tenants, he has a duty to all those on the premises of legal right to use ordinary care and diligence to maintain the retained parts in a reasonably safe condition.

[1] While Levine v. Katz dealt with a physical defect in the building leading to plaintiff's injury, the rationale as applied to predictable criminal acts by third parties is the same.[5] The duty is the landlord's because by his control of the areas of common use and common danger he is the only party who has the *power* to make the necessary repairs or to provide the necessary protection.

As a general rule, a private person does not have a duty to protect another from a criminal attack by a third person. We recognize that this rule has sometimes in the past been applied in landlord-tenant law, even by this court.[6] Among the reasons for the application of this rule to landlords are: judicial reluctance to tamper with the traditional common law concept of the landlord-tenant relationship; the notion that the act of a third person in committing an intentional tort or crime is a superseding cause of the harm to another resulting therefrom; the oftentime difficult problem of determining foreseeability of criminal acts; the vagueness of the standard which the landlord must meet; the economic consequences of the imposition of the duty; and conflict with the public policy allocating the duty of protecting citizens from criminal acts to the government rather than the private sector.

[2, 3] But the rationale of this very broad general rule falters when it is applied to the conditions of mod-

ern day urban apartment living, particularly in the circumstances of this case. The rationale of the general rule exonerating a third party from any duty to protect another from a criminal attack has no applicability to the landlord-tenant relationship in multiple dwelling houses. The landlord is no insurer of his tenants' safety, but he certainly is no bystander. And where, as here, the landlord has notice of repeated criminal assaults and robberies, has notice that these crimes occurred in the portion of the premises exclusively within his control, has every reason to expect like crimes to happen again, and has the exclusive power to take preventive action, it does not seem unfair to place upon the landlord a duty to take those steps which are within his power to minimize the predictable risk to his tenants.

This court has recently had occasion to review landlord-tenant law as applied to multiple family urban dwellings. In Javins v. First National Realty Corporation,[7] the traditional analysis of a lease as being a conveyance of an interest in land—with all the medieval connotations this often brings—was reappraised, and found lacking in several respects. This court noted that the value of the lease to the modern apartment dweller is that it gives him "a well known package of goods and services—a package which includes not merely walls and ceilings, but also adequate heat, light and ventilation, serviceable plumbing facilities, *secure windows and doors*, proper sanitation, and proper maintenance."[8] It does not give him the land itself, and to the tenant as a practical matter this is supremely unimportant. Speaking for the court, Judge Wright then went on to state, "In our judgment the trend toward treating leases as contracts is wise and well considered. Our holding in this case reflects a belief that leases of urban dwelling units should be interpreted and construed like any other contract."[9]

Treating the modern day urban lease as a contract, this court in *Javins, supra,* recognized, among other things, that repair of the leased premises in a multiple dwelling unit may require access to equipment in areas in the control of the landlord, and skills which no urban tenant possesses. Accordingly, this court delineated the landlord's duty to repair as including continued maintenance of the rented apartment throughout the term of the lease, rightfully placing the duty to maintain the premises upon the

---

5. Kendall v. Gore Properties, 98 U.S.App.D.C. 378, 236 F.2d 673 (1956).

6. Appelbaum v. Kidwell, 56 App.D.C. 311, 12 F.2d 846 (1926); Goldberg v. Housing Authority of Newark, 38 N.J. 578, 186 A.2d 291, 10 A.L.R.3d 595 (1962); *but see* Ramsay v. Morrissette, D.C.App., 252 A.2d 509 (1969) and Kendall v. Gore Properties, *supra*, note 5.

7. 138 U.S.App.D.C. 369, 428 F.2d 1071 (1970).

8. *Id.* 138 U.S.App.D.C. at 372, 428 F.2d at 1074, (emphasis added).

9. *Id.* 138 U.S.App.D.C. at 373, 428 F.2d at 1075.

party to the lease contract having the capacity to do so, based upon an implied warranty of habitability.[10]

[4] In the case at bar we place the duty of taking protective measures guarding the entire premises and the areas peculiarly under the landlord's control against the perpetration of criminal acts upon the landlord, the party to the lease contract who has the effective capacity to perform these necessary acts.

As a footnote to *Javins, supra*, Judge Wright, in clearing away some of the legal underbrush from medieval common law obscuring the modern landlord-tenant relationship, referred to an innkeeper's liability in comparison with that of the landlord to his tenant. "Even the old common law courts responded with a different rule for a landlord-tenant relationship which did not conform to the model of the usual agrarian lease. Much more substantial obligations were placed upon the keepers of inns (the only multiple dwelling houses known to the common law)."

Specifically, innkeepers have been held liable for assaults which have been committed upon their guests by third parties, if they have breached a duty which is imposed by reason of the innkeeper-guest relationship. By this duty, the innkeeper is generally bound to exercise reasonable care to protect the guest from abuse or molestation from third parties, be they innkeeper's employees, fellow guests, or intruders, if the attack could, or in the exercise of reasonable care, should have been anticipated.[11]

Liability in the innkeeper-guest relationship is based as a matter of law either upon the innkeeper's supervision, care, or control of the premises,[12] or by reason of a contract which some courts have implied from the entrustment by the guest of his personal comfort and safety to the innkeeper. In the latter analysis, the contract is held to give the guest the right to expect a standard of treatment at the hands of the innkeeper which includes an obligation on the part of the latter to exercise reasonable care in protecting the guest.[13]

Other relationships in which similar duties have been imposed include landowner-invitee, businessman-patron, employer-employee, school district-pupil, hospital-patient, and carrier-passenger.[14] In all, the theory of liability is essentially the same: that since the ability of one of the parties to provide for his own protection has been limited in some way by his submission to the control of the other, a duty should be imposed upon the one possessing control (and thus the power to act) to take reasonable precautions to protect the other one from assaults by third parties which, at least, could reasonably have been anticipated. However, there is no liability normally imposed upon the one having the power to act if the violence is sudden and unexpected provided that the source of the violence is not an employee of the one in control.[15]

We are aware of various cases in other jurisdictions following a different line of reasoning, conceiving of the landlord and tenant relationship along more traditional common law lines, and on varying fact situations reaching a different result from that we reach here. Typical of these is a much cited (although only a 4–3) decision of the Supreme Court of New Jersey, Goldberg v. Housing Authority of Newark, *supra* relied on by appellee landlord here. There the court said:

> Everyone can foresee the commission of crime virtually anywhere and at any time. If foreseeability itself gave rise to a duty to provide "police" protection for others, every residential curtilage, every shop, every store, every manufacturing plant would have to be patrolled by the private arm of the owner. And since hijacking and attack upon occupants of motor vehicles are also foreseeable, it would be the duty of every motorist to provide armed protection for his passengers and the property of others. Of course, none of this is at all palatable.[16]

---

10. The landlord's duty to repair was held to include the leased premises in Whetzel v. Jess Fisher Management Co., 108 U.S.App.D.C. 385, 282 F.2d 943 (1960). In that case, we held that the Housing Regulations altered the old common law rule, and further, that the injured tenant had a cause of action in *tort* against the landlord for his failure to discharge his duty to repair the premises. Our recent decision in Kanelos v. Kettler, 132 U.S.App.D.C. 133, 406 F.2d 951 (1968), reaffirms the position taken in *Whetzel*.

11. An excellent discussion of the innkeeper's duty to his guest, including citations to relevant case material, is found in: Annot., 70 A.L.R.2d 621 (1960).

12. Gurren v. Casperon, 147 Wash. 257, 265 P. 472 (1928). *See also* Fortney v. Hotel Rancroft, Inc., 5 Ill.App.2d 327, 125 N.E.2d 544 (1955).

13. McKee v. Sheraton-Russell, Inc., 268 F.2d 669 (1959) (applying New York law).

14. Cases involving these relationships are collected and summarized in Goldberg v. Housing Authority of Newark, 38 N.J. 578, 186 A.2d 291, 10 A.L.R.3d 595 (1962).

15. *See:* Central of Georgia R. Co. v. Hopkins, 18 Ga.App. 230, 89 S.E. 186 (1916); Martincich v. Guardian Cab Co., 10 N.Y.S.2d 308 (1938, City Ct. N.Y.); and Callender v. Wilson, La.App., 162 So.2d 203, writ refused 246 La. 351, 164 So.2d 352 (1964).

16. 38 N.J. 578, 186 A.2d 291, 293, 10 A.L.R.3d 595, 601 (1962).

This language seems to indicate that the court was using the word *foreseeable* interchangeably with the word *possible*. In that context, the statement is quite correct. It would be folly to impose liability for mere possibilities. But we must reach the question of liability for attacks which are foreseeable in the sense that they are *probable* and *predictable*. Thus, the United States Supreme Court, in Lillie v. Thompson[17] encountered no difficulty in finding that the defendant-employer was liable to the employee because it "was aware of conditions which created a likelihood" of criminal attack.

[5] In the instant case, the landlord had notice, both actual and constructive, that the tenants were being subjected to crimes against their persons and their property in and from the common hallways. For the period just prior to the time of the assault upon appellant Kline the record contains unrefuted evidence that the apartment building was undergoing a rising wave of crime. Under these conditions, we can only conclude that the landlord here "was aware of conditions which created a likelihood" (actually, almost a certainty) that further criminal attacks upon tenants would occur.

Upon consideration of all pertinent factors, we find that there is a duty of protection owed by the landlord to the tenant in an urban multiple unit apartment dwelling.

Summarizing our analysis, we find that this duty of protection arises, first of all, from the logic of the situation itself. If we were answering without the benefit of any prior precedent the issue as posed by the appellee landlord here, "whether a duty should be placed on a landlord to take steps to protect tenants from foreseeable criminal acts committed by third parties," we should have no hesitancy in answering it affirmatively, at least on the basis of the facts of this case.

As between tenant and landlord, the landlord is the only one in the position to take the necessary acts of protection required. He is not an insurer, but he is obligated to minimize the risk to his tenants. Not only as between landlord and tenant is the landlord best equipped to guard against the predictable risk of intruders, but even as between landlord and the police power of government, the landlord is in the best position to take the necessary protective measures. Municipal police cannot patrol the entryways and the hallways, the garages and the basements of private multiple unit apartment dwellings. They are neither equipped, manned, nor empowered to do so. In the area of the predictable risk which materialized in this case, only the landlord could have taken measures which might have prevented the injuries suffered by appellant.

We note that in the fight against crime the police are not expected to do it all;[18] every segment of society has obligations to aid in law enforcement and to minimize the opportunities for crime. The average citizen is ceaselessly warned to remove keys from automobiles and, in this jurisdiction, may be liable in tort for any injury caused in the operation of his car by a thief if he fails to do so, notwithstanding the intervening criminal act of the thief, a third party. Gaither v. Myers, 131 U.S.App.D.C. 216, 404 F.2d 216 (1968). In addition, auto manufacturers are persuaded to install special locking devices and buzzer alarms, and real estate developers, residential communities, and industrial areas are asked to install especially bright lights to deter the criminally inclined. It is only just that the obligations of landlords in their sphere be acknowledged and enforced.[19]

---

17. 332 U.S. 459, 68 S.Ct. 140, 92 L.Ed. 73 (1947).

---

18. In this regard, we observe that in some of the relationships in which a duty of protection has been found, the courts display no compunction in requiring the use of security guards or special police, where their use is reasonably necessary to see to the safety of those under the control of another. Thus, in Dilley v. Baltimore Transit Co., 183 Md. 557, 39 A.2d 469 (1944), the court said:

Carriers are not required to furnish a police force sufficient to overcome all violence of other passengers or strangers, when such violence is not to be reasonably expected; but the carrier is required to furnish *sufficient police force to protect its passengers* from the assaults or violence of other passengers or strangers which might reasonably be expected, and to see that its police perform their duty. (Emphasis supplied.)

See also Amoruso v. New York City Transit Authority, 12 A.D.2d 11, 207 N.Y.S.2d 855 (1960); and Dean v. Hotel Greenwich Corp., 21 Misc.2d 702, 193 N.Y.S.2d 712 (1959).

19. In Kendall v. Gore Properties, *supra*, note 3, this court recognized that the obligation of the landlord to his tenant includes the duty to protect him against the criminal acts of third parties. The District of Columbia Court of Appeals, noting this in Ramsay v. Morrissette, *supra*, said of the imposition of this duty on the landlord:

Such a duty was found in Kendall v. Gore Properties, 98 U.S.App.D.C. 378, 236 F.2d 673 (1956), where the landlord's employee, alleged to be of unsound mind, strangled to death a tenant whose apartment he was painting. The negligence in *Kendall*, however, was the failure to make any investigation whatever of the employee before hiring him to work, without supervision, in the apartment of a young woman, living alone. The court did say that the tenant, under her lease, paid both for shelter and protection. It said further: "We have heretofore made clear as to apartment houses, the reasons which underlie the landlord's duty under modern conditions and which,

[6] Secondly, on the rationale of this court in Levine v. Katz, Kendall v. Gore Properties, and Javins v. First National Realty Corporation, *supra*, there is implied in the contract between landlord and tenant an obligation on the landlord to provide those protective measures which are within his reasonable capacity. Here the protective measures which were in effect in October 1959 when appellant first signed a lease were drastically reduced. She continued after the expiration of the first term of the lease on a month to month tenancy. As this court pointed out in *Javins*, *supra*, "Since the lessees continue to pay the same rent, they were entitled to expect that the landlord would continue to keep the premises in their beginning condition during the lease term. It is precisely such expectations that the law now recognizes as deserving of formal, legal protection."[20]

Thirdly, if we reach back to see the precedents of common law, on the question of whether there exists or does not exist a duty on the owner of the premises to provide protection against criminal acts by third parties, the most analogous relationship to that of the modern day urban apartment house dweller is not that of a landlord and tenant, but that of innkeeper and

guest. We can also consider other relationships, cited above, in which an analogous duty has been found to exist.

IV

We now turn to the standard of care which should be applied in judging if the landlord has fulfilled his duty of protection to the tenant. Although in many cases the language speaks as if the standard of care itself varies, in the last analysis the standard of care is the same—reasonable care in all the circumstances.[21] The specific measures to achieve this standard vary with the individual circumstances. It may be impossible to describe in detail for all situations of landlord-tenant relationships, and evidence of custom amongst landlords of the same class of building may play a significant role in determining if the standard has been met.

In the case at bar, appellant's repeated efforts to introduce evidence as to the standard of protection commonly provided in apartment buildings of the same character and class as 1500 Massachusetts Avenue at the time of the assault upon Miss Kline were invariably frustrated by the objections of opposing counsel and the impatience of the trial judge. At one

---

19. *(continued)*

as to various hazards call for at least 'reasonable or ordinary care, which means reasonably safe conduct, but there is no sufficient reason for requiring less.' True, the landlord does not become a guarantor of the safety of his tenant. But, if he knows, or in the exercise of ordinary care ought to know, of a possibly dangerous situation and fails to take such steps as an ordinarily prudent person, in view of existing circumstances, would have exercised to avoid injury to his tenant, he may be liable, (citations omitted)"

The court also stressed that '*particular* conduct, *depending upon circumstances*, can raise an issue for the jury to decide in terms of negligence and proximate cause.' Id. at 384, 236 F.2d at 679. (Footnotes omitted)

The language that the District of Columbia Court of Appeals quoted from *Kendall* signals the extension of a rule theretofore applied only to injuries caused by defects or obstacles in areas under the landlord's control (see Levine v. Katz, *supra*), to criminal acts of third parties. By our decision today, we merely amplify and refine our reasoning in *Kendall*.

---

20. Javins v. First National Realty Corp., *supra*, note 7, 138 U.S.App.D.C. 377, 428 F.2d 1079. With reference to some duties imposed by law upon the landlord for the benefit of the tenant, it may not be possible for landlords to contract out of their obligations. It has been held that a lease clause is invalid if it would insulate landlords from the consequences of violations of their duties to the public under both the common law and the District of Columbia Building Code * * *." Tenants Council of Tiber Island—Carolsburg Square v. DeFranceaux, 305 F.Supp. 560, 563 (D.C. D.C.1969).

21. Kermarec v. Compagnie Generale, 358 U.S. 625, 631, 79 S.Ct. 406, 3 L.Ed.2d 550 (1959); Hecht Co. v. Jacobsen, 86 U.S.App.D.C. 81, 83, 180 F.2d 13, 15 (1950).

To refer to only one factor as illustrative, we recognize that the obligations to which landlords of various types of property are held may well increase as the individual tenant's control over his own safety on the landlord's premises decreases; conversely, as the tenant's control over his own safety increases, the landlord's obligations should decrease. Possibly because of the great degree of control exercised by a carrier over a passenger, many courts have held carriers to the exercise of the greatest measure of care with respect to the safety of their passengers, and in some instances, have held carriers to have the liability of insurers. Yet when the passenger is injured at a terminal or station (where the passenger has more, and the carrier has less, control over the safety of his person), the obligations of the carrier are less. In this regard compare McPherson v. Tamiami Trail Tours, 383 F.2d 527 (5 Cir. 1967) with Neering v. Illinois Central Railway Co., 383 Ill. 366, 50 N.E.2d 497, conformed to 321 Ill.App. 625, 53 N.E.2d 271 (1943). *See also* Federal Insurance Company v. Colon, 392 F.2d 662, 665 (1968), where the U.S. Court of Appeals for the First Circuit, upon referring to the plaintiff's assertion that a public carrier owes its patrons the greatest measure of care, said:

[T]his applies only to passengers who are in the actual course of travel or who are boarding or alighting. The overwhelming majority rule is that it does not apply to the carrier's premises generally. * * * (citing cases)

For the imposition of more stringent obligations constituting a standard of reasonable care in the innkeeper-guest relationship, *see* Fortney v. Hotel Rancroft, Inc., 5 Ill.App.2d 327, 125 N.E.2d 544 (1955).

point during appellant's futile attempts, the judge commented with respect to the degree of proof required to show a custom: "I think the old proverb that one swallow does not make a summer applies. If you can get 100 swallows, you say this must be summertime."

Later, but still during appellant's efforts on this point, the judge commented to opposing counsel,

> [M]ay I remind you that it is very dangerous to win a case by excluding the other side's testimony because the Court of Appeals might say that testimony should have been admitted even though you might have won the case with the testimony in.

Appellant then attempted to offer evidence of individual apartment houses with which she was familiar. The trial judge became impatient with the swallow by swallow approach, and needled by opposing counsel's objections, disregarded his own admonition and cut short appellant's efforts in this direction. The record as to custom is thus unsatisfactory, but its deficiencies are directly chargeable to defendant's counsel and the trial judge, not appellant.

[7] We therefore hold in this case that the applicable standard of care in providing protection for the tenant is that standard which this landlord himself was employing in October 1959 when the appellant became a resident on the premises at 1500 Massachusetts Avenue. The tenant was led to expect that she could rely upon this degree of protection. While we do not say that the precise measures for security which were then in vogue should have been kept up (e.g., the number of people at the main entrances might have been reduced if a tenant-controlled intercom-automatic latch system had been installed in the common entryways),[22] we do hold that the same relative degree of security should have been maintained.

The appellant tenant was entitled to performance by the landlord measured by this standard of protection whether the landlord's obligation be viewed as grounded in contract or in tort. As we have pointed out, this standard of protection was implied as an obligation of the lease contract from the beginning. Likewise, on a tort basis, this standard of protection may be taken as that commonly provided in apartments of this character and type in this community, and this is a reasonable standard of care on which to judge the conduct of the landlord here.[23]

---

22. *See* text at 478, *supra.*

23. The record indicates that just prior to the poor people's campaign, the landlord caused an electric security system to be installed at the subject apartment building.

V

Given this duty of protection, and the standard of care as defined, it is clear that the appellee landlord breached its duty toward the appellant tenant here.[24] The risk of criminal assault and robbery on any tenant was clearly predictable, a risk of which the appellee landlord had specific notice, a risk which became reality with increasing frequency, and this risk materialized on the very premises peculiarly under the control, and therefore the protection, of the landlord to the injury of the appellant tenant. The question then for the District Court becomes one of damages only. To us the liability is clear.

Having said this, it would be well to state what is *not* said by this decision. We do not hold that the

---

24. In an apparent attempt to show that, regardless of the amount of care exercised, the landlord here could not possibly have prevented an assault such as that which had befallen the plaintiff, the following cross examination of Miss Kline was undertaken:

Q. Is it also correct that this apartment building also houses office apartments?

A. As the years went by they were putting more and more offices into the building, yes, sir.

Q. What types of offices would they be?

A. Well, I understood they were supposed to be professional offices because I tried to get my name listed once.

Q. Irrespective of whether you tried to get your name listed or not, did you observe the offices?

A. Yes, I worked for some of them.

Q. What type of organizations had their offices there?

A. Manufacturing representatives; there was a lawyer's office, maybe two; there were some engineers; there were some tour salesmen. That is all I can think of right now.

Q. So that there would be then in the course of a normal day clients going in and out of the lawyers' offices or customers going in and out of the other types offices, would that be correct?

A. Yes.

Q. And they would be able to walk in even if there was a doorman there?

A. Yes.

Q. And one would only speculate as to whether or not anyone could ever leave or not leave, isn't that also correct?

A. What do you mean, speculate if one could leave or not leave?

To which the trial court commented:

THE COURT: Well, we assume the general public would come into any office building or in any big apartment house.

*   *   *   *   *

THE COURT: The point is though that an intruder who commits this kind of an assault is apt to act a little different from the rest of the public although it does not always follow, you never know. Of course an intruder is not likely to come in through a public entrance either.

landlord is by any means an insurer of the safety of his tenants. His duty is to take those measures of protection which are within his power and capacity to take, and which can reasonably be expected to mitigate the risk of intruders assaulting and robbing tenants. The landlord is not expected to provide protection commonly owed by a municipal police department; but as illustrated in this case, he is obligated to protect those parts of his premises which are not usually subject to periodic patrol and inspection by the municipal police. We do not say that every multiple unit apartment house in the District of Columbia should have those same measures of protection which 1500 Massachusetts Avenue enjoyed in 1959, nor do we say that 1500 Massachusetts Avenue should have precisely those same measures in effect at the present time. Alternative and more up-to-date methods may be equally or even more effective.

Granted, the discharge of this duty of protection by landlords will cause, in many instances, the expenditure of large sums for additional equipment and services, and granted, the cost will be ultimately passed on to the tenant in the form of increased rents. This prospect, in itself, however, is not deterrent to our acknowledging and giving force to the duty, since without protection the tenant already pays in losses from theft, physical assault and increased insurance premiums.

The landlord is entirely justified in passing on the cost of increased protective measures to his tenants, but the rationale of compelling the landlord to do it in the first place is that he is the only one who is in a position to take the necessary protective measures for overall protection of the premises, which he owns in whole and rents in parts to individual tenants.

Reversed and remanded to the District Court for the determination of damages.

---

24. (*continued*)

To this we add our own comment that it is unlikely in any case that a patron of one of the businesses, even if disposed to criminal conduct, would have waited for five hours after the usual closing time to perpetrate his crime — especially one of a violent nature. Further, although it is not essential to our decision in this case, we point out that it is not at all clear that a landlord who permits a portion of his premises to be used for business purposes and the remainder for apartments would be free from liability to a tenant injured by the criminal act of a lingering patron of one of the businesses. If the risk of such injury is foreseeable, then the landlord may be liable for failing to take reasonable measures to protect his tenant from it.

We note parenthetically that no argument regarding any change in the character of the building or its tenants was pursued on appeal.

---

1. Case Identification

Identify the following aspects of a case in the **case identification** section of a case brief.

- Name of case

- Year case was decided

- Level of court hearing the case

- Jurisdiction of the court

These features help not only to identify the parties but also to establish the historical context of the case and determine its precedential value. A court of appeals decision, for example, may not be binding authority. A decision in a jurisdiction other than that relevant to your case is persuasive authority only.

A brief of *Kline* would have the following identifiers.

Kline v. 1500 Massachusetts Ave. Apartment Corp. (D.C. Cir. 1970).

Note that the status of the parties (whether they are an appellant, appellee, respondent, plaintiff, or defendant) is not indicated, although it certainly would not be wrong to do so. The "Cir." indicates that a circuit court heard the case; the "D.C." shows that the circuit court is located in the District of Columbia.

FIGURE 6.2
Kline Brief

KLINE BRIEF

Kline v. 1500 Massachusetts Ave. Apartment Corp. (D.C. Cir. 1970)

Procedural History: Tenant sued Landlord for negligently failing to protect Tenant from criminal acts of third parties. Landlord argued no duty to protect existed. District Court held in favor of Landlord.

Facts: Tenant was robbed in the common hallway at her apartment building. When Tenant moved into the apartment, several security measures were in place, but these measures were discontinued despite an increasing number of crimes being perpetrated against various tenants. Two months prior to Tenant being robbed, another tenant had been attacked in the same commonway. Only Landlord had the capacity to prevent or at least minimize the risk of criminal assaults by preventing unauthorized entries onto the premises.

Issues: (1) Does a landlord who is aware of ongoing criminal attacks on tenants, who provides and then discontinues security measures, and who has the sole capacity to protect tenants from criminal attacks, owe a duty of care to a tenant who is robbed in a common hallway?
(2) If the landlord owes a tenant a duty of care, what is that duty?

Holdings: (1) Yes.
(2) The standard of care is that standard used by the landlord when the tenant moved in. The standard set by similarly situated landlords in the community may also be taken into consideration.

Rationale: (1) Landlords' duty to protect tenants from probable and predictable criminal attacks by third parties arises first from the fact that landlords are in a better position than tenants to protect against intruders. Second, the obligation to provide protection that is within the reasonable capacity of landlords is implicit in the landlord-tenant contract. Third, an analogous duty exists between innkeepers and guests.

   (2) The standard of care to which a landlord will be held is based on the standard of care provided by a landlord when a tenant first became a resident, because this is the standard of care on which the tenant reasonably relied when moving in. The standard of protection commonly provided at similarly situated apartments in the community may also be used in establishing the reasonable standard of care of the residence in question.

SYNTHESIS OF *KLINE* AND *TURNER*:
Where there is a special relationship between parties, as between a landlord and a tenant, the defendant owes the plaintiff a duty of protection against criminal attack if the defendant is in a better position than the plaintiff to prevent such an attack, if the community standard is to provide such protection, and if criminal attacks are reasonably foreseeable. Where there is no special relationship, where the defendant is adhering to the community standard of care, and where the defendant has no actual or constructive knowledge of the imminent probability of attack upon the plaintiff, no duty to protect exists.

Practice Pointer	The abbreviations used here and throughout the book conform to *A Uniform System of Citation* (the bluebook). If you are unfamiliar with the bluebook, you may have to use whatever abbreviations are meaningful to you. On the other hand, you may want to use this opportunity to familiarize yourself with the rules of proper citation using the bluebook. Although conforming to correct citation rules is very important, remember that for purposes of preparing case briefs, at least, the emphasis should be on functionality and not on formality.

An alternative to picking particular information from the case is simply copying the complete citation and using that as your identifier.

Kline v. 1500 Massachusetts Ave. Apartment Corp., 439 F.2d 477 (D.C. Cir. 1970).

In this way, you have the information you need if you decide to consult the case again. The advantage of pulling out the key data from the citation is that merely making the conscious effort to do so draws your attention to these details and heightens your awareness as to when and by whom the case was decided. Simply copying a citation does not generally bring about such an awareness. If you do not write the complete citation, however, be sure to keep a copy of the case or write the complete cite somewhere so that you can readily relocate the case if necessary.

PUTTING IT INTO PRACTICE

Prepare the case identification for *Isaacs v. Powell* (found on pp. 323–325 in Appendix A) and *Donner v. Arkwright-Boston Manufacturers Mutual Ins. Co.* (found on pp. 325–329 in Appendix A).

2. Procedural History

In the procedural history, include the following.

- Claims made by the parties
- Defenses made and relief sought by the parties
- Disposition of the lower tribunals

By including claims and defenses made by the parties, you can establish clearly in your mind what the parties attempted to do at the trial court level. Such an understanding is essential in some cases if one is to clearly comprehend the reasoning of the appellate court and the legal doctrine thus established.

The disposition of a case, you may remember, reflects the practical directive of the court. An appellate court may, for example, "reverse and remand for further

Practice Pointer	Knowing whether to put information in the procedural history section or the facts section can sometimes be confusing. Procedural facts relate to actions taken by the parties in regard to litigation after the dispute between them arose. Facts that belong in the facts section pertain to actions taken by the parties leading up to the dispute. Procedural facts should be included in the facts section only when procedural issues are being litigated. If, for example, the defendant claims that the plaintiff did not conform to the rules of civil procedure, then the procedural steps followed by the plaintiff are relevant to the facts and must be included in that section.

proceeding" or "affirm" or "vacate," while a trial court may "dismiss" an action or "grant summary judgment for plaintiff."

Committing the procedural history to writing is especially important when the procedural gyrations at the trial court level are particularly convoluted or when a case has been up and down the appellate ladder a few times, having been appealed, remanded, and appealed again. The more you can visualize the steps taken by the parties and the judges as well as the reasoning behind those steps, the more clearly you will be able to comprehend the decision of the appellate court.

In *Kline*, the following procedural history would be appropriate.

Prior Proceedings: Tenant sued Landlord for negligently failing to protect Tenant from criminal acts of third parties. Landlord argued no duty to protect existed. District Court held in favor of Landlord.

Current Proceedings: Tenant is appealing holding of District Court.

For a more complete discussion of procedural history, see Chapter Two.

PUTTING IT INTO PRACTICE
....

Write out the procedural history for *Isaacs v. Powell* (found on pp. 323–325 in Appendix A) and *Donner v. Arkwright-Boston Manufacturers Mutual Ins. Co.* (found on pp. 325–329 in Appendix A).
....

---

3. Facts

Remember that facts are the backbone of case law. If the relevant facts change, the holding may change. Therefore, do not skim lightly over the facts. Include all facts that are critical to the court's decision. Focus on the relationships between parties and the events that led to the dispute or problem being considered on appeal. Use those relationships to identify the parties rather than their proper names. Refer to a party as "Tenant," for example, rather than as Ms. Kline.

Notice that the *Kline* court (as most courts do) provided the facts pertinent to its decision. But notice also that the following summary is more succinct than that provided by the court.

Practice Pointer	Any facts discussed in the rationale or included in the issue statement must be included in the facts section. When in doubt about whether to include a fact, do so. It is better to be overinclusive rather than underinclusive. Sometimes courts scatter relevant facts throughout the opinion instead of isolating them at the beginning. Be on the alert, therefore, for essential and relevant facts anywhere in an opinion.

Tenant was robbed in the common hallway at her apartment building. When Tenant moved into the apartment, several security measures were in place, but these measures were discontinued despite an increasing number of crimes being perpetrated against various tenants. Two months prior to Tenant being robbed, another tenant had been attacked in the same commonway. Only Landlord had the capacity to prevent or at least minimize the risk of criminal assaults by preventing unauthorized entries onto the premises.

For more information on the facts to be included in a brief, see Chapter Three.

PUTTING IT INTO PRACTICE

Write out the facts for *Isaacs v. Powell* (found on pp. 323–325 in Appendix A) and *Donner v. Arkwright-Boston Manufacturers Mutual Ins. Co.* (found on pp. 325–329 in Appendix A).

---

4. Issues

Facts/rule of law

The question(s) before the court, i.e., the issue(s), should be stated in a single sentence in the form of a question. Remember that the issue should be stated narrowly and should include facts that were essential to the decision. If possible, issues should be stated in such a way that the holding can be given as a yes or no answer. A case may contain more than one issue. The court's holding is often a good source for a recapitulation of the issue. By transforming the court's holding into a question, you can frequently create a good issue statement.

In *Kline*, the issues might read as follows:

(1) Does a landlord who is aware of ongoing criminal attacks on tenants, who provides and then discontinues security measures, and who has the sole capacity to protect tenants from criminal attacks, owe a duty of care to a tenant who is robbed in a common hallway?

(2) If the landlord owes a tenant a duty of care, what is that duty?

Chapter Four contains more information on issues.

Practice Pointer	To make a case brief easier to read, number the issues, holdings, and rationale. In other words, issue (1) should correspond to holding (1) and rationale (1), issue (2) should correspond to holding (2) and rationale (2), and so on. Doing this will not only help distinguish issues but will clarify which line of reasoning the court used in reference to which issue.

5. Holdings

The holding is the answer to the question posed in the issue statement, and ideally it should be stated as a yes or no. In some cases, a yes or no answer may not be feasible or advisable. In such cases, give whatever explanation is necessary in as concise a manner as possible.

Although one of the holdings in *Kline* can be confined to a simple yes, the other issue demands a more complete answer. The holdings might be stated as follows.

(1) Yes.

(2) The standard of care is that standard used by the landlord when the tenant moved in. The standard set by similarly situated landlords in the community may also be taken into consideration.

See Chapter Four for a more in-depth discussion of holdings.

PUTTING IT INTO PRACTICE

Write out the issues and holdings for *Isaacs v. Powell* (found on pp. 323–325 in Appendix A) and *Donner v. Arkwright-Boston Manufacturers Mutual Ins. Co.* (found on pp. 325–329 in Appendix A).

6. Rationale

To continue with our anatomical metaphor, if the facts are the backbone of a case, then the rationale is its heart. The desire to understand courts' rationale is what drives legal analysis. You cannot claim to have fully mastered a case until you are able to explain how the court arrived at its decision. A court's reasoning reflects reliance on a variety of factors, including other court decisions, public policy, significant facts, and/or compelling legal principles.

When preparing a memorandum, you will look to the rationale section of your briefs to articulate the "rules" applicable to your case. (See Chapter Nine for a discussion of the "rules," which is the "R" in the acronym "IRAC." IRAC stands for Issue, Rule, Application, and Conclusion and reflects the method of analysis used by lawyers.) A court's reasoning establishes a "rule" of sorts, because it provides an explanation as to how it reached a conclusion. Opinions signal litigants as to the application of reasoning that can be expected for similarly situated parties.

Practice Pointer	Sometimes students confuse a court's holding with its reasoning. A holding is **what** a court decided; the rationale is **why** the court decided what it did. The rationale summarizes the reasoning process used by the court, i.e., how the court used prior case law, public policy, or legislative mandates to reach its conclusion. The rationale should, in a nutshell, give the reader a clear insight into the court's logic.

Therefore, careful attention must be given to the rationale when briefing a case. Make sure you capture the essence of the court's argument. Avoid including any biases or interpretations of your own.

The rationale of the *Kline* court was multifaceted but might be summarized as follows.

(1) Landlords' duty to protect tenants from probable and predictable criminal attacks by third parties arises first from the fact that landlords are in a better position than tenants to protect against intruders. Second, the obligation to provide protection that is within the reasonable capacity of landlords is implicit in the landlord-tenant contract. Third, an analogous duty exists between innkeepers and guests.

(2) The standard of care to which a landlord will be held is based on the standard of care provided by a landlord when a tenant first became a resident, because this is the standard of care on which the tenant reasonably relied when moving in. The standard of protection commonly provided at similarly situated apartments in the community may also be used in establishing the reasonable standard of care of the residence in question.

For more information on courts' rationale, see Chapter Five.

PUTTING IT INTO PRACTICE

Summarize the rationale used by the court in *Isaacs v. Powell* (found on pp. 323–325 in Appendix A) and in *Donner v. Arkwright-Boston Manufacturers Ins. Co.* (found on pp. 325–329 in Appendix A).

7. Synthesis

One additional element to include when briefing two or more cases involving the same issue is the synthesis. Essentially, the synthesis captures the rules of law that can be derived from the cases. To ascertain those rules, you need to review the issues and rationale considered in each case. How do the issues compare? Do they involve similar or dissimilar fact patterns? What reasoning process did each court use, and how do those reasoning processes compare?

FIGURE 6.3
Synthesis

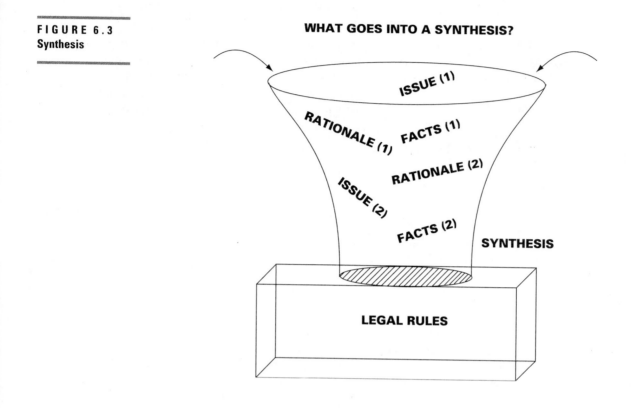

WHAT GOES INTO A SYNTHESIS?

ISSUE (1)

RATIONALE (1)   FACTS (1)

RATIONALE (2)

ISSUE (2)

FACTS (2)

SYNTHESIS

LEGAL RULES

The synthesis is not simply a restatement of the courts' holdings. It compares the outcomes of the cases and attempts to harmonize these outcomes into a set of logically consistent rules of law.

Synthesis prods you to see the interrelationships among cases. After reading several cases dealing with the same issue, you may be hard pressed to see the similarities and dissimilarities. Through synthesis, you begin to see a consistent pattern and formulate a general principle applicable in similar scenarios. Or, to the contrary, you may see a divergence in rationale and then may be able to identify some criteria for distinguishing cases.

In synthesis, you will begin to understand why courts with similar fact patterns arrive at dissimilar results. You will also see connections between cases that are ostensibly unrelated factually.

Consider this analogy. Before synthesis, cases stand alone in unrelated succession, much like a list of family members whose relationships are not designated. After synthesis, case law takes on the appearance of a family tree, where the interrelationships and connections between family members can be readily understood.

Case synthesis is the crux of legal analysis. Without it, legal research is reduced to merely stockpiling cases. If you cannot synthesize what you have gathered, you will never go beyond merely having an impressive collection of cases. Ferreting out relevant case law is an important skill, but if you cannot synthesize these cases on the basis of their similarities and dissimilarities, your value to an attorney is indeed limited. Therefore, synthesis is a skill you would be well advised to develop.

So how do you synthesize cases? Look at the facts first. How do those facts compare? Isolate the factual similarities and dissimilarities. If two courts come to apparently contradictory conclusions, did they do so because of a relevant factual

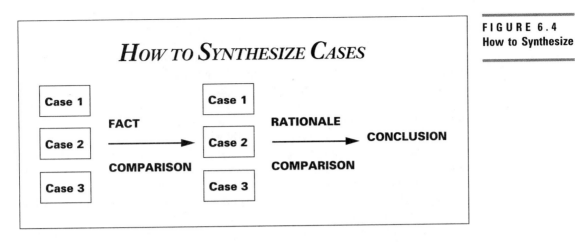

FIGURE 6.4
How to Synthesize

difference? Next, consider the rationale. How do the reasoning processes utilized by the courts compare? Did one court adhere closely to the principle of *stare decisis*, while the other court turned to public policy to justify its conclusion? Did the courts look to different statutes, administrative regulations, or constitutional provisions, or did they simply disagree as to how those enactments should be interpreted?

Suppose, for example, that you read other cases dealing with landlords' duty to protect tenants from criminal acts and that the holdings of some of those cases were consistent with *Kline* while others were not. Your task in synthesizing the case law would be to find a rational basis on which to distinguish cases that were inconsistent with *Kline* and to find connections among those cases that concurred with *Kline*.

Skim over *Turner v. United States* on pp. 329–332 in Appendix A. In this case, the plaintiff was assaulted while working at the Department of Agriculture building, which is owned by the U.S. government. She sued the federal government for negligence, alleging that her attack was foreseeable and that the government breached its duty of care toward her by leaving the entrances to the building unguarded and by lowering the lighting in the building for conservation purposes. In negligence theory, one's duty of care is determined by foreseeability.

The court analogizes to *Kline* but then distinguishes that case from the facts before it. The court notes that "the degree of security which the Government must

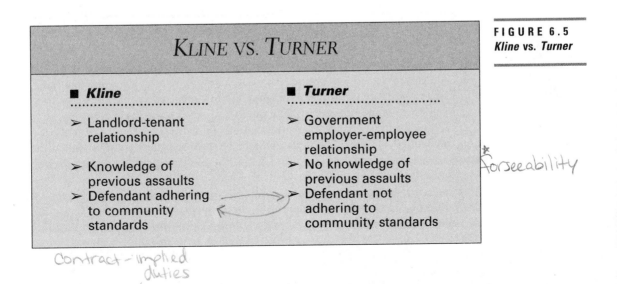

FIGURE 6.5
Kline **vs.** *Turner*

KLINE VS. TURNER

■ *Kline*
- Landlord-tenant relationship
- Knowledge of previous assaults
- Defendant adhering to community standards

■ *Turner*
- Government employer-employee relationship
- No knowledge of previous assaults
- Defendant not adhering to community standards

provide in its building with respect to non-structural dangers raises different considerations than were addressed by the Court of Appeals in *Kline* ... where a landlord-tenant relationship created a variety of implied contract... In the absence of any like relationship, there is no implied guarantee of safety against the occurrence of violence in a government building." Although the court concedes that "[g]iven the prevalence of crime in the District of Columbia, it is, of course, always 'foreseeable' that harm could come to an occupant of a government building," it concludes that a duty to protect arises only when there is "actual or constructive knowledge of an imminent probability of that particular type of harm." The court concludes that the government had complied with the community standard of care and that no facts compelled it to adhere to a higher standard.

A synthesis of *Kline* and *Turner* would attempt to reconcile the contrasting holdings by focusing on the essential facts that each court relied on (the relationship of the parties and the foreseeability of criminal attack). The synthesis might be written as follows.

> Where there is a special relationship between parties, as between a landlord and a tenant, the defendant owes the plaintiff a duty of protection against criminal attack if the defendant is in a better position than the plaintiff to prevent such an attack, if the community standard is to provide such protection, and if criminal attacks are reasonably foreseeable. Where there is no special relationship, where the defendant is adhering to the community standard of care, and where the defendant has no actual or constructive knowledge of the imminent probability of attack upon the plaintiff, no duty to protect exists.

PUTTING IT INTO PRACTICE

Synthesize *Isaacs v. Powell* (found on pp. 323–325 in Appendix A) and *Donner v. Arkwright-Boston Manufacturers Mutual Ins. Co.* (found on pp. 325–329 in Appendix A).

CHAPTER SUMMARY

Briefing cases allows you to quickly determine the essential facts of a case, the proceedings leading up to the case, the issue before the court, the court's holding, and its rationale. It requires you to become actively engaged in the reading process and heightens your understanding of case law.

Although the format of case briefs varies, most briefs contain case identification, procedural history, facts, issues, holdings, rationale, and synthesis. Since the crux of legal analysis is case synthesis, the synthesis section of a case brief is often the most critical portion. The synthesis connects cases by identifying general legal principles that arise from the cases. Synthesis can also help identify criteria for distinguishing cases. The case identification section contains the case name, the year the case was decided, the level of the court hearing the case, and the jurisdiction of the court. The other elements were described in previous chapters.

KEY TERMS

case identification   synthesis

COGNITIVE CALISTHENICS

1. Read *Doe v. Dominion Bank of Washington* (found in Instructor's Manual). Brief the case and then synthesize it along with *Turner* and *Kline*.

2. Brief the following cases and synthesize them. (Answers are found in Appendix B on page 357.)
   (a) *Nienstedt v. Wetzel*, 133 Ariz. 348 (Ct. App. 1982)
   (b) *Linthicum v. Nationwide*, 150 Ariz. 326 (1986)
   (c) *White v. Mitchell*, 157 Ariz. 523 (Ct. App. 1988)
   (d) *Olson v. Walker*, 162 Ariz. 174 (Ct. App. 1089)

3. Brief the following cases and synthesize each pair of related cases.
   (a) *Cundick v. Broadbent* and *Ruffini v. Avara*
   (b) *Matter of Estate of Swenson* and *Parrisella v. Fotopulos*
   (c) *BenShalom v. Marsh* and *U.S. v. Watkins* (concurring opinion of J. Norris only)
   (d) *Minnesota v. Dickerson* and *Arizona v. Hicks*

CHAPTER SEVEN

COMPARING CASE LAW

Chapter Objectives

In this chapter you will learn:

- How to recognize the tensions inherent in the application of *stare decisis.*

- The factors that determine whether a case will be distinguished.

- How to compare the facts of cases.

- How to compare the reasoning of cases.

In school, you have no doubt noticed differences in teachers as far as their adherence to classroom rules and school policies. Some believe that if a rule has been established, then it must be applied systematically to everyone. They do not make exceptions, because they believe that to do so would be unfair. Others see rules and policies more as guidelines than as constraints. They deviate from these guidelines when the situation seems to call for flexibility, because they believe that fairness requires responsiveness to individual needs.

The difference in these approaches is apparent when you, as a student, request something that is in opposition to the rules. You ask to be given a makeup exam when the rules forbid it; you ask to be excused from a class or an activity that requires your attendance; you give an answer that is at odds with the most commonly acceptable answer. The teacher is then faced with the dilemma of treating you with consistency by simply following the applicable rule or bending to meet your particular needs if the situation suggests some flexibility.

Courts face this same dilemma. They strive to provide consistency so that people can reasonably foresee the consequences of certain actions. At the same time, they attempt to meet the needs of individuals in their unique circumstances. In essence, the law seeks to provide both consistency and flexibility. But, as you can probably imagine, these ideals are sometimes in conflict.

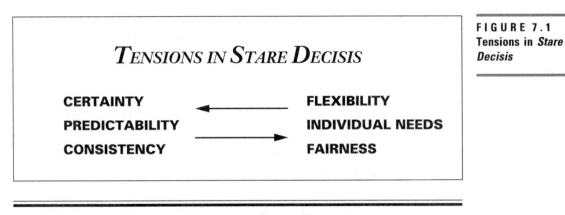

FIGURE 7.1
Tensions in *Stare Decisis*

POLICIES BEHIND *STARE DECISIS*

You must appreciate this tension in the law if you are to truly understand the principle of *stare decisis*. *Stare decisis* requires courts to honor their previous decisions as well as the decisions of higher courts in that jurisdiction. This principle obviously strives to promote consistency in legal practice, to eliminate capriciousness and elitism, and to foster certainty and predictability. In other words, this principle ensures individuals that no matter what their economic status or their level of sophistication, they are entitled to the same protections and held to the same standards as everyone else in their society.

No matter how laudable these goals of predictability and certainty may be, they can lead to a rigid practice of law that fails to yield to individual vagaries. To ameliorate some of this rigidity, principles have been introduced that allow judges and litigants to deviate from strict adherence to case precedent if they can find justification for not applying prior case law, i.e., for **distinguishing** a case. The primary reason for distinguishing a case is a substantial difference in the fact pattern. For example, if a constitutional decision allows the search of a high school student's purse without having probable cause, a court faced with a similar search of a college student may reach a different conclusion because of the arguably significant fact difference in reference to the environment in which the search is being conducted.

Finding substantial differences in fact patterns revolves around the classification of critical facts. You may remember that in Chapter Three we distinguished significant facts from essential facts on the basis of whether the fact in question affected the outcome of the case. If the deletion or modification of a particular fact would most likely have altered the court's holding, that fact is considered an essential fact. In order to distinguish case law, one must argue that the essential facts in a court opinion differ from the facts in the case at hand. Any factual differences that are not critical will be viewed as minor variations and will require conformance with existing case law. Therefore, considerable energies need to be directed toward fact differentiation if one is to convincingly distinguish a relevant case.

What sometimes underlies the distinguishing of cases by judges is a difference in judicial policy. Nowhere is this more evident than with the United States Supreme Court in the area of criminal procedure. The Burger and Rehnquist Courts (named after the Chief Justices of the Court at that time and both considered relatively pro-law-enforcement courts) have found ingenious ways of distinguishing cases decided by the more individual-rights-oriented Warren Court. In *United States v. Chadwick*, for example, the Warren Court disallowed a warrantless search of a footlocker, thus creating the general rule that a search of a container requires a

FIGURE 7.2
Distinguishing
Cases

FACTORS INVOLVED IN DISTINGUISHING CASES

■ **FACT DIFFERENCES**
....

➤ Do fact differences involve essential or material facts?

■ **PARTY'S POSITION**
....

➤ Does case support or negate party's position?

■ **JUDICIAL POLICY**
....

➤ Does reviewing court agree with precedent?

warrant (unless some exigent circumstance exists). However, in *United States v. Ross*, the Burger Court allowed the warrantless search of a suitcase. The distinguishing factor was that the police observed the suitcase being placed in the trunk of a vehicle, thereby creating the general rule that a search of a container requires a search warrant unless that container is found in a vehicle. Although the Court justified its distinction on the basis of the nature of the probable cause that existed (probable cause to believe that contraband was in a container versus probable cause to believe that contraband was in a vehicle), it appears fairly apparent that the Court was searching for a way to circumvent precedent without overruling it.

STARE DECISIS IN PRACTICE

How loosely or narrowly one interprets prior case decisions depends on your position in a particular litigation. If you find case law that supports your client's position, you will want to interpret it very loosely, so that even if the facts are somewhat different from your client's facts, you can convince the trier of fact that the case is applicable. If, on the other hand, the case is contrary to your client's position, you will want to interpret it very narrowly, arguing that the case is not applicable because of the difference in fact patterns.

Suppose, for example, that an attorney represented a tenant who had been sexually assaulted in her apartment complex. Assume that no previous criminal assaults had occurred in the complex but that the crime rate in the area was relatively high. If *Kline* (discussed and found on pp. 111–119 of Chapter Six) were the controlling case, the attorney representing the tenant would minimize the factual difference (previous assaults in *Kline* versus no previous assaults in the case at hand) and argue that the landlord's duty of care did not hinge on a knowledge of previous crimes in the complex. The attorney for the landlord, on the other hand, would use this fact difference to distinguish *Kline*, arguing that the court's holding did require knowledge of previous criminal activity and that in the absence of such knowledge no duty of care exists. Notice how the breadth of interpretation (and, therefore, the classification of facts as essential or significant) would vary depending on the party's position.

The facts in a client's case are rarely the same as those found in case law. (If the facts are identical, no ambiguity exists and litigation is unnecessary.) Therefore, most legal arguments center around analogizing to or distinguishing from existing case law. This process is the heart of legal analysis.

Making arguments that case law either should or should not apply is the essence of what lawyers do. Learning how to make such arguments is essential if you plan to work in the legal arena. Legal gamesmanship is not unlike any sport. It requires that you be able to anticipate and respond to your opponent's moves so that you can effectively block them. Therefore, you will find that the construction of counterarguments is essential to legal analysis. For every argument, you must try to create a counterargument. After a while, this practice will become second nature to you. You will find yourself making statements and immediately taking the counterposition to rebut your original position. Although your friends and family may find this distressing, you should be pleased to know that you are building your legal skills.

PUTTING IT INTO PRACTICE

....

Suppose your client, CBS Records, produced a recording by a famous rock singer, "Ozzy" Osbourne. A troubled young man, who suffered from severe emotional problems as well as alcohol abuse, committed suicide while listening to the album by Osbourne. The young man had repeatedly played several of Osbourne's albums, including one which encouraged suicide. Your client has been sued by the young man's estate for negligently causing his death. [These facts are taken from an actual case, *McCollum v. CBS, Inc.*, 249 Cal. Rptr. 187 (1988).]

Assume that *Weirum v. RKO General, Inc.* (found on pp. 252–257) is the only controlling case. What position should you take toward this case?

....

COMPARING FACTS

The first step in analyzing relevant case law is to examine the facts. Decide which facts are essential. (See the discussion in Chapter Three.) Remember, deciding what is or is not an essential fact is a subjective decision that will vary depending on your perspective and your reasoning. One might say that essential facts, like beauty, are in the eye of the beholder.

Once you have identified the essential facts, you must compare those facts to the facts of your client's case. To help objectify this comparison, make three columns on a sheet of paper. Label one column "Similar Facts," another "Dissimilar Facts," and another "Unknown Facts." Doing this will help you visualize the extent of the differences that exist. Having done this, you must then evaluate the relative importance of the similarities, dissimilarities, and unknowns. If, for example, the factual similarities involve relatively unimportant facts, while the dissimilarities or unknowns pertain to critical facts, then you may be hard pressed to convince a court to apply the case. If the essential facts are for the most part similar and the dissimilarities and unknowns are relatively trivial, then a court will be likely to apply the case to your facts.

Let us look at *Neil v. Biggers* to put this process of comparison into practice. As you read *Biggers*, focus primarily on the facts.

---

409 U.S. 188, 34 L.Ed.2d 401
William S. NEIL, Warden,
v.
Archie Nathaniel BIGGERS.
No. 71–586.
Argued Oct. 18 and 19, 1972.
Decided Dec. 6, 1972.

Habeas corpus proceeding by state prisoner. The United States District Court for the Middle District of Tennessee, Nashville Division, entered judgment grating writ, and the state appealed. The Court of Appeals, 448 F.2d 91, affirmed, and certiorari was granted. The Supreme Court, Mr. Justice Powell, held that United States Supreme Court's equally divided affirmance of petitioner's state court conviction was not an "actual adjudication" barring subsequent consideration on habeas corpus. The Court further held that even though station house showup may have been suggestive, and notwithstanding lapse of seven months between crime and the confrontation, there was no substantial likelihood of misidentification and evidence concerning the out-of-court identification by victim was admissible, where victim spent up to half an hour with her assailant, victim was with assailant under adequate artificial light in her house and under a full moon outdoors and at least twice faced him directly and intimately, victim's description to police included her assailant's approximate age, height, weight, complexion, skin texture, build, and voice, victim had "no doubt" that defendant was person who raped her, and victim made no previous identification at any of the showups, lineups, or photographic showings.

Affirmed in part, reversed in part, and remanded.

Mr. Justice Marshall took no part in consideration or decision of case.

Mr. Justice Brennan concurred in part and dissented in part and filed opinion in which Mr. Justice Douglas and Mr. Justice Stewart concurred.

1. **Habeas Corpus k117(1)** Statute providing that, in a habeas corpus proceeding by a state prisoner, a prior judgment of the United States Supreme Court

shall be conclusive as to all issues of fact or law actually adjudicated by the Supreme Court, embodies a recognition that if the Supreme Court has actually adjudicated a claim on direct appeal or certiorari, a state prisoner has had federal redetermination to which he is entitled. 28 U.S.C.A. § 2244 (c).

2. **Appeal and Error k1123**
Courts k89 Affirmance by an equally divided United States Supreme Court merely ends process of direct review, settles no issue of law and is not entitled to precedential weight.

3. **Habeas Corpus k117(1)** United States Supreme Court's equally divided affirmance of petitioner's state court conviction was not an "actual adjudication" barring subsequent consideration on habeas corpus under statute providing that, in a habeas corpus proceeding by a state prisoner, a prior judgment of the United States Supreme Court shall be conclusive as to all issues of fact or law actually adjudicated by the Supreme Court. 28 U.S.C.A. § 2244(c).

See publication Words and Phrases for other judicial constructions and definitions.

4. **Appeal and Error k1094(2)** Rule of practice, under which the United States Supreme Court does not lightly overturn concurrent findings of fact of two lower federal courts, is a salutary one to be followed where applicable.

5. **Habeas Corpus k113(12)** Rule of practice, under which the United States Supreme Court does not lightly overturn concurrent findings of fact of

two lower federal courts, was inapplicable where dispute between parties was not so much over elemental facts as over constitutional significance to be attached to them, and also in light of fact the case was a habeas corpus case in which facts were contained primarily in state court record and evidentiary hearing in federal district court purported to be confined to two specific issues which the Supreme Court deemed not controlling.

6. **Constitutional Law k266(3)**   With respect to scope of due process protection against admission of evidence derived from suggestive identification procedures, primary evil to be avoided is a very substantial likelihood of irreparable misidentification.

7. **Criminal Law k339**   Phrase "a very substantial likelihood of irreparable misidentification," while coined as a standard for determining whether an in-court identification would be admissible in the wake of a suggestive out-of-court identification, serves equally well, with deletion of "irreparable," as a standard for admissibility of testimony concerning out-of-court identification itself.

8. **Criminal Law k1169.1(5)**   If testimony concerning out-of-court identification at a station house showup was inadmissible because of likelihood of misidentification, conviction must be overturned.

9. **Constitutional Law k266(3)**   With regard to scope of due process protection against admission of evidence derived from suggestive identification procedures, it is likelihood of misidentification which violates defendant's right to due process.

10. **Criminal Law k339**   Suggestive confrontations are disapproved because they increase likelihood of misidentification, and unnecessarily suggestive ones are condemned for further reason that increased chance of misidentification is gratuitous.

11. **Constitutional Law k266(3)**   Admission of evidence of a showup without more does not violate due process.

12. **Criminal Law k339**   A strict rule barring evidence of unnecessarily suggestive confrontations would be inappropriate, where both confrontation and trial preceded United States Supreme Court decision which first gave notice that suggestiveness of confrontation procedures was anything other than a matter to be argued to the jury.

13. **Criminal Law k339**   Factors to be considered in evaluating likelihood of misidentification because

of suggestiveness of confrontation procedures, for purpose of determining admissibility of testimony concerning out-of-court identification, include opportunity of witness to view criminal at time of crime, witness' degree of attention, accuracy of witness' prior description of the criminal, level of certainty demonstrated by witness at the confrontation, and length of time between the crime and the confrontation.

14. **Criminal Law k339**   Even though station house showup may have been suggestive, and notwithstanding lapse of seven months between crime and the confrontation, there was no substantial likelihood of misidentification and evidence concerning the out-of-court identification by victim was admissible, where victim spent up to half an hour with her assailant, victim was with assailant under adequate artificial light in her house and under a full moon outdoors and at least twice faced him directly and intimately, victim's description to police included her assailant's approximate age, height, weight, complexion, skin texture, build, and voice, victim had "no doubt" that defendant was person who raped her, and victim made no previous identification at any of the showups, lineups, or photographic showings.

*Syllabus**
Respondent was convicted of rape on evidence that consisted in part of testimony concerning the victim's visual and voice identification of respondent at a station-house showup that occurred seven months after the rape. The victim, who had been in the presence of her assailant a considerable time and had directly observed him indoors and under a full moon outdoors, testified that she had "no doubt" that respondent was her assailant. She had previously given the police a description of her assailant, which was confirmed by a police officer. Before the showup where she identified respondent, the victim had made no identification of others who were presented at previous showups, lineups, or through photographs. The police asserted that they used the showup technique because they had difficulty in finding for a lineup other individuals generally fitting respondent's description as given by the victim. The Tennessee Supreme Court's affirmance of the conviction was affirmed here by an equally divided Court. 390 U.S. 404, 88 S.Ct.

---

* The syllabus constitutes no part of the opinion of the Court but has been prepared by the Reporter of Decisions for the convenience of the reader. See United States v. Detroit Timber & Lumber Co., 200 U.S. 321, 337, 26 S.Ct. 282, 287, 50 L.Ed. 499.

979, 19 L.Ed.2d 1267. Respondent then brought a habeas corpus action in District Court. After rejecting the petitioner's contention that this Court's affirmance constituted an actual adjudication within the meaning of 28 U.S.C. § 2244(c) and thus barred further review of the showup identification in a federal habeas corpus proceeding, the District Court, noting that a lineup is relatively more reliable than a showup, held that the confrontation here was so suggestive as to violate due process. The Court of Appeals affirmed. *Held:*

1. This Court's equally divided affirmance of respondent's state court conviction does not, under 28 U.S.C. § 2244(c), bar further federal relief by habeas corpus, since such an affirmance merely ends the process of direct review but settles no issue of law. P. 378.

2. While the station-house identification may have been suggestive, under the totality of the circumstances the victim's identification of respondent was reliable and was properly allowed to go to the jury. Pp. 380–383. 448 F.2d 91, affirmed in part, reversed in part, and remanded.

Bart C. Durham III, Nashville, Tenn., for petitioner.

Michael Meltsner, New York City, for respondent.

Mr. Justice POWELL delivered the opinion of the Court.

In 1965, after a jury trial in a Tennessee court, respondent was convicted of rape and was sentenced to 20 years' imprisonment. The State's evidence consisted in part of testimony concerning a station-house identification of respondent by the victim. The Tennessee Supreme Court affirmed. Biggers v. State, 219 Tenn. 553, 411 S.W.2d 696 (1967). On certiorari, the judgment of the Tennessee Supreme Court was affirmed by an equally divided Court. Biggers v. Tennessee, 390 U.S. 404, 88 S.Ct. 979, 19 L.Ed.2d 1267 (1968) (Marshall, J., not participating). Respondent then brought a federal habeas corpus action raising several claims. In reply, petitioner contended that the claims were barred by 28 U.S.C. § 2244(c), which provides in pertinent part:

"In a habeas corpus proceeding brought in behalf of a person in custody pursuant to the judgment of a State court, a prior judgment of the Supreme Court of the United States on an appeal or review by a writ of certiorari at the instance of the prisoner of the decision of such State court, shall be conclusive as to all issues of fact or law with respect to an asserted denial of a Federal right which constitutes ground for discharge in a habeas corpus proceeding, actually adjudicated by the Supreme Court therein. . ."

The District Court held that the claims were not barred and, after a hearing, held in an unreported opinion that the station-house identification procedure was so suggestive as to violate due process. The Court of Appeals affirmed. 6 Cir., 448 F.2d 91 (1971). We granted certiorari to decide whether an affirmance by an equally divided Court is an actual adjudication barring subsequent consideration on habeas corpus, and, if not whether the identification procedure violated due process. 405 U.S. 954, 92 S.Ct. 1167, 31 L.Ed.2d 230 (1972).

[Habeas corpus discussion omitted.]

II

[4,5] We proceed, then, to consider respondent's due process claim.[3] As the claim turns upon the facts, we must first review the relevant testimony at the jury trial and at the habeas corpus hearing regarding the rape and the identification. The victim testified at trial that on the evening of January 22, 1965, a youth with a butcher knife grabbed her in the doorway to her kitchen:

---

3. The dissent would have us decline to address the merits because the District Court, after an evidentiary hearing, found due process to have been violated, and the Court of Appeals—after reviewing the entire record—found that "the conclusions of fact of the District Judge are [not] clearly erroneous." 448 F.2d 91, 95. It is said that we should not depart from "our long-established practice not to reverse findings of fact concurred in by two lower courts unless shown to be clearly erroneous." *Post*, at 383. This rule of practice, under which the Court does not lightly overturn the concurrent findings of fact of two lower federal courts, is a salutary one to be followed where applicable. We think it inapplicable here where the dispute between the parties is not so much over the elemental facts as over the constitutional significance to be attached to them. Moreover, this is a habeas corpus case in which the facts are contained primarily in the state court record (equally available to use as to the federal courts below) and where the evidentiary hearing in the District Court purported to be "confined" to two specific issues which we deem not controlling. Of the nine cases cited in the dissenting opinion in support of the rule of practice urged upon us, eight of them involved civil litigation in the federal system. Only one of the cases cited, Boulden v. Holman, 394 U.S. 478, 89 S.Ct. 1138, 22 L.Ed.2d 433 (1969), involved a habeas corpus review and the Court simply held—on the basis of "an independent study of the entire record"—that the conclusion reached by the District Court and the Court of Appeals "was justified." 394 U.S., at 480, 89 S.Ct., at 1140.

"A. [H]e grabbed me from behind, and grappled—twisted me on the floor. Threw me down on the floor.

"Q. And there was no light in that kitchen?

"A. Not in the kitchen.

"Q. So you couldn't have seen him then?

"A. Yes, I could see him, when I looked up in his face.

"Q. In the dark?

"A. He was right in the doorway—it was enough light from the bedroom shining through. Yes, I could see who he was.

"Q. You could see? No light? And you could see him and know him then?

"A. Yes." Tr. of Rec. in No. 237, O.T.1967, pp. 33–34.

When the victim screamed, her 12-year-old daughter came out of her bedroom and also began to scream. The assailant directed the victim to "tell her [the daughter] to shut up, or I'll kill you both." She did so, and was then walked at knifepoint about two blocks along a railroad track, taken into a woods, and raped there. She testified that "the moon was shining brightly, full moon." After the rape, the assailant ran off, and she returned home, the whole incident having taken between 15 minues and half an hour.

She then gave the police what the Federal District Court characterized as "only a very general description," describing him as "being fat and flabby with smooth skin, bushy hair and a youthful voice." Additionally, though not mentioned by the District Court, she testified at the habeas corpus hearing that she had described her assailant as being between 16 and 18 years old and between five feet ten inches and six feet tall, as weighing between 180 and 200 pounds, and as having a dark brown complexion. This testimony was substantially corroborated by that of a police officer who was testifying from his notes.

On several occasions over the course of the next seven months, she viewed suspects in her home or at the police station, some in lineups and others in showups, and was shown between 30 and 40 photographs. She told the police that a man pictured in one of the photographs had features similar to those of her assailant, but identified none of the suspects. On August 17, the police called her to the station to view respondent, who was being detained on another charge. In an effort to construct a suitable lineup, the police checked the city jail and the city juvenile home. Finding no one at either place fitting respondent's unusual physical description, they conducted a showup instead.

The showup itself consisted of two detectives walking respondent past the victim. At the victim's re-

quest, the police directed respondent to say "shut up or I'll kill you." The testimony at trial was not altogether clear as to whether the victim first identified him and then asked that he repeat the words or made her identification after he had spoken.[4] In any event, the victim testified that she had "no doubt" about her identification. At the habeas corpus hearing, she elaborated in response to questioning.

"A. That I have no doubt, I mean that I am sure that when I—see, when I first laid eyes on him, I knew that it was the individual, because his face—well, there was just something that I don't think I could ever forget. I believe—

"Q. You say when you first laid eyes on him, which time are you refereing to?

"A. When I identified him—when I seen him in the courthouse when I was took up to view the suspect." App. 127.

We must decide whether, as the courts below held, this identification and the circumstances, surrounding it failed to comport with due process requirements.

III

We have considered on four occasions the scope of due process protection against the admission of evidence deriving from suggestive identification procedures. In Stovall v. Denno, 388 U.S. 293, 87 S.Ct. 1967, 18 L.Ed.2d 1199 (1967), the Court held that the defendant could claim that "the confrontation conducted ... was so unnecessarily suggestive and conducive to irreparable mistaken identification that he was denied due process of law." *Id.*, at 301–302, 87 S.Ct., at 1972. This we held, must be determined "on the totality of the circumstances." We went on to find that on the facts of the case then before us, due process was not violated, emphasizing that the critical condition of the injured witness justified a showup in

---

4. At trial, one of the police officers present at the identification testified explicitly that the words were spoken after the identification. The victim testified:

"Q. What physical characteristics, if any, caused you to be able to identify him?

"A. First of all,—uh—his size,—next I could remember his voice.

"Q. What about his voice? Describe his voice to the Jury.

"A. Well, he has the voice of an immature youth—I call it an immature youth. I have teen-age boys. And that was the first thing that made me think it was the boy." Tr. of Rec. in No. 237, O.T.1967, p. 17.

The colloquy continued, with the victim describing the voice and other physical characteristics. At the habeas corpus hearing, the victim and all of the police witnesses testified that a visual identification preceded the voice identification. App. 80, 123, 134.

her hospital room. At trial, the witness, whose view of the suspect at the time of the crime was brief, testified to the out-of-court identification, as did several police officers present in her hospital room, and also made an in-court identification.

Subsequently, in a case where the witnesses made in-court identifications arguably stemming from previous exposure to a suggestive photographic array, the Court restated the governing test:

> "[W]e hold that each case must be considered on its own facts, and that convictions based on eyewitness identification at trial following a pretrial identification by photograph will be set aside on that ground only if the photographic identification procedure was so impermissibly suggestive as to give rise to a very substantial likelihood of irreparable misidentification." Simmons v. United States, 390 U.S. 377, 384, 88 S.Ct. 967, 971, 19 L.Ed.2d 1247 (1968).

Again we found the identification procedure to be supportable, relying both on the need for prompt utilization of other investigative leads and on the likelihood that the photographic identifications were reliable, the witnesses having viewed the bank robbers for periods of up to five miutes under good lighting conditions at the time of the robbery.

The only case to date in which this Court has found identification procedures to be violative of due process is Foster v. California, 394 U.S. 440, 442, 89 S.Ct. 1127, 1128, 22 L.Ed.2d 402 (1969). There, the witness failed to identify Foster the first time he confronted him, despite a suggestive lineup. The police then arranged a showup, at which the witness could make only a tentative identification. Ultimately, at yet another confrontation, this time a lineup, the witness was able to muster a definite identification. We held all of the identifications inadmissible, observing that the identifications were "all but inevitable" under the circumstances. Id., at 443, 89 S.Ct., at 1129.

In the most recent case of Coleman v. Alabama, 399 U.S. 1, 90 S.Ct. 1999, 26 L.Ed.2d 387 (1970), we held admissible an in-court identification by a witness who had a fleeting but "real good look" at his assailant in the headlights of a passing car. The witness testified at a pretrial suppression hearing that he identified one of the petitioners among the participants in the lineup before the police placed the participants in a formal line. Mr. Justice Brennan for four members of the Court stated that this evidence could support a finding that the in-court identification was "entirely based upon observations at the time of the assault and not at all induced by the conduct of the lineup." Id., at 5–6, 90 S.Ct., at 2001.

[6–11] Some general guidelines emerge from these cases as to the relationship between suggestiveness and misidentification. It is, first of all, apparent that the primary evil to be avoided is "a very substantial likelihood of irreparable misidentification." Simmons v. United States, 390 U.S., at 384, 88 S.Ct., at 971. While the phrase was coined as a standard for determining whether an in-court identification would be admissible in the wake of a suggestive out-of-court identification, with the deletion of "irreparable" it serves equally well as a standard for the admissibility of testimony concerning the out-of-court identification itself.[5] It is the likelihood of misidentification which violates a defendant's right to due process, and it is this which was the basis of the exclusion of evidence in *Foster.* Suggestive confrontations are disapproved because they increase the likelihood of misidentification, and unnecessarily suggestive ones are condemned for the further reason that the increased chance of misidentification is gratuitous. But as *Stovall* makes clear, the admission of evidence of a showup without more does not violate due process.

[12] What is less clear from our cases is whether, as intimated by the District Court, unnecessary suggestiveness alone requires the exclusion of evidence.[6] While we are inclined to agree with the courts below that the police did not exhaust all possibilities in seeking persons physically comparable to respondent, we do not think that the evidence must therefore be excluded. The purpose of a strict rule barring evidence of unnecessarily suggestive confrontations would be to deter the police from using a less reliable procedure where a more reliable one may be available, and would not be based on the assumption that in every instance the admission of evidence of such a confrontation offends due process. Clemons v. United States, 133 U.S.App.D.C. 27, 48, 408 F.2d 1230, 1251 (1968)

---

5. See Clemons v. United States, 133 U.S. App.D.C. 27, 47, 408 F.2d 1230, 1250 (1968) (McGowan, J., for the court *en banc*), cert. denied, 394 U.S. 964, 89 S.Ct. 1318, 22 L.Ed.2d 567 (1969). In the present case, there has been controversy, in our view irrelevant, over whether, as she testified at the habeas corpus hearing, the victim actually made an in-court identification. While we think it evident from the many testimonial links between her out-of-court identification and "the defendant" before her in court that the answer is "yes," we recognize that if the testimony concerning the out-of-court identification was inadmissible, the conviction must be overturned.

6. The District Court stated:
   "In this case it appears to the Court that a line-up, which both sides admit is generally more reliable than a show-up, could have been arranged. The fact that this was not done tended needlessly to decrease the fairness of the identification process to which petitioner was subjected." App. 42.

(Leventhal, J., concurring); cf. Gilbert v. California, 388 U.S. 263, 273, 87 S.Ct. 1951, 1957, 18 L.Ed.2d 1178 (1967); Mapp v. Ohio, 367 U.S. 643, 81 S.Ct. 1684, 6 L.Ed.2d 1081 (1961). Such a rule would have no place in the present case, since both the confrontation and the trial preceded Stovall v. Denno, *supra*, when we first gave notice that the suggestiveness of confrontation procedures was anything other than a matter to be argued to the jury.

[13] We turn, then, to the central question, whether under the "totality of the circumstances" the identification was reliable even though the confrontation procedure was suggestive. As indicated by our cases, the factors to be considered in evaluating the likelihood of misidentification include the opportunity of the witness to view the criminal at the time of the crime, the witness' degree of attention, the accuracy of the witness' prior description of the criminal, the level of certainty demonstrated by the witness at the confrontation, and the length of time between the crime and the confrontation. Applying these factors, we disagree with the District Court's conclusion.

In part, as discussed above, we think the District Court focused unduly on the relative reliability of a lineup as opposed to a showup, the issue on which expert testimony was taken at the evidentiary hearing. It must be kept in mind also that the trial was conducted before *Stovall* and that therefore the incentive was lacking for the parties to make a record at trial of facts corroborating or undermining the identification. The testimony was addressed to the jury, and the jury apparently found the identification reliable. Some of the State's testimony at the federal evidentiary hearing may well have been self-serving in that it too neatly fit the case law, but it surely does nothing to undermine the state record, which itself fully corroborated the identification.

We find that the District Court's conclusions on the critical facts are unsupported by the record and clearly erroneous. The victim spent a considerable period of time with her assailant, up to half an hour. She was with him under adequate artificial light in her house and under a full moon outdoors, and at least twice, once in the house and later in the woods, faced him directly and intimately. She was no casual observer, but rather the victim of one of the most personally humiliating of all crimes.[7] Her description to the police, which included the assailant's approximate age, height, weight, complexion, skin texture, build, and voice, might not have satisfied Proust but was more than ordinarily thorough. She had "no doubt" that respondent was the person who raped her. In the nature of the crime, there are rarely witnesses to a rape other than the victim, who often has a limited opportunity of observation.[8] The victim here, a practical nurse by profession, had an unusual opportunity to observe and identify her assailant. She testified at the habeas corpus hearing that there was something about his face. "I don't think I could ever forget." App. 127.

[14] There was, to be sure, a lapse of seven months between the rape and the confrontation. This would be a seriously negative factor in most cases. Here, however, the testimony is undisputed that the victim made no previous identification at any of the showups, lineups, or photographic showings. Her record for reliability was thus a good one, as she had previously resisted whatever suggestiveness inheres in a showup. Weighing all the factors, we find no substantial likelihood of misidentification. The evidence was properly allowed to go to the jury.[9]

Affirmed in part, reversed in part, and remanded.

Mr. Justice MARSHALL took no part in the consideration or decision of this case.

Mr. Justice BRENNAN, with whom Mr. Justice DOUGLAS and Mr. Justice STEWART concur, concurring in part and dissenting in part.

[Dissent omitted.]

---

7. See United States ex rel. Phipps v. Follette, 428 F.2d 912, 915–916 (CA2) (Friendly, J.), cert. denied, 400 U.S. 908, 91 S.Ct. 151, 27 L.Ed.2d 146 (1970).

8. Respondent attaches some weight to the failure of the victim's daughter to identify him. Apart from the fact that this does not bear directly on the reliability of her mother's identification the girl was only 12 years old and had as best we can tell only a very brief view of the assailant from across the room.

9. Respondent's habeas corpus petition raised a number of other claims, including one challenging the legality of his detention at the time he was viewed by the victim. The courts below did not address these claims, nor do we.

Notice that in *Biggers* the Court considered several factors in deciding that the state's method of identifying the defendant was not "unnecessarily suggestive." The victim/witness was a nurse, who arguably would be alert to subtle details in a person's appearance. She was able to observe the defendant for a reasonably long time (30 minutes) in close proximity (by nature of being raped) in good light (full moon), and she was very certain of her identification. On the other hand, a relatively long time elapsed between the incident and her identification (seven months), and the show-up used to identify the defendant was no doubt suggestive, since the defendant was the only suspect presented to the victim.

Now let us suppose that we have a client who has been accused of theft. Like the defendant in *Biggers*, our client was identified by his alleged victim in a show-up seven months after the crime. The state has looked to *Biggers* to justify the show-up, but we want to distinguish *Biggers* because of the following fact differences. In our case, the victim is a legal secretary who observed the defendant fleetingly when he approached her from behind and stole her purse. She caught only a glimpse of his face (side view) but noticed that he had an unusual scar on his right cheek. She chased after him for about a block and was able to give the police a detailed description of his clothing. She also noticed that his hair was blond and in a pony-tail. The theft occurred around dusk.

The question boils down to whether the fact differences between our case and *Biggers are substantial enough that we can convince the court to distinguish Biggers* and find the show-up constitutionally unsound. Let us start by making a chart of the similarities, dissimilarities, and unknowns.

Two of the similarities involve facts that make the identification problematic, namely, that both cases involve show-ups (which are by their very nature suggestive) and that the out-of-court identifications occur seven months after the crime (which casts doubt on the accuracy of the identification). The other similarity (that both crimes involve personal attacks) tends to lend some credence to the identification because of the close range in which the victim observed the defendant.

FIGURE 7.3
Neil v. Biggers
Compared to
Our Case

FACTS OF BIGGERS COMPARED TO OUR CASE

■ SIMILARITIES

➢ Seven-month delay in identification
➢ Show-up
➢ Personal attack

■ DISSIMILARITIES

➢ Thirty-minute observation	➢ Glimpse
➢ Moonlight	➢ Dusk
➢ Rape	➢ Theft
➢ Nurse	➢ Secretary

■ UNKNOWNS

➢ No unusual markings mentioned	➢ Scar
➢ No clothing mentioned	➢ Clothing identified
➢ Voice identification	➢ No known voice identification
➢ Certainty of identification	➢ Unknown level of certainty of identification

Some of the facts relied on by the *Biggers* Court are unknown in our case. The victim in *Biggers* was able to identify the defendant by virtue of his voice as well as his physical characteristics, and she strengthened her identification by the certainty with which she offered it. If we discover that comparable facts exist in our case, *Biggers* will be more difficult to distinguish than if we find differences in regard to these factors. On the other hand, our victim's identification possesses two elements not discussed by the *Biggers* Court in that she observed a scar, arguably a unique feature, and described her assailant's clothing in detail. These two factors tend to make our victim's identification more compelling.

Fortunately for us, the dissimilarities for the most part involve essential facts that the *Biggers* Court relied on in reaching its determination. The attack in our case was less invasive and provided the victim with much less opportunity to observe the defendant. Instead of facing the defendant at close range for thirty minutes, the victim in our case caught only a fleeting glimpse of the defendant and then only from the side. Significantly, the lighting in our case was much less conducive to accurate identification since the incident occurred at dusk rather than under a bright moon. We have no indication in our case that the victim's identification was as certain as the one given by the victim in *Biggers*, a fact that the *Biggers* Court seemed to find important. Finally, our victim was a secretary rather than a nurse. Although not necessarily true, a secretary is arguably less observant of details about the body than a nurse because a nurse is trained and required to carefully note physical symptoms and to monitor changes in those symptoms.

Going back to the fact gaps, however, the state may argue that our victim's observation of a very unusual scar and her detailed description of the defendant's clothing (although we have no indication as to how accurate that description was) point to the excellent observation powers of the victim. These facts also make the defendant's identification more reliable since such a scar would make it less likely that the defendant might be confused with others. The state might also argue that the victim in our case was less frightened than the victim in *Biggers*, as evidenced by the fact that she chased the defendant. Her lack of fear could conceivably strengthen her ability to observe and recall. Finally, her detailed description arguably could offset in the court's mind the fact that she had minimal contact with the defendant and that she observed him under poor lighting conditions at a side angle.

PUTTING IT INTO PRACTICE
....

Comparing Facts
Assume the same facts as in the previous "Putting It into Practice." What essential facts will you use to distinguish *Weirum* from your client's case? In other words, on what basis would you argue that *Weirum* should not be controlling in your case?

....

COMPARING REASONING

Coming to any conclusion with regard to the arguments raised above would be difficult without knowing the reasoning used by the Court. How can we determine what factual differences are important until we first understand why the Court included the facts that it did? Before we can compare our case to *Biggers*, we must probe the *Biggers* rationale.

The Court indicates that the "primary evil to be avoided" in cases involving out-of-court identifications is "a very substantial likelihood of irreparable misidentification." The Court says, "Suggestive confrontations are disapproved because they increase the likelihood of misidentification, and unnecessarily suggestive ones are condemned for the further reason that the increased chance of misidentification is gratuitous." The Court goes on to clarify, however, that unnecessary suggestiveness alone does not require the exclusion of evidence. It applies the "totality of the circumstances" approach to a suggestive identification procedure. It then enumerates those factors that should be considered in determining whether the procedure is constitutionally reliable—"the opportunity of the witness to view the criminal at the time of the crime, the witness' degree of attention, the accuracy of the witness' prior description of the criminal, the level of certainty demonstrated by the witness at the confrontation, and the length of time between the crime and the confrontation." Weighing all of these factors, the Court concludes that despite the suggestiveness of the show-up and the extensive time lapse between the crime and the identification, the out-of-court identification was reliable.

To successfully distinguish *Biggers*, we must apply the balancing test to our facts and demonstrate that the factual differences tip the balance in the direction of unreliability. We must emphasize that the witness in our case lacked the personal, prolonged contact in good lighting that the victim had in *Biggers*. We should argue that our victim's mere glance afforded her an opportunity to give only the most general of descriptions and that the poor lighting cast doubt on her ability to perceive anything but the most obvious of features. We must point out that the primary similarities (the unnecessarily suggestive nature of the show-up and the long time between the crime and the identification) both lean in the direction of misidentification. We could then reason that the facts shared in common with *Biggers* are those that tip the balance in favor of misidentification and that, in terms

FIGURE 7.4
Reasoning Used in *Biggers*

KEY REASONING USED IN NEIL V. BIGGERS

Evil to be avoided is "very substantial likelihood of irreparable misidentification."

"Unnecessarily suggestive" confrontations are to be avoided but unnecessary suggestiveness alone does not require exclusion of evidence.

Under the "totality of the circumstances" approach to a suggestive identification, one should consider:
- ➤ Opportunity of the witness to view the criminal.
- ➤ Witness' degree of attention.
- ➤ Accuracy of the witness' prior description.
- ➤ Certainty of witness at the confrontation.
- ➤ Time between crime and confrontation.

of dissimilarities, more facts in our case point toward misidentification than in *Biggers*. The logical conclusion flowing from a tallying of all these factors would be an increased likelihood of misidentification.

A good advocate must also anticipate the arguments of an opponent, so we must reflect on the likely rebuttals that the state would make. The state would probably focus on the accuracy of the victim's identification and the uniqueness of the suspect's description (the scar). It would use these factors to tip the scales back in favor of reliability, pointing out that while the victim's encounter with the suspect may have been brief, she was still able to gather sufficient information to individualize him.

Notice that in this case, the state would minimize the fact differences and focus the court's attention on the similarities between its case and *Biggers*, while the defense would do just the opposite. Choosing one's alignment with case law is the basis of legal advocacy. While such fluctuation in positions may on the surface appear to be capricious and unprincipled, it is essential to the advocacy process. When ambiguities or unanswered questions in the law exist, attorneys are required to raise any reasonable arguments that support their client's position. Judges are then called upon to use reason and wisdom in discerning which argument prevails. When no reasonable argument can be made by one party or the other, the legal game comes to an abrupt halt. But until such time, attorneys are ethically obligated to engage in logical attacks and counterattacks against their opponents' position.

PUTTING IT INTO PRACTICE
....

Comparing Reasoning
Assume the facts given in the first "Putting It into Practice" in this chapter. What reasoning would you extract from *Weirum* to argue that your client owed no duty of care to the plaintiff?

....

CHAPTER SUMMARY

Stare decisis promotes consistency and predictability in the law but can lead to some degree of rigidity. To avoid this rigidity, litigants and judges can distinguish cases if substantial differences in essential facts exist. Judges who disagree with the judicial policies of their predecessors can distinguish cases to avoid following precedent. Litigants choose to distinguish cases that do not support their position; they do so by interpreting case law as narrowly as possible. To compare case law, factual similarities, dissimilarities, and unknowns must be identified in the context of the reasoning used by the courts. Good legal gamesmanship also requires anticipating arguments that opponents are likely to make.

KEY TERMS

distinguish

COGNITIVE CALISTHENICS

1. The following scenarios have slightly different fact patterns than the cases you have read in previous chapters. Construct an argument in each case that would support distinguishing the new fact pattern from the court opinion. (Suggested responses found in Appendix B.)

   (a) The facts are the same as those in *Nienstedt v. Wetzel* (found on pp. 274–279 of Appendix A), except that the defendants in the abuse of process case introduce evidence of their financial status.

   (b) The facts are the same as those in *Linthicum v. Nationwide Life Ins. Co.* (found on pp. 262–268 of Appendix A), except that two of the people reviewing the denial conclude that the claim is **not** preexisting. The senior claims examiner then disagrees with their conclusions and advises that the Linthicums' claim be denied.

   (c) The facts are the same as those in *White v. Mitchell* (found on pp. 268–274 of Appendix A), except that the trucking company inspects the driver's vehicle and orders him to get his brakes fixed before going back on the road but does not take steps to ensure that he does so. Because of the inspector's failure to advise the driver's supervisor of his defective brakes, the driver is inadvertently given the load that he is transporting at the time of the accident.

   (d) The facts are the same as those in *Olson v. Walker* (found on pp. 257–262 in Appendix A), except that the defendant's blood alcohol level at the time of the accident is 0.090 (below the presumptive level of intoxication in Arizona).

2. The following scenarios have slightly different fact patterns than the cases you have read in previous chapters. Construct an argument in each case that would support distinguishing the new fact pattern from the court opinion.

   (a) The facts are the same as those in *Cundick v. Broadbent* (found on pp. 279–286 of Appendix A), except that the plaintiff is diagnosed as having Alzheimer's and is unrepresented by counsel during his transactions with the defendant.

   (b) The facts are the same as those in *Matter of Estate of Swenson* (found on pp. 286–288 of Appendix A), except that the defendant never urges the decedent to seek counsel different from the one she had used to draft her first two wills. In fact, it is the decedent who makes this choice because she is unhappy with the service she received from her first attorney.

   (c) The facts are the same as those in *Ben Shalom v. Marsh* (found on pp. 288–293 of Appendix A), except that an Army officer testifies that she once observed the plaintiff and another female "embracing." When this "embrace" is observed, the plaintiff is in civilian clothes, is off duty, and is in a town near the military installation where she works.

   (d) The facts are the same as those in *Minnesota v. Dickerson* (found on pp. 293–301 of Appendix A), except that the officer has reasonable suspicion that the defendant has committed an armed robbery. In the process of frisking him for weapons, the officer feels a soft lump in the defendant's pants pocket which he testifies he immediately recognized as a baggie of marijuana.

3. Compare the facts of the scenario below with *Olson v. Walker* (found on pp. 257–262 of Appendix A). List the factual similarities, dissimilarities, and unknowns. Construct an argument that punitive damages should be awarded in this case and then prepare a rebuttal argument. Structure your argument around one factual dissimilarity rather than trying to cover all the factual differences. (Suggested response found in Appendix B.)

   After having a fight with his wife, George calls his best friend and meets him at a local tavern, where he consumes ten beers. Because of his obnoxious behavior, George is asked to leave. Before getting in his car, he decides to "steady his nerves" for the drive home by smoking a joint of marijuana. Once on the road, George becomes engaged in a verbal dispute with another driver because the other driver claims he is driving too slow. (He is in fact driving approximately 20 mph below the speed limit of 45 mph according to another driver who witnesses the dispute.) Because George is not paying attention to his driving, he runs into the rear of another vehicle, causing the driver to lose control of the vehicle and run into a pole.

When the police arrive at the scene, they observe George sitting on his car hood and talking incoherently. They take him to the police station where a test reveals his blood alcohol level to be 0.11 (above the presumptive level of intoxication of 0.10). George is cited and released into the custody of a friend.

An expert toxicologist testifies at trial that George must have consumed at least eight twelve-ounce beers to reach a blood alcohol level of 0.11. He also testifies that George's blood alcohol level at the time of the accident was at least 0.12 percent. After a jury trial in which the plaintiff is awarded $100,000 in compensatory damages and $100,000 in punitive damages, George requests a remittitur. When that is denied, he appeals.

4. Compare the facts of the scenario below with *Matter of Estate of Swenson* (found on pp. 286–288 of Appendix A). List the factual similarities, dissimilarities, and unknowns. Con-

struct an argument that the will was not the product of undue influence and then prepare a rebuttal argument. Structure your argument around one factual dissimilarity rather than trying to cover all the factual differences.

Martha is a hospice volunteer who devotedly and lovingly cares for the decedent during the last six months of her life. When Martha becomes aware of the callousness with which the decedents' daughters treat their mother, she begins questioning the decedent about "whether she has her affairs in order." Martha casually mentions to the decedent some of the comments she has heard the daughters make about their mother. She is aware that this information might precipitate some disputes between the decedent and her daughters but believes the decedent will benefit in the long run from such confrontations.

After one particularly violent exchange, the decedent asks Martha to locate an attorney for her so that she can rewrite her will. Martha, knowing that the end is near, contacts her own attorney the next day and is at the decedent's home but not present in her room when the attorney talks with the decedent. Two days later the decedent signs her new will, in which she disinherits her daughters and leaves what would have been their portion of the estate to Martha. Within a week, the decedent dies and Martha, to her surprise, is left a considerable sum of money.

CHAPTER EIGHT

STATUTORY LAW

Chapter Objectives

In this chapter you will learn:

- How to determine legislative intent.

- How to analyze statutes.

- How to analyze administrative regulations.

You can't play any game unless you know the rules, but rules are subject to interpretation. Have you ever gone to someone's house and played Ping-Pong, for example? Did you discover that your rules and your host's rules differed somewhat? Did you perhaps get into a dispute over who won a critical point because of your difference in rule interpretation?

The game of law is also based on rules. No more consensus exists around the rules of law than around the rules of Ping-Pong. As the champions of rule interpretation, lawyers are often called upon to referee when parties disagree about what the "rules" are. Most of the debate revolves around the meaning of specific words. Because the meaning of words has been debated by philosophers, linguists, and theologians for millennia without a consensus being reached, we can hardly expect agreement among lawyers.

In many respects, you will find the analysis of statutes to be similar to the analysis of case law. We will discuss them separately for two reasons. First, because so much of legal practice is devoted to statutory interpretation, it merits special attention. Second, the analysis of statutes demands even greater attention to subtle differences in language and the context of that language than does the analysis of case law, and we will use this chapter to focus on those subtleties.

LEGISLATIVE INTENT

Your study of statutes will largely be devoted to decoding vague or ambiguous words or phrases. To do this, you must determine the purpose of the statute, that is, the **legislative intent** behind it. Was the legislature attempting to remedy some social ill? Was it trying to close a loophole? Were the legislators addressing a particular

FIGURE 8.1
Determination of
Legislative Intent

DETERMINING LEGISLATIVE INTENT

■ **Definitions Section of Statute**

■ **Plain Meaning**

■ **Context of Other Statutes**

■ **Public Policy**

■ **Case Law**

■ **Legislative History**

■ **Canons of Construction**

FIGURE 8.1
Determination of Legislative Intent

problem, or were they trying to write a statute general enough to apply to a wide variety of circumstances? Were they attempting to thwart some future acts that they anticipated might be a problem? Was this legislation part of a package designed to remedy a common problem?

To illustrate the determination of legislative intent, consider a criminal code that defines a particular degree of arson as arson of an "occupied" structure. Does this statute apply to abandoned or vacant houses? In other words, must an "occupied" structure for purposes of this statute be occupied in the commonsense meaning of the term?

Definitions Section of Statute

To answer this question, you would first consult the definitions section of the statute. As you can see from Figure 8.2, the definitions precede the body of the statute and are included for terms that have a technical meaning that differs from ordinary usage. In this case, the term "occupied structure" includes a structure that is abandoned or vacant.

Plain Meaning

If no definitions are available (which is frequently the case), you would consider the **plain meaning** (everyday meaning) of the word "occupied." The rules of statutory construction require adherence to the language used by the legislature, and other sources cannot be consulted unless the language is ambiguous or some inconsistency exists within the statute. In other words, since the term "occupied" clearly suggests that humans must inhabit the structure (and if no definition indicates otherwise), the plain meaning suggests that the statute does not apply to abandoned structures.

ARSON

Section
13–1701. Definitions.
13–1702. Reckless burning; classification.
13–1703. Arson of a structure or property; classification.
13–1704. Arson of an occupied structure; classification.
13–1705. Arson of an occupied jail or prison facility;
　　　　　classification.

*A combined index appears following the
juvenile court procedure rules text.*

WESTLAW Computer Assisted Legal Research
WESTLAW supplements your legal research in many ways.
WESTLAW allows you to
　● update your research with the most current infor-
　　mation
　● expand your library with additional resources
　● retrieve direct history, precedential history and
　　parallel citations with the Insta-Cite service
For more information on using WESTLAW to supplement your
research, see the WESTLAW Electronic Research Guide, which
follows the Preface.

*Chapter 17, consisting of §§ 13–1701 to
13–1704, was added by Laws 1977, Ch. 142,
§ 71, effective October 1, 1978.*

§ 13–1701. Definitions

In this chapter, unless the context otherwise requires:

1. "Damage" means any physical or visual impairment of any surface.

2. "Occupied structure" means any structure as
defined in paragraph 4 in which one or more
human beings either is or is likely to be present or
so near as to be in equivalent danger at the time
the fire or explosion occurs. The term includes
any dwelling house, whether occupied, unoccupied
or vacant.

3. "Property" means anything other than a
structure which has value, tangible or intangible,
public or private, real or personal, including documents evidencing value or ownership.

4. "Structure" means any building, object, vehicle, watercraft, aircraft or place with sides and a
floor, separately securable from any other structure

attached to it and used for lodging, business, transportation, recreation or storage.
Added by Laws 1977, Ch. 142, § 71, eff. Oct. 1, 1978.

§ 13–1702. Reckless burning; classification

A. A person commits reckless burning by recklessly causing a fire or explosion which results in
damage to an occupied structure, a structure or
property.

B. Reckless burning is a class 1 misdemeanor.
Added by Laws 1977, Ch. 142, § 71, eff. Oct. 1, 1978.

**§ 13–1703. Arson of a structure or property;
classification**

A. A person commits arson of a structure or
property by knowingly and unlawfully damaging a
structure or property by knowingly causing a fire
or explosion.

B. Arson of a structure is a class 4 felony.
Arson of property is a class 4 felony if the property
had a value of more than one thousand dollars.
Arson of property is a class 5 felony if the property
had a value of more than one hundred dollars but
not more than one thousand dollars. Arson of
property is a class 1 misdemeanor if the property
had a value of one hundred dollars or less.
Added by Laws 1977, Ch. 142, § 71, eff. Oct. 1, 1978.
Amended by Laws 1978, Ch. 164, § 7, eff. Oct. 1, 1978;
Laws 1980, Ch. 229, § 18, eff. April 23, 1980; Laws 1987,
Ch. 169, § 1.

**§ 13–1704. Arson of an occupied structure;
classification**

A. A person commits arson of an occupied
structure by knowingly and unlawfully damaging
an occupied structure by knowingly causing a fire
or explosion.

B. Arson of an occupied structure is a class 2
felony.
Added by Laws 1977, Ch. 142, § 71, eff. Oct. 1, 1978.
Amended by Laws 1980, Ch. 229, § 19, eff. April 23,
1980; Laws 1987, Ch. 169, § 2.

Context of Other Statutes

If the plain meaning is subject to equally reasonable but different interpretations,
then plain meaning does not solve the dilemma. In those cases, the statutory context
must be considered. How is the term used in other sections of the statute or other
statutes addressing the same issue?

In reference to the term "occupied," we might refer to another section of the
criminal code that uses the term. If the burglary statute, for example, defines "occupied," we might apply that definition to the arson statute. Of course, the legislative intent behind each statute may be different, in which case the definitions
would not be interchangeable.

Public Policy

Alternatively, the historical context of the statute may be enlightening. The events
and conditions that shaped the passage of the statute may reveal the legislature's

motivation. These public policy considerations may be found in other statutes, in case law, or in the legislative history (discussed below).

Public policy might help us interpret the term "occupied" by giving us some insight into the legislature's motivation in passing the arson statutes. If their intent was to broaden the concept of arson to include any structure whose burning could possibly endanger human life, then they may have envisioned "occupied" structures as including any structure that could have been occupied even if it was actually unoccupied at the time of the arson.

Case Law

Interpretations by other courts, administrative agencies, or legal scholars may also shed light on the legislature's intent. If other courts within your jurisdiction have interpreted the terms at issue, their conclusions will guide you. If courts in other jurisdictions have interpreted the terms, their conclusions may be persuasive but not binding. In other words, a California court opinion may not control a Texas court's interpretation of a statute although the Texas court may certainly consider the California court's reasoning and holdings.

Using case law to interpret statutes can be a tricky business, however. If the same statutes are involved, you can fairly easily apply the court's interpretation. But if a different statute is at issue, the analytical path becomes more treacherous. How do you know, for example, that the legislature had the same intent in mind when writing the two statutes? If the legislative purpose for drafting each statute was different, the language used may have very different meanings.

For example, as we saw in Vo (discussed in Chapter Five), the term "human being" took on different meanings depending on whether it was used in the civil or criminal context. A fetus fell within the realm of human beings for purposes of a wrongful death statute but not for purposes of a criminal statute. Among other reasons, the Vo court noted that the wrongful death statute was remedial in nature and, therefore, was to be construed liberally to "advance the remedy," whereas the criminal statute had to give "fair warning" to the public. Therefore, "human being" as defined in the civil context could not be superimposed on the criminal statute.

Legislative History

If none of these endeavors yields the legislature's intent in passing the statute, the **legislative history** of the statute should be examined. This history includes the events that took place before the statute's passage and during its consideration (statements made by legislators during debates or committee reports discussing its passage) that reflect on the bill's purpose.

A statute's legislative history does not, however, necessarily impart the legislative intent behind the statute. Determining the collective intent of any group of people is difficult, but determining such intent in the context of political agendas is almost impossible. Legislators vote to pass bills for a variety of reasons, and their actual motivation is often known only by them. Furthermore, legislators are ill-equipped to predict the future, and frequently situations arise that they never contemplated when they passed the bill. Such novel situations demand creative interpretations of applicable laws.

To determine the meaning of the term "occupied" in regard to a structure, we might consult the hearing and debate records and committee reports surround-

FIGURE 8.3
Vo—Civil vs.
Criminal Statutes

418   Ariz.   **836 PACIFIC REPORTER, 2d SERIES**

cannot expand the scope of the crime of murder based on evolving common law principles. Furthermore, we cannot consider the wisdom or soundness of policy of legislative enactments, because such matters are clearly addressed to the legislature, not to the courts. *See, e.g., Schrey v. Allison Steel Mfg. Co.,* 75 Ariz. 282, 286, 255 P.2d 604, 606 (1953). We do agree, however, with the *Cass* and *Horne* courts that due process problems might arise in this case if we applied the first degree murder statute to a fetal murder in view of the lack of prior authority. This is particularly true given that the manslaughter statute, which is the only homicide statute that specifically prohibits the "death of an unborn child," has been construed to require a separate criminal intent toward the fetus. *See Amaya–Ruiz,* 166 Ariz. at 172–73, 800 P.2d at 1280–81.[11]

V. *Application of Summerfield to the Murder Statute*

Based on our previous discussion, we reject the state's argument and the trial court's conclusion that the *Summerfield* holding that a viable fetus is a "person" within the meaning of our wrongful death statute expands the common law definition of "person" within the penal murder statute. We also do not believe the *Summerfield* decision applies in the criminal context for several other reasons.

First, the *Summerfield* court clearly rejected any analogy between civil tort liability and criminal liability for causing death, noting that the common law probably did not recognize murder of a fetus. 144 Ariz. at 474, 698 P.2d at 719. Second, we point out that the wrongful death statute, unlike the murder statute, is a remedial statute in derogation of the common law that should be liberally construed to "advance the remedy" not provided by the common law that it abrogated. *See Carrow Co. v. Lusby,*

167 Ariz. 18, 804 P.2d 747 (1990); *Terry v. Linscott Hotel Corp.,* 126 Ariz. 548, 617 P.2d 56 (App.1980). The criminal statutes, however, must be interpreted to give "fair warning." A.R.S. § 13–101(2). Third, as the *Summerfield* court pointed out, "The issue of recovery for tort law damage to the fetus has come within the province of common law development." 144 Ariz. at 479, 698 P.2d at 724. As we have already explained, the development of the criminal law through common law principles has been abolished in Arizona. A.R.S. § 13–103. Fourth, the *Summerfield* court noted that the Arizona legislature had not provided a definition of the word "person" as used in A.R.S. § 12–611. 144 Ariz. at 475, 698 P.2d at 720. However, the legislature has defined "person" within the meaning of the homicide statutes as "a human being," A.R.S. § 13–1101(3), and has otherwise included a fetus within the protection of the manslaughter statute as "unborn child." A.R.S. § 13–1105(A)(1).

Finally, we recognize, as did the *Summerfield* court, that "[t]he word 'person' can mean different things in different contexts." 144 Ariz. at 478, 698 P.2d at 723. The court concluded that the holding of *Roe v. Wade,* 410 U.S. 113, 93 S.Ct. 705, 35 L.Ed.2d 147 (1973), that a fetus is not a "person" within the meaning of the fourteenth amendment, "neither prohibits nor compels" the inclusion of a fetus as a "person" in the context of the wrongful death statute. *Summerfield,* 144 Ariz. at 478, 698 P.2d at 723; *see also* D. Kader, *The Law of Tortious Prenatal Death Since Roe v. Wade,* 45 Mo.L.Rev. 639 (1980). Nor do we believe *Roe v. Wade* controls the issue before us for the same reasons as those expressed in *Summerfield.*

Based on these distinctions between the tort issues involved in *Summerfield* and the criminal issue involved here, we agree with other courts that have held that tort

---

11. In *Amaya–Ruiz,* the court noted, although it did not decide, that the statutory language of the manslaughter statute, " '*if* the death of the mother *had occurred,*' might also support an argument that the statute is inapplicable if the woman is murdered, and is only applicable if she survives." 166 Ariz. at 173 n. 1, 800 P.2d at 1281 n. 1 (emphasis in original). We express no

opinion regarding the application of the manslaughter statute to the limited facts before us. *But see State v. Brewer,* 170 Ariz. 486, 507–508, 826 P.2d 783, 804–05 (Ariz.1992), (upholding trial court's ruling that state was free to proceed with manslaughter charge for death of a fetus when mother also died).

<table>
<tr><td>

Practice Pointer

</td><td>

At the federal level, proposed legislation is referred to as a bill. Each bill is assigned a number that reflects which legislative body (House or Senate) introduced it as well as the order in which it was introduced. The bill is referred to an appropriate subcommittee, where it is scrutinized. Administrative agencies interested in the bill may submit reports, and public hearings may be held. Records of such hearings may be useful in determining legislative intent. The subcommittee submits a report to the full committee, which in turn votes to reject or recommend the bill to the entire legislative body. A bill that is recommended is accompanied by a committee report describing the bill's purpose, why it should be enacted, committee amendments, and an analysis of each section. In the House or Senate, the bill is debated and a record of those debates is maintained. Although less helpful than committee reports and hearing records, debate records may give some insight into legislative intent.

When a bill passes both the House and the Senate, it is assigned a new number called a "public law number" and is published as a "slip law" (available in the *United States Code Service Advance* pamphlets). At the end of each congressional session, the slip laws are compiled into one or more chronologically ordered volumes called "session laws," which are published in the *United States Statutes at Large*. Session laws are then arranged according to subject matter called "codes." Codified federal law is found in the *United States Code* (official version), the *United States Code Annotated* (unofficial version published by West Publishing), and the *United States Code Service* (unofficial version published by Lawyers' Cooperative).

</td></tr>
</table>

ing the passage of the arson statutes. Hopefully, one or all of these records might discuss the legislature's intent in enacting this statute and might enlighten us as to the reasoning in choosing the word "occupied."

Canons of Construction

Although the pursuit of legislative history is a worthy and sometimes fruitful quest, you may have to enlist the **canons of construction** in the process of interpreting a statute. These canons are rules that guide courts in interpreting statutes and include the following.

- Words and phrases should be construed in the context of the statute of which they are a part.

- Statutes should be construed in light of the harm the legislature intended to address.

Practice Pointer

Sources for the legislative history of federal statutes include the *United States Code Congressional and Administrative News* (better known as U.S.C.C.A.N.), the *Congressional Information Service* (C.I.S.), and the *Congressional Record* (*Cong. Rec.*). The latter is published on a daily basis while Congress is in session.

- Statutes on the same subject should be construed together.

- Statutes should be construed in such a way as to preserve their constitutionality.

- Statutes in conflict with the common law should be construed narrowly.

FIGURE 8.4
Canons of Construction

VO v. SUPERIOR COURT   Ariz. **413**
Cite as 836 P.2d 408 (Ariz.App. Div. 1 1992)

II. *Rules of Criminal Statutory Construction in Arizona*

[2] The legislature has abolished the common law rule of strict construction of criminal laws, and has provided that criminal laws "must be construed according to the fair meaning of their terms to promote justice and effect the objects of the law, including the purposes stated in A.R.S. § 13–101." A.R.S. § 13–104; *see also State v. Tramble*, 144 Ariz. 48, 695 P.2d 737 (1985). Among the purposes of the criminal law in Arizona, the legislature has included the following:

It is declared the public policy of this state and the general purposes of the provisions of this title are:

. . . .

2. To give fair warning of the nature of the conduct proscribed and of the sentences authorized upon conviction. . . .

A.R.S. § 13–101(2). Although the rule of strict construction of criminal statutes no longer applies, where the meaning of a statute is unclear, the "rule of lenity" requires us to resolve any doubt in a defendant's favor. *State v. Pena*, 140 Ariz. 545, 683 P.2d 744 (App.1983), *approved* 140 Ariz. 544, 683 P.2d 743 (1984); *State v. Sirny*, 160 Ariz. 292, 772 P.2d 1145 (App. 1989).

determine whether the Arizona legislature intended to include a fetus within the definition of a "person" within the homicide statutes as "a human being." *See* A.R.S. § 13–1101(3).

[4] In determining this intent, we look first to the way in which the words of the statute were understood at the time the legislation was enacted. *Kriz v. Buckeye Petroleum Co.*, 145 Ariz. 374, 701 P.2d 1182 (1985). Although there are no common law crimes in Arizona, when a crime such as murder is enacted by its common law name, we assume the legislature was aware of the common law meanings of the words in that statute and intended their use. *See Engle v. State*, 53 Ariz. 458, 90 P.2d 988 (1939); *State v. Bowling*, 5 Ariz. App. 436, 427 P.2d 928 (1967). *See also Keeler v. Superior Court*, 2 Cal.3d at 628, 470 P.2d at 622, 87 Cal.Rptr. at 486; *People v. Greer*, 79 Ill.2d 103, 106, 37 Ill.Dec. 313, 319, 402 N.E.2d 203, 209 (1980); *State v. Amaro*, 448 A.2d 1257, 1259 (R.I.1982) ("the Legislature would have expressly deviated from the common-law born-alive meaning of 'person' had it meant to do so.").

PUTTING IT INTO PRACTICE
· ·

Consider the following burglary statute.

A person commits burglary in the second degree by entering
or remaining unlawfully in or on a residential structure with
the intent to commit any theft or any felony therein.

Assume that this statute is based on the Model Penal Code. How
would you determine the meaning of "structure"? How would you
determine, for example, whether the statute applied to an
automobile in which someone was living?
· ·

STATUTORY ANALYSIS IN PRACTICE

Having reviewed several means of determining legislative intent, let us look at a
specific statute to more concretely demonstrate the problems inherent in statutory
interpretation. Suppose a statute prohibits driving or being in "actual physical control" of a vehicle while under the influence of alcohol. Say that we have a client
who was discovered passed out in the front seat of his vehicle with his keys in the
ignition. Was he in "actual physical control" of the vehicle?

Assume that neither the statute nor the department of transportation (an administrative agency) defines the critical language. We must then look to the plain
meaning rule. What does "actual physical control" mean on its face? Does it mean
that such drivers must have their keys in their hand or in the ignition, or can the
keys be in the driver's pocket? Must the ignition be turned on, or must the vehicle
simply be operational? Must drivers be conscious, or must they simply have the
potential to regain consciousness? These questions make it apparent that we cannot
find our answer in the plain meaning rule. We must look to legislative intent. Why
did the legislature add the words "actual physical control"? What does this phrase
encompass that "driving" does not?

Comparing Different Statutes

Reckless Driving Statute vs. Drunk Driving Statute
Suppose further research reveals that our courts have interpreted "physical control"
in reference to a reckless driving statute. This statute assigns responsibility for reckless driving to the individual(s) in "physical control" of the vehicle. Legislative
committee reports and hearing records reveal that the legislature wrote the statute
in response to a series of accidents in which a driver and one or more passengers
engaging in horseplay resulted in the driver losing control of the vehicle. In the
litigation arising from one such accident, the question was whether the passenger
was in "physical control" of the vehicle. The court defined being in "physical
control" for purposes of this statute as "operating the steering and/or braking mech-
anism of a vehicle."

Note that the language of the two statutes is not identical. Our statute refers
to "actual physical control," while the reckless driving statute refers to "physical

control." Is the term "actual" a critical addition? Does it change the meaning of the phrase? Arguably, "actual physical control" is more precise than "physical control," and perhaps the legislature intended to distinguish the two phrases. On the other hand, the key words may be "physical control," and the term "actual" may be superfluous.

The primary question, however, is whether the legislature had the same purpose in mind when drafting these two statutes. The purpose of the reckless driving statute seems to be expanding criminal responsibility for reckless driving beyond the person in the driver's seat to all those engaged in the driving process. Even a passenger in the back seat could conceivably be in "physical control" of a vehicle and, therefore, legally responsible for the operation of the vehicle. The policy served seems to be to discourage passengers from interfering with the operation of the vehicle they are in.

Suppose that case law shows that the purpose of the drunk driving statute is to authorize the police to remove intoxicated individuals when they pose a potential threat to the community's safety. Its purpose, then, would not be to expand the scope of responsible persons but to expand the scope of drunk driving. Therefore, while the reckless driving statute anticipates movement of vehicles, the drunk driving statute does not necessarily require movement and may, in fact, be designed to prevent any such movement.

Since the purpose of the statutes appears to be dissimilar, we will probably not be successful in looking to the reckless driving statute to define the phrase "actual physical control." Not only is the language slightly different but the public policies involved (expanding scope of liability versus expanding scope of crime) are also different. Therefore, making any comparison is suspect.

Drunk Riding Statute vs. Drunk Driving Statute

Suppose that another statute criminalizes riding or being in "actual physical control" of a horse or any other type of livestock while under the influence of alcohol. Can we apply this statute's definition of "actual physical control"? Let us consider the public policy behind including these words in the statute. Might we imagine that the legislature intended to criminalize all conduct that could potentially result in someone under the influence of alcohol endangering an animal, self, or others? Did the legislature want to expand the scope of "riding" beyond its traditional interpretation to include those scenarios in which the individual on the horse was

FIGURE 8.5
Comparing
Statutes

COMPARING STATUTES

■ **Do the statutes share a common language?**

■ **Is there a common public policy behind the statutes?**

■ **Do the statutes share a common purpose?**

not actually riding but had the potential to do so? Would the same public policy apply to operating a motor vehicle?

Suppose a court in our jurisdiction was asked to interpret the phrase "actual physical control" in reference to a rider who had passed out while riding his horse home and was found lying across the horse's neck with the reins dropped to the ground. Suppose further that the court found the rider to be in "actual physical control" of his horse because he had the "apparent ability to move" the animal when he regained consciousness. Could the same definition be applied to our client? Like the rider, he had the "apparent ability to move" his vehicle even though he was passed out and did not have the ignition turned on (similar to having the reins in his hand).

You could certainly argue that the statutes were intended to deal with different types of dangerous behavior (drunk driving versus drunk riding) and are, therefore, dissimilar in purpose. But, on the other hand, third persons are arguably more endangered by drivers driving while under the influence than by riders riding while under the influence. Therefore, if the legislature so broadly defined "riding," we can reasonably assume that it intended at least as broad an interpretation of "driving."

Notice that the drunk riding statute is more similar in purpose to the drunk driving statute than is the reckless driving statute. Although our comparison of statutory language does not lead to a definitive conclusion in either case, we can assume that statutes that share a similar purpose and language share a more common legislative intent than those that are dissimilar in purpose and language.

Comparing Cases Involving the Same Statute

If a comparison of different statutes containing the same or similar language can lead to ambiguous results, perhaps a comparison of case law interpreting the same statute will be more clear-cut. Let us look at a case that defines "actual physical control."

STATE of Arizona ex rel. Roderick G. McDOUGALL, Phoenix City Attorney, Petitioner,

v.

SUPERIOR COURT OF the State of Arizona, In and For the COUNTY OF MARICOPA, the Honorable Frederick J. Martone, a judge thereof, Respondent Judge,

Dean Dwight SCHRADER, Real Party in Interest.

No. 1 CA-SA 91-328.

Court of Appeals of Arizona,

Division 1, Department B.

Sept. 10, 1992.

Reconsideration Denied Oct. 21, 1992.

Petition for Review Granted Feb. 17, 1993.*

Review Dismissed April 27, 1993.**

---

*Martone, J., of the Supreme Court, recused himself and did not participate in the determination of this matter.

**Editor's Note: The Arizona Supreme Court's April 27, 1993 Order is published at 849 P.2d 1373.

Defendant was convicted in the Phoenix City Court, John L. Wiehn, J., of being in actual physical control of vehicle while under influence of intoxicating liquor and with blood alcohol content of 0.10 percent or grater, and he appealed. The Maricopa County Superior Court, Frederick J. Martone, J., No. 91–00473, reversed, and state petitioned for special action. The Court of Appeals, Garbarino, J., held that defendant was in "actual physical control" of vehicle.

Reversed and remanded.

1. **Automobiles k332** Defendant's subjective intent to drive vehicle is not relevant to determination of whether defendant was in "actual physical control" of vehicle under statutes which make it unlawful for person to drive or be in actual physical control of vehicle while under influence of intoxicating liquor or with blood alcohol content of 0.10 percent or greater. A.R.S. § 28–692, subd. A, pars. 1, 2.

2. **Automobiles k332** To avoid conviction for "actual physical control" of vehicle while intoxicated, driver must pull off the roadway and turn off the ignition. A.R.S. § 28–692, subd. A, pars. 1, 2.

See publication Words and Phrases for other judicial constructions and definitions.

3. **Automobiles k332** Defendant who had pulled off the roadway into parking lot and was sleeping in vehicle with engine running was in "actual physical control" of vehicle, as required to support convictions for being in actual physical control of vehicle while under the influence of intoxicating liquor and with blood alcohol content of 0.10 percent or greater. A.R.S. § 28–692, subd. A, pars. 1, 2.

Roderick G. McDougall, Phoenix City Atty. by Gregory S. Williams, Asst. City Prosecutor, Phoenix, for petitioner.

Basil G. Diamos, Phoenix, for real party in interest.

OPINION

GARBARINO, Judge.

Appellant Dean Dwight Schrader (the defendant) was arrested and charged with violating Ariz.Rev. Stat.Ann. (A.R.S.) section 28–692(A)(1) and (A)(2) which makes it unlawful for any person to drive or be in actual physical control of any vehicle within the state while under the influence of intoxicating liquor if the person is impaired to the slightest degree or with a blood alcohol content of .10 or greater within two hours of driving or being in actual physical control of the vehicle.

The defendant waived his right to a jury trial, and the case was tried to the Phoenix Municipal Court. The only issue before the municipal court was whether the defendant was in actual physical control of his vehicle. The court found the defendant guilty of being in actual physical control while under the influence of alcohol, and while having a blood alcohol concentration of .10 or more within two hours. The defendant appealed to the Maricopa County Superior Court. The superior court, sitting as an intermediate appellate court, reversed on appeal and remanded to the Phoenix Municipal Court, with directions to enter a verdict of acquittal on each of the charges. The state filed a petition for special action contesting this ruling. We accepted jurisdiction and granted relief with an opinion to follow. This is that opinion.

JURISDICTION

Our jurisdiction of this special action is governed by A.R.S. section 12–120.21(A)(4), which provides:

A. The court of appeals shall have: . . . .

4. Jurisdiction to hear and determine petitions for special action brought pursuant to the rules of procedure for special actions, without regard to its appellate jurisdiction.

Based upon the foregoing statute and the fact that this case is of statewide importance, we accept jurisdiction and grant relief.

ISSUE

The sole issue for our consideration in this special action is whether the superior court erred in finding that the defendant was not in "actual physical control" of his vehicle pursuant to A.R.S. section 28–692(A)(1) and (2).

FACTS AND PROCEDURAL HISTORY

The facts in this case are essentially undisputed. The defendant was arrested on February 3, 1991, at 8:30 p.m. in Phoenix, Arizona. He had been at a party drinking alcohol since approximately noon. At approximately 7 p.m., the defendant left the party and went to his vehicle which was parked in a paved parking lot of a cabin park. The property contained driveways which turned onto a public street. The defendant's vehicle was not on a roadway. When the defendant entered the vehicle he turned on the engine and the heater. Two local residents heard the motor running for approximately one hour. When the residents went to investigate, the defendant was sitting slumped over the wheel and he was sleeping. One of the residents attempted to awaken the defendant, but he did not respond. The resident turned the ignition off, took the keys with him, and called 911. When the police arrived at approximately 8:30 p.m., the defendant was disoriented and belligerent. The police observed that the defendant had symptoms of intoxication. No field sobriety tests were administered, but a Gas Chromatograph Intoxilizer (GCI) test performed at the police station established that the defendant had a blood alcohol content of .19. The defendant was arrested and charged with violating A.R.S. section 28–692(A)(1) and (2).

The municipal court found that the defendant did not intend to drive the vehicle, that he was out of traffic, but that he had his engine running. The court noted that the facts of this case differ from the facts in *State v. Zavala*, 136 Ariz. 356, 666 P.2d 456 (1983), the distinguishing factor being that in *Zavala* the defendant was found *not* to be in actual physical control of his vehicle because the engine was *not* running. Therefore, based upon our supreme court's holding in *Zavala*, the municipal court found the defendant to be in "actual physical control" of his vehicle, in violation of the statute. The defendant was sentenced to alcohol abuse screening and a $430 fine. The sentence was imposed on both citations, to run concurrently.

The defendant appealed to the Maricopa County Superior Court. He asserted that he was never in "actual physical control" of his vehicle because he never intended to drive the vehicle and he was well off the roadway in a parking lot at the time he was arrested. The state argued that the defendant had placed himself in the driver's seat of the vehicle with the engine running and then fell asleep. Therefore, he never "voluntarily ceased to exercise control over the vehicle prior to losing consciousness" as required by *Zavala*. 136 Ariz. 359, 666 P.2d at 459. Additionally, the state argued that the intent of the defendant was irrelevant. The superior court reversed the municipal court's judgment and remanded the case to that court with directions to enter a verdict of acquittal on each of the charges. The superior court stated:

> While the bright line test of having an ignition on or off may ordinarily be dispositive, and while intent to drive need not be proven, where, as here, the undisputed facts indicate that the defendant did not intend to drive and had not been driving, and that the engine had been on to keep the defendant warm, the bright line test must yield to a result which advances the purposes sought to be served by *Zavala*.

The court further stated that the purpose of the court's holding in *Zavala* was to allow intoxicated persons to stay in their nonmoving cars until they "sleep it off."

DISCUSSION

Arizona Revised Statutes Annotated section 28–692(A) states:

> A. It is unlawful and punishable as provided in § 28–692.01 for any person to drive or be in actual physical control of any vehicle within this state under any of the following circumstances:
> 1. While under the influence of intoxicating liquor, any drug, a vapor releasing substance containing a toxic substance or any combination of liquor, drugs or vapor releasing substances if the person is impaired to the slightest degree.
> 2. If the person has an alcohol concentration of 0.10 or more within two hours of driving or being in actual physical control of the vehicle.

While our legislature has not defined the term "actual physical control," our supreme court has stated that the 1950 amendment to the statute which added the words "or be in actual physical control" manifests a legislative intent that the law apply to persons having control of a vehicle while not actually driving it or having it in motion. *State v. Webb*, 78 Ariz. 8, 10, 274 P.2d 338, 339 (1954).

In *Webb*, the defendant was discovered in his truck, parked in a lane of traffic with the headlights on, and the motor running. 78 Ariz. at 9–10, 274 P.2d at 338–39. The police found the defendant asleep and intoxicated with both hands and his head resting on the steering wheel. *Id.* On appeal, the defendant conceded that he was under the influence of intoxicating liquor, but argued that the statute did not encompass his conduct. 78 Ariz. at 10, 274 P.2d at 339. He asserted that the statute did not apply to the facts of his case where the vehicle was not moving and he was asleep or unconscious. *Id.* Our supreme court held that the defendant was in "actual physical control" of his vehicle, in violation of the statute. 78 Ariz. at 11, 274 P.2d at 340. The court in *Webb* focused on 2 circumstances present at the time of the arrest: the fact that the vehicle's engine was running and the position of the truck in a lane of traffic. 78 Ariz. at 11, 274 P.2d at 340. In holding that these facts established a violation of the statute, the court stated:

> An intoxicated person seated behind the steering wheel of a motor vehicle is a threat to the safety and welfare of the public. The danger is less than that involved when the vehicle is actually moving, but it does exist. While at the precise moment the defendant was apprehended he may

have been exercising no conscious volition with regard to the vehicle, still there is a legitimate inference to be drawn that defendant had of his choice placed himself behind the wheel thereof, and had either started the motor or permitted it to run. He therefore had the "actual physical control" of that vehicle, even though the manner in which such control was exercised resulted in the vehicle's remaining motionless at the time of the apprehension.

78 Ariz. at 11, 274 P.2d at 340.

The *Webb* court clearly articulated that even if the driver is exercising "no conscious volition" at the moment of apprehension he did have "actual physical control" even though his vehicle remained motionless. Therefore, even if the driver did not intend to drive, he was still in "actual physical control." 78 Ariz. at 11, 274 P.2d at 340.

The question of "actual physical control" was next considered by our supreme court in *State v. Zavala*, 136 Ariz. 356, 666 P.2d 456 (1983). In *Zavala*, the defendant was found asleep in his vehicle, which was stopped in the emergency lane of the freeway with the key in the ignition. 136 Ariz. at 357, 666 P.2d at 457. However, the motor was *not* running. *Id.* The court stated that the element of "actual physical control" is shown where defendant has " 'the apparent ability to start and move the vehicle.' " 136 Ariz. at 359, 666 P.2d at 459. The court focused on the identical factors the *Webb* court focused upon when it determined whether the defendant was in "actual physical control": the fact that the motor was running, and the position of the defendant's vehicle in a traffic lane. *Id.* at 358, 666 P.2d at 458. The court found that since neither of those circumstances were present, the defendant was not in "actual physical control" of the vehicle pursuant to the statute. *Id.* at 359, 666 P.2d at 459. The court set forth a 2-prong test which must be met to find that a defendant is not in "actual physical control" pursuant to the statute: The impaired driver must remove his vehicle from the roadway *and* the driver must turn the engine off. 136 Ariz. at 358–59, 666 P.2d at 458–59. The court explained that its interpretation of the language of A.R.S. section 28–692(A) encouraged a driver who felt impaired to completely pull off the highway, turn off the key, and sleep until he is sober without fear of being arrested for being in "actual physical control." 136 Ariz. at 359, 666 P.2d at 459. "To hold otherwise might encourage a drunk driver, apprehensive about being arrested, to attempt to reach his destination while endangering others on the highway." *Id.*

Following *Zavala*, this court held that as a matter of law, a person is in "actual physical control" of his vehicle if the ignition is turned to the "on" position, even though the engine is not running. *State v. Del Vermuele*, 160 Ariz. 295, 297, 992 P.2d 1148, 1150 (App.1989). In *Del Vermuele*, the defendant was parked illegally on a curbside adjacent to a bar. 160 Ariz. at 296, 772 P.2d at 1149. Upon approaching the vehicle, the police observed the defendant lose his balance and they noticed that his speech was slurred. *Id.* When the defendant entered his vehicle, he turned the ignition switch to the "on" position. *Id.* The dashboard lights were on but the engine was not running. *Id.* The defendant was confronted by the police, ordered out of the vehicle and subsequently arrested for being in "actual physical control" of his vehicle while having a BAC of .10 or more, pursuant to A.R.S. section 28–692(A). The defendant contended that he had turned the ignition key on so that his mobile phone would become operative in order that he could secure a ride home. 160 Ariz. at 297, 772 P.2d at 1150. The court found that *Webb* and *Zavala* were factually distinguishable, primarily because the drivers of those vehicles at the time of their apprehension were asleep. *Id.* The court reasoned that the findings in those cases of the defendants being in "actual physical control" were related to their ability to maneuver the vehicles out into the stream of traffic. *Id.* The court focused upon the fact that in this case the defendant was not asleep and was readily capable of placing his vehicle into the stream of traffic. *Id.* The court held that the defendant was clearly in "actual physical control" of his vehicle. *Id.* The court noted that "[t]he officers would have been derelict in their duties had they allowed appellee to start the engine and operate the vehicle." *Id.*

Courts in other jurisdictions have held intoxicated motorists to be in "actual physical control" of a vehicle while asleep or passed out behind the steering wheel. *Commonwealth v. Kloch*, 230 Pa.Super. 563, 327 A.2d 375 (1974); *City of Kansas City v. Troutner*, 544 S.W.2d 295 (Mo.App. 1976). In so holding, these courts have viewed the motorist as being in a position to regulate the vehicle's movements or as having the authority to manage the vehicle.

The state first asserts that the superior court misapplied the 2-prong test set forth in *Zavala* by considering the defendant's subjective intent as to whether he intended to drive the vehicle. Citing *State v. Goseyun*, 153 Ariz. 119, 122, 735 P.2d 149, 152 (App.1987) the state contends that this court rejected a subjective intent test when it stated:

We believe our supreme court in *Webb* and *Zavala* rejected a test which turns on the subjective intent of the driver and chose a determination based on the actual circumstances present at the time his vehicle is discovered by the authorities.

[1] We find that portion of the superior court's ruling which gave effect to the finding that the defendant did not intend to drive the vehicle to be in error. Our supreme court's holdings in *Webb* and *Zavala* are controlling in this case. In both *Webb* and *Zavala* our supreme court refused to consider the subjective intent of the defendant. Rather, the court focused upon whether the defendant had pulled off the road and had turned off the ignition, indicating that the defendant voluntarily ceased to exercise control over the vehicle prior to losing consciousness.

The state also contends that the superior court simply misapplied the 2-prong test articulated in *Zavala*. The state asserts that the defendant did not take affirmative steps to lower the life-treatening risks to the public as required by *Zavala*. The defendant did not remove himself from the flow of traffic at the time he knew he was impaired. Rather, he placed himself in actual physical control of his vehicle by affirmatively getting into his vehicle and sitting behind the steering wheel. The defendant also turned on the engine, thereby raising the risk of danger to the traveling public. The state argues that *Zavala* requires the defendant to remove the vehicle from the roadway outside the flow of traffic *and* to turn off the ignition to show that the defendant voluntarily ceased to exercise control over the vehicle prior to losing consciousness. The state contends that because both of these factors were not met, the trial court erred in finding that the defendant was not in "actual physical control" of his vehicle. We agree, and find fault only with the state's characterization that the defendant was restricting or interfering with the flow of traffic.

[2,3] The facts indicate that the defendant was pulled off of a roadway in a parking lot and was sleeping. However, regardless of this fact, *Zavala* holds that for a driver to be found not in "actual physical control" of his vehicle he must place his vehicle away from the road pavement outside the flow of traffic *and* turn off the ignition. 136 Ariz. at 358–59, 666 P.2d at 458–59. We believe the acts of the defendant were sufficient to support the defendant's conviction of being in "actual physical control" of a vehicle while intoxicated pursuant to *Zavala*. Therefore, the superior court erred in finding to the contrary.

There is no question that an intoxicated person sitting behind the steering wheel of a motor vehicle is a threat to the public safety and welfare. We believe that as long as the defendant is physically able to assert dominion, in the sense of movement, then he has as much control over the vehicle as he would if he were actually driving the vehicle. It is not dispositive that the defendant's car was not moving, and that the defendant was not making an effort to move it when the police arrived. There is a legitimate inference to be drawn from the fact that since the defendant placed himself behind the wheel of the vehicle with the engine running, he could have at any time driven away. He therefore had "actual physical control" of the vehicle within the meaning of the statute.

Finally, the state asserts that the superior court erred when it stated that "this case seems to fit *Zavala's* purpose of allowing inebriated persons to stay in their nonmoving cars until they sleep it off." The state argues that *Zavala's* purpose is not to allow impaired persons to take affirmative steps to get into their car and operate the controls. Rather, the court's purpose in *Zavala* was to encourage drivers to pull off the road and to turn off the engine without fear of being arrested for being in control. The *Zavala* policy requires affirmative steps to lessen potential life-threatening risk to the motoring public.

The real purpose of A.R.S. section 28–692(1), (2) and (3) is to deter individuals who have been drinking intoxicating liquor from operating their vehicles while in an intoxicated state. The "actual physical control" offense is a preventative measure intended to deter the drunk driver. One who has been drinking intoxicating liquor should not be encouraged to test his driving ability on any road, where his life and the lives of other motorists are at stake.

CONCLUSION

The order of the superior court is reversed, and this case is remanded for proceedings consistent with this opinion.

KLEINSCHMIDT, Acting P.J., and SHELLEY, J.**, concur.

**The Honorable Melvyn T. Shelley was authorized to participate in this case by the Chief Justice of the Arizona Supreme Court pursuant to Arizona Constitution article VI, section 20.

In *McDougall v. Arizona*, the defendant was found by two people who heard the motor of his vehicle running and who found him slumped over the wheel asleep. When they could not awaken him, they called 911. The police arrived and observed him to be belligerent, disoriented, and apparently intoxicated. The defendant argued that he was not in "actual physical control" because he never intended to drive and was parked off the roadway at the time of his arrest.

The state relied on the definition set forth in *State v. Zavala* to rebut the defendant's claim. In that case, the defendant had his key in the ignition but the motor was not running, and the vehicle in which he was found asleep was parked in the emergency lane of the freeway. The court defined "actual physical control" as having the "apparent ability to start and move the vehicle." Based on the fact that the motor was not running and that the vehicle was removed from the roadway, the court concluded that the defendant was not in "actual physical control."

In *McDougall*, the state urged the court to distinguish *Zavala* because the motor in this case was running and, therefore, the defendant had an opportunity to move the vehicle. The court concurred and concluded that since the defendant had the "apparent capacity to move or start the vehicle," he was in "actual physical control." The court also clarified that *Zavala* did not consider the subjective intent of the driver and that the defendant's testimony that he did not intend to drive was irrelevant.

The difference in outcome between *Zavala* and *McDougall* can be attributed primarily to a factual distinction (whether the motor was running). In another case discussed by the *McDougall* court, however, policy considerations more than factual differences determined the difference in outcome. In *Del Vermuele*, the defendant was confronted by the police after entering his vehicle and turning his ignition switch "on." Although the defendant claimed his only intent was to activate his mobile phone in order to contact someone to drive him home, the court found him to be in "actual physical control." The court observed that the purpose of *Zavala*, which was to encourage inebriated drivers to pull off the road and sleep until sober without fear of being arrested, was not served in this case because the driver was awake. Therefore, even though the engine was not running and the driver

---

FIGURE 8.6
Defining "Actual Physical Control"

DEFINING "ACTUAL PHYSICAL CONTROL"

■ ZAVALA

➤ Motor not running; driver asleep; parked in emergency lane.
CONCLUSION: Driver was not in "actual physical control."

■ DEL VERMUELE

➤ Ignition switch on; driver awake; pulled off roadway.
CONCLUSION: Driver was in "actual physical control."

■ McDOUGALL

➤ Motor running; driver asleep; parked off roadway.
CONCLUSION: Driver was in "actual physical control."

was pulled off the roadway (as was true in *Zavala*), the defendant was readily able to pull into traffic because he was awake.

The lesson to be derived from these cases is that you must be alert to slight factual differences even when dealing with statutory interpretation. The difference in the cases dealing with "actual physical control" hinged on whether the motor was running, a difference that might not seem important except when you consider the policy considerations underlying this case law. Although the courts applied the same definition in each case, they came to different conclusions because of these factual distinctions.

PUTTING IT INTO PRACTICE

What would the Arizona court conclude if the police discovered the defendant slumped over the wheel, unconscious, and the vehicle pulled over to the side of a heavily traveled road? Assume that medical testimony indicates that injuries sustained by the defendant in addition to his high level of intoxication rendered him incapable of driving.

Comparing Statutes from Different Jurisdictions

The problem of trying to determine legislative intent is further compounded when dealing with statutes from different jurisdictions. A valid comparison of statutes requires language that is similar if not identical. The primary factor that complicates such comparison, however, is that you are dealing with different legislative bodies. You have no doubt observed that ascertaining the intent of one legislature is difficult. Determining the intent of two legislative bodies is even more precarious. Therefore, if at all possible, avoid using case law in one jurisdiction to interpret statutes in another jurisdiction.

Statutes that are based on **uniform** or **model acts**, such as the Uniform Commercial Code and the Model Penal Code, can more legitimately be compared because you can infer that the purpose of the statutes is the same. Uniform and model acts are drafted for the purpose of standardizing statutory law across the United States. Legislation based on a uniform or model act can be interpreted by reviewing the drafters' comments as well as case law interpreting other jurisdictions' statutes based on the same uniform or model act. If the California courts, for example, interpret a controversial section of the Uniform Commercial Code, you are justified in citing this interpretation to a court that has also adopted the Uniform Commercial Code.

This is not to say that courts never consider the statutory construction offered by other jurisdictions. In *Vo*, for example, which was discussed in Chapter Five (pp. 88–97), the court looked to other courts for validation. Notice, however, that after citing the jurisdictions that were in accord with the *Vo* court's definition of "person," the court also distinguished the result reached by two common law states. Explaining that as a "code" state, Arizona courts could not usurp the role of the legislature by creating new crimes (as was the prerogative of the common law courts), the court relegated its role to that of interpreter. Even though the *Vo* court

FIGURE 8.7
Vo—Comparing
Case Law from
other Jurisdictions

Only two courts have judicially determined that a fetus was within the protection of homicide statutes based on common law principles.[9] *See Commonwealth v. Cass*, 392 Mass. 799, 467 N.E.2d 1324 (1984) (8½ month fetus is a "person" within intent of vehicular homicide statute); *State v. Horne*, 282 S.C. 444, 319 S.E.2d 703 (1984) (nine-month fetus is a "person" within meaning of statutory definition of murder).

In both *Cass* and *Horne*, the court expanded the criminal law through principles of common law interpretation that are not available to this court in the present case. For example, in *Horne*, the South Carolina Supreme Court reasoned as follows:

> This court has the right and the duty to develop the common law of South Carolina to better change an everchanging society as a whole. In this regard, the criminal law has been the subject of change.... The fact that this particular issue has not been raised or ruled on before does not mean we are prevented from declaring the common law as it should be.

319 S.E.2d at 704. In *Cass*, the court reasoned:

[W]e reject the notion that we are unable to develop common law rules of criminal law because the Legislature has occupied the entire field of criminal law. While this may be true in code jurisdictions, it is not true in this Commonwealth, where our criminal law is largely common law. 467 N.E.2d at 1327. This distinction, between "code states," which have abolished common law crimes and provide that no crime can be defined other than by the legislature, and "common law states," which recognize common law crimes and allow judicial decisions to fashion expanded definitions of crimes, is critical. *See, e.g., State v. Soto*, 378 N.W.2d at 627–30 (rejecting the reasoning of *Cass* and *Horne* because, although Massachusetts and South Carolina are "common law states," Minnesota is a "code state").

[6] Arizona is a "code state," and this court is legislatively precluded from creating new crimes by expanding the common law through judicial decision. A.R.S. § 13–103. Our function, therefore, is limited to interpreting what the legislature has prohibited in light of its intent, rather than expanding the criminal law based on our own sense of changing societal perceptions of what the law should be. Unlike the courts in *Cass* and *Horne*,[10] therefore, we

cannot expand the scope of the crime of murder based on evolving common law principles. Furthermore, we cannot consider the wisdom or soundness of policy of legislative enactments, because such matters are clearly addressed to the legislature, not to the courts. *See, e.g., Schrey v.*

167 Ariz. 18, 804 P.2d 747 (1990); *Terry v. Linscott Hotel Corp.*, 126 Ariz. 548, 617 P.2d 56 (App.1980). The criminal statutes, however, must be interpreted to give "fair warning." A.R.S. § 13–101(2). Third, as the *Summerfield* court pointed out, "The issue of recovery for tort law damage to

considered other jurisdictions, it did so only after examining the legislative history of the statutes in question as well as the relevant case law within its own jurisdiction.

Conflicting Statutes

You do not have to look to different jurisdictions to find ambiguity in legislative intent. Sometimes a single legislative body writes statutes containing apparently conflicting provisions. In an effort to harmonize such statutes, courts assume that the legislature did not intend to create conflict. Let us consider two courts that dealt with conflicting statutes and interpreted them differently. We will examine

FIGURE 8.8
Statutes from *Hernandez*

STATUTES PERTAINING TO LIABILITY OF THOSE WHO SERVE ALCOHOL

A.R.S. Sec. 4–301
Liability limitation; social host
A person other than a licensee . . . is not liable in damages to any person who is injured, or to the survivors of any person killed, or for damage to property, which is alleged to have been caused in whole or in part by reason of the furnishing or serving of spirituous liquor to a person of the legal drinking age.

A.R.S. Sec. 4–311
Liability for serving intoxicated person or minor; definition
A. A licensee is liable for property damage and personal injuries or is liable to a person who may bring an action for wrongful death pursuant to Sec. 12–612 if a court or jury finds the following:
1. The licensee sold spirituous liquor either to a purchaser who was obviously intoxicated, or to a purchaser under the legal drinking age without requesting identification containing proof of age or with knowledge that the person was under the legal drinking age. . .

A.R.S. Sec. 4–312(B)
Liability limitation
Subject to the provisions of subsection A of this section and except as provided in Sec. 4–311, a person, firm, corporation or licensee is not liable in damages to any person who is injured, or to the survivors of any person killed, or for damage to property which is alleged to have been caused in whole or in part by reason of the sale, furnishing or serving of spirituous liquor.

the reasoning of each as illustration of how reasonable minds can logically arrive at contrasting conclusions.

Read first *Hernandez v. Arizona Board of Regents*, which was rendered by the Arizona Court of Appeals. When you have thoroughly digested this opinion, read the following opinion by the Arizona Supreme Court.

The ESTATE OF Ruben A. HERNANDEZ, by Elizabeth L. HERNANDEZ-WHEELER, his personal representative, for and on behalf of Ruben R. HERNANDEZ, Elizabeth L. Hernandez-Wheeler, and Catherine Rose Poli, Plaintiffs/Appellants,
vs.
ARIZONA BOARD OF REGENTS, a body corporate, Delta Tau Delta Fraternity, a New York corporation, Epsilon Epsilon Chapter of Delta Tau Delta Fraternity, Inc., an Arizona corporation, Epsilon Epsilon Educational Foundation, an Arizona corporation, Brett Harper Anderson, Bradley Reed Bergamo, Paul Jude Biondolillo,

Joshua Christopher Bliss, Matthew James Bosco, Steven Penn Bryan, Anthony Charles P. Caputo, Thomas David Carlson, Stephen Michael Carpenter, Jeffrey David Catlin, Nathaniel Louis Derby, Albert Edward Dietrich IV, Clo Earl Edgington, Karam Elias Farah, Christopher Todd Flavio, Gerritt Andrew Gehan, Barry James Ginch, Steven Hare, David James Henshall, Markus Rudolph Holtby, Mark Thomas Hopkins, David Laurence Ison, Douglas Edward Jameson, Gregory Richard Janis, Rex Edward Jorgensen, Jay Adam Josephs, Craig Landon, Sean David Leahy, Dale R. Lemon, John Christopher Manross, John Conrad Miller, Christopher J. Molloy, Harrison Lane Morton, Kurt Richard Munzinger, Paige Ray Peterson, Kenneth S. Plache, Daniel Lee Rasmus, Scott Allen Remington, Paul Anthony Reynolds, James Samuel Rigberg, Gary Edward Rink, Erick Jon Roberts, Michael Daniel Roth, George Evangelos Roussos, Charles Dana Sacks, Thomas McKinlay Schwarze, William John Sheoris, Douglas Todd Sims, Clifford Lawrence Smith, Kristopher James Stathakis, Roger Sanford Stinnett, Douglas Matthew Stoss, Anthony Charles Suriano, Eric Joseph Szoke, Nelson Sterlin Udstuen, James Frank Uppendahl, Scott Urban, Larry Wagner, Todd Eric Wallis, Jonathan Blakeslee Woodard, Michael Patrick Woodward, Jeffrey Ryan Wyne, and David Hall Yohe, Defendants/Appellees

Nos. 2 CA–CV 90–0191, 2 CA–CV 90–0219, 2 CA–CV 90–0252, 2 CA–CV 90–0257
Court of Appeals of Arizona, Division Two, Department B
838 P.2d 1283, 172 Ariz. 522, 101 Ariz. Adv. Rep. 87
November 29, 1991
Appeal from the Superior Court of Pima County. Cause No. 255362.
Honorable Lina S. Rodriguez, Judge
Review Granted on Issues 1, 2, 5, and 6, and Denied on all other Issues
November 3, 1992.

COUNSEL

Risner & Graham by Kenneth K. Graham and William J. Risner, Tucson, for plaintiff/appellant.

Grant Woods, Atty. Gen. by Bruce J. MacDonald and Nancy M. Coomer, Tucson, for defendants/appellees Arizona Board of Regents and Steven Hare.

Fish, Duffield, Miller, Young, Adamson & Alfred, P.C. by Samuel D. Alfred, Tucson, for defendant/appellee Delta Tau Delta Fraternity.

Murphy, Goering, Roberts & Berkman, P.C. by Michael F. McNamara and William L. Rubin, Tucson, for defendants/appellees Epsilon Epsilon Chapter of Delta Tau Delta Fraternity, Epsilon Epsilon Educational Foundation and Certain Individuals.

Ridenour, Swenson, Cleere & Evans by Harold H. Swenson, Richard H. Oplinger, and Robert R. Byrne, Phoenix, for defendant/appellees Douglas Matthew Stoss and John Christopher Manross.

Law Offices of Kevin E. Miniat by Kevin E. Miniat, Tucson, for defendant/appellee James Frank Uppendahl.

JUDGES

Fernandez, Judge. Roll, P.J., concurs. Hathaway, Judge, dissenting.

AUTHOR: FERNANDEZ

OPINION

This case presents the issues of the validity of A.R.S. § 4–312(B) and the potential liability of members of a University of Arizona fraternity, the local fraternity chapter, its house corporation, the national fraternity, and the Arizona Board of Regents for the serious injury and subsequent death of a motorist involved in a collision with an underage, intoxicated fraternity member who had recently driven away from a fraternity party. The trial court granted summary judgment in favor of appellees, and the personal representative of the deceased motorist's estate appeals. We affirm.

Because the case was decided on summary judgment, we view the facts in the light most favorable to the personal representative, the party opposing the motions. *Gulf Insurance Co. v. Grisham*, 126 Ariz. 123, 613 P.2d 283 (1980). On August 27, 1988, appellee Epsilon Epsilon Chapter of Delta Tau Delta Fraternity, Inc. (Epsilon Epsilon) at the University of Arizona held a bid party to welcome pledges who had been through "Rush Week" and had agreed as of 6:00 p.m. that evening to join Epsilon Epsilon.

Approximately 63% of the members of the fraternity that fall semester were under the age of 21, the legal drinking age in Arizona. A.R.S. § 4–101(16). The fraternity kept records of its members' birth dates. All members, regardless of age, could contribute to a fund maintained by the social fund chair. The chair, a member over 21, kept the members' contributions in a separate checking account outside the normal operation of the fraternity's treasury and used the money to purchase alcohol to be served at fraternity parties. For the fall semester 1988, each member who contributed to the fund paid $80. All members who contributed to the fund, regardless of their ages, were entitled to drink the purchased alcohol at fraternity parties; they were not permitted to take their own alcohol.

Extensive discovery was conducted in this case. The evidence was that the fraternity purchased between six and eight kegs of beer for the party on August 27. It owned the equipment to have four kegs operating at the same time. A member testified that the fraternity generally began its parties with four kegs operating and then served from two kegs at a time the rest of the evening. Several hundred people generally attended the fraternity's parties, most of them underaged females.

On August 27, John Rayner, a fraternity member, was twenty years, five and one-half months old. He attended the party and was seen drinking there. The party ended at 1:00 a.m. At 1:45a.m., Rayner's vehicle crashed into a vehicle driven by Ruben Hernandez. Rayner was traveling at least 43 miles per hour in a 25-mile-per-hour zone. His blood alcohol level at 2:30 a.m. was .15 percent. Hernandez was rendered blind, brain-damaged, and quadriplegic. He died in July 1990.

Hernandez sued Rayner for his injuries, and Hernandez's three adult children sued for their loss of consortium. The complaint was later amended to add as defendants each member of the fraternity who had contributed to the social fund that fall semester; Epsilon Epsilon; Epsilon Epsilon Educational Foundation, the corporation formed to lease the property on which the fraternity house is located; Delta Tau Delta Fraternity, the national fraternity organization; the Arizona Board of Regents; and Steven Hare, a university student assigned to Epsilon Epsilon pursuant to a university program aimed at reducing alcohol problems among fraternities and sororities. After Hernandez's death, his personal representative was substituted as plaintiff. Rayner settled with the estate and has been dismissed from the suit.

THE COMPLAINT ALLEGATIONS

The complaint alleged that the individual fraternity members and Epsilon Epsilon were joint venturers who furnished or aided or abetted the furnishing of alcohol to those under the age of 21 either by contributing to the social fund or by serving alcoholic beverages at the party on August 27. Epsilon Epsilon was also alleged to be responsible under the doctrine of respondeat superior and for breach of its duty to control the activities of its members.

The national fraternity is alleged to have breached its duty to supervise the local chapter so as to assure its compliance with university rules and regulations. It is also alleged to be liable under the doctrine of respondeat superior for the negligent conduct of the local chapter adviser, who is alleged to be an agent of the national organization.

Epsilon Epsilon Educational Foundation (the house corporation) leases the fraternity house property from its owner, the Arizona Board of Regents. The house corporation was established to constitute a continuing entity for leasing the property because the Board of Regents will not lease directly to transient fraternity members. The house corporation is alleged to have breached its duty to use reasonable care in entrusting its property to the chapter because it knew or should have known that the site was regularly used for fraternity parties at which alcohol was served to those under the legal drinking age.

The Board of Regents is alleged to have been negligent in continuing to lease the premises to the house corporation when it knew that the fraternity served alcoholic beverages to persons under the legal drinking age. Steven Hare is alleged to have gratuitously undertaken the responsibility to educate the members of Epsilon Epsilon on university regulations about the consumption of alcohol, to monitor the chapter's compliance with those regulations, and to report any violations of those regulations. The complaint alleges that he failed to exercise reasonable care in carrying out that undertaking. Hare is also alleged to have acted as an agent of the Board of Regents, and the Board is alleged to be liable both under the doctrine of respondeat superior and for its negligent supervision of Hare.

The basis for appellant's allegations against Hare is the following: In January 1987 a Greek Relationship Statement was approved by the university, which recognized that the fraternity/sorority system is an integral part of the institution's entire educational program. The statement notes that the university employs a professional staff member who is responsible for the administration of university policies relating to fraternity/sorority activities. The statement also requires all chapters to comply with all "federal, state and local laws, and University of Arizona regulations, guidelines, and procedures concerning student and student organizations' conduct." One of the items on which local chapters are required to have educational policies is alcohol use.

In the spring of 1988, meetings were held for the purpose of creating an organization entitled "University of Arizona Greeks Advocating Mature Management of Alcohol" (GAMMA). The purposes of GAMMA were stated to be:

A. To provide continuous education regarding Greek social functions.

B. To aid planning of social functions.

C. To regulate Greek events where alcohol is involved.

D. To increase awareness and allow the Greek system to take responsibility for it's [sic] own actions.

The members of GAMMA are fraternity and sorority members who are full-time students classified as sophomores or higher with a good grade point average. GAMMA has two co-chairs and one member for each two fraternity or sorority organizations. Each GAMMA member is assigned to a specific fraternity or sorority. Among his or her responsibilities is assisting in the planning of all alcohol-related events sponsored by the chapter, educating the chapter about university alcohol regulations and state laws on alcohol, and reporting alleged violations to GAMMA. GAMMA's bylaws expressly provide that the fraternity and sorority chapters retain sole responsibility for obtaining proof of legal drinking age at their functions.

At the beginning of rush activities in fall 1988, an assembly was held for all those participating in rush. At that assembly, at least two speakers talked about alcohol issues and the rules and laws applicable to fraternities and sororities. Steven Hare was the GAMMA member assigned to Epsilon Epsilon during fall 1988. He is not a member of Epsilon Epsilon. He stated in an affidavit that he attended the bid party on August 27, 1988 for a time and that he saw no underage fraternity members drinking while he was there.

APPLICATION OF A.R.S. § 4–312(B)

In granting summary judgment to the individual fraternity members, the trial court found that they are immune from liability pursuant to A.R.S. § 4–312(B). Appellant contends that the court erred in granting judgment, arguing that § 4–312(B) does not apply to this case and, alternatively, if it does apply, that it is unconstitutional. Section 4–312 reads as follows:

Liability limitation
    A. A licensee is not liable in damages to any consumer or purchaser of spirituous liquor over the legal drinking age who is injured or whose property is damaged, or to survivors of such a person, if the injury or damage is alleged to have been caused in whole or in part by reason of the sale, furnishing or serving of spirituous liquor to that person. A licensee is not liable in damages to any other adult person who is injured or whose property is damaged, or to the survivors of such a person, who was present with the person who consumed the spirituous liquor at the time the spirituous liquor was consumed and who knew of the impaired condition of the person, if the injury or damage is alleged to have been caused in whole or in part by reason of the sale, furnishing or serving of spirituous liquor.

    B. Subject to the provisions of subsection A of this section and except as provided in § 4–311, a person, firm, corporation or licensee is not liable in damages to any person who is injured, or to the survivors of any person killed, or for damage to property which is alleged to have been caused in whole or in part by reason of the sale, furnishing or serving of spirituous liquor.

The trial court found that § 4–312(B) renders a social host immune from liability to anyone injured or killed by reason of the serving of spirituous liquor to any person, regardless of age. The court also stated that it was bound by the decision of this court in *Kent v. Mar-Fran Enterprises, Inc.*, 49 Ariz. Adv. Rep. 61 (App. December 12, 1989), that § 4–312(B) is constitutional. That case, however, held only that § 4–312(A) was constitutional; the opinion was subsequently redesignated a memorandum decision. Meanwhile, in April 1990 the Supreme Court ruled that § 4–312(A) is unconstitutional because it takes from the jury the questions of contributory negligence and assumption of risk. *Schwab v. Matley*, 164 Ariz. 421, 793 P.2d 1088 (1990). In light of that ruling, therefore, we must determine the constitutionality of subsection (B).

The court's specific ruling in *Schwab* cannot apply to subsection (B), because no issues of either contributory negligence or assumption of the risk could be involved in suits resulting in injury or damage to third persons. The only question then is whether subsection (B) is severable from subsection (A).

SEVERABILITY

The rule on severability is that the remaining part of a statute will be held valid if it is "so separate and distinct that it is clear or may be presumed that the legislature would have enacted the former without the latter, if it had known of the invalidity . . ." *Millett v. Frohmiller*, 66 Ariz. 339, 342, 188 P.2d 457, 460 (1948), quoting 59 C.J. Statutes § 206.

Appellant contends that the subsections are not severable because (B) refers to (A), citing *Industrial*

Commission v. C & D Pipeline, 125 Ariz. 64, 607 P.2d 383 (App.1979). The mere fact, however, that (B) refers to (A) does not render (B) a dependent provision of (A). Nor is the language of (B) so inextricably intertwined with the provisions of (A) that it can be said with confidence that the legislature would not have enacted (B) if it had known that (A) was invalid. *Benjamin v. Arizona Department of Revenue*, 163 Ariz. 182, 786 P.2d 1033 (App.1989).

We conclude, therefore, that subsection (B) is severable from (A) and that the ruling in *Schwab* had no effect on (B). Our determination that (B) is severable from (A), however, does not settle the issue of whether (B) is constitutional. A determination of that issue requires further examination.

RELATIONSHIP OF § 4–312(B) AND § 4–301

Section 4–312 is part of title 4, which is entitled "Alcoholic Beverages." Chapter 3 of title 4 is entitled "Civil Liability of Licensees and Other Persons." It is a short chapter consisting of only two articles, each of which contains only two sections.

Article 1 of chapter 3, entitled "Liability Limitation," includes § 4–301, which reads as follows:

Liability limitation; social host

A person other than a licensee or an employee of a licensee acting during the employer's working hours or in connection with such employment is not liable in damages to any person who is injured, or to the survivors of any person killed, or for damage to property, which is alleged to have been caused in whole or in part by reason of the furnishing or serving of spirituous liquor to a person of the legal drinking age.

The second section of article 1 applies only to licensees, as does the first section of article 2. Section 312 is the second section of article 2.

As appellant notes, § 4–301 clearly provides immunity to a social host only if the person furnished or served alcohol is over 21. If that were the only statute before us, we might rule that there is no immunity for persons who furnish or serve alcohol to those under 21 because of the specificity of the statutory language. However, we cannot ignore the fact that the same Thirty-seventh Legislature that enacted § 4–301 in 1985 also enacted § 4–312 the very next year. By its express language, § 4–312(B) provides immunity to anyone who furnishes alcohol to another, regardless of age, who subsequently causes injury or death to a third person. Both statutes thus appear to address the same issue in different ways, and we must resolve the apparent conflict between them.

There are a number of applicable rules of statutory construction to guide us in that endeavor. First, statutes are to be liberally construed "to effect their objects and to promote justice." A.R.S. § 1–211(B). We must construe a statute "in the context of related provisions and in light of its place in the statutory scheme." *City of Phoenix v. Superior Court*, 144 Ariz. 172, 176, 696 P.2d 724, 728 (App.1985). When two statutes seemingly conflict, we must harmonize them if possible, "in the absence of a manifest legislative intent to the contrary." *Mead, Samuel & Co. v. Dyar*, 127 Ariz. 565, 568, 622 P.2d 512, 515 (App.1980). That effort to harmonize them requires us to find the legislative intent of both by examining "the words, context, subject matter, effects and consequences, reason, and spirit of the law." *Arnold Construction Co. v. Arizona Board of Regents*, 109 Ariz. 495, 498, 512 P.2d 1229, 1232 (1973). When we determine, however, that two statutes are "in irreconcilable conflict, the general rule is that the more recent one prevails." *Mead*, 127 Ariz. at 568, 622 P.2d at 515.

An examination of the issue of civil liability for the furnishing or serving of alcoholic beverages begins with the cases of *Ontiveros v. Borak*, 136 Ariz. 500, 667 P.2d 200 (1983), and *Brannigan v. Raybuck*, 136 Ariz. 513, 667 P.2d 213 (1983). Prior to 1983, tavern owners were not liable for damages that resulted from the serving of liquor. In *Ontiveros*, the Supreme Court abolished that common law doctrine as to an intoxicated adult who left a tavern and injured a third person. It did the same in *Brannigan* as to intoxicated sixteen- and seventeen-year-olds who left a tavern and crashed into a wall. Neither case addressed the issue of social host liability.

In April 1985, the legislature enacted § 4–301, presumably in response to those cases, to prevent the extension of such liability to social hosts. The act that included § 4–301 also amended A.R.S. § 4–244, which proscribes various acts related to the sale of spirituous liquors. That act was adopted as an emergency measure and became effective immediately. A week later, this court held that a social host was not liable to a third person who was injured by an intoxicated guest, over the age of 21, who had been furnished alcohol by the social host. *Keckonen v. Robles*, 146 Ariz. 268, 705 P.2d 945 (App.1985).

The act that includes § 4–312 was approved by the governor in May 1986. 1986 Ariz. Sess. Laws ch. 329. It contains only two sections, 4–311 and 4–312. Section 4–311 provides that a licensee is liable for personal injury, property damage, and/or wrongful death that results from the licensee's sale of liquor to an obviously intoxicated purchaser or to a person whom the licensee either knows is under 21 or from whom the licensee has failed to request proof of age.

If we were to interpret § 4–312(B) to apply only to licensees, as appellant contends we should, we would render the words "person, firm, [and] corporation" meaningless, thus violating the rules of statutory construction. *State v. Superior Court*, 113 Ariz. 248, 550 P.2d 626 (1976); *City of Phoenix v. Yates*, 69 Ariz. 68, 208 P.2d 1147 (1949). We would also ignore the apparent legislative intent to address the liability of both licensees and social hosts in a single section.

The only reasonable conclusion that we can reach from a review of the applicable statutes and the contemporaneous case law is that § 4–312(B) implicitly repealed § 4–301 by rendering it essentially redundant. Apparently the legislature, on an emergency basis, intended to provide for social host immunity at the same time that it amended the statute listing various liquor sale violations. By the next year, in a nonemergency measure, the legislature enacted a more thorough bill that enumerates specific areas of li-

censee liability and nonliability and that provides comprehensive immunity for social hosts, regardless of the age of the person served or furnished the alcohol.

Although we acknowledge our duty to harmonize statutes and to avoid finding that a more recent statute has implicitly repealed an earlier one, we must make such a finding when the two statutes "are so in conflict that they cannot stand together upon any reasonable construction." *State ex rel. Purcell v. Superior Court*, 107 Ariz. 224, 227, 485 P.2d 549, 552 (1971). We note, however, that our conclusion is consistent with the spirit of both statutes. Although § 4–301 is thereby rendered redundant, the subject that it addresses is nevertheless encompassed within § 4–312(B). The implicit repeal, therefore, does not result in any drastic alteration of the law of § 4–301; instead, its scope is merely expanded to include underage persons within the social host immunity.

The ESTATE OF Ruben A. HERNANDEZ, by Elizabeth L. HERNANDEZ-WHEELER, his personal representative, for and on behalf of Ruben R. Hernandez, Elizabeth L. Hernandez-Wheeler and Catherine Rose Poli, Plaintiffs/Appellants,

v.

ARIZONA BOARD OF REGENTS, a body corporate, Delta Tau Delta Fraternity, a New York corporation, Epsilon Epsilon Chapter of Delta Tau Delta Fraternity, Inc., an Arizona corporation, Epsilon Epsilon Educational Foundation, an Arizona corporation, Brett Harper Anderson, Bradley Reed Bergamo, Paul Jude Biondolillo, Joshua Christopher Bliss, Matthew James Bosco, Steven Penn Bryan, Anthony Charles P. Caputo, Thomas David Carlson, Stephen Michael Carpenter, Jeffrey David Catlin, Nathaniel Louis Derby, Albert Edward Dietrich IV, Clo Earl Edgington, Karam Elias Farah, Christopher Todd Flavio, Gerritt Andrew Gehan, Barry James Ginch, Steven Hare, David James Henshall, Markus Rudolph Holtby, Mark Thomas Hopkins, David Laurence Ison, Douglas Edward Jameson, Gregory Richard Janis, Rex Edward Jorgensen, Jay Adam Josephs, Craig Landon, Sean David Leahy, Dale R. Lemon, John Christopher Manross, John Conrad Miller, Christopher J. Molloy, Harrison Lane Morton, Kurt Richard Munzinger, Paige Ray Peterson, Kenneth S. Plache, Daniel Lee Rasmus, Scott Allen Remington, Paul Anthony Reynolds, James Samuel Rigberg, Gary Edward Rink, Erick Jon Roberts, Michael Daniel Roth, George Evangelos Roussos, Charles Dana Sacks, Thomas McKinlay Schwarze, William John Sheoris, Douglas Todd Sims, Clifford Lawrence Smith, Kristopher James Stathakis, Roger Sanford Stinnett, Douglas Matthew Stoss, Anthony Charles Suriano, Eric Joseph Szoke, Nelson Sterlin Udstuen, James Frank Uppendahl, Scott Urban, Larry Wagner, Todd Eric Wallis, Jonathan Blakeslee Woodard, Michael Patrick Woodward, Jeffrey Ryan Wyne, and David Hall Yohe, Defendants/Appellees.

No. CV–92–0079–PR.

Supreme Court of Arizona, En Banc.
Jan. 13, 1994.
Reconsideration Denied March 3, 1994.

Personal representative of deceased motorist who was killed in automobile accident with fraternity member following fraternity party brought personal injury action against fraternity, each fraternity member who contributed to social fund used to purchase alcohol for party, lessor of property on which fraternity house was located, national fraternity organization, state Board of Regents, and student assigned to fraternity through university student education program aimed at reducing alcohol-related problems among fraternities and sororities. The Superior Court, Pima County, No. 255362, Lina S. Rodriguez, J., granted summary judgment for defendants, and personal representative appealed. The Court of Appeals, 172 Ariz. 522, 838 P.2d 1283, affirmed. Personal representative appealed. The Supreme Court, Feldman, C.J., held that: (1) defendants were not protected by any statutory immunity, and (2) defendants had duty of care to avoid furnishing alcohol to underage consumers.

Reversed and remanded.

1. **Appeal and Error k934(1)**   When reviewing grant of summary judgment, Supreme Court examines facts in light most favorable to party opposing motion.

2. **Intoxicating Liquors k286, 299**   Statute applicable to social hosts, which immunizes from liability licensees who furnish or serve alcohol to person of legal drinking age, grants no immunity when nonlicensee furnishes liquor to underage person. A.R.S. § 4–301.

3. **Statutes k158**   Law does not favor construing statute as repealing earlier statute by implication.

4. **Statutes k223.1**   Whenever possible, Supreme Court interprets two apparently conflicting statutes in way that harmonizes them and gives rational meaning to both.

5. **Statutes k188**   When determining legislative intent, courts must apply ordinary meaning of words used, unless it appears from context or otherwise that different meaning should control.

6. **Statutes k211**   Section headings contained in statute are not part of substantive law, but they aid interpretation when uncertainty exists. A.R.S. § 1–212.

7. **Statutes k213**   Little weight is generally give to nonlegislative testimony when determining legislative

intent, unless there is some indication that such evidence reflects legislators' views.

8. **Statutes k184**   When text of statute is capable of more than one construction or result, legislative intent on specific issue is unascertainable, and more than one interpretation is plausible, Supreme Court ordinarily interprets statute in such a way as to achieve general goals that can be adduced from body of legislation in question.

9. **Intoxicating Liquors k299**   Term "person, firm or corporation" in statute which provides that, except as provided in statute regarding licensee's liability for serving alcohol to intoxicated person or minor, "person, firm or corporation or licensee is not liable * * * by reason of the sale, furnishing or serving of spirituous liquor" is intended to protect from liability only licensees and their associates who conduct transaction permitted under license for "sale, furnishing or serving" of alcohol. A.R.S. §§ 4–311, subd. A, 4–312, subd. B.

10. **Intoxicating Liquors k299**   Statute which provides that, except as provided in statute regarding licensee's liability for serving alcohol to intoxicated person or minor, "person, firm or corporation or licensee is not liable * * * by reason of the sale, furnishing or serving of spirituous liquor" has no effect on nonlicensee liability under statute regarding immunity for damages caused by furnishing of liquor to person of legal drinking age by social host. A.R.S. §§ 4–301, 4–312, subd. B.

11. **Intoxicating Liquors k286**   No statutory immunity protected nonlicensees who, at fraternity party, furnished alcohol to minor, who subsequently was involved in automobile accident. A.R.S. §§ 4–301, 4–311, subd. A., 4–312, subd. B.

12. **Intoxicating Liquors k286, 299**   By granting statutory immunity in connection with provision of alcohol by social hosts only to those nonlicensees who furnish or serve alcohol to "person of legal drinking age," legislature left Supreme Court to determine liability, if any, of social hosts who furnish or serve alcohol to those under legal drinking age. A.R.S. § 4–301.

13. **Negligence k6**   Criminal statute may establish tort duty if statute is designed to protect class of persons, in which plaintiff is included, against risk of

type of harm which has in fact occurred as result of its violation.

14. Intoxicating Liquors k299, 302   Fraternity, each fraternity member who contributed to social fund used to purchase alcohol for party, lessor of property on which fraternity house was located, national fraternity organization, state Board of Regents, and student assigned to fraternity through university student education program aimed at reducing alcohol-related problems among fraternities and sororities had duty of care to avoid furnishing alcohol to underage consumers.

15. Intoxicating Liquors k286, 299   Arizona courts will entertain action for damages against nonlicensee who negligently furnishes alcohol to those under legal drinking age when that act is cause of injury to third person.

Risner & Graham by Kenneth K. Graham, William J. Risner, Tucson, for plaintiffs/appellants.

Grant Woods, Atty. Gen. of Arizona by Bruce G. McDonald, Nancy M. Coomer, Tucson, for defendants/appellees Arizona Board of Regents, Steven Hare.

Fish, Duffield, Miller, Young, Adamson & Alfred, P.C. by Samuel D. Alfred, Tucson, for defendant/appellee Delta Tau Delta Fraternity.

Murphy, Goering, Roberts & Berkman by Michael F. McNamara, William L. Rubin, Tucson, for defendants/appellees Epsilon Epsilon Chapter of Delta Tau Delta Fraternity, Epsilon Epsilon Educational Foundation, Brett Harper Anderson, Bradley Reed Bergamo, Paul Jude Biondolillo, Joshua Christopher Bliss, Matthew James Bosco, Steven Penn Bryan, Anthony Charles P. Caputo, Thomas David Carlson, Stephen Michael Carpenter, Jeffrey David Catlin, Nathaniel Louis Derby, Albert Edward Dietrich IV, Clo Earl Edgington, Karam Elias Farah, Christopher Todd Flavio, Gerritt Andrew Gehan, Barry James Ginch, David James Henshall, Markus Rudolph Holtby, Mark Thomas Hopkins, David Laurence Ison, Douglas Edward Jameson, Gregory Richard Janis, Rex Edward Jorgensen, Jay Adam Josephs, Craig Landon, Sean David Leahy, Dale R. Lemon, John Conrad Miller, Christopher J. Molloy, Harrison Lane Morton, Kurt Richard Munzinger, Paige Ray Peterson, Kenneth S. Plache, Daniel Lee Rasmus, Scott Allen Remington, Paul Anthony Reynolds, James Samuel Rigberg, Gary Edward Rink, Erick Jon Roberts, Michael Daniel Roth, George Evangelos Roussos, Charles Dana Sacks, Thomas McKinlay Schwarze, William John Sheoris, Douglas Todd Sims, Clifford Lawrence Smith, Kristopher James Stathakis, Roger Sanford Stinnett, Anthony Charles Suriano, Eric Joseph Szoke, Nelson Sterlin Udstuen, Scott Urban, Larry Wagner, Todd Eric Wallis, Jonathan

Blakeslee Woodard, Michael Patrick Woodward, Jeffrey Ryan Wyne, and David Hall Yohe.

Ridenour, Swenson, Cleere & Evans by Harold H. Swenson, Richard H. Oplinger, Robert R. Byrne, Phoenix, for defendants/appellees John Christopher Manross and Douglas Matthew Stoss.

Law Office of Kevin E. Miniat by Kevin E. Miniat, Tucson, for defendant/appellee James Frank Uppendahl.

Begam, Lewis, Marks, Wolfe & Dasse, P.A. by Stanley J. Marks, Michael J. D'Amelio, Phoenix, for amicus curiae Mothers Against Drunk Driving (MADD).

OPINION

FELDMAN, Chief Justice.

We review a court of appeals opinion affirming summary judgment for defendants. The trial court held that A.R.S. § 4–312(B) immunizes a social host from liability for serving alcohol to a minor who became intoxicated and injured an innocent third party. The court of appeals affirmed. *Estate of Hernandez v. Arizona Board of Regents*, 172 Ariz. 522, 838 P.2d 1283 (Ct.App.1991). It held A.R.S. § 4–312(B) severable from A.R.S. § 4–312(A), which we declared unconstitutional in *Schwab v. Matley*, 164 Ariz. 421, 793 P.2d 1088 (1990). The court of appeals also found that A.R.S. § 4–312(B) did not violate the anti-abrogation provisions of Ariz. Const. art. 18, § 6.

We have jurisdiction under Ariz. Const. art. 6, § 5(3) and A.R.S. § 12–120.24. We granted review to determine whether a nonlicensee can be liable for damages for furnishing alcohol to a person under the legal drinking age who subsequently harms a third party.[1] *See* Ariz.R.Civ.P. 23(c)(4).

FACTS

[1] When reviewing a grant of summary judgment, we examine the facts in the light most favorable to the party opposing the motion. *Gulf Ins. Co. v. Grisham*, 126 Ariz. 123, 124, 613 P.2d 283, 284 (1980).

On August 27, 1988, a University of Arizona fraternity welcomed new members with a bid party. As was customary, the fraternity served alcohol. To purchase alcohol for social events, the fraternity maintained a separate fund to which all imbibing members contributed. The social fund chair, a member over the age of twenty-one, collected and held the liquor

---

1. We consolidated this case for oral argument with *Petolicchio v. Santa Cruz County Fair & Rodeo Ass'n*, No. CV–92–1098–PR, and *Simental v. Magma Copper Co.*, No. CV–92–0036–PR, which present related issues.

money, and ensured that noncontributing members did not drink at parties.

The fraternity's officers kept background records on all members and were aware of their ages. As of August 27, 1988, a majority of the members were under the legal drinking age of twenty-one. However, all members, regardless of age, could contribute to the fund; and contribution was the sole criterion to drink at parties. Several hundred people generally attended these functions, but the fraternity checked neither members nor non-members for proof of age.

John Rayner, a contributing fraternity member under twenty-one, drank at the bid party that night. At 1:45 a.m., Rayner's car crashed into a vehicle driven by Ruben Hernandez. Rayner was driving over forty in a twenty-five mile-per-hour zone. At 2:30 a.m., his blood alcohol level was .15, exceeding the limit set by A.R.S. § 28–692(A)(2). The crash left Hernandez blind, severely brain-damaged, and quadriplegic.

Hernandez brought an action against Rayner for personal injuries, and his three adult children joined in the action to recover loss of consortium. Hernandez later amended the complaint to add as defendants: (1) the fraternity; (2) each fraternity member who contributed to the social fund that semester; (3) the lessor of the property on which the fraternity house was located; (4) the national fraternity organization; (5) the Arizona Board of Regents; and (6) a student assigned to the fraternity through a university student education program aimed at reducing alcohol-related problems among fraternities and sororities. Hernandez died in July 1990, and his personal representative was substituted as a plaintiff. Rayner settled and was dismissed from the suit. We refer to the remaining defendants collectively as "Defendants."

LEGISLATIVE BACKGROUND

At one time, Arizona arguably did not recognize civil liability for those who furnished or sold alcohol that was a contributing factor in a later accident.[2] *See, e.g., Lewis v. Wolf,* 122 Ariz. 567, 568, 596 P.2d 705, 706 (Ct.App.1979); *Profitt v. Canez,* 118 Ariz. 235, 236, 575 P.2d 1261, 1262 (Ct.App.1978). In 1983, however, we held that a licensed tavern owner could be liable to third persons injured by an intoxicated patron. *See Ontiveros v. Borak,* 136 Ariz. 500, 667 P.2d

200 (1983). We also held that the tavern owner could be liable to a minor who was furnished alcohol and, as a result, injured himself. *See Brannigan v. Raybuck,* 136 Ariz. 513, 667 P.2d 213 (1983).

Following these decisions, in April 1985, the Arizona Legislature enacted A.R.S. § 4–301, dealing with "social hosts" and granting civil immunity to nonlicensees who serve alcohol to a person *over* the legal drinking age. One obvious purpose of § 4–301 was to limit any extension of *Ontiveros* and *Brannigan* to nonlicensees. The statute reads:

Liability limitation; social host

> A person other than a licensee . . . *is not liable* in damages to any person who is injured, or to the survivors of any person killed, or for damage to property, which is alleged to have been caused in whole or in part *by reason of the furnishing* or serving of *spirituous liquor to a person of the legal drinking age.*

A.R.S. § 4–301 (emphasis added).

The following year the legislature enacted 1986 Ariz.Sess. Laws ch. 329, entitled "Illegal Sale of Spirituous Liquor." This act had only two sections, designated §§ 4–311 and 4–312. In pertinent part, the first provides:

Liability for serving intoxicated person or minor; definition

> A. A *licensee* is liable for property damage and personal injuries or is liable to a person who may bring an action for wrongful death pursuant to § 12–612 if a court or jury finds the following:
>
> 1. The licensee sold spirituous liquor either to a purchaser who was obviously intoxicated, or to a purchaser under the legal drinking age without requesting identification containing proof of age or with knowledge that the person was under the legal drinking age. . . .

A.R.S. § 4–311(A) (emphasis added).

The other provision, § 4–312(B), reads:

Liability limitation

> Subject to the provisions of subsection A of this section[3] and *except as provided in section 4–*

---

2. *But see McFarlin v. Hall,* 127 Ariz. 220, 619 P.2d 729 (1980) (court found liability when bar owner continued to serve intoxicated patron with knowledge of patron's violent temper, and failed to warn or protect fellow patrons, one of whom the intoxicated patron shot in parking lot); *Pratt v. Daly,* 55 Ariz. 535, 104 P.2d 147 (1940) (court found liability based on server's knowledge of imbiber's alcoholism).

3. A.R.S. § 4–312(A) limited liability by preventing intoxicated persons and their companions from suing the *licensee* provider of the alcohol. In *Schwab,* we found this section unconstitutional because it mandated a finding of contributory negligence and assumption of the risk, impermissibly infringing on the jury's right to decide the question in "all cases" as guaranteed under the Arizona Constitution. *Schwab,* 164 Ariz. at 425, 793 P.2d at 1092; Ariz. Const. art. 18 § 5; *see generally* Richard Gordon, Note, *Schwab v. Matley: The Constitutionality of the Legislative Attempt to Limit Dramshop Liability in Arizona,* 33 ARIZ.L.REV. 955 (1991).

311, a person, firm, corporation or licensee is not liable in damages to any person who is injured, or to the survivors of any person killed, or for damage to property which is alleged to have been caused in whole or in part *by reason of the sale, furnishing or serving of spirituous liquor.*

(Emphasis added). In *Schwab* we did not address the scope and effect of the immunity purportedly granted by § 4–312(B), but we must do so now.

DISCUSSION

A. *Does A.R.S. § 4–312(B) provide immunity to nonlicensees who illegally furnish alcohol to persons under the legal drinking age?*

Defendants argue that they are protected under the language of § 4–312(B), which immunizes all persons, firms, or corporations not liable under § 4–311. Under Defendants' reading, therefore, § 4–312(B) confers blanket immunity on everyone except those *licensees* who may be liable, in certain instances, under § 4–311. If correct, this theory would immunize Defendants and all nonlicensees, including social hosts, under all circumstances.

1. *The effect of A.R.S. § 4–301*

[2] Defendants' argument stretches § 4–312(B) much too far for two reasons. First, it overlooks § 4–301, which is in the same chapter as §§ 4–311 and 4–312. By its title, § 4–301 is applicable to social hosts and immunizes only those nonlicensees who furnish or serve alcohol "to a person of legal drinking age." Conspicuously absent from § 4–301 is any provision immunizing nonlicensees who serve those under the legal drinking age. It is a familiar if overused rule that a statute's expression of one or more items of a class indicates legislative intent to exclude unexpressed items of the same class. *Pima County v. Heinfeld*, 134 Ariz. 133, 134, 654 P.2d 281, 282 (1982); *Wells Fargo Credit Corp. v. Arizona Property & Cas. Ins. Guar. Fund*, 165 Ariz. 567, 571, 799 P.2d 908, 912 (Ct.App.1990).

Second, and as important, common sense tells us that when, in dealing with a very controversial subject,[4] the legislature took the trouble to expressly grant immunity for furnishing alcohol to persons of legal drinking age, it meant to exclude from its largesse those who furnish alcohol to persons below that age. We see no other rational construction of § 4–301, nor

has any been suggested. We conclude, therefore, that § 4–301 covers non-licensee liability and grants no immunity when, as in this case, a non-licensee furnishes liquor to an underaged person. Defendants concede this interpretation but argue that § 4–301 was repealed.

2. *Implied repeal*

Notwithstanding the lack of express repeal, Defendants claim that § 4–301 is no longer in effect because it conflicts with the provisions of § 4–312(B), which grants immunity to all persons, firms, or corporations except those licensees liable under § 4–311. Because § 4–312 was passed after § 4–301, Defendants argue we must resolve the conflict in the statutes by construing § 4–312 as repealing § 4–301. *Lemons v. Superior Court*, 141 Ariz. 502, 505, 687 P.2d 1257, 1260 (1984). We disagree.

[3,4] The law does not favor construing a statute as repealing an earlier one by implication. *Pima County v. Maya Construction Co.*, 158 Ariz. 151, 155, 761 P.2d 1055, 1059 (1988); *Mead, Samuel & Co., Inc. v. Dyar*, 127 Ariz. 565, 568, 622 P.2d 512, 515 (Ct.App.1980). Rather, whenever possible, this court interprets two apparently conflicting statutes in a way that harmonizes them and gives rational meaning to both. *Id.* We can do so here with a construction that both fulfills legislative intent and furthers legislative goals.

a. *"Plain wording"*

[5] Defendants submit that the words of § 4–312(B)—"a person, firm, corporation or licensee is not liable,"—are plain and must be applied accordingly. They read the words as granting immunity to *every* person, firm, or corporation, licensed or not, except those *licensees* liable under § 4–311 for sale to intoxicated or underaged persons. When determining legislative intent, they argue, courts must apply the ordinary meaning of the words used. This, of course, is true "unless it appears from the *context* or otherwise that a different meaning should control." *State v. Raffaele*, 113 Ariz. 259, 262, 550 P.2d 1060, 1063 (1976) (emphasis added).

[6] If read in isolation, the provisions of § 4–312(B) may seem unambiguous. However, given § 4–301, Defendants' broad interpretation is insupportable. We believe the section headings are telling. Although section headings are not part of the substantive law, *see* § 1–212, they aid interpretation when uncertainty exists. *State v. Barnett*, 142 Ariz. 592, 597, 691 P.2d 683, 688 (1984).

All three statutes are in chapter 3 of title 4. The chapter is entitled "Civil Liability of Licensees and Other Persons." The legislature first addressed "other persons"—nonlicensee, non-sale liability—in article 1

---

4. The subject of this legislation was hotly debated. *See, e.g., New law takes aim at teen-age 'keg parties,'* Ariz. Daily Star, *May 4, 1985,* § B, at 6.

of chapter 3, denominated as § 4–301, "Liability limitation; *social hosts*" (emphasis added). The following year, the legislature added article 2 to chapter 3, entitled "Illegal *Sale* of Spirituous Liquor" (emphasis added). These headings at least indicate that the legislature intended the first article (consisting of § 4–301) to apply to transactions other than sales and the second article (§ § 4–311 and 4–312) to apply to sales under a license.

b. *Legislative intent*

We would be reluctant, of course, to base construction of such important statutes on chapter headings and section titles. However, Defendants' argument that the conflict in the statutes indicates legislative intent to repeal the earlier statute has yet another fatal flaw. We believe that we would not only defy common sense if we were to conclude that § 4–301 was repealed by implication on adoption of § 4–312 but would attack legislative competence as well.

Section 4–301 is not a technical provision that could be overlooked and impliedly repealed by a legislative committee engaged in the revision of some obscure portion of the code. Although such oversights may occur with legislative bodies and others, we deal here with three statutes passed by the same legislature. These statutes were contained in the same chapter and dealt with a subject that, after *Ontiveros* and *Brannigan*, was one of the most controversial before the legislature.[5] In essence, Defendants ask us to assume that in 1986, when the legislature added article 2 (§ § 4–311 and 4–312) to chapter 3, it forgot that just the previous year it had adopted article 1 of that chapter, expressly providing for only a partial limitation of social host liability. We do not assume so easily that the legislature was unaware of its own actions. Nor does the legislature's own language admit of such a conclusion.

In 1985, when enacting § 4–301, the legislature's stated purpose was "in no way [to modify] existing law with respect to the principles of civil liability applicable to licensees who sell, furnish or serve spirituous liquor." A.R.S. § 4–301, Historical Note. We believe the only rational conclusion is that in 1985 the legislature enacted a provision (§ 4–301) dealing only with the liability of non-licensees, and in 1986, the same

legislature, after further debate and thought, followed with two complementary provisions (§ § 4–311 and 4–312) regulating only licensee liability. We believe common sense makes this conclusion much more likely than the "legislature forgot" argument that we would otherwise have to adopt if we found an implied repeal.

[7] The legislative record further indicates the lawmakers' intent to address only licensees by the 1986 enactments. Legislative committee members considering § 4–312 discussed "barowners" and "liquor establishments," but *never* even mentioned social hosts or non-licensees in reference to the statute. *See* Minutes, Committee on Judiciary, H.B. 2376, March 3, 1986. They referred to the proposed law as "dramshop legislation." *Id.* The legislative minutes also contain numerous comments by bar and restaurant owners, and the Arizona Licensed Beverage Association,[6] indicating that the purpose of the 1986 legislation was to alleviate commercial vendors' difficulties in obtaining affordable liquor liability insurance. *Id.* The owner of one Tempe establishment testified that his insurance premiums had jumped from $43,000 in 1983 (when there was almost *no* common-law liability) to $113,000 in 1985. *Id.* This testimony was typical of that given by several other individuals in the restaurant and bar industry. *Id.*

Some further history helps to clarify legislative intent. After passing § § 4–311 and 4–312, citizens groups attempted to place the legislation on the November 1986 general election ballot as Proposition 301. *See* Proposition 301, Publicity Pamphlet. The measure evidently did not qualify. *See* State of Arizona Official Canvass, Nov. 4, 1986 (an official list of all measures that were actually on the ballot). Proposition 301 does not appear on the canvass—presumably because the sponsor did not collect the required signatures—but the Arizona Attorney General's Office published the necessary publicity pamphlet.

---

5. For example, in one of several articles, the Arizona Daily Star called *Ontiveros* and *Brannigan* "landmark decisions." The paper, quoting a legislator about resulting legislation, stated "[a]nytime you get into legislation that involves alcohol, you get into a lot of discussion." *See Bars liable for patrons, state justices rule*, ARIZ. DAILY STAR, July 7, 1983, at 9.

---

6. We consider this testimony in conjunction with the legislators' own comments and only to discern the subject matter. Little weight is generally given to non-legislative testimony when determining legislative intent, unless there is some indication that such evidence reflects the legislators' views. *See Turner v. Prod*, 707 F.2d 1109, 1119 (9th Cir.1983) ("[T]estimony of witnesses before congressional committees prior to passage of legislation generally constitutes only 'weak evidence' of legislative intent.") (citing 2A C.D. **SANDS, STATUTES AND STATUTORY CONSTRUCTION, A REVISION OF THE THIRD EDITION OF SUTHERLAND ON STATUTORY CONSTRUCTION** § 48.10 (4th ed. 1973), *rev'd on other grounds*, *Heckler v. Turner*, 470 U.S. 184, 105 S.Ct. 1138, 84 L.Ed.2d 138 (1985).

As required by § 19–124,[7] a simple analysis and a "pro" and "con" argument written by the Arizona Legislative Council, with input from informed and interested legislators, accompanied Proposition 301 in the publicity pamphlet. This analysis of Proposition 301 discussed *only* licensee liability, and in reference to § 4–312(B) states, "if the conditions listed in paragraphs 1, 2 and 3 above [§ 4–311] do not exist, then the *liquor licensee* is not liable." Proposition 301, Publicity Pamphlet (emphasis added). In its supporting statement, the council even gave meaning to the terms "person," "firm," and "corporation" in the context of a liquor licensee. When discussing the "server" of liquor it stated, "every time a server pours a drink, he is exposing *himself* and the *owner of the business* to possible liability that can wipe out the business." *Id.* (emphasis added). Hence, we believe that the legislature's intent with respect to a person, firm, or corporation was to protect those associated with licensees. Our reading is reinforced by the wording of § 4–301, which excludes from immunity an employee of a licensee acting in connection with employment. This illustrates the legislature's belief that the word "licensee" is broad enough to encompass those beyond the actual license holder.

In short, every aspect of the statute's history indicates a legislative intent to regulate nonlicensee liability under § 4–301 and licensee liability under §§ 4–311 and 4–312.

c. *Overall legislative scheme*

[8] As this court has stated, "[w]hen the text of a statute is capable of more than one construction or result, legislative intent on the specific issue is unascertainable, and more than one interpretation is plausible, we ordinarily interpret the statute in such a way as to achieve the general goals that can be adduced from the body of legislation in question." *Dietz v. General Elect. Co.*, 169 Ariz. 505, 510, 821 P.2d 166, 171 (1991); *see also City of Phoenix v. Superior Court*, 144 Ariz. 172, 175–76, 696 P.2d 724, 727–28 (Ct.App.1985).

The legislature's goals are clear. As pointed out in an amicus curiae brief, the legislature has re-

sponded to the tragic problem of underaged drinking[8] with a strong policy of deterrence. The statutory scheme includes § 4–244(9), which creates criminal penalties for both *minors* who possess alcohol and licensees *or others* who serve alcohol to anyone *under the legal drinking age*; § 4–241(A), which requires a licensee *or other person* to demand identification before serving liquor to a person *who appears underage*; § 4–301, which grants immunity to social hosts only when serving those *of the legal drinking age*; § 4–312(A), which implies, among other things, that licensees are liable for injuries resulting from a licensee's service *to a minor*; and § 8–249 (the "not a drop" law), which allows courts to suspend the driver's license of a minor who drives while possessing or consuming *any* alcohol.

As a whole, this body of legislation reveals a definite scheme. The legislature has imposed criminal and other sanctions on all persons who, whether licensed or not, furnish alcohol to minors. Given this, it is unreasonable to assume that the legislature would provide civil relief to those who act illegally by serving alcohol to minors. Such a reading of § 4–312(B) would give civil immunity to someone whose conduct could even result in a charge of manslaughter. *See State v. Marty*, 166 Ariz. 233, 801 P.2d 468 (Ct.App.1990) (defendant can be guilty of manslaughter by supplying drugs and alcohol to driver who subsequently dies in accident).

The parties have not cited, and we cannot find, any instance where the legislature has expressed such an intent. We can see no indication that the legislature wanted to abandon its comprehensive fight against the cost and carnage created by underage drinking and driving by granting immunity to those who illegally furnish alcohol to minors.

3. *Resolution*

We conclude, therefore, that the most plausible interpretation of § 4–312(B) is that the immunity it grants applies solely to liquor licensees and their associates. In the statute, the word "person" must refer to a licensee's agent or employee, while "firm or corporation" refers to any entity associated with the li-

---

7. The version of § 19–124 in effect in 1986 stated:
B. Not later than sixty days preceding the regular primary election the legislative council, after providing *reasonable opportunity for comments by all legislators*, shall prepare and file with the secretary of state an analysis of the provisions of each ballot proposal of a measure or proposed amendment. . . .
(Emphasis added.)

8. The statistics are alarming. In 1990, about 30.8% of fatally injured 16- to 20-year-old drivers were intoxicated at the time of the accident. More than 43% of all deaths of 16- to 20-year-olds in 1990 resulted from automobile accidents. Almost half of those were alcohol-related. Of all persons arrested for DUI/DWI nationally, approximately 26% were under the age of 25. Alcohol is a factor in 21% of all college dropouts and that likely costs nearly $210 million in tuition in 1991. MADD Amicus Curiae Brief, Appendix A.

censee, such as a partner, landlord, subsidiary corporation, or the like. The most reasonable construction is that by enacting § 4–312(B), the legislature protected only licensees and those associated with a licensee's permitted activities from personal liability, "subject to" the common-law liability expressed in *Ontiveros* and *Brannigan* and codified in § 4–311.

This interpretation harmonizes all three statutes. It leaves § 4–301 intact, reconciles potentially conflicting wording in all three statutes, and implements the overall intent expressed in the chapter's title, the legislative history, and the entire body of Arizona law on alcohol and minors.

[9–11] We hold, therefore, that the term "person, firm or corporation" in § 4–312(B) is intended to protect from liability only licensees and their associates who conduct a transaction permitted under a license for the "sale, furnishing or serving" of alcohol. We further hold that § 4–312(B) has no effect on non-licensee liability under § 4–301. The statutory immunity granted by § 4–301 applies only when a non-licensee furnishes alcohol to "a person of legal drinking age." Thus, no statutory immunity protects Defendants—all of whom are non-licensees who furnished alcohol to a minor.

This holding obviates the need to determine the constitutionality of A.R.S. § 4–312 under Ariz. Const. art. 18, § 6 or other issues such as severability, de facto licensee, and retroactivity. Having determined that Defendants are not protected by any statutory immunity, we turn now to the question of common-law liability.

B. Is there a common-law cause of action against a social host who serves alcohol to a minor?

1. *The effect of A.R.S. § 4-301*

[12] Defendants argue that if we sustain Hernandez' claim, we create a new cause of action, infringing on the legislature's realm. Given the noted statutory provisions, we see no infringement on legislative prerogative. Indeed, we believe that by granting immunity in A.R.S. § 4–301 only to those nonlicensees who furnish or serve alcohol "to a person of the legal drinking age," the legislature left this court to determine the liability, if any, of social hosts who furnish or serve alcohol to those under the legal drinking age. We see no other explanation for legislative action immunizing non-licensees who serve those of legal age and legislative silence on the question that then comes into focus: what about the liability of those who serve underaged drinkers?

Thus, we see no reason to "pass the buck" to the legislature. By the words of § 4–301, the lawmakers have obviously left resolution of this issue to us, and we would abdicate our responsibility by refusing to decide it.

2. *The effect of criminal statutes*

[13] The common-law rule of non-liability was based on either a lack of causation or a lack of duty. The existence of a statute criminalizing conduct is one aspect of Arizona law supporting the recognition of duty in this cause of action. Like other states,[9] Arizona has a statute making it a criminal offense to furnish alcohol to a minor. A.R.S. § 4–244(9). A criminal statute may establish a tort duty if the statute is "designed to protect the class of persons, in which the plaintiff is included, against the risk of the type of harm which has in fact occurred as a result of its violation. . . ." W. PAGE KEETON ET AL., PROSSER AND KEETON ON THE LAW OF TORTS § 36, at 229–30 (5th ed. 1984).

We have previously relied on § 4–244 to sustain a cause of action against those who furnish alcohol to minors.

> We believe that A.R.S. § 4–244(9) . . . constitute[s] legislative recognition of the foreseeable danger to both the patron and third parties, and an effort to meet that danger by enactment of laws designed to regulate the industry, to protect third persons, and to protect those who are underage from themselves.

Brannigan, 136 Ariz. at 517, 667 P.2d at 217.

Although *Brannigan* addressed licensee liability, § 4–244(9) makes it a crime for *anyone* to furnish alcohol to a minor. We believe the rationale of *Brannigan* is certainly broad enough to apply to the facts of this case.[10] Here, as in *Ontiveros* and *Brannigan*, we find Defendants' violation of the statute further supports a civil cause of action. These provisions are not new. The statutory prohibition against furnishing alcohol to a minor is long settled in Arizona. It was a crime as early as 1887. "Every person who shall directly or indirectly, knowingly . . . give away any intoxicating liquor to any minor . . . without the consent of [the minor's] guardian or parent, shall be deemed guilty of a misdemeanor, . . ." Arizona Penal Code § 514 (1887); *see also* Arizona Penal Code § 270 (1901) (adopting the same ban). Based on past and

---

9. *Cf.* Michael P. Rosenthal, *The Minimum Drinking Age for Young People: an Observation*, 92 DICK.L.REV. 649, 656 n. 62 (1988) ("every state bans sales [of alcohol] to minors").

10. We contrast these facts with those in *Keckonen v. Robles*, 146 Ariz. 268, 705 P.2d 945 (Ct.App.1985), where the court of appeals found no duty upon which to extend liability to social hosts. In *Keckonen*, a social host furnished alcohol to an intoxicated adult. The court expressly excluded minors from the scope of its decision. *Id.* at 269 n. 1, 705 P.2d at 946 n. 1.

present statutes, we see no constriction of the duty of social hosts under the facts of this case.

3. *Duty based on common-law principles*

Many state courts faced with a claim against a social host who served alcohol to a minor have found this to be a valid cause of action properly before the judiciary. *Cravens v. Inman,* 223 Ill.App.3d 1059, 166 Ill. Dec. 409, 586 N.E.2d 367 (Ill.Ct.App.1991) (citing cases), *rev. granted,* 143 Ill.2d 637, 167 Ill.Dec. 398, 587 N.E.2d 1013 (1992), *appeal dismissed,* 168 Ill.Dec. 19, 589 N.E.2d 133 (1992). *See generally* Edward L. Raymond, Jr., Annotation, *Social Hosts Liability for Injuries Incurred by Third Parties as a Result of Intoxicated Guest's Negligence,* 62 A.L.R. 4th 16 (1988). A minority of courts have left this problem to their legislatures for various reasons. *See, e.g., Cravens,* 166 Ill.Dec. at 420, 586 N.E.2d at 375–78. Most have deferred because their legislatures had "entered the field" and they felt the "policy decision" were better left to them. *See, e.g., Bankston v. Brennan,* 507 So.2d 1385, 1387 (Fla.1987). As noted above, we believe that the legislature invited this court to decide the question of liability for those who furnish alcohol to minors by declaring an immunity extending only to adults. *See* A.R.S. § 4–301.

It is especially appropriate for this court to address this issue because, under Ariz. Const. art. 18, § 6, Arizona's judiciary shares responsibility for the evolution of the law of torts. *Law v. Superior Court of State of Arizona,* 157 Ariz. 147, 156, 755 P.2d 1135, 1143 (1993), ("[T]his court has an obligation to participate in the evolution of tort law so that it may reflect societal and technological changes.") (citing *Summerfield v. Superior Court,* 144 Ariz. 467, 698 P.2d 712 (1985)). This court is a proper forum in which to resolve this important issue. As we have held:

> [T]he common law, which is judge-made and judge-applied, can and will be changed when changed conditions and circumstances establish that it is unjust or has become bad public policy. In reevaluating previous decisions in light of present facts and circumstances, we do not depart from the proper role of the judiciary.

Ontiveros, 135 Ariz. at 504, 667 P.2d at 204.

Before 1983, this court arguably recognized the common-law rule of non-liability for tavern owners and, presumably and *a fortiori,* for social hosts. *Id.* Traditional authority held that when "an able-bodied man"[11] caused harm because of his intoxication, the

act from which liability arose was the consuming not the furnishing of alcohol. *See also Megge v. United States,* 344 F.2d 31, 32 (6th Cir.), *cert. denied,* 382 U.S. 831, 86 S.Ct. 69, 15 L.Ed.2d 74 (1965); 45 Am.Jur.2d *Intoxicating Liquors* § 553 (1969).

However, the common law also provides that:

> One who supplies . . . a chattel for the use of another whom the supplier knows or has reason to know to be likely because of his youth, inexperience, or otherwise . . . to use it in a manner involving unreasonable risk of physical harm to himself and others . . . is subject to liability for physical harm resulting to them.

RESTATEMENT (SECOND) OF TORTS § 390 (1965) (hereinafter RESTATEMENT). Arizona's courts have repeatedly followed the RESTATEMENT'S analysis in this area. *See Powell v. Langford,* 58 Ariz. 281, 119 P.2d 230 (1941) (lending car to intoxicated driver); *Lutfy v. Lockhart,* 37 Ariz. 488, 295 P. 975 (1931) (giving automobile to incompetent driver); *see also Ontiveros,* 136 Ariz. at 508, 667 P.2d at 208 (same analysis as RESTATEMENT § 390).

Even in an earlier era, it was actionable negligence to furnish a minor with a dangerous instrument. For example, in *Anderson v. Settergren,* 100 Minn. 294, 111 N.W. 279 (1907), relying on a criminal statute making it illegal for one under the age of fourteen to possess a gun, the Minnesota Supreme Court held the defendant liable for damage resulting from furnishing a thirteen-year-old with a gun. The court stated: " 'Every man must be taken to contemplate the probable consequence of the act he does.' " *Id.* 111 N.W. at 280–81 (quoting *Townsend v. Wathen,* 103 Eng.Rep. 579, 580–81 (1808)).[12]

This principle, like RESTATEMENT § 390, found common application in cases involving furnishing cars to inexperienced, youthful, or intoxicated drivers. *Se Engleman v. Traeger,* 136 So. 527, 530 (Fla.1931) ("every court in the land has recognized" liability for entrusting a car to a person who is drinking); *Ransom v. City of Garden City,* 113 Idaho 202, 743 P.2d 70 (1987) (city can be liable when police officer entrusted keys to intoxicated person who then caused an automobile accident).

---

11. *See Cruse v. Aden,* 127 Ill. 231, 20 N.E. 73, 74 (1889) ("It was not a tort at common law to either sell or give intoxicating liquor to 'a strong and able-bodied man' ").

12. *See also Binford v. Johnston,* 82 Ind. 426 (1882) (holding defendant liable for harm caused from giving toy pistol loaded with gunpowder and ball to two boys, ages 10 and 12); *Carter Towne,* 98 Mass. 567 (1868) (holding licensed gunpowder seller liable for harm caused by providing gunpowder to 8-year-old child); *Lynch v. Nurdin,* 1 Q.B. 30, 113 Eng.Rep. 1041 (1841) (finding that defendant negligently left horse and cart in street, causing child to be injured when he climbed into cart).

We perceive little difference in principle between liability for giving a car to an intoxicated youth and liability for giving drinks to a youth with a car. If there should be a difference between duty in the former and the latter, no case cited has explained it to us, and we perceive none. If the recipient is known to be incompetent to receive the dangerous instrument, it is irrelevant whether it is a loaded gun, a car, or alcohol. The theory of recovery is the same and was well-established long ago. This, perhaps, is the unarticulated rationale explaining why so many states now impose either common-law or statutory liability in cases such as this. *See Cravens*, 586 N.E.2d at 374 (listing states). Perhaps these states have interpreted common-law concepts of duty as broad enough to encompass the liability of one who furnishes alcohol to a minor. *See, e.g., Wiener v. Gamma Pi*, 258 Or. 632, 485 P.2d 18 (1971); *Congini v. Portersville Valve Co.*, 504 Pa. 157, 470 A.2d 515 (1983); *Koback v. Crook*, 123 Wis.2d 259, 366 N.W.2d 857 (1985).

4. *Duty based on prior Arizona case law*

In 1940, this court sustained a claim for a wife's loss of consortium against defendants who had supplied liquor to her husband, despite knowing he was alcoholic. *Pratt v. Daly*, 55 Ariz. 535, 104 P.2d 147 (1940). Although it recognized that Arizona held that there is a duty not to provide liquor to persons known to have subnormal ability to control their actions. *Id.* at 546, 104 P.2d at 151. As in the present case, the defendants in *Pratt* argued there was no Arizona precedent for such a decision and no common law to sustain the action, and therefore the court would be legislating if it allowed the claim to proceed. With great wisdom, Judge Alfred C. Lockwood replied:

Every requested application of the principles of the common law to a new set of circumstances is originally without precedent, and some court must be the first one to make the proper application.

In answer to the second question, ... [w]e are asked to declare what the common law is and always has been, and a declaration by us that it has always *permitted* such an action, even though none has ever actually been brought, is no more legislation than would be a declaration that it does not.

Id. at 545–46, 104 P.2d at 151.

A minor is similar to an adult who has diminished judgment and capacity to control his alcohol consumption. Moreover, unlike *Pratt*, where the tortious conduct was legal, here it is illegal to furnish alcohol to a minor.

In *Brannigan*, this court sustained an analogous claim, basing its decision on the duty, foreseeability,

and causation issues related to furnishing alcohol to a minor. We held in relevant part:

A growing number of cases, however, have recognized that one of the very hazards that makes it negligent to furnish liquor to a minor ... is the foreseeable prospect that the [youthful] patron will become drunk and injure himself or others. Accordingly, modern authority has increasingly recognized that one who furnishes liquor to a minor ... breaches a common law duty owed ... to innocent third parties who may be injured.

Brannigan, 136 Ariz. at 516, 667 P.2d at 216 (citations omitted). Although *Brannigan* dealt with a licensee, the common-law concept of the duty of reasonable care logically applies whether the individual furnishing alcohol to an underage person is a licensee or social host.

Nor are considerations of proximate causation a reason to conclude there is no liability as a matter of law in all cases. *See Ontiveros*, 136 Ariz. at 505, 667 P.2d at 205 (finding that both furnishing and drinking alcohol contributed to the cause of the subsequent accident). Furnishing alcohol to underaged consumers creates an obvious and significant risk to the public. The facts of this case and its two companion cases are illustrative. We are hard pressed to find a setting where the risk of an alcohol-related injury is more likely than from underaged drinking at a university fraternity party the first week of the new college year.

CONCLUSION

The factors we have considered on the issue of recognizing the common-law liability of those who provide alcohol to persons under the legal drinking age point to a single conclusion. Furnishing alcohol to underaged drinkers violates numerous statutes. It is outside the area of immunity from civil liability described by the legislature in A.R.S. §§ 4–301 and 4–312. It is within the area left by the legislature to judicial decision. The conduct in question violates well-established common-law principles that recognize a duty to avoid furnishing dangerous items to those known to have diminished capacity to use them safely. These principles are embodied in Arizona authority and in the majority of cases that have examined the question of common-law duty.

[14] We join the majority of other states, therefore, and conclude that as to Plaintiffs and the public in general, Defendants had a duty of care to avoid furnishing alcohol to underaged consumers.[13] We

---

13. In speaking of duty here, we include not only the concepts of duty as described in most cases, see, e.g., *Markowitz*

understand the need to specify in this area of tort law what we hold and what we do not. We hold only that the so-called traditional rule—if ever there was one—of non-liability when a nonlicensee serves alcohol to minors does not exist in Arizona. We do *not*, in this opinion, lay down any rule of absolute liability for serving alcohol to minors. We also expressly refrain

from addressing, considering, or deciding in any way the liability of nonlicensees for serving adults or the validity of A.R.S. § 4–301 under Ariz. Const. art. 18, § 6.

[15] Arizona courts, therefore, will entertain an action for damages against a nonlicensee who negligently furnishes alcohol to those under the legal drinking age when that act is a cause of injury to a third person.

We vacate the court of appeals' opinion and reverse the trial court's judgment. Because we do not, at this stage in the case, reach the questions of negligence or cause in fact, we simply remand to the trial court for further proceedings.

MOELLER, V.C.J., and CORCORAN, ZLAKET and MARTONE, JJ., concur.

---

13. (*continued*)
v. Arizona Parks Board, 146 Ariz. 352, 706 P.2d 364 (1985), but also the concept of proximate cause, or the so-called able-bodied man theory, that was mixed with the duty issue in some of the older cases, such as *Cruse*. *See supra*, n. 10. In doing so, however, we do not address fact-intensive questions involving proximate cause or any question of negligence or cause in fact.

The conflict dealt with in these cases arises out of provisions in A.R.S. Sec. 4–301, Sec. 4–311, and Sect. 4–312(B). A.R.S. Sec. 4–301 provides in relevant part that "a person *other than a licensee* is not liable in damages . . . which [are] alleged to have been caused in whole or in part by reason of the furnishing or serving of spirituous liquor to a person of the legal drinking age." [emphasis added] A.R.S. Sec. 4–311 establishes liability for licensees who serve to those obviously intoxicated or to minors without requesting identification or with knowledge that they are under age. Sec. 4–312(B) provides that "a person, firm, corporation or licensee is not liable" for damages resulting from the serving of alcohol. In essence, Sec. 4–301 provides immunity to a social host (but not to a licensee) serving liquor to someone over 21 while Sec. 4–312(B) provides such immunity to licensees furnishing alcohol to a third person regardless of age.

The defendants in *Hernandez* (a fraternity) argued that Sec. 4–312(B) conflicts with Sec. 4–301 because it grants immunity to all persons (including social hosts) and therefore implicitly repeals Sec. 4–301. The defendants wanted Sec. 4–301 repealed because it does not immunize social hosts who serve alcohol to minors (which the defendants were alleged to have done). Under their reading of Sec. 4–312(B), they as "persons" were not liable for damages resulting from serving alcohol, and under Sec. 4–311, they as nonlicensees were not liable.

The Court of Appeals began its attempt to resolve the apparent conflict regarding the liability of nonlicensees by looking to the legislative history and noting that Sec. 4–301 was enacted in response to some Arizona Supreme Court decisions that abolished common law immunity for tavern owners. Concerned that the Court would extend its decision to social hosts, the legislature immediately enacted legislation that precluded social host liability. After reviewing this history, the appellate court concluded that Sec. 4–301 and Sec. 4–312(B) were redundant and agreed with the defendants that the subsequent passage of Sec. 4–312(B) implicitly repealed Sec. 4–301. Reasoning that Sec. 4–301 was an emergency measure that was superseded by a more thorough measure the following years in the form of Sec. 4–312, the court concluded that Sec. 4–312(B) expanded the scope of Sec. 4–301 by including minors within the parameters of social host immunity.

The Supreme Court responded to this reasoning by pointing out that the law "does not favor construing a statute as repealing an earlier one by implication." The Court refused to accept that the legislature merely overlooked the inconsistency in the statutes, assuming instead that it was aware of its actions. After reviewing the minutes from committee hearings, a publicity pamphlet explaining the legislation, and the overall legislative scheme, the Court concluded that the legislature intended Sec. 4–301 to apply only to social hosts and Sec. 4–312 to apply only to licensees. The Court held that Sec. 4–312 had no effect on nonlicensee (social host) nonliability and that Sec. 4–301 applied only when social hosts serve liquor to those of legal drinking age. Therefore, because the defendants furnished liquor to minors, they were not protected by statutory immunity.

Notice that the Court of Appeals looked at the conflict and, assuming sloppiness in legislative enactments, reasoned that repeal must have been the intent. The Supreme Court, on the other hand, carefully reviewed the legislative history in the context of political events and prior court decisions and reached a conclusion that assumed meaningful behavior on the part of the legislature. Both conclusions are logically defensible and demonstrate two approaches to resolving apparent inconsistencies in statutes.

PUTTING IT INTO PRACTICE
....

Answer the following questions about the Court of Appeals decision, *Hernandez v. Arizona Board of Regents.*

1. What rules of statutory construction does the court cite?

2. Why did the legislature enact Sec. 4–301, according to the Court of Appeals?

3. Why does the court believe that it cannot interpret Sec. 4–301 to apply only to licensees?

4. What reasoning does the court use to conclude that Sec. 4–312(B) implicitly repealed Sec. 4–301?

Answer the following questions about the Supreme Court decision, *Hernandez v. Arizona Board of Regents.*

1. On what basis do the defendants argue that they are immunized?

2. Why does the Court reject this argument?

3. Why does the Court reject the argument that Sec. 4–312 repeals Sec. 4–301?

4. Why does the Court reject the defendants' plain meaning argument?

5. Where does the Court look to determine legislative intent?

(continued)

Putting It into Practice *(continued)*

6. How does the legislative scheme conflict with the defendants' argument that the legislature intended to grant immunity to those who illegally provide liquor to minors?

7. How does the Court interpret the word "person"?

8. What does the Court hold?

Which of these opinions do you find more persuasive? Why?

ADMINISTRATIVE REGULATIONS

Administrative regulations, like statutes, often require interpretation, and the basic principles discussed above can be applied. A problem unique to administrative law, however, is created by virtue of the relationship between administrative agencies and the legislative body that created them. **Enabling statutes** create administrative agencies and establish the parameters within which they must operate. Such statutes set forth the general purpose of the law and then delegate power to the administrative agencies to carry out that purpose. Conflict arises when an agency creates regulations that are inconsistent with the enabling legislation.

In *Ferguson v. Arizona Dept. of Economic Security* (starting on page 346), for example, the appellant contended that an administrative regulation created by the Department of Economic Security (DES) conflicted with the purposes of the Arizona Employment Security Act. This act provides for unemployment compensation for those "involuntarily unemployed" but "available for work." The administrative regulation promulgated by DES disqualifies individuals for compensation if they leave work "voluntarily without good cause." "Good cause" requires being able to show that remaining at work would have required the individual to "suffer substantial detriment" or that the person quit to "accept a definite offer of work."

The court found no inconsistency between the act and the regulation and summarily concluded that the regulation was both reasonable and congruent with the purposes of the Employment Security Act. This case lays out the rules that are generally used to determine the validity of an administrative regulation. As the court recited, a regulation must be "reasonably related to the purposes of the enabling legislation" and must not be "inconsistent with or contrary to the provision of . . . the statute it seeks to effectuate."

While regulations may define or implement the provisions of a statute, they may not limit or in any way modify these provisions. This principle is illustrated in *St. Joseph's Hospital and Medical Center v. Maricopa County* (beginning on page 348). In this case, the county Department of Health Services added the word "legal" to the statutory residency requirements establishing eligibility for those receiving subsidized health care. In so doing, the department limited the concept of residency. Noting that administrative regulations are "subordinate to the terms of the statute and in aid of its provisions," the court concluded that the department's addition of the legality requirement limited the county's duty of reimbursement by denying eligibility to undocumented aliens. The court further pointed out that the legislature was undoubtedly aware of the massive number of undocumented aliens and could easily have chosen to limit its obligations by restricting its care to legal residents.

PUTTING IT INTO PRACTICE

Suppose that the Department of Health Services denied eligibility for subsidized health care to convicted felons. Based on the reasoning stated in *St. Joseph's Hospital and Medical Center v. Maricopa County* (see pp. 348–351 in Appendix A), would the regulation stand?

A number of other factors limit administrative agencies, but the primary reason behind the invalidity of a regulation is its inconsistency with a statute. Therefore, your task in reconciling regulations and statutes is determining the purpose of the statute and then ascertaining whether that purpose is furthered by the regulation in question.

CHAPTER SUMMARY

Statutory interpretation is largely based on determining legislative intent. Such intent can be gleaned from the definitions section of statutes, the plain meaning of the term or concept in question, the context of other statutes, public policy considerations, case law, legislative history, and the canons of construction. Ambiguous terms or concepts can be interpreted by comparing different statutes within the same jurisdiction that use the same terms or concepts as well as case law interpreting the same statutes. Statutes from other jurisdictions can also be compared, although such comparison is suspect unless both statutes are based on a common uniform or model act. The question in all cases of comparison is whether the legislative intent was the same for both statutes. Sometimes statutes written by the same legislature appear to conflict and courts must make every effort to harmonize them. Administrative regulations must be reviewed in the context of the enabling statutes that created the agency, for regulations must not conflict with enabling legislation.

Practice Pointer	Federal administrative regulations can be found in the *Code of Federal Regulations* (C.F.R.) and in the *Federal Register* (Fed. Reg.). The latter is published on a daily basis and so is preferable to the C.F.R. when dealing with new or amended regulations.

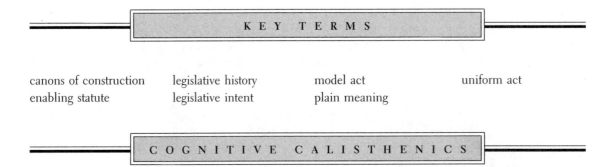

KEY TERMS

canons of construction	legislative history	model act	uniform act
enabling statute	legislative intent	plain meaning	

COGNITIVE CALISTHENICS

1. The police find our client slumped over the steering wheel and asleep. His keys are in the ignition, and the switch is in the "on" position. He has a mobile phone which he indicates he intended to activate when he turned on the ignition because he wanted to contact his wife and have her drive him home. He says he fell asleep, however, before being able to do so. His vehicle is parked on a side street adjacent to the bar at which he had been drinking.

   We want to argue that our client was not in "actual physical control" of his vehicle based on the case law discussed in *McDougall* (found on pp. 155–159). Construct such an argument based on factual elements and policy considerations. Then prepare a counterargument that you think the state will make.

2. Read *Bruce v. Chas Roberts Air Conditioning, Inc.*, (in Instructor's Manual) and decide whether the majority or dissent makes a more compelling argument as to whether A.R.S. Section 4–301 forecloses liability for an employer who observes an employee drinking during work hours if that employee later injures someone. Explain why you think this is the superior argument. What, if any, policy considerations influenced your decision?

3. The following statute is in effect in our state.

   (a) A person is justified in threatening or using both physical force and deadly physical force against another if and to the extent the person reasonably believes that physical force or deadly physical force is immediately necessary to prevent the other's commission of arson of an occupied structure under Sec. 13–1704, burglary in the second or first degree under Sec. 13–1507 or Sec. 13–1508, kidnapping under Sec. 13–1304, manslaughter under Sec. 13–1103, second or first degree murder under Sec. 13–1104 or Sec. 13–1105, sexual conduct with a minor under Sec. 13–1405, armed robbery under Sec. 13–1904, child molestation under Sec. 13–1410, or aggravated assault under Sec. 13–1204, subsection A, paragraphs 1 and 2.

   (b) There is no duty to retreat before threatening or using deadly physical force justified by subsection A of this section.

   (c) A person is presumed to be acting reasonably for the purposes of this section if he is acting to prevent the commission of any of the offenses listed in subsection A of this section.

   The defendant claims that she and her husband, who had fought throughout their marriage, were engaged in an altercation after both had been drinking. After he grabbed her hair and dragged her, she feared he would strangle her, and so, after escaping him, she grabbed a kitchen knife and stabbed him in the stomach. She then went to a neighbor's house, leaving him to bleed to death. She argues that she used deadly physical force to defend herself against an aggravated assault and that under subsection (C) she should be presumed conclusively to have acted reasonably. In other words, since she intended to prevent the crime of aggravated assault, her actions were inherently reasonable. The state argues that subsection (C) must be read in conjunction with subsection (A), which requires that the actor reasonably believe that deadly force is immediately necessary, thereby necessitating an objective standard (based on conduct of a reasonable person).

How would you go about reconciling the apparent conflict in these subsections? What information would you want to gather? What arguments might you make to support the defendant? What arguments might you make to support the state?

To find how this case was resolved, see *Korzep v. Ellsworth,* 103 Ariz. Adv. Rep. 17 (1992).

4. An illegal alien who has lived in the United States for three years is assaulted and severely beaten by three youths. He files a claim for assistance under the Victims of Violent Crimes Act. The State Board of Control denies his claim because he is not a resident of the state as defined by its regulation, which provides: "Resident, for purposes of this article, means citizen of this state . . . or an alien residing in this state who is in possession of a document issued by the United States Immigration and Naturalization Service which authorizes such person to reside in this state." The Victims of Violent Crimes Act does not define "resident."

Is the board's regulation an unauthorized amendment of the act? In other words, does the regulation modify the act or simply clarify it? What arguments can you give to support your assertion?

To see how this case was resolved, see *Cabral v. State of California Board of Control,* 112 Cal.App.3d 1012, 169 Cal. Rptr. 604 (1981).

5. Jailers employed by the city police department are injured on the job. They seek disability benefits allowed under the labor code for city police and other city personnel whose jobs "clearly fall within the scope of active law enforcement service." The city argues that the duties of jailers do not "clearly fall within the scope of active law enforcement service." To support its argument, the city looks to a case in which the state supreme court interpreted a provision in the government code pertaining to the receipt of retirement benefits. The court held that jailers were not engaged in "active law enforcement."

Construct an argument that the statutory interpretation given under the government code should be applied to the labor code and that the jailers should not be deemed to be in "active law enforcement." Then prepare a counterargument. Which of these two arguments do you find more persuasive? Why?

To find how this case was resolved, see *United Public Employees, Local 790, SEIU, AFL-CIO v. City of Oakland,* (1994).

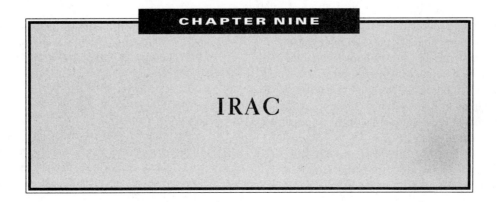

CHAPTER NINE

IRAC

Chapter Objectives

In this chapter you will learn:

■ How to use the IRAC format for legal analysis.

■ How to avoid some common errors of legal analysis.

Football is an alien sport to some people. Its rules and regulations defy their comprehension. They are never sure whether to boo or cheer their team. In fact, they are never quite sure who exactly is on their team. And so they are left amazed and bewildered by all the hoopla that surrounds football season and its heroes. Perhaps ignorance is the primary cause of their apathy.

Just as these people's lack of understanding of the rules of football inhibits their appreciation of the game and would most certainly interfere with their playing it, so too can your lack of understanding of legal analysis interfere with your ability to play the game of law. Attorneys are taught the essentials of legal analysis during their first year in law school. Even if they are not consciously aware of the elements of legal analysis, they have absorbed these elements into their legal writing practice by the end of their first year of schooling.

The importance of legal analysis cannot be overestimated. If you want to penetrate the legal mind, you must adopt the thinking process of lawyers (a frightening prospect, perhaps, but necessary nevertheless). Lawyers want to be apprised of the legal issue up front, guided by the applicable rules, given suggestions as to how those rules should be applied to the issue, and offered a plausible conclusion. If one of these elements is omitted or presented out of order, lawyers/readers will react negatively, feeling a sense of frustration or irritation. Even though they may not be able to articulate what specifically bothers them about the writing, they will, at the very least, label it as ineffective.

To paraphrase a well-known aphorism, "When in the law, do as lawyers do." Reserve your creativity for your arguments. When structuring your legal analysis, follow the path established by the millions of practitioners who have preceded you. By doing so, you will find that you and those with whom you work will be better able to communicate.

What Is IRAC?

Legal analysis (the thinking process of lawyers) can be reduced to four essential elements, as expressed in the acronym IRAC. IRAC stands for:

I = ISSUE

R = RULE

A = APPLICATION

C = CONCLUSION

In analyzing a legal question, the issue must first be clearly and accurately stated. Second, the applicable rules must be identified. These rules include relevant statutes, case law, constitutions, and regulations. Third, the rules must be applied to the issue, and, fourth, a logical conclusion must be reached. Regardless of its format, a legal argument must possess these elements or it is incomplete. Let us consider each of these elements separately and contemplate the potential problems that each one presents.

Issue

No one can sensibly respond to any question until that question is understood. Although this statement may seem self-evident, stating the issue is often a stumbling

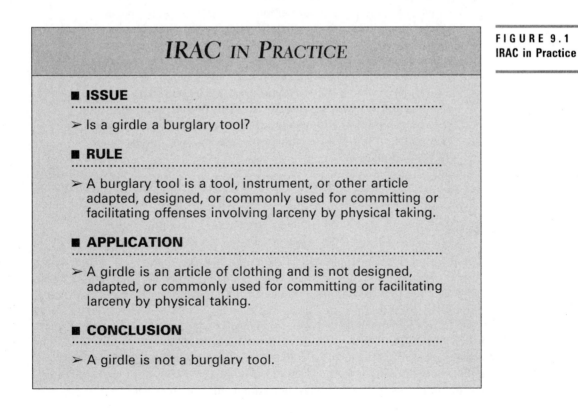

FIGURE 9.1
IRAC in Practice

IRAC in Practice

■ **ISSUE**

➤ Is a girdle a burglary tool?

■ **RULE**

➤ A burglary tool is a tool, instrument, or other article adapted, designed, or commonly used for committing or facilitating offenses involving larceny by physical taking.

■ **APPLICATION**

➤ A girdle is an article of clothing and is not designed, adapted, or commonly used for committing or facilitating larceny by physical taking.

■ **CONCLUSION**

➤ A girdle is not a burglary tool.

block for those learning legal analysis and a point of contention for those engaging in the litigation process. Therefore, as discussed in Chapter Four (Issues and Holdings), do not treat the process of constructing an issue statement lightly.

An improperly phrased issue statement can lead to erroneous or misleading conclusions. Consider the investigation of some infamous murder cases that led to the conviction of defendants later proved to be innocent. Many of these misguided investigations got off to a bad start because the investigators asked the wrong question. They asked "How can I prove that suspect X committed this murder?" instead of "Who committed this murder?" The former phrasing of the question diverted investigators down pathways that a more neutral phrasing would have avoided.

When writing a legal argument, you need not restate the issue every time you consider a different rule or apply the rule in a different manner. If, for example, the question you are addressing is whether the parties entered into a contract, you need not state that as an issue every time you consider each of the elements of a contract. Of course, if several issues are involved or an issue has various subparts, then you must distinguish those issues and clearly identify which issue you are addressing.

PUTTING IT INTO PRACTICE

Issue
Assume the same facts as were used in the Chapter Seven "Putting It into Practice." Your client is CBS Records, who produced a recording by Ozzy Osbourne, a famous rock singer. A troubled young man, beset by severe emotional problems and alcohol abuse, committed suicide while listening to the recording by Osbourne. He had listened to several of Osbourne's records, one of which encouraged suicide. The young man's parents have sued your client for negligently causing their son's death. *Weirum v. RKO General, Inc.* is the only case on point. The primary issue is whether CBS Records owes a duty of care to the young man; that duty hinges primarily on whether the young man's suicide was foreseeable. Write the issue statement as it would appear in a memorandum.

Rules

The rules involved in legal analysis are much like the rules in any game. These rules establish the confines in which you must operate. For purposes of legal analysis, these rules include statutes, ordinances and regulations, case law, court procedural rules, constitutional provisions, and executive orders.

In most memoranda, a large percentage of the analysis is devoted to establishing the rules. Before you can even consider the problems presented in your situation, you must logically and systematically set forth the principles that will guide your reasoning process. Therefore, any memorandum must open with a discussion of pertinent case holdings, procedural rules, statutes, etc.

PUTTING IT INTO PRACTICE
....

Rules
Assuming the same facts as in the previous "Putting It into Practice," write out the rules from *Weirum* that you would use in analyzing the issue of foreseeability of suicide resulting from listening to a recording that encouraged suicide.

....

Application

Once you have identified the rules, you must apply them to the facts in your situation using either inductive or deductive reasoning. (See discussion in Chapter Five.) Suppose, for example, that a statute relieves social hosts of any liability should one of their guests injure a third party. If your client served liquor at a party and one of the guests injured someone in a motor vehicle accident as a result of being intoxicated, you would use the IRAC method to determine your client's liability. You would begin by citing the rule (statute) and applying it. Using deductive reasoning, you would argue that the statute precludes liability for social hosts (major premise) and, since your client was a social host (minor premise), the client had no duty of care toward the injured party (conclusion). If your client's son set up the party without your client's knowledge and your client's status as a social host were in question, you might have to use inductive reasoning to determine liability. If no case law dealing with parental liability existed, you would have to examine factually similar cases and determine which were most analogous to yours.

Usually, application of the rules will not be quite this straightforward. Conflicting or ambiguous rules will often be involved, and you will have to determine which is most applicable. You may, for example, have a group of related cases, none of whose holdings directly resolve the question in your case. After explaining each case and discussing the similarities and dissimilarities between cases, you will have to explain which holding is most analogous to your case and, therefore, dictates a certain outcome.

If the application of rules can lead to conflicting outcomes, how neutral should you be when constructing your arguments? The answer depends on your purpose in writing the memorandum. If you are preparing it for an attorney for informational purposes or for a professor for instructional purposes, you should apply the rules in every imaginable way. Since you are not trying to persuade your reader to reach a certain outcome, you should consider every reasonably conceivable argument. This way the reader can anticipate likely arguments of opponents and mull over likely rebuttals. If, on the other hand, your audience is a court and your intent is to persuade, you should present your arguments in a manner that best reflects your client's position.

In this text, our focus is more on informational memos than on persuasive memos. Therefore, you will need to present all sides of every issue. When first learning to construct legal arguments, prepare a counterargument for every argument. If you argue that an ambiguous statute should be applied to your fact situation, immediately present reasons why the statute should not be applied. If relevant

Practice Pointer

To assist you in becoming more aware of writing counter-arguments, review the first draft of your memos and identify each argument with an "A" and each counterargument with a "C/A." Doing this will immediately alert you to any one-sided arguments.

case law suggests that the plaintiff should prevail, prepare a counterargument that the defendant should prevail. Getting in the habit of contemplating counter-arguments will prevent you from becoming too one-sided in your thinking.

PUTTING IT INTO PRACTICE

Application

Assume the same facts as in the first "Putting It into Practice" in this chapter. Notice that one primary fact difference between your case and *Weirum* is that the radio station in *Weirum* incited listeners to act irresponsibly by speeding from one location to another, while the record company did not urge those who purchased the recording to engage in any particular activity. Write an argument that this fact difference distinguishes your case from *Weirum* and justifiably relieves CBS Records of liability. Then prepare a counterargument. Use the rules from *Weirum* as the basis for your arguments.

Conclusion

Having pondered all sides of an issue, you may find yourself paralyzed when you must finally render a conclusion. Nevertheless, good legal analysis requires a conclusion. You can hedge by indicating that you lack all the facts and, therefore, can offer only a tentative conclusion. You can suggest the possibility of several conclusions, depending on a number of variables. But you must come to some sort of conclusion, tentative or not.

Failing to reach or state a conclusion is a common failing of initiates to legal analysis. Having become comfortable with making arguments and counter-arguments, they seem to find something distasteful about drawing a conclusion. They often complain that they cannot reach a conclusion because they lack suffi-cient data. How, they argue, can a realistic conclusion be reached if they don't know all the facts?

Two answers come to mind. First, in the actual practice of law, you frequently have to draw conclusions without knowing the whole picture. Until the discovery process is completed, you have a one-sided perception of the problem at hand because all your information comes from your client. Even after discovery is com-pleted, factual questions may be unresolved as the parties continue to disagree about what happened. Second, conclusions drawn from incomplete data can be acknowl-edged as tentative. You can admit that you are not privy to certain critical infor-

Practice Pointer	To assist you in making sure that you draw conclusions, identify conclusions in your memos using a "C." As you read through your first draft, check to make sure that a conclusion follows every argument and counterargument.

mation. If the unknown facts turn out one way, your conclusion will be X, but if they turn out another way, your conclusion will be Y. In this way, the reader knows that you have considered all the contingencies. The bottom line, however, is that you must reach a conclusion—no excuses.

At the end of your memorandum, you must come to an ultimate conclusion. This conclusion will be based on the intermediate conclusions you reached throughout your analysis.

PUTTING IT INTO PRACTICE

Conclusion

Consider the two arguments you wrote in the previous "Putting It into Practice." Which do you find more persuasive? Write your conclusion and explain why you selected the argument you did.

IRAC IN PRACTICE

To put the IRAC method into practice, let us use the following hypothetical case (also found in the third exercise of the "Cognitive Calisthenics" in Chapter Seven).

> After having a fight with his wife, George calls his best friend and meets him at a local tavern, where he consumes ten beers. Because of his obnoxious behavior, George is asked to leave. Before getting in his car, he decides to "steady his nerves" for the drive home by smoking a joint of marijuana. Once on the road, George becomes engaged in a verbal dispute with another driver because the other driver claims he is driving too slow. (He is in fact driving approximately 20 mph below the speed limit of 45 mph according to another driver who witnesses the dispute.) Because George is not paying attention to his driving, he runs into the rear of another vehicle, causing the driver to lose control of the vehicle and run into a pole.
>
> When the police arrive at the scene, they observe George sitting on his car hood and talking incoherently. They take him to the police station where a test reveals his blood alcohol level to be 0.11 (above the presumptive level of intoxication of 0.10). George is cited and released into the custody of a friend.
>
> An expert toxicologist testifies at trial that George must have consumed at least eight twelve-ounce beers to reach a blood alcohol level of

FIGURE 9.2
Labeling Arguments and Conclusions

LABELING ARGUMENTS AND CONCLUSIONS

AVOIDING ONE-SIDED ARGUMENTS AND LACK OF CONCLUSIONS

LABELING ARGUMENTS AND CONCLUSIONS

A { A burglary tool is defined as a tool, instrument, or other article adapted, designed, or commonly used for committing or facilitating offenses involving larceny by physical taking. A girdle is neither a tool, instrument, nor article adapted, designed, or commonly used for purposes of committing larceny. It is simply an article of clothing.

C/A { Some would argue, however, that a girdle may indeed be adapted for purposes of larceny. Because of its design, it is especially helpful in committing shoplifting since it provides the perfect place for hiding clothing and relatively small items.

C { The legislative intent of Sec. 140.35 of the Penal Law was to include tools used to take items but to exclude tools used to hide them. Even though burglary tools could logically include girdles, the legislature apparently did not intend to do so. Therefore, for purposes of our penal code, a girdle is not considered a burglary tool.

0.11. He also testifies that George's blood alcohol level at the time of the accident was at least 0.12 percent. After a jury trial in which the plaintiff is awarded $100,000 in compensatory damages and $100,000 in punitive damages, George requests a remittitur. When that is denied, he appeals.

Notice that the facts of this scenario differ somewhat from the facts in *Olson v. Walker*. In the third exercise of the "Cognitive Calisthenics" in Chapter Seven, you were asked to prepare a list of similarities and dissimilarities. Focus your attention on the dissimilarities. Imagine that this set of facts is given to you by your supervising attorney. She asks you to prepare a memorandum in which you compare your case to *Olson v. Walker* and advise her as to the possibility of your client (the plaintiff) being able to collect punitive damages.

Example of Issue Statement

Assuming that you are intimately familiar with *Olson*, begin by preparing the issue statement. Although the attorney has identified the issue she wants you to address, you need to incorporate the essential facts of the case into the issue statement. The pertinent facts are those factors that the court considered essential in *Olson*, namely, the blood alcohol level of the defendant, the drugs he had consumed, and his driving behavior.

With those facts in mind, we might phrase the issue statement as follows.

Is a plaintiff, injured after being rear-ended by someone engaging in a dispute with another driver while driving under the speed limit and under the influence of marijuana as well as having a blood alcohol content of approximately 0.12 percent, entitled to an award of punitive damages?

Example of Rules

In order to write the rules section, you need to look back at *Olson* to capture the essence of the court's argument regarding punitive damages and its justification for that award. Find key language the court used so you can incorporate those phrases into your arguments. Notice that the court defines the "evil mind" required for punitive damages and then points out that such mind can be "inferred by outrageous conduct." It then looks at specific conduct of the defendant (the large amount of alcohol he had consumed as well as the Valium he had ingested) and concludes that "a person would have known it was unsafe to drive after drinking ten beers in an hour."

The court then contrasts its facts with those in *Baker v. Marcus* (cited by the defendant) and concludes that this case can be distinguished because the defendant was merely negligent as compared to the recklessness of Walker. No evidence in *Baker* indicated that the defendant's intoxication was the cause of the accident, whereas the accident in Walker's case "occurred solely because he was intoxicated." Furthermore, Baker's intoxication was "borderline," whereas Walker's was "well beyond borderline." The court reflects on other cases as well and synthesizes them by saying, "Intoxication alone, in the absence of other compelling circumstances, may not warrant punitive damages." By contrast, Walker, the court points out, had, in addition to being intoxicated, consumed Valium, driven recklessly, and caused an accident by virtue of his intoxication.

In light of the above discussion, the rules section might be written as follows.

> Punitive damages require the showing of an evil mind, which is evidenced by an intent to injure another or by a defendant "consciously pursue[ing] a course of conduct knowing that it create[s] a substantial risk of harm to others." Such a mind can be inferred by "egregious or outrageous conduct."
>
> In *Olson v. Walker*, the defendant consumed a large amount of alcohol (at least ten beers within an hour), leading to a blood alcohol level of approximately 0.15 percent at the time of the accident, ingested 20 mg of Valium, and drove recklessly (speeding and causing other drivers to take evasive action). The court concluded that an evil mind could be inferred from such outrageous conduct.
>
> The *Olson* court contrasted the facts before it with other cases. In these cases, the defendant's intoxication was "borderline," his/her driving was negligent rather than reckless, and the defendant's intoxication was not shown to be the cause of the accident. The court noted that "[i]ntoxication alone, in the absence of other compelling circumstances, may not warrant punitive damages," but then concluded that "circumstances beyond intoxication were clearly shown" by the facts before it. Those facts were Walker's intoxication (which went beyond "borderline"), his combining of Valium and alcohol, and his reckless driving.

Example of Application

Having established the rules, you must now apply them. Here the list of factual similarities, dissimilarities, and unknowns comes in handy. You can assume that the factual similarities will compel a court to follow *Olson*, but each dissimilarity and unknown could induce the court to distinguish your case. Therefore, you must apply the rules established by the *Olson* court to each factual dissimilarity and conclude whether the difference is substantial enough to justify a difference in outcome.

Comparison of Blood Alcohol Level

Begin by comparing the blood alcohol level of the defendant in your case (estimated at 0.12 percent) with that of Walker (estimated at 0.155 percent). Is the lower blood alcohol level enough to distinguish your case from *Olson*? The *Olson* court indicated that 0.155 percent was "beyond borderline," but is 0.12 percent more "borderline" because it is closer to the presumptive level of 0.10 percent? In other words, is a twenty percent difference in blood alcohol content significant? Although blood alcohol levels taken out of the context of behavior are relatively meaningless (because other factors, such as slurred speech, unsteady gait, and slowed reaction time more accurately reflect intoxication levels), does the difference in the levels alone distinguish the defendants' conduct? One person with a blood alcohol level of 0.12 percent may be mildly intoxicated, while another person with the same level may be on the verge of passing out. The mere fact that your defendant's blood alcohol level is twenty percent less than Walker's probably does not, by itself, distinguish your case from *Olson*. Nevertheless, in conjunction with other fact differences, the

FIGURE 9.3
Fact Comparison—Walker v. Our Defendant

FACT COMPARISON—WALKER V. OUR DEFENDANT

FACT COMPARISON
WALKER v. OUR DEFENDANT

WALKER	OUR DEFENDANT
BLOOD ALCOHOL	
0.155%	0.12%
DRIVING BEHAVIOR	
10–15 mph over speed limit	20 mph under speed limit
Swerving	No evidence of swerving
Lost control of vehicle	Rear-ended vehicle
No altercations with other drivers	Altercation with other driver
DRUG CONSUMPTION	
Alcohol and Valium	Alcohol and marijuana
BEHAVIOR AFTER ACCIDENT	
Tried to leave scene	Sat on hood of car, talking incoherently

lower blood alcohol level may make it easier for the defendant in your case to argue that his conduct was less outrageous than Walker's and that he should not have to pay punitive damages.

On the other hand, the defendants in both cases consumed ten beers an hour before driving. The fact that the defendant in your case had a lower blood alcohol level indicates that he probably weighed more than the defendant in *Olson*, but, regardless of his weight, ten beers indicates substantial consumption in a relatively short time frame (probably more than the average drinker is accustomed to imbibing). Therefore, despite the differences in blood alcohol levels, the defendant in your case arguably acted just as outrageously as the defendant in *Olson*.

Drivers' Behavior

Since the *Olson* court indicated that mere intoxication alone does not justify punitive damages, you must examine the defendants' driving behavior. That behavior must go beyond negligence if your client is to be able to prove the existence of an evil mind. Was the defendant in your case more or less reckless than the defendant in *Olson*? The latter defendant drive ten to fifteen miles per hour over the speed limit, swerved in and out of traffic, cut off at least one driver, lost control of his vehicle, and tried to leave the scene of the accident. In contrast, the defendant in your case was driving twenty miles per hour under the speed limit and became involved in an accident because he was not paying attention.

You might first contend that the defendant in your case was just as reckless as the defendant in *Olson*. Arguably, driving excessively slow is just as dangerous as speeding and may indicate driver impairment as much or perhaps even more than speeding. Police officers often testify that they are more suspicious of slow drivers than of their speedier counterparts because alcohol, as a depressant, slows reaction time. Because of their impaired reaction time, drivers often slow down to be able to respond to stimuli. Although the defendant in your case did not endanger others by swerving in and out of traffic, he arguably created just as much of a threat by engaging in a verbal dispute while driving. In fact, this lack of attentiveness caused the accident. His driving behavior paints a picture of one who "consciously pursued a course of conduct knowing that it created a substantial risk of harm to others." His conduct was both outrageous and egregious and indicative of an evil mind.

On the other hand, you might argue that while your defendant's driving behavior may have been annoying to other drivers, it did not constitute the same degree of recklessness and risk to others that Walker's excessive speeding and swerving did. You can also point out that verbal altercations between drivers are not reserved to the intoxicated and, in fact, are a frequent occurrence on our streets today. Although immature and disruptive behavior, it does not rise to the level of egregious conduct that justifies punitive damages. Taken as a whole, the defendant's behavior (slow driving and arguing with other drivers) arguably depicts negligence more than extreme recklessness. You would argue that while he was certainly liable for any damages he caused, he did not engage in the type of conduct that warrants punitive damages.

Other Fact Differences

Another major variable to consider is your defendant's use of marijuana in contrast with Walker's use of Valium. Are these two drugs comparable in effect when combined with alcohol, or is one substantially more dangerous? Also, the drivers' behavior after the accident differed. The defendant in your case sat on his car and talked incoherently, while Walker tried to flee the scene. Which behavior is more outrageous, or are they comparable?

Unknown Factors

To complete the discussion, you would have to look at the unknown factors and reflect on how they might affect your case. You do not know, for example, whether your defendant engaged in any dangerous behavior other than arguing with another driver. Was he weaving or changing lanes frequently or driving in two lanes simultaneously? You also do not know when he smoked his joint, so you cannot be certain whether he was actually driving under the influence of marijuana. Although nothing indicates that your defendant tried to leave the scene, you do not know how he reacted to the accident. His behavior at that time is yet another variable that could work for or against you.

Discuss One Variable at a Time

Several factual differences distinguish your case from *Olson v. Walker.* You may be tempted to discuss all of these variables simultaneously and may, in fact, argue that each variable affects every other variable. In other words, you may reason that driving behavior and drug consumption cannot be discussed independently of blood alcohol level because each one affects the other. While their interdependence is indisputable, attempting to deal with them simultaneously leads to a very confusing discussion. For clarity's sake, discuss one variable at a time. In other words, prepare arguments and counterarguments pertaining to the differences in blood alcohol levels only; then do the same for driving behavior, drug consumption, and any other variables you wish to include. In the conclusion section of your memo, you will have an opportunity to pull everything together.

Application of Rules in Olson

To get a sense of how an application of the rules might appear in a memorandum, consider the following comparison of driving behavior. Notice that only driving behavior is discussed. Later sections would be devoted to the other variables.

Practice Pointer	Use your imagination in crafting arguments. Do not restrict yourself to known facts. Arguing that if the facts are A, then the consequence will likely be C, while if the facts are B, then the consequence is more likely to be D, is acceptable speculation. Suppose you know nothing about the effects of a marijuana/alcohol combination as compared to a Valium/alcohol combination. You could still argue that if marijuana affects muscular coordination and reaction time as much as Valium does, then combining marijuana with alcohol is probably as dangerous as combining Valium with alcohol. If, however, marijuana counteracts some of the depressant effects of alcohol, then combining marijuana with alcohol may not be as dangerous as combining Valium with alcohol. In other words, raise all possible lines of reasoning that you think should be explored. Do not be intimidated by your inability to resolve the questions you raise.

Mere intoxication alone may not justify the award of punitive damages. *Olson v. Walker*, 162 Ariz. 174 (App. 1989). In *Olson*, the defendant manifested signs of recklessness in addition to being intoxicated. He drove 10 to 15 mph over the speed limit, he swerved in and out of traffic, forcing other drivers to take evasive action, and he lost control of his vehicle. By contrast, the driver in the instant case drove 20 mph under the speed limit and argued with another driver, ultimately resulting in him running into the plaintiff's vehicle because he was not paying attention.

On the one hand, we might argue that the defendant in our case was less reckless than the defendant in *Olson*. He did not endanger others by speeding, nor did he interfere with other drivers by cutting them off. His loss of attention did not rise to the same level of recklessness evidenced by Walker losing control of his vehicle.

On the other hand, driving under the speed limit (especially when one's speed is substantially below that of other drivers) is arguably just as likely to cause accidents as speeding. The frustration that other drivers experience often leads them to take chances and engage in reckless behavior that they might otherwise avoid. It is certainly conceivable that the dispute between the defendant and the other driver was initiated because of just such frustration. Furthermore, driving much slower than the speed limit is a factor that officers typically consider when they suspect someone of driving under the influence. Therefore, while our defendant may not have manifested the same type of manic behavior that Walker did, his driving was nevertheless consistent with someone who was severely intoxicated.

Example of Conclusion

You may have noticed that what the excerpt above lacks is a conclusion. While arguments are raised on both sides of the issue (whether the defendant's conduct was reckless enough to justify the awarding of punitive damages), no conclusion is reached. You must decide whether your defendant's conduct in reference to his driving behavior alone is as flagrant as Walker's.

In addition to offering a conclusion, you need to explain the reasoning behind it. To omit your reasoning leaves the reader hanging, wondering why that particular conclusion was drawn. Your conclusion must not appear to be the result of a coin toss. To give the reader confidence in your decision, you must provide a rationale.

In the preceding section, opposing arguments were given as to whether the facts in your situation were as outrageous as those in *Olson v. Walker*. Now you must stop hedging and decide which of your arguments is superior. Most importantly, you must explain how you decided between the two sets of arguments.

Consider the following conclusion. Remember that you could just as logically have reached the opposite conclusion. Your conclusion need only be a valid conclusion; it need not be the **only** valid conclusion.

Is the defendant's conduct so egregious that it can be inferred that the defendant "consciously disregarded the substantial risk of harm" to others? Although we do not know to what extent the defendant endangered others by his driving, we do know that he angered at least one other driver and that he caused injury to the plaintiff. While his conduct may not have been as overtly dangerous as Walker's, he, in fact, created as great a risk of harm to others, and perhaps even more, because of the tensions his inordinately slow driving created in others. Although my conclusion may be weakened or strengthened by additional information I receive pertaining to his driving behavior, I believe that the defendant's driving in our case is just as reckless as Walker's driving and is every bit as deserving of a punitive damage award.

COMMON PROBLEMS IN MEMO WRITING

Conclusory Writing

One of the most common errors committed by students in their first memos is **conclusory writing.** In this type of writing, a conclusion is given with no explanation or discussion. The writer simply states the problem and offers a conclusion but does not engage in any analysis.

Law school exams illustrate the pitfalls of conclusory writing. Those who think that "knowing the answer" is the key to success quickly discover otherwise. Students must do more than spot issues and resolve them; they must explain their reasoning. Those who do not offer any explanation quickly learn that this omission adversely affects their grade. Legal analysis requires consideration of a possible argument and reflection on one or more counterarguments. Only after reflecting on both sides of an issue can a conclusion be reached.

Consider the following example of conclusory writing.

In *Olson v. Walker,* the defendant drove recklessly, endangering the lives of others. Because of his erratic driving and his consumption of alcohol in

FIGURE 9.4
Errors in Legal Analysis

ERRORS IN LEGAL ANALYSIS

■ **Conclusory writing**

■ **Lack of conclusion**

■ **Failing to tie argument to issue**

■ **Making the same argument twice**

■ **Illogical conclusions**

■ **Analyzing multiple variables simultaneously**

combination with Valium, a jury concluded that his behavior warranted an award of punitive damages. Instead of speeding and driving recklessly, the defendant in our case was driving under the speed limit. Therefore, his conduct did not merit an award of punitive damages.

What arguments did the writer consider? Were any counterarguments offered? The writer offers no explanation about the thought process. The reader knows only that the defendants behaved differently and that the writer felt that this difference warranted a difference in outcome. The reader has no idea why the writer reached this conclusion.

Compare that paragraph with the next one.

In *Olson v. Walker*, the defendant drove recklessly, endangering the lives of others. Because of his erratic driving and his consumption of alcohol in combination with Valium, a jury concluded that his behavior warranted an award of punitive damages. Instead of speeding and driving recklessly, the defendant in our case was driving under the speed limit. Arguably, his conduct was not as egregious as that of the defendant in *Olson*, <u>because </u>he did not create as substantial a risk of injury to others by driving slowly as he would have had he been speeding. Someone driving under the speed limit has greater control over his vehicle. On the other hand, he may have been driving slowly simply because he was so inebriated that he could barely maintain control over his vehicle. In other words, his slow driving may have been a surer sign of impairment than speeding. I conclude that our client is just as deserving of a punitive damage award as the plaintiff in *Olson*.

While this paragraph is certainly better than the first one in that it provides some arguments and counterarguments, it still lacks an explanation as to how the writer reached the conclusion. On the surface, both arguments appear plausible, so how did the writer decide between the two? To resolve the reader's quandary, the writer might add the following paragraph.

If we discover evidence that the defendant in our case was driving slowly because of his excessive impairment and that, in fact, he was unable to maintain control of his vehicle at a higher speed, then I believe that his conduct was just as deserving of punitive damages as that of the defendant in *Olson*. If, on the other hand, no evidence indicates excessive impairment and he was simply driving slower to be safe, then I believe his conduct was less egregious than that of the defendant in *Olson* and does not merit punitive damages.

Now you can understand how the writer reached the conclusion. You can agree or disagree with the conclusion by examining the reasoning. If you find fault with the reasoning, you can find fault with the conclusion. With the previous paragraphs, you would be hard pressed to either agree or disagree with the writer's conclusion, since you would not know how it evolved.

No Conclusion

Another common failing of beginning legal writers is the omission of a conclusion. Hopefully, you understand now that legal writers must draw some kind of conclusion even if it is tentative. You can "waffle" by making your conclusion contingent on the existence of certain facts, but you still must come to a conclusion.

Remember the suggestion earlier in this chapter that you identify each argument, counterargument, and conclusion in the rough draft of your memos. Consciously marking these elements will lessen the chance that you will omit any of them.

Failure to Tie Argument to Issue

While making arguments is crucial to legal analysis, you must not forget why you are making these arguments. Students often correctly identify factual differences between their reference case and their client's case only to make arguments without ever referring to the issue at hand. The following paragraph illustrates this point.

> The defendant in *Olson* was speeding and driving recklessly. Because of his imprudent driving behavior, he caused an accident that resulted in injury to the plaintiff. He even tried to leave the scene of the accident, further illustrating his indifference to the well-being of others. The defendant in our case, on the other hand, was driving under the speed limit and became involved in an accident only because his attention was momentarily diverted. He remained at the accident scene and otherwise demonstrated concern for the welfare of others. I conclude that the defendant in our case did not behave as badly as the defendant in *Olson*.

The question is not who behaved worse—the defendant in our case or the defendant in *Olson*. The question is whether the conduct of the defendant in our case justifies punitive damages to the same extent as the conduct of the defendant in *Olson*. The conclusion and the arguments must constantly be tied back to the legal rules set forth in *Olson*.

In *Olson*, the court tied punitive damages to conduct that indicated a "substantial creation of imminent risk to others" and colored the defendant's conduct as "egregious" and "outrageous." We must do the same in characterizing the conduct of the defendant in our case. The question is whether his conduct was "egregious," "outrageous," or "created a substantial risk of injury to others." Therefore, a better conclusion for the above paragraph would be:

> I conclude that the conduct of the defendant in our case was not as egregious as the conduct of the defendant in *Olson*. The defendant in our case did not create a "substantial risk of harm to others" by driving slowly. His conduct is more accurately described as negligent rather than as "outrageous." Therefore, based on this factor alone, I do not believe the jury was justified in awarding the plaintiff punitive damages.

Making the Same Argument Twice

Some students go through the motions of making a counterargument, but closer examination reveals that they have really made the same argument twice. Consider the following example.

> In *Olson*, the defendant combined alcohol with Valium, whereas the defendant in our case combined alcohol with marijuana. The question is whether the conduct of the defendant in our case was as dangerous as that of the defendant in *Olson* and was, therefore, as deserving of a punitive

Practice Pointer	Pay careful attention to key language used by the court, and repeat that language in your arguments. Students are sometimes reluctant to copy a court's words and choose instead to paraphrase because they do not want to be accused of plagiarism. As long as quotation marks are used, plagiarism is not a problem. To the contrary, the sign of a good legal analyst is the ability to spot phrases and terminology central to a court's decision and use the same phrases and terminology in constructing arguments relevant to the legal issue at stake.

damage award. While marijuana may be an illegal drug, it does not multiply the depressant effects of alcohol as Valium does. On the other hand, Valium has more effect on a person's reaction time than marijuana does and is more likely to interfere with drivers' ability to avoid an accident. Therefore, I conclude that combining alcohol with Valium is more dangerous than combining alcohol with marijuana. Consequently, the conduct of the defendant in our case in this regard was less egregious than the conduct of the defendant in *Olson* and was therefore less deserving of punitive damages.

Notice that even though on the surface the writer appears to have made a counterargument (using the words "on the other hand"), the same argument has actually been made twice. The writer argues first that marijuana is less dangerous than Valium and second that Valium is more dangerous than marijuana (the same argument), making the conclusion a foregone one. This problem involves a lack of logic, which can be avoided by carefully reviewing arguments.

Illogical Conclusions

A similar problem involves conclusions that do not follow from the arguments given. If the writer above, for example, had come to the conclusion that marijuana is more dangerous than Valium, the conclusion would be inconsistent with the arguments. Again, this type of inconsistency involves a flaw in logic that can be eliminated by careful editing.

Tackling Multiple Variables Simultaneously

Legal reasoning is often complex enough without trying to further complicate it by tackling multiple variables at the same time. As in scientific inquiries, only one factor should be dealt with at a time. When that factor is thoroughly examined, the next factor should be considered, and so on, until all of the factors are analyzed. Then, and only then, should all of the factors be reviewed in combination and their effects on one another contemplated.

Notice that we have visited this concept before. So many students violate this basic principle, however, that it bears repeating.

CHAPTER SUMMARY

Legal analysis can be reduced to four essential elements, as depicted in the acronym IRAC: issue, rule, application, and conclusion. A good legal analysis requires an accurate, properly phrased issue statement followed by a complete summary of the applicable rules (statutes, constitutional provisions, court rules, case law, etc.). These rules must then be applied to the facts at hand. Informational memoranda require consideration of all reasonable arguments regarding the application of the rules. For every fact difference, an argument regarding the application of the rule should be made, followed by a counterargument and ending with a conclusion. Legal analysis requires the drawing of at least tentative conclusions even when data is lacking.

Good legal analysis requires analyzing one variable at a time, avoiding conclusory writing or writing that lacks any conclusion, relating arguments to the legal issue at hand, and adhering to the rules of logic.

KEY TERMS

conclusory writing
IRAC

COGNITIVE CALISTHENICS

1. What problems can you identify in each of the following excerpts?
   (a) We might argue that the defendant in our case was less reckless than Walker. He did not endanger others by speeding, nor did he interfere with other drivers by cutting them off. His loss of attention did not rise to the same level of recklessness evidenced by Walker losing control of his vehicle.

   On the other hand, driving under the speed limit is arguably just as likely to cause accidents as speeding. The frustration that other drivers experience often leads them to take chances and engage in reckless behavior they might otherwise avoid. Conceivably, the dispute between our defendant and the other driver started because of just such frustration. Therefore, while our defendant may not

   have shown the same type of manic behavior that Walker did, his driving was, nevertheless, consistent with someone who was severely intoxicated.

   (b) In *Olson v. Walker*, Walker attempted to leave the scene. Our defendant sat on the hood of his car after the accident. This shows that our defendant was at least coherent enough to know not to leave the scene.

   On the other hand, our defendant may have been too intoxicated to try to leave the scene. Although we do not know to what extent our defendant endangered others by his driving, we do know that he angered at least one other driver and that he caused injury to our client. While his conduct may not have been as overtly dangerous as Walker's, he created as great a risk of harm to others because of the tension his slow driving created in others.

(c) The defendant may argue that it was his altercation with another driver that distracted him from driving. Distractions, such as retrieving a dropped cigarette or talking to a passenger, may be negligent but do not rise to the level of "outrageousness."

We may argue, however, that drivers must give their full attention to protecting people and property. Not taking care to avoid distractions does constitute "outrageous" behavior, especially when the driver is intoxicated.

According to the case law cited in *Olson v. Walker*, inattentiveness can be the cause of an accident even if the driver is intoxicated. Inattentiveness constitutes negligence but not outrageousness.

(d) Arguably, it is worse to combine marijuana with alcohol than to combine Valium with alcohol. Marijuana is an illegal drug, and its effects are unpredictable. If the legislature saw fit to prohibit its use, then anyone who uses it, especially in a driving situation, is acting "outrageously."

On the other hand, Valium is used legally to help individuals deal with anxiety and emotional upsets. Thousands of people use Valium under doctors' orders to help them cope with the stresses of their lives. Taking a drug under these conditions is not as reprehensible as taking a drug just to get "high."

Therefore, the defendant in our case will have a hard time arguing that his consumption of marijuana was not as bad as Walker's consumption of Valium. Because of the illegality of marijuana, its use in any public setting is unjustifiable.

2. Consider the following facts (the same as those used in the third exercise of the "Cognitive Calisthenics" in Chapter Seven). Pick three essential facts that differentiate this case from *Olson v. Walker* (found on pp. 257–262 of Appendix A). Analyze each of these three fact differences using the IRAC format. Prepare an argument, counterargument, and conclu-

sion for each fact difference. **Hint:** To help you get accustomed to the IRAC format, copy (by hand) the analysis used in this chapter relating to the fact difference regarding driving behavior. By doing this, you will literally get the feel of this analytical format and will find it easier to write your own arguments.

After having a fight with his wife, George calls his best friend and meets him at a local tavern, where he consumes ten beers. Because of his obnoxious behavior, George is asked to leave. Before getting in his car, he decides to "steady his nerves" for the drive home by smoking a joint of marijuana. Once on the road, George becomes engaged in a verbal dispute with another driver because the other driver claims he is driving too slowly. (He is in fact driving approximately 20 mph below the speed limit of 45 mph according to another driver who witnesses the dispute.) Because George is not paying attention to his driving, he runs into the rear of another vehicle, causing the driver to lose control of the vehicle and run into a pole.

When the police arrive at the scene, they observe George sitting on his car hood and talking incoherently. They take him to the police station where a test reveals his blood alcohol level to be 0.11 (above the presumptive level of intoxication of 0.10). George is cited and released into the custody of a friend.

An expert toxicologist testifies at trial that George must have consumed at least eight twelve-ounce beers to reach a blood alcohol level of 0.11. He also testifies that George's blood alcohol level at the time of the accident was at least 0.12 percent. After a jury trial in which the plaintiff is awarded $100,000 in compensatory damages and $100,000 in punitive damages, George requests a remittitur. When that is denied, he appeals.

3. Add the following facts to the scenario set forth in the above exercise. Assume that George wants to appeal the punitive damage award on the grounds that it was excessive. Identify at least two facts from the facts below that differentiate George's case from *Olson v. Walker*.

Analyze each of these fact differences using the IRAC format. Prepare an argument, counter-argument, and conclusion for each fact.

George discloses to us that his annual salary as a construction worker was around $40,000 but that he has been out of work for at least six months and has no immediate prospects for a job. He is currently receiving unemployment benefits.

He concedes that his conduct may have justified punitive damages, but he believes that the award was excessive and wants to appeal on that basis.

CHAPTER TEN

STRUCTURE OF A MEMORANDUM

Chapter Objectives

In this chapter you will learn:

- How to differentiate between an internal memorandum and an advocacy memorandum.

- A variety of possible memorandum formats.

- How to prepare each element of a memorandum.

- A variety of organizational schemes for the analysis section of a memorandum.

At last, the moment has arrived for you to drag out all the information bits you have been given in the previous chapters and assemble a memorandum. Take a peek at page 206 to get a feel for what it is you are about to construct. Perhaps it looks a bit intimidating. To make it less intimidating, we are going to dissect a memorandum into its discrete parts and examine each part in detail. Having confronted each section individually, you will find the memorandum as a whole to be much more manageable.

One of the greatest challenges of memo writing is organization of your analysis. Trying to organize an analysis is like trying to decide where to put furniture in a huge room where the potential arrangements appear limitless. You often have to try several different placements before you discover the pattern that is most functional and aesthetically pleasing. One way to do this is by physically moving the furniture into each configuration. Another way is to draw different placements, choose the optimal one, and move the furniture once.

In this chapter, we will use the latter approach. Rather than requiring you to write an entire analysis using a particular type of organization only to discover that that organization does not work, we will survey outlines of various approaches. You can then select an outline, apply it to your analysis, and determine whether that outline allows you to present your arguments in as clear and as rational a manner as possible. In like manner, you can try several alternative outlines until you find the one that is optimal. This process circumvents some of the laborious process of rewriting by allowing you to consider options mentally without actually committing everything to paper.

ADVOCACY MEMORANDA V. INTERNAL MEMORANDA

But wait—what is your purpose in doing this? Do you intend to persuade your readers to adopt your position, or do you merely want to provide information? The answer depends on who your audience is. If you are writing to an attorney in your office, your purpose is to inform. If you are writing to the trial court, hearing judge, or appellate court, your purpose is clearly to persuade. Persuasive memoranda are frequently referred to as **advocacy memoranda** (since you are advocating a particular position). They are also referred to as "points and authority memoranda" or "trial memoranda."

A memorandum written for an attorney by a paralegal, law clerk, or associate is called an **office memorandum** or **internal memorandum.** Because the purpose of such a memo is largely to inform, both sides of every issue must be presented. For every argument made, a reasonable counterargument should be considered. The attorney needs to be apprised of every possible position that opposing counsel could take. As in any game, the player must be able to anticipate the opponent's moves. Your job in writing an internal memorandum is to advise the attorney what moves the opponent is most likely to make and which are most likely to be successful.

While it is important to recognize that a balanced analysis must be given, you must not totally abandon your advocacy position. Too often novices to the law forfeit the game before it is even begun. After researching a question and deciding that the law clearly favors the opposition, they give up all hope of mounting any kind of defense and suggest surrender as the only realistic option. If any viable arguments exist, they must be explored and creative applications of legal principles should be pondered. Realistic assessment of the weaknesses of a case is good, but premature abandonment of a position (and therefore of a client) is unprofessional.

In this book, the focus of our discussion is internal memoranda. If you are asked to prepare an advocacy memo, remember that you will want to omit, or at the very least minimize, the weaknesses in your case while highlighting your strongest arguments and facts. You will also need to review the rules of the court to which you are addressing the memo to ensure that you conform to its structural requirements.

FORMATS OF MEMORANDA

As with case briefs, several organizational formats exist for legal memoranda. A few variations will be presented for your consideration, but remember that your choice of format will be dictated largely by the preferences of the attorney for whom you are preparing the memo.

FORMAT A	FORMAT B	FORMAT C
Heading	Heading	Heading
Overview	Issue	Issue
Facts	Answer	Conclusion
Issue; Answer	Facts	Facts
Analysis	Analysis	Analysis
Conclusion	Conclusion	
Recommendations		

The advantage of format A is that the readers are given an overview of the case and the pertinent facts before being presented with all of the details. The readers are better able then to recognize the relevance of the facts and connect them with the pertinent legal issues. This format also leaves the readers with recommendations to consider in terms of further research, investigation that may need to be conducted, or procedural options that might be pursued.

Format B allows the readers to be apprised of the legal issues before sifting through the facts. The answers to the issues may be more detailed than in format A simply because the readers have not had the advantage of reading the overview provided by format A. In format C, the answers to the questions in the issue section are replaced by a conclusion. The advantage of such placement is that the readers are afforded an immediate answer to the questions. On the other hand, such placement arguably exposes the readers prematurely to a conclusion that cannot be fully appreciated until the analysis is completed. Placing the conclusion at the end of the memo also provides readers with a natural sense of completion that is lacking when the memo ends with a discussion of the application of legal principles.

Since format A encompasses all of the elements of formats B and C, we will use it as the basis for the following discussion. The sample memo in Figure 10.1 illustrates the essential elements of a memorandum.

ELEMENTS OF A MEMORANDUM

Heading

The heading of a memo contains basic identifying information—your name, the name of the person to whom the memo is being addressed, the date the memo was submitted, the case name, the office file number, and the court docket number. A "re" statement in the right-hand corner of the memo identifies the basic subject matter being discussed. This statement allows anyone looking through a case file to quickly identify the subject matter of the memo and facilitates the filing of the memo if it is stored in the law office library. Therefore, the information in this statement must be detailed enough to distinguish this memorandum from others.

Overview

The overview provides a brief summary of the memo. Before diving into the forest of facts and legal principles, the readers are afforded an aerial view of the memo's

FIGURE 10.1
Sample Memo

SAMPLE MEMO

To: Kim Pallay
From: Janis Bailey

Date: August 2, 1995

Case: Lester v. Reilly
Office File Number: T95-567
Docket Number: CA 95-85282

RE: Whether punitive damages can be awarded when the driver who caused the accident was under the influence of alcohol and marijuana and was driving under the speed limit

OVERVIEW

In the only relevant authority, *Olson v. Walker*, the court held that a driver under the influence of alcohol and Valium and driving recklessly demonstrated sufficient evidence of an "evil mind" to justify the awarding of punitive damages. Likewise, in our case, the defendant, George, was under the influence of alcohol (although his blood alcohol content was 20 percent lower than the blood alcohol content of the defendant in *Olson*). George, however, smoked marijuana rather than consuming Valium and drove 20 mph under the speed limit rather than speeding and driving recklessly. Although the circumstances in our case differ somewhat from those in *Olson*, sufficient similarities exist to show that George "consciously pursued a course of conduct knowing that it created a substantial risk of harm to others." His conduct was, therefore, just as egregious as the conduct of the defendant in *Olson v. Walker* and just as deserving of punitive damages.

FACTS

After getting into an argument with his wife, George went to a local bar. In about an hour, he consumed approximately ten beers. He was thrown out of the bar because of his obnoxious behavior. Before driving, he smoked a joint of marijuana to "steady his nerves." George drove 20 mph under the speed limit and ultimately became involved in a verbal dispute with another driver because of his slowness. Because George was not paying attention, he rear-ended our client. When the police arrived, George was sitting on his car hood, talking incoherently. He was taken to the police station, where his blood alcohol level was determined to be 0.11 percent. At trial, a toxiocologist testified that George's blood alcohol level at the time of the accident was 0.12 percent and that he had consumed at least ten twelve-ounce beers in the hour preceding the accident. The jury ordered George to pay $100,000 in compensatory damages and $100,000 in punitive damages. George's request for a remittitur was denied. He is now appealing the punitive damage award.

ISSUE AND ANSWER

Issue: Is a plaintiff injured by a driver who was driving under the speed limit and who was under the influence of alcohol and marijuana entitled to an award of punitive damages?
Answer: Yes.

FIGURE 10.1
Sample Memo *continued*

ANALYSIS
Overview of *Olson v. Walker*

The only relevant authority in our jurisdiction in reference to punitive damage awards is *Olson v. Walker*. While the facts of *Olson* differ somewhat from ours, important similarities exist. In both cases, the defendants were under the influence of alcohol and another drug, both caused an accident because of their inappropriate behavior, and both exhibited driving behavior that deviated from the norm.

In *Olson*, defendant Walker had gone to a bar with friends to discuss business and relax after work. He and his friends drank alcohol and played pool for about two hours. About thirty minutes before driving, Walker took 20 mg of Valium. He drove 10 to 15 mph over the speed limit, swerving in and out of traffic, and cutting off at least one other driver. He lost control of his vehicle and rear-ended the plaintiff's car. Walker did not immediately stop, but when he did, he was staggering, smelled strongly of alcohol, had bloodshot eyes and slurred speech, and had trouble standing up. He attempted to leave the scene but was restrained by two witnesses.

At trial, a toxicologist testified that Walker's blood alcohol level at the time of the accident was 0.155 percent and that he must have consumed at least ten twelve-ounce beers before the accident. A jury awarded the plaintiff $133,000 in compensatory damages and $100,000 in punitive damages. Walker appealed the punitive damage award.

While noting that mere intoxication alone is not enough to warrant punitive damages, the court found sufficient evidence of an "evil mind" to warrant a punitive damage award. Pointing out that an "evil mind" exists where the defendant, although not intending to cause injury, "consciously pursued a course of conduct knowing that it created a substantial risk of injury or significant harm to others," the court looked at a combination of factors in reaching its conclusion that the defendant evidenced an "evil mind." Looking at Walker's consumption of ten beers within an hour of driving, resulting in a blood alcohol level of 0.155 percent (a level the court indicated went "well beyond borderline"), along with his consumption of 20 mg of Valium, the court reasoned that the defendant reasonably should have known that his ability to drive safely was impaired. These factors, in addition to his reckless driving and speeding and his failure to take any steps to avoid the accident, indicated the presence of an "evil mind" and, in the court's assessment, overrode the defendant's testimony that he was not aware that his actions could cause harm to others.

COMPARISON BETWEEN WALKER'S AND GEORGE'S CONDUCT
Driving Behavior

Mere intoxication alone may not justify the award of punitive damages, but in *Olson* the defendant manifested signs of recklessness in addition to being intoxicated. He drove 10 to 15 mph over the speed limit, swerved in and out of traffic, forcing other drivers to take evasive action, and lost control of his vehicle. By contrast, the driver in the instant case drove 20 mph under the speed limit and argued with another driver, causing him to run into the plaintiff's vehicle because he was not paying attention.

On the one hand, we might argue that defendant George was less reckless than defendant Walker. He did not endanger others by speeding nor did he interfere with other drivers by cutting them off. His loss of attention did not rise to the same level of recklessness evidenced by Walker losing control of his vehicle.

FIGURE 10.1
Sample Memo *continued*

On the other hand, driving under the speed limit (especially when one's speed is substantially below that of other drivers) is arguably just as likely to cause accidents as speeding. The frustration that other drivers experience often leads them to take chances and engage in reckless behavior that they might otherwise avoid. It is certainly conceivable that the dispute between George and the other driver was initiated because of just such frustration. Furthermore, driving much slower than the speed limit is a factor that officers typically consider when they suspect someone of driving under the influence. Therefore, while George may not have manifested the same type of manic behavior that Walker did, his driving was nevertheless consistent with someone who was severely intoxicated.

Is George's conduct so egregious that it can be inferred that he "consciously disregarded the substantial risk of harm" to others? Although we do not know to what extent George endangered others by his driving, we do know that he aggravated at least one other driver and that he caused injury to the plaintiff. While his conduct may not have been as overtly dangerous as Walker's, he in fact created as great a risk of harm to others and perhaps even more because of the tensions his inordinately slow driving created in others. Although my conclusion may be weakened or strengthened by additional information I receive pertaining to his driving behavior, I believe that George's driving is deserving of a punitive damage award.

Blood Alcohol Level

Was George's blood alcohol level sufficiently high to merit an award of punitive damages? In *Olson*, defendant Walker's blood alcohol level of .155 percent (which was well beyond borderline) indicated that he drank at least ten beers in a one-hour period. He consumed this alcohol in a relaxed social environment. After the accident occurred, Walker staggered, smelled strongly of alcohol, and had trouble standing, all of which are obvious signs of severe intoxication. Consuming such a large amount of alcohol in a short period of time supports an inference that he intended to become intoxicated or at least knew that would be the result. Any reasonable person would have known it was unsafe to drive after drinking ten beers, yet Walker drove and became involved in an accident that was a direct result of his intoxication. Walker disregarded the fact that his impaired ability to drive created a substantial risk of significant harm to others.

By contrast, according to the toxicologist's testimony, George consumed eight beers, resulting in a blood alcohol level of 0.12 percent, 20 percent lower than Walker's. When the police arrived at the scene, George was sitting on the hood of his car and talking incoherently but was not staggering.

We might argue that George drank less than Walker did, resulting in a lower blood alcohol level that might be considered "borderline" since it was barely over the legal limit. George did not exhibit the typical symptoms of severe intoxication that Walker did. Therefore, he may not have had reason to believe he was severely intoxicated. Although he appeared incoherent, that may have been due to the accident itself rather than intoxication. If George did not knowingly drink to excess and then drive, he could not have known he was creating a risk of harm to others. From the facts, we cannot be sure that the accident was a result of intoxication rather than simple inattentiveness.

FIGURE 10.1
Sample Memo *continued*

On the other hand, George's blood alcohol level was above the legal standard of .10 percent. Although he did not exhibit the typical signs of intoxication, those symptoms may have been diminished by other factors. The mere fact that blood alcohol levels differ by 20 percent is insufficient to show that George was less intoxicated than Walker or less likely to have had reason to believe he was creating a risk of substantial harm to others.

Since blood alcohol levels taken out of context mean little, we will have to look at other factors, such as behavior, to determine the true degree of intoxication. One person with a blood alcohol level of .12 percent may appear falling down drunk, while another may seem perfectly normal. The fact that George had a lower blood alcohol level although he admits to drinking the same number of beers as Walker may be the result of a larger body size, the amount of food eaten, and other factors of which I am unaware. I need additional information regarding the defendant's height, weight, and food intake before I can realistically assess the difference in blood alcohol levels, but without that information I believe that George's blood alcohol level is less conclusive of his level of intoxication than his outward symptoms of intoxication. Since George's overt conduct was not as outrageous as Walker's (George was not staggering, did not have blood-shot eyes, and did not attempt to leave the accident scene), I believe that punitive damages are not as clearly justified as they were in Walker's case.

Valium v. Marijuana

Does the use of marijuana in combination with alcohol constitute conduct as egregious as the use of Valium with alcohol? Valium and alcohol combined multiply the intensities of one another. In *Olson*, this factor was part of the court's reasoning that the defendant's conduct was outrageous. The effects of alcohol and marijuana, on the other hand, are additive rather than synergistic. Because we do not know how much marijuana George smoked or how potent the marijuana was, our discussion is, to some extent, speculative.

Looking at outward conduct only, Walker seems to have been more impaired than George. Walker took no precautions to make his driving safer, whereas George at least drove more slowly, presumably in an effort to be more cautious because of the drugs he had consumed. The mere fact that George became involved in a verbal dispute was not necessarily a result of his consumption of alcohol and marijuana, since drivers do not need drugs to be provoked into altercations. George's conduct, while negligent, is arguably not as outrageous as Walker's conduct and, therefore, not as deserving of punitive damages.

On the other hand, both Valium and marijuana alter an individual's behavior and when combined with alcohol intensify the effects on the body. Whether one drug is worse than the other is irrelevant. The simple fact that both George and Walker chose not only to drink but to ingest a drug is outrageous in so far as their disregard for the safety of others. Although their impairment was manifested in different forms (reckless driving and speeding as opposed to slow driving and arguing with others), they both demonstrated irresponsible and outrageous behavior. The consequences of their drug consumption rather than their choice of drugs is what is most important. Therefore, George, like Walker, should have punitive damages awarded against him.

FIGURE 10.1
Sample Memo *continued*

Although Valium and marijuana interact differently with alcohol, they both adversely affect driving ability. It was the combination of alcohol and Valium that the *Olson* court considered in coming to its conclusion that Walker's conduct was outrageous. The degree to which one drug enhances the detrimental influence of alcohol seems irrelevant. Drinking and driving is irresponsible, but mixing drugs (when the resultant effect is by necessity unknown) and driving goes beyond the realm of negligence and falls within the purview of an "evil mind." George's choice of marijuana rather than Valium does not justify his being treated any differently than Walker. The plaintiff in our case is just as deserving of punitive damages as was Olson.

CONCLUSION

Based on *Olson v. Walker*, sufficient evidence exists in our case to justify the award of punitive damages. Although George drove under the speed limit rather than speeding (as Walker did), he created just as great a risk of harm to others because of the tensions his slow driving induced in others. Similarly, while George ingested marijuana with alcohol and Walker took Valium with alcohol, both drugs exacerbate the debilitating effects of alcohol. Even though Valium may intensify the depressant effects of alcohol more than marijuana does, both impair driving behavior, and driving under their influence constitutes outrageous behavior. The only fact difference I considered in which I concluded that punitive damages were not clearly justified was that George's blood alcohol level was 20 percent lower than Walker's. This difference may, however, be due to differences in height and weight and other factors rather than differences in alcohol consumption. Overt conduct seems to be a more reliable indicator of intoxication than blood alcohol level. Therefore, since George's overt conduct was not as outrageous as Walker's in terms of his appearance at the accident scene, I concluded that punitive damages in reference to this factor alone were not as clearly justified as they were in Walker's case.

All other factors, however, pointed to the conclusion that George displayed evidence of an "evil mind" and that the plaintiff deserved to receive punitive damages. Although George will most certainly argue to the contrary, his decision to drive while under the influence of alcohol and marijuana displayed a blatant disregard for the well-being of others and shows that he "consciously pursued a course of conduct knowing that it created a substantial risk of harm to others." His slow driving and his participation in a verbal dispute with another driver were further evidence of his incapacitation to drive. George made a conscious decision to drive and in doing so put the lives of others in jeopardy. That decision exemplifies the classic "evil mind" envisioned by those who created the concept of punitive damages.

RECOMMENDATIONS

Additional information should be gathered in reference to the marijuana that George smoked. We should find out the potency of the marijuana, the size of the cigarette he smoked, and when he smoked it. We also need to ascertain more about his physical appearance at the accident scene to determine if he demonstrated any overt symptoms of intoxication. Finally, we should interview any witnesses to the accident and to the dispute between George and the other driver to discover any additional evidence of his impairment.

I think our chances are very good of prevailing on appeal and recommend that we advise Mr. Lester accordingly.

contents. This synopsis allows the readers to know what issues are presented and how they are resolved. The readers can then decide whether they need to read the entire memo or can skim through it with an eye as to what the outcome is. While you may argue that giving away the conclusion at the beginning takes away some of its impact, remember that you are writing a memo and not a suspense novel. You do not want to shock or amaze your readers. You want to convey ideas as systematically and as painlessly as possible.

In the overview, you should include the issues discussed in your analysis, your resolution of each issue, and, ever so briefly, the reasoning used to arrive at your conclusion. The overview should be restricted to one or two paragraphs. If you write much more, you defeat the purpose of providing a brief summary.

Facts

Although the attorney is no doubt familiar with the pertinent facts, you must commit them to paper nevertheless. Doing so will not only refresh the attorney's memory but will help you clarify which facts are important to the case. Additionally, memos are filed in the office and read later by parties who lack any familiarity with the case. Providing a detailed discussion of the facts puts the legal issue into a meaningful context for future readers.

Any fact that you discuss in your analysis must be included in the statement of facts. To help you honor this fundamental rule of memo writing, review your analysis after you have completed it to ensure that every fact you have discussed in the analysis is recorded in the statement of facts.

The facts section should not only be comprehensive in terms of containing all the relevant facts, but it should also be as concise as possible. Eliminate any facts that are irrelevant to the issues at hand. Even more importantly, use precise, powerful terminology that clearly and accurately portrays the events that occurred leading up to litigation.

Issue and Answer

The issue should be stated as completely as possible. It should contain the legal question at stake, but it should be clothed in the factual context that makes the issue unique to the case at hand. As discussed in Chapter Four, avoid writing an issue statement that is so broad that the legal principles cannot be discerned. "Is the will valid?" is not an adequate formulation of the issue, because we do not know the circumstances under which the will was created or executed.

Issues should be written in such a way that they can be universalized. In other words, the way the issue is written should indicate that the legal principles are applicable to persons other than the parties in the case. An issue such as "Did Mr. Smith breach the contract when he failed to begin construction on the date specified in the contract?" is too narrow in that it focuses on Mr. Smith. A better statement of the issue would be "Is the failure to begin construction on the date specified in a contract a breach of that contract?"

Since the reader has already been apprised as to the resolution of the issues in the overview, a very brief answer to the question raised in the issue is appropriate. A simple yes or no may be sufficient. If the issue was not clearly resolved but involves some contingencies, those contingencies should be identified in the answer. Brevity should be the watchword. Remember that the reader can go to the analysis and conclusion sections for more detail.

Analysis

IRAC is the linchpin for analysis. Begin every discussion of an issue with a disclosure of all the relevant case law, statutes, constitutions, and other "rules." After clearly articulating the "rules," offer an argument as to how the rules might be applied and explain which rules are most persuasive. Present any reasonable counterarguments, followed by a conclusion explaining which argument you find most persuasive and why.

Explain Your Reasoning

Remember that the soundness of your reasoning is the criterion by which your arguments will be evaluated by the attorney. Therefore, you must do more than suggest arguments. You must explain in as much detail as possible how each argument emanates from the legal rules and how you arrived at your conclusion. In essence, you must construct a mental footpath for your readers to follow. Each stone must be carefully laid and pointed out to your readers to prevent them from stumbling. Your goal is to see that your readers arrive at the same destination (conclusion) you do. To ensure this, eliminate any gaps in your mental walkway. Your readers should not have to leap from point A to point B but should simply be able to trace the logical path you laid and arrive with as little effort as possible at the end point you intended.

Notice how difficult it is to follow the reasoning in this excerpt.

> The Arizona Court of Appeals upheld an officer's search of a suspect's wallet because the wallet contained a "hard" object that the officer could reasonably believe contained a weapon. *State v. Clevidence*, 736 P.2d 379 (Ariz. Ct. App. 1987). The Washington Supreme Court, on the other hand, rejected a search with which the officer continued, after feeling two "spongy" objects in the suspect's pockets. The court reasoned that the officer could not have feared that the "spongy" objects were weapons. Based on these court decisions, I conclude that the search of our client's pockets will be deemed unconstitutional and the heroin will be inadmissible.

Not only is the reliance on two case decisions from different jurisdictions misplaced, but absolutely no reasoning is offered to substantiate the writer's conclusion. What general rule did the writer glean from the two cases? How did the writer apply that rule to the facts of the client's case? The readers are hard-pressed to evaluate a conclusion when the reasoning supporting it is unknown.

Some people are afraid to explain their reasoning in too great a detail out of fear of appearing patronizing to the readers. Remember that you are typically writing about complex and abstract ideas, some of which may be completely foreign to the readers. If the readers find your conclusions obvious because your presentation is so clearly logical, you have achieved your goal of effective communication and have not threatened the readers' egos in the process.

Opening Your Analysis

Open your analysis with a brief (one paragraph) explanation of the primary considerations involved in resolving the issues at stake. Much like a prologue to a play, this paragraph should set the scene by focusing the readers on the problems that lie ahead. Suppose the question, for example, is whether a seller misrepresented the house he was selling and the case revolves around whether the defect in the house was a latent defect. The introductory paragraph should explain that sellers are liable for failure to disclose latent defects and should identify the nature of the defect as the key factor upon which the outcome of the case hinges. This paragraph should also indicate how you expect this issue will be resolved and why. Notice that this paragraph differs from the overview in that it highlights the decisive factors in the case, i.e., the factors that will determine the outcome of the case. The overview summarizes all of the issues in the case rather than focusing on those issues around which the case revolves.

Having laid the foundation, you must now decide the order in which to discuss all the pertinent cases and other legal references. Choosing an organizational scheme is one of the greatest challenges of writing an analysis. Several organizational schemes are possible, as you will see. Obviously, you want the scheme that most logically and clearly leads to the conclusion toward which you are building.

Suggested Organizational Schemes

The analysis can generally be organized according to the IRAC model.

Issue (I)

General rule of law (R)

Application of rule of law to facts (A)

Conclusion (C)

This basic format requires further organization into subparts. The rule of law, application, and conclusion sections can be organized in a number of different ways. Let us use the problems in the "Cognitive Calisthenics" to illustrate the different schemes possible. After considering these specific topics, we will generalize and propose some basic guidelines you can look to when writing memos.

Swenson and *Cundick*

Read part (a) of Cognitive Calisthenics 1 and 2.

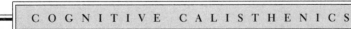

C O G N I T I V E   C A L I S T H E N I C S

1. Frederick had been married for ten years when he finally could no longer bear the pretense of a heterosexual relationship. He separated from his wife and two children and soon after became involved in a relationship with Jacob, who was ten years his junior and a law school student. Frederick's wife, who was greatly embittered by these events, refused to allow Frederick to see his children and caused his entire family to turn against him.

Within a year of their breakup, Frederick became very ill and was eventually diagnosed as having AIDS. Believing that he would die soon, Frederick asked Jacob to draw up a will. Jacob, who had just graduated from law school, was reluctant to draft the will but acceded to Frederick's pleas because he knew Frederick was in financially desperate straits. Jacob fully honored Frederick's requests in preparing the will and offered no advice except when Frederick asked him about the legal implications of his decisions. After preparing a draft, Jacob asked an attorney friend of his to review the will and finalize it.

Frustrated by his family's refusal to acknowledge his relationship with Jacob and hurt by his children's hateful attitude toward him, Frederick decided to leave to Jacob his only valuable possession, a ranch left to him by his father. He knew that Jacob, who loved the lore of the West, would probably live on the ranch after Frederick's death. Frederick also knew that the only value anyone in his family would see in the ranch was its resale price, and he wanted to give the ranch to someone who would cherish it as his father had.

When Frederick died and his former wife became aware of the provisions of his will, she was incensed that her children had received nothing. Convinced that Jacob was the instigator of Frederick's having executed such a will, she sought legal counsel, who suggested that the will may have been the product of undue influence. Your firm has been retained by Jacob. You need to determine the likelihood of the will being invalidated on the grounds of undue influence. Focus on the homosexual and quasi-attorney relationship between the testator and beneficiary.

(a) Based on *Swenson*, determine whether undue influence exists in this case.

(b) Based on the case law in your state, determine whether undue influence exists in this case.

2. Wilma recently purchased a restored home in a district of town devoted to the preservation of historic buildings. Although Wilma was thrilled at her purchase, her brother became livid when he discovered what she had paid for it. He has brought Wilma to our firm and asked us to determine whether there are grounds upon which the contract can be voided.

He claims that Wilma has been "addle-brained" for several years and that she had engaged in "unwise transactions" in the past.

After recently being diagnosed as having Alzheimer's, she had a legal guardian appointed. The doctors do not know for certain how long she has had the disease but suspect its onset was several years ago. All of the doctors who have evaluated or treated Wilma believe that she becomes befuddled at times and has momentary memory losses. None of them believes that she currently has the capacity to conduct her financial affairs, but they are not certain as to whether she was incapacitated at the time she entered into the contract to purchase the house.

While Wilma's brother asserts that Wilma is clearly unable to manage her own affairs at this time, he did not believe that to be true at the time she bought the house. At that time, he says, she acted "peculiarly" sometimes, but he did not believe that she was disabled. Some of her friends, however, have recently told him about buying sprees in which she purchased items for which she had absolutely no need. They also recounted times when she became disoriented and could not remember where she lived. She begged them not to tell her brother for fear that he would institutionalize her, and so they declined to relate these incidents to him.

Based on the ludicrous purchase price and the fact that the house closely resembles the one Wilma grew up in, Wilma's brother believes that she was confused about what she was doing at the time she entered into the contract. After reviewing the law regarding capacity to contract, you must determine whether Wilma was legally incapacitated when she bought the house.

(a) Using *Cundick v. Broadbent* as your reference, determine whether Wilma had the capacity to enter into the contract.

(b) Based on the case law in your jurisdiction, determine whether Wilma had the capacity to enter into the contract.

Part (a) ▪ Cognitive Calisthenic 1 (*Swenson*), involving undue influence in the context of a will, and 2 (*Cundick*), involving the capacity to enter into a contract, can be organized in a similar fashion. With part (a) of both questions, begin by summarizing your reference case (*Swenson* or *Cundick*). Briefly state the facts, issue(s), holding(s), and reasoning. Although these summaries contain the same elements as a case brief, do not merely copy from your case brief. Capture the essence of these cases in as brief a synopsis as possible. Then discuss the law in your reference case and apply it to the case as a whole or apply the rules set forth in *Swenson* or *Cundick* to each element separately. *Swenson*, for example, outlines seven elements of undue influence. You could discuss all seven elements first and then apply the rules to the facts of your case, reaching a conclusion for each element separately.

ALTERNATIVE ONE
I. *Swenson*
   A. Facts
   B. Issue
   C. Holding
II. Rules regarding undue influence derived from *Swenson*
   A. Element 1
   B. Element 2
   C. Element 3
   D. Element 4
   E. Element 5
   F. Element 6
   G. Element 7
III. Application of rules of law
   A. Element 1
      1. Argument
      2. Counterargument
   B. Element 2
      1. Argument
      2. Counterargument

         *   *   *

   G. Element 7
      1. Argument
      2. Counterargument
IV. Conclusions
   A. Element 1
   B. Element 2
   C. Element 3
   D. Element 4
   E. Element 5
   F. Element 6
   G. Element 7

On the other hand, you could combine your application and conclusion sections, coming to a conclusion for one element before moving on to a discussion of the next element.

ALTERNATIVE TWO
II. Rules regarding undue influence derived from *Swenson*
   A. Element 1
   B. Element 2
   C. Element 3
   D. Element 4
   E. Element 5

     F. Element 6
     G. Element 7
III. Application and conclusion
     A. Element 1
        1. Argument
        2. Counterargument
        3. Conclusion
     B. Element 2
        1. Argument
        2. Counterargument
        3. Conclusion

                *   *   *

     G. Element 7
        1. Argument
        2. Counterargument
        3. Conclusion

Alternatively, you could discuss the rules of law for element 1, apply those rules to your case, and come to a conclusion before moving on to element 2.

       ALTERNATIVE THREE

I. *Swenson*
     A. Facts
     B. Issue
     C. Holding
II. Rule 1 regarding undue influence derived from *Swenson*
     A. Explanation of rule of law
     B. Application of rule of law to facts
        1. Argument
        2. Counterargument
     C. Conclusion
III. Rule 2 regarding undue influence derived from *Swenson*
     A. Explanation of rule of law
     B. Application of rule of law to facts
        1. Argument
        2. Counterargument
     C. Conclusion

    Which of these formats you choose depends on the complexity and interdependence of the elements you are discussing. If the readers need to understand all the elements before they can fully understand how the law could be applied in reference to element 1, the first or second alternative is preferable. If, on the other hand, element 1 will likely determine the outcome of the case, therefore requiring extensive analysis, whereas elements 2 and 3 are relatively straightforward, necessitating little discussion, the third alternative is probably preferable.

    As discussed in the previous chapter, your application of the rules of law to the facts requires you to make all reasonable arguments and counterarguments. The factual differences could lead to different conclusions from those drawn in the reference case, and the nature of an internal memo compels you to consider all possibilities. Of course, if you cannot pose a reasonable counterargument, you are not expected to retreat into the realm of the absurd. But allow your creative side to reign as you construct your arguments, just as you allow your practical side to prevail when drawing conclusions.

PUTTING IT INTO PRACTICE
....

Which outline would you use for your analysis of *Cundick* [question 2(a)] and why? Write the first sentence for each part of the outline.

....

Read part (b) of Cognitive Calisthenics 1 and 2.

Part (b) ▪ The organization for memos having only one reference case is relatively straightforward, but part (b) of exercises 1 and 2 requires handling several cases. What is the best way to organize this more complex discussion?

Swenson sets forth seven elements of undue influence. You could discuss these elements in the order in which they appear in the case law, or you could first isolate the most important elements (those that determine the outcome of the case). Suppose that the existence of a confidential relationship is imperative to a finding of undue influence. After opening your analysis with a brief overview of the case, you would want to discuss the pivotal nature of the element of confidential relationship, explaining how the court's finding in reference to this element would dictate the outcome of the case. Because of the importance of confidential relations, you would probably delve into great detail in this area. You would then narrow your discussion to confidential relations in the context of homosexual relationships. In order to formulate public policy, you would need to review any legal commentary about the development of the law in this area.

I. Confidential relations
    A. Case law in general
    B. Case law in reference to homosexuals
    C. Public policy
    D. Conclusion as to how your jurisdiction will treat homosexual relationships

Having come to a conclusion as to how the court in your jurisdiction will treat homosexual relationships in reference to confidential relations, you could either apply that conclusion to your facts or examine the other elements of undue influence. In other words, you could use the outlines discussed in reference to part (a) of this exercise to organize the remainder of your memo.

BenShalom
Read part (a) of Cognitive Calisthenics 3.

COGNITIVE CALISTHENICS

3. In an attempt to control the AIDS problem, which has reached epidemic proportions in your state, your legislature recently mandated the registration of all homosexuals with the Department of Health Services (DHS). The rationale for the statute is that having the names of high-risk people will allow DHS to more easily monitor the contacts these people

have with health-care facilities. Another provision in the statute requires all health-care providers to conduct a test for HIV on any person whose name is on the DHS list and who comes to them for medical care. Failure to register with DHS is a felony with mandatory prison time. One of your clients, David, has been charged with violation of this statute.

(a) Based on *BenShalom*, determine whether this statute violates the equal protection clause.

(b) Review the case law in your jurisdiction and determine how you think your court will classify homosexuals. Then subject both provisions in the statute to the varying levels of review to which the court might submit them and conclude whether they will be able to survive any of these levels of review.

Part (a) ▪ Part (a) of Cognitive Calisthenics 3 (*BenShalom*) involves an equal protection analysis of a statute. Begin by educating the reader about the general principles of equal protection analysis before applying the principles to your facts. The *BenShalom* court's conclusion that homosexuals belong to a suspect class was based on the plaintiff's status rather than her conduct. Therefore, your analysis would revolve around whether the statute in question applied to homosexuals in general or only those who engaged in homosexual conduct. The answer would determine the level of review the court would give the statute, since those statutes involving a suspect class (for purposes of equal protection analysis) are given strict scrutiny (a level of review that few statutes pass) while those involving a non-suspect class are given a rational basis review (a level of review that most statutes pass). The second half of your analysis would examine whether the statute would survive strict scrutiny or a rational basis review.

An outline might look as follows.

I.   Homosexuals as a suspect class
    A. Homosexual status
    B. Homosexual conduct
II.   Equal protection analysis of statute
    A. Strict scrutiny
        1. Argument
        2. Counterargument
        3. Conclusion
    B. Rational basis
        1. Argument
        2. Counterargument
        3. Conclusion

PUTTING IT INTO PRACTICE

Write out the first sentence for each part of the outline for exercise 3 (a) of the *BenShalom* assignment.

Read part (b) of Cognitive Calisthenics 3.

Part (b) ▪ Part (b) of this exercise would also require laying the foundation for equal protection analysis in general and would include a discussion of quasi-suspect class (a classification not mentioned in *BenShalom* and one which requires intermediate scrutiny, a level of scrutiny less than strict scrutiny but greater than rational basis review). An analysis of case law and legal commentary illustrating each classification and level of review as applied to other groups would have to precede any consideration of case law and commentary in reference to homosexuals.

I. Classification under equal protection
   A. Suspect class
   B. Quasi-suspect class
   C. Non-suspect class
II. Levels of review
   A. Strict scrutiny
   B. Intermediate scrutiny
   C. Rational basis

Alternatively, classification and level of review could be discussed together.

I. Equal protection analysis
   A. Suspect class and strict scrutiny
   B. Quasi-suspect class and intermediate scrutiny
   C. Non-suspect class and rational basis

With that foundation laid, the rules could then be applied to the statute in question.

I. Equal protection analysis of statute
   A. How are homosexuals likely to be classified?
      1. Suspect class
      2. Quasi-suspect class
      3. Non-suspect class
   B. Conclusion regarding classification
   C. Will the statute pass any level of review?
      1. Strict scrutiny
      2. Intermediate scrutiny
      3. Rational basis
   D. Conclusion regarding survival of statute

Of course, your discussion of each level of classification and scrutiny would have to include any plausible arguments and counterarguments. The conclusions reached regarding the survival of the statute would need to reflect the subconclusions reached regarding the classification of homosexuals.

Dickerson
Read part (a) of Cognitive Calisthenics 4.

COGNITIVE CALISTHENICS

4. Susie, a local nightclub performer, was walking in the vicinity of a well-known crack house when she observed a patrol car. Becoming nervous because of her recent encounters with the vice squad (none of which had resulted in arrest but which did involve extensive questioning), she turned around and walked quickly in the opposite direction.

As the patrol car sped up, so did Susie. Her heels made it difficult for her to run, and she tripped. After she fell to the sidewalk, one of the officers approached her and observed her put her hand to her right breast in an apparent attempt to remove something. Although Susie protested that she was simply adjusting her bra, the officer suspected that she might have a weapon and conducted a pat-down search. When the officer came to the right breast, he felt an object that he believed to be a packet of crack cocaine. When he removed the object, he found it to be a baggie of condoms containing heroin. After being arrested for possession of heroin, Susie retained your law firm.

(a) If your state follows the lead of *Dickerson*, determine whether you can distinguish the facts of your case and convincingly argue that the evidence of the pat-down should be suppressed.

(b) After reviewing the case law in your state in reference to stop-and-frisks, determine whether you think your state court will follow *Minnesota v. Dickerson* and accept the rationale of the "plain feel" rule set forth in that case. Then ascertain whether you can distinguish the facts of your case from *Dickerson* and convincingly argue that the evidence of the pat-down should be suppressed.

Part (a) ▪ Part (a) of this exercise requires a comparison between the facts of the reference case (*Dickerson*) and our facts. Therefore, discuss the facts, holdings, and rationale of *Dickerson* in detail before contemplating any kind of comparison. Having done this, focus on the factual dissimilarities between the two cases, considering each one in turn. For each fact difference, construct an argument that this difference could affect the outcome of the case, consider a counterargument, and come to a conclusion. After reviewing all the fact differences, compare your subconclusions and arrive at an ultimate conclusion.

I. *Dickerson*
    A. Facts
    B. Issue
    C. Holding
    D. Rationale
II. Comparison between our case and *Dickerson*
    A. Identification of dissimilarity 1
        1. Argument that dissimilarity 1 may affect outcome of case
        2. Counterargument
        3. Conclusion
    B. Identification of dissimilarity 2
        1. Argument that dissimilarity 2 may affect outcome of case
        2. Counterargument
        3. Conclusion
III. Conclusion

PUTTING IT INTO PRACTICE

Write the first sentence for each section of the outline for part (a) of the *Dickerson* assignment.

Read part (b) of Cognitive Calisthenics 4.

Part (b) ▪ In part (b) of this exercise, begin with a thorough analysis of *Dickerson* (the "plain feel" rule) and then discuss whether the courts in your jurisdiction would adopt this rule. This question, in essence, dictates the organization of the memo.

After discussing *Dickerson* at length, review any cases in your jurisdiction that have dealt with this rule and then look to courts outside your jurisdiction that have either adopted or rejected the rule. If you discern any pattern to their reasoning, you can use this pattern to structure your analysis. In other words, if some courts adopted a plain feel rule for one reason and others adopted it for another reason, use their reasoning as a format for your analysis. Ultimately, you will have to predict whether your jurisdiction will follow *Dickerson*, which can be done by reviewing the trend of your courts in the areas of plain feel, plain view, and stop-and-frisk. To better depict any trends, present these cases in chronological order. In this way, changes in the direction your court is taking will be more obvious. Your final task is to apply the rules of *Dickerson* to your facts [as you did in part (a)].

I. Analysis of *Dickerson*
  A. Facts
  B. Issue
  C. Holding
  D. Reasoning
II. Status of plain feel in our jurisdiction
III. Status of plain feel in other jurisdictions
  A. Reasoning used by courts that have adopted plain feel
  B. Reasoning used by courts that have rejected plain feel
IV. Conclusion as to your jurisdiction's response to *Dickerson*
  A. Trend of decisions in regard to stop-and-frisk
  B. Trend of decisions in regard to plain view
  C. Trend of decisions in regard to plain feel
V. Application of *Dickerson* to your facts

Why not simply skip to section V of the outline if your jurisdiction has accepted some variation of the plain feel doctrine? You cannot assume that just because your court accepted the plain feel rule in the past your current court will do so. Perhaps, for example, your court has changed its judicial philosophy. Remember that one of the purposes of an internal memo is to explore all possible options and then advise the attorney as to which ones are most likely to occur. For that reason, you will have to apply *Dickerson* to your facts even if you conclude that your jurisdiction is unlikely to accept it. A complete analysis requires contemplation of all possible contingencies.

Hernandez
Read part (a) of Cognitive Calisthenics 5.

C O G N I T I V E   C A L I S T H E N I C S

5. Hall, who is 21, went to a graduation party for his friend, Matt, who is 18. Most of the guests were over 21, but a few were under the legal drinking age. All guests had to pay a

dollar to cover the cost of the beer. Hal had only a few beers, but another guest, Stu, who was also 21, became very intoxicated and hit Hal in the jaw. Several other guests pulled Stu off Hal before he could inflict any more damage, but Hal sustained a broken jaw. Matt's parents were on the premises during the party but stayed in a back room watching TV because they did not want to interfere. They were not aware of the altercation at the time it occurred. Hal has come to your firm seeking compensation for his medical damages and his pain and suffering.

Assume that the following statute is in place in our state.

A.R.S. Sect. 4–301 Liability limitation; social host

A person other than a licensee . . . is not liable in damages to any person who is injured, or to the survivors of any person killed, or for damage to property, which is alleged to have been caused in whole or in part by reason of the furnishing or serving of spiritous liquor to a person of the legal drinking age.

A.R.S. Sect. 4–311(A) Liability for serving intoxicated person or minor; definition

A. A licensee is liable for property damage and personal injuries or is liable to a person who may bring an action for wrongful death pursuant to Sect. 13–612 if a court or jury finds the following:

1. The licensee sold spiritous liquor either to a purchaser who was obviously intoxicated, or to a purchaser under the legal drinking age without requesting identification containing proof of age or with knowledge that the person was under the legal drinking age.

A.R.S. Sect. 4–312(B) Liability limitation

B. Subject to the provisions of subsection A of this section and except as provided in section 4–311, a person, firm, corporation, or licensee is not liable in damages to any person who is injured, or to the survivors of any person killed, or for damage to property which is alleged to have been caused in whole or in part by reason of the sale, furnishing, or serving of spiritous liquor.

(a) Based on these statutes and the Arizona Supreme Court decision *Hernandez v. Arizona Board of Regents* (found on page 000 in Appendix A), do you think Hal has a cause of action against Matt's parents?

(b) Based on a review of the case law in your state, do you think Hal has either a statutory or common law cause of action? Use the discussion in *Hernandez* to guide your analysis of the common law issue. You will need to determine whether Matt's parents owed a duty of care to Hal, whether they breached that duty, and whether that breach was the cause of Hal's injuries.

Part (a) ■ Exercise 5(a) requires statutory analysis. Therefore, initiate the discussion by quoting statutes and pointing out the key provisions in each. You can use the discussion in *Hernandez* to illustrate the apparent statutory conflict and to explain how the court harmonized the statutes after examining legislative history, the plain meaning of the statutes' provisions, and public policy. Then compare the facts of your case to *Hernandez* and show why your client's situation raises a somewhat different question. Relying on public policy arguments and legislative intent, you can postulate how the court will resolve the liability issue.

I. Statutory analysis
   A. Statutory provisions
   B. Conflict between statutes
   C. Interpretation of legislative intent by *Hernandez* court
      1. Legislative history
      2. Plain meaning
      3. Public policy

II. Application of *Hernandez* to your case
   A. Fact comparison
   B. Arguments that defendants should be liable
   C. Counterarguments
   D. Conclusion

PUTTING IT INTO PRACTICE

Write out the first sentence for each part of the outline for exercise 5(a) of the *Hernandez* assignment.

Read part (b) of Cognitive Calisthenics 5.

Part (b) ▪ *Hernandez* went on to discuss whether the defendants had a common law cause of action. Use the format of that discussion as the basis of your outline for exercise 5(b). After explaining the court's rationale for finding a duty based on the common law, analyze whether the same rationale should apply to your facts. Examine other case law dealing with causation to determine the likelihood that any statutory violations by the defendants in your case would be considered the proximate cause of your client's injuries. As with any fact comparison, consider arguments and counterarguments before arriving at a conclusion.

The second half of your analysis might look as follows.

I. Duty under common law
   A. Analysis by *Hernandez*
   B. Application of *Hernandez* rationale to our facts
      1. Arguments
      2. Counterarguments
      3. Conclusion
II. Causation under common law
   A. Case law dealing with causation
   B. Application of rationale to our facts
      1. Arguments
      2. Counterarguments
      3. Conclusion

Organizational Schemes in General

Now that we have examined organizational outlines for specific questions, let us generalize. If you are asked to look at one case, compare your facts to it, and decide if your outcome will be the same, you can often use this outline.

I. Reference case
   A. Facts
   B. Issue
   C. Holding
   D. Rationale
II. Application of rules of reference case to our case
   A. Element 1

  1. Argument
  2. Counterargument
  3. Conclusion
 B. Element 2
  1. Argument
  2. Counterargument
  3. Conclusion
III. Conclusion

If your task is to decide whether your jurisdiction will adopt persuasive authority, you will want to examine trends in your jurisdiction and other jurisdictions. Therefore, this outline might be appropriate.

I. Reaction of your jurisdiction to persuasive authority
 A. Reasoning of persuasive authority
 B. Comparison with authority in your jurisdiction
  1. Similarities
  2. Dissimilarities
  3. Public policy
 C. Trend in your jurisdiction
 D. Conclusion as to reaction of your jurisdiction

If you are asked to consider more than one case, your outline will probably look as follows.

I. Case law in general
 A. Holdings (facts, if pertinent)
 B. Reasoning
 C. Public policy
II. Case law in reference to specific issue
 A. Holdings (facts, if pertinent)
 B. Reasoning
 C. Public policy
III. Conclusions as to how law will be applied to your case
IV. Application of rules of law to your case

When groups of cases are discussed, they can be organized chronologically, either beginning with the most recent case and working back to the origin of the body of law or starting with the oldest case and moving forward to demonstrate the evolution of the law.

Alternatively, you can organize case law according to patterns—patterns based on holdings, facts, reasoning, or public policy. For example, if you discern a pattern in courts' holdings or if you observe that the holdings are dependent on certain facts, you can use those patterns to structure your discussion.

You can also organize around a seminal case (a case such as *Miranda* or *Roe v. Wade*, around which the remainder of case law revolves). Using this case as the center point for discussion, you can show how the courts have either expanded or restricted the law after this case.

Finally, you can organize case law from the general to the specific. Discuss general principles of law and then zoom in for a closer examination of a more restricted area of the law. In exercise 1 of the "Cognitive Calisthenics," for example, we discussed undue influence in general and then narrowed it to undue influence in the context of homosexual testators and beneficiaries.

Analysis of statutory law differs somewhat from analysis of case law; consequently, the organization differs as well. A discussion of statutory law typically opens with quotation of the pertinent sections of the statute(s), followed by definition of key terms and identification of the ambiguous/vague terms in question or the conflicting provisions within statutes. Legislative history is explored, and statutes in other jurisdictions are considered as well as related statutes in the litigants' jurisdiction. The facts at hand are subjected to all possible interpretations of the statute, and a conclusion is reached as to which interpretation is most in line with legislative intent.

I.   Statutory analysis
    A.   Key provisions
    B.   Ambiguous/vague terms or conflicts between statutes
    C.   Plain meaning
    D.   Legislative history
    E.   Comparison with other statutes in same jurisdiction
    F.   Comparison with statutes in other jurisdictions
    G.   Public policy considerations
II.   Application of statute to facts of case
    A.   Arguments
    B.   Counterarguments
    C.   Conclusion

Conclusion

Although it may seem repetitious, summarize your resolution of each issue in your conclusion (what you decided and how you decided it). Why restate what you have already said in your analysis? The conclusion section may be the only section the readers actually read. In the frantic pace of law practice, attorneys frequently skim over materials in an attempt to "cut to the chase." Initially, they may be interested only in how you resolved the legal issues and may thoroughly digest the "hows" of your reasoning later. You can fulfill this need for instant information by succinctly paraphrasing the discussion in your analysis. Highlight the conclusion you reached for each subissue and explain briefly, if necessary, what facts and/or reasoning dictated the outcome of your decision. The identification of the facts that affected your decision-making process may be particularly important, since in the discovery process those facts may change. Knowing which facts dictate the outcome of a case is essential to any attorney in the negotiation and litigation phases of a case.

In your concluding paragraph, come to an overall conclusion. Explain how you arrived at that conclusion, particularly if your subconclusions suggest conflicting final conclusions. An explanation of your reasoning process is essential if the readers are to evaluate the soundness of your conclusion.

Make sure that your subconclusions are consistent with your ultimate conclusion. Before writing your conclusion, review the arguments in your analysis and summarize them, first in your mind and then on paper. Then, and only then, commit your ultimate conclusion to paper.

Recommendations

In the last section of the memo, recommend how you think the case should be handled. You might, for example, recommend that the case be settled or that a claim be filed. This is the appropriate place to indicate where further investigation is needed and what specific factual questions need to be addressed. In your analysis, you undoubtedly had to draw tentative conclusions in the absence of sufficient data. Before writing the recommendations section, review your analysis and take note of every unknown factor. Use this section as a platform for drawing attention to all unknown variables that need clarification.

CHAPTER SUMMARY

Memoranda can be written either to persuade (advocacy memoranda) or to inform (office or internal memoranda). They can be organized according to a variety of formats but typically include a heading, an overview, a facts section, an issue and answer section, an analysis, a conclusion, and recommendations. The heading contains basic identifying information, while the overview provides a brief summary of the memo. The facts section identifies the relevant facts, and the issue and answer section identifies the issues at stake and provides a brief answer to the question posed in the issue statement. The analysis is organized according to IRAC and explains the writer's reasoning process in detail. All analyses should open with an introductory paragraph that serves as a prologue but may be structured according to a variety of organizational schemes. The conclusion section summarizes the resolution of each issue and provides an overall conclusion, with an explanation as to how that conclusion was reached. In the recommendations, the writer suggests how the case should be handled and indicates questions that need to be further explored.

KEY TERMS

Advocacy memorandum
Internal memorandum
Office memorandum

COGNITIVE CALISTHENICS

The Cognitive Calisthenics for this chapter are included within the chapter rather than at the end.

For each Cognitive Calisthenic in the chapter, write an internal memorandum addressing the questions raised in the scenario(s). Each exercise has a part (a) and a part (b). Part (a) can be answered using the case law provided in this text, while part (b) requires outside references.

CHAPTER ELEVEN

WRITING TIPS

Chapter Objectives

In this chapter you will learn:

- How to organize your writing by using thesis sentences, topic sentences, transitions, and headings.

- How to clarify your writing by explaining your thought process, seeking simplicity and brevity, and expressing important ideas at the beginning of sentences.

- How to avoid quoting extensively and using the "In X v. Y" construction too frequently.

- The use of proper tense.

- The importance of proper spelling and grammar and a professional appearance.

Have you ever had an inspiring experience that you just couldn't wait to share with a friend or loved one, only to have your revelation received with a blank stare? Frustrating, wasn't it? As wondrous as your experience was, you could not share it until you were able to express it in such a way that it literally could be transplanted into the mind of another. That's what good communication is all about—creating the same mental image in the mind of another that is in your mind. To the extent that the person with whom you are communicating receives a picture that is different in any way, a breakdown in communication occurs.

The best communicators are those who are able to efficiently and accurately transmit information to others, minimizing the conveyance of misunderstood words and concepts. While communication is no doubt a two-way task, the responsibility for eliminating ambiguity and unnecessary complexity lies with the individual expressing the ideas.

FIGURE 11.1
Good
Communication

GOOD COMMUNICATION

SENDER

RECEIVER

   Simplicity and clarity are the keys to good legal writing. Legal concepts and comparisons are often complex and abstract. To explain them in a concise, clear manner requires more thought and skill than to present them in a convoluted, obtuse way that, while superficially impressive, tends to confuse the reader. This is an important point, so please do not gloss over it. We have a tendency to revere those who express ideas in such an obscure manner that we do not understand them; we assume that such people must have a superior intellect. But think about that assumption. Are not clarity and simplicity signs of a superior mind? Reflect for a moment on the greatest teachers and orators. Are they not famous because they used simple, poignant phrases or parables to make their points?

   Your perception of the law will typically go from simplicity to complexity to clarity. When doing legal research, for example, you may perceive a legal problem as being rather straightforward until you begin to appreciate the multitude of issues raised. Then you may feel hopelessly lost in a quagmire of legal principles and rules and policies and not know where to turn. After considerable effort, however, you will probably begin to see the commonality underlying the diversity and will see the clarity arise out of the complexity. Your ultimate challenge is to help your readers avoid the quagmire and see only the clarity. If you are successful, you will have accomplished the same feat as the great teachers and orators referred to above. You will have made the complex appear simple.

ORGANIZING YOUR WRITING

The best way to organize your writing is to offer your readers a verbal road map as a guide. Tell the readers every step of the way where you are going and how you propose to get there. Using transitional words and phrases, lead the readers from one paragraph to another, assist them to see the connection between one thought and the next, and make these connections and transitions seem so natural that the readers are not even aware that they are being led.

Above all, keep in mind the "golden rule" of writing. **Write to others as you would prefer they write to you.** If you do not like to read material that is dense and confusing, do not write that way.

Thesis Sentence

Begin leading your readers by opening your memo with a **thesis sentence.** This sentence (as you may remember from your English classes) announces the subject of the memo. You are not writing a mystery, so do not leave your readers in suspense until the end of the memo. Reveal immediately what the problem is and how you think it will be resolved. This way the readers know what to focus on while reading the memo and which concepts are particularly important.

In the following introductory paragraph, the readers are told what the issue is in the first sentence and how the writer expects to resolve the issue in the last sentence. The readers know immediately the subject matter and outcome of the memo.

> The issue before us is whether the punitive damages awarded against our client, Mr. Dougall, were justified. In the only case on point, *Olson v. Walker*, 162 Ariz. 174 (Ct. App. 1989), the court determined that the punitive damages awarded against the defendant were warranted. Having compared the blood alcohol levels, driving behavior, and drug consumption of our client and Mr. Walker, I have concluded that punitive damages are likely to be awarded in our case.

Compare this introduction with the next paragraph. Note that the first sentence in the next paragraph gives the readers no clue what relevance *Olson v. Walker* has. Even though in the last sentence the writer apprises the readers of what will be discussed in the memo, the outcome is not indicated, so the readers do not know where to focus their attention as they read about the relevant points of comparison.

> In *Olson v. Walker*, 162 Ariz. 174 (Ct. App. 1989), the plaintiff was awarded punitive damages after being injured by the defendant in a motor vehicle accident. Prior to the accident, the defendant had consumed 20 mg of

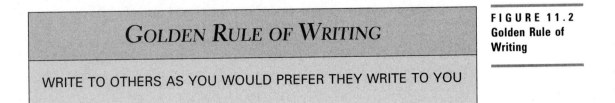

FIGURE 11.2
Golden Rule of Writing

GOLDEN RULE OF WRITING

WRITE TO OTHERS AS YOU WOULD PREFER THEY WRITE TO YOU

Valium, had a blood alcohol level of 0.155%, and had been driving 10 to 15 mph over the speed limit. In this memo, I will compare the facts in this case to the facts of our case to determine if punitive damages were justified in being awarded against our client.

Topic Sentences

Having forewarned the readers about what to anticipate in the memo, continue to provide guidance by opening each paragraph with a **topic sentence**. This sentence tells the readers about the subject matter to be discussed in that paragraph. In essence, it is a thesis sentence for a paragraph, and its purpose is to prepare the readers so they know what to focus on while reading the paragraph.

The topic sentence that introduces the following paragraph immediately draws the readers' attention to the significance of the case being discussed.

> Intoxication alone may not justify punitive damages. *Baker v. Marcus*, 114 S.E.2d 617 (Ct. App. 1960). The *Baker* court concluded that even though the defendant's intoxication was "borderline," such conduct was negligent and did not warrant punitive damages because no surrounding circumstances indicated the malice necessary to impose punitive damages.

Compare that paragraph with the following, in which the readers must infer why the writer is discussing *Baker v. Marcus.* This "In X. v. Y" format is often tempting to beginning legal writers but should be avoided whenever possible. Legal concepts can be expressed far more clearly and succinctly in other formats.

> In *Baker v. Marcus*, 114 S.E.2d 617 (Ct. App. 1960), the defendant's level of intoxication was considered "borderline." The court concluded that even though the defendant's conduct was negligent, such conduct did not warrant punitive damages because no surrounding circumstances indicated the malice necessary to impose punitive damages.

PUTTING IT INTO PRACTICE

Thesis and Topic Sentences

Suppose we have a client who wants to challenge the validity of a contract she entered into. The facts surrounding her case are similar to those in *Cundick v. Broadbent,* except that she has recently been diagnosed as suffering from Alzheimer's disease and she had no lawyer representing her interests at the time she entered into the contract. The doctor who diagnosed her Alzheimer's disease is not sure when it began and cannot definitively say that she was suffering from the disease at the time she signed the contract.

Assume that you are going to write a memo comparing our case to *Cundick.* Write the thesis sentence for the analysis section and then write a few of the topic sentences you think would be appropriate in your analysis.

Transitions

The thesis and topic sentences forewarn the readers of what is to be discussed, but the readers must also know how one paragraph is connected to another. You must not confer the responsibility for connecting one thought to the next upon the readers. It is all too easy to assume that the readers will understand why you shifted from one idea to another. After all, by the time you commit your thoughts to writing, your thought process is so self-evident to you that explanation seems unnecessary. Remember that the readers have not been privy to your analytical maneuvering. They need direction every step of the way.

Use transitional words and phrases to provide that direction. Imagine that you are laying a footpath for the readers to follow. Every step should be clearly set so that all the readers have to do is to follow your verbal signs. Look over the following examples of some of those verbal signs.

Additionally	Moreover
Although	Next
Because	On the other hand
Even though	Therefore
First (second, third, etc.)	To illustrate
For example	To the contrary
Furthermore	Whereas
However	While
In spite of	

Incorporate these words into your writing. Use them at the beginning of paragraphs and to make a transition from one thought to the next within a paragraph. Ask yourself as you go from one paragraph to the next what the connection between the two paragraphs is and then use the appropriate word or phrase to indicate that connection.

Notice the use of transitions in the following example.

> We contend that the search of our client's jacket was impermissible because it exceeded the bounds of *Terry*. Traditionally, *Terry* limited a "stop and frisk" to a search for weapons under the rationale that officers must be allowed to protect themselves and others from what they reasonably believe is imminent harm. Because the officer in our case felt a soft object, he had no reason to suspect that our client had a weapon. Therefore, his continuing search violated the precepts of *Terry*.
>
> The state, on the other hand, looks to *Dickerson* to support its argument that a "stop and frisk" that leads to evidence other than weapons is constitutional as long as the incriminating nature of the object is immediately apparent to the officer. Moreover, the state uses this so-called "plain feel" doctrine to justify the officer's seizure of cocaine from our client even though the officer's identification of the drug was initially erroneous.

You can also assist your readers in moving from one idea to the next by summarizing what you have just said. This summary gives the readers some closure

FIGURE 11.3
Transitions

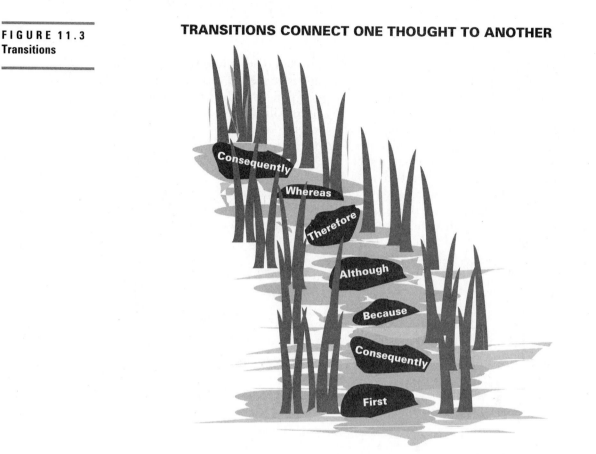

TRANSITIONS CONNECT ONE THOUGHT TO ANOTHER

Consequently

Whereas

Therefore

Although

Because

Consequently

First

STREAM OF THOUGHT

and allows them to assimilate what has been discussed in capsule form. Frequent summaries assist you in "teaching" your readers the material previously presented before confronting them with new information.

Notice how the writer in the next excerpt summarizes the essential content of the first paragraph in the first sentence of the second paragraph.

The officer who conducted the pat-down of our client indicated that he felt an object he immediately believed to be a packet of cocaine. He did not squeeze or in any way manipulate the object he detected. His actions are in direct contrast to the officer in *Dickerson*. In that case, the officer detected the contraband only after squeezing, sliding, and manipulating the contents of the defendant's pocket. The *Dickerson* court characterized his actions as an additional search that it deemed unconstitutional.

Since there is no indication that the officer in our case squeezed or manipulated the object he found in our client's jacket, the state will likely maintain that the search was constitutional. It will argue that the incriminating nature of the object was immediately apparent to the officer and was therefore within the bounds established by *Dickerson*. If our court adopts the *Dickerson* rationale, we must turn to another line of reasoning if we are to prevail.

Similarly, you may anticipate what you are going to discuss by offering the readers a brief preview. Such a preview allows the readers to glean the essence of what is to be discussed in detail. This technique allows the readers to make a transition into new territory with less trepidation, because they have been prepared in advance. They also know specifically what to look for in their reading.

In the example below, the writer forewarns the readers that before addressing the notion of "general acceptance," the phrase "scientific community" must be defined. The readers then know that the discussion about "scientific community" lays the foundation for the discussion about "general acceptance."

> Before we can address whether the technique used by our experts has received "general acceptance" of the scientific community, we must first ascertain what the relevant scientific community is. If the scientific community includes only criminalists, for example, then general acceptance will be much easier for us to prove than if it includes the community of geneticists, statisticians, and criminalists.
>
> How have the courts defined "scientific community"? . . .

PUTTING IT INTO PRACTICE

Transitions
Provide transitions where helpful in the following selection.

> Punitive damages are awarded to deter future misconduct of others and to punish wrongdoers. A jury may consider a defendant's wealth and his conduct when awarding punitive damages. An award "must not financially kill the defendant" and cannot be the result of "passion or prejudice" or "shock the conscience of the court." In *Olson,* an identical punitive damage award was not found to be excessive when that defendant had almost the same income as our client. Judge Gerber in his dissenting opinion balanced the "long-term needs of society" against "destroying an individual" by poverty and debt. The defendant's family in that case played a significant role in Judge Gerber's decision that a punitive damage award of $50,000 would have been more appropriate.
>
> We may argue that the punitive damage award "financially kills" our client because he cannot begin to pay it now or in the near future. If he has no income, he cannot pay any debt, no matter what its source. The punitive damage award should "shock the conscience of the court" because our client has no money. The award is excessive.

(continued)

> **Putting It into Practice** *(continued)*
>
> The plaintiff may state that our client's conduct was found to be "outrageous" and in so being justifies any punitive damage award without "passion or prejudice." His wealth is a factor the jury may consider, but it is not mandatory to do so. The judgment against the defendant in *Olson* was upheld on appeal, and he was more sympathetic than our client in that he had three dependents. The punitive damage award is not excessive.
>
> I conclude that the punitive damage award against our client will not be altered on appeal. His current financial situation is parallel to but less sympathetic than the defendant's in *Olson.* Judge Gerber's dissent is more realistic than the majority opinion, but since our client has no dependents, the dissent has little value for us. Proving "passion or prejudice" would be the only way to persuade a majority of the court to reverse the award. Our client's chances of reversing the punitive damages award are slim as there is no evidence of "passion or prejudice."

Headings

Headings are additional signs that you can offer your readers to make their journey through your thoughts more pleasant. The more headings and subheadings you provide, the easier the journey will be. Headings allow the readers to know at a glance what is being discussed. Moreover, they allow the readers to skim your writing quickly and get a feel for the primary issues being discussed.

A more subtle asset of headings is their introduction of white space between all those rows of black type. If you think giving the readers a reprieve is inconsequential, ask yourself how you feel about reading a text that is devoid of headings. Do you like plowing through pages and pages of text with no relief in sight? Or do you prefer a text that is replete with headings and subheadings? White space gives the eyes a momentary rest and serves as a psychological buffer for the readers. Be kind to your readers. Give them a reading break, and provide them with direction by posting road signs along the way. Notice the liberal use of headings in the sample memo on page 206.

CLARIFYING YOUR WRITING

Explain Your Thinking Process

Although transitional phrases, topic sentences, and headings provide road signs for your readers to follow, you still must consciously focus on explaining your thought process every step of the way. Lack of explanation is one of the primary flaws in

APPEARANCE OF A WELL-ORGANIZED PAPER

FIGURE 11.4
Appearance of
Well-Organized
Writing

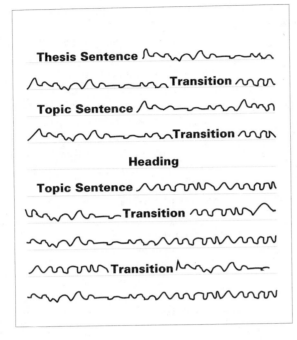

student writing. Once the writer has thoroughly researched and pondered an issue, the tendency is to forget the cognitive steps taken in reaching the conclusion and to assume that anyone would necessarily follow the same steps.

Good writing is just like any other art. It should appear simple to the observer. Figure skaters, dancers, gymnasts, and other athletes and performers who are highly skilled are a joy to watch because what they do looks deceptively easy. Good writing shares that deception. Because the readers find the reasoning simple to follow, they conclude that the subject matter is simple and that the conclusions are inescapable.

Think about it. Aren't well-written instructions easy to follow, making the whole process of whatever you are trying to do seem simple? By the same token, can't confusing instructions make the simplest task seem almost impossible? If your purpose is to educate your readers, then can't you best achieve that by explaining each step so that the readers cannot possibly go astray? Do you want your readers wondering how you went from step A to B, or do you want to so clearly and plainly lay out your thinking that even a novice to the law could understand your reasoning?

Consider the following discussion of a relatively complex concept, and note the systematic explanation given to describe each step. The author is generous in the use of transitional words and as much as possible uses terse sentences with simple subject-verb construction. The explanations are clear, and the conclusions seem obvious. Notice too how the author uses concrete examples to illustrate each factor that is considered. The citations have been deleted to more clearly illustrate the court's concise but thorough writing.

I now address the merits of Watkins' argument that the Army's regulations must be subjected to strict scrutiny because homosexuals constitute a suspect class under equal protection jurisprudence. The Supreme Court has identified several factors that guide our suspect class inquiry. I now turn to each of these factors.

The first factor the Supreme Court generally considers is whether the group at issue has suffered a history of purposeful discrimination. . . As the Army concedes, it is indisputable that "homosexuals have historically been the object of pernicious and sustained hostility" . . . Recently courts have echoed the same harsh truth: "Lesbians and gays have been the object of some of the deepest prejudice and hatred in American society" . . .

Discrimination against homosexuals has been pervasive in both the public and private sectors. Legislative bodies have excluded homosexuals from certain jobs and schools and have prevented homosexual marriage. In the private sphere, homosexuals continue to face discrimination in jobs, housing, and churches. . .Moreover, reports of violence against homosexuals have become commonplace in our society. In sum, the discrimination faced by homosexuals is plainly no less pernicious or intense than the discrimination faced by other groups already treated as suspect classes, such as aliens or people of a particular national origin. . .

The second factor that the Supreme Court considers in suspect class analysis is difficult to capsulize and may in fact represent a cluster of factors grouped around a central idea—whether the discrimination embodies a gross unfairness that is sufficiently inconsistent with the ideals of equal protection to term it "invidious." Consideration of this additional factor makes sense. After all, discrimination exists against some groups because the animus is warranted—no one could seriously argue that burglars form a suspect class. . . In giving content to this concept of gross unfairness, the Court has considered (1) whether the disadvantaged class is defined by a trait that "frequently bears no relation to ability to perform or contribute to society" . . . (2) whether the class has been saddled with unique disabilities because of prejudice or inaccurate stereotypes; and (3) whether the trait defining the class is immutable. . . I consider these questions in turn.

Sexual orientation plainly has no relevance to a person's "ability to perform or contribute to society." Sergeant Watkins' exemplary record of military service stands as a testament to quite the opposite. Moreover, as the Army itself concluded, there is not a scintilla of evidence that Watkins' avowed homosexuality "had either a degrading effect upon unit performance, morale, or discipline, or upon his own performance". . .

This irrelevance of sexual orientation to the quality of a person's contribution to society also suggests that classifications based on sexual orientation reflect prejudice and inaccurate stereotypes—the second indicium of a classification's gross unfairness. . . I agree with Justice Brennan that "discrimination against homosexuals is 'likely . . . to reflect deep-seated prejudice rather than . . . rationality.' ". . .

The Army suggests that the opprobrium directed toward gays does not constitute prejudice in the pejorative sense of the word but rather is simply appropriate public disapproval of persons who engage in immoral behavior. . . . The Army equates homosexuals with sodomists and justifies its regulations as simply reflecting a rational bias against a class of persons who engage in criminal acts of sodomy. In essence, the Army argues that homosexuals, like burglars, cannot form a suspect class because they are criminals.

The Army's argument rests on two false premises. First, as I have noted throughout this opinion, the class burdened by the regulations at issue in this case is defined by the sexual orientation of its members, not by their sexual conduct... To my knowledge, homosexual orientation itself has never been criminalized in this country. Moreover, any attempt to criminalize the status of an individual's sexual orientation would present grave constitutional problems...

Second, little of the homosexual conduct covered by the regulations is criminal. The regulations reach many forms of homosexual conduct other than sodomy, such as kissing, hand-holding, caressing, and hand-genital contact. Yet, sodomy is the only consensual adult sexual conduct that Congress has criminalized... Indeed, the Army points to no law, federal or state, which criminalizes any form of private consensual homosexual behavior other than sodomy. The Army's argument that its regulations merely ban a class of criminals might be relevant, although not necessarily persuasive, if the class at issue were limited to sodomists. But the class banned from Army service is not composed of sodomists, or even of homosexual sodomists; the class is composed of persons of homosexual orientation whether or not they have engaged in sodomy.

Watkins v. U.S. Army, 847 F.2d 1329 (9th Cir. 1988).

PUTTING IT INTO PRACTICE

Explain Your Thinking Process

The following selection contains arguments and counterarguments but no explanation for the conclusion. Write an explanation for the conclusion reached.

In *Olson v. Walker,* the defendant combined alcohol with Valium, whereas our client combined alcohol with marijuana. Arguably the combination of Valium and alcohol is more dangerous than the combination of marijuana and alcohol because of the synergistic (multiplicative) effects of Valium and alcohol. When two depressants, such as Valium and alcohol, are taken together, they interact in such a way that their combined effects are greater than the sum of their individual effects. In other words, if the effect of alcohol is 1 and the effect of Valium is 1, their combined effect may be 10 rather than 2. Marijuana, on the other hand, has depressant, stimulant, and hallucinogenic qualities. Users do not experience a synergistic effect when taking it in conjunction with alcohol.

Despite its lack of a synergistic effect, however, marijuana is dangerous either by itself or in combination with alcohol when used before or during driving. Its effects are arguably less predictable than the effects of Valium, because the potency (i.e., the THC content) of marijuana is so variable. Both THC, the primary psychoactive component of marijuana, and Valium impair a driver's reaction time, ability to make decisions, and perception of distance. Which causes more impairment is largely a matter of dosage, and since THC potency is an unknown (since it, unlike Valium, is not prescribed in milligram dosages), the effects of marijuana in combination with alcohol cannot be easily predicted.

(continued)

Putting It into Practice *(continued)*

....

I conclude that our client's consumption of marijuana and alcohol made his conduct just as outrageous as the defendant's conduct in *Olson v. Walker*.

....

Keep It Short

If the aim is to educate your readers with the least amount of effort on their part, then brevity should be your motto. Keep your paragraphs as short as possible. Paragraphs that run on for pages are intimidating to readers. Long paragraphs tend to have too many ideas and can be difficult for the readers to assimilate even if you provide wonderful transitions and lead the readers through every step of the analysis.

Long paragraphs add to the complexity of legal concepts. You should strive to express difficult concepts in as concise and succinct a manner as possible. Again, turn to your own experience for verification. When you are learning a foreign concept, do you appreciate short paragraphs with brief, to-the-point explanations? Or do you enjoy sifting through lengthy paragraphs with ponderous explanations? Write as you prefer to be written to.

Sentences too should be as short as possible without sacrificing content. Sometimes you will find it necessary to write relatively long sentences, because to break up the thought into separate sentences would interfere with your explanation. Just remember that long sentences are not a sign of superior intellect. More often they are a sign of laziness—of a writer who failed to take the time to rewrite. Keep in mind as well that your most powerful sentences will probably be your shortest sentences. When you really want to make a lasting impression, use a short sentence.

To reinforce this concept of brevity, think for a moment of some of the most powerful oratorical statements—"I have a dream," "Physician, heal thyself," "The unexamined life is not worth living." What makes these statements so memorable? In part, the fact that they are short and yet meaningful. Advertising slogans are another prime example of the power of brevity. Effective communicators are masters of verbal efficiency.

You can, however, take brevity to an extreme and make every sentence short. To make your writing more interesting and powerful, vary your sentence length. Short sentences are not powerful if every sentence is short. They gain power because they stand apart from the other sentences. In a nutshell, avoid writing interminably long, convoluted sentences that have to be read several times before they can be understood. And when you have an important point to make, make it using a short sentence.

Notice the effective use of short sentences in the following example. While some of the sentences are intermediate in length, the court expresses its conclusion in short, direct sentences. From this concise summary, the reader is able to glean the gist of the foregoing discussion and immediately comprehend how the court reached its conclusion.

In sum, no federal appellate court has decided the critical issue raised by Watkins' claim: whether persons of homosexual orientation constitute a suspect class under the equal protection doctrine. To be sure, *Hardwick* forecloses Watkins from making a due process claim that the Army's regulations impinge on an asserted fundamental right to engage in homosexual sodomy. But Watkins makes no such claim. Rather, he claims only that the Army's regulations discriminate against him because of his membership in a disfavored group—homosexuals. This claim is not barred by precedent.

Watkins v. U.S. Army, 847 F.2d 1329 (9th Cir. 1988).

PUTTING IT INTO PRACTICE

Keep It Short

Shorten the sentences in the following paragraph without changing the meaning. If you think it needs to be subdivided into more than one paragraph for ease of understanding, do so.

We have to establish "general acceptance" through the court's review of published and peer-reviewed scientific journals and law reviews that are presented to the court by our experts from the relevant scientific communities named above, plus the court would do its own research. There are several points that we must keep in mind when presenting evidence to the court. First, the scientific communities we choose to present to the court must be relevant to DNA theories and procedural uses; at the same time, the relevant scientific community that must be shown to have accepted a new scientific procedure is often self-selecting and yet scientists who have no interest in novel scientific principles are unlikely to evaluate them even though the court determines they are a part of the relevant scientific community. Second, there is no head count as to the number of published and peer-reviewed scientific journals needed to show that "general acceptance" exists. Third, "general acceptance" does not require a showing of universal acceptance of the reliability of the scientific principles and procedures; at the same time, the procedures and principles do not need to be absolutely accurate or certain.

Keep It Simple

In keeping with the theme of brevity, simplicity is another goal toward which to strive. Nothing is served if you write short paragraphs and sentences and use convoluted language in the process. Choose your words carefully and selectively, opting for words that effectively and simply convey ideas. The ideas you are presenting are often complex enough. Do not complicate the matter by using complex terminology.

Simplicity does not require weak words, however. To the contrary, powerful words that conjure up vivid images are preferred. Such words are efficient, in that they create mental images with a minimal use of words, and they are accurate, in that they are likely to create the same mental image in the readers' minds that exists in the writer's mind. For example, if a man is described as "ambling," a clearer

FIGURE 11.5
Words and
Phrases to Avoid

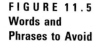

WORDS AND PHRASES TO AVOID

■ **On or before**
....

■ **Heretofore**
....

■ **Herein**
....

■ **For the purpose of**
....

■ **Aforesaid**
....

■ **Hereunto**
....

■ **Per annum**
....

mental image is created than if he is described as "walking slowly and aimlessly." The writer has created a clearer image and used fewer words.

Choose your words, especially your verbs and adjectives, as carefully as you do your wardrobe. You select clothes to convey an image of professionalism or casualness or elegance. Your vocabulary creates an image as well. If you want to bore your readers, you say over and over "The court held," but if you want to create a stronger image in the readers' minds, you choose your verbs more carefully. You might say that "The court articulated" or "The court explained" or "The court pontificated" or "The court bemoaned" or "The court accentuated." If you want to create a vague mental image, you say "It was hot that day." But if you want to create a vivid mental image, you say "The searing sun blistered their skin in a few minutes." The client isn't merely "upset"; the client is "tormented" or "agitated." Your opposition doesn't just "argue"; it "strains to argue" or it "lamely argues." The words you choose must accurately portray what you are describing, but they should be vivid. Accurate, vivid words are more powerful than bland, generic words.

Another aspect of simplicity is the avoidance of extraneous words—words that take up space but whose absence will not affect the meaning of what you are conveying. Legalisms abound in extraneous words—heretofore, aforesaid, herein, thereunto, etc. Eliminate these words from your vocabulary. Do not operate under the delusion that you are more "lawyerly" if you adopt such archaic jargon. When you consider incorporating such a phrase as "in excess of," ask yourself if you couldn't as easily say "more than." Isn't "annually" just as good as "per annum"? Isn't "for" just as effective as "for the purpose of," "by" more concise than "on or before," and "use" more succinct than "utilize"? Must you tell someone you are giving them your "honest opinion"? Can't we assume that any opinion you give will be honest? Why say "In the case of *X v. Y*" when you can simply say "In *X v. Y*"?

When reviewing your writing, take on the role of an efficiency expert. Imagine that each word costs you money. Then eliminate every word that is duplicative, archaic, or otherwise unnecessary. Be tough with yourself but fair. Do not eliminate important words in the name of efficiency, and do not change the meaning in the process.

PUTTING IT INTO PRACTICE

Keep It Simple
Simplify the following sentences, eliminating unnecessary words.

1. With respect to the apparent age of the sample, it is accepted that age is one of the problems that can arise in extracting DNA.

2. In trying to construct a defense for our client by convincingly arguing that the heroin seized from him during a pat-down search should be inadmissible, it will first be necessary to try to determine whether or not the Arizona Supreme Court will follow the "plain feel" rule first set forth in *Minnesota v. Dickerson*,— U.S.—, 113 S.Ct. 2130 (1993), or rely on its own past opinion that there is no "plain feel" exception to the Fourth Amendment as it is stated in *State v. Collins*, 139 Ariz. 434, 679 P.2d 80 (App. 1983).

3. While heretofore we might have argued that inasmuch as strict scrutiny was reserved for ethnic and racial groups, we must for purposes of our discussion concede that in the light of such cases as *Watkins v. U.S. Army* in the not-too-distant future this same demanding level of review will be brought to the forefront for the purpose of reviewing cases involving socially stigmatized groups.

4. There is no doubt in my mind that after all is said and done the Supreme Court will stick to its guns and refuse to entertain even the possibility that it overturn precedent in this area.

Say What Is Important First

Reserve the beginning of sentences for the most important part of your message. Do not stash the subject of the sentence away in the middle or leave it to the end. Say it up front. Consider the following example.

> The court had to resolve the issue of whether or not subject matter jurisdiction existed.

The writer is trying to convey the nature of the issue the court had to resolve. Why not let the readers know in the first few words what this issue was?

> Subject matter jurisdiction was the issue the court had to resolve.

Here is another example.

> We must identify the appropriate scientific community whose general acceptance of the DNA theory and testing technique is required in order to satisfy the "general acceptance" test of *Frye*.

Again, you are not aware of the subject matter until the end of the sentence. How much easier on the readers to apprise them up front.

To satisfy the "general acceptance" test of *Frye*, we must identify the appropriate scientific community whose general acceptance of the DNA theory and testing technique is required.

PUTTING IT INTO PRACTICE

Say What Is Important First
Make the following sentences easier to read by putting the most important part of the sentence at the beginning.

1. Lack of legislative accountability is a major criticism of underinclusive statutes.

2. What is accepted at one time may be found to be completely wrong at a later time because science is not a collection of facts but rather an ongoing search for truth.

3. Due to the suspect's reaching inside his coat pocket, the officer had reason to believe that the suspect had a weapon.

4. Because of the likelihood that substantive flaws in methodology will be detected, a testing technique should be subjected to peer review and publication.

AVOIDING LONG QUOTATIONS

Do you enjoy reading extensive quotations? Or do you have a tendency to skip over those quotations, hoping that they are not crucial to your understanding? Going back to the "golden rule" of good writing, do not inflict on others what you would not have inflicted on yourself. Few people have the discipline required to read through lengthy quotations. Therefore, if you feel you must quote, pick out the essential phrases or words and express the remainder in your own words. If you absolutely cannot forego the quote (on the grounds that the court or legal commentator said it so much better than you could), then either before or after the quote explain what they said in your own words. Such paraphrasing will discourage you from too easily succumbing to the temptation to quote. You will find that there are few expressions that are so eloquent that they must be quoted.

On the other hand, in some cases quoting is necessary. If you are discussing a statute, ordinance, or regulation, you must quote the relevant parts. If you are discussing a contract, you should quote the sections at issue. If you need to convey a court's or party's exact words, especially if legal terms are being used, then you should quote. The latter is a judgment call. If you are not sure that you could accurately paraphrase what is being said, first quote and then paraphrase. The readers can then decide if you have paraphrased accurately.

EXAMPLE OF EXTENSIVE USE OF QUOTES

FIGURE 11.6
Avoiding
Extensive Quoting

■ Misrepresentation

➤ "A contract may be rescinded for material misrepresentations of fact which have been relied upon by the parties seeking rescission." *Hilburn v. General Electric Credit Corp.*, 442 P.2d 547 (Ariz. App. 1968). "Notwithstanding the absence of an intent to deceive, an action for rescission may be found upon a mispresentation innocently or negligently made." *Hubbs v. Costello*, 528 P.2d 1257 (Ariz. App. 1974). To establish fraudulent mispresentation "plaintiff must prove representation, its falsity, its materiality, speaker's knowledge of its falsity or ignorance of its truth, his intent that it should be acted upon by and in manner reasonably contemplated, hearer's ignorance of falsity, his reliance on its truth, his right to rely thereon, and his consequent and proximate injury; and if one or more of such elements are not present case must fail." *Godfrey v. Navratil*, 440 P.2d 665 (Ariz. App. 1966). "A promise to do something in the future, made with a present intent not to perform, will give rise to an action in fraud; such promissory fraud lies not in the subsequent failure to perform but in the misrepresentation of present state of mind." *Berry v. Roberta*, 443 P.2d 461 (Ariz. App. 1969).

AVOIDING THE "IN X V. Y" CONSTRUCTION

Tempting as it may be to begin each sentence "In *U.S. v. White*, the court held . . . while in *U.S. v. Black*, the court held . . .," avoid this configuration as much as possible. A preferable way to discuss case law is to set forth the holding of the court in terms that make its relevance to the case at hand clear and to then identify the court using a citation at the end of the sentence.

> When a court is faced with an equal protection claim, it must use one of three levels of review. *City of Cleburne v. Cleburne Living Center*, 473 U.S. 432 (1985). To determine the appropriate level of review, the court must first decide whether the statute affects a suspect class. *Id.* at 439. A suspect class is one that has endured a history of purposeful and invidious discrimination and lacks the political power to obtain redress from the political branches of government. *Watkins v. U.S. Army*, 875 F.2d 699 (9th Cir. 1989).

Notice how this paragraph reads much more fluently than the following paragraph.

In *City of Cleburne v. Cleburne Living Center,* 473 U.S. 432 (1985), the Court held that equal protection claims require the use of one of three levels of review. The Court also held that before determining the appropriate level of review, a court must first decide whether the statute affects a suspect class. In *Watkins v. U.S. Army,* 875 F.2d 699 (9th Cir. 1989), the court held that a suspect class is one that has endured a history of purposeful and invidious discrimination and that lacks the political power to obtain redress from the political branches of government.

Citations at the beginning of sentences tend to interfere with the legal concepts being presented. They grab the readers' attention and divert it away from the more important concepts presented within the sentence.

You will find it tempting to use the "In X *v.* Y, the court held . . ." construction because it relieves you of the responsibility of connecting one case to another. Transitions tend to disappear, and your memo becomes a string of cases discussed one after another with no mention of how they are all related. You can avoid this trap by incorporating transitional words into your writing and always asking "Why am I discussing this case?" and "How does this case relate to the previous case and the next case?"

PUTTING IT INTO PRACTICE

Avoiding the "In *X v. Y*" Construction

Rewrite the following selection, putting citations at the ends of sentences wherever possible.

According to Laurence Tribe, *American Constitutional Law,* Sec. 1440 n. 4 (2d ed. 1988), the Court rarely invalidates underinclusive laws. In *Railway Express Agency v. New York,* 336 U.S. 106 (1949), the Court allowed an underinclusive classification to pass the rational basis test. The ordinance at issue demanded that vehicles displaying advertising be banned as traffic distractions but excluded vehicles advertising their own products. The rationale of the majority was that equal protection does not demand that "all evil of the same genus be eradicated or none at all." *Id.* at 109. In other cases, such as *Minnesota v. Clover Leaf,* 449 U.S. at 446 (1976), and *Katzenbach v. Morgan,* 384 U.S. 641 (1966), the courts have allowed this step-by-step method of addressing legislative concerns. On the other hand, in *Rinaldi v. Yeagar,* 384 U.S. 305 (1966), an underinclusive statute failed rational basis review. In this case, a New Jersey statute required unsuccessful appellants who were subsequently imprisoned to repay the cost of trial transcript preparation. Other categories of unsuccessful appellants sentenced to probation or fined were not required to reimburse the state's expenses. The Court concluded that despite the state's legitimate interest in reimbursement, the statute's underinclusiveness belied its assertion that its actual purpose was not invidious discrimination.

MECHANICS OF GOOD WRITING

Proper Tense

While it may not seem to be a major concern when you have all of the foregoing factors to consider, improper tense can be annoying to the reader. The following conventions are observed in legal writing.

When discussing a case that has already been decided, use the past tense.

> The *Blake* court held that general acceptance does not require acceptance by everyone in the relevant scientific community.

When writing about the facts of your case, use the past tense if those events occurred in the past but use the present tense if the events are still ongoing.

> While the plaintiff may have overreacted at the time of the incident, she continues to fear for her safety.

Discussion of statutes or rules should be in the present tense as long as they are still in effect.

> The Model Penal Code provides for the punishment of corporate officials who commit crimes within the scope of their duties.

Your own arguments as well as your opponent's arguments should be phrased in the present tense.

> While the respondents maintain that no confidential relationship existed, we can identify several factors that point to the existence of confidential relations.

PUTTING IT INTO PRACTICE
. . . .

Proper Tense
Correct the tense errors in the following sentences.

1. In *Olson v. Walker,* the defendant drives under the influence of alcohol in combination with Valium, causing an accident because of his reckless driving. Our client, on the other hand, drove under the influence of alcohol and marijuana. The *Olson* court reasons that intoxication alone does not justify the award of punitive damages, but the plaintiff in our case argued that our client was not only intoxicated but drove in such an outrageous manner that he created a substantial risk of injury to others.

2. In *Dickerson,* the police continue their pat-down search of the defendant because they feel a small lump in the defendant's pocket. After manipulating, squeezing, and pushing the lump, they deduce that the lump is crack cocaine. The Court refuses to allow the admission of the cocaine into evidence because it finds that the search exceeds the bounds of *Terry.*

(continued)

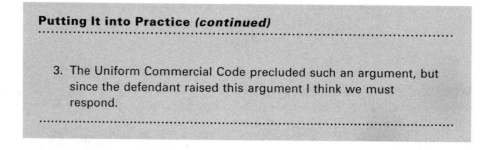

Putting It into Practice *(continued)*

3. The Uniform Commercial Code precluded such an argument, but since the defendant raised this argument I think we must respond.

Spelling

Avoid spelling errors—they make you appear ignorant. Even the most brilliant prose appears substandard if it is littered with spelling errors. Use computer aids to check your spelling. Have knowledgeable readers edit your work, looking for spelling errors. If your spelling proficiency is questionable, begin by making sure that you can at least accurately differentiate between all of the paired words in the following list. Then consider pursuing a course of study or practice that will assist you in gradually expanding the list of words that you have mastered.

Advice; advise

Affect; effect

Already; all ready

Are; our

Cite; site

Conscious; conscience

Defendants; defendant's; defendants' (and similar nouns such as court, plaintiff, etc.)

Infer; imply

Its; it's

Preceding; proceeding

Principal; principle

Rational; rationale

Reckless; wreck

Then; than

There; their; they're

Note that some of these words involve the proper use of the apostrophe. If you have forgotten the rules regarding the use of apostrophes, review them at once.

Grammar

The scope of this text precludes a review of grammatical rules. The most common grammatical errors I have seen involve run-on sentences, sentence fragments (incomplete sentences), lack of parallelism, and lack of subject-verb agreement. If you have reason to suspect that you might need to refresh your recollection of the rules of grammar, please do so before submitting a writing sample to an attorney or instructor. Command of the English language includes a command of its rules. At this level of education, those who read your writing are not unreasonable in expecting that you have mastered the rules of grammar.

General Appearance

Lawyers are accustomed to receiving memos and other writings that are professional in appearance. What does a professional appearance entail? The document should be neat and unsoiled. (Stains, wrinkles, tears, etc., are unacceptable.) Corrections should be invisible to the naked eye (which means that white-out should be avoided). In this day of readily available technology, memos should be printed out on word processors rather than conventional typewriters.

FIGURE 11.7
Corollaries of Golden Rule of Good Writing

COROLLARIES OF GOLDEN RULE OF GOOD WRITING

1. **Use thesis and topic sentences to introduce topics.**

2. **Use transitions to connect sentences and paragraphs.**

3. **Use headings to guide the reader.**

4. **Explain your thought process.**

5. **Keep sentences and paragraphs as short as possible.**

6. **Use simple, powerful language and avoid extraneous verbiage.**

7. **Express important ideas first.**

8. **Avoid long quotations.**

9. **Avoid the "In *X* v. *Y*" construction.**

10. **Use proper tense, spelling, and grammar.**

Good Writing in a Nutshell

Good legal writing, as any good writing, is concise and clear. It leads the readers easily and relatively effortlessly through a maze of legal principles using precise but powerful language. It does not deliberately confuse or distract the readers. It has no spelling or grammatical errors. The legal citations blend into the writing and are presented in such a way that they inform rather than divert the readers from the subject being discussed. Above all, good legal writing reflects the "golden rule" of writing—write as you would prefer to be written to.

Chapter Summary

Simplicity and clarity are the keys to good legal writing. Clarity is best achieved by giving the reader a verbal road map. Such a road map can be constructed using thesis and topic sentences, transitions, and headings. Explaining your thought processes also assists the reader in tracking your reasoning. Simplicity can be achieved by making sentences and paragraphs as short as possible, by carefully choosing powerful but efficient language, and by avoiding extraneous verbiage. Expressing important ideas at the beginning of sentences, avoiding extensive quoting, and minimizing the use of the " In X v. Y" construction will also improve the quality of your writing, as will the use of proper tense, spelling, and grammar.

KEY TERMS

thesis sentence
topic sentence

COGNITIVE CALISTHENICS

1. Read over the paragraph below and make the following corrections.
   (a) Add a topic sentence.
   (b) Add transitions.
   (c) Shorten the sentences, if possible, and modify any language you find unclear.

   In *Daubert*, the Court focuses on whether or not the evidence is reliable, relevant, valid, and assists the trier of the fact in determining the issue at hand. In *Frye*, the court focuses on whether or not there is "general acceptance" within the relevant scientific communities. In *Daubert*, "general acceptance" is not dispositive of the evidence being admissible. Under *Frye*, relatively new or novel scientific evidence won't be recognized if there is not sufficient general acceptance within the relevant scientific communities. Under *Daubert*, new or novel scientific evidence will be allowed on the basis of the expert's qualifications, reliability, and the validity of the theory and/or technique which will be established through the expert who is qualified as reliable and then presented to the trier of fact who then compares the probative value of the evidence to the prejudicial weight of the evidence before deciding upon its admissibility. Under *Daubert*, the evidentiary gatekeeper is the court, but under *Frye*, the evidentiary gatekeeper is the relevant scientific communities.

2. Read the following selection to gain an understanding of the concepts being presented. Once you think you grasp the basic ideas, consider how they could be presented in a simpler manner and rewrite the selection. Focus on simplicity and brevity. Eliminate any unnecessary repetition and reorganize if necessary.

   The rational basis test is a highly deferential standard of review for equal protection claims. Key words at that level are that there must be a "legitimate government interest" and that the statutory means selected by the legislature must be "rationally related" to that interest. This level of review is appropriate for social and economic legislation where states are allowed wide latitude.

   Although states may accord more rights to their citizens under their respective constitutions, the correct standard for a state court to use when evaluating a statute under the Fourteenth Amendment of the U.S. Constitution is that standard that would be used by the U.S. Supreme Court. Therefore, to deviate from this mandatory authority is to risk reversal by the U.S. Supreme Court.

   In discussion of the rational basis test, fact deference is to the state legislature's determination. A court may look at the actual purpose of the legislature's actions or any hypothetical purpose to determine if the legislature's actions were arbitrary. Therefore, it appears as if the rational basis test is essentially a rubber stamp to validate legislative laws.

   A resulting inequality is not grounds upon which to find a statute invalid when applying the rational basis test. Therefore, the most unfairness is found at this level of review.

   Upon examination of an overinclusive statute, that is, one affecting more people than necessary, it appears as if a government interest must be more compelling than merely legitimate. Therefore, an overinclusive statute is less likely than other inequities to be found constitutional at this level of review.

   On the other hand, underinclusive statutes are more likely to pass the rational basis test. Because the legislature is permitted to experiment and take one step at a time in addressing an issue, courts have consistently upheld statutes in this category. Therefore, most underinclusive statutes are constitutional if they address a legitimate government interest.

   A legitimate government interest can be found almost anywhere under the rational basis test. Because a court is free to hypothesize, a legitimate interest can be found even where perhaps none existed at either the time of a statute's inception or at the time the legislation is being examined. It is unlikely that a legitimate government interest will not be found by a court when examining a statute at this level of review.

   Additionally, the connection between the means and the objective of the statute can be quite loose. It does not matter if in reality the statute is not working toward achieving its actual or hypothetical objective. And it does not matter if the objective is no longer a valid one. So long as the court perceives that the legislature could have seen a connection at the time a statute came into being, the statute will not offend the constitution under the rational basis test. The rationale for this is that unjustness will be remedied by the democratic process. Therefore, the connection between a statute's means and objective can be loose, although not totally arbitrary.

3. Read over the following selection to gain an understanding of the concepts being presented. Once you think you have grasped the basic ideas, rewrite the selection using shorter sentences and changing the tense where appropriate. Reorganize if you find it necessary, and indicate what information is missing that you think should have been included to allow the reader to better understand the standard set forth by the *Daubert* Court.

   In determining admissibility of scientific evidence under *Daubert*, a court should weigh general acceptance in the relevant scientific community along with the following factors: whether the evidence will assist the trier of fact to understand the evidence or to determine a fact at issue; whether the evidence will add to the common understanding of the jury; whether the underlying theory is generally accepted as valid; whether the procedures used are generally accepted as reliable if performed properly; and whether the procedures were applied and conducted properly in the present instance, and the court should then consider whether admitting the evidence will be more probative than prejudicial.

Relevancy of the subject matter (a standard discussed in *Daubert*) must be proven, however, "general acceptance" is not a necessary precondition to the admissibility of scientific evidence under the Federal Rules of Evidence, but the Rules of Evidence—especially Rule 702—do assign to the trial judge the task of ensuring that an expert's testimony both rests on a reliable foundation and is relevant to the task at hand.

The *Daubert* Court does not explicitly define scientific validity or apply its new teaching to the evidence at issue in that case, but it does begin to draw the parameters of this inquiry by providing the following nonexclusive list of factors, which can be considered to be the elements that must be proven until said time that the list is further modified by adjudication.

- The theory or technique can be (and has been) used.

- The theory or technique has been subjected to peer review publication.

- The known or potential rate of error in using a particular scientific technique and the existence and maintenance of standards controlling the technique's operation exist.

- The theory or technique has been generally accepted in the particular scientific field.

The *Daubert* Court has instructed the courts that they are not to be concerned with the reliability of the conclusions generated by valid methods, principles, and reasoning. Rather, they are only to determine whether the principles and methodology underlying the testimony itself are valid. If the principles, methodology, and reasoning are scientifically valid, then it follows that the inferences, assertions, and conclusions derived therefrom are scientifically valid as well.

4. Write out the directions from your house to your favorite restaurant. Concentrate on making the directions concise and clear. Give the directions to someone who is not familiar with the restaurant of your choice and ask for feedback on their clarity.

5. Choose a controversial subject (abortion, gun control, capital punishment, etc.) and explain your position on it. Anticipate the responses of your opponents and include your rebuttal to the anticipated arguments. Have someone else review what you have written and ask them to summarize your position. Then assess how clearly you stated your position.

APPENDIX A

Contents

Ronald A. WEIRUM et al., Plaintiffs and Appellants,
v.
RKO GENERAL, INC., Defendant and Appellant, Marsha L. Baime, Defendant and Appellant.
L.A. 30452.
Supreme Court of California.
Aug. 21, 1975.

An action was brought for wrongful death of plaintiff's decedent who was killed when his automobile was negligently forced off a highway by a listener to defendant's radio station which was conducting a contest rewarding the first contestant to locate a peripatetic disc jockey. The District Court, Ventura County, Marvin H. Lewis, J., entered judgment for plaintiffs against radio broadcaster and it appealed. The Supreme Court, Mosk, J., held that evidence supported jury finding of foreseeability of injury or death in that it was foreseeable that broadcaster's youthful listeners, finding the prize had eluded them at one location, would race to arrive first at the next site and in their haste disregard demands of highway safety; the court further held that broadcaster was not insulated from such liability on basis of deference due society's interest in the First Amendment; it was further held that broadcaster could not escape liability on basis that it had no duty to control conduct of third parties, in view of fact broadcaster's liability was grounded upon an affirmative act of misfeasance creating an undue risk of harm, and not upon mere nonfeasance.

Judgment and orders affirmed.

Opinion, Cal.App., 119 Cal.Rptr. 151 vacated.

1. **Negligence k136(2)**   The determination of existence of a duty of due care is primarily a question of law.

2. **Negligence k2**   Any number of considerations may justify imposition of a duty of due care in particular circumstances, including guidance of history, refined concepts of morals and justice, convenience of the rule, and social judgment as to where loss should fall.

3. **Negligence k2**   While question of whether one owes a duty of due care to another must be decided on a case-by-case basis, every case is governed by rule of general application that all persons are required to use ordinary care to prevent others from being injured as the result of their conduct.

4. **Negligence k10**   Foreseeability of risk is a primary consideration in establishing element of duty of due care.

5. **Negligence 136(16)**   While existence of duty of due care is a question of law, foreseeability of risk of harm from an activity is a question of fact for the jury.

6. **Appeal and Error k1001(1), 1002**   Review of implied jury finding of foreseeability of risk of harm was limited to a determination of whether there was any substantial evidence, contradicted or uncontradicted, supporting the finding.

7. **Automobiles k244(22)**   Evidence, in action for wrongful death arising out of an automobile collision allegedly caused by negligence of defendant radio station in conducting a contest wherein contestants had to drive their automobiles and be the first to locate a peripatetic disc jockey, supported jury finding of foreseeability of injury or death in that it was foreseeable that broadcaster's youthful listeners, finding the prize had eluded them at one location, would race to arrive first at the next site and in their haste disregard demands of highway safety.

8. **Automobiles k197(1)**   A radio broadcaster was not excused from liability for negligence in sponsoring a radio contest under which it was foreseeable that listeners, in order to win a prize, would race about in their automobiles to be first to arrive at a certain site wherein a disc jockey of the broadcaster would appear, on basis that harm, if any, to other

persons would be inflicted by third parties acting negligently; such concept is valid, only to extent intervening concept cannot be anticipated.

9. **Negligence k10**   If the likelihood that a third person may react in a particular manner is a hazard which makes the actor negligent, such reaction whether innocent or negligent does not prevent the actor from being liable for the harm caused thereby.

10. **Negligence k1**   Liability for negligence is imposed only if the risk of harm resulting from the act is deemed unreasonable—that is, if the gravity and likelihood of the danger outweigh the utility of the conduct involved.

11. **Constitutional Law k90.1(9)**   A radio broadcaster's liability for negligence in conducting a giveaway contest in such manner as to create a high risk of injury or death to motorists and pedestrians was not insulated from such liability on basis of deference due society's interest in the First Amendment. U.S.C.A.Const. Amend. 1.

12. **Automobiles k197(1)**   Imposition of duty of due care upon a radio broadcaster in regard to conducting of a contest requiring listeners to move about in their automobiles and find a certain disc jockey would not be denied upon basis that it might lead to unwarranted extensions of liability to other entrepreneurs.

13. **Automobiles k197(1)**   A radio broadcaster which sponsored a contest rewarding first contestant locating a peripatetic disc jockey, could not escape liability on basis that it had no duty to control conduct of third parties in manner in which they drove their automobiles, in view of fact broadcaster's liability was grounded upon an affirmative act of misfeasance creating an undue risk of harm, and not upon mere nonfeasance.

14. **Appeal and Error k882(12)**   Defendant could not attack substance of instruction requested by plaintiff where defendant himself proposed a similar instruction.

15. **Trial k312(1)**   A trial court possesses inherent right on its own motion to recall jurors for further instructions.

16. **Appeal and Error k1069.3**   Recalling of jury in a negligence action during third day of its deliberations for reading to it of an unintentionally omitted instruction would not be considered prejudicial on basis of overemphasis where prefatory remarks of trial judge minimized any such tendency and where defendant failed to request either additional cautionary instructions or a rereading of all related instructions.

Robert O. Angle, Hollister & Brace, and Richard C. Monk, Santa Barbara, for plaintiffs and appellants.

Stearns & Nelson, Stearns, Nelson & LeBerthon, Robert S. Stearns, Hollywood, Lascher & Radar, Edward L. Lascher and Wendy Cole Wilner, Ventura, for defendant and appellant.

Benton, Orr, Duval, Buckingham and James F. McGahan, Ventura, for defendant and respondents.

MOSK, Justice.   *crucial to negligence*

A rock radio station with an extensive teenage audience conducted a contest which rewarded the first contestant to locate a peripatetic disc jockey. Two minors driving in separate automobiles attempted to follow the disc jockey's automobile to its next stop. In the course of their pursuit, one of the minors negligently forced a car off the highway, killing its sole occupant. In a suit filed by the surviving wife and children of the decedent, the jury rendered a verdict against the radio station. We now must determine whether the station owed decedent a duty of due care.

The facts are not disputed. Radio station KHJ is a successful Los Angeles broadcaster with a large teenage following. At the time of the accident, KHJ commanded a 48 percent plurality of the teenage audience in the Los Angeles area. In contrast, its nearest rival during the same period was able to capture only 13 percent of the teenage listeners. In order to attract an even larger portion of the available audience and thus increase advertising revenue, KHJ inaugurated in July of 1970 a promotion entitled "The Super Summer Spectacular." The "spectacular," with a budget of approximately $40,000 for the month, was specifically designed to make the radio station "more exciting." Among the programs included in the "spectacular" was a contest broadcast on July 16, 1970, the date of the accident.

On that day, Donald Steele Revert, known professionally as "The Real Don Steele," a KHJ disc jockey and television personality, traveled in a conspicuous red automobile to a number of locations in the Los Angeles metropolitan area. Periodically, he apprised KHJ of his whereabouts and his intended destination, and the station broadcast the information to its listeners. The first person to physically locate Steele and fulfill a specified condition received a cash prize. In addition, the winning contestant participated in a brief interview on the air with "The Real Don Steele." The following excerpts from the July 16 broadcast illustrate the tenor of the contest announcements:

certain time and place

1. The conditions varied from the giving of a correct response to a question to the possession of particular items of clothing.

"9:30 and The Real Don Steele is back on his feet again with some money and he is headed for the Valley. Thought I would give you a warning so that you can get your kids out of the street."

"The Real Don Steele is out driving on— could be in your neighborhood at any time and he's got bread to spread, so be on the lookout for him."

"The Real Don Steele is moving into Canoga Park—so be on the lookout for him. I'll tell you what will happen if you get to The Real Don Steele. He's got twenty-five dollars to give away if you can get it . . . and baby, all signed and sealed and delivered and wrapped up."

"10:54—The Real Don Steele is in the Valley near the intersection of Topanga and Roscoe Boulevard, right by the Loew's Holiday Theater—you know where that is at, and he's standing there with a little money he would like to give away to the first person to arrive and tell him what type car I helped Robert W. Morgan give away yesterday morning at KHJ. What was the make of the car. If you know that, split. Intersection of Topanga and Roscoe Boulevard— right nearby the Loew's Holiday Theater—you will find The Real Don Steele. Tell him and pick up the bread."

In Van Nuys, a 17-year-old Robert Sentner was listening to KHJ in his car while searching for "The Real Don Steele." Upon hearing that "The Real Don Steele" was proceeding to Canoga Park, he immediately drove to that vicinity. Meanwhile in Northridge, 19-year-old Marsha Baime heard and responded to the same information. Both of them arrived at the Holiday Theater in Canoga Park to find that someone had already claimed the prize. Without knowledge of the other, each decided to follow the Steele vehicle to its next stop and thus be the first to arrive when the next contest question or condition was announced.

For the next few miles the Sentner and Baime cars jockeyed for position closest to the Steele vehicle, reaching speeds up to 80 miles an hour.[2] About a mile and a half from the Westlake offramp the two teenagers heard the following broadcast:

"11:13—The Real Don Steele with bread is heading for Thousand Oaks to give it away. Keep listening to KHJ . . . The Real Don Steele out on the highway—with bread to give away—be on the lookout, he may stop in Thousand Oaks and may stop along the way. . . . Looks like it may be a

good stop Steele—drop some bread to those folks."

The Steele vehicle left the freeway at the Westlake offramp. Either Baime or Sentner, in attempting to follow, forced decedent's car onto the center divider, where it overturned. Baime stopped to report the accident. Sentner, after pausing momentarily to relate the tragedy to a passing peace officer, continued to pursue Steele, successfully located him and collected a cash prize.

Decedent's wife and children brought an action for wrongful death against Sentner, Baime, RKO General, Inc. as owner of KHJ, and the maker of decedent's car. Sentner settled prior to the commencement of trial for the limits of his insurance policy. The jury returned a verdict against Baime and KHJ in the amount of $300,000 and found in favor of the manufacturer of decedent's car. KHJ appeals from the ensuing judgment and from an order denying its motion for judgment notwithstanding the verdict. Baime did not appeal.[3]

[1–4] The primary question for our determination is whether defendant owed a duty to decedent arising out of its broadcast of the giveaway contest. The determination of duty is primarily a question of law. (*Amaya v. Home Ice, Fuel & Supply Co.* (1963) 59 Cal.2d 295, 307, 29 Cal.Rptr. 33, 379 P.2d 513 (overruled on other grounds in *Dillon v. Legg* (1968) 68 Cal.2d 728, 748, 69 Cal.Rptr. 72, 441 P.2d 912).) It is the court's "expression of the sum total of those considerations of policy which lead the law to say that the particular plaintiff is entitled to protection." (Prosser, Law of Torts (4th ed. 1971) pp. 325–326.) Any number of considerations may justify the imposition of duty in particular circumstances, including the guidance of history, our continually refined concepts of morals and justice, the convenience of the rule, and social judgment as to where the loss should fall. (Prosser, *Palsgraf Revisited* (1953) 52 Mich.L.Rev. 1, 15.) While the question whether one owes a duty to another must be decided on a case-by-case basis,[4] every

---

2. It is not contended that the Steele vehicle at any time exceeded the speed limit.

---

3. Plaintiffs filed a cross-appeal from an order entered after judgment denying them certain costs against Baime and KHJ. They do not assert before this court that the order was erroneous, and we shall therefore affirm the order on the cross-appeal.

---

4. Defendant urges that we apply the factors enumerated in *Connor v. Great Western Savings and Loan Association* (1968) 69 Cal.2d 850, 865, 73 Cal.Rptr. 369, 447 P.2d 609, in determining whether it owed a duty to a decedent. In that case, however, the primary issue was whether a duty was to be imposed upon the defendant notwithstanding the absence

case is governed by the rule of general application that all persons are required to use ordinary care to prevent others from being injured as the result of their conduct. (*Hilyar v. Union Ice Co.* (1955) 45 Cal.2d 30, 36, 286 P.2d 21.) However, foreseeability of the risk is a primary consideration in establishing the element of duty. (*Dillon v. Legg, supra,* 68 Cal.2d 728, 739, 69 Cal.Rptr. 72, 441 P.2d 912) Defendant asserts that the record here does not support a conclusion that a risk of harm to decedent was foreseeable.

[5,6] While duty is a question of law, foreseeability is a question of fact for the jury. (*Wright v. Arcade School Dist.* (1964) 230 Cal.App.2d 272, 277, 40 Cal.Rptr. 812.) The verdict in plaintiffs' favor here necessarily embraced a finding that decedent was exposed to a foreseeable risk of harm. It is elementary that our review of this finding is limited to the determination whether there is any substantial evidence, contradicted or uncontradicted, which will support the conclusion reached by the jury.

[7] We conclude that the record amply supports the finding of foreseeability. These tragic events unfolded in the middle of a Los Angeles summer, a time when young people were free from the constraints of school and responsive to relief from vacation tedium. Seeking to attract new listeners, KHJ devised an "exciting" promotion. Money and a small measure of momentary notoriety awaited the swiftest response. It was foreseeable that defendant's youthful listeners, finding the prize had eluded them at one location, would race to arrive first at the next site and in their haste would disregard the demands of highway safety.

Indeed, "The Real Don Steele" testified that he had in the past noticed vehicles following him from location to location. He was further aware that the same contestants sometimes appeared at consecutive stops. This knowledge is not rendered irrelevant, as defendant suggests, by the absence of any prior injury. Such an argument confuses foreseeability with hindsight, and amounts to a contention that the injuries of the first victim are not compensable. "The mere fact that a particular kind of an accident has not happened before does not ... show that such accident is one which might not reasonably have been anticipated." (*Ridley v. Grifall Trucking Co.* (1955) 136 Cal.App.2d

682, 686, 289 P.2d 31, 34.) Thus, the fortuitous absence of prior injury does not justify relieving defendant from responsibility for the foreseeable consequences of its acts.

[8,9] It is of no consequence that the harm to decedent was inflicted by third parties acting negligently. Defendant invokes the maxim that an actor is entitled to assume that others will not act negligently. (*Porter v. California Jockey Club, Inc.* (1955) 134 Cal.App.2d 158, 160, 285 P.2d 60.) This concept is valid, however, only to the extent the intervening conduct was not to be anticipated. (*Premo v. Grigg* (1965) 237 Cal.App.2d 192, 195, 46 Cal.Rptr. 683.) If the likelihood that a third person may react in a particular manner is a hazard which makes the actor negligent, such reaction whether innocent or negligent does not prevent the actor from being liable for the harm caused thereby. (*Richardson v. Ham* (1955) 44 Cal.2d 772, 777, 285 P.2d 269.) Here, reckless conduct by youthful contestants, stimulated by defendant's broadcast, constituted the hazard to which decedent was exposed.

[10] It is true, of course, that virtually every act involves some conceivable danger. Liability is imposed only if the risk of harm resulting from the act is deemed unreasonable—i.e., if the gravity and likelihood of the danger outweigh the utility of the conduct involved. (See Prosser, Law of Torts (4th ed. 1971) pp. 146–149.)

We need not belabor the grave danger inherent in the contest broadcast by defendant. The risk of a high speed automobile chase is the risk of death or serious injury. Obviously, neither the entertainment afforded by the contest nor its commercial rewards can justify the creation of such a grave risk. Defendant could have accomplished its objectives of entertaining its listeners and increasing advertising revenues by adopting a contest format which would have avoided danger to the motoring public.

[11] Defendant's contention that the giveaway contest must be afforded the deference due society's interest in the First Amendment is clearly without merit. The issue here is civil accountability for the foreseeable results of a broadcast which created an undue risk of harm to decedent. The First Amendment does not sanction the infliction of physical injury merely because achieved by word, rather than act.

[12] We are not persuaded that the imposition of a duty here will lead to unwarranted extensions of liability. Defendant is fearful that entrepreneurs will henceforth be burdened with an avalanche of obligations: an athletic department will owe a duty to an ardent sports fan injured while hastening to purchase one of a limited number of tickets; a department store will be liable to injuries incurred in response to a

---

of privity, and we therefore examined considerations appropriate to that contractual framework. For example, the first of the enumerated elements was the extent to which the transaction was intended to affect the plaintiff. Such a consideration manifestly fails to illuminate our inquiry in the present case. Generally speaking, standards relevant to the determination of duty in one particular situation may not be applied mechanically to other cases.

"while-they-last" sale. This argument, however, suffers from a myopic view of the facts presented here. The giveaway contest was no commonplace invitation to an attraction available on a limited basis. It was a competitive scramble in which the thrill of the chase to be the one and only victor was intensified by the live broadcasts which accompanied the pursuit. In the assertedly analogous situations described by defendant, any haste involved in the purchase of the commodity is an incidental and unavoidable result of the scarcity of the commodity itself. In such situations there is no attempt, as here, to generate a competitive pursuit on public streets, accelerated by repeated importuning by radio to be the very first to arrive at a particular destination. Manifestly the "spectacular" bears little resemblance to daily commercial activities.

[13] Defendant, relying upon the rule stated in section 315 of the Restatment Second of Torts, urges that it owed no duty of care to decedent. The section provides that, absent a special relationship, an actor is under no duty to control the conduct of third parties. As explained hereinafter, this rule has no application if the plaintiff's complaint, as here, is grounded upon an affirmative act of defendant which created an undue risk of harm.

The rule stated in section 315 is merely a refinement of the general principle embodied in section 314[5] that one is not obligated to act as a "good samaritan." (Rest.2d Torts, § 314, com. (a); James, *Scope of Duty in Negligence Cases* (1953) 47 Nw.U.L.Rev. 778, 803.) This doctrine is rooted in the common law distinction between action and inaction, or misfeasance and nonfeasance. Misfeasance exists when the defendant is responsible for making the plaintiff's position worse, i.e., defendant has created a risk. Conversely, nonfeasance is found when the defendant has failed to aid plaintiff through beneficial intervention. As section 315 illustrates, liability for nonfeasance is largely limited to those circumstances in which some special relationship can be established. If, on the other hand, the act complained of is one of misfeasance, the question of duty is governed by the standards of ordinary care discussed above.

Here, there can be little doubt that we review an act of misfeasance to which section 315 is inapplicable. Liability is not predicated upon defendant's failure to intervene for the benefit of decedent but rather upon its creation of an unreasonable risk of harm to him. (*See Shafer v. Keeley Ice Cream Co.* (1925), 65

Utah 46, 234 P. 300.)[6] Defendant's reliance upon cases which involve the failure to prevent harm to another is therefore misplaced, e.g., *Wright v. Arcade School Distr., supra*, 230 Cal.App.2d 272, 40 Cal.Rptr. 812 (school district held free of a duty of care to children injured on their way to and from school).

Finally, we address the propriety of an allegedly erroneous and prejudicial instruction. The challenged instruction, though approved by the trial judge after submission by plaintiffs, was inadvertently omitted from the charge to the jury. Although plaintiffs immediately called the oversight to the judge's attention, the absence of a court reporter prevented verification of the omission until the morning of the jury's third day of deliberations. Thereupon, the judge recalled the jury, explained his inadvertent error, and read the instruction, which stated: "One who undertakes to direct the action of another has a duty to do so with due care."

[14] Defendant contends that the instruction was argumentative in that it focused exclusively on KHJ and no other defendant. We need not examine the merit of this assertion for defendant itself requested and received an instruction to substantially the same effect. That instruction began, "Every person who engages in a business activity which directs or influences the conduct of others and who, while so engaged exercises ordinary care. . . ."[7] It is well settled that a party

---

6. In *Shafer* defendant entered a float in a commercial parade and as the float traveled down the street, employees threw candy to the crowd. Children running to collect the candy injured a spectator. The court distinguished cases in which the conduct of the person who immediately caused the accident was not set in motion by any act of the defendant on the ground that the defendant, in throwing the candy, induced the response of the children which resulted in the plaintiff's injuries.

Contrary to defendant's assertion, *Shafer* is not distinguishable because there the defendant had *actual* knowledge children were following the float and scrambling for candy. Such knowledge only obviated the need for a determination that the acts of the children were foreseeable. In the present case, as we have seen, the jury's determination that the accident was foreseeable is supported by the evidence.

---

7. The entire instruction read: "Every person who engages in a business activity which directs or influences the conduct of others and who, while so engaged, exercises ordinary care (in the manner in which said activity is conducted) has a right to assume that every other person will perform his duty and obey the law, and in the absence of reasonable cause for thinking otherwise or actual notice to the contrary, it is not negligence for such person to fail to anticipate an accident which can be occasioned only by a violation of law or duty by another person (or persons).

---

5. Section 314 states: "The fact that the actor realizes or should realize that action on his part is necessary for another's aid or protection does not of itself impose upon him a duty to take such action."

cannot attack the substance of an instruction if he himself proposed similar instructions. (*Smith v. Americania Motor Lodge* (1974) 39 Cal.App.3d 1, 7, 113 Cal.Rptr. 771.) For the same reason, we reject defendant's contentions that there was no support in the record for the challenged instruction and that it was ambiguous.

Additionally, defendant claims that independent prejudice arose from the tardy and isolated manner in which the instruction was given. The jury, it is asserted, attached undue importance to the instruction because it was given by itself on the third day of deliberations. We do not agree.

[15,16] The trial court possesses the inherent right on its own motion to recall the jurors for further instructions. (*People v. Wester* (1965) 237 Cal.App.2d 232, 238, 46 Cal.Rptr. 699; *People v. Hewitt* (1936) 11 Cal.App.2d 197, 199, 53 P.2d 365.) In *Davis v. Erickson* (1960) 53 Cal.2d 860, 3 Cal.Rptr. 567, 350 P.2d 535, we stated if a court recalls the jury for the purpose of reading unintentionally omitted instructions the danger that the instruction will be overemphasized may be avoided if the court admonishes the jury not to attach any particular emphasis to the fact that it is reading certain instructions which had been inadvertently omitted in its first reading or by rereading all the instructions. Here the prefatory remarks of the trial judge minimized any tendency of the jury to be unduly impressed by the circumstances under which the instruction was given.

Moreover, defendant failed to request either additional cautionary instructions or a rereading of all related instructions. Under similar circumstances, it was held in *Stoddard v. Rheem* (1961) 192 Cal.App.2d 49, 13 Cal.Rptr. 496 that the defendant should not be permitted to stand silently by, giving the appearance of acquiescence in the manner in which an instruction was given and be later heard to complain, too late for curative measures to be taken.

The judgment and the orders appealed from are affirmed. Plaintiffs shall recover their costs on appeal. The parties shall bear their own costs on the cross-appeal.

WRIGHT, C. J., and McCOMB, TOBRINER, SULLIVAN, CLARK and RICHARDSON, JJ., concur.

---

781 P.2d 1015
12 A.L.R. 5th 1020
(Cite as: 162 Ariz. 174, 781 P.2d 1015)
Thomas Allen OLSON, an individual, Plaintiff-Appellee,
v.
Jerry H. WALKER and Rachelle Walker, husband and wife, Defendants-Appellants.
No. 1 Ca-CV 88-316.
Court of Appeals of Arizona, Division 1, Department D.
June 27, 1989.
Review Denied Nov. 21, 1989.*

Defendant appealed from an order of the Superior Court of Maricopa County, Cause No. C-600994, Cheryl K. Hendrix, J., which rendered judgment for plaintiff in personal injury action and awarded punitive damages. The Court of Appeals, Grant, C.J., held that: (1) evidence was sufficient to warrant punitive damages; (2) punitive damage award was not excessive; (3) punitive damage award did not violate due process, prohibition against excessive fines or double jeopardy; and (4) trial court did not abuse discretion in refusing to instruct jury to disregard expert testimony regarding arthritic changes in plaintiff's back.

Affirmed.

Gerber, J., dissented and filed opinion.

1. **Damages k87(1)**　Punitive damages are awarded primarily to punish wrongdoer and deter others from similar conduct and thus, award of punitive damages is limited to situations where these objectives can be furthered.

2. **Damages k184**　Award of punitive damages against intoxicated driver may only be had upon clear and convincing evidence of driver's evil mind.

---

*Moeller, J., of the Supreme Court, voted to grant review as to Issues B, C and D.

3. **Damages k91(1)**   Award of punitive damages against intoxicated driver was appropriate where evidence showed that driver drank at least ten beers within one-hour period prior to accident, that driver took 20 milligrams of valium prior to accident and that driver was driving recklessly and was speeding in middle turn lane.

4. **Damages k91(1)**   Intoxicated driver was not required to know that his conduct was so egregious that it created substantial risk of harm to others in order to be liable for punitive damages, but rather it was sufficient that driver should have known nature of his conduct.

5. **Damages k181**   Defendant's wealth and nature of his conduct may be considered in awarding punitive damages.

6. **Damages k94**   Punitive damage award of $100,000 against intoxicated driver was not excessive, despite contention that award represented approximately two and one-half times his gross annual income.

* * *

Harrison, Harper, Christian & Dichter, P.C. by Douglas L. Christian and Gregg H. Temple, Phoenix, for defendants-appellants.

Berry & Martori by Frederick C. Berry, Jr., Phoenix, for plaintiff-appellee.

OPINION

GRANT, Chief Judge

This appeal primarily concerns the award of punitive damages in a personal injury action. A secondary issue concerns the trial court's refusal to strike certain expert testimony. For the reasons explained below, we affirm.

FACTS

We view the facts most favorably to upholding the jury verdict. *Venerias v. Johnson*, 127 Ariz. 496, 622 P.2d 55 (App.1980). Thomas Allen Olson and Jerry H. Walker were involved in a motor vehicle accident at approximately 6:30 P.M. on October 30, 1985. Immediately prior to the accident, Walker spent approximately two hours at a bar with his accountant and one other acquaintance. During that time, the three men played pool and drank at least two pitchers of beer between approximately 4:30 P.M. and 5:30 P.M. When they left the bar, the accountant drove to a community college where he taught an accounting class. Walker drove east on Bell Road, which has a posted speed

limit of 40 miles per hour. A witness testified that Walker was traveling at least 50–55 miles per hour, that he swerved in and out of traffic, that he cut the witness off, and that he lost control of his vehicle.

Meanwhile, Olson was driving his motorcycle to pick up a pizza. He was almost stopped in the left-hand lane on Bell Road, waiting for traffic to clear so he could turn left, when Walker's vehicle rear-ended him. Walker did not immediately stop, but when he did get out of his car, he staggered, smelled strongly of alcohol, and had trouble standing. He had bloodshot eyes and slurred speech. A witness testified that Walker attempted to leave the scene, but was stopped by two bystanders. Walker was arrested for driving while intoxicated. See A.R.S. § 28–692. As a result, he ultimately paid a fine of $372.50 and had his driver's license temporarily suspended.

Based upon his blood-alcohol level approximately one hour after the accident, an expert toxicologist testified that Walker's blood-alcohol level at time of the accident was .155 percent. He also testified that Walker must have consumed ten or more twelve-ounce cans of beer during the one-hour period he was drinking. There was also disputed testimony that Walker took 20 mg. of Valium approximately one-half hour before the accident. The toxicologist testified that the Valium and alcohol would have intensified the effect of each other.

A jury trial resulted in an award of $133,000 compensatory damages and $100,000 punitive damages to Olson. After the trial court denied his motion for a new trial or, in the alternative, remittitur, Walker brought this appeal.

ISSUES

Walker raises the following issues: (1) Whether the evidence at trial was insufficient to warrant punitive damages; (2) Whether the $100,000 punitive damages award is excessive and the result of passion and prejudice; (3) Whether the punitive damages award is unconstitutional because it violates Walker's due process rights, is an excessive fine, or constitutes double jeopardy; and (4) Whether the trial court erred by refusing to instruct the jury to disregard certain testimony regarding arthritic changes in Olson's lower back. Additional facts will be added as necessary for the discussion of each issue.

I. PUNITIVE DAMAGES AWARD

Walker argues that the evidence at trial was insufficient to warrant a punitive damages instruction. Specifically, he argues that there was no evidence that Walker intended to injure Olson or that he knowingly and consciously disregarded a substantial risk of harm to Olson or others.

Although an award of punitive damages should be upheld if there is any reasonable evidence to support it, an award may be reversed when the punitive damages issue has been submitted to the jury on slight and inconclusive evidence. *Filasky v. Preferred Risk Mutual Ins. Co.*, 152 Ariz. 591, 599, 734 P.2d 76, 84 (1987). To properly analyze Walker's argument, we must examine the punitive damages standard that has evolved in recent years and then determine whether there was more than slight or inconclusive evidence to warrant an award.

A. Punitive Damages Standard

[1] Punitive damages are awarded primarily to punish the wrongdoer and deter others from similar conduct. *Linthicum v. Nationwide Life Ins. Co.*, 150 Ariz. 326, 330, 723 P.2d 675, 679 (1986). The award of punitive damages is limited to situations where these objectives can be furthered. *Gurule v. Illinois Mutual Life and Casualty Co.*, 152 Ariz. 600, 601, 734 P.2d 85, 86 (1987). Punitive damages are therefore awarded only where the defendant's wrongful conduct is the result of an "evil mind," something more than the mere commission of a tort. *Linthicum*, 150 Ariz. at 330, 723 P.2d at 679. Accordingly, the primary inquiry is based on the wrongdoer's state of mind or attitude. Id. An evil mind is found where the defendant intended to injure the plaintiff, or where the defendant, not intending to cause injury, "consciously pursued a course of conduct knowing that it created a substantial risk of significant harm to others." *Rawlings v. Apodaca*, 151 Ariz. 149, 162, 726 P.2d 565, 578 (1986). An evil mind can be inferred when the defendant's conduct is so outrageous or egregious that it can be assumed he intended to injure or that he consciously disregarded the substantial risk of harm created by his conduct. *Gurule*, 152 Ariz. at 602, 734 P.2d at 87; *Rawlings*, 151 Ariz. at 162–63, 726 P.2d at 578–79.

The Arizona Supreme Court first announced the standard described above in insurance bad-faith cases. See *Rawlings*; *Linthicum*. The court correspondingly imposed a more stringent standard of proof, thereby allowing the recovery of punitive damages only upon clear and convincing evidence of the defendant's evil mind. *Linthicum*, 150 Ariz. at 332, 723 P.2d at 681; see also *Gurule*. These standards have since been applied to other types of cases, including products liability, see *Volz v. Coleman Co.*, 155 Ariz. 567, 748 P.2d 1191 (1987), and personal injury actions. See *Ranburger v. Southern Pacific Transportation Co.*, 157 Ariz. 551, 760 P.2d 551 (1988).

[2] Previously, the question of punitive damages against intoxicated drivers was allowed to go to the jury upon a showing of gross or wanton negligence. E.g.,

Smith v. Chapman, 115 Ariz. 211, 564 P.2d 900 (1977); *Rustin v. Cook*, 143 Ariz. 486, 694 P.2d 316 (App.1984). The current standard for awarding punitive damages developed by recent case law applies to these types of cases and must be utilized in determining whether punitive damages are recoverable in this case.

B. Sufficiency of the Evidence

We must next determine whether the evidence was clear and convincing that Walker acted with an "evil mind," in that he consciously pursued a course of conduct knowing it created a substantial risk of significant harm to others.

In support of the punitive damages award, Olson points to Walker's testimony that he knew that it was dangerous to drive while intoxicated, and that intoxicated drivers create a substantial risk of harm to others. Olson also refers us to the following evidence:

1. Walker's intoxilyzer test results were .14 and .15 percent one hour after the accident. An expert toxicologist testified that Walker consumed at least ten beers during the hour he admits he was drinking and that his blood alcohol level would have been at least .155 percent at the time of the accident;

2. There was testimony that Walker took 20 mg. of Valium 25 minutes before the accident. The Valium and alcohol would have enhanced the effects of each other;

3. Walker drove recklessly before the accident and caused another driver to take evasive action;

4. Walker was speeding at the time of the accident;

5. Walker did not brake or take other evasive action until after he collided with Olson's motorcycle;

6. Walker attempted to flee the scene and was physically restrained by two bystanders; and

7. Walker was agitated after he was arrested and stated that he needed more Valium.

Although Olson suggests that a determination of voluntary intoxication is sufficient to warrant a punitive damages instruction, he claims there is abundant additional evidence showing Walker's "evil mind" and the punitive damages award should therefore be affirmed.

Walker, on the other hand, contends that a plaintiff must show more than defendant's voluntary intoxication; he must show that when the defendant got into his car to drive, he either knew he was too intoxicated to drive safely, or that he deliberately became intoxicated knowing he would later drive. Walker points to his own testimony that he did not feel that his driving ability was impaired when he left the bar and that he did not know he might be creating a substantial risk of significant harm to others by driving. There is no evidence, he claims, that he became intoxicated knowing he would later create a substantial risk of harm to others by driving. He points to undisputed testimony that he met with his two companions to discuss business and to relax after work, as opposed to becoming intoxicated, and that one of his companions taught an accounting class after consuming the same amount of alcohol as Walker.

[3] We do not agree with Walker's ultimate conclusion that there was no evidence to support a punitive damages jury instruction. Walker ignores the fact that an evil mind can be inferred by egregious or outrageous conduct. We believe there was sufficient evidence that Walker's conduct was so outrageous that an evil mind could be inferred.

Preliminarily, we note that we are looking beyond the undisputed evidence that Walker was negligent, or even grossly negligent, as he candidly admits. Viewing the evidence most favorably to supporting the verdict, Walker's blood-alcohol level indicated that he drank at least ten beers within the one-hour period he admits he was drinking. This large amount of alcohol in a short period of time supports an inference that he intended to become intoxicated or at least knew that would be the result. In addition, he took 20 mg. of Valium. Even assuming Walker did not know he was intoxicated when he sat behind the wheel of his car, he does not claim he did not know he had been drinking. Between the drinking and the Valium, it can be readily inferred that Walker disregarded the fact that his ability to drive safely was impaired, thereby creating a substantial risk of significant harm to others. Walker drove to the bar, and he does not suggest he intended to leave by another method. When he left, he drove recklessly and was speeding in the middle turn lane, instead of driving cautiously in an attempt to minimize the risk to others.

This evidence amply supports a finding of an evil mind. To hold otherwise based on Walker's testimony that he neither knew nor consciously disregarded the substantial risk he was creating would be tantamount to determining punitive damages exclusively on a defendant's own testimony of his lack of an evil mind, even when his conduct indicates otherwise. The mental states of intent and knowledge cannot be disproved on a defendant's mere denial of them.

[4] It is sufficient that Walker should have known that his conduct was so egregious that it created a substantial risk of harm to others. *See Linthicum*, 150 Ariz. at 330, 723 P.2d at 679 ("It is only when the wrongdoer should be consciously aware . . . that his conduct is so outrageous, oppressive or intolerable.

. . .") (emphasis added). In *White v. Mitchell*, 157 Ariz. 523, 759 P.2d 1327 (App.1988), this court upheld a punitive damages award against a truck driver based upon testimony that an experienced driver would have known the brakes were unsafe. We concluded that even though the evidence was circumstantial, the jury could have found that the driver knew the truck was unsafe, giving rise to a substantial risk of serious injury to other drivers and pedestrians. *Id.* at 529, 759 P.2d at 1333. In this case, a person who knows it is unsafe to drink and drive would have known it was unsafe to drive after drinking ten beers in an hour.

Walker's reliance on case law from other jurisdictions is misplaced. For example, he cites *Baker v. Marcus*, 201 Va. 905, 114 S.E.2d 617 (Ct.App.1960) in which a Virginia court refused to sustain a punitive damages award against an intoxicated driver. The reason for the court's holding, however, was that the facts did not indicate the accident was the result of the defendant's intoxication, as opposed to simple negligence when she momentarily took her eyes off the road. *Id.* at 910, 114 S.E.2d at 621. The defendant's degree of intoxication was considered "borderline" and she was only charged with reckless driving. *Id.* at 907, 114 S.E.2d at 619; see also *Miskin v. Carter*, 761 P.2d 1378 (Utah 1988). Similarly, in *Detling v. Chockley*, 70 Ohio St.2d 134, 139, 436 N.E.2d 208, 212 (1982), the court held that punitive damages were not recoverable against a drunk driver where there were no surrounding circumstances demonstrating the malice required to impose punitive damages. In *Gesselein v. Britton*, 175 Kan. 661, 266 P.2d 263 (1954), the court refused to allow a claim for punitive damages based on the defendant's intoxication alone because the plaintiff had failed to allege any facts showing "gross and wanton negligence." The fact that the defendant drove while intoxicated was insufficient standing alone to award punitive damages. *Id.* at 664, 266 P.2d at 265.

By contrast, here there was clear and convincing evidence that Walker's intoxication was well beyond borderline and that the accident occurred solely because he was intoxicated. In addition, Walker had taken Valium and was driving recklessly in excess of the speed limit. Intoxication alone, in the absence of other compelling circumstances, may not warrant punitive damages. E.g., *Biswell v. Duncan*, 742 P.2d 80 (Utah Ct.App.1987). In this case, however, additional circumstances beyond intoxication were clearly shown. The trial court properly allowed the question of punitive damages to go to the jury.

II. AMOUNT OF PUNITIVE DAMAGES

Walker next argues that the $100,000 punitive damages award is excessive and that the jury acted out of passion or prejudice. Such an award, he argues, will destroy him financially. At the time of trial, Walker claimed his business was in bankruptcy, that he supported his wife and two children on an annual income of $38,000, that he had about $4,000 in the bank, and after paying bills had approximately $500 left over every month. He contends that $100,000 is well beyond the average working person's ability to pay. He points out that, even assuming he had $500 to pay at the end of every month, it would take him nearly seventeen years to pay the award, excluding any interest.

Olson responds that although Walker's employer was in bankruptcy, there was no evidence that Walker had ever filed bankruptcy. He also points out that Walker's income the year previous to trial was $44,356 and that Walker owns his own home.

As a general rule, the amount of a punitive damages award is within the fact finder's discretion and will not be disturbed on appeal, unless it is so unreasonable that it is the product of passion or prejudice. *Nielson v. Flashberg*, 101 Ariz. 335, 341, 419 P.2d 514, 520 (1966); *Nienstedt v. Wetzel*, 133 Ariz. 348, 357, 651 P.2d 876, 885 (App.1982). The test is whether the verdict is "so manifestly unfair, unreasonable and outrageous as to shock the conscience of the Court." *Acheson v. Shafter*, 107 Ariz. 576, 579, 490 P.2d 832, 835 (1971) (citing *Young Candy & Tobacco Co. v. Montoya*, 91 Ariz. 363, 370, 372 P.2d 703, 707 (1962)); *see also Hawkins v. Allstate Ins. Co.*, 152 Ariz. 490, 501, 733 P.2d 1073, 1084, *cert. denied*, 484 U.S. 874, 108 S.Ct. 212, 98 L.Ed.2d 177, *reh'g denied*, 484 U.S. 972, 108 S.Ct. 477, 98 L.Ed.2d 414 (1987). The amount of the award alone is insufficient evidence that a jury acted with passion or prejudice. *Hawkins*, 152 Ariz. at 501, 733 P.2d at 1084.

[5] One factor that may be considered in awarding punitive damages is the defendant's wealth. The wealthier the defendant, the greater the amount of the award needed to punish him. *Id.* At the same time, however, the award "must not financially kill the defendant." *Id.*; *see also Maxwell v. Aetna Life Ins. Co.*, 143 Ariz. 205, 219, 693 P.2d 348, 362 (App.1984).

Another factor the jury can consider is the nature of the defendant's conduct. *Hawkins*, 152 Ariz. at 502, 733 P.2d 1085. Thus, "the more reprehensible the defendant's conduct and the more serious the harm likely to occur, the larger the appropriate punishment." *Id.*

In support of his contention that the $100,000 punitive damages award will financially kill him, Walker relies on Hawkins, in which the court determined that a $3.5 million punitive damages award was not excessive because it represented only 1/25 of one percent of the corporate defendant's total assets and net income of approximately 3½ days. In contrast, the $100,000 award against Walker represents approxi-

mately two and one-half times his gross annual income. Division 2 of this court, however, upheld a punitive damages award of more than $53,000 against a defendant with an annual income of $22,000, who lived from paycheck to paycheck. *Rustin v. Cook*, 143 Ariz. 486, 694 P.2d 316 (App.1984). The court concluded that the size of the award was not so excessive as to show passion or prejudice and decided that the court would not interfere with the jury's determination, which had also been approved by the trial court. *Id.* at 491, 694 P.2d at 321; see also *Puz v. McDonald*, 140 Ariz. 77, 79, 680 P.2d 213, 215 (App.1984) (an award in excess of the defendant's assets is not sufficient grounds to set it aside).

[6] Turning to this case, evidence was presented concerning Walker's occupation, income, and assets. Presumably, the jury considered this evidence, as well as the evidence regarding Walker's conduct and the strong likelihood that it could (and did) result in serious harm. Taking these factors into consideration, the jury could have concluded that Walker's conduct was so egregious that a large punitive damages award was necessary to punish him. A high award also serves the public by deterring others from similar conduct, a concern of paramount importance, as the problem of intoxicated drivers has grown in recent years.

We cannot agree with Walker's contention that a $100,000 punitive damages award "shocks the conscience." Undeniably, it is a steep punishment not easily absorbed by Walker. However, the purpose of punitive damages—to punish the wrongdoer and deter others—would be little furthered by an award easily paid by a defendant. *See Hawkins*, 152 Ariz. at 497, 733 P.2d at 1080 ("[T]he goals of punishment and deterrence would be circumvented if the financial position of the defendant allowed it to comfortably absorb the award"). The growing public concern and increasing deaths and injuries caused by intoxicated drivers justify an award which will hopefully deter others from similar conduct.

* * *

CONCLUSION

In conclusion, there was sufficient evidence to support the punitive damage instruction to the jury. The resulting award was not excessive. We reject Walker's arguments that the punitive damage award is unconstitutional. Finally, the trial court did not err by refusing to strike the portion of Dr. LaBarre's testimony of which Walker complains, or by refusing to declare a mistrial.

The judgment of the trial court is affirmed.

SILVERMAN, J., concurs.
NOTE: The Honorable BARRY G. SILVERMAN of the Maricopa County Superior Court, State of Ari-

zona, has been authorized to participate in this matter by the Chief Justice of the Arizona Supreme Court, pursuant to Ariz. Const. Art. VI, § 3.

GERBER, Judge, dissenting:

I dissent from that portion of the majority opinion upholding the $100,000 punitive damage award. While there is no showing of passion or prejudice, the award is simply excessive for this wrongdoer and, in a larger sense, for all of us. I would grant a remittitur as I believe the trial court should have done under A.R.S. 12–2104, to reduce that sum to something in the neighborhood of $50,000.

Hawkins v. Allstate Insur. Co., 152 Ariz. 490, 501, 733 P.2d 1073, 1084 (1987) counsels that the wealthier a defendant, the greater may be the punitive damages; the obverse of this principle is that the less wealthy a defendant, the lower should be the punitive damages. Hawkins also advises that punitive damages should not destroy an individual. In my opinion, that will happen here. The destruction will go beyond this culpable individual to innocent family members and may well come back to bite society—all of us—in the heel.

This defendant is a young, relatively newly married man with a non-employed wife, with two children who, at trial time, were five years and one month old respectively. He had lost his job in bankruptcy proceedings. His income in the year in question was $38,000; in the prior year it was approximately $44,000. He is the sole support of his family. In addition to suffering compensatory damages of $133,000, he is now saddled with an additional $100,000 in punitive damages.

The $100,000 punitive damage award is two to two and one-half times his family's annual income. It is not speculative to envision that its effects go well beyond punishing simply this defendant. For him to pay off the $100,000 out of savings, even at the harsh rate of $500 per month, without any payment of interest, would require 17 years; when interest is added, it could take almost twice as long, possibly his entire remaining life. This punishment spreads beyond this wrongdoer; it punishes his three innocent family members as well and could readily deny or seriously impair education for the children, force the wife or husband to work second or third jobs, cause deprivation of basic family needs, and put the marriage itself to the test.

The law's deterrent desires regarding this defendant's drinking problem need be balanced against other social values. Deterrence needs to be measured against the long term effects upon society at large when the debilitation of this family taxes all of us on the rebound. It little profits us as a society to deter so mightily as to cause greater disasters. While I have not a shred of sympathy for this defendant's conduct and find some punitive damages well warranted, I regret the court's failure to consider the larger picture. Pulverizing defendants for outrageous conduct can lead to social fall-out beyond the punitive satisfaction of the moment. It is a narrow view to consider simply the true but worn refrain of "sending a message" of deterrence; we also need to embrace the larger view of the effects of disproportionate punitive damage assessments on a family and our larger society when its members are destroyed by poverty, debt, or even unyielding cynicism. Unfortunately, in my opinion, the arctic winter of punishment has here encroached on prudence, leaving one to ponder Clausewitz's comment that, at times, the law becomes plunder without the excuse of war.

Sandra LINTHICUM, widow, surviving wife and Personal Representative of the Estate of Jerry Linthicum, deceased, Plaintiff-Appellee,

v.

NATIONWIDE LIFE INSURANCE CO., an Ohio corporation, and Dan R. Wagnon and Associates, Inc., an Arizona corporation, Defendants-Appellants.

No. CV 86-0061-PR.

Supreme Court of Arizona, In Banc.

July 23, 1986.

Reconsideration Denied Sept. 9, 1986.

Suit was brought against insurer and its claims agency for breach of contract and bad faith. The Superior Court, Maricopa County, Cause No. C-446562, Robert Hertzberg, J., awarded compensatory and punitive damages. The Court of Appeals, 150 Ariz. 354, 723 P.2d 703, reversed the punitive damage award, but affirmed on all other issues, and review was granted. The Supreme Court, Cameron, J., held that while insurer may not have dealt with the insureds in good faith, there was not sufficient evidence of an evil mind, illustrating a desire to harm or consciously disregard insureds' rights and therefore punitive damages were not warranted.

Reversed in part and affirmed in part.

1. **Damages k 87(1)** Exemplary or punitive damages are those damages awarded in excess of full compensation to victim in order to punish the wrongdoer and to deter others from emulating his conduct.

2. **Damages k 91(1)** In deciding whether punitive damages are awardable, inquiry should be focused upon the wrongdoer's mental state; wrongdoer must be consciously aware of the wrongfulness or harmfulness of his conduct and yet continue to act in the same manner in deliberate controvention to the rights of the victim.

3. **Damages k 184** Before a jury may award punitive damages there must be evidence of an "evil mind" and aggravated and outrageous conduct.

4. **Damages k 184** Burden of proof for punitive damages is by clear and convincing evidence.

5. **Insurance k 602.2(1)** Punitive damages are recoverable in a bad-faith action where defendant's conduct is aggravated, outrageous, malicious or fraudulent, combined with an evil mind as evidenced by showing that defendant was consciously aware of the needs and rights of the insured and nevertheless ignored its obligations.

6. **Insurance k 602.2(1)** While insurer may not have dealt with the insureds in good faith, there was not sufficient evidence of an evil mind, illustrating a desire to harm or consciously disregard insureds' rights and therefore punitive damages were not warranted in a bad-faith action.

Hofmann, Salcito, Stevens & Myers by Robert D. Myers and Leroy W. Hofmann, Phoenix, for plaintiff-appellee.

McCord & Howe by Warren S. McCord, Scottsdale, and Kornblum, Kelly & Herlihy by Guy O. Kornblum and Abigail S. Kelly, San Francisco, Cal., for defendants-appellants.

Streich, Lang, Weeks & Cardon by Louis A. Stahl, William S. Hawgood, II and Susan Gaylord Gale, Phoenix, for amicus curiae American Council of Life Ins. and Health Ins. Assoc. of America.

Langerman, Begam, Lewis and Marks by Amy G. Langerman, Phoenix, for amicus curiae Arizona Trial Lawyers Assoc.

CAMERON, Justice.

This is a petition for review of a decision and opinion of the court of appeals which affirmed a jury award of compensatory damages for bad faith against Nationwide Life Insurance Company, but reversed the award of two million dollars in punitive damages. *Linthicum v. Nationwide Life Insurance Company*—Ariz.—, 723 P.2d 703, (App.1985). We have jurisdiction pursuant to art. 6 § 5(3) of the Arizona Constitution, A.R.S. § 12–120.24 and Rule 23, Ariz.R.Civ.App.P., 17A A.R.S.

We granted oral argument on the petition for review and asked that counsel direct their attention to the following questions:

1. Assuming that indifference to or failure to consider the interests of the insured is sufficient grounds for award of tort damages in a bad faith case, what additional requirement or standard is appropriate to justify an award of punitive damages?

2. Does the evidence in this case meet or fail to meet that standard?

After oral argument we granted the petition for review as to the issue of punitive damages only. We affirm the decision and opinion of the court of appeals as to the other issues considered by that court.

The facts follow. In September 1979, Jerry Linthicum (Jerry) was hospitalized by his family physician, Dr. James Skinner. A tumor on one of his parathyroid glands[1] was surgically removed by Dr. Robert A. Brock on 28 September 1979. At that time, Jerry's physicians, Dr. Skinner and Dr. Brock, plus the pathologist at Phoenix General Hospital, Dr. Voit, determined based upon tissue samples that it was parathyroid *adenoma*, ie. a benign tumor. However, as these tumors can be differently interpreted, some representative slides were sent to the Mayo Clinic for verification. A pathologist at the Mayo Clinic, Dr. Edward Soule, also diagnosed it as parathyroid adenoma. The final diagnosis in the summary addendum of Phoenix General Hospital, prepared by Dr. Vericolli, also states parathyroid adenoma.

Following his surgery, Jerry was required to see Dr. Skinner monthly to have his blood tested for any

---

1. There are four parathyroid glands located within the thyroid gland. The parathyroid glands secrete a hormone which regulates the amount of calcium in the body.

surgery induced hypocalcemia (low blood calcium) or a reoccurrence of his prior symptoms. He also returned to work, gained twenty-five pounds, and resumed his active lifestyle.

Effective 1 April 1980, Sandra Linthicum (Sandra) obtained medical insurance from Nationwide Life Insurance Company (Nationwide) through a group insurance policy issued to her employer, Arizona Optical Company. The policy was also to include coverage for her husband, Jerry, as a dependent. Sandra never received a copy of this policy, but instead was simply added as a certificate-holder of the policy issued to Arizona Optical Company. Both the group policy and the certificate contained the following limitation as to preexisting illness:

> Eligible expenses do not include any charges incurred . . .(7) for an illness for which the Insured Person received medical care or treatment within the 90 days preceding the effective date of his insurance hereunder. . . . The term "treatment" includes the taking of any drug prescribed by a physician.

During the ninety day period prior to Sandra's insurance becoming effective, Dr. Skinner saw Jerry on 16 January, 25 January and 18 March 1980, for blood tests. The March blood test revealed that his blood pressure and calcium level were both slightly elevated (hypertension and hypercalcemia). Dr. Skinner prescribed a blood pressure medication, Enduronyl Forte. Jerry also received treatment from a Dr. Emerson, during February, for a shoulder injury.

On 12 June 1980, Jerry became ill while playing softball. Dr. Skinner had Jerry admitted to Phoenix General Hospital and later transferred him to the Hospital of the Good Samaritan in Los Angeles, California, under the care of Dr. Leonard Rosoff. At both hospitals, Sandra gave the Nationwide policy number as part of the requested insurance information.

On 11 July 1980, Dr. Rosoff operated on Jerry and discovered extensive metastatic carcinoma (cancer) of the parathyroid glands. Dr. Rosoff removed the entire thyroid gland, including the three remaining parathyroid glands, but he was unable to remove all the cancer as it had spread throughout the neck and into the chest area. Dr. Rosoff and Dr. Roger Terry, a Los Angeles pathologist, examined the records and tissue samples from Jerry's 1979 surgery. They disagreed with the previous diagnosis and concluded that the tumor discovered in 1979 had been malignant and not benign.

The bills from Phoenix General Hospital and the Hospital of the Good Samaritan were submitted to Nationwide. The claim was processed by Ms. Georgia Nihoff, senior claims examiner. Ms. Nihoff testified

that she followed Nationwide's normal procedure concerning claims by new insureds and initiated an investigation to determine if the claim was valid or excludable as a preexisting illness. Mr. Richard Schlade, another claims examiner, testified that one of the first bills submitted to Nationwide was from a radiologist and referred to the earlier surgery for parathyroid adenoma. A form letter was sent to Arizona Optical requesting the names and addresses of all doctors that had seen Jerry since 1 January 1980, and further requesting the Linthicums to give authorization for Nationwide to obtain medical information from these doctors. This letter did not state that the medical information sought was part of an investigation concerning whether the claim should be denied as a preexisting illness.

Upon receipt of the authorization and list of doctors, Nationwide sent each physician a "Dear Doctor" letter. These form letters requested information concerning any contact the doctor had with Jerry, either in person or by telephone. The letters also sought: any symptoms Jerry exhibited, diagnosis by the doctor, medications prescribed or services rendered, fees charged and finally any information on treatment rendered by any other doctors.

Dr. Skinner responded to such a letter by stating that he had moved his practice and that all Jerry's medical records were in the possession of his former employer, Dr. Luke. Dr. Luke, however, claimed that he did not have the records. Ms. Nihoff then sent another form letter to Dr. Skinner for "reconsideration". Dr. Skinner again stated that Dr. Luke had the medical records. Dr. Skinner also stated that Jerry's case was "complicated" and that Nationwide should call him if they had any questions. Dr. Luke, in response to a second letter, provided dates, diagnosis, (hyperparathyroidism with hypercalcemia, hypertension), medication and charges for Jerry's monthly office visits during January, February and March 1980. Dr. Luke also indicated that these visits were follow-up care from his 1979 surgery and that Jerry was a patient of Dr. Skinner's during this time, not his.

Dr. Rosoff responded to a similar inquiry from Nationwide. Dr. Rosoff stated that Jerry had parathyroid carcinoma but that his treating physicians did not know this prior to July 1980. He submitted discharge summaries to this effect prepared by himself and Dr. Bruce Larson, an endocrinologist, who also treated Jerry at the Hospital of the Good Samaritan in Los Angeles. At trial, Dr. Skinner testified that, in hindsight, he now believes the tumor removed in 1979 was probably cancerous.

Nationwide also received the admitting records and discharge summaries from Jerry's 1979 surgery at Phoenix General Hospital. These records contained the conclusion that the 1979 parathyroid tumor was benign. However, the confirmation letter from Dr. Soule at the Mayo Clinic concerning the tumor is absent from the Nationwide file.

Ms. Nihoff made the final decision to deny Jerry's claim based upon her determination that he had been receiving treatment for cancer during the ninety day exclusionary period even though the cancer was un-diagnosed at that time. Ms. Nihoff testified that the treatment consisted of the office visits and blood tests. She further stated that it was her understanding of Nationwide policy that treatment could include any contact with a doctor, such as visiting his office or talking with him on the telephone.

On 20 October 1980, a denial letter was sent to Arizona Optical. This letter stated that Jerry's claim was denied because he had received treatment "for this illness" within ninety days of the policy's effective date. It further stated that a review of the denial was possible upon request. The denial letter was sent only to Arizona Optical, as the policyholder, even though Nationwide knew that Sandra Linthicum no longer worked there. Sandra did not receive a copy of this letter and states she was not informed of the denial.

Jerry was hospitalized again at Phoenix General Hospital on 28 October 1980. When Sandra gave the admitting personnel her insurance information, she was informed that Jerry's previous hospital bill had not been paid. Upon telephoning Nationwide from the hospital, Sandra states, she was informed by Ms. Nih-off for the first time that the claim had been denied on the basis of a preexisting illness. Subsequently, Jerry was transferred to Mercy Clinic at St. Joseph's Hospital as a charity patient. From October 1980 until his death in February 1982, Jerry remained a charity patient at Mercy Clinic, receiving out-patient treatment between hospital stays. Dr. Skinner testified that it was his opinion that Jerry eventually became para-lyzed due to the delay involved in obtaining treatment through Mercy Clinic. Dr. Skinner felt the paralysis was avoidable, and could have been prevented if Jerry could have afforded private care. Additionally, Sandra, her twelve year old son, other family members, and friends administered medications and cared for Jerry at his home.

After an inquiry by a Phoenix newspaper column, "Answerline", Nationwide reviewed its denial in April 1981. Mr. Richard Schlade, after reviewing the file, concluded that the denial was justified. Mr. Schlade was persuaded by Dr. Rosoff's determination that Jerry had cancer in 1979 and that his previous doctors had misdiagnosed it. Further, Mr. Schlade testified that Dr. Larson's discharge summary indicated that hyper-calcemia and hypertension were secondary to or caused by parathyroid carcinoma. From this, Mr.

Schlade drew a causational link to the hypercalcemia and hypertension reported in the records of Dr. Luke and determined Jerry had parathyroid cancer and had received treatment for it or a symptom caused by it during the ninety days prior to the effective date of Nationwide's policy.

Later, Ms. Mary Beth Miller, the claims department supervisor, conducted another review of Jerry's claim. She also concluded that Jerry had been treated for cancer or a symptom of it during the ninety day exclusionary period, based upon Dr. Larson's report that hypercalcemia and hypertension are due to parathyroid carcinoma. Ms. Miller, however, showed some uncertainty about this conclusion and therefore, sent the file to the home office, where it was referred to Mr. Richard Kokesh, the Group Filed Services Manager for Nationwide.

Prior to Mr. Kokesh reviewing the file, it was initially examined by his assistant Ms. Pat Tweeton, a senior claims examiner. She wrote on the file:

> Rich, I think they did an excellent job on this file. I re-reviewed the whole thing and came to the same conclusion they did.
>
> I feel the claim is preexisting. The problem is, if it is a problem, that the doctors doing the 1979 surgery did not diagnose as cancer. So neither doctor or patient knew this.
>
> * * *
>
> My suggestion would be to stick to denial and advise Wagnon not to discuss with media.

In his review Mr. Kokesh agreed, concluding primarily on the basis of the opinions of Drs. Rosoff and Terry, that the denial was justified.

After Jerry's death, Sandra brought suit against Nationwide and its claim agency, Wagnon, for breach of contract and bad faith. A jury awarded Sandra $14,951.13 for breach of contract, $150,000 for bad faith, and $2,000,000 in punitive damages. The court of appeals reversed the punitive damage award but affirmed on all other issues. We granted review to examine the issue of punitive damages.

THE STANDARD FOR IMPOSITION OF PUNITIVE DAMAGES

A. When Punitive Damages May Be Imposed
[1] Exemplary or punitive damages are those damages awarded in excess of full compensation to the victim in order to punish the wrongdoer and to deter others from emulating his conduct. *Cassel v. Schacht*, 140 Ariz. 495, 496, 683 P.2d 294, 295 (1984); Prosser & Keeton, The Law of Torts § 2 at 9 (5th ed. 1984); Dobbs, Handbook on the Law of Remedies § 3.9 at

204 (1973); Restatement (Second) of Torts § 908. Other rationales, besides punishment and deterrence, utilized as justification for punitive damages include preserving the peace, inducing private law enforcement, compensating victims for otherwise unrecoverable losses, and financing the costs of litigation. Ellis, Fairness and Efficiency in the Law of Punitive Damages, 56 So. Cal.L.Rev. 1, 3 (1982).

[2] In deciding whether punitive damages are awardable, the inquiry should be focused upon the wrongdoer's mental state. Dobbs, *supra*. To recover punitive damages something more is required over and above the "mere commission of a tort." *Rawlings v. Apodaca*, 151 Ariz.— —, 726 P.2d 565, 578 [1986]; *Prosser & Keeton, supra*, § 2 at 9–10. The wrongdoer must be consciously aware of the wrongfulness or harmfulness of his conduct and yet continue to act in the same manner in deliberate contravention to the rights of the victim. *Rawlings v. Apodaca, supra*, 151 Ariz. at —, 726 P.2d at 578. It is only when the wrongdoer should be consciously aware of the evil of his actions, of the spitefulness of his motives or that his conduct is so outrageous, oppressive or intolerable in that it creates a substantial risk of tremendous harm to others that the evil mind required for the imposition of punitive damages may be found. *Id.*

This court and the court of appeals have attempted to express and illustrate the type of "evil mind" necessary for punitive damages in many ways and in a myriad of contexts. Unfortunately, this has resulted in an ambiguous, overbroad list of "catch phrases" from which attorneys pick and choose in an effort to obtain punitive damages. The various characterizations of conduct allowing recovery of punitive damages include:

(1) *Malice—express or implied, Arizona Publishing Co. v. Harris*, 20 Ariz. 446, 181 P. 373 (1919); *Magma Copper Co. v. Shuster*, 118 Ariz. 151, 575 P.2d 350 (App.1977);

(2) *Spite* or *ill will, State Farm Mutual Insurance Co. v. St. Joseph's Hospital*, 107 Ariz. 498, 489 P.2d 837 (1971);

(3) *Evil intent or bad motive, Smith v. Chapman*, 115 Ariz. 211, 564 P.2d 900 (1977); *McNelis v. Bruce*, 90 Ariz. 261, 367 P.2d 625 (1962);

(4) *Gross negligence, Gila Water Co. v. Gila Land and Cattle Co.*, 30 Ariz. 569, 249 P. 751 (1926); *Iaeger v. Metcalf*, 11 Ariz. 283, 94 P. 1094 (1908);

(5) *Wanton, reckless or willful acts, Lutfy v. R.D. Roper & Sons Motor Co.*, 57 Ariz. 495, 115 P.2d 161 (1941);

(6) *Intentional misconduct, Id.; Wetzel v. Gulf Oil Corp.*, 455 F.2d 857 (9th Cir.1972);

(7) *Fraud, Jenkins v. Skelton*, 21 Ariz. 663, 192 P. 249 (1920);

(8) *Oppression, Id.; Salt River Water Users' Association v. Giglio*, 113 Ariz. 190, 549 P.2d 162 (1976); *Jerman v. O'Leary*, 145 Ariz. 397, 701 P.2d 1205 (App.1985);

(9) *Extreme, aggravated or outrageous conduct, Lerner v. Brettschneider*, 123 Ariz. 152, 598 P.2d 515 (App.1979);

(10) *Conduct involving an unreasonable risk of causing distress, Wetzel v. Gulf Oil Corp., supra.;*

(11) *Reckless disregard for or indifference to the rights, interests or safety of others, Smith v. Chapman, supra; Salt River Water Users' Association v. Giglio, supra; Sellinger v. Freeway Mobile Homes Sales, Inc.*, 110 Ariz. 573, 521 P.2d 1119 (1976); *Neilson v. Flashberg*, 101 Ariz. 335, 419 P.2d 514 (1966); *McNelis v. Bruce, supra; Schmidt v. American Leasco*, 139 Ariz. 509, 679 P.2d 532 (App.1983);

(12) *Criminal acts or conduct, Puz v. McDonald*, 140 Ariz. 77, 680 P.2d 213 (App.1984);

(13) *Acts done in bad faith, Huggins v. Deinhard*, 127 Ariz. 358, 621 P.2d 45 (App.1980).

The numerous expressions of the conduct and mental state required for punitive damages has broadened its scope but loosened its impact.

[C]ourts have developed a large vocabulary to describe the kind of mental state required—the defendant must be "malicious", "reckless", "oppressive", "evil", "wicked", or guilty of "wanton misconduct", or "morally culpable" conduct. Since all of these words refer to the same underlying culpable state of mind, and since courts have not been at all concerned with any shades of difference that might be found between, say, malice and recklessness, almost any term that describes misconduct coupled with a bad state of mind will describe the case for punitive damages.

Dobbs, Handbook on the Law of Remedies, § 3.9 at 205. Having juries decide whether to award compensatory vs. punitive damages based on vague verbal distinctions between mere negligence, gross negligence and reckless indifference is often futile and nothing more than semantic jousting by opposing attorneys.

Further, it leads to misapplication of the extraordinary civil remedy of punitive damages which should be appropriately restricted to only the most egregious of wrongs. "A standard that allows exemplary awards based upon gross negligence or mere reckless disregard of the circumstances overextends the availability of punitive damages, and dulls the potentially keen edge of the doctrine as an effective deterrent of truly reprehensible conduct." *Tuttle v. Raymond,* 494 A.2d 1353, 1361 (Me.1985).

We find ourselves in agreement with the Supreme Judicial Court of Maine and "perceive cogent reasons for avoiding an overbroad application of the [punitive damages] doctrine." *Tuttle v. Raymond,* 494 A.2d at 1360. The type of tortious conduct justifying punitive damages should be only those limited classes of consciously malicious or outrageous acts of misconduct where punishment and deterrence is both paramount and likely to be achieved.

[3] We, therefore, conclude that a less broad standard for punitive damages is needed. As discussed earlier, it is the "evil mind" that distinguishes action justifying the imposition of punitive damages. *See Rawlings v. Apodaca, supra.* In whatever way the requisite mental state is expressed, the conduct must also be aggravated and outrageous. It is conscious action of a reprehensible character. The key is the wrongdoer's intent to injure the plaintiff or his deliberate interference with the rights of others, consciously disregarding the unjustifiably substantial risk of significant harm to them. *Rawlings v. Apodaca,* 151 Ariz. at —, 726 P.2d at 576. While the necessary "evil mind" may be inferred, it is still this "evil mind" in addition to outwardly aggravated, outrageous, malicious, or fraudulent conduct which is required for punitive damages. We hold that before a jury may award punitive damages there must be evidence of an "evil mind" and aggravated and outrageous conduct.

B. Burden of Proof For Punitive Damages
[4] In examining the currently broad scope of punitive damages, we reach a related issue, the burden of proof in a claim for punitive damages. As this remedy is only to be awarded in the most egregious of cases, where there is reprehensible conduct combined with an evil mind over and above that required for commission of a tort, we believe it is appropriate to impose a more stringent standard of proof. When punitive damages are loosely assessed, they become onerous not only to defendants but the public as a whole. Additionally, its deterrent impact is lessened. Therefore, while a plaintiff may collect compensatory damages upon proof by a preponderance of the evidence of his injuries due to the tort of another, we conclude that recovery of punitive damages should be awardable only upon clear and convincing evidence of the defendant's evil mind. *See Tuttle v. Raymond,* 494 A.2d at 1362–1363. In making this distinction, we are not alone. *See e.g. Tuttle v. Raymond, supra; Travelers Indemnity Co. v. Armstrong,* 442 N.E.2d 349 (Ind.1982); *Wangen v. Ford Motor Co.,* 97 Wis.2d 260, 294 N.W.2d 437 (1980); Or.Rev.Stat. § 30.925 (1981); Minn.Stat.Ann. § 549.20 (1984); *See also* Colo.Rev.Stat. § 13–25–127(2) (1973) (proof beyond a reasonable doubt); Wheeler, *The Constitutional Case for Reforming Punitive Damages Procedures,* 69 Va.L.Rev. 269, 296–298 (1983) (recommending such a higher standard). We hold that the burden of proof for punitive damages is by clear and convincing evidence.

C. Punitive Damages in Bad Faith Claims
[5] In the instant case, we consider whether punitive damages may be awarded in a case involving the tort of bad faith. This question was recently answered by this court in *Rawlings v. Apodaca, supra.* In a bad faith tort case, as with all other torts, punitive damages are not awardable unless there is something more than the conduct required to establish the tort. *Rawlings v. Apodaca,* 151 Ariz. at —, 726 P.2d at 578; *Farr v. Transamerica Occidental Life Insurance Co.,* 145 Ariz. 1, 8, 699 P.2d 376, 384 (1984). However, as we stated in *Rawlings, supra,* punitive damages are recoverable in a bad faith action when the defendant's conduct is "aggravated, outrageous, malicious or fraudulent" combined with an evil mind as evidenced by a showing that the defendant was consciously aware of the needs and rights of the insured and nevertheless ignored its obligations. 151 Ariz. at —, 726 P.2d at 578. We hold that punitive damages may be awarded in a bad faith case. *Rawlings, supra.*

IS THERE SUFFICIENT EVIDENCE TO AWARD PUNITIVE DAMAGES IN THIS CASE?

[6] In the case before us, the court of appeals held that the award of punitive damages was not justified. We agree.

While Nationwide may not have dealt with the Linthicums in good faith, there is not sufficient evidence of an evil mind, illustrating a desire to harm or consciously disregard the Linthicum's rights, as is necessary to warrant punitive damages. We reach this conclusion irrespective of whether the burden of proof is clear and convincing evidence or the lesser standard of a preponderance of the evidence.

Initially, we note, as did the court of appeals, that "certain of the alleged acts of misconduct [by Nationwide] were specifically approved by Arizona law. For example, the practice of issuing an insurance certificate to summarize the terms and conditions of the policy, and transmitting that certificate to the insured through her employer, is authorized by . . . A.R.S. § 20–1402." *Linthicum v. Nationwide Life Insurance Company*, 723 P.2d at 714.

Other acts of misconduct alleged by the Linthicums to warrant punitive damages include: sending a denial of claim letter only to Arizona Optical and not to Sandra; not disclosing the medical basis for the denial; investigating all dependent claims filed in the first year of coverage for potential denial; not directly asking any of Jerry's doctors whether he had treated Jerry during the ninety day exclusionary period before issuing its denial; strictly construing its policy against the insured; conducting only fake reviews of the claim denial after a newspaper inquiry; refusing to provide Sandra with a copy of the policy; knowing the harm a denial would cause the Linthicums and denying the claim anyway. While we do not entirely agree with the court of appeals characterization of these facts as "procedural errors on the part of Nationwide", neither do we find them sufficient to support an award of punitive damages. *Linthicum v. Nationwide Life Ins. Co.*, 723 P.2d at 714.

Admittedly, Nationwide does appear to construe its policy strictly in its own favor. Investigating all dependent claims filed within the first year for potential denial and denying all claims upon any possible supportable basis is definitely not in the insured's interest. These facts are definitely relevant to a claim for bad faith; however, without evidence of an "evil mind" there is not a claim for punitive damages. Nationwide follows a tough claims policy but it is not "aggravated, outrageous, oppressive or fraudulent".

The knowledge of the harm its denial was causing the Linthicums is definitely relevant to proving an "evil mind". If it had been shown that there was a deliberate ignoring of the Linthicums' rights and needs, then punitive damages might have been awardable. In the instant case, Nationwide reviewed the file several times because of the gravity of the situation. While the petitioner may not be satisfied with the procedures utilized in these reviews, they do not appear to be designed to deny valid claims. We do not find sufficient evidence to affirm the punitive damage award.

We reverse and vacate the award for punitive damages and affirm the remainder of the judgment of the trial court and the opinion of the court of appeals.

HOLOHAN, C.J., GORDON, V.C.J., and HAYS and FELDMAN, JJ., concur.

Copr. (C) West 1995 No claim to orig. U.S. govt. works
759 P.2d 1327
(Cite as: 157 Ariz. 523, 759 P.2d 1327)
Henry WHITE and Sandra White, his wife, Plaintiffs-Appellees,

v.

Christopher MITCHELL and Deborah Mitchell, his wife; D.L. Sitton Motor Lines, Inc., a foreign corporation, Defendants-Appellants.
No. 1 CA-CIV 9687.
Court of Appeals of Arizona, Division 1, Department A.
Aug. 4, 1988.

Driver of automobile and his wife sued owner and driver of truck for personal injuries to automobile driver resulting from collision with truck. Following jury verdict, the Superior Court, Maricopa County, William P. Sargeant, III, J., entered judgment in favor of automobile driver, and owner and driver of truck appealed. The Court of Appeals, Eubank, J., held that: (1) owner and driver of truck failed to preserve for appeal their challenge to wording of punitive damages instruction; (2) instruction as to punitive damages against driver of truck was proper; (3) instruction as to punitive damages against owner of truck was improper and award would be vacated; (4) determination of amount of punitive damages against driver of truck was supported by evidence; and (5) instruction on comparative negligence between owner and driver of truck was proper.

Reversed in part; affirmed in part.

1. **Appeal and Error k231(9)** Appellant's failure to raise specific ground of objection to instruction court precludes arguing that ground on appeal.

2. **Trial k255(1)** Party who is dissatisfied with instructions trial court proposes to give is under duty to submit other instructions for trial court's consideration.

3. **Appeal and Error k232(3)** Owner and driver of truck failed to preserve for appeal their challenge to wording of punitive damage instruction that it failed to convey "evil mind" requirement for recovery of punitive damages; objection to instruction was based only on contention that evidence was insufficient to submit issue of punitive damages to jury.

4. **Damages k91(1)** Driver of automobile could recover punitive damages from driver of truck based on evidence that driver of truck consciously pursued course of conduct knowing that it created substantial risk of significant harm to others; poor condition of truck's brakes was obvious.

5. **Damages k91(3)** Driver of automobile could not recover punitive damages from owner of tractor trailer truck for personal injuries sustained when truck collided with automobile absent evidence that owner was aware of and consciously disregarded substantial and unjustifiable risk that significant harm would occur, even though owner's retention of driver and its failure to ensure regular and adequate inspection of driver and its failure to ensure regular and adequate inspection of truck or exercise due care to prevent driver from operating dangerous vehicle constituted gross wantonly negligent conduct.

6. **Damages k184** Plaintiff in punitive damages case need only introduce evidence sufficient to allow trier of fact to calculate an award that is reasonable under the circumstances.

7. **Damages k94** Jury award to driver of automobile of $30,000 punitive damages against driver of truck which collided with automobile was supported by evidence that driver owned tractor involved in accident, even though no comprehensive information was introduced concerning driver's financial circumstances.

8. **Damages k208(8)** Jury could intelligently evaluate nature of truck driver's conduct as element of proof of punitive damages, including reprehensibility of conduct and severity of harm likely to result, in action for personal injuries arising from collision of truck with automobile.

9. **Automobiles k245(28)** Jury could find that driver of truck was employee of owner of truck and was driving errand for owner at time of accident, so that owner was liable for driver's negligence, if any, in personal injury action arising from collision of truck with automobile.

10. **Automobiles k245(30)** Jury could find that driver of truck was employee of owner of truck and was driving errand for owner at time of accident, so that owner was liable for driver's negligence, if any, in personal injury action arising from collision of truck with automobile.

**1328 *524 Vermeire & Turley, P.C. by Kent E. Turley, Phoenix, for plaintiffs-appellees.

Sorenson, Moore, Evens & Burke by George R. Sorenson and John S. Schaper, Phoenix, for defendants-appellants.

OPINION

EUBANK, Judge.
Christopher Mitchell and D.L. Sitton Motor Lines, Inc. appeal from an adverse judgment for compensatory and punitive damages entered on a jury's verdict and from the denial of their motion for new trial in Henry and Sandra White's action for personal injuries sustained by Henry White. Appellants raise the following issues for our consideration: (1) whether the jury was erroneously instructed on punitive damages; and (2) whether the instructions to the jury were conflicting, confusing, and inconsistent with the verdict form. We have jurisdiction pursuant to A.R.S. § 12–2101(B) and (F)(1).

Facts and Procedural History
Henry White was driving his automobile east on Thomas Road in Phoenix at about 5:30 P.M. on March 25, 1985. He intended to turn left on 51st Avenue and proceed north. Immediately ahead of him was a vehicle driven by Denise Bauer, who also intended to turn left at 51st Avenue.

Bauer entered the intersection while the traffic light was green for traffic on Thomas. While the light remained green, Bauer was unable to turn left because there was too much oncoming traffic. When the traffic signal turned yellow, Bauer observed two cars and a truck approaching the intersection from the east on Thomas Road. The two cars were almost stopped at the crosswalk, and the truck, which was farther back, looked as if it would have been able to slow down. Bauer testified: Q: Why did you think he was going to slow down? A: Well, because he was behind those other cars and they had came to a stop. I don't know how hard it is to stop a truck. He was a ways back there. I thought he had plenty of time to stop and slow down because he didn't seem like he was going all that fast that he had to go through the yellow. After Bauer had been in the intersection "a couple seconds" after the light had turned yellow, she turned left. Bauer estimated the truck's speed to be at least 35 miles per hour. Another second or two after Bauer turned left, she observed the truck hit the car behind her in her rearview mirror.

White's car was beyond the west crosswalk in the left turn lane waiting behind Bauer's car. When the traffic signal turned yellow and Bauer began her left turn, White was about a car length behind her. As the light was changing to yellow, White observed a car in the first westbound lane next to the left-turn lane coming to a halt. Farther down the road, about 250 to 300 feet, he saw a truck. It appeared to him to be proceeding at about the speed limit. Because the light had changed to yellow and the car in the first westbound lane had stopped, White concluded that the truck was going to stop. White commenced making a normal left turn about two seconds after Bauer commenced hers. When White was across the middle of the intersection and approaching the northern crosswalk along Thomas, he looked to his right and saw the truck bearing down on him. The truck hit the right front side of his car, causing his left hand to hit the steering wheel and injuring it severely.

The tractor portion of the semi tractor-trailer truck that hit White's car was owned by appellant Christopher Mitchell, its driver, who leased it to appellant D.L. Sitton Motor Lines, Inc. The van-trailer portion was owned by Sitton.

On March 25, 1985, following the accident, diesel mechanic Billy Byrd had inspected Mitchell's tractor. He testified that the tractor's brakes did not have the ability to stop the truck to their maximum capacity and that the condition of the tractor indicated it had been totally neglected as to inspection and maintenance. He noted that all of the rear brake shoes were worn out, the brake drums were also worn, that some of the slack adjusters were near or beyond the maximum distance they were designed to go, that the brake shoes had been worn out before the accident, that the brakes had not been adjusted for about 30,000 miles, and that the rivets on the brake shoes were exposed and digging into the brake drums. Byrd further testified that given the condition of the brakes, stopping the truck would take one-third more distance than if the brakes were in good condition, and that that distance would increase if the truck was loaded. He testified he would not expect that all the brakes would be able to lock up.

Byrd also testified that trucks should be inspected daily, repaired as necessary and checked over thoroughly at least weekly. Checking a truck every 90 days is not often enough. He also testified that all one would have to do to see the condition of the brakes on the tractor would be to get under it. In some cases even that would not be necessary, and on this truck one could have seen from the side of the truck that the brakes were worn out. Byrd testified that any experienced driver would know that the brake shoes and drums on this truck were not in a safe and reasonable condition.

Howard Purdy, Byrd's former supervisor, testified that Mitchell's tractor's brake shoes were less than three-eighths of an inch thick, where new shoes would have been one and three-sixteenth inches thick. The rivets in the brake shoes were scoring the brake drums and causing glazing of the brake pads, which resulted in metal-to-metal contact and reduced the tractor's braking. All eight of the brake shoes on the tractor were worn out. Purdy testified that the brake shoes were so far out of adjustment that they would travel up to the maximum of three inches before making contact with the brake drum. This would reduce the pressure that the shoes were capable of applying to the drums, and would make wheel lock-up less likely. At a minimum, brakes on an eighteen-wheeler should be adjusted every 10,000 miles under industry practice.

White's accident reconstructionist, Richard Roller, testified that in his opinion Mitchell was about 423 feet from the easternmost crosswalk along 51st Avenue when the traffic signal turned yellow, about 300 feet from that point when Bauer made her left turn two seconds into the yellow light, and about 133 feet away when the traffic signal turned red. He testified that Mitchell was traveling at 45–50 miles per hour before he began to skid. If Mitchell's tractor had had good brakes, a reasonable speed under the circumstances would have been no more than 40 miles per hour. Roller testified that given the actual condition of Mitchell's brakes, a reasonable speed would have been 0 miles per hour, because the truck should not have been on the road.

Roller testified:

Q: Can you speak to where the driver of this vehicle, assuming he drove from Joplin, Missouri, to Phoenix and was on his way to California to get another load, and the accident happened— assuming that to be the case, the man was an experienced driver—anyway, he would not have known his brakes were out of adjustment, there was this extra lag time?

A: In my opinion, there would be no possible way he would be unaware of the brake conditions.

Q: How about as to somebody knowledgeable in inspecting the brakes? Would there be any difficulty knowing, seeing the brakes were out of adjustment, the drums were worn?

A: No. The reason is, first of all, you don't have to—like on passenger cars, you don't have to jack the car up and get it adjusted. . . . The air brake system [on a truck] is exposed and you can see the shoes, the drums, and you can see the push rods and everything. The adjustment, for example, the drums you don't even need to get down and look. You can merely put your hand behind there and feel the wear on the drums. You can easily see the push rods are out of adjustment.

Roller also testified that if Michell's truck's brakes had not been worn out and out of adjustment, Michell could have avoided the accident, because it was the lag time in the effective operation of his brakes that kept Mitchell's evasive action from being successful.

Sitton first took Mitchell on as a driver on May 17, 1983. The day before, Stanley Edens, supervisor of trailer maintenance for Sitton, gave Mitchell a road test, which included stop lights, left turns, right turns, two-lane roads, four-lane roads, railroad crossings and general traffic. In Edens' judgment, Mitchell satisfactorily passed all those tests. Eight days after Sitton hired Mitchell, Sitton received a report on Mitchell's driving record indicating that his license had been suspended for three months in September of 1982 for three speeding tickets. Although Mitchell's employment application had asserted that his driver's license had not previously been suspended, Sitton did not discharge Mitchell at that time.

A further motor vehicle report on Mitchell should have been ordered for January of 1984, but was apparently not received. Sitton ordered no motor vehicle report on Mitchell for January of 1985. If it had done so, it would have been informed that Mitchell committed three more speeding violations from March through December of 1984.

Edens testified that according to federal regulations, tractors driven by Sitton's owner-operators were to go through Sitton's shop every 90 days for a complete inspection of all systems. Sitton actually inspected Mitchell's tractor on May 9, 1983; December 16, 1983; June 15, 1984; January 23, 1985; and July 23, 1985. Edens could not say why seven months elapsed between the June 1984 and January 1985 inspections, and testified that this should not have occurred. He testified that if one of Sitton's vehicles got on the road without being inspected after 90 days, that would be contrary to the policy of Sitton's inspection department.

Sitton's inspection report from January 23, 1985, two months before the accident, indicated "[n]o defects as to brakes." If a systematic maintenance inspection had revealed that the brakes on Mitchell's truck had brake pads worn out almost to the rivets, Sitton would have noted this on the inspection sheet and would have declined to issue Mitchell a load until the brakes were fixed. Further, if Mitchell's truck had been inspected in early March 1985 and had been in the condition that Billy Byrd's post-accident inspection had revealed, the truck would have been "deadlined."

On March 19, 1985, six days before the accident, a motor vehicle report was run on Mitchell. Diana Burkhart, Driver Personnel Director for Sitton, received the report on March 21, 1985. It indicated that Mitchell's driver's license had been suspended for 60 days beginning February 10, 1985, but had been reinstated nine days later. Burkhart told Safety Director Jerry Cornwell about this, and also spoke to Mitchell. Although Burkhart testified that the reinstatement of Mitchell's license was more than likely the result of a hardship application made by Mitchell, Mitchell told Burkhart he was not aware his license had been suspended. Burkhart did not instruct Mitchell to return to Joplin immediately, though she had authority to do so. Instead, Burkhart "told him we needed to work him back into Joplin." Mitchell was to return to straighten out his license.

White and his wife brought this action against Mitchell and his wife and Sitton on November 27, 1985. It was tried before a nine-person jury, which returned a seven-person majority verdict as follows on January 14, 1987: We, the Jury, duly empaneled and sworn in the above entitled action, upon our oaths, do find in favor of the Plaintiff, HENRY WHITE, and find the damages to be $330,000.00 and SANDRA WHITE $10,000.00. We find the relative degrees of fault to be:

Defendant Sitton 70%
Defendant Mitchell 30%
100 %

We assess punitive damages against Defendant Sitton in the amount of $100,000.00. We assess punitive damages against Defendant Mitchell in the amount of $30,000.00. (Underlined portions filled in by jury.) The trial court entered judgment in accordance with the verdict on January 27, 1987. By formal order entered March 18, 1987, the trial court denied appellants' motion for remittitur and motion for new trial. This timely appeal followed.

Should the Trial Court Have Instructed the Jury on Punitive Damages?

[1][2][3] We first examine appellants' argument that the trial court's instruction on punitive damages was an inaccurate statement of the law. The trial court instructed: Only if you have awarded compensatory damages, you may also consider whether to award plaintiffs White punitive damages against defendants Mitchell and/or D.L. Sitton, Inc. Such damages are awarded in excess of full compensation to the plaintiff in order to punish the defendant and to deter others from emulating his conduct. Such damages are exemplary or punitive damages. To recover exemplary or punitive damages, plaintiffs White must prove by clear and convincing evidence that said defendants consciously pursued a course of conduct knowing that it created a substantial risk of significant harm to others. They must also prove aggravated and outrageous conduct by the defendants. Appellants now contend that the wording of this instruction failed to convey the "evil mind" requirement for recovery of punitive damages under *Rawlings v. Apodaca*, 151 Ariz. 149, 726 P.2d 565 (1986) and *Linthicum v. Nationwide Life Insurance Co.*, 150 Ariz. 326, 723 P.2d 675 (1986). In the trial court, however, appellants' counsel objected to the giving of the trial court's instruction based only on the contention that the evidence was insufficient to warrant submitting the issue of punitive damages to the jury. Moreover, appellants' counsel not only failed to challenge the correctness of the proposed instruction's text, but also repeated part of that instruction almost verbatim in stating his understanding of the then current criteria for punitive damages under Arizona law. Rule 51(a), Arizona Rules of Civil Procedure (Rule), provides in part: No party may assign as error the giving or the failure to give an instruction unless he objects thereto before the jury retires to consider its verdict, stating distinctly the matter to which he objects and the grounds of his objection. An appellant's failure to raise a specific ground of objection to an instruction before the trial court precludes him from arguing that ground on appeal. *Long v. Corvo*, 131 Ariz. 216, 639 P.2d 1041 (App.1981); *Watson Construction Co. v. Amfac Mortgage Corp.*, 124 Ariz. 570, 606 P.2d 421 (App.1979). Further, a party who is dissatisfied with instructions the trial court proposes to give is under a duty to submit other instructions for the trial court's consideration. *See Dubreuil v. Gard-*

ner, 99 Ariz. 312, 409 P.2d 23 (1965). In our opinion appellants failed to preserve on appeal their challenge to the wording of the trial court's punitive damages instruction. Moreover, unlike appellants, we do not read Rule 59(c)(3), to provide that a party's mere assertion, in a motion for new trial, that error was made in instructing the jury requires either the trial court or this court "to review the propriety of all instructions" where the party has failed to comply with Rule 51(a).

We next address appellants' contention that the evidence did not justify a punitive damages instruction as to either Mitchell or D.L. Sitton Motor Lines, Inc. In a line of cases beginning with *Rawlings v. Apodaca*, our supreme court narrowed and restated the circumstances under which punitive damages may be awarded in Arizona. *See generally* Schmidt, *Punitive Damages in Arizona: The Reports of Their Death Are Greatly Exaggerated*, 29 Ariz.L.Rev. 599 (1987). In *Rawlings* the court stated: We do not believe that the concept of punitive damages should be stretched. We restrict its availability to those cases in which the defendant's wrongful conduct was guided by evil motives. Thus, to obtain punitive damages, plaintiff must prove that defendant's evil hand was guided by an evil mind. The evil mind which will justify the imposition of punitive damages may be manifested in either of two ways. It may be found where defendant intended to injure the plaintiff. It may also be found where, although not intending to cause injury, defendant consciously pursued a course of conduct knowing that it created a substantial risk of significant harm to others. *See Grimshaw v. Ford Motor Co.*, 119 Cal.App.3d 757, 809. 174 Cal.Rptr. 348, 381 (1981). It has been stated that action justifying the award of punitive damages is "conduct involving some element of outrage similar to that usually found in crime." Restatement (Second) of Torts § 908 comment b; *see also* W. Prosser & W. Keeton, [The Law of Torts,] § 2 at 9. Applying this analogy, punitive damages will be awarded on proof from which the jury may find that the defendant was "aware of and consciously disregard[ed] a substantial and unjustifiable risk that" significant harm would occur. *See* A.R.S. § 13–105(5)(c), defining criminal recklessness. 151 Ariz. at 162, 726 P.2d at 578. In *Linthicum v. Nationwide Life Insurance Co.*, the court further defined the "evil mind" prong of the test for punitive damages under Rawlings. The court stated: As discussed earlier, it is the "evil mind" that distinguishes action justifying the imposition of punitive damages. *See Rawlings v. Apodaca, supra.* In whatever way the requisite mental state is expressed, the conduct must also be aggravated and outrageous. It is conscious action of a reprehensible character. The key is the wrongdoer's intent to injure the plaintiff or his deliberate interference with the rights of others, consciously disregarding the unjustifiably substantial risk of significant harm to them. *Rawlings v. Apodaca*, 151 Ariz. 161, 726 P.2d at 577. While the necessary "evil mind" may be inferred, it is still this "evil mind" in addition to outwardly aggravated, outrageous, malicious or fraudulent conduct which is required for punitive damages. We hold that before a jury may award punitive damages there must be evidence of an "evil mind" and aggravated and outrageous conduct. 150 Ariz. at 331, 723 P.2d at 680.

The supreme court further extended its analysis in *Gurule v. Illinois Mutual Life and Casualty Co.*, 152 Ariz. 600, 734 P.2d 85 (1987). There the court stated: In summary, the propriety of awarding punitive damages turns upon the defendant's state of mind. Intent to injure or defraud, or pursuit of wrongful conduct with conscious disregard of the probability of some injury or damage to the rights and interests of others all qualify as forms of "evil mind," justifying imposition of punitive damages. We abandon such terms as "gross," "reckless," and "wanton" conduct. They convey little, and fail to focus the jury's attention on the important question—the defendant's motives. The quality of defendant's conduct is relevant and important only because it provides one form of evidence from which defendant's motives may be inferred. The more outrageous or egregious the conduct, the more compelling will be the inference of "evil mind." Of course, defendant's state of mind may be evidenced by other factors and may be established or inferred even if defendant's conduct was outwardly unexceptional. The inquiry in every punitive damage case focuses on the defendants' state of mind, which may be established by either direct or circumstantial evidence. 152 Ariz. at 602, 734 P.2d at 87. *See also Volz v. The Coleman Company, Inc.*, 155 Ariz. 567, 748 P.2d 1191 (1987); *Bradshaw v. State Farm Mutual Automobile Ins. Co.*, 157 Ariz. 411, 758 P.2d 1313 (May 18, 1988); *Ranburger v. Southern Pacific Transportation Co.*, — Ariz.—, 760 P.2d 551, (1988). In addition, the supreme court has made it clear that a jury will not be permitted to consider an award of punitive damages if the evidence supporting such an award is only slight and inconclusive. *See Filasky v. Preferred Risk Mutual Insurance Co.*, 152 Ariz. 591, 599, 734 P.2d 76, 84 (1987); *Farr v. Transamerica Occidental Life Insurance Co.*, 145 Ariz. 1, 9, 699 P.2d 376, 384 (App.1984) (approved in *Rawlings v. Apodaca*, 151 Ariz. at 161, 163, 726 P.2d at 577, 579).

[4] In our opinion the evidence presented at trial was sufficient to justify a punitive damages instruction as to Mitchell's conduct. Though the evidence was largely circumstantial, the jury could have found that Mitchell was well aware he was driving a tractor-trailer rig that was in such dangerous condition that its continued operation gave rise to a very substantial risk of causing serious personal injury or death to pedestrians or other motorists, and yet deliberately persisted in doing so over a long period of time. The trial court correctly instructed the jury on the issue of punitive damages as to Mitchell.

[5] We reach the opposite conclusion, however, with respect to punitive damages against appellant D.L. Sitton Motor Lines, Inc. The evidence would unquestionably have supported a finding that Sitton's retention of Mitchell as a driver, and its failure to ensure regular and adequate inspection of his truck or exercise due care to prevent him from operating a dangerous vehicle, constituted gross, wantonly negligent conduct. *See Nichols v. Baker*, 101 Ariz. 151, 416 P.2d 584 (1966). There was, however, no sufficient evidence from which any jury could reasonably have found that Sitton, like Mitchell, was aware of and consciously disregarded a substantial and unjustifiable risk that significant harm would occur, such that it could be characterized as having acted with the requisite "evil mind." *Rawlings v. Apodaca*, 151 Ariz. at 162, 726 P.2d at 578. In contrast to the situation with Mitchell, the case for punitive damages against Sitton was no more than slight and inconclusive. *Farr v. Transamerica Occidental Life Insurance Co.*, 145 Ariz. at 9, 699 P.2d at 384. Further, the supreme court has expressly barred awards of punitive damages based on gross negligence or mere reckless disregard of the circumstances. *Volz v. The Coleman Company, Inc.*, 155 Ariz. at 570, 748 P.2d at 1194. The award of $100,000 punitive damages against Sitton must accordingly be vacated.

[6,7] We reject Mitchell's argument that White failed to introduce sufficient evidence from which the jury could have determined an appropriate amount of punitive damages to award against him. Contrary to Mitchell's argument, *Hawkins v. Allstate Insurance Co.*, 152 Ariz. 490, 733 P.2d 1073 (1987) does not require specific proof of Mitchell's "wealth, property, income, education, earning capacity, debts, savings, or credit." The plaintiff, in a punitive damages case, need only introduce evidence sufficient to allow the trier of fact to calculate an award that is reasonable under the circumstances. *Hawkins v. Allstate Insurance Co.*, 152 Ariz. at 497, 733 P.2d at 1080. It is true that Hawkins listed the defendant's financial position among the elements of relevant proof on this point, but it did not hold that such evidence was always required. Here, though no comprehensive information was introduced concerning Mitchell's financial cir-

cumstances, it was at least clear from the evidence that he owned the tractor involved in the accident.

[8] Another element of relevant proof Hawkins mentioned was "the nature of the defendant's conduct, including the reprehensibility of the conduct and the severity of the harm likely to result, as well as the harm that has occurred. . . ." *Id.* at 497, 733 P.2d at 1080. The record contains ample evidence from which the jury in this case could have intelligently evaluated that factor in its deliberations.

* * *

The judgment is reversed to the extent it awards $100,000 punitive damages against Sitton, and is otherwise affirmed.

CONTRERAS, P.J., and JACOBSON, J., concur.

Philip R. NIENSTEDT and Barbara Nienstedt, husband and wife, Plaintiffs — Appellees,

v.

Manfred R. WETZEL and Nancy Wetzel, husband and wife, Defendants — Appellants.

No. 1 CA-CIV 5106.

Court of Appeals of Arizona, Division 1, Department A.

July 8, 1982.

Rehearing Denied Aug. 25, 1982.

Review Denied Sept. 28, 1982.

Action was brought to recover damages allegedly sustained as result of abuse of process by defendants in prior litigation between the parties. The Superior Court, Maricopa County, Cause No. C-351561, Warren C. Ridge, J., rendered judgment on jury verdict awarding punitive and compensatory damages, and defendants appealed. The Court of Appeals, Haire, J., held that (1) word "process" as used in the tort abuse of process is not restricted to the narrow sense of that term but encompasses entire range of procedures incident to litigation process and includes such matters as notice of depositions, entry of defaults and motions to compel production, etc.; (2) showing that wrongful use of process has resulted in seizure of plaintiff's person or property is not required; (3) evidence was for jury; (4) award of attorney fees in prior action was not res judicata of instant claim that purpose of alleged abuse of process was to subject defendants to unreasonable attorney fees; (4) testimony concerning defendant husband's suspension from practice was relevant; and (5) award of $50,000 punitive damages was not excessive.

Affirmed.

1. **Process k168**   Word "process" as used in the tort of abuse of process is not restricted to the nar-

row sense of that term but has been interpreted broadly and encompasses the entire range of procedures incident to the litigation process and the tort is not restricted to utilization of process in the nature of attachment, garnishment or warrants of arrest. A.R.S. § 1–215, subd. 26. See publication Words and Phrases for other judicial constructions and definitions.

2. **Process k168**   For purpose of tort of abuse of process, "process" included noticing of depositions, entry of defaults and utilization of various motions such as motions to compel production, for protective orders, for change of judges, for sanctions and for continuances.

3. **Process k168**   To establish a claim for abuse of process there must be a showing that defendant has used a legal process against plaintiff primarily to accomplish a purpose for which the process was not designed and that harm has been caused to plaintiff by such misuse of process.

4. **Process k168**   Essential elements of tort of abuse of process include a willful act in the use of judicial process for an ulterior purpose not proper in the regular conduct of the proceedings.

5. **Process k168**   Showing that wrongful use of process has resulted in seizure of plaintiff's person or property is not an element of the tort of abuse of process.

6. **Process k168**   Gist of the tort of abuse of process is the misuse of process, justified in itself, for an end other than that which it was designed to accomplish.

7. **Process k168**   It is immaterial that process may have been properly obtained or issued as a normal incident of litigation as it is the subsequent misuse which constitutes the misconduct for which liability is imposed under the tort of abuse of process.

8. **Process k168**   There is no liability for abuse of process when defendant has done nothing more than legitimately utilize the process for its authorized purposes, even though with bad intention.

9. **Process k171**   Evidence in abuse of process action warranted conclusion that in many instances the ulterior collateral purpose of defendant to subject plaintiff to excessive litigation expenses in prior suit was in fact his primary purpose and that his use of various legal processes was not for legitimate or reasonably justifiable purposes of advancing his interest in the prior litigation.

10. **Process k168**   General abuse of process principles apply to the situation where the ulterior or collateral purpose involved has been to expose the injured party to excessive attorney fees and legal expenses.

11. **Process k168**   Liability for abuse of process does not result from either indifference or intense satisfaction in utilizing the legal machinery and liability should result only when the sense of awareness progresses to a sense of purpose and, in addition the utilization of the procedure for the purposes for which it was designed becomes so lacking in justification as to lose its legitimate function as a reasonably justifiable litigation procedure.

* * *

21. **Damages k94**   There is no compensatory-punitive damage ratio limit.

22. **Damages k94**   Whether punitive damages are excessive is based solely on the circumstances and one of the factors a jury may consider is defendant's wealth, although wealth is not a necessary prerequisite to an award of punitive damages.

23. **Appeal and Error k205**   A defendant attacking a punitive damages award may not complain of absence of evidence of his wealth when he has made no effort to introduce such evidence.

24. **Damages k208(8)**   Amount of punitive damages is a matter of discretion with the trier of fact.

25. **Appeal and Error k1004(11)**   Punitive damages award will not be disturbed unless it is so unreasonable in light of circumstances as to show influence of passion or prejudice.

26. **Appeal and Error k1004(11)**   Size of punitive damage verdict alone is not sufficient evidence of passion or prejudice to warrant setting aside.

27. **Damages k91(1)**   Punitive damages are allowed where conduct of the wrongdoer is wanton, reckless or shows spite or ill will.

28. **Appeal and Error k1004(13)**   Where the trial court has refused to interfere with jury's determination of punitive damages the reviewing court cannot interpose its own judgment unless convinced that the verdict is so excessive as to suggest passion or prejudice.

29. **Process k171**   Award of $50,000 punitive damages for tort of abuse of process was not so excessive as to suggest passion or prejudice as jury could reasonably conclude that defendants' conduct in prior litigation reflected spite, ill will and reckless indifference to the interests of plaintiffs.

Law Offices of Donald Maxwell, P. C. by Donald Maxwell and William G. Poach, Jr., Scottsdale, for plaintiffs-appellees.

Black, Robertshaw, Frederick, Copple & Wright, P. C. by Jon R. Pozgay, Phoenix, for defendants-appellants.

OPINION

HAIRE, Judge.

Appellees, Philip R. and Barbara Nienstedt, husband and wife, commenced this action in Maricopa County Superior Court to recover damages allegedly sustained as a result of abuse of process by appellants Manfred R. and Nancy Wetzel, husband wife, in prior litigation between the parties. A jury verdict awarded the Nienstedts $7,350 as compensatory damages and $50,000 as punitive damages. The Wetzels have appealed from the judgment entered on that verdict.

Although several issues have been raised on appeal, we will first address appellants' contentions concerning the applicability of abuse of process concepts to the claim involved here, as well as the contention that the evidence was insufficient to justify submission of the claim to the jury.

ABUSE OF PROCESS

Viewing the evidence in a light most favorable to supporting the judgment, we find that the following facts were established at trial.

In February 1975, Manfred Wetzel, then an attorney licensed to practice law in Arizona, filed a complaint against the Nienstedts in Maricopa County Cause No. C-307988 for breach of an alleged oral contract, fraud and defamation.[1] Appellants and the Nienstedts were neighbors when this complaint was filed and the lawsuit involved an alleged oral contract pursuant to which the parties were to share the cost of building a retaining wall on appellants' property adjacent to the Nienstedts' property. The Nienstedts' liability under the alleged oral contract would have amounted to $780.69. Appellant Manfred Wetzel had purchased the home prior to his marriage to Nancy Wetzel and brought suit solely in his name. The Nienstedts answered the complaint and counterclaimed against both of the appellants on the assumption that Nancy Wetzel, even though not named as a plaintiff in the complaint, might have a legal interest in the home. In his capacity as the Wetzels' attorney, Manfred Wetzel thereafter filed a pleading entitled a "Counter-counterclaim" on behalf of his wife. This pleading was essentially a reiteration of the original complaint naming Nancy Wetzel as the "Counter-counterclaimant."

On May 13, 1975, the Nienstedts filed a motion to dismiss and strike the counter-counterclaim as an improper pleading. On January 29, 1976, the Nienstedts, not having filed an answer or a reply, appellants entered their default on the counter-counterclaim. On February 27, 1976, a default hearing before a superior court judge was conducted at which time the default was set aside and the court set April 2, 1976, as the time for hearing the Nienstedts' motion to dismiss and strike, as well as other pending motions. On that date the court, by minute entry order, denied the motion to dismiss and strike, and stated that following completion of discovery the court would consider realignment of the parties.

On April 27, 1976, appellants entered another default against the Nienstedts on the counter-counterclaim and noticed a default hearing before a court

commissioner for May 27, 1976. The Nienstedts filed a motion to quash the default hearing, and at the hearing on this motion the trial court vacated the default hearing and realigned the parties denominating Nancy Wetzel as a plaintiff. The court further joined the counter-counterclaim with the complaint and held that the answer previously filed by the Nienstedts would be considered as an answer to the counter-counterclaim and that the counterclaim previously filed by the Nienstedts would be considered as a counterclaim against both appellants.

Numerous discovery motions were filed by both parties. At one point the trial court imposed sanctions for what it described as obstructionist activities of appellants.

In August 1976, one day prior to the scheduled trial, appellant Manfred Wetzel moved for a continuance. The motion stated that he was committed to represent a client at another trial scheduled on the same day on a matter having a lower cause number. In response, the Nienstedts filed an affidavit stating that appellant Manfred Wetzel did not appear as the counsel of record on that particular case. However, appellant Manfred Wetzel filed an uncontroverted affidavit stating that although his brother's name appeared as the attorney of record, he and his brother had associated on the case and he was in fact trying the case.

In response to one of the Nienstedts' motions to produce, appellants filed a motion for a protective order to prevent disclosure of two tape recordings allegedly containing conversations of the Nienstedts which Manfred Wetzel had filed with the court in a sealed envelope. Manfred Wetzel had indicated to the Nienstedts that these tapes proved the existence of an oral contract, and if played at trial, could be used to prove perjury by the Nienstedts. He represented to the court that these tape recordings were to be used for impeachment purposes and also were subject to protection because they constituted his work product as an attorney inasmuch as the questions on the tape "were structured" by him. He further requested that the court review the tapes in chambers and determine whether they were privileged as his work product. At the hearing on appellants' motion for the protective order appellants were represented by counsel other than Manfred Wetzel. Following the court's denial of his motion for a protective order, Manfred Wetzel admitted to the court that the tapes were blank, contrary to his prior express affirmation to the court that the tapes contained questions structured by him. The court then found that appellant Manfred Wetzel had deceived the court, had willfully and intentionally failed to comply with the Nienstedts' motion for production, and had filed motions for enlargement of

---

1. The disposition in that action is also on appeal to this court, 1 CA-CIV 5685. It is a separate appeal and is not considered in this opinion.

time and for a protective order which were a sham and unjustified. Consequently, the court dismissed appellants' complaint as a sanction pursuant to Rule 37, Arizona Rules of Civil Procedure, 16 A.R.S. The court further awarded the Nienstedts $500 in attorney's fees incurred on their motion to produce and their response to appellants' motion for protective order, plus their total costs incurred in that action.

The Nienstedts then commenced this litigation against appellants claiming that abuse of process in the prior litigation had occurred when appellants: sought recovery of punitive damages in a contract action; filed a motion to continue by reason of another pending action in which appellant Manfred Wetzel did not appear as attorney of record; entered default on an improper pleading; entered a second default and scheduled a hearing before a court commissioner when the appellants knew that the trial judge had set aside an identical default and contemplated realignment of the parties; and failed to act in good faith in discovery proceedings. The Nienstedts contended that in engaging in the aforementioned procedures, the primary goal of the appellants was to utilize processes of the court to harass the Nienstedts by purposely subjecting them to excessive legal fees in defending against appellants' claims. In this connection, there was evidence that during discovery proceedings appellant Manfred Wetzel told the Nienstedts that through this case he was going to make the Nienstedts' attorney a rich man; that he (Wetzel) could break people financially (impliedly through subjecting them to legal fees and expenses); and, that because he was a lawyer representing himself it would not be necessary for him to incur similar fees and expenses.

[1][2] Against this factual background we now address the legal requirements necessary for the establishment of an abuse of process claim. First, we note that through developing case law the word "process" as used in the tort "abuse of process" is not restricted to the narrow sense of that term.[2] Rather, it has been interpreted broadly, and encompasses the entire range of procedures incident to the litigation process. *Barquis v. Merchants Collection Association of Oakland, Inc.*, 7 Cal.3d 94, 496 P.2d 817, 101 Cal.Rptr. 745 (1972); *Thornton v. Rhoden*, 245 Cal.App.2d 80, 53 Cal.Rptr. 706 (1966); *Younger v. Solomon*, 38 Cal.App.3d 289, 113 Cal.Rptr. 113 (1974); *Foothill Industrial Bank v. Mikkelson*, 623 P.2d 748 (Wyo.1981). Thus it has been held that a request for admissions will, under appropriate circumstances, support a complaint for abuse of process, *Twyford v. Twy-*

ford, 63 Cal.App.3d 916, 134 Cal.Rptr. 145 (1976). *See also Hopper v. Drysdale*, 524 F.Supp. 1039 (D.Mont.1981) (the noticing of depositions). As applied to this case, we therefore consider as "processes" of the court for abuse of process purposes, the noticing of depositions, the entry of defaults, and the utilization of various motions such as motions to compel production, for protective orders, for change of judge, for sanctions and for continuances.

[3] Concerning whether the utilization of any of these processes singly or collectively constitutes an abuse of the court's processes, the Restatement (Second) of Torts (1977), states the general principle as follows: "§ 682. General principle "One who uses a legal process, whether criminal or civil, against another primarily to accomplish a purpose for which it is not designed, is subject to liability to the other for harm caused by the abuse of process." Under this view, to establish a claim for abuse of process there must be a showing that the defendant has (1) used a legal process against the plaintiff; (2) primarily to accomplish a purpose for which the process was not designed; and, (3) harm has been caused to the plaintiff by such misuse of process.

[4] Although Arizona case law relating to the tort of abuse of process is not extensive, it appears to be in accord with the Restatement's view, recognizing that the essential elements of the tort include (1) a willful act in the use of judicial process; (2) for an ulterior purpose not proper in the regular conduct of the proceedings. We consider this second requirement to be essentially equivalent to the Restatement's element requiring a showing that the process has been used primarily to accomplish a purpose for which the process was not designed. *See Bird v. Rothman*, 128 Ariz. 599, 627 P.2d 1097 (App.), *cert. denied*, 454 U.S. 865, 102 S.Ct. 327, 70 L.Ed.2d 166 (1981); *Rondelli v. County of Pima*, 120 Ariz. 483, 586 P.2d 1295 (App.1978); *Joseph v. Markovitz*, 27 Ariz.App. 122, 551 P.2d 571 (1976); *Gray v. Kolhase*, 18 Ariz.App. 368, 502 P.2d 169 (1972); *Blue Goose Growers, Inc. v. Yuma Groves, Inc.*, 641 F.2d 695 (9th Cir. 1981).

[5] We reject appellants' suggestion that we adopt the position taken by some courts which require as an additional element of an abuse of process claim, a showing that the wrongful use of the court's process has resulted in the seizure of plaintiffs' person or property. See *Funk v. Cable*, 251 F.Supp. 598 (N.D.Pa. 1966); *Sachs v. Levy*, 216 F.Supp. 538 (D.Or.1960). Such a requirement has not been set forth in prior Arizona decisions or in the Restatement, and, in essence, would limit the scope of the tort to those instances involving the use of "process" in the strictest sense of that term. As previously indicated, the later authorities interpret "process" as encompassing the en-

---

2. See A.R.S. § 1–215(26) which, for statutory interpretation purposes, gives a restricted definition of the word "process."

tire range of court procedures incident to the litigation process, and do not restrict the tort to the utilization of process in the nature of attachment, garnishment or warrants of arrest.

[6][7][8] Arizona case law recognizes that the gist of the tort is the misuse of process, justified in itself, for an end other than that which it was designed to accomplish. *Rondelli v. County of Pima,* supra; *see also* Prosser, The Law of Torts, § 121 (4th ed. 1971). It is immaterial that the process may have been properly obtained or issued as a normal incident of the litigation involved. It is the subsequent misuse which constitutes the misconduct for which liability is imposed. See Restatement (Second) of Torts § 682, Comment (a) (1977). On the other hand, the authorities recognize that there is no liability when the defendant has done nothing more than legitimately utilize the process for its authorized purposes, even though with bad intentions. See generally, Prosser, Law of Torts, § 121, p. 857 (4th ed. 1971). This same concept is implied in the Restatement's § 682's use of the word "primarily," which is explained in Comment (b): "b. 'Primarily.' The significance of this word is that there is no action for abuse of process when the process is used for the purpose for which it is intended, but there is an incidental motive of spite or an ulterior purpose of benefit to the defendant."

[9] Seizing upon the above-quoted language of Comment (b), the appellants contend that even if it is assumed that appellant Manfred Wetzel had an incidental motive or ulterior purpose to cause the Nienstedts to incur substantial legal expenses, nevertheless there can be no liability because appellants merely used the legal procedures available in this litigation for the very purposes for which they were intended. We would agree with appellants' position if the evidence presented in the trial court was such as to require the conclusion that the complained of processes were in fact invoked for legitimate and reasonably justifiable litigation purposes. However, there is evidence from which a trier of fact could have concluded that in many instances the ulterior or collateral purpose of appellant Manfred Wetzel to subject the Nienstedts to excessive litigation expenses was in fact his primary purpose, and that his use of various legal processes was not for legitimate or reasonably justifiable purposes of advancing appellants' interests in the ongoing litigation.

[10] Although our research has not revealed any cases in which liability for abuse of process has been imposed where the ulterior or collateral purpose involved has been to expose the injured party to excessive attorney's fees and legal expenses, we can perceive no reason why general abuse of process principles should not apply to such circumstances. *Cf. Ginsberg*

v. Ginsberg, 84 A.D.2d 573, 443 N.Y.S.2d 439 (1981) (abuse of process liability imposed when party repeatedly used subpoena processes for the purpose of exhausting the opponent's financial resources); *Board of Education of Farmingdale Union Free School District v. Farmingdale Classroom Teachers Association, Inc.,* 38 N.Y.2d 397, 343 N.E.2d 278, 380 N.Y.S.2d 635 (1975) (involving the use of witness subpoena power for 87 teachers so as to impose financial hardship); *Dishaw v. Wadleigh,* 15 A.D. 205, 44 N.Y.S. 207 (1897) (involving assignment of collection claims to an associate in a distant part of the state, thereby purposely exposing debtors to the inconvenience and expense of attending a distant court).

[11] We recognize that the utilization of virtually any available litigation procedure by an attorney will generally be accompanied by an awareness on that attorney's part that his action will necessarily subject the opposing party to additional legal expenses. The range of feeling in the initiating attorney evoked by that awareness might well vary from instances of actual indifference to instances of intense satisfaction. By our holding in this case we do not intend to suggest that liability for abuse of process should result from either of the said instances alone. Liability should result only when the sense of awareness progresses to a sense of purpose, and, in addition the utilization of the procedure for the purposes for which it was designed becomes so lacking in justification as to lose its legitimate function as a reasonably justifiable litigation procedure. As previously stated, there was evidence presented here of many instances from which a trier of fact could have concluded that the ulterior or collateral purpose of appellant Manfred Wetzel to subject the Nienstedts to excessive litigation expenses was in fact his primary purpose, and that his use of various legal processes was not justified or used for legitimate or reasonably justifiable purposes of advancing appellants' interests in ongoing litigation.

* * *

EXCESSIVE VERDICT

Appellants do not contest the award of $7,350 as actual damages except on the basis that the actual damages were precluded by the res judicata effect of the superior court decision in Maricopa County Case No. C-307988. As previously discussed, the award of attorney's fees in the prior action related only to the award of fees relative to appellees' motion to produce and response to appellants' motion for protective order. The record in this matter contains testimony that the attorney's fees sought in the present action were fees incurred in excess of the amount awarded in the prior action. Appellees also sought compensatory damages in the present action for mental suffering. The jury verdict does not specify in its award of actual damages the amounts granted for attorney's fees or mental suffering. Therefore, we make no assumption with respect to the amounts allocable to these claims.

Appellants' argument on appeal concerning excessive damages is limited to an attack on the award of $50,000 punitive damages which they claim was the result of passion or prejudice. The only arguments asserted in support of this claim are that the failure of appellees to introduce evidence relative to appellants' wealth or financial resources resulted in the jury having no way of relating punitive damages to appellants' economic status. Additionally, it is urged that the amount of punitive damages was excessive in comparison to the actual damages awarded. Appellants speculate that the excessive punitive damages award was caused by the introduction of evidence relative to appellant Wetzel's suspension from the practice of law.

[21][22][23] In Arizona, there is no compensatory-punitive damage ratio limit. Whether punitive damages are excessive is based solely on the circumstances of each case and one of the factors that the jury may consider in assessing the degree of punishment is the wealth of the defendant. *Dodge City Motors, Inc. v. Rogers*, 16 Ariz.App.24, 490 P.2d 853 (1971). However, we are aware of no authority, nor has appellant cited any authority, indicating that evidence of the wealth of a defendant is a necessary prerequisite to an award of punitive damages. For cases holding that such evidence is not required, *see Rinaldi v. Aaron*, 314 So.2d 762 (Fla.1975); *Carrick v. McFadden*, 216 Kan. 683, 533 P.2d 1249 (1975); *Fahrenberg v. Tengel*, 96 Wis.2d 211, 291 N.W.2d 516

(1980); *Rogers v. Florence Printing Company*, 233 S.C. 567, 106 S.E.2d 258 (1958). In any event, a defendant may not complain of the absence of evidence of his wealth when he has made no effort to introduce such evidence. *Rogers v. Florence Printing Company*, supra; *Rinaldi v. Aaron*, supra.

[24][25][26][27] The amount of an award for punitive damages is a matter of discretion with the trier of fact, and such award will not be disturbed unless it is so unreasonable in regard to the circumstances as to show influence of passion or prejudice. *Nielson v. Flashberg*, 101 Ariz. 335, 419 P.2d 514 (1966). The size of the verdict alone is not sufficient evidence of passion or prejudice on the part of the jury. *Jackson v. Mearig*, 17 Ariz.App. 94, 495 P.2d 864 (1972). Punitive damages are allowed where the conduct of the wrongdoer is wanton, reckless or shows spite or ill will. E.g., *Salt River Valley Water Users Association v. Giglio*, 113 Ariz. 190, 549 P.2d 162 (1976); *Country Escrow Service v. Janes*, 121 Ariz. 511, 591 P.2d 999 (App.1979).

[28][29] Where the trial court has refused to interfere with the jury's determination of damages, this court cannot interpose its own judgment on the issue unless convinced that the verdict is so excessive as to suggest passion or prejudice. *Frontier Motors, Inc. v. Horrall*, 17 Ariz.App. 198, 496 P.2d 624 (1972). The record in this matter contains testimony from which a jury could conclude that appellants' conduct reflected spite, ill will and reckless indifference to the interest of appellees. We do not find the verdict so excessive as to suggest passion or prejudice.

The judgment of the trial court is affirmed.

CONTRERAS, Acting P. J., Department A, and OGG, J., concur.

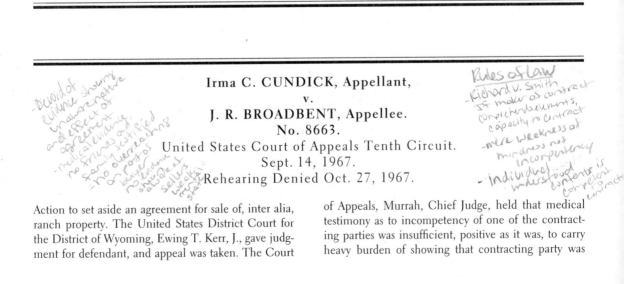

Irma C. CUNDICK, Appellant,

v.

J. R. BROADBENT, Appellee.

No. 8663.

United States Court of Appeals Tenth Circuit.

Sept. 14, 1967.

Rehearing Denied Oct. 27, 1967.

Action to set aside an agreement for sale of, inter alia, ranch property. The United States District Court for the District of Wyoming, Ewing T. Kerr, J., gave judgment for defendant, and appeal was taken. The Court

of Appeals, Murrah, Chief Judge, held that medical testimony as to incompetency of one of the contracting parties was insufficient, positive as it was, to carry heavy burden of showing that contracting party was incompetent, that is, that he did not know the extent and condition of his property, how he was disposing of it, and to whom and upon what considerations, when weighed against affirmative evidence of contracting party's normal behavior during period of the transaction.

Affirmed.

Hill, Circuit Judge, dissented.

1. **Mental Health k373**   Contractual act by one claiming to be mentally deficient, but not under guardianship, absent fraud or knowledge of such asserted incapacity by other contracting party, is not a void act but at most only voidable at instance of the deficient party, and then only in accordance with certain equitable principles.

2. **Contracts k92**   Mental capacity to contract depends upon whether the allegedly disabled person possesses sufficient reason to enable him to understand the nature and effect of the act in issue; even average intelligence is not essential to a valid bargain.

3. **Contracts k92**   If a maker of a contract has sufficient mental capacity to retain in his memory without prompting the extent and condition of his property and to comprehend how he is disposing of it and to whom and upon what consideration, then he possesses sufficient mental capacity to execute such instrument.

4. **Contracts k92, 94(1)**   Under Wyoming law, either weakness of body or mind, or of both, do not constitute "mental incompetency" sufficient to render a contract voidable; a condition which may be described by a physician as senile dementia may not be insanity in a legal sense, but a weak mind is highly relevant in determining whether deficient party was overreached and defrauded.

See publication Words and Phrases for other judicial constructions and definitions.

5. **Contracts k99(1)**   Burden is on the one asserting incompetency and fraud at crucial time of making of challenged agreement.

6. **Evidence k570**   Expert evidence does not foreclose lay testimony concerning same matter which is within knowledge and comprehension of lay witness.

7. **Contracts k99(2)**   Nature and circumstances of transaction are relevant evidence of capacity of parties to contract.

8. **Courts k406.3(2)**   Trial judge who heard and saw witnesses is the first and best judge of weight and value to be given to all the evidence, both expert and non-expert.

9. **Evidence k571(2)**   Medical testimony in action to set aside agreement, as to incompetency of one of the contracting parties, was insufficient, positive as it was, to carry heavy burden of showing that contracting party was "incompetent", that is, that he did not know the extent and condition of his property, how he was disposing of it, and to whom and upon what considerations, when weighed against affirmative evidence of contracting party's normal behavior during period of the transaction.

See publication Words and Phrases for other judicial constructions and definitions.

10. **Vendor and Purchaser k44**   Evidence supported finding that party to contract relating to, inter alia, sale of ranch property, who was allegedly incompetent, was not deceived or overreached by other contracting party.

11. **Corporations k316(3)**   Under Wyoming law, a director does not stand in a fiduciary relationship to a shareholder with regard to his stock; he has the right to purchase a shareholder's stock, and mere failure on part of director to disclose inside information does not compel an inference of fraud.

12. **Vendor and Purchaser k44**   Evidence supported finding that contract to, inter alia, sell ranch property, as amended, was not unconscionable, unfair or inequitable.

John J. Rooney, Cheyenne, Wyo., for appellant.

Edward T. Lazear, of Loomis, Lazear, Wilson & Pickett, Cheyenne, Wyo., for appellee.

Before MURRAH, Chief Judge, and BREITENSTEIN and HILL, Circuit Judges.

MURRAH, Chief Judge.   *—where case begins—law*

Irma Cundick, guardian ad litem for her husband, Darwin Cundick, brought this diversity suit in Wyoming to set aside an agreement for the sale of (1) livestock and equipment; (2) shares of stock in a development company; and (3) base range land in Wyoming. The alleged grounds for nullification were that at the time of the transaction Cundick was mentally incompetent to execute the agreement; that Broadbent, knowing of such incompetency, fraudulently represented to Cundick that the purchase price for the property described in the agreement was fair and just and that Cundick relied upon the false representations when he executed the agreement and transferred the property. The complaint further states that the guardian ad litem had offered to restore and does now offer to do so, but Broadbent has refused.

Upon a trial of the case without a jury, Judge Kerr made findings of fact in which he narrated the details of the months-long transaction. Specifically, he found that the various papers and documents embodying the agreement between the parties were prepared by Cundick's counsel and signed by Cundick in the presence of his counsel and his wife with her consent and approval; that the purchase price was paid and the transaction carried out between the date on which the agreement was executed, September 2, 1963, and the middle of February, 1964; that during this time neither Cundick nor his wife ever complained that he was incompetent or mentally incapable of transacting his own affairs, or that he was unable to understand and appreciate the effect of the transaction in which he had participated. He further found that Cundick's conduct during the critical time was the conduct and behavior of a competent person and there was no indication or evidence of any kind that Cundick was defrauded, imposed upon, deceived or overreached; that Cundick's election to rescind the agreement was not made until March, 1964, at which time the contract had been practically carried out; and that the election to rescind was not, therefore, sufficiently prompt.

The court concluded that Cundick failed to sustain the burden of proving that at the time of the transaction he was mentally incapable of managing his affairs; or that Broadbent knew of any mental deficiency when they entered into the agreement; or that Broadbent knowingly overreached him. The appeal is from a judgment dismissing the action. For reasons we shall state, the judgment is affirmed.

The contentions on appeal are twofold and stated alternatively: (1) that at the time of the transaction Cundick was totally incompetent to contract; that the agreement between the parties was therefore void ab initio, hence incapable of ratification; and (2) that in any event Cundick was mentally infirm and Broadbent knowingly overreached him; that the contract was therefore voidable, was not ratified—hence rescindable.

[1] At one time, in this country and in England, it was the law that since a lunatic or non compos mentis had no mind with which to make an agreement, his contract was wholly void and incapable of ratification. But, if his mind was merely confused or weak so that he knew what he was doing yet was incapable of fully understanding the terms and effect of his agreement, he could indeed contract, but such contract would be voidable at his option. *See Dexter v. Hall*, 15 Wall. 9, 82 U.S. 9, 21 L.Ed. 73; *see also* Principles of Contract by Sir Fredrick Pollock, 4th ed.

1888, p. 158. But in recent times courts have tended away from the concept of absolutely void contracts toward the notion that even though a contract be said to be void for lack of capacity to make it, it is nevertheless ratifiable at the instance of the incompetent party. The modern rule, and the weight of authority, seems to be as stated in 2 Jaeger's Williston on Contracts, 3d ed., § 251, in which an Eighth Circuit case is cited and quoted to the effect that "* * * the contractual act by one claiming to be mentally deficient, but not under guardianship, absent fraud, or knowledge of such asserted incapacity by the other contracting party, is not a void act but at most only voidable at the instance of the deficient party; and then only in accordance with certain equitable principles." *Rubenstein v. Dr. Pepper Co.*, 8 Cir., 228 F.2d 528. *See also* Williston, Secs. 253 and 254.

[2–4] In recognition of different degrees of mental competency the weight of authority seems to hold that mental capacity to contract depends upon whether the allegedly disabled person possessed sufficient reason to enable him to understand the nature and effect of the act in issue. Even average intelligence is not essential to a valid bargain. Williston on Contracts, 2d ed., § 256. In amplification of this principle, it has been said that if a maker of a contract "* * * has sufficient mental capacity to retain in his memory without prompting the extent and condition of his property and to comprehend how he is disposing of it and to whom and upon what consideration, then he possesses sufficient mental capacity to execute such instrument." *Richard v. Smith*, 235 Ark. 752, 361 S.W.2d 741, 742, *citing and quoting Donaldson v. Johnson*, 235 Ark. 348, 359 S.W.2d 810, 813; *see also Conerly v. Lewis*, 238 Miss. 68, 117 So.2d 460; *Matthews v. Acacia Mutual Life Insurance Co.*, Okl., 392 P.2d 369; *Berry v. Berry*, 269 Ala. 623, 114 So.2d 916. The Wyoming court adheres to the general principle that "Mere weakness of body or mind, or of both, do not constitute what the law regards as mental incompetency sufficient to render a contract voidable. * * * A condition which may be described by a physician as senile dementia may not be insanity in a legal sense." *Kaleb v. Modern Woodmen of America*, 51 Wyo. 116, 64 P.2d 605, 607. Weakmindedness is, however, highly relevant in determining whether the deficient party was overreached and defrauded. *See* Williston on Contracts, 3d ed., § 256 and cases collected there.

[5] From all this it may be said with reasonable assurance that if Cundick was utterly incapable of knowing the nature and effect of the transaction, the agreement is, without more, invalid, though capable of ratification by his representative or by him during lucid intervals. But, if the degree of disability was such

that he was capable of contracting, yet his mental condition rendered him susceptible of being overreached by an unscrupulous superior, his complaint comes under the heading of fraud to be proved as such. The burden is, of course, on the one asserting incompetency and fraud at the crucial time of the making of the challenged agreement.

Cundick was never judicially adjudged incompetent and his guardian ad litem apparently assumes the burden and accepts, as she must, the proposition that if the court's findings are supported by the record, they are conclusively binding here. She meets the issue squarely with the emphatic contention that the findings of the court are utterly without support in the record; that the evidence is all one way to the effect that at the time of the execution of the writings Cundick was mentally incompetent to make a valid contract. But, even if he was legally capable of doing so, she contends the evidence conclusively proves that he was weak-minded and that Broadbent defrauded him. It is suggested that the court significantly failed to make an affirmative finding on the issue of competency in the face of positive medical expert testimony to the effect that he was mentally incapable of conducting his affairs, particularly the sale and disposition of all his property.

All of the physicians who examined Cundick between 1961 and 1965 testified that in their judgment he was incapable of entering into the contract. When in December, 1960, Cundick first went to his family physician his condition was diagnosed as "depressive psychosis" and he was referred to a psychiatrist in Salt Lake City. While the Salt Lake City physician's report is not in evidence, the family physician apparently was informed by letter that Cundick had been given shock treatments. When Cundick returned to the family physician more than two years later, he was treated for sore throat and bronchitis. From that time until October, 1965, the family physician saw Cundick about 25 times and treated him for everything from a sore throat to a heart attack suffered in March, 1964, but nothing was said or done about a mental condition. Apparently after this suit was filed and upon order of the court Cundick was examined in March, 1964, by two neurosurgeons in Cheyenne. By extensive tests it was established that Cundick was suffering from an atrophy of the frontal lobes of his brain diagnosed as pre-senile or premature arteriosclerosis. Both physicians used different language to say that from their examination in March, 1964, they were of the opinion that on the date of the transaction, i. e. September 2, 1963, Cundick was a "confused and befuddled man with very poor judgment", and although there were things he could do, he was, in their opinion, unable to handle his affairs at the time of the transaction. A

psychologist to whom Cundick was referred in March by the Cheyenne neurosurgeons also testified that in his judgment Cundick was incapable of transacting his important business affairs in September of 1963. There was no medical testimony to the contrary. There was also lay testimony on behalf of Cundick to the effect that he was a quiet, reserved personality; that in approximately 1962 his personality changed from one of friendliness to inattentiveness and that during 1963 he was unable to make decisions with respect to the conduct of his ranching business.

[6–8] This unimpeached testimony may not be disregarded and the trier of the fact is bound to honor it in the absence of countervailing evidence—expert or non-expert—upon which to rest a contrary finding. "But, expert evidence does not foreclose lay testimony concerning the same matter which is within the knowledge and comprehension of the lay witness. A lay witness may tell all he knows about a matter in issue even though it may tend to impugn the conclusions of the expert." *Stafos v. Missouri Pacific Railroad Company*, 10 Cir., 367 F.2d 314, 317, and cases cited. The trier of the fact is not concluded by expert proof if other facts and circumstances of the case tend to cast doubt on its credibility. *See Perlmutter v. C.I.R.*, 10 Cir., 373 F.2d 45, and cases cited; and *see also Dayton P. & L. Co. v. Public Utilities Comm.*, 292 U.S. 290, 54 S.Ct. 647, 78 L.Ed. 1267. It has even been said that opinion evidence in cases of this kind is "* * * generally considered low grade, and not entitled to much weight against positive testimony of actual facts." *See In re Meyers*, 410 Pa. 455, 189 A.2d 852, 860.[1] The nature and circumstances of the transaction are certainly relevant evidence of the capacity

---

1. In the comprehensive opinion in the Meyers case the Supreme Court of Pennsylvania recognized at p. 862 three classes of testimony in determining mental competency, "(1) the testimony of those who observed the speech and conduct of the person on the day of execution of the instrument whose validity is challenged; (2) the testimony of those who observed the speech and conduct of the person a reasonable time before and after the day of execution of the instrument; (3) the testimony of those who never observed the speech and conduct of the person. In the first two classes, every witness, whether lay or expert, recites what he or she observed and then draws from the observation of such behavior an inference as to competency or incompetency which is called an opinion. In the last class, the inference is drawn after reading or hearing someone's recital of the person's speech and conduct, reliance being placed not on the observations of the witness but on the observations of another party. Obviously, the last class of testimony is not entitled to much weight." *See also Cyrus v. Tharp*, 147 W.Va. 110, 126 S.E.2d 31.

of the parties to contract. The trial judge who heard and saw the witnesses and felt the pulse beat of the lawsuit is, to be sure, the first and best judge of the weight and value to be given to all of the evidence, both expert and non-expert.

Against the background of medical and lay evidence tending to show Cundick's incompetency on the crucial date, there is positive evidence to the effect that at the time in question he was 59 years old, married and operating a sheep ranch in Wyoming; that in previous years he had sold his lamb crop to Broadbent and on a date prior to this transaction the parties met at a midway point for the purpose of selling the current lamb crop. Although there is innuendo concerning what transpired at the meeting, neither party testified and no one else was present. We do know that the meeting resulted in a one page contract signed by both parties in which Cundick agreed to sell all of his ranching properties to Broadbent. It is undisputed that Cundick and his wife thereafter took this one page contract to their lawyer in Salt Lake City who refined and amplified it into an eleven page contract providing in detail the terms by which the sale was to be consummated. The contract was signed in the lawyer's office by Cundick and Broadbent in the presence of Cundick's wife and the lawyer. The lawyer testified that the contract had been explained in detail and that all parties apparently understood it.

Thereafter and on September 23, pursuant to the terms of the contract Cundick and Broadbent met at the Cundick ranch and the lamb crop was delivered to Broadbent who in turn delivered them to another purchaser. All of the arrangements for the delivery of the lamb crop were made by Cundick, and he and Broadbent worked the scales together and tallied the weights. Later, and on October 4, 1963, Cundick wrote to Broadbent notifying him that he was ready to deliver the remainder of the sheep on October 10. This date was unsatisfactory to Broadbent and the parties agreed to a postponement until October 17, Broadbent agreeing to pay all of the expenses caused by the delay. The parties met at the Cundick corral, as agreed, on October 17. Cundick and Broadbent, aided by their ranch hands, mouthed, separated, checked and counted the ewes according to age. Cundick participated in this operation and no one seemed to notice anything unusual about him, except that in the process of mouthing the sheep Cundick missed a number of the old ewes placing them with the young to his advantage.

Cundick's lawyer who drafted the contract testified concerning an office memorandum dated October 18 which recited that Mrs. Cundick had called him that day saying the sheep had been delivered and that Broadbent had made part payment on account of

the contract including a check for the expenses incurred by Cundick due to the delay in taking delivery of the sheep. The memorandum recited that Broadbent had offered to call off the whole deal but that Cundick had refused.[2] The office memorandum further stated that Broadbent had given Cundick a signed memo providing "1. Cundick will waive interest on balance of amount due on contract for one year and Broadbent will add $5 per acre on the land. 2. Any income from oil or gas royalties, or leases or private lands, or oil and gas, or minerals will be paid to seller." The office memorandum went on to state the increase in the sale price resulting from this modification.[3] Thereafter Mr. and Mrs. Cundick took the memo to their lawyer and he prepared a supplemental agreement covering the changes reflected in the memo. This supplemental agreement was signed in the lawyer's office on October 24 after discussion between the parties. Thereafter and between October 24 and February, 1964, Cundick signed and delivered all the instruments including assignments, receipts and proxies necessary to fully complete the transactions in accordance with the contract as amended.

[9] As we have seen Cundick was not treated nor did he consult a physician for his mental condition from the time he returned from Salt Lake City in early 1961, until he was examined apparently by order of the court in March, 1964, after this suit was commenced. There was, to be sure, evidence of a change in his personality and attitude toward his business affairs during this period. But the record is conspicuously silent concerning any discussion of his mental condition among his family and friends in the com-

---

2. There was corroborated testimony that while the sheep were being "shaped up" and delivered, Mrs. Cundick was heard to say to Broadbent that "she didn't like the deal", and that Broadbent replied "Up to this point no one is hurt, the outfit is intact and if you don't like it you can have it." Mrs. Cundick then said "* * * A deal [is] a deal and we can go along with it." Curiously enough neither Broadbent nor Mrs. Cundick took the stand to testify in this case. But it was stipulated that if she testified she would deny that "an offer was made to rescind the full contract"; that instead "the offer was to rescind that portion of the contract which had to do with the base lands only * * *." It was also stipulated that if Broadbent took the stand he would testify that "the offer was made."

---

3. Trial counsel objected to the Salt Lake City lawyer's reading from this memo and "other notes and data" contained in his files. But there is nothing in these files, notes and data in the form of a communication which could properly be the subject of a confidential disclosure. *See Wilcoxon v. United States*, 10 Cir., 231 F.2d 384.

munity where he lived and operated his ranch. Certainly, the record is barren of any discussion or comment in Broadbent's presence. It seems incredible that Cundick could have been utterly incapable of transacting his business affairs, yet such condition be unknown on this record to his family and friends, especially his wife who lived and worked with him and participated in the months-long transaction which she now contends was fraudulently conceived and perpetrated. All this record silence, together with the affirmative evidence of normal behavior during the period of the transaction speaks loudly in support of the court's finding that Cundick's acts "* * *" were the acts, conduct and behavior of a person competent to manage his affairs * * *." As applied to the critical issue of incompetency, this finding leads us to the conclusion reached by the trial judge that when the medical testimony, positive as it may be, is considered in the context of all that was said and done, it does not carry the heavy burden of proving that Cundick was incompetent, i.e., he did not know the extent and condition of his property, how he was disposing of it, to whom and upon what consideration.

[10,11] The narrated facts of this case amply support the trial court's finding to the effect that Broadbent did not deceive or overreach Cundick. In the absence of any evidence that Broadbent knew of Cundick's mental deficiency, the only evidence from which it can be said that Broadbent took advantage or overreached him is the proof concerning the value of the property sold under the contract. As to that, there is positive evidence that the property was worth very much more than what Broadbent paid for it. But as we have noted, there was evidence to the effect that after the original contract was signed and some complaint made about the purchase price, the parties agreed to raise the price and the contract was so modified. The trial court found that the contract was supported by adequate consideration and specifically that the price paid for the shares of stock in the development company far exceeded the amount for which it sold from 1957 to 1962. It is suggested that fraudulent implications should be drawn from the fact that a substantial dividend was paid to the shareholders of the development company within a year from the date of the subject transaction; that as a director Broadbent had knowledge of a corporate transaction which contributed at least in part to the dividend and that Cundick had no such knowledge. But, there is nothing on this record from which it can be said with assurance that Broadbent possessed any knowledge of corporate affairs or transactions which was unavailable to Cundick or any other shareholder. Moreover, under applicable Wyoming law, a director does not stand in a fiducial relationship to a shareholder with regard to his stock. He has a right to purchase a shareholder's

stock, and mere failure on the part of the director to disclose inside information does not compel an inference of fraud. *See Morrison v. State Bank of Wheatland*, 58 Wyo. 138, 126 P.2d 793; *But Cf. Blazer v. Black*, 10 Cir., 196 F.2d 139.

[12] The Court finally concluded that the contract as amended was not unconscionable, unfair or inequitable. From the whole record we cannot say its conclusions in that respect are unsupported by the evidence. In this view of the case we have no occasion to consider whether the contract, if voidable, was in fact ratified.

Affirmed.

HILL, Circuit Judge (dissenting):

I am compelled to disagree with my distinguished associates. A careful review of the entire record before us leaves me with a firm and definite conviction that not only has a mistake been made by the very able trial judge but it is my feeling that a gross miscarriage of justice has taken place.

The evidence relied upon by the trial court and by the majority is actually trivial and inconsequential as compared with the undisputed medical testimony in the record as to the mental competency of Cundick to comprehend and understand the nature of the transactions in which he was involved.

Viewing all of the evidence adduced by appellee in a light most favorable to him, I cannot say that it meets the test of substantial evidence and I must conclude that it actually has little or no probative value. Much of this evidence pertains to the "mouthing" or separating of sheep by Cundick in the consummation of the deal. Five witnesses testified about this matter. One such witness admitted he did not have an opportunity to observe Cundick's ability to handle detailed business transactions. Another testified about mistakes made by Cundick in performing this simple "mouthing" operation. To me, none of this evidence even vaguely approaches the crucial issue of mental competency. Another Broadbent witness, an 89 year old lawyer from Evanston, Wyoming, admitted he "didn't have any occasion to make any observation about Cundick's ability to conduct his own business." The concluding evidence on behalf of Broadbent came from the deposition of lawyer Mark, who had prepared the legal documents in connection with the transaction in question. The fact that Mark testified only by deposition precludes the application of the rule that because of the trial judge's opportunity to observe and hear a witness personally testify, he is in a much better position to evaluate such testimony than is an appellate court. In this case, so far as the testimony of Mark is concerned, we are on an equal footing with the trial court and free to make our own independent evaluation. Mark was not asked to express his opinion as to the mental competency of Cundick. From all four corners of Mark's deposition it is plain that Mrs. Cundick, not Mr. Cundick, was the one actively participating in the conferences with Mark, and the one who was actually handling the consummation of the sale to Broadbent. What little participation is shown by Mr. Cundick was only through the guiding hand of Mrs. Cundick or Mark. This conclusion goes also to every act shown by the evidence to have been performed by Cundick in furtherance of the sale.

The one page longhand written agreement between Cundick and Broadbent was undisputedly written by Broadbent with only the two contracting parties present. It is significant to me that after every event that transpired in performance of the contract to sell, Cundick was relying upon another person for directions as to what he should do.

Both the trial court and my brothers seem to put some stress upon Mrs. Cundick's participation in the transaction. To me, what she did or said is immaterial. She is actually a stranger to the transaction and her mental competency and understanding of the import of what was taking place cannot be a substitute for the required mental competency and understanding on the part of Mr. Cundick. The same may be said as to the materiality and importance of the testimony of lawyer Mark.

The trial court made no specific finding as to the mental competency of Cundick as of the date of the contract but did find generally "The acts and conduct of Cundick between September 2, 1963, and the middle of February, 1964, were the acts, conduct and behavior of a person competent to manage his affairs and cognizant of the effect of his actions." To me, there is no evidence in the record to support this sweeping finding. The evidence, as I have pointed out, shows without contradiction that during the above period of time every pertinent act by Cundick was performed under the guiding hand of either his wife, his lawyer or some other person.

The opinion of the majority accurately reflects the expert testimony adduced by appellant on the issue of the mental competency of Cundick to make the questioned contract. It was positive, convincing and undisputed. Under the law of this Circuit the trial judge was compelled to honor it.[1] Upon his failure to follow these cases, we should reverse.

Finally, on the question of whether Broadbent,

in a legal sense, overreached Cundick, the evidence is uncontradicted that he did.

The evidence as to the true value of the property covered by the contract is uncontroverted. The 2252 acres of land involved sold for $39,510.00. A qualified expert on land values in the vicinity fixed the value at $86,189.00. Cundick's interest in Uinta Development Company sold for $46,750.00. Witness Spaulding for appellee testified this interest had a value of $73,743.45 and the three witnesses for appellant valued it at $184,358.63, $105,491.38 and $184,358.63. It is noteworthy that within a year after the date of the contract a dividend of $20,000.00 became payable upon Cundick's interest in the company and that Broadbent was one of the directors of Uinta on the date of the contract of sale and was in a position to have special knowledge about the company affairs and the value of its stocks.

It is well recognized by the authorities that transactions by a person of weak understanding are subject to close scrutiny. This principle recognizes the fact that advantage could quite easily be taken of such people. Therefore, evidence of weakness of mind and circumstances showing unfair dealing and inadequacy of consideration may present a situation where transactions taken should be rescinded. Williston, Contracts, § 256; 23 Am.Jur., Fraud and Deceit, § 15; 17 C.J.S. Contracts § 133(1). The majority recognizes this principle but does not, I feel, apply it to this case. It has been clearly established here that even if Cundick was not incompetent he was in a weakened mental condition. The gross inadequacy of the consideration was set out above. These factors clearly establish the basis for the application of the above principle. A strikingly similar case occurred in Colorado where an elderly rancher was persuaded by a person with whom he had had frequent livestock transactions to sell his ranch and cattle, having a worth of approximately $20,000.00, for about $8,000.00. Although the trial court found, on the basis of psychiatric evidence taken after the sale, that the rancher was incompetent, an alternative basis for the decision was: "Even though a mental condition may not amount to legal insanity, it may be sufficient to result in an inequality between the parties properly to be considered in connection with circumstances of unfair dealing and inadequacy of the consideration in determining whether a transaction vitiated by fraud, either actual or constructive." *Ruffini v. Avara*, 121 Colo. 567, 220 P.2d 355 at 358. It is significant to note that no mention was made of whether the purchasers had any knowledge of the seller's lack of capacity. The court felt that "the circumstances [of the sale] in themselves would seem to indicate a lack of capacity to manage property * * *." *Ibid.* I believe the instant case fits within the above quoted principle.

---

1. *Stafos v. Missouri Pacific Ry. Co.*, 10 Cir., 367 F.2d 314; *Browning v. Crouse*, 10 Cir., 356 F.2d 178, *cert. denied*, 384 U.S. 973, 86 S.Ct. 1864, 16 L.Ed.2d 683; *Potucek v. Cordeleria Lourdes*, 10 Cir., 310 F.2d 527, *cert. denied*, 372 U.S. 930, 83 S.Ct. 875, 9 L.Ed.2d 734; *Nicholas v. Davis*, 10 Cir., 204 F.2d 200.

It is inconceivable to me that any mentally competent person, with a lifetime of experience as a successful and substantial rancher and stockman, would dispose of his ranch interests at a price equal to less than one-half of the actual value. I would reverse and direct the entry of judgment in favor of appellant as prayed for.

In the Matter of the ESTATE of Grace SWENSON, Deceased.
Jane TROYER, and Urinda Laura Lee Russell, Respondents,
v.
Cora PLACKETT, Personal Representative of the Estate of Grace Swenson, Appellant.
No. 128786; CA No. 16071.
Court of Appeals of Oregon.
Argued and Submitted July 23, 1980.
Decided Sept. 29, 1980.

Daughters of decedent instituted proceeding to contest decedent's will, alleging that will was product of undue influence exerted by sole beneficiary. The Circuit Court, Multnomah County, William S. McLennan, J., entered order declaring will null and void, and beneficiary appealed. The Court of Appeals, Warden, J., held that evidence was sufficient to support determination that sole beneficiary, who had been acquainted with decedent less than two months prior to execution of will in which decedent disinherited her two daughters, exerted undue influence in making of will.

Affirmed.

1. **Wills k163(1)**   Burden of proving undue influence is upon will contestants.

2. **Wills k163(2)**   Confidential relationship between testator and beneficiary, considered together with other suspicious circumstances, may require beneficiary to carry burden of proof and to present evidence to overcome adverse inference of undue influence.

3. **Wills k157**   Individual who was decedent's "friend," bathed decedent, gave her drugs, shopped for her, wrote her checks and transported her, bore "confidential relationship" to decedent requisite to proving case of undue influence.

See publication Words and Phrases for other judicial constructions and definitions.

4. **Wills k158**   Factors to be considered in determining whether undue influence is exercised are participation of beneficiary in preparation of will, testator's receipt of independent advice in preparation of will, secrecy and haste in will preparation, change in attitude of decedent toward others, change in decedent's plan of disposing of property, unnatural or unjust gift by decedent, and decedent's susceptibility to influence.

5. **Wills k157**   Beneficiary who participates in preparation of will and occupies confidential relationship to testator has duty to see that testator receives independent, disinterested advice.

6. **Wills k166(5)**   Evidence in proceeding to contest will was sufficient to support determination that sole beneficiary, who had been acquainted with decedent less than two months prior to execution of will disinheriting decedent's two daughters, exerted undue influence in making of will.

Robert J. Riecke, Philomath, argued the cause and filed the briefs for appellant.

Robert D. Dayton, Portland, argued the cause for respondents. With him on the brief were Schwabe, Williamson, Wyatt, Moore & Roberts, and Ridgway K. Foley, Jr., Portland.

Before JOSEPH, P. J., and WARDEN and WARREN, JJ.

WARDEN, Judge.

This is a proceeding to contest the will of Grace Swenson brought by Jane Troyer and Urinda Laura Lee "Betty" Russell, daughters of the deceased. They contend that decedent lacked testamentary capacity and that the will was the product of undue influence exerted by the sole beneficiary, Cora Plackett.

The will was admitted to probate on March 20, 1978. Contestants filed objections to probate on July 20, 1978. After a hearing on those objections on July 23, 24 and 25, 1979, the trial court, on September 24, 1979, issued a letter opinion finding that at the time of the execution of the will decedent lacked testamentary capacity and, further, that the will was the result of the undue influence of Cora Plackett. By order entered October 12, 1979, the court made formal findings in accordance with its letter opinion, sustained the objections to probate, declared the will null and void, decreed the order admitting the will to probate set aside and revoked the appointment of Cora Plackett as personal representative of the estate of Grace Swenson. Cora Plackett appeals this order. Our review is de novo. We affirm the trial court, finding that the will of Grace Swenson dated July 21, 1977, was the product of undue influence of Cora Plackett.

We abstain from the usual lengthy recitation of the facts in this type of case. We will recite facts in our discussion of the issue of undue influence which control our decision.

In *In Re Reddaway's Estate*, 214 Or. 410, 419–20, 329 P.2d 886 (1958), the Supreme Court said:

> "Definitions of undue influence couched in terms of the testator's freedom of will are subject to criticism in that they invite us to think in terms of coercion and duress, when the emphasis should be on the unfairness of the advantage which is reaped as the result of wrongful conduct. 'Undue influence does not negative consent by the donor. Equity acts because there is want of conscience on the part of the donee, not want of consent on the part of the donor.' 3 Modern L.Rev. 97, 100 (1939). Said in another way, undue influence has a closer kinship to fraud than to duress. It has been characterized as a 'species of fraud.'"

[1–3] The burden of proving undue influence is upon the contestants. *In Re Southman's Estate*, 178 Or. 462, 168 P.2d 572 (1946). A confidential relationship between the testator and a beneficiary, considered together with other suspicious circumstances, may require the beneficiary to carry the burden of proof and present evidence to overcome the adverse inference of undue influence. *In Re Reddaway's Estate, supra*; *In Re Southman's Estate, supra*; and *Carlton v. Wolf*, 21 Or.App. 476, 535 P.2d 119 (1975). Cora Plackett bore a confidential relationship to decedent. She was decedent's "friend"; she bathed decedent, gave her drugs, shopped for her, wrote her checks and transported her.

[4] The factors to be considered in determining whether undue influence is exercised were set out by the Supreme Court in *In Re Reddaway's Estate, supra*, and reiterated by this court in *Carlton v. Wolf, supra*.

The first of these factors is procurement, that is, participation of the beneficiary in the preparation of the will. Cora Plackett, after learning that decedent intended to disinherit both her daughters and shortly after being told by decedent that decedent was thinking of leaving her entire estate to her, urged decedent to make a new will. She gave decedent the phone book, made the phone call to the attorney for her, talked to the attorney at the time of his first conference with the decedent and escorted the decedent to the attorney's office for purposes of execution of the will on July 21, 1977. (It is also at least interesting to note that Cora Plackett did not list that date in her diary as one of the days on which she worked for decedent.)

[5] The second factor is independent advice. A beneficiary who participates in preparation of a will and occupies a confidential relationship to the testator has a duty to see that the testator receives independent, disinterested advice. *In Re Reddaway's Estate supra*; *In Re Estate of Manillus Day*, 198 Or. 518, 257 P.2d 609 (1953). Cora Plackett did not seek to have decedent call either Mr. Hammond or Mr. Herbrand, attorneys, each of whom had drawn a will for decedent within ten months immediately preceding the drawing of this will. Instead, she helped the decedent contact a lawyer unknown to decedent. The attorney chosen had been in the practice of law less than two years and he relied in part on misinformation provided him by either decedent or Cora Plackett. The record discloses that he acted as little more than a scrivener. No effort was made by Cora Plackett to communicate with either of decedent's daughters, with other relatives or friends of the decedent, with doctors or with representatives of social agencies serving decedent to secure independent advice.

The third factor is secrecy and haste. No notice was given to the decedent's family members, close friends, or social service personnel. Decedent's true condition was kept from her daughter, Jane Troyer, when she made inquiry of her mother's condition on June 27, 1977, after a cousin, who had visited decedent for a week, phoned Jane telling her that her mother needed help, was being taken advantage of, and was on "dope." The services of an attorney who did not know decedent were sought, rather than those of attorneys to whom she was known. Cora Plackett urged the decedent to change her will and acted to assist her in changing her will within a week after Cora Plackett learned from decedent that decedent was considering making her her sole beneficiary.

The fourth factor is change in attitude toward others. Decedent had made two wills in the ten months prior to making this will. In September, 1976, she made a will leaving her entire estate to her two daughters to be shared equally. In February, 1977, by a second will, she left her entire estate to both daughters, with one receiving but $5 and the residue going to the other. Though Cora Plackett testified that she did not seek to have decedent leave her entire estate to her, the record is also entirely void of any effort by her to urge upon decedent any reconciliation with her daughter, Jane Troyer, from whom she had become estranged. Jane Troyer was a friend of Cora Plackett's sister and had engaged Cora Plackett's services for the decedent.

The fifth factor is a change in the decedent's plan of disposing of her property. The two prior wills left decedent's entire estate to her daughters. This will disinherited them and gave the estate to a virtual stranger.

The sixth factor is that of an unnatural or unjust gift. The decedent disowned her two daughters, the natural subject of her bounty, and gave her entire estate to an acquaintance of less than two months duration. Decedent's original contact with the lawyer who drew the will was made only 33 days after Cora Plackett entered her home.

The seventh and final factor is susceptibility to influence. Decedent was physically sick, suffering from numerous ailments and injuries. She was unable to walk without help. She could not drive an automobile. She was dependent upon drugs and frequently used alcohol to excess. She had recently lost her husband of 40 years. She mistakenly accused one of her daughters of stealing her property. Her susceptibility to being taken advantage of was amply demonstrated by her dealings with a husband and wife, realtors, who befriended her and then took advantage of her in a series of transactions.

There are substantial conflicts in the testimony in this case. It is apparent from the record and the trial judge's decision that he did not accept the testimony of Cora Plackett as credible. As we have often stated, we give substantial weight to the findings of the trier of fact who saw and observed the witnesses.

[6] We are satisfied from this record that Cora Plackett, the beneficiary of the July 21, 1977 will of Grace Swenson, exerted undue influence in the making of that will. Because we decide the case favorably to contestants on this issue, we do not address the question of the decedent's testamentary capacity. The judgment of the trial court is affirmed.

Miriam BenSHALOM, Plaintiff,

v.

John O. MARSH, Jr., Secretary of the U.S. Army; Commanding Officer H.Q., 84th Division, U.S. Army Reserve; Commanding Officer 5091st U.S. Army Reception Battalion, Defendants.

No. 88–C–468.

United States District Court, E.D. Wisconsin.

Jan. 10, 1989.

Servicemember who was denied reenlistment brought action challenging army reserve regulation that barred reenlistment to any servicemember who declared himself or herself to have homosexual orientation, without regard to whether servicemember engaged in homosexual conduct. On motions for summary judgment, the District Court, Myron L. Gordon, Senior District Judge, held that: (1) regulation unreasonably chilled servicemember's right to freedom of speech in violation of First Amendment, and (2) regulation did not further compelling government interest and, thus, violated principles of equal protection.

Plaintiff's motion granted.

* * *

2. **Constitutional Law k213.1(1)**   Homosexuals, as defined by status of having particular sexual orientation, without regard to whether they have engaged in any homosexual conduct, are suspect class for purposes of equal protection doctrine. U.S.C.A. Const.Amends. 5, 14.

3. **Armed Services k24** Army reserve regulation that barred reenlistment to any servicemember who declared himself or herself to have homosexual orientation violated servicemember's Fifth Amendment right to equal protection of law; although government interests sought to be protected by regulation were compelling, they were not rationally advanced by regulation distinguishing military personnel on basis of their sexual orientation, without regard to sexual conduct, so that regulation failed even most deferential standard of review. AR 140–111; U.S.C.A. Const. Amend. 5.

4. **United States k147(20)** Position taken by government in defending army reserve regulation barring reenlistment to any servicemember who declared himself or herself to have homosexual orientation was not substantially justified and, thus, servicemember challenging regulation was entitled to recover attorney fees incurred in having regulation declared void as violating First and Fifth Amendments. AR 140–111; 28 U.S.C.A. §§ 2412, 2412(d)(1)(B); U.S.C.A. Const.Amends. 1, 5.

*1373 Angermeier & Rogers by Patrick T. Berigan, Milwaukee, Wis., for plaintiff.

Kenneth C. Kohl, Civil Div., Dept. of Justice, Washington, D.C., Francis D. Schmitz, Asst. U.S. Atty., Milwaukee, Wis., for defendants.

DECISION AND ORDER

MYRON L. GORDON, Senior District Judge.

Sergeant Miriam BenShalom has filed this action seeking to have declared as unconstitutional the Army Reserve Regulation, AR 140–111, Table 4–2, that bars reenlistment to any serviceperson who declares himself or herself to have a homosexual orientation. Sergeant BenShalom is a self-declared lesbian who, on the basis of that declaration, was denied reenlistment by the Army Reserves. The matter is before the court on cross motions for summary judgment. For reasons stated herein, the court finds that Army Reserve Regulation AF 140–111, Table 4–2, violates the plaintiff's first and fifth amendment rights and, therefore, is constitutionally void on its face.

BACKGROUND

The facts are uncontested. Sergeant BenShalom enlisted in the Army Reserve in November 1974. At various times during her enlistment, she publicly acknowledged that she is a lesbian. On December 1, 1976, she was discharged solely because of her status as a person with a homosexual orientation.

The discharge was effectuated under Army Reserve Regulation AR 135–178, P 7–56(E), which allowed for the discharge of any soldier who "evidences homosexual tendencies, desire, or interest, but is without overt homosexual acts." There was no proof that Sergeant BenShalom had engaged in homosexual acts or had done anything that could be interpreted as a homosexual advance toward another female soldier. By all indications, Sergeant BenShalom was an excellent soldier with an exemplary military record.

Sergeant BenShalom successfully brought a mandamus action seeking reinstatement. Another branch of the district court held that the army regulations then at issue violated her first amendment rights of free speech and association as well as her constitutionally protected right to privacy. *BenShalom v. Secretary of Army*, 489 F.Sup. 964, 976 (E.D.Wis.1980) (hereafter BenShalom I). Vindication, however, was slow in coming. As late as August 1987, seven years after the district court ordered reinstatement, the Army resisted the reinstatement on the ground that the original regulations under which she had been discharged had been reworded. In ordering her reinstatement, the court of appeals for the seventh circuit stated: When BenShalom is returned to the Army, the Army is prohibited from discriminating against her because she professes to be a lesbian ... A change in the Army regulations, which the Secretary now claims would prohibit BenShalom from serving in the Reserves, cannot alter the right of BenShalom which was established in Judge Evans' 1980 opinion. *BenShalom v. Secretary of Army*, 826 F.2d 722, 724 (7th Cir.1987).

Sergeant BenShalom was finally reinstated in September 1987, almost eleven years after she had been unconstitutionally discharged. Her enlistment period was due to expire on August 11, 1988, and she timely requested reenlistment for a six year term; that request was denied on April 7, 1988. The revised regulations which the Army applied to bar her reenlistment made the status of homosexual a "nonwaivable moral and administrative disqualification." AR 140–111, Table 4–2. Sergeant BenShalom was denied reenlistment on the basis of the same earlier verbal declarations that had previously been the cause of her unlawful discharge.

Sergeant BenShalom filed the instant lawsuit on May 3, 1988. In an effort to preserve the status quo pending resolution of this action, she also filed a motion for a preliminary injunction. The motion was granted on August 3, 1988, 690 F.Supp. 774, and the Army was directed to consider Sergeant BenShalom's reenlistment without regard to her sexual orientation. In response to this court's August 3, 1988, order, the Army considered Sergeant BenShalom's reenlistment request without regard to her sexual orientation and determined that she otherwise satisfies all criteria for reenlistment. Nevertheless, the Army refused to reenlist her; instead, they chose to extend her prior enlistment. After being adjudged in contempt of court on September 1, 1988, the Army finally reenlisted Sergeant BenShalom pending the outcome of this case.

The uncontested factual situation today is very similar to that of 1980. The only real differences are the rewording of the regulations at issue and the fact that Sergeant BenShalom was denied reenlistment instead of being discharged. The basic policy remains the same: the Army considers those people with the status of having a homosexual orientation to be incompatible with military service because the Army believes such people, by their statements, demonstrate a propensity to engage in homosexual conduct. Today, as in 1980, there is no allegation that Sergeant Ben-Shalom has engaged in or attempted to engage in homosexual conduct of any type.

The Army regulation in question contains a list of numerous "nonwaivable moral and administrative disqualifications" to reenlistment. In that context, Table 4–2 of AR 140–111 places homosexuality in the following category: Rule E: Disqualification: Questionable moral character, history of antisocial behavior, sexual perversion, homosexuality (includes an individual who is an admitted homosexual but as to whom there is no evidence that they have engaged in homosexual acts either before or during military service, or has committed homosexual acts), or having frequent difficulties with law enforcement agencies. (see note 1.) The regulation defines a homosexual as "an individual, regardless of sex, who desires bodily contact between persons of the same sex, actively undertaken or passively permitted, with the intent of obtaining or giving sexual gratification. Any official, private, or public profession of homosexuality may be considered in determining whether an individual is an admitted homosexual." AR 140–111, Table 4–2, note 1. A homosexual act is defined as "bodily contact between persons of the same sex, actively undertaken or passively permitted, with the intent of obtaining or giving sexual gratification, or any proposal, solicitation or attempt to perform such an act." Id.

The regulation in question defines a homosexual on the basis of one's sexual desires. Neither the actual commission of a homosexual act nor the intent to commit one is an element of the definition. If a person, such as Sergeant BenShalom, has the status of having a homosexual orientation and that person engages in speech which discloses or otherwise acknowledges that status, then that person is subject to an automatic, nonwaivable disqualification to reenlistment, regardless whether that person has engaged in or intends to engage in actual homosexual conduct.

The regulation also includes the following caveat: Individuals who have been involved in homosexual acts in an apparently isolated episode, stemming solely from immaturity, curiosity, or intoxication, and absent other evidence that the individual is a homosexual, normally will not be excluded from service. AR 140–111, Table 4–2, note 1.

It follows that the regulation in question does not penalize the commission of homosexual acts per se. If a person with a heterosexual orientation engages in homosexual conduct, that person can avoid the consequences of AR 140–111 upon proof of his or her heterosexual orientation. In other words, status based on heterosexual orientation may be a defense to the commission of homosexual acts, and a person with a heterosexual orientation may engage in conduct which is prohibited on the part of a person with a homosexual orientation.

* * *

EQUAL PROTECTION

[2] Sergeant BenShalom claims that her fifth amendment right to equal protection of the law is violated by Army Reserve Regulation AR 140–111, Table 4–2. She argues that the regulation is subject to heightened scrutiny because homosexuals, as defined by the status of having a particular sexual orientation and absent any allegations of sexual misconduct, constitute a suspect class. A regulation based on such a classification, she argues, must fail because it is not necessary to achieve a compelling state end. Alternatively, Sergeant BenShalom argues that the regulation fails rationally to further a legitimate, articulated state purpose.

The Secretary argues that homosexuals are not a suspect class. But in the event that homosexuals are held to be a suspect class, the Secretary contends that the regulation does not violate the equal protection clause because it satisfies the test of heightened scrutiny since it furthers compelling government interests. Finally, the Secretary asserts that the correct approach is to uphold the constitutionality of the regulation under the traditional test of deferential scrutiny because the regulation rationally furthers several legitimate state interests.

The equal protection clause of the fourteenth amendment directs that no state shall "deny to any person within its jurisdiction the equal protection of the laws." The equal protection clause is made binding upon the federal government by the fifth amendment's due process clause, *Bolling v. Sharpe*, 347 U.S. 497, 498–99, 74 S.Ct. 693, 694, 98 L.Ed. 884 (1953), and "fifth amendment equal protection claims are treated precisely the same as equal protection claims under the fourteenth amendment." *Weinberger v. Wie-*

senfeld, 420 U.S. 636, 638 n. 2, 95 S.Ct. 1225, 1228 n. 2, 43 L.Ed.2d 514 (1975).

It is a general rule that government regulations will be presumed to be valid under the equal protection clause as long as the classification drawn by the regulation "rationally furthers some legitimate, articulated state purpose." *McGinnis v. Royster*, 410 U.S. 263, 270, 93 S.Ct. 1055, 1059, 35 L.Ed.2d 282 (1972). Under this deferential standard of scrutiny, the classification is tested for a general relationship to the articulated state purpose, and it matters not that an individual member of the burdened class proves to be an exception. *Massachusetts Board of Retirement v. Murgia*, 427 U.S. 307, 310–11, 96 S.Ct. 2562, 2565–66, 49 L.Ed.2d 520 (1975). This judicial deference is grounded in a constitutional presumption that "improvident [classifications] will eventually be rectified by the democratic processes." *Cleburne v. Cleburne Living Center Inc.*, 473 U.S. 432, 440, 105 S.Ct. 3249, 3254, 87 L.Ed.2d 313 (1984).

When a regulation creates classifications based on race, alienage or national origin, judicial deference gives way to heightened scrutiny. These classifications are considered suspect because they are based on "factors which are so seldom relevant to the achievement of any legitimate state interest that laws grounded in such considerations are deemed to reflect prejudice and antipathy." *Cleburne*, 473 U.S. at 440, 105 S.Ct. at 3254.

The debate over whether sexual orientation constitutes a suspect or quasi-suspect classification has been blurred by a failure adequately to differentiate between classifications based on conduct and those based on status. The regulation at issue in this case creates a classification based entirely on status. AR 140–111, Table 4–2, cannot be characterized as a classification based on conduct. The issue before the court is whether homosexuals, defined by the status of having a particular sexual orientation and absent any allegations of sexual misconduct, constitute a suspect or quasi-suspect class.

In *Bowers v. Hardwick*, 478 U.S. 186, 106 S.Ct. 2841, 92 L.Ed.2d 140 (1986), the Court held that there is no constitutionally protected privacy right to engage in consensual acts of homosexual sodomy. The court of appeals for the ninth circuit has noted that: [A]lthough *Hardwick* held that the due process clause does not prevent states from criminalizing acts of homosexual sodomy, [cite omitted], nothing in *Hardwick* actually holds that the state may make invidious distinctions when regulating sexual conduct. . . . While it is not our role to question Hardwick's concerns about substantive due process and specifically the right to privacy, these concerns have little relevance to equal protection doctrine. The right to equal protection of the laws has a clear basis in the text of the Constitution. *Watkins v. U.S. Army*, 847 F.2d 1329, 1340, 1341 (9th Cir.1988).

In *Padula v. Webster*, 822 F.2d 97, 102 (D.C.Cir.1987), the court decided that homosexuals were not a suspect or quasi-suspect class "when defined as persons who engage in homosexual conduct." The court was careful to stress that the classification then under scrutiny "focus[ed] only on homosexual conduct, not homosexual status." *Id.* The *Padula* court held that the Supreme Court's decision in *Hardwick* foreclosed efforts to make practicing homosexuals a suspect class. *Padula*, 822 F.2d at 103.

In an equal protection context, *Padula* and *Hardwick* can only be reasonably construed as standing for the proposition that classifications are not subject to strict scrutiny when defined by homosexual conduct that rises to the level of criminal sodomy. *Doe v. Casey*, 796 F.2d 1508, 1522 (D.C.Cir.1986) ("[*Hardwick*] did not reach the difficult issue of whether an agency of the federal government can discriminate against individuals merely because of sexual orientation.") (emphasis in the original). In *Baker v. Wade*, 769 F.2d 289, 292 (5th Cir.1985), the court rejected an equal protection claim challenging a Texas statute that criminalized homosexual sodomy. The court declined to hold that homosexuals, defined by conduct, constituted a suspect or quasi-suspect class. *Id.* In denying a petition for rehearing en banc, the court took care to distinguish between conduct and status by noting that "[t]he statute is directed at certain conduct, not a class of people." *Baker v. Wade*, 774 F.2d 1285, 1287 (5th Cir.1985).

In *Watkins v. U.S. Army*, 847 F.2d 1329, 1349 (9th Cir.1988), *reh'g en banc ordered*, 847 F.2d 1362 (9th Cir.1988), the court held that homosexuals constitute a suspect class when defined by status. The facts in Watkins are very similar to those in the instant case; both cases involved essentially the same army regulation that makes homosexuality a nonwaivable bar to reenlistment.

Homosexuals have suffered a history of purposeful discrimination. Justice Brennan has noted that "homosexuals have historically been the object of pernicious and sustained hostility, and it is fair to say that discrimination against homosexuals is 'likely . . . to reflect deep-seated prejudice rather than . . . rationality.'" *Rowland v. Mad River Local School District*, 470 U.S. 1009, 1014, 105 S.Ct. 1373, 1377, 84 L.Ed.2d 392 (1985) (dissenting from denial of cert.). Such hostility is evident in the very pleadings in this case wherein homosexuals are analogized to kleptomaniacs and arsonists. *See* Defendants' Memorandum in Reply to Plaintiff's Brief in Opposition to Motion to Dismiss, p. 10.

The Secretary has continuously characterized homosexuals as a group defined by the desire and intent to engage in criminal acts of sodomy. Yet not one shred of evidence has been presented to the court to show that homosexuals as a group share a compelling desire to commit that particular form of sexual conduct. The court is asked by the Secretary to hold that homosexual orientation is inherently intertwined with a desire and intent to commit criminal acts of sodomy. To do so is to create a class based on prejudicial notions of what homosexuals are supposedly like. This type of discrimination, based on unsupported stereotypes, is precisely the type of discrimination that requires enhanced judicial scrutiny. *Cleburne*, 473 U.S. at 440, 105 S.Ct. at 3245; *High Tech Gays v. Defense Indust. Sec. Clear. Off.*, 668 F.Supp. 1361, 1369 (N.D.Cal.1987).

It is also clear that a class based on homosexual orientation is defined by a trait that bears no relationship to an individual's ability to contribute to the good of society. In *BenShalom I*, Judge Evans held that: [T]he record is clear that [BenShalom's] sexual preferences made no difference to her immediate supervisors or her students. The court is satisfied from the record that her sexual preferences had as much relevance to her military skills as did her gender or the color of her skin. *BenShalom I, supra*, 489 F.Supp. at 973–74; *accord, Watkins, supra*, 847 F.2d at 1346; *High Tech Gays, supra*, 668 F.Supp. at 1369–70.

In only a very few communities do homosexuals possess the political power effectively to obtain redress from invidious discriminations in the political arena. It is estimated that homosexuals constitute between 8% and 15% of the population. *Rowland v. Mad River Local School District*, 470 U.S. 1009, 1014 n. 7, 105 S.Ct. 1373, 1377 n. 7, 84 L.Ed.2d 392 (1985) (Brennan, J., dissenting from denial of cert.). Homosexuals constitute a discrete and insular group subject to potential prejudicial political power. *Watkins, supra*, 847 F.2d at 1348–49.

The court concludes that homosexuals, as defined by the status of having a particular sexual orientation, constitute a suspect class for the purposes of the equal protection doctrine. However, it is unnecessary for the court to subject the classification to strict scrutiny because the court finds that the classification fails even the most deferential standard of review. The classification is not rationally related to any articulated legitimate government interest. *McGinnis v. Royster*, 410 U.S. 263, 270, 93 S.Ct. 1055, 1059, 35 L.Ed.2d 282 (1972).

[3] The court recognizes that the government interests articulated by the Secretary are indeed compelling. The problem is that none are rationally advanced by an Army regulation which distinguishes military personnel on the basis of their sexual orientation. The elimination of all soldiers with homosex-

ual orientations from the ranks of the Army is not rationally related to the advancement of any compelling government interest. It has already been noted that sexual orientation is a trait that bears no relationship to an individual's ability to perform or contribute to the military, and it is not rational to hold that there is a general relationship between the trait upon which the classification is based and the advancement of any of the articulated military interests.

The military does have a legitimate interest in the regulation of sexual conduct of service personnel. It is reasonable to say that regulation of sexual behavior is rationally related to each of the articulated government interests. But such regulation must be targeted at the conduct itself and cannot be based on prejudicial stereotypes of what people with certain orientations are like.

The challenged regulation can survive deferential scrutiny only if the Secretary is correct in the assertion that the status-conduct distinction is bogus. The Secretary insists that the regulation is aimed at conduct and that we must presume a correlation between orientation and conduct. I disagree.

In *Baker v. Wade*, 774 F.2d 1285, 1287 (5th Cir.1985), the court noted that "[t]hough the conduct be the desire of the bisexually or homosexually inclined, there is no necessity that they engage in it." In *Cyr v. Walls*, 439 F.Supp. 697, 702 (N.D.Tex.1977), the court stated that it "can take notice of the logical distinction between gay individuals who simply prefer the companionship of members of their own sex and homosexual individuals who actively practice homosexual conduct."

[4] A prevailing party in any civil action against the United States, or any agency or any official of the United States acting in his or her official capacity, is entitled to a reasonable attorney's fee unless the position of the United States was substantially justified or other conditions exist which would make an award unjust. 28 U.S.C. § 2412. In the case at bar, the plaintiff is clearly the prevailing party in all respects. It is equally clear that the position taken by the United States was not substantially justified. Accordingly, the plaintiff will be allowed 30 days from the date of this decision and order to serve and file her application for fees and other expenses in accordance with 28 U.S.C. § 2412(d)(1)(B). The government will be allowed 10 business days from the date of the filing of the application to serve and file its objections, if any, concerning the reasonableness of the requested amount.

CONCLUSION

Therefore, IT IS ORDERED that the defendants' motion for summary judgment be and hereby is denied.

IT IS ALSO ORDERED that the plaintiff's cross motion for summary judgment be and hereby is granted.

IT IS FURTHER ORDERED that Army Reserve Regulation AR 140–111, Table 4–2, be and hereby is declared unconstitutional on its face.

IT IS FURTHER ORDERED that the defendants be and hereby are directed to continue Sergeant BenShalom's reenlistment without regard to her sexual orientation.

IT IS FURTHER ORDERED that the clerk of this court enter judgment in favor of the plaintiff, with costs.

END OF DOCUMENT

MINNESOTA, Petitioner,
v.
Timothy DICKERSON.
No. 91–2019.
Argued March 3, 1993.
Decided June 7, 1993.

Defendant's motion to suppress seizure of crack cocaine from defendant's person was denied by the District Court, Hennepin County, and defendant appealed. The Minnesota Court of Appeals, 469 N.W.2d 462, reversed. The State appealed. The Minnesota Supreme Court, 481 N.W.2d 840, affirmed. The State's petition for certiorari was granted. The Supreme Court, Justice White, held that: (1) police may seize nonthreatening contraband detected through the sense of touch during protective patdown search so long as the search stays within the bounds marked by *Terry*, and (2) search of defendant's jacket exceeded lawful bounds marked by *Terry* when officer determined that the lump was contraband only after squeezing, sliding and otherwise manipulating the contents of the defendant's pocket, which officer already knew contained no weapon.

Affirmed.

Justice Scalia filed a concurring opinion.

The Chief Justice filed an opinion concurring in part and dissenting in part, in which Justice Blackmun and Justice Thomas joined.

1. Criminal Law k1134(3)   Defendant's constitutional challenge to validity of patdown search as not moot even though, under Minnesota law, diversionary sentence would not be considered a conviction; there was possibility of reinstatement of the record of the charges in subsequent state or federal proceedings that would carry collateral legal consequences. U.S.C.A. Const.Amend. 4; M.S.A. § 152.18.

2. Arrest k63.5(9)   A *Terry* protective search—permitted without a warrant and on basis of reasonable suspicion less than probable cause—must be strictly limited to that which is necessary for the discovery of weapons which might be used to harm the officer or others nearby. U.S.C.A. Const.Amend. 4.

3. Arrest k63.5(9)   If the *Terry* protective search goes beyond what is necessary to determine if the suspect is armed, it is no longer valid and its fruits will be suppressed. U.S.C.A. Const.Amend. 4.

4. Arrest k63.5(9)   Police officers may seize nonthreatening contraband detected during a patdown search for weapons so long as the officer's search stays within the bounds marked by *Terry*. U.S.C.A. Const.Amend. 4.

5. Searches and Seizures k47.1, 49   Under "plain-view" doctrine, if police are lawfully in a position from which they view an object, if its incriminating character is immediately apparent, and if the officers have lawful right of access to the object, they may seize it without a warrant, but if the police lack probable cause to believe that an object in plain view is contraband without conducting some further search of the object, i.e., if its incriminating character is not immediately apparent, the "plain-view" doctrine cannot justify its seizure. U.S.C.A. Const.Amend. 4.

6. Searches and Seizures k47.1   "Plain-view" doctrine has obvious application by analogy to cases in which an officer discovers contraband through the sense of touch during an otherwise lawful search. U.S.C.A. Const.Amend. 4.

7. **Searches and Seizures k16** Rationale of "plain-view" doctrine is that if contraband is left in open view and is observed by police officer from lawful vantage point, there has been no invasion of legitimate expectation of privacy and thus no "search" within meaning of the Fourth Amendment. U.S.C.A. Const.Amend. 4.

8. **Searches and Seizures k47.1** Warrantless seizure of contraband that is in plain view is deemed justified by realization that resort to neutral magistrate under such circumstances would often be impracticable and would do little to promote objectives of Fourth Amendment. U.S.C.A. Const.Amend. 4.

9. **Searches and Seizures k47.1, 49** If police officer lawfully pats down a suspect's outer clothing and feels an object whose contour or mass makes its identity immediately apparent, there has been no invasion of the suspect's privacy beyond that already authorized by the officer's search for weapons; if the object is contraband, its warrantless seizure would be justified by the same practical considerations that inhere in the plain view context. U.S.C.A. Const.Amend. 4.

10. **Searches and Seizures k49** Regardless of whether during *Terry* stop and patdown search the officer detects the contraband by sight (plain-view) or by touch (plain-feel), the Fourth Amendment's requirement that the officer have probable cause to believe that the item is contraband before seizing it ensures against excessively speculative seizures. U.S.C.A. Const.Amend. 4.

11. **Searches and Seizures k49** The seizure during *Terry* patdown search of an item whose identity is already known occasions no further invasion of privacy and thus suspect's privacy interests are not advanced by categorical rule barring seizure of contraband plainly detected through sense of touch. U.S.C.A. Const.Amend. 4.

12. **Arrest k63.5(9)** Police officer overstepped lawful bounds marked by *Terry* when officer determined that lump in pocket of defendant's jacket was contraband crack cocaine only after squeezing, sliding and otherwise manipulating the contents of the defendant's pocket which the officer already knew contained no weapon. U.S.C.A. Const.Amend. 4.

13. **Searches and Seizures k47.1, 147.1** Where an officer who is executing a valid search for one item seizes a different item, Supreme Court is sensitive to the danger that officers will enlarge specific authorization, furnished by warrant or an exigency, into the equivalent of a general warrant to rummage or seize at will. U.S.C.A. Const.Amend. 4.

14. **Arrest k63.5(9) Searches and Seizures k49** Although police officer was lawfully in a position to feel lump in defendant's jacket pocket, because *Terry* entitled him to place his hands upon defendant's jacket, the incriminating character of the object was not immediately apparent to officer and was determined to be contraband only after officer conducted further search, one not authorized by *Terry* or by any other exception to the warrant requirement, and thus further search of defendant's pocket was constitutionally invalid; seizure of the cocaine that followed was likewise unconstitutional.

*Syllabus**

Based upon respondent's seemingly evasive actions when approached by police officers and the fact that he had just left a building known for cocaine traffic, the officers decided to investigate further and ordered respondent to submit to a patdown search. The search revealed no weapons, but the officer conducting it testified that he felt a small lump in respondent's jacket pocket, believed it to be a lump of crack cocaine upon examining it with his fingers, and then reached into the pocket and retrieved a small bag of cocaine. The state trial court denied respondent's motion to suppress the cocaine, and he was found guilty of possession of a controlled substance. The Minnesota Court of Appeals reversed. In affirming, the State Supreme Court held that both the stop and the frisk of respondent were valid under *Terry v. Ohio*, 392 U.S. 1, 88 S.Ct. 1868, 20 L.Ed.2d 889, but found the seizure of the cocaine to be unconstitutional. Refusing to enlarge the "plain view" exception to the Fourth Amendment's warrant requirement, the court appeared to adopt a categorical rule barring the seizure of any contraband detected by an officer through the sense of touch during a patdown search. The court further noted that, even if it recognized such a "plain feel" exception, the search in this case would not qualify because it went far beyond what is permissible under *Terry*.

Held:

1. The police may seize nonthreatening contraband detected through the sense of touch during a protective patdown search of the sort permitted by *Terry*, so long as the search stays within the bounds marked by *Terry*. Pp. 2135–2138.

---

*The syllabus constitutes no part of the opinion of the Court but has been prepared by the Reporter of Decisions for the convenience of the reader. See *United States v. Detroit Lumber Co.*, 200 U.S. 321, 337, 26 S.Ct. 282, 287, 50 L.Ed. 499.

(a) *Terry* permits a brief stop of a person whose suspicious conduct leads an officer to conclude in light of his experience that criminal activity may be afoot, and a patdown search of the person for weapons when the officer is justified in believing that the person may be armed and presently dangerous. This protective search—permitted without a warrant and on the basis of reasonable suspicion less than probable cause—is not meant to discover evidence of crime, but must be strictly limited to that which is necessary for the discovery of weapons which might be used to harm the officer or others. If the protective search goes beyond what is necessary to determine if the suspect is armed, it is no longer valid under *Terry* and its fruits will be suppressed. *Sibron v. New York*, 392 U.S. 40, 65–66, 88 S.Ct. 1889, 1904, 20 L.Ed.2d 917. Pp. 2135–2136.

(b) In *Michigan v. Long*, 463 U.S. 1032, 1050, 103 S.Ct. 3469, 3481, 77 L.Ed.2d 1201, the seizure of contraband other than weapons during a lawful *Terry* search was justified by reference to the Court's cases under the "plain-view" doctrine. That doctrine—which permits police to seize an object without a warrant if they are lawfully in a position to view it, if its incriminating character is immediately apparent, and if they have a lawful right of access to it—has an obvious application by analogy to cases in which an officer discovers contraband through the sense of touch during an otherwise lawful search. Thus, if an officer lawfully pats down a suspect's outer clothing and feels an object whose contour or mass makes its identity immediately apparent, there has been no invasion of the suspect's privacy beyond that already authorized by the officer's search for weapons. *Cf., e.g., Illinois v. Andreas*, 463 U.S. 765, 771, 103 S.Ct. 3319, 3324, 77 L.Ed.2d 1003. If the object is contraband, its warrantless seizure would be justified by the realization that resort to a neutral magistrate under such circumstances would be impracticable and would do little to promote the Fourth Amendment's objectives. *Cf., e.g., Arizona v. Hicks*, 480 U.S. 321, 326–327, 107 S.Ct. 1149, 1153–1154, 94 L.Ed.2d 347. Pp. 2135–2138.

2. Application of the foregoing principles to the facts of this case demonstrates that the officer who conducted the search was not acting within the lawful bounds marked by *Terry* at the time he gained probable cause to believe that the lump in respondent's jacket was contraband. Under the State Supreme Court's interpretation of the record, the officer never thought that the lump was a weapon, but did not immediately recognize it as cocaine. Rather, he determined that it was contraband only after he squeezed, slid, and otherwise manipulated the pocket's contents. While *Terry* entitled him to

place his hands on respondent's jacket and to feel the lump in the pocket, his continued exploration of the pocket after he concluded that it contained no weapon was unrelated to the sole justification for the search under *Terry*. Because this further search was constitutionally invalid, the seizure of the cocaine that followed is likewise unconstitutional. Pp. 2138–2139.

481 N.W.2d 840, (Minn.1992) affirmed.

WHITE, J., delivered the opinion for a unanimous Court with respect to Parts I and II, and the opinion of the Court with respect to Parts III and IV, in which STEVENS, O'CONNOR, SCALIA, KENNEDY, and SOUTER, JJ., joined. SCALIA, J., filed a concurring opinion. REHNQUIST, C.J., filed an opinion concurring in part and dissenting in part, in which BLACKMUN and THOMAS, JJ., joined.

Michael O. Freeman, Hennepin Co. Atty., Beverly J. Wolfe, Asst. Co. Atty., Minneapolis, MN, for petitioner.

Richard H. Seamon, Washington, DC, for the U.S., as amicus curiae by special leave of Court.

Peter W. Gorman, Minneapolis, MN, for respondent.

Justice WHITE delivered the opinion of the Court.

In this case, we consider whether the Fourth Amendment permits the seizure of contraband detected through a police officer's sense of touch during a protective patdown search.

I

On the evening of November 9, 1989, two Minneapolis police officers were patrolling an area on the city's north side in a marked squad car. At about 8:15 p.m., one of the officers observed respondent leaving a 12-unit apartment building on Morgan Avenue North. The officer, having previously responded to complaints of drug sales in the building's hallways and having executed several search warrants on the premises, considered the building to be a notorious "crack house." According to testimony credited by the trial court, respondent began walking toward the police but, upon spotting the squad car and making eye contact with one of the officers, abruptly halted and began walking in the opposite direction. His suspicion aroused, this officer watched as respondent turned and entered an alley on the other side of the apartment building. Based upon respondent's seemingly evasive actions and the fact that he had just left a building known for cocaine traffic, the officers decided to stop respondent and investigate further.

The officers pulled their squad car into the alley and ordered respondent to stop and submit to a pat-down search. The search revealed no weapons, but the officer conducting the search did take an interest in a small lump in respondent's nylon jacket. The officer later testified:

"[A]s I pat-searched the front of his body, I felt a lump, a small lump, in the front pocket. I examined it with my fingers and it slid and it felt to be a lump of crack cocaine in cellophane." Tr. 9 (Feb. 20, 1990).

The officer then reached into respondent's pocket and retrieved a small plastic bag containing one fifth of one gram of crack cocaine. Respondent was arrested and charged in Hennepin County District Court with possession of a controlled substance.

Before trial, respondent moved to suppress the cocaine. The trial court first concluded that the officers were justified under *Terry v. Ohio*, 392 U.S. 1, 88 S.Ct. 1868, 20 L.Ed.2d 889 (1968), in stopping respondent to investigate whether he might be engaged in criminal activity. The court further found that the officers were justified in frisking respondent to ensure that he was not carrying a weapon. Finally, analogizing to the "plain-view" doctrine, under which officers may make a warrantless seizure of contraband found in plain view during a lawful search for other items, the trial court ruled that the officers' seizure of the cocaine did not violate the Fourth Amendment:

"To this Court there is no distinction as to which sensory perception the officer uses to conclude that the material is contraband. An experienced officer may rely upon his sense of smell in DWI stops or in recognizing the smell of burning marijuana in an automobile. The sound of a shotgun being racked would clearly support certain reactions by an officer. The sense of touch, grounded in experience and training, is as reliable as perceptions drawn from other senses. 'Plain feel,' therefore, is no different than plain view and will equally support the seizure here." App. to Pet. for Cert. C–5.

His suppression motion having failed, respondent proceeded to trial and was found guilty.

On appeal, the Minnesota Court of Appeals reversed. The court agreed with the trial court that the investigative stop and protective patdown search of respondent were lawful under *Terry* because the officers had a reasonable belief based on specific and articulable facts that respondent was engaged in criminal behavior and that he might be armed and dangerous. The court concluded, however, that the officers had overstepped the bounds allowed by *Terry* in seizing the cocaine. In doing so, the Court of Appeals "decline[d] to adopt the plain feel exception" to the warrant requirement. 469 N.W.2d 462, 466 (1991).

The Minnesota Supreme Court affirmed. Like the Court of Appeals, the State Supreme Court held that both the stop and the frisk of respondent were valid under *Terry*, but found the seizure of the cocaine to be unconstitutional. The court expressly refused "to extend the plain view doctrine to the sense of touch" on the grounds that "the sense of touch is inherently less immediate and less reliable than the sense of sight" and that "the sense of touch is far more intrusive into the personal privacy that is at the core of the [F]ourth [A]mendment." 481 N.W.2d 840, 845 (1992). The court thus appeared to adopt a categorical rule barring the seizure of any contraband detected by an officer through the sense of touch during a pat-down search for weapons. The court further noted that "[e]ven if we recognized a 'plain feel' exception, the search in this case would not qualify" because "[t]he pat search of the defendant went far beyond what is permissible under *Terry*." *Id*., at 843 and 844, n. 1. As the State Supreme Court read the record, the officer conducting the search ascertained that the lump in respondent's jacket was contraband only after probing and investigating what he certainly knew was not a weapon. See *Id*., at 844.

[1] We granted certiorari, 506 U.S. —, 113 S.Ct. 53, 121 L.Ed.2d 22 (1992), to resolve a conflict among the state and federal courts over whether contraband detected through the sense of touch during a patdown search may be admitted into evidence.[1] We now affirm.[2]

---

1. Most state and federal courts have recognized a so-called "plain feel" or "plain touch" corollary to the plain-view doctrine. See *United States v. Coleman*, 969 F.2d 126, 132 (CA5 1992); *United States v. Salazar*, 945 F.2d 47, 51 (CA2 1991), cert. denied, 504 U.S. —, 112 S.Ct. 1975, 118 L.Ed.2d 574 (1992); *United States v. Buchannon*, 878 F.2d 1065, 1067 (CA8 1989); *United States v. Williams*, 262 U.S.App.D.C. 112, 119–124, 822 F.2d 1174, 1181–1186 (1987); *United States v. Norman*, 701 F.2d 295, 297 (CA4), *cert. denied*, 464 U.S. 820, 104 S.Ct. 82, 78 L.Ed.2d 92 (1983); *People v. Chavers*, 33 Cal.3d 462, 471–473, 658 P.2d 96, 102–104 (1983); *Dickerson v. State*, 1993 WL 22025, *2, 1993 Del.LEXIS 12, *3–*4 (Jan. 26, 1993); *State v. Guy*, 172 Wis.2d 86, 101–102, 492 N.W.2d 311, 317–318 (1992). Some state courts, however, like the Minnesota court in this case, have rejected such a corollary. See *People v. Diaz*, 81 N.Y.2d 106, 595 N.Y.S.2d 940, 612 N.E.2d 298 (1993); *State v. Collins*, 139 Ariz. 434, 435–438, 679 P.2d 80, 81–84 (Ct.App.1983); *People v. McCarty*, 11 Ill.App.3d 421, 422, 296 N.E.2d 862, 863 (1973); *State v. Rhodes*, 788 P.2d 1380, 1381 (Okla.Crim.App.1990); *State v. Broadnax*, 98 Wash.2d

II

A

The Fourth Amendment, made applicable to the States by way of the Fourteenth Amendment, *Mapp v. Ohio*, 367 U.S. 643, 81 S.Ct. 1684, 6 L.Ed.2d 1081 (1961), guarantees "[t]he right of the people to be secure in their persons, houses, papers, and effects, against unreasonable searches and seizures." Time and again, this Court has observed that searches and seizures " 'conducted outside the judicial process,

---

289, 296–301, 654 P.2d 96, 101–103 (1982); *cf. Commonwealth v. Marconi*, 408 Pa.Super. 601, 611–615, and n. 17, 597 A.2d 616, 621–623, and n. 17 (1991), *appeal denied*, 531 Pa. 638, 611 A.2d 711 (1992).

---

2. Before reaching the merits of the Fourth Amendment issue, we must address respondent's contention that the case is moot. After respondent was found guilty of the drug possession charge, the trial court sentenced respondent under a diversionary sentencing statute to a 2-year period of probation. As allowed by the diversionary scheme, no judgment of conviction was entered and, upon respondent's successful completion of probation, the original charges were dismissed. *See* Minn.Stat. § 152.18 (1992). Respondent argues that the case has been rendered moot by the dismissal of the original criminal charges. We often have observed, however, that "the possibility of a criminal defendant's suffering 'collateral legal consequences' from a sentence already served" precludes a finding of mootness. *Pennsylvania v. Mimms*, 434 U.S. 106, 108, no. 3, 98 S.Ct. 330, 332, n. 3, 54 L.Ed.2d 331 (1977) (*per curiam*); *see also Evitts v. Lucey*, 469 U.S. 387, 391, no. 4, 105 S.Ct. 830, 833, no. 4, 83 L.Ed.2d 821 (1985); *Sibraon v. New York*, 392 U.S. 40, 53–58, 88 S.Ct. 1889, 1897–1900, 20 L.Ed.2d 917 (1968). In this case, Minnesota law provides that the proceeding which culminated in finding respondent guilty "shall not be deemed a conviction for purposes of disqualifications or disabilities imposed by law upon conviction of a crime or for any other purpose." Minn.Stat. § 152.18 (1992). The statute also provides, however, that a nonpublic record of the charges dismissed pursuant to the statute "shall be retained by the department of public safety for the purpose of use by the courts in determining the merits of subsequent proceedings" against the respondent. *Ibid.* Construing this provision, the Minnesota Supreme Court has held that "[t]he statute contemplates use of the record should [a] defendant have 'future difficulties with the law.' " *State v. Goodrich*, 256 N.W.2d 506, 512 (1977). Moreover, the Court of Appeals for the Eighth Circuit has held that a diversionary disposition under § 152.18 may be included in calculating a defendant's criminal history category in the event of a subsequent federal conviction. *United States v. Frank*, 932 F.2d 700, 701 (1991). Thus, we must conclude that reinstatement of the record of the charges against respondent would carry collateral legal consequences and that, therefore, a live controversy remains.

without prior approval by judge or magistrate, are *per se* unreasonable under the Fourth Amendment—subject only to a few specifically established and well delineated exceptions.' " *Thompson v. Louisiana*, 469 U.S. 17, 19–20, 105 S.Ct. 409, 410, 83 L.Ed.2d 246 (1984) (*per curiam*) (quoting *Katz v. United States*, 389 U.S. 347, 357, 88 S.Ct. 507, 514, 19 L.Ed.2d 576 (1967) (footnotes omitted)); *Mincey v. Arizona*, 437 U.S. 385, 390, 98 S.Ct. 2408, 2412, 57 L.Ed.2d 290 (1978); *see also United States v. Place*, 462 U.S. 696, 701, 103 S.Ct. 2637, 2641, 77 L.Ed.2d 110 (1983). One such exception was recognized in *Terry v. Ohio*, 392 U.S. 1, 88 S.Ct. 1868, 20 L.Ed.2d 889 (1968), which held that "where a police officer observes unusual conduct which leads him reasonably to conclude in light of his experience that criminal activity may be afoot" the officer may briefly stop the suspicious person and make "reasonable inquiries" aimed at confirming or dispelling his suspicions. *Id.*, 392 U.S., at 30, 88 S.Ct., at 1884; *see also Adams v. Williams*, 407 U.S. 143, 145–146, 92 S.Ct. 1921, 1922–1923, 32 L.Ed.2d 612 (1972).

[2,3] *Terry* further held that "[w]hen an officer is justified in believing that the individual whose suspicious behavior he is investigating at close range is armed and presently dangerous to the officer or to others," the officer may conduct a patdown search "to determine whether the person is in fact carrying a weapon." 392 U.S., at 24, 88 S.Ct., at 1881. "The purpose of this limited search is not to discover evidence of crime, but to allow the officer to pursue his investigation without fear of violence. . . ." *Adams, supra*, at 146, 92 S.Ct., at 1923. Rather, a protective search—permitted without a warrant and on the basis of reasonable suspicion less than probable cause—must be strictly "limited to that which is necessary for the discovery of weapons which might be used to harm the officer or others nearby." *Terry, supra*, at 26, 88 S.Ct., at 1882; *see also Michigan v. Long*, 463 U.S. 1032, 1049, and 1952, n. 16, 103 S.Ct. 3469, 3480–3481, and 3482, n. 16, 77 L.Ed.2d 1201 (1983); *Ybarra v. Illinois*, 444 U.S. 85, 93–94, 100 S.Ct. 338, 343–344, 62 L.Ed.2d 238 (1979). If the protective search goes beyond what is necessary to determine if the suspect is armed, it is no longer valid under *Terry* and its fruits will be suppressed. *Sibron v. New York*, 392 U.S. 40, 65–66, 88 S.Ct. 1889, 1904, 20 L.Ed.2d 917 (1968).

[4] These principles were settled 25 years ago when, on the same day, the Court announced its decisions in *Terry* and *Sibron*. The question presented today is whether police officers may seize nonthreatening contraband detected during a protective patdown search of the sort permitted by *Terry*. We think the answer is clearly that they may, so long as the

officer's search stays within the bounds marked by *Terry*.

B

We have already held that police officers, at least under certain circumstances, may seize contraband detected during the lawful execution of a *Terry* search. In *Michigan v. Long, supra,* for example, police approached a man who had driven his car into a ditch and who appeared to be under the influence of some intoxicant. As the man moved to reenter the car from the roadside, police spotted a knife on the floorboard. The officers stopped the man, subjected him to a patdown search, and then inspected the interior of the vehicle for other weapons. During the search of the passenger compartment, the police discovered an open pouch containing marijuana and seized it. This Court upheld the validity of the search and seizure under *Terry.* The Court held first that, in the context of a roadside encounter, where police have reasonable suspicion based on specific and articulable facts to believe that a driver may be armed and dangerous, they may conduct a protective search for weapons not only of the driver's person but also of the passenger compartment of the automobile. 463 U.S., at 1049, 103 S.Ct., at 3480–3481. Of course, the protective search of the vehicle, being justified solely by the danger that weapons stored there could be used against the officers or bystanders, must be "limted to those areas in which a weapon may be placed or hidden." *Ibid.* The Court then held: "If, while conducting a legitimate *Terry* search of the interior of the automobile, the officer should, as here, discover contraband other than weapons, he clearly cannot be required to ignore the contraband, and the Fourth Amendment does not require its suppression in such circumstances." *Id.,* at 1050, 103 S.Ct., at 3481; *accord, Sibron,* 392 U.S., at 69–70, 88 S.Ct., at 1905–1906 (WHITE, J., concurring); *Id.,* at 79, 88 S.Ct., at 1910 (Harlan, J., concurring in result).

[5] The Court in *Long* justified this latter holding by reference to our cases under the "plain-view" doctrine. *See Long, supra,* at 1050, 103 S.Ct., at 3481; *see also United States v. Hensley,* 469 U.S. 221, 235, 105 S.Ct. 675, 683–684, 83 L.Ed.2d 604 (1985) (upholding plain-view seizure in context of *Terry* stop). Under that doctrine, if police are lawfully in a position from which they view an object, if its incriminating character is immediately apparent, and if the officers have a lawful right of access to the object, they may seize it without a warrant. *See Horton v. California,* 496 U.S. 128, 136–137, 110 S.Ct. 2301, 2307–2308, 110 L.Ed.2d 112 (1990); *Texas v. Brown,* 460 U.S. 730, 739, 103 S.Ct. 1535, 1541–1542, 75 L.Ed.2d 502 (1983) (plurality opinion). If, however, the police lack

probable cause to believe that an object in plain view is contraband without conducting some further search of the object—*i.e.,* if "its criminating character [is not] 'immediately apparent.' " *Horton, supra,* at 136, 110 S.Ct., at 2308—the plain-view doctrine cannot justify its seizure. *Arizona v. Hicks,* 480 U.S. 321, 107 S.Ct. 1149, 94 L.Ed.2d 347 (1987).

[6–9] We think that this doctrine has an obvious application by analogy to cases in which an officer discovers contraband through the sense of touch during an otherwise lawful search. The rationale of the plain view doctrine is that if contraband is left in open view and is observed by a police officer from a lawful vantage point, there has been no invasion of a legitimate expectation of privacy and thus no "search" within the meaning of the Fourth Amendment—or at least no search independent of the initial intrusion that gave the officers their vantage point. *See Illinois v. Andreas,* 463 U.S. 765, 771, 103 S.Ct. 3319, 3324, 77 L.Ed.2d 1003 (1983); *Texas v. Brown, supra,* at 740, 103 S.Ct., at 1542. The warrantless seizure of contraband that presents itself in this manner is deemed justified by the realization that resort to a neutral magistrate under such circumstances would often be impracticable and would do little to promote the objectives of the Fourth Amendment. *See Hicks, supra,* at 326–327, 107 S.Ct., at 1153; *Coolidge v. New Hampshire,* 403 U.S. 443, 467–468, 469–470, 91 S.Ct. 2022, 2028–2029, 2040, 29 L.Ed.2d 564 (1971) (opinion of Stewart, J.). The same can be said of tactile discoveries of contraband. If a police officer lawfully pats down a suspect's outer clothing and feels an object whose contour or mass makes its identity immediately apparent, there has been no invasion of the suspect's privacy beyond that already authorized by the officer's search for weapons; if the object is contraband, its warrantless seizure would be justified by the same practical considerations that inhere in the plain view context.[3]

[10,11] The Minnesota Supreme Court rejected an analogy to the plain-view doctrine on two grounds: first, its belief that "the sense of touch is inherently less immediate and less reliable than the sense of sight," and second, that "the sense of touch is far more intrusive into the personal privacy that is at the core of the [F]ourth [A]mendment." 481 N.W.2d, at 845.

---

3. "[T]he police officer in each [case would have] had a prior justification for an intrusion in the course of which he came inadvertently across a piece of evidence incriminating the accused. The doctrine serves to supplement the prior justification . . . and permits the warrantless seizures." *Coolidge v. New Hampshire,* 403 U.S. 443, 466, 91 S.Ct. 2022, 2038, 29 L.Ed.2d 564 (1971) (opinion of Stewart, J.).

We have a somewhat different view. First, *Terry* itself demonstrates that the sense of touch is capable of revealing the nature of an object with sufficient reliability to support a seizure. The very premise of *Terry*, after all, is that officers will be able to detect the presence of weapons through the sense of touch and *Terry* upheld precisely such a seizure. Even if it were true that the sense of touch is generally less reliable than the sense of sight, that only suggests that officers will less often be able to justify seizures of unseen contraband. Regardless of whether the officer detects the contraband by sight or by touch, however, the Fourth Amendment's requirement that the officer have probable cause to believe that the item is contraband before seizing it ensures against excessively speculative seizures.[4] The court's second concern—that touch is more intrusive into privacy than is sight—is inapposite in light of the fact that the intrusion the court fears has already been authorized by the lawful search for weapons. The seizure of an item whose identity is already known occasions no further invasion of privacy. *See Soldal v. Cook County*, 506 U.S. —, —, 113 S.Ct. 538, —, 121 L.Ed.2d 450 (1992), *Horton, supra*, at 141, 110 S.Ct., at 2310; *United States v. Jacobsen*, 466 U.S. 109, 120, 104 S.Ct. 1652, 1660, 80 L.Ed.2d 85 (1984). Accordingly, the suspect's privacy interests are not advanced by a categorical rule barring the seizure

---

4. We also note that this Court's opinion in *Ybarra v. Illinois*, 444 U.S. 85, 100 S.Ct. 338, 62 L.Ed.2d 238 (1979), appeared to contemplate the possibility that police officers could obtain probable cause justifying a seizure of contraband through the sense of touch. In that case, police officers had entered a tavern and subjected its patrons to patdown searches. While patting down the petitioner Ybarra, an "officer felt what he described as 'a cigarette pack with objects in it,'" seized it, and discovered heroin inside. *Id.*, at 88–89, 100 S.Ct., at 340–342. The State argued that the seizure was constitutional on the grounds that the officer obtained probable cause to believe that Ybarra was carrying contraband during the course of a lawful *Terry* frisk. *Ybarra, supra*, at 92, 100 S.Ct., at 342–343. This Court rejected that argument on the grounds that "[t]he initial frisk of Ybarra was simply not supported by a reasonable belief that he was armed and presently dangerous," as required by *Terry*. 444 U.S., at 92–93, 100 S.Ct., at 343. The Court added, "[s]ince we conclude that the initial patdown of Ybarra was not justified under the Fourth and Fourteenth Amendments, we need not decide whether or not the presence on Ybarra's person of 'a cigarette pack with objects in it' yielded probable cause to believe that Ybarra was carrying any illegal substance." *Id.*, at 93, no. 5, 100 S.Ct., at 343, no. 5. The Court's analysis does not suggest, and indeed seems inconsistent with, the existence of a categorical bar against seizures of contraband detected manually during a *Terry* patdown search.

of contraband plainly detected through the sense of touch.

III

[12] It remains to apply these principles to the facts of this case. Respondent has not challenged the finding made by the trial court and affirmed by both the Court of Appeals and the State Supreme Court that the police were justified under *Terry* in stopping him and frisking him for weapons. Thus, the dispositive question before this Court is whether the officer who conducted the search was acting within the lawful bounds marked by *Terry* at the time he gained probable cause to believe that the lump in respondent's jacket was contraband. The State District Court did not make precise findings on this point, instead finding simply that the officer, after feeling "a small, hard object wrapped in plastic" in respondent's pocket, "formed the opinion that the object . . . was crack . . . cocaine." App. to Pet. for Cert. C–2. The District Court also noted that the officer made "no claim that he suspected this object to be a weapon," *Id.*, at C–5, a finding affirmed on appeal, *see* 469 N.W.2d, at 464 (the officer "never thought the lump was a weapon"). The Minnesota Supreme Court, after "a close examination of the record," held that the officer's own testimony "belies any notion that he 'immediately'" recognized the lump as crack cocaine. *See* 481 N.W.2d, at 844. Rather, the court concluded, the officer determined that the lump was contraband only after "squeezing, sliding and otherwise manipulating the contents of the defendant's pocket"—a pocket which the officer already knew contained no weapon. *Ibid.*

[13] Under the State Supreme Court's interpretation of the record before it, it is clear that the court was correct in holding that the police officer in this case overstepped the bounds of the "strictly circumscribed" search for weapons allowed under *Terry*. *See Terry*, 392 U.S., at 26, 88 S.Ct., at 1882. Where, as here, "an officer who is executing a valid search for one item seizes a different item," this Court rightly "has been sensitive to the danger . . . that officers will enlarge a specific authorization, furnished by a warrant or an exigency, into the equivalent of a general warrant to rummage and seize at will." *Texas v. Brown*, 460 U.S., at 748, 103 S.Ct., at 1546–1547 (STEVENS, J., concurring in judgment). Here, the officer's continued exploration of respondent's pocket after having concluded that it contained no weapon was unrelated to "[t]he sole justification of the search [under *Terry*:] . . . the protection of the police officer and others nearby." 392 U.S., at 29, 88 S.Ct., at 1884. It therefore amounted to the sort of evidentiary search that *Terry* expressly refused to authorize, *see Id.*, at 26, 88 S.Ct., at 1882, and that we have condemned in subsequent

cases. *See Michigan v. Long*, 463 U.S., at 1049, n. 14, 103 S.Ct., at 3480–3481; *Sibron*, 392 U.S., at 65–66, 88 S.Ct., at 1904.

[14] Once again, the analogy to the plain-view doctrine is apt. In *Arizona v. Hicks*, 480 U.S. 321, 107 S.Ct. 1149, 94 L.Ed.2d 347 (1987), this Court held invalid the seizure of stolen stereo equipment found by police while executing a valid search warrant for other evidence. Although the police were lawfully on the premises pursuant to the search warrant, they obtained probable cause to believe that the stereo equipment was contraband only after moving the equipment to permit officers to read its serial numbers. The subsequent seizure of the equipment could not be justified by the plain-view doctrine, this Court explained, because the incriminating character of the stereo equipment was not immediately apparent; rather, probable cause to believe that the equipment was stolen arose only as a result of a further search — the moving of the equipment — that was not authorized by the search warrant or by any exception to the warrant requirement. The facts of this case are very similar. Although the officer was lawfully in a position to feel the lump in respondent's pocket, because *Terry* entitled him to place his hands upon respondent's jacket, the court below determined that the incriminating character of the object was not immediately apparent to him. Rather, the officer determined that the item was contraband only after conducting a further search, one not authorized by *Terry* or by any other exception to the warrant requirement. Because this further search of respondent's pocket was constitutionally invalid, the seizure of the cocaine that followed is likewise unconstitutional. *Horton*, 496 U.S., at 140, 110 S.Ct., at 2309–2310.

IV

For these reasons, the judgment of the Minnesota Supreme Court is

Affirmed.

Justice SCALLIA, concurring.

I take it to be a fundamental principle of constitutional adjudication that the terms in the Constitution must be given the meaning ascribed to them at the time of their ratification. Thus, when the Fourth Amendment provides that "[t]he right of the people to be secure in their persons, houses, papers, and effects, against *unreasonable searches and seizures*, shall not be violated" (emphasis added), it "is to be construed in the light of what was deemed an unreasonable search and seizure when it was adopted," *Carroll v. United States*, 267 U.S. 132, 149, 45 S.Ct. 280, 284, 69 L.Ed. 543 (1925); *see also California v. Acevedo*, 500 U.S. —, —, 111 S.Ct., at 982, —, 114 L.Ed.2d 619 (1991) (SCALIA, J., concurring in judgment). The purpose of the provision, in other words, is to preserve that degree of respect for the privacy of persons and the inviolability of their property that existed when the provision was adopted — even if a later, less virtuous age should become accustomed to considering all sorts of intrusion "reasonable."

My problem with the present case is that I am not entirely sure that the physical search — the "frisk" — that produced the evidence at issue here complied with that constitutional standard. The decision of ours that gave approval to such searches, *Terry v. Ohio*, 392 U.S. 1, 88 S.Ct. 1868, 20 L.Ed.2d 889 (1968), made no serious attempt to determine compliance with traditional standards, but rather, according to the style of this Court at the time, simply adjudged that such a search was "reasonable" by current estimations. *Id.*, at 22–27, 88 S.Ct., at 1880–1883.

There is good evidence, I think, that the "stop" portion of the *Terry* "stop-and-frisk" holding accords with the common law — that it had long been considered reasonable to detain suspicious persons for the purpose of demanding that they give an account of themselves. This is suggested, in particular, by the so-called night-walker statutes, and their common-law antecedents. *See* Statute of Winchester, 13 Edw. I, Stat. 2, ch. 4 (1285); Statute of 5 Edw. III, ch. 14 (1331); 2 W. Hawkins, Pleas of the Crown c. 13, § 6, p. 129 (8th ed. 1824) ("It is holden that this statute was made in affirmance of the common law, and that every private person may by the common law arrest any suspicious night-walker, and detain him till he give a good account of himself"); 1 E. East, Pleas of the Crown ch. 5, § 70, p. 303 (1803) ("It is said . . . that every private person may by the common law arrest any suspicious night-walker, and detain him till he give a good account of himself"); *see also* M. Dalton, The Country Justice ch. 104, pp. 352–353 (1727); A. Costello, Our Police Protestors: History of the New York Police 25 (1885) (quoting 1681 New York City regulation); 2 Perpetual Laws of Massachusetts 1788–1798, ch. 82, § 2, p. 410 (1797 Massachusetts statute).

I am unaware, however, of any precedent for a physical search of a person thus temporarily detained for questioning. Sometimes, of course, the temporary detention of a suspicious character would be elevated to a full custodial arrest on probable cause — as, for instance, when a suspect was unable to provide a sufficient accounting of himself. At *that* point, it is clear that the common law would permit not just a protective "frisk," but a full physical search incident to the arrest. When, however, the detention did not rise to the level of a full-blown arrest (and was not supported by the degree of cause needful for that purpose), there appears to be no clear support at common law for physically searching the suspect. *See* Warner, *The Uniform Arrest Act,* 28 Va.L.Rev. 315, 324 (1942) ("At common law, if a watchman came upon a suspiciously acting nightwalker, he might arrest him and then search him for weapons, but he had no right to search before arrest"); Williams, Police Detention and Arrest Privileges—England, 51 J.Crim.L., C. & P.S. 413, 418 (1960) ("Where a suspected criminal is also suspected of being offensively armed, can the police search him for arms, by tapping his pockets, before making up their minds whether to arrest him? There is no English authority. . . .").

I frankly doubt, moreover, whether the fiercely proud men who adopted our Fourth Amendment would have allowed themselves to be subjected, on mere *suspicion* of being armed and dangerous, to such indignity—which is described as follows in a police manual:

> "Check the subject's neck and collar. A check should be made under the subject's arm. Next a check should be made of the upper back. The lower back should also be checked.
>
> "A check should be made of the upper part of the man's chest and the lower region around the stomach. The belt, a favorite concealment spot, should be checked. The inside thigh and crotch area also should be searched. The legs should be checked for possible weapons. The last items to be checked are the shoes and cuffs of the subject." J. Moynahan, Police Searching Procedures 7 (1963) (citations omitted).

On the other hand, even if a "frisk" prior to arrest would have been considered impermissible in 1791, perhaps it was considered permissible by 1868, when the Fourteenth Amendment (the basis for applying the Fourth Amendment to the States) was adopted. Or perhaps it is only since that time that concealed weapons capable of harming the interrogator quickly and from beyond arm's reach have become common—which might alter the judgment of what is "reasonable" under the original standard. But technological changes were no more discussed in *Terry* than was the original state of the law.

If I were of the view that *Terry* was (insofar as the power to "frisk" is concerned) incorrectly decided, I

might—even if I felt bound to adhere to that case—vote to exclude the evidence incidentally discovered, on the theory that half a constitutional guarantee is better than none. I might also vote to exclude if it I agreed with the original-meaning-is-relevant, good-policy-is-constitutional-law school of jurisprudence that the *Terry* opinion represents. As a policy matter, it may be desirable to *permit* "frisks" for weapons, but not to *encourage* "frisks" for drugs by admitting evidence other than weapons.

I adhere to original meaning, however. And though I do not favor the mode of analysis in *Terry,* I cannot say that its result was wrong. Constitutionality of the "frisk" in the present case was neither challenged nor argued. Assuming, therefore, that the search was lawful, I agree with the Court's premise that any evidence incidentally discovered in the course of it would be admissible, and join the Court's opinion in its entirety.

Chief Justice REHNQUIST, with whom Justice BLACKMUN and Justice THOMAS join, concurring in part and dissenting in part.

I join Parts I and II of the Court's opinion. Unlike the Court, however, I would vacate the judgment of the Supreme Court of Minnesota and remand the case to that court for further proceedings.

The Court, correctly in my view, states that "the dispositive question before this Court is whether the officer who conducted the search was acting within the lawful bonds marked by *Terry* [*v. Ohio,* 392 U.S. 1, 88 S.Ct. 1868, 20 L.Ed.2d 889 (1968),*]* at the time he gained probable cause to believe that the lump in respondent's jacket was contraband." *Ante,* at 2138. The Court then goes on to point out that the state trial court did not make precise findings on this point, but accepts the appellate findings made by the Supreme Court of Minnesota. I believe that these findings, like those of the trial court, are imprecise and not directed expressly to the question of the officer's probable cause to believe that the lump was contraband. Because the Supreme Court of Minnesota employed a Fourth Amendment analysis which differs significantly from that now adopted by this Court, I would vacate its judgment and remand the case for further proceedings there in the light of this Court's opinion.

In the Matter of CHARLOTTE K., Age 15, A Person Alleged to be a Juvenile Delinquent, Respondent.
Family Court, Richmond County.
April 1980.

In a delinquency proceeding charging respondent juvenile with possession of burglar's tools, the Richmond County Family Court, Daniel D. Leddy, Jr., J., held that girdle, into which respondent dropped shoplifted items, was not a "burglar's tool" within the meaning of statute prohibiting possession of burglar's tools.

Dismissed.

Burglary k12 Her girdle, into which respondent dropped shoplifted items, was not a "burglar's tool" within the meaning of statute prohibiting possession of burglar's tools. Penal Law § 140.35.

See publication Words and Phrases for other judicial constructions and definitions.

Allen G. Schwartz, Corp. Counsel, New York City by Archibald H. Broomfield, Staten Island, for petitioner.

Charles Schinitsky, Legal Aid Society, Brooklyn by Rhoda Cohen, Staten Island, Law Guardian for Child.

DANIEL D. LEDDY, Jr., Judge.

Is a girdle a burglar's tool or is that stretching the plain meaning of Penal Law Sec. 140.35? This elastic issue of first impression arises out of a charge that the respondent shoplifted certain items from Macy's Department Store by dropping them into her girdle.

Basically, Corporation Counsel argues that respondent used her girdle as a Kangaroo does her pouch, thus adapting it beyond its maiden form.

The Law Guardian snaps back charging that with this artificial expansion of Sec. 140.35's meaning, the foundation of Corporation Counsel's argument plainly sags. The Law Guardian admits that respondent's tight security was an attempt to evade the store's own tight security. And yet, it was not a tool, instrument or other article adapted, designed or commonly used for committing or facilitating offenses involving larceny by physical taking. It was, instead, an article of clothing, which, being worn under all, was, after all, a place to hide all. It was no more a burglar's tool than a pocket, or maybe even a kangaroo's pouch.

The tools, instruments or other articles envisioned by Penal Law Sec. 140.35 are those used in taking an item and not in hiding it thereafter. They are the handy gadgets used to break in and pick up, and not the bags for carrying out. Such is the legislative intent of this section, as is evident from the *Commission Staff Comments on the Revised Penal Law of 1965.* Title I, Article 140, N Sec. 140.35, which reads in relevant part:

> "The new section, by reference to instruments 'involving larceny' . . . expands the crime to include possession of numerous other *tools*, such as those used for breaking into motor vehicles, stealing from public telephone coin boxes, tampering with gas and electric meters, and the like." (Emphasis added.)

The Court has decided this issue mindful of the heavy burden that a contrary decision would place upon retail merchants. Thus is avoided the real bind of having customers check not only their packages, but their girdles too, at the department store's door.

The Court must also wonder whether such a contrary decision would not create a spate of unreasonable bulges that would let loose the floodgates of stop and frisk cases, with the result of putting the squeeze on court resources already overextended in this era of trim governmental budgets.

Accordingly, the instant allegation of possession of burglar's tools is dismissed.

Sergeant Perry WATKINS, Plaintiff-Appellant,
v.
UNITED STATES ARMY, et al., Defendants-Appellees.
No. 85–4006.
United States Court of Appeals, Ninth Circuit.
Argued En Banc and Submitted Oct. 12, 1988.
Decided May 3, 1989.

Soldier brought action challenging revocation of security clearance and seeking to prevent discharge from the Army. The United States District Court for the Western District of Washington, 551 F.Supp. 212, Barbara J. Rothstein, Chief Judge, held that the Army was estopped from relying on Army regulation which made homosexuality nonwaivable disqualification for reenlistment as bar to soldier's reenlistment. The Army appealed. The Court of Appeals, 721 F.2d 687, reversed. On remand the District Court held that the Army's regulations were not repugnant to the Constitution or statutory authority. Soldier appealed. The Court of Appeals, 847 F.2d 1329, reversed and remanded, and full court review was granted. The Court of Appeals, Pregerson, Circuit Judge, held that the Army was estopped from barring soldier's reenlistment solely because of his acknowledged homosexuality.

Opinions at 721 F.2d 687 and 847 F.2d 1329 withdrawn; District Court order of June 17, 1985 vacated; and District Court order of October 5, 1982, 551 F.Supp. 212, affirmed.

William A. Norris, Circuit Judge, concurred in the judgment and filed opinion.

Canby, Circuit Judge, concurred and filed opinion.

Cynthia Holcomb Hall, Circuit Judge, dissented and filed opinion in which Trott, Circuit Judge, concurred and Goodwin, Chief Judge, and Beezer, Circuit Judge, concurred in part.

* * *

James E. Lobsenz, Wolfe, Lobsenz & Cullen, American Civil Liberties Union—Washington State, Seattle, Wash., for plaintiff-appellant.

E. Roy Hawkens, Asst. Atty. Gen., Civil Div., U.S. Dept. of Justice, Washington, D.C., for defendants-appellees.

Appeal from the United States District Court for the Western District of Washington.

Before GOODWIN, Chief Judge, SCHROEDER, PREGERSON, ALARCON, NELSON, CANBY, NORRIS, BEEZER, HALL, O'SCANNLAIN, and TROTT, Circuit Judges.

PREGERSON, Circuit Judge:

The United States Army denied Sgt. Perry J. Watkins reenlistment solely because he is a homosexual. The Army refused to reenlist Watkins, a 14-year veteran, even though he had been completely candid about his homosexuality from the start of his Army career, even though he is in all respects an outstanding soldier, and even though the Army, with full knowledge of his homosexuality, had repeatedly permitted him to reenlist in the past. The Army did so despite its longstanding policy that homosexuality was a nonwaivable disqualification for reenlistment. The issue before the en banc court is whether the Army may deny reenlistment to Watkins solely because of his acknowledged homosexuality.

I. FACTUAL AND PROCEDURAL BACKGROUND[1]

In August 1967, at the age of 19, Perry Watkins was drafted into the United States Army. In filling out the Army's preinduction medical form, he marked "yes" in response to a question asking whether he had homosexual tendencies. The Army nonetheless found Watkins "qualified for admission" and inducted him into its ranks.

During Watkins' initial three-year tour of military duty, he served in the United States and Korea as a chaplain's assistant, personnel specialist, and company clerk. A year after his induction, in 1968, Watkins signed an affidavit stating that he had been a homosexual from the age of 13 and that, since his enlistment, he had engaged in sodomy with two other servicemen, a crime under military law. The Army, which received this affidavit as part of a criminal in-

---

1. These facts are taken largely from this court's opinion in *Watkins v. United States Army*, 847 F.2d 1329, 1330–34 (9th Cir.1988), as well as from other prior opinions in this case. *See* 721 F.2d 687 (9th Cir.1983); 551 F.Supp. 212 (W.D.Wash.1982); 541 F.Supp. 249 (W.D.Wash.1982).

vestigation into Watkins' sexual conduct, dropped the investigation because of insufficient evidence.

When his first enlistment period expired in 1970, Watkins received an honorable discharge, but his reenlistment eligibility code was listed as "unknown." In 1971, Watkins requested correction of the reenlistment designation and the Army corrected the code to category 1, "eligible for reentry on active duty." Shortly thereafter, he reenlisted for a second three-year term. In 1972, Watkins was denied a security clearance because of his homosexuality, and the Army again investigated him for allegedly committing sodomy and again terminated the investigation for insufficient evidence. Following another honorable discharge in 1974, the Army accepted Watkins' application for a six-year reenlistment.

In 1975, the Army convened a board of officers to determine whether Watkins should be discharged because of his homosexual tendencies. On this occasion his commanding officer, Captain Bast, testified that Watkins was "the best clerk I have known," that he did "a fantastic job—excellent," and that Watkins' homosexuality did not affect the company. A sergeant testified that Watkins' homosexuality was well-known but caused no problems and generated no complaints from other soldiers. The four officers on the board unanimously found that "Watkins is suitable for retention in the military service" and stated, "In view of the findings, the Board recommends that SP5 Perry J. Watkins be retained in the military service because there is no evidence suggesting that his behavior has had either a degrading effect upon unit performance, morale or discipline, or upon his own job performance. SP5 Watkins is suited for duty in administrative positions and progression through Specialist rating." The board's recommendation became the final decision of the Secretary of the Army.

In November 1977, the United States Army Artillery Group (the USAAG) granted Watkins a security clearance for information classified as "Secret." His application for a position in the Nuclear Surety Personnel Reliability Program (the PRP), however, was initially rejected because his records—specifically, his own admissions—showed that he had homosexual tendencies. After this initial rejection, Watkins' commanding officer in the USAAG, Captain Pastain, requested that Watkins be requalified for the position. Captain Pastain stated, "From daily personal contacts I can attest to the outstanding professional attitude, integrity, and suitability for assignment within the PRP, of SP5 Watkins. In the 6 months he has been assigned to this unit SP5 Watkins has had no problems what-so-ever in dealing with other assigned members. He has, in fact, become one of our most respected

and trusted soldiers, both by his superiors and his subordinates." An examining Army physician concluded that Watkins' homosexuality appeared to cause no problem in his work, and the decision to deny Watkins a position in the Nuclear Surety Personnel Reliability Program was reversed.

Watkins worked under a security clearance without incident until he again stated, in an interview on March 15, 1979, that he was homosexual. This prompted yet another Army investigation which, in July 1980, culminated in the revocation of Watkins' security clearance. As the notification of revocation makes clear, the Army based this revocation on Watkins' 1979 admission of homosexuality, on medical records containing Watkins' 1968 affidavit stating that he had engaged in homosexual conduct, and on his history of performing (with the permission of his commanding officer) as a female impersonator in various revues. The Army did not rely on any evidence of homosexual conduct other than Watkins' 1968 affidavit. In October 1979, the Army accepted Watkins' application for another three-year reenlistment.

In 1981 the Army promulgated Army Regulation (AR) 635–200, chpt. 15, which mandated the discharge of all homosexuals regardless of merit. Pursuant to this new discharge regulation, another Army board convened to consider discharging Watkins. Although this board explicitly rejected the evidence before it that Watkins had engaged in homosexual conduct after 1968, the board recommended that Watkins be separated from the service "because he has stated that he is a homosexual." Major General Elton, the discharge authority overseeing the board, approved this finding and recommendation and directed that Watkins be discharged.[2]

In May 1982, after the Army board voted in favor of Watkins' discharge, but before the discharge actually issued, District Judge Rothstein enjoined the Army from discharging Watkins on the basis of his statements admitting his homosexuality. 541 F.Supp.

---

2. Major General Elton, on his own initiative, made an additional finding that Watkins had engaged in homosexual acts with other soldiers. The district court ruled both that Major General Elton lacked the regulatory authority to make supplemental findings, *Watkins v. United States Army*, 541 F.Supp. 249, 259 (W.D.Wash.1982), and that the evidence presented at the discharge hearing could not support a specific finding that Watkins had engaged in any homosexual conduct after 1968. *Id.* at 257. The Army has not contested either of these rulings, and, on appeal, cites only Watkins' 1968 affidavit as evidence of homosexual conduct.

at 259.[3] The district court reasoned that the discharge proceedings were barred by the Army's regulation against double jeopardy, AR 635–200, ¶ 1–19(b), because they essentially repeated the discharge proceedings of 1975. *Id.* at 258–59.[4]

During oral argument before the district court, counsel for the Army declared that if the Army were enjoined from discharging Watkins, it would deny Watkins reenlistment, pursuant to AR 601–280, ¶ 2–21(c),[5] when his current tour of duty expired in October 1982.[6] This reenlistment regulation, which was promulgated in 1981 along with the discharge regulation AR 635–200, chapt. 15, is simply a clarification of the earlier regulation which had always made homosexuality a nonwaivable disqualification for reenlistment. The district court nonetheless enjoined Watkins' discharge, and the Army fulfilled its promise by rejecting Watkins' reenlistment application "[b]ecause of self admitted homosexuality as well as homosexual acts."

On October 5, 1982, the district court enjoined the Army from refusing to reenlist Watkins because of his admitted homosexuality, holding that the Army was equitably estopped from relying on the nonwaivable disqualification provisions of AR 601–280, ¶ 2–21(c). *Watkins v. United States Army*, 551 F.Supp. 212, 223 (W.D.Wash.1982).[7] The Army reenlisted Watkins for a six-year term on November 1, 1982, with the proviso that the reenlistment would be voided if the district court's injunction were not upheld on appeal.

While the Army's appeal of the district court injunction was pending, the Army rated Watkins' performance and professionalism. He received 85 out of 85 possible points. His ratings included perfect scores for "Earns respect," "Integrity," "Loyalty," "Moral Courage," "Self-discipline," "Military Appearance," "Demonstrates Initiative," "Performs under pressure," "Attains results," "Displays sound judgment," "Communicates effectively," "Develops subordinates," "Demonstrates technical skills," and "Physical fitness." His military evaluators unanimously recommended that he be promoted ahead of his peers. The Army's written evaluation of Watkins' performance and potential stated:

> SSG Watkins is without exception, one of the finest Personnel Action Center Supervisors I have encountered. Through his diligent efforts, the Battalion Personnel Action Center achieved a near perfect processing rate for SIPDERS transactions. During this training period, SSG Watkins has been totally reliable and a wealth of knowledge. He requires no supervision, and with his "can do" attitude, always exceeds the requirements and demands placed upon him. I would gladly welcome another opportunity to serve with him, and firmly believe that he will be an asset to any unit to which he is assigned.
>
> SSG Watkins should be selected to attend ANCOC and placed in a Platoon Sergeant position. [Rater's Evaluation of Watkins' performance and potential.]
>
> SSG Watkins' duty performance has been outstanding in every regard. His section continues to set the standard within the Brigade for submission of accurate, timely personnel and financial transactions. Keeping abreast of ever-

---

3. Watkins had originally brought suit in August 1981 to have his security clearance reinstated, alleging various constitutional violations. After receiving notice that discharge proceedings would be convened, he amended his complaint in October to seek an injunction against his discharge. The district court declined to reach the issue whether the Army could revoke Watkins' security clearance, reasoning that the issue was not yet ripe because Watkins had an administrative appeal pending. *See* 541 F.Supp. at 259; *see also Watkins v. United States Army*, 551 F.Supp. at 223. Watkins' security clearance dispute is thus not before us on appeal.

---

4. The district court held that evidence could not support a finding that Watkins engaged in homosexual conduct subsequent to the 1975 discharge proceedings and that the Army's double jeopardy provision barred the Army from basing Watkins' discharge on statements that merely reiterated what Watkins had stated in the 1975 discharge proceedings—that he was homosexual. *See* 541 F.Supp. at 257–59.

---

5. This reenlistment regulation, unlike the new discharge regulation, is simply a clarification of the pre-1981 reenlistment regulation. Throughout Watkins' 14 years in the Army, homosexuality was always a nonwaivable disqualification for reenlistment.

---

6. At that time, the regulation appeared at ¶ 2–24(c). However, for convenience, this opinion will refer to all Army regulations by the paragraph numbers used in the Army's September 15, 1986 update, unless a different date is explicitly noted.

---

7. This case does not involve a claim that courts can exercise general review of the Army's reenlistment decisions. Watkins does not seek a judicial determination of the merits of his reenlistment application. He merely seeks a judicial determination that the Army must consider his reenlistment application on its merits without regard to his homosexuality. *See* 551 F.Supp. at 218.

changing personnel regulations and directives, SSG Watkins has provided sound advice to the commanded as well as to the soldiers within the command. His suggestion to separate S–1 and Personnel Action Center functions and to colocate the Personnel Action Center with the Company Orderly Rooms was adopted and immediately resulted in improved service by both offices. SSG Watkins' positive influence has been felt throughout the Battalion and will be sorely missed.

SSG Watkins' potential is unlimited. He has consistently demonstrated the capacity to manage numerous complex responsibilities concurrently. He is qualified for promotion now and should be selected for attendance at ANCOES at the earliest opportunity. [Indorser's Evaluation of Watkins' performance and potential.]

[1] On appeal, a panel of this court reversed the district court's injunction. *Watkins v. United States Army*, 721 F.2d 687, 691 (9th Cir.1983) [hereinafter *Watkins I*]. The panel reasoned that the equity powers of the federal courts could not be exercised to order military officials to violate their own regulations absent a determination that the regulations were repugnant to the Constitution or to the military's statutory authority. *Id.* On remand, the district court held that the Army's regulations were not repugnant to the Constitution or to statutory authority and accordingly denied Watkins' motion for summary judgment and granted summary judgment in favor of the Army. Watkins again appealed and a divided panel of this court reversed the district court's ruling. The panel held that the Army's reenlistment regulations violate the constitutional guarantee of equal protection of the laws because they discriminate against persons of homosexual orientation and because the regulations are not necessary to promote a legitimate compelling governmental interest. *Watkins v. United States Army*, 847 F.2d 1329, 1352–53 (9th Cir.1988) [hereinafter *Watkins II*]. The full court granted review to address the issues raised in *Watkins I*[8] and *Watkins II*. We hold that the Army is estopped from barring Watkins' reenlistment on the basis of his homosexuality. Accordingly, *Watkins I* no longer states the law of this circuit.

Moreover, it is unnecessary to reach the constitutional issues raised in *Watkins II*.

II. EXHAUSTION OF REMEDIES

[Discussion of Exhaustion of Remedies is omitted]

* * *

III. EQUITABLE ESTOPPEL

[Discussion of Equitable Estoppel is omitted.]

* * *

IV. CONCLUSION

This is a case where equity cries out and demands that the Army be estopped from refusing to reenlist Watkins on the basis of his homosexuality. We therefore reinstate the district court's October 5, 1982 Order estopping the Army from relying on its reenlistment regulation, AR 601–280 ¶ 2–24(c), as a bar to Sgt. Watkins' reenlistment. *See* 551 F.Supp. at 223.[18]

Our opinions in *Watkins I* and *Watkins II* are withdrawn. The district court Order of June 17, 1985 is vacated and the district court Order of October 5, 1982 is AFFIRMED.

433, 436–37 n. 9 (2d Cir.1978) (en banc) (law of the case doctrine cannot immunize panel decisions from review by the court en banc), *aff'd*, 444 U.S. 472, 100 S.Ct. 745, 62 L.Ed.2d 676 (1980); *cf. United States v. Mills*, 810 F.2d 907, 909 (9th Cir.1987) (stating that law of the case is a discretionary doctrine and declining to apply the doctrine), *cert. denied*, — U.S. —, 108 S.Ct. 107, 98 L.Ed.2d 67 (1987).

---

8. The law of the case doctrine does not, as the Army suggests, prevent us from reconsidering the issues raised in *Watkins I. See, e.g., Shimman v. International Union of Operating Engineers, Local 18*, 744 F.2d 1226, 1229 n. 3 (6th Cir.1984) (en banc) ("The law of the case doctrine . . . does not impair the power of an en banc court to overrule any panel decision."), *cert. denied*, 469 U.S. 1215, 105 S.Ct. 1191, 84 L.Ed.2d 337 (1985); *Van Gemert v. Boeing Co.*, 590 F.2d

18. Our holding does not mean and should not be read to imply that Watkins has a right to commit acts that Congress has declared illegal. *See Watkins*, 551 F.Supp. at 225. We do nevertheless reiterate the point made in the district court's October 28, 1982 Order "that the Army cannot, consistent with the [district] court's October 5 Order, use plaintiff's homosexuality as an open door through which to probe for possible misconduct, when it has no grounds to believe such misconduct exists." 551 F.Supp. at 225.

In addition, we note that the district court found that the Army's attempt to discharge Watkins in 1982 was barred by the Army's regulation against double jeopardy, AR 635–200, ¶ 1–19(b)(2), because the 1982 discharge proceedings essentially repeated the 1975 discharge proceedings against Watkins. 541 F.Supp. at 257–58. The Army did not appeal from that judgment. Therefore, the Army may not attempt to discharge Watkins for any alleged homosexual acts that were the subject of past discharge proceedings or for any past or future statements by Watkins acknowledging his homosexuality.

NORRIS, Circuit Judge, concurring in the judgment:

I

I concur in the judgment requiring the Army to reconsider Sgt. Watkins' reenlistment application without regard to his homosexuality. I cannot join the majority's opinion, however, because I agree with the dissent that the judgment cannot rest on the doctrine of equitable estoppel. The Supreme Court has declined to approve the invocation of equitable estoppel against the government even in cases where the facts are no less sympathetic than the facts in Sgt. Watkins' case. *See, e.g., INS v. Miranda,* 459 U.S. 14, 17–19, 103 S.Ct. 281, 282–84, 74 L.Ed.2d 12 (1982) (per curiam) (reversing Ninth Circuit decision equitably estopping INS from denying resident status to alien spouse of citizen when petitioner became ineligible during INS delay in processing application); *INS v. Hibi,* 414 U.S. 5, 94 S.Ct. 19, 38 L.Ed.2d 7 (1973) (per curiam) (reversing Ninth Circuit decision equitably estopping INS from denying citizenship to Filipino war veteran); *Montana v. Kennedy,* 366 U.S. 308, 314–15, 81 S.Ct. 1336, 1340–41, 6 L.Ed.2d 313 (1961) (government not estopped to deny citizenship to child of U.S. citizen born while his mother was living abroad, even though government official advised her that she could not return to the U.S. to have her baby). Indeed, the Supreme Court has expressed uncertainty as to whether equitable estoppel can ever be invoked against the government. *See Heckler v. Community Health Servs.,* 467 U.S. 51, 60–61, 104 S.Ct. 2218, 2224, 81 L.Ed.2d 42 (1984). In any event, I see no justification for invoking the doctrine on the facts of this case.

In my view, Watkins is entitled to relief because the Army denied him the equal protection of the laws by discharging and refusing to reenlist him solely on the basis of his homosexuality. Before addressing Watkins' claim that the Army's regulations on homosexuality violate equal protection, however, I must address Watkins' non-constitutional claim—that the Army's discharge and reenlistment regulations are arbitrary and capricious under the Administrative Procedure Act, 5 U.S.C. § 706(2)(A).[1] I reject this claim because Watkins does not argue that the Army's regulations on homosexuality themselves violate the Administrative

Procedure Act; rather he argues only that the regulations are arbitrary as applied to the facts of his case. Because he does not argue that the regulations on their face are arbitrary or capricious, Watkins' APA claim must fail. *See Watkins I,* 721 F.2d at 690–91.

I now turn to Watkins' claim that the Army's regulations deny him equal protection of the laws in violation of the Fifth Amendment.[2] Watkins argues that the Army's regulations constitute an invidious discrimination based on sexual orientation.[3] To evaluate this claim I must engage in a three-stage inquiry. First, I must decide whether the regulations in fact discriminate on the basis of sexual orientation. Second, I must decide which level of judicial scrutiny applies by asking whether discrimination based on sexual orientation burdens a suspect or quasi-suspect class,[4] which

---

[1]. Because I would grant Watkins the relief he seeks on the basis of his equal protection claim, I need not address in this concurring opinion Watkins' other constitutional claims involving the free speech clause, the petition clause, and the due process entrapment doctrine.

---

[2]. The equal protection component of the Fifth Amendment imposes precisely the same constitutional requirements on the federal government as the equal protection clause of the Fourteenth Amendment imposes on state governments. *See, e.g., Weinberger v. Wiesenfeld,* 420 U.S. 636, 638 n. 2, 95 S.Ct. 1225, 1228 n. 2, 43 L.Ed.2d 514 (1975).

---

[3]. In this opinion I use the term "sexual orientation" to refer to the orientation of an individual's sexual preference, not to his actual sexual conduct. Individuals whose sexual orientation creates in them a desire for sexual relationships with persons of the opposite sex have a heterosexual orientation. Individuals whose sexual orientation creates in them a desire for sexual relationships with persons of the same sex have a homosexual orientation.

In contrast, I use the terms "homosexual conduct" and "homosexual acts" to refer to sexual activity between two members of the same sex whether their orientations are homosexual, heterosexual, or bisexual, and we use the terms "heterosexual conduct" and "heterosexual acts" to refer to sexual activity between two members of the opposite sex whether their orientations are homosexual, heterosexual, or bisexual.

Throughout this opinion, the terms "gay" and "homosexual" will be used synonymously to denote persons of homosexual orientation.

---

[4]. Discriminations that burden some despised or politically powerless groups are so likely to reflect antipathy against those groups that the classifications are inherently suspect and must be strictly scrutinized. *See, e.g., Plyler v. Doe,* 457 U.S. 202, 216 n. 14, 102 S.Ct. 2382, 2394 n. 14, 72 L.Ed.2d 786 (1982). Such groups are generally termed "suspect classes." The Supreme Court has identified other groups whose history of past discrimination entitles them to intermediate scrutiny protection under equal protection doctrine. Such groups are termed "quasi-suspect" classes. *See generally,* Nowak, Rotunda & Young, *Constitutional Law,* Ch. 16, § 1, at 593 (2d ed. 1983).

would make it subject, respectively, to strict or intermediate scrutiny. *See City of Cleburne v. Cleburne Living Center*, 473 U.S. 432, 439–41, 105 S.Ct. 3249, 3253–55, 87 L.Ed.2d 313 (1985). If the discrimination burdens no such class, it is subject to ordinary rationality review. *Id*. Finally, I must decide whether the challenged regulations survive the applicable level of scrutiny by deciding whether, under strict scrutiny, the legal classification is necessary to serve a compelling governmental interest; whether, under intermediate scrutiny, the classification is substantially related to an important governmental interest; or whether, under rationality review, the classification is rationally related to a legitimate governmental interest. *See Id*.

II

I turn first to the threshold question raised by Watkins' equal protection claim: Do the Army's regulations discriminate on the basis of sexual orientation? The portion of the Army's reenlistment regulation that bars homosexuals from reenlisting states in full:

> Applicants to whom the disqualifications below apply are ineligible for RA [Regular Army] reenlistment at any time and requests for waiver or exception to policy will not be submitted. . . .
>
> c. Persons of questionable moral character and a history of antisocial behavior, sexual perversion or homosexuality. A person who has committed homosexual acts or is an admitted homosexual but as to whom there is no evidence that they have engaged in homosexual acts either before or during military services is included. (See note 1). . . .
>
> k. Persons being discharged under AR 635–200 for homosexuality. . . .
>
> *Note:* Homosexual acts consist of bodily contact between persons of the same sex, actively undertaken or passively permitted, with the intent of obtaining or giving sexual satisfaction, or any proposal, solicitation, or attempt to perform such an act. Persons who have been involved in homosexual acts in an apparently isolated episode, stemming solely from immaturity, curiosity [sic], or intoxication, and in the absence of other evidence that the person is a homosexual, normally will not be excluded from reenlistment. A homosexual is a person, regardless of sex, who desires bodily contact between persons of the same sex, actively undertaken or passively permitted, with the intent to obtain or give sexual gratification. Any official, private, or public profession of homosexuality, may be considered in determining whether a person is an admitted homosexual.

AR 601–280, ¶ 2–21. Although worded in somewhat greater detail, the Army's regulation mandating the separation of homosexual soldiers from service (discharge), AR 635–200, is essentially the same in substance.[5]

---

5. AR 635–200 provides:

15–2 Definitions . . .

> a. Homosexual means a person, regardless of sex, who engages in, desires to engage in, or intends to engage in homosexual acts.
>
> b. Bisexual means a person who engages in, desires to engage in, or intends to engage in homosexual and heterosexual acts.
>
> c. A homosexual act means bodily contact, actively undertaken or passively permitted, between soldiers of the same sex for sexual satisfaction.

15–3 Criteria

The basis for separation may include preservice, prior service, or current service conduct or statements. A soldier will be separated per this chapter if one or more of the following approved findings is made:

> a. The soldier has engaged in, attempted to engage in, or solicited another to engage in a homosexual act unless there are further approved findings that—

(1) Such conduct is a departure from the soldier's usual and customary behavior; and

(2) Such conduct is unlikely to recur because it is shown, for example, that the act occurred because of immaturity, intoxication, coercion, or a desire to avoid military service; and

(3) Such conduct was not accomplished by use of force, coercion, or intimidation by the soldier during a period of military service; and

(4) Under the particular circumstances of the case, the soldier's continued presence in the Army is consistent with the interest of the Army in proper discipline, good order, and morale; and

(5) The soldier does not desire to engage in or intend to engage in homosexual acts.

Note: To warrant retention of a soldier after finding that he or she engaged in, attempted to engage in, or solicited another to engage in a homosexual act, the board's findings must specifically include all *five* findings listed in a (1) through (5) above. In making these additional findings, boards should reasonably consider the evidence presented. For example, engagement in homosexual acts over a long period of time could hardly be considered "a departure from the soldier's usual and customary behavior." The intent of this policy is to permit retention *only* of *nonhomosexual* soldiers who, because of extenuating circumstances (as demonstrated by findings required by para 15–3a(1) through (5)) engaged in, attempted to engage in, or solicited a homosexual act.

> b. The soldier has stated that he or she is a homosexual or bisexual, unless there is a further finding that the soldier is not a homosexual or bisexual.

On their face, these regulations discriminate against homosexuals on the basis of their sexual orientation. Under the regulations any homosexual act or statement of homosexuality gives rise to a presumption of homosexual orientation, and anyone who fails to rebut that presumption is conclusively barred from Army service. In other words, the regulations target homosexual orientation itself. The homosexual acts and statements are merely relevant, and rebuttable, indicators of that orientation.

In spite of these facial appearances, the Army argues that its regulations target homosexual conduct rather than orientation. I cannot agree. A close reading of the complex regulations leaves no room for doubt that the regulations target orientation rather than conduct.

Under the Army's regulations, "homosexuality," not sexual conduct, is clearly the operative trait for disqualification. AR 601–280, ¶ 2–21(c), *see also* AR 635–200, ¶ 15–1(a) (articulating the same goal). For example, the regulations ban homosexuals who have done nothing more than acknowledge their homosexual orientation even in the absence of evidence that the persons ever engaged in any form of sexual conduct. The reenlistment regulation disqualifies any "admitted homosexual"—a status that can be proved by "[a]ny official, private, or public profession of homosexuality" even if "there is no evidence that they have engaged in homosexual acts either before or during military service." AR 601–280, ¶ 2–21(c) & note; *see also* AR 635–200, ¶ 15–3(b). Since the regulations define a "homosexual" as "a person, regardless of sex, who *desires* bodily contact between persons of the same sex, actively undertaken or passively permitted, with the intent to obtain or give sexual gratification,"

a person can be demed homosexual under the regulations without ever engaging in a homosexual act. 601–280, ¶ 2–21(c) & note (emphasis added); *see also* A.R. 635–200, 15–2(a) (same desire sufficient to make one homosexual). Thus, no matter what statements a person has made, and what conduct he or she has engaged in, the ultimate evidentiary issue is whether he or she has a homosexual orientation. Under the reenlistment regulation, persons are disqualified from reenlisting only if, based on any "profession of homosexuality" they have made, they are found to have a homosexual orientation. AR 601–280, ¶ 2–21(c) & note. Similarly, under the discharge regulation a soldier must be discharged if "[t]he soldier has stated that he or she is a homosexual or bisexual, *unless* there is a further finding that the solider is not a homosexual or bisexual." AR 635–200, ¶ 15–3(b) (emphasis added). In short, the regulations do not penalize all statements of sexual desire, or even only statements of homosexual desire; they penalize only homosexuals who declare their homosexual orientation.

True, a "person who has committed homosexual acts" is also presumptively "included" under the reenlistment regulation as a person excludable for "homosexuality." AR 601–280, ¶ 2–21(c); *see also* AR 635–200, ¶ 15–3(a). But it is clear that this provision is merely designed to round out the possible evidentiary grounds for inferring a homosexual orientation. The regulations define "homosexual acts" to encompass any "bodily contact between persons of the same sex, actively undertaken or passively permitted, with the intent of obtaining or giving sexual satisfaction, or any proposal, solicitation, or attempt to perform such an act." AR 601–280, ¶ 2–21(c) & note; *see also* AR 635–200, ¶¶ 15–2(c) & 15–3(a) (stating the same in slightly different order). Thus, the regulations barring homosexuals from the Army cover any form of bodily contact between persons of the same sex that gives sexual satisfaction—from oral and anal intercourse to holding hands, kissing, caressing, and any number of other sexual acts. Indeed, in this case the Army tried to prove at Watkins' discharge proceedings that he had committed a homosexual act described as squeezing the knee of a male soldier, but failed to prove it was Watkins who did the alleged knee-squeezing. Moreover, even non-sexual conduct can trigger a presumption of homosexuality: The regulations provide for the discharge of soldiers who have "married or attempted to marry a person known to be of the same sex . . . *unless* there are further findings that the soldier is not a homosexual or bisexual." AR 635–200, ¶ 15–3(c) (emphasis added). With all the acts and statements that can serve as presumptive evidence of homosexuality under the regulations, it is hard to think of any grounds for inferring homosexual orientation

---

c. The soldier has married or attempted to marry a person known to be of the same biological sex (as evidenced by the external anatomy of the person involved) unless there are further findings that the soldier is not a homosexual or bisexual (such as, where the purpose of the marriage or attempt to marry was the avoidance or termination of military service).

AR 635–200, ¶¶ 15–2 & 15–3 (emphasis in original).

Although it is the Army's refusal to reenlist Watkins because of his homosexuality that is directly at issue, Watkins' challenge to the Army's regulation on discharge is relevant to this appeal for two reasons: (1) persons being validly discharged for homosexuality at the time of reenlistment, as Watkins was, cannot reenlist under 601–280 ¶ 2–21(k); (2) enjoining the Army to consider Watkins' reenlistment application without regard to his homosexuality will provide no effective relief if he would be subject to mandatory discharge because of homosexuality as soon as he was reenlisted. I thus consider Watkins' challenge to the constitutionality of the Army's discharge regulation as well as its reenlistment regulation.

that are *not* included.[6] The fact remains, however, that homosexual orientation, not homosexual conduct, is plainly the object of the Army's regulations.

Moreover, under the regulations a person is not automatically disqualified from Army service just because he or she committed a homosexual act. Persons may still qualify for the Army despite their homosexual conduct if they prove to the satisfaction of Army officials that their *orientation* is heterosexual rather than homosexual. To illustrate, the discharge regulation provides that a soldier who engages in homosexual acts can escape discharge if he can show that the conduct was "a departure from the soldier's usual and customary behavior" that "is unlikely to recur because it is shown, for example, that the act occurred because of immaturity, intoxication, coercion, or a desire to avoid military service" *and* that the "soldier does not desire to engage in or intend to engage in homosexual acts." AR 635–200, ¶ 15–3(a). The regulation expressly states, "The intent of this policy is to permit retention *only* of *nonhomosexual* soldiers who, because of extenuating circumstances engaged in, attempted to engage in, or solicited a homosexual act." *Id.* at note (emphasis in original). Similarly, the Army's ban on reenlisting persons who have committed homosexual acts does not apply to "[p]ersons who have been involved in homosexual acts in an apparently isolated episode, stemming solely from immaturity, curiosity [sic], or intoxication, and in the absence of other evidence that the person is a homosexual." AR 601–280, ¶ 2–21 note. If a straight soldier and a gay soldier of the same sex engage in homosexual acts because they are drunk,

immature or curious, the straight soldier may remain in the Army while the gay soldier is automatically terminated. In short, the regulations do not penalize soldiers for engaging in homosexual acts; they penalize soldiers who have engaged in homosexual acts only when the Army decides that those soldiers are actually gay.[7]

In sum, the discrimination against homosexual orientation under these regulations is about as complete as one could imagine. The regulations make any act or statement that might conceivably indicate a homosexual orientation evidence of homosexuality; that evidence is in turn weighed against any evidence of a heterosexual orientation. It is thus clear in answer to my threshold equal protection inquiry that the regulations directly burden the class consisting of persons or homosexual orientation.

III

A

Before reaching the question of the level of scrutiny applicable to discrimination based on sexual orientation and the question whether the Army's regulations survive the applicable level of scrutiny, I first address the Army's argument that *Bowers v. Hardwick*, 478 U.S. 186, 106 S.Ct. 2841, 92 L.Ed.2d 140 (1986), forecloses Watkins' equal protection claim. In *Hardwick*, the Court rejected a claim by a homosexual that a Georgia statute criminalizing sodomy deprived him of his liberty without due process of law in violation of the Fourteenth Amendment. More specifically, the Court held that the constitutionally protected right to privacy—recognized in cases such as *Griswold v. Connecticut*, 381 U.S. 479, 85 S.Ct. 1678, 14 L.Ed.2d 510 (1965), and *Eisenstadt v. Baird*, 405 U.S. 438, 92 S.Ct. 1029, 31 L.Ed.2d 349 (1972)—does not extend to acts

---

6. In stark contrast to the breadth and focus of the regulations, the only statute Congress has enacted regulating the private consensual sexual activity of military personnel covers only sodomy, not other forms of sexual conduct, and covers sodomy whether engaged in by homosexuals or heterosexuals. 10 U.S.C. § 925 (1982) provides:

> (a) Any person subject to this chapter who engages in unnatural carnal copulation with another person of the same or opposite sex or with an animal is guilty of sodomy. Penetration, however slight, is sufficient to complete the offense.
> (b) Any person found guilty of sodomy shall be punished as a court-martial may direct.

Although the statute does not define "sodomy" or "unnatural carnal copulation," the statute does require proof of "penetration," which apparently limits sodomy to oral and anal copulation. *See United States v. Harris*, 8 M.J. 52, 53–59 (C.M.A.1979).

The Army has never made a finding that Watkins ever engaged in an act of sodomy in violation of section 925. Indeed, the Army twice investigated Watkins for allegedly committing sodomy in violation of section 925 and had to drop both investigations because of "insufficient evidence."

---

7. This reading of the regulations is supported by the Army's treatment of Watkins himself. The only evidence that Watkins ever engaged in homosexual conduct is a statement he made during a 1968 investigation that he committed homosexual acts with two other servicemen. When these two servicemen denied engaging in homosexual acts with Watkins, the Army discontinued the investigation without making a finding that Watkins had committed homosexual acts. The Army did not decide to discharge Watkins (and deny him reenlistment) until 1981. In the meantime, Watkins openly and repeatedly acknowledged his homosexual orientation without admitting to any homosexual acts. It strains credulity to think that the Army decided to discharge Watkins and deny him reenlistment solely on the basis of his contradicted statement in 1968 that he had committed homosexual acts. Plainly it is Watkins' homosexual orientation—rather than evidence of any conduct—that explains the Army's decision to end Watkins' Army career.

of consensual homosexual sodomy.[8] *See id.* 478 U.S. at 190–96, 106 S.Ct. at 2843–46. The Court's holding was limited to this due process question. The parties did not argue and the Court explicitly did not decide the question whether the Georgia sodomy statute might violate the equal protection clause. *See id.* at 196, n. 8,[9] 106 S.Ct. at 2846 n. 8.

The Army nonetheless argues that it would be "incongruous" to hold that its regulations deprive gays of equal protection of the laws when *Hardwick* holds that there is no constitutionally protected privacy right to engage in homosexual sodomy. Army's Second Supp. Brief at 19. I could not disagree more. First, while *Hardwick* does indeed hold that the due process clause provides no substantive privacy protection for acts of private homosexual sodomy, nothing in *Hardwick* suggests that the state may penalize gays merely for their sexual orientation. *Cf. Robinson v. California,* 370 U.S. 660, 82 S.Ct. 1417, 8 L.Ed.2d 758 (1962) (holding that state violated due process by criminalizing the status of narcotics addiction, even though the state could criminalize the use of the narcotics—conduct in which narcotics addicts by definition are prone to engage). In other words, the class of persons involved in *Hardwick*—those who engage in homosexual sodomy—is not congruous with the class of persons targeted by the Army's regulations—those with a ho-

mosexual orientation. *Hardwick* was a "conduct" case; *Watkins'* is an "orientation" case.[10]

Second, and more importantly, *Hardwick* does not foreclose *Watkins'* claim because *Hardwick* was a *due process,* not an *equal protection* case.[11] Although the Army acknowledges, as it must, that *Hardwick* does not discuss equal protection explicitly, the Army nonetheless argues that *Hardwick's* discussion of due process has equal protection implications. Specifically, the Army argues that the *Hardwick* Court, in holding that the criminalization of homosexual sodomy does not violate due process, decided *sub silentio* that the criminalization of *heterosexual* sodomy *would* violate due process. The Army concludes from this that *Hardwick* is controlling precedent that the government may discriminate against homosexuals without violating equal protection.

Both the premise and the conclusion of the Army's argument are mistaken. In the first place, *Hardwick* did not decide *sub silentio* that heterosexual sodomy is constitutionally protected. Indeed, the Court expressly refused to take a position on whether heterosexual sodomy was protected by the due process

---

8. Under the Court's analysis, because the Constitution's protection of the right to privacy does not extend to homosexual sodomy, a judgment by the state that sodomy is immoral provides a sufficiently rational basis for sodomy laws to satisfy the requirements of substantive due process. *See Hardwick* at 196, 106 S.Ct. at 2846.

---

9. *See also Hardwick,* 478 U.S. at 201, 106 S.Ct. at 2849 (Blackmun, J., dissenting) (Court "refused to consider" equal protection clause); *Doe v. Casey,* 796 F.2d 1508, 1522 (D.C.Cir.1986), *aff'd in part, rev'd in part sub. nom, Webster v. Doe,* — U.S. —, 108 S.Ct. 2047, 100 L.Ed.2d 632 (1988) ("Although . . . the Supreme Court's recent decision in *Bowers v. Hardwick* [held] that homosexual *conduct* is not constitutionally protected, the Court did not reach the different issue of whether an agency of the federal government can discriminate against individuals merely because of sexual *orientation*." (Footnotes omitted and emphasis in the original.)); *Swift v. United States,* 649 F.Supp. 596, 42 FEP Cases (BNA) 787, 790 (D.D.C.1987) ("*this Circuit has declined to read [Hardwick]* as barring claims of discrimination based on sexual preference"); *but cf. Padula v. Webster,* 822 F.2d 97 (D.C.Cir.1987) ("reasoning in *Hardwick* forecloses . . . suspect class status for practicing homosexuals").

---

10. One commentator and one district court have already agreed with *Watkins II* that the conduct-orientation dichotomy is a valid way of distinguishing *Watkins'* case from *Hardwick.* As Professor Sunstein has written, "this feature [the conduct/orientation distinction] serves to distinguish [*Watkins* from] *Hardwick* in a persuasive way. . . ." Sunstein, Sexual Orientation and the Constitution: A Note on the Relationship Between Due Process and Equal Protection, 55 U.Chi.L.Rev. 1161, 1162 n. 9 (1988).

In *BenShalom v. Secretary of Army,* 703 F.Supp. 1372 (1989), the District Court for the Eastern District of Wisconsin prevented the Army from denying reenlistment to Sergeant BenShalom under the same regulations Watkins challenges. The district court based this decision on both the First Amendment and the equal protection component of the Fifth Amendment. In analyzing BenShalom's equal protection claim, the district court tracked the equal protection analysis of *Watkins II,* relying heavily on the conduct/orientation distinction.

---

11. Thus, whether the Army's regulations are "conduct-based" or "orientation-based," *Hardwick* cannot be read to foreclose *Watkins'* equal protection claim. Professor Sunstein agrees, noting that "*Hardwick* . . . was interpreted correctly in the majority opinion in *Watkins* [*II*], and misread in . . . Judge Reinhardt's opinion in *Watkins* [*II*] . . . [Because *Hardwick* involved due process rather than equal protection], *Watkins* can be distinguished from *Hardwick* even if the former decision were to be applied to a class of people including some, many or all who engage in the conduct at issue in *Hardwick.*" Sunstein, *supra* note 10, at 1162 & n. 9.

clause.[12] Second, even if we accept, *arguendo*, the Army's premise that the *Hardwick* Court drew a distinction between homosexual sodomy and heterosexual sodomy for due process purposes, such a distinction under the *due process* clause would have no bearing on whether the *equal protection* clause nonetheless prohibits official discrimination against homosexuals. I discuss these points in turn.

Implicit in the Army's position is the proposition that the Court in *Hardwick* somehow *did* decide that the due process clause prohibits a state from criminalizing heterosexual sodomy. That is, the Army reads Justice White's opinion in *Hardwick* as extending the zone of privacy first recognized in *Griswold* to heterosexual sodomy, thus drawing a due process line between heterosexual and homosexual sodomy. That reading of *Hardwick* flies directly in the face of footnote 2, which expressly reserves the question of the constitutionality of the Georgia statute as applied to heterosexual sodomy. *See* 478 U.S. at 188 n. 2, 106 S.Ct. at 2842 n. 2.[13]

Even apart from the Court's express reservation of this question, the Army's reading of *Hardwick* is untenable. I see no basis for reading *Hardwick* as holding *sub silentio* that a right to engage in heterosexual sodomy is "deeply rooted in this Nation's history and tradition" or "implicit in the concept of ordered liberty"—which would be necessary for heterosexual sodomy to qualify for due process protection under *Hardwick*'s analysis.[14] Note that when the Court found the suggestion that homosexual sodomy qualified for due process protection to be "at best, facetious," 478 U.S. at 194, 106 S.Ct. at 2846, it relied upon the historical fact that sodomy was a criminal offense at common law, under the laws of all 13 colonies, and, until 1961, under the laws of all 50 states. 478 U.S. at 192–94, 106 S.Ct. at 2844–46. Note further that the Court did *not* find it significant that these laws, as Justice

Stevens pointed out in his dissent, drew no distinction between homosexual and heterosexual sodomy. *See* 478 U.S. at 214–15, 106 S.Ct. at 2856–57.[15] They outlawed all acts of sodomy, both homosexual and heterosexual.

In light of the historical record relied upon by the Court, there is no way to read *Hardwick* as establishing that heterosexual sodomy is "deeply rooted in this Nation's history and tradition" while homosexual sodomy is not. I find it untenable, then, to interpret *Harwick* as extending due process protection to heterosexual conduct while denying such protection to homosexual conduct. It is hard to imagine that the Court in *Hardwick* intended to suggest that acts of heterosexual sodomy implicate higher constitutional values than acts of homosexual sodomy.

Even if, as the Army implicitly argues, *Hardwick* did in fact extend constitutional protection to heterosexual sodomy while denying it to heterosexual sodomy, such a differentiation between heterosexual and homosexual sodomy for *due process* purposes would have no bearing—none—on the entirely separate question whether official discrimination against homosexuals violates the *equal protection* clause. The relevant inquiry in equal protection jurisprudence is fundamentally different from the relevant due process inquiry. The due process clause, as the Court recognized in *Hardwick*, protects practices which are "deeply rooted in this Nation's history and tradition." The equal protection clause, in contrast, protects minorities from discriminatory treatment at the hands of the majority. Its purpose is not to protect traditional values and practices, but to *call into question* such values and practices when they operate to burden disadvantaged minorities. As Professor Sunstein puts it:

> From its inception, the Due Process Clause has been interpreted largely (though not exclusively) to protect traditional practices against short-run departures. The clause has therefore been associated with a particular conception of judicial review, one that sees the courts as safeguards against novel developments brought about by temporary majorities who are insufficiently sensitive to the claims of history.

---

12. *See Hardwick*, 478 U.S. at 188 n. 2, 106 S.Ct. at 2842 n. 2.

---

13. "The only claim properly before the Court . . . is Hardwick's challenge to the Georgia statute as applied to consensual homosexual sodomy. *We express no opinion on the constitutionality of the Georgia statute as applied to other acts of sodomy.*" *Hardwick*, 478 U.S. at 188 n. 2, 106 S.Ct. at 2842 n. 2. (emphasis added).

---

14. *See Hardwick*, 478 U.S. at 191–92, 106 S.Ct. at 2844 (*quoting Palko v. Connecticut*, 302 U.S. 319, 325, 58 S.Ct. 149, 152, 82 L.Ed. 288 (1937) and *Moore v. East Cleveland*, 431 U.S. 494, 503, 97 S.Ct. 1932, 1937, 52 L.Ed.2d 531 (1977) (Opinion of Powell, J.)).

---

15. *See also* Anne Goldstein, History, Homosexuality, and Political Values: Searching for the Hidden Determinants of *Bowers v. Hardwick* 97 Yale L.J. 1073, 1084–85 (1988) (state laws relied upon by majority outlawed all sodomy, whether homosexual or heterosexual). Moreover, Congress has not distinguished between heterosexual and homosexual sodomy in proscribing acts of sodomy by members of the armed forces. *See supra* note 6.

The Equal Protection Clause, by contrast, has been understood as an attempt to protect disadvantaged groups from discriminatory practices, however deeply engrained and longstanding. The Due Process Clause often looks backward; it is highly relevant to the Due Process issue whether an existing or time-honored convention, described at the appropriate level of generality, is violated by the practice under attack. By contrast, the Equal Protection Clause looks forward, serving to invalidate practices that were widespread at the time of its ratification and that were expected to endure. The two clauses therefore operate along different tracks.

Sunstein, *supra* note 10, at 1163.

The Supreme Court did not decide in *Hardwick*—and indeed has never decided in any case—whether discrimination against homosexuals violates equal protection. All *Hardwick* decided is that homosexual sodomy is not a practice so "deeply rooted in this Nation's history and tradition" that it falls within the zone of personal privacy protected by the due process clause. It is perfectly consistent to say that homosexual sodomy is not a practice so deeply rooted in our traditions as to merit due process protection, and at the same time to say, for example, that because homosexuals have historically been subject to invidious discrimination, laws which burden homosexuals as a class should be subjected to heightened scrutiny under the equal protection clause. Indeed, the two propositions may be complementary: In all probability, homosexuality is not considered a deeply-rooted part of our traditions *precisely because* homosexuals have historically been subjected to invidious discrimination. In any case, homosexuals do not become "fair game" for discrimination simply because their sexual practices are not considered part of our mainstream traditions.

A hypothetical may help make the point. Suppose a city passed a "single family occupancy" housing ordinance allowing only members of the immediate, nuclear family to live in the same house.[16] Suppose further that a disproportionate number of black families in the community lived together in extended families that included, for example, cousins and grandparents.[17] Finally, suppose the ordinance was motivated by a racially discriminatory purpose.[18] A black family challenging the ordinance could raise a due process claim, arguing that the ordinance impermissibly intruded on "deeply rooted" family traditions. In real life, the Court found such a due process claim persuasive.[19] But suppose the Court had rejected the due process claim. Suppose the Court had instead agreed with the city of East Cleveland that the privacy interests protected by the Constitution do not include extended family relationships—that the due process clause does not "give grandmothers any fundamental rights with respect to grandsons."[20] In that event, the black family could still challenge the ordinance on equal protection grounds, arguing that the ordinance discriminated against blacks. Could anyone seriously maintain that the Court's hypothetical refusal to give *due process* protection to "extended family" living would have any bearing on the black family's *equal protection* claim? Of course not. And the black family's equal protection claim would be no less viable even if the Court in the hypothetical had ruled that due process *does* protect the nuclear family (in the hypothetical, the form disproportionately favored by the whites in the community) but *does not* protect the extended family (disproportionately favored by blacks).

The relationship between *Hardwick* and Watkins' case is exactly the same as the relationship between the due process and equal protection claims in this hypothetical. Whether homosexual conduct is protected by the due process clause is an entirely separate question from whether the equal protection clause prohibits discrimination against homosexuals. And in answering this latter question, it makes no difference whether the *Hardwick* Court intended to extend *due process* protection to heterosexual conduct, but not homosexual conduct. In sum, the equal protection question presented by Sgt. Watkins simply is not answered—not in the slightest—by *Hardwick*.

The Army also argues that *Hardwick's* concern "about the limits of the Court's role in carrying out its constitutional mandate," 478 U.S. at 190, 106 S.Ct. at 2843, should prevent courts from holding that equal protection doctrine protects homosexuals from discrimination. To be sure, the Court in *Hardwick* jus-

---

16. This example is loosely drawn from *Moore v. City of East Cleveland*, 431 U.S. 494, 97 S.Ct. 1932, 52 L.Ed.2d 531 (1977).

17. *See Moore*, 431 U.S. at 509, 97 S.Ct. at 1940 (Brennan, J., concurring) (indicating this was the case in East Cleveland).

18. I should make clear that this was not shown to be the case in *Moore*. *See* 431 U.S. at 510, 97 S.Ct. at 1941 (Brennan, J., concurring).

19. *See Moore*, 431 U.S. at 505–06, 97 S.Ct. at 1938–39 (plurality opinion).

20. *See* 431 U.S. at 500, 97 S.Ct. at 1936 (plurality opinion) (quoting city's argument).

tified its decision to cabin the right to privacy largely by pointing to the problems allegedly created when judges recognize constitutional "rights not readily identifiable in the Constitution's text" and "having little or no cognizable roots in the language or design of the Constitution." 478 U.S. at 191, 194, 106 S.Ct. at 2844, 2846. The Court stressed its concern that such rights might be perceived as involving "the imposition of the Justices' own choice of values on the States and the Federal Government" and that this antidemocratic perception might undermine the legitimacy of the Court. *Id.* Finally, the Court expressed the more specific concern about potential difficulties in defining the contours of the right to privacy. *See Id.* at 195–96, 106 S.Ct. at 2846–47.

Whatever one might think about the *Hardwick* Court's concerns about substantive due process in general and the right of privacy in particular, these concerns have little if any relevance to equal protection doctrine.[21] The right to equal protection of the laws has a clear basis in the text of the Constitution. This principle of equal treatment, when imposed against majoritarian rule, arises from the Constitution itself, not from judicial fiat. Moreover, equal protection doctrine does not prevent the majority from enacting laws based on its substantive value choices. Equal protection simply requires that the majority apply its values evenhandedly. Indeed, equal protection doctrine plays an important role in perfecting, rather than frustrating, the democratic process. The constitutional requirement of evenhandedness advances the political legitimacy of majority rule by safeguarding minorities from majoritarian oppression. The requirement of evenhandedness also facilitates a representation of minorities in government that advances the operation of representative democracy.[22] Finally, the practical difficulties of defining the requirements imposed by equal protection, while not insignificant, do not involve the judiciary in the same degree of value-based line-drawing that the Supreme Court in *Hardwick* found so troublesome in defining the contours of substantive due process. In sum, the driving force behind *Hardwick* is the Court's ongoing concern with the expansion of rights under substantive due process, not an unbounded antipathy toward a disfavored group.

B

The Army also relies upon *Beller v. Middendorf,* 632 F.2d 788 (9th Cir.1980), *cert. denied,* 452 U.S. 905, 101 S.Ct. 3030, 69 L.Ed.2d 405 (1981), *Hatheway v. Secretary of the Army,* 641 F.2d 1376 (9th Cir.), *cert. denied,* 454 U.S. 864, 102 S.Ct. 324, 70 L.Ed.2d 164 (1981), and *DeSantis v. Pacific Tel. & Tel. Co.,* 608 F.2d 327 (9th Cir.1979), to argue that the Ninth Circuit has already rejected the kind of equal protection attack Watkins makes. In my view, the equal protection question Watkins raises—whether the Army's regulations should be subjected to strict scrutiny because homosexuals constitute a suspect class—was not addressed in any of these Ninth Circuit cases.

The Army's reliance on *Beller* is misplaced because *Beller,* like *Hardwick,* is a substantive due process case, not an equal protection case. In rejecting a substantive due process challenge to Navy regulations providing for the discharge of personnel who engaged in homosexual acts, our court held in *Beller* that substantive due process required only that courts balance the governmental and individual interests at stake in a fashion similar to intermediate scrutiny. *Beller,* 632 F.2d at 805–12. As now-Justice Kennedy's carefully tailored opinion makes clear, Beller's appeal did "not require us to address the question whether consensual private homosexual conduct is a fundamental right as that term is used in equal protection . . . [and was] not presented to us as implicating a suspect or quasi-suspect classification. . . . Substantive due process, not equal protection, was the basis of the constitutional claim, and we address the case in those terms." *Id.* at 807. Thus, *Beller,* like *Hardwick,* has no relevance to Watkins' claim that the challenged governmental regulations discriminate against a suspect class in violation of equal protection doctrine. *See Sethy v. Alameda County Water Dist.,* 545 F.2d 1157, 1159–60 (9th Cir.1976) (en banc) (a prior decision is not precedent on issues that were neither raised by counsel nor discussed in the opinion of the court); *Sakamoto v. Duty Free Shoppers,* 764 F.2d 1285, 1288 (9th Cir.1985) (same).

The Army's reliance on *Hatheway v. Secretary of the Army,* 641 F.2d 1376 (9th Cir.), *cert. denied,* 454 U.S. 864, 102 S.Ct. 324, 70 L.Ed.2d 164 (1981), is

---

21. Professor John Hart Ely, for example, has severely criticized the Supreme Court's substantive due process analysis in *Roe v. Wade,* 410 U.S. 113, 93 S.Ct. 705, 35 L.Ed.2d 147 (1973), while at the same time expressing the view that governmental classifications burdening homosexuals merit heightened scrutiny under the equal protection clause. *Compare* J. Ely, Democracy and Distrust 248 n. 52 (1980), *with Id.* at 162–64.

---

22. *See generally* J. Ely, *supra* note 21, at 101–02 ("unlike an approach geared to the judicial imposition of 'fundamental values,' the representation-reinforcing [approach] . . . is not inconsistent with, but to the contrary is entirely supportive of, the American system of representative democracy. It recognizes the unacceptability of the claim that appointed and life-tenured judges are better reflectors of conventional values than elected representatives, devoting itself instead to policing the mechanisms by which the system seeks to ensure that our elected representatives will actually represent.").

also misplaced. In *Beller*, our court reserved two distinct equal protection questions: first, whether the challenged regulations penalizing homosexual conduct burdened the exercise of a fundamental or important substantive right to engage in certain conduct; second, whether the challenged regulations discriminated against a suspect or quasi-suspect class. As explained below, in *Hatheway* we clearly answered the first of these discrete equal protection questions. The Army argues, however, that *Hatheway* also decided the second question reserved in *Beller*—the question raised in Watkins' claim—whether homosexuals constitute a suspect or quasi-suspect class.[23]

Hatheway, a soldier convicted of committing sodomy in violation of 10 U.S.C. § 925, claimed that the Army was prosecuting cases involving homosexual sodomy while refusing to prosecute cases involving heterosexual sodomy. Our court "understood Hatheway's claim (that the commission of a homosexual act is an impermissible basis for prosecution) to be an equal protection argument," *Hatheway*, 641 F.2d at 1382, which we treated as resting on the branch of equal protection doctrine concerned with whether a governmental classification burdens a fundamental or important substantive right to engage in certain conduct. Thus, we explicitly characterized Hatheway's claim "that the commission of a homosexual act is an impermissible basis for prosecution" to be the sort of equal protection claim that "implicate[d] the 'right to be free . . . from unwarranted intrusions into one's privacy.'" 641 F.2d at 1382 (quoting *Stanley v. Georgia*, 394 U.S. 557, 564, 89 S.Ct. 1243, 1247–48, 22 L.Ed.2d 542 (1969)). We then reasoned that the interest at stake in *Hatheway* was similar to the substantive interest at stake in *Beller*. 641 F.2d at 1382. Because in *Beller* we decided that under the due process clause the right to engage in homosexual conduct merited "heightened solicitude," but not strict scrutiny, in *Hatheway* we adopted this assessment for the purposes of our fundamental rights equal protection analysis. Accordingly, we applied intermediate scrutiny to the Army's actions and held that "the selection of cases involving homosexual acts for Article 125 prosecutions" was permissible because such prosecu-

tions bore "a substantial relationship to an important government interest." *Id.* Thus, we rejected Hatheway's claim based on an analysis of the fundamental rights branch of equal protection doctrine, the branch of equal protection doctrine upon which Watkins *does not* rely.

The Army argues that *Hatheway* should nonetheless be read as having decided the suspect class question. In support of this argument, the Army relies upon a single sentence in a footnote—the opinion's only reference to suspect class analysis. In footnote 6 we wrote: "Though '[t]he courts have not designated homosexuals a "suspect" or "quasi-suspect" classification so as to require more exacting scrutiny,' *DeSantis v. Pacific Tel. & Tel. Co.*, 608 F.2d 327, 333 (9th Cir.1979), heightened scrutiny is independently required where a classification penalizes the exercise of a fundamental right. *See Shapiro v. Thompson*, 394 U.S. 618, 634, 89 S.Ct. 1322, 1331, 22 L.Ed.2d 600 (1969)." 641 F.2d at 1382 n. 6. Although I recognize that the intended purpose of this footnote is not entirely clear, I cannot fairly read this passing reference as an adjudication of the important and unresolved constitutional question whether homosexuals constitute a suspect or quasi-suspect class for the purpose of equal protection analysis. Rather, I read footnote 6 as simply clarifying the distinction between the suspect class and fundamental rights branches of equal protection doctrine while acknowledging that at the time of the *Hatheway* decision courts had not yet decided whether homosexuals constitute a suspect or quasi-suspect class. That the critical language in footnote 6 is taken directly from our opinion in *DeSantis*, 608 F.2d at 327, informs our reading. In *DeSantis*, we acknowledged that our court had not yet designated homosexuals as a suspect or quasi-suspect class, but we did not decide that homosexuals should not be so designated. *See infra* at 722–23. Similarly, in footnote 6 of *Hatheway*, we remarked on the existing state of the law with respect to homosexuals without deciding the open question whether homosexuals constitute a suspect or quasi-suspect class. In other words, I read *Hatheway* as interpreting the equal protection claim presented as resting solely on the fundamental rights branch of equal protection analysis. *Hatheway* is also distinguishable from this case because, like both *Hardwick* and *Beller*, *Hatheway* involved a classification based on homosexual conduct, not homosexual orientation. As I note throughout my opinion, this distinction is relevant to an analysis of Watkins' particular equal protection claim.

Because I read *Hatheway* as not deciding the suspect class issue, and because the suspect class and fundamental rights branches of equal protection doctrine involve very separate inquiries, *see e.g., San Antonio*

---

23. Under equal protection doctrine, heightened scrutiny not only applies to legal classifications that burden suspect or quasi-suspect classes but also applies to classifications that burden the exercise of fundamental or important substantive rights to engage in certain conduct. *See, e.g., Plyler v. Doe*, 457 U.S. 202, 216–17 & nn. 14–15, 102 S.Ct. 2382, 2394–95 & nn. 14–15, 72 L.Ed.2d 786 (1982); *Maher v. Roe*, 432 U.S. 464, 470–78, 97 S.Ct. 2376, 2380–85, 53 L.Ed.2d 484 (1977); L. Tribe, American Constitutional Law § 16–7, at 1002–03, § 16–31, at 1089–90 & n. 1 (1978).

School Indep. District v. Rodriguez, 411 U.S. 1, 18–39, 93 S.Ct. 1278, 1288–1300, 36 L.Ed.2d 16 (1973); Perry, *Modern Equal Protection*, 79 Column.L.Rev. 1023, 1074–83 (1979); *Developments in the Law—Equal Protection*, 82 Harv.L.Rev. 1065, 1087–1131 (1969),*Hatheway* does not stand in the way of Watkins' equal protection claim.[24]

Finally, I must reject the Army's contention that in *DeSantis v. Pacific Tel. & Tel. Co.*, 608 F.2d 327 (9th Cir.1979), our court held that homosexuals do not constitute a suspect or quasi-suspect class. In *DeSantis*, we considered whether homosexuals were a protected class within the meaning of 42 U.S.C. § 1985(3), which secures a right of action against private parties who conspire to deprive "any person or class of persons of the equal protection of the laws." We held that section 1985(3) protects only those groups that *have been* previously determined by Congress or the courts to need special Federal assistance in protecting their civil rights. 608 F.2d at 333.[25] Applying this standard, we concluded that homosexuals could not receive the protection of section 1985(3), in part because "[t]he courts *have not* designated homosexuals a 'suspect' or 'quasi-suspect' classification," 608 F.2d at 333 (emphasis added). We did not, and did not need to, consider whether homosexuals *should be* considered a suspect class. Thus, our decision that section 1985(3) did not protect homosexuals turned simply on the point that courts had not *yet* designated homosexuals a suspect class. Although *DeSantis* does not articulate the reasons that section 1985(3) requires a *prior* governmental determination, it seems likely—since section 1985(3) authorizes suits against private individuals and requires no state action—that our court's interpretation of the statute was animated by concerns about providing potential defendants with sufficient notice of the statute's scope. *Cf. Marks v. United States*, 430 U.S. 188, 192, 97 S.Ct. 990, 993, 51 L.Ed.2d 260 (1977) (judicial enlargement of the scope of criminal statute without fair notice violates due process).

C

While neither the Supreme Court nor the Ninth Circuit has decided the question presented in Watkins' appeal—whether persons of homosexual orientation constitute a suspect class under equal protection doctrine—several other circuits have considered the different but related question whether laws burdening the class of individuals engaging in homosexual *conduct* trigger heightened scrutiny under the equal protection clause. Only one circuit, however, has given the issue more than cursory treatment.[26] In *Padula v. Webster*, 822 F.2d 97 (D.C.Cir.1987), the District of Columbia Circuit rejected an equal protection challenge to the FBI's policy of discriminating against "practicing homosexuals" in its hiring decisions. The D.C. Circuit did not analyze whether the class of persons engaging in homosexual conduct satisfies the traditional indicia of suspectness, *see infra* at 723–728, but rather concluded summarily (as the Army urges us to do here) that "[i]t would be quite anomalous, on its face, to declare status defined by conduct that states may constitutionally criminalize as deserving of strict scrutiny under the equal protection clause." *Id.* at 103. The D.C. Circuit reasoned that "[i]f the [Supreme] Court [in *Hardwick*] was unwilling to object to state laws that criminalize the behavior that defines the class, it is hardly open to a lower court to conclude that state sponsored discrimination against the class is invidious. After all, there can hardly be more palpable discrimination against a class than making the conduct that defines the class criminal." *Id.*

---

26. The Fifth and Tenth circuits have also considered this question. *Baker v. Wade*, 769 F.2d 289, 292 (5th Cir.1985) (en banc), (stressing that statute at issue was "directed at certain conduct, not at a class of people"), *cert. denied*, 478 U.S. 1022, 106 S.Ct. 3337, 92 L.Ed.2d 742 (1986); *National Gay Task Force v. Board of Educ.*, 729 F.2d 1270, 1273 (10th Cir.1984) (statute at issue proscribes "public homosexual activity" by teachers), *aff'd without opinion by an equally divided Court*, 470 U.S. 903, 105 S.Ct. 1858, 84 L.Ed.2d 776 (1985). Both of these circuits held that discrimination based on homosexual conduct does not merit heightened scrutiny under the equal protection clause, but neither circuit attempted any serious analysis of the issue. *See Baker v. Wade*, 769 F.2d at 292 (noting merely that the plaintiff "has not cited any cases holding, and we refuse to hold, that homosexuals constitute a suspect or quasi-suspect classification"); *National Gay Task Force*, 729 F.2d at 1273 (stating summarily that classification based on choice of sexual partners could not be suspect because Supreme Court has not held gender to be a suspect classification); *see also Rich v. Secretary of the Army*, 735 F.2d 1220, 1229 (10th Cir.1984) (citing without explanation *National Gay Task Force*, *Hatheway*, and *DeSantis* for the proposition that a "classification based on one's choice of sexual partners is not suspect").

---

24. If *Hatheway* had decided that homosexuals do not constitute a suspect class, I would vote to have this *en banc* panel overrule it.

---

25. Along with subsequent cases, *DeSantis* has established that there are only two ways of making this showing under § 1985(3): (1) proving that Congress *has* enacted statutes offering special protection to the class; or (2) proving that courts *have* offered special protection to the class by designating it a suspect or quasi-suspect class. *Id.*, *see also Schultz v. Sundberg*, 759 F.2d 714, 718 (9th Cir.1985).

Padula's reasoning rests on the false premise that *Hardwick* issues a blanket approval for discrimination against homosexuals. To repeat what I said above, *Hardwick* held only that the constitutionally protected right to privacy does not extend to homosexual sodomy. The case had nothing to do with equal protection. I see no principled way to transmogrify the Court's holding that the due process clause permits states to criminalize specific sexual conduct commonly engaged in by homosexuals into a holding that the equal protection clause gives states a license to pass "homosexual laws"—laws imposing special restrictions on gays because they are gay. Thus, I find *Padula* unpersuasive. Moreover, as I have reiterated throughout this opinion, the regulations at issue here target orientation, not conduct—the trait at issue in *Padula.*

In sum, no federal appellate court[27] has decided the critical issue raised by Watkins' claim: whether persons of homosexual orientation constitute a suspect class under equal protection doctrine. To be sure, *Hardwick* forecloses Watkins from making a due process claim that the Army's regulations impinge on an asserted fundamental right to engage in homosexual sodomy. But Watkins makes no such claim. Rather, he claims only that the Army's regulations discriminate against him because of his membership in a disfavored group—homosexuals. This claim is not barred by precedent.

IV

I now address the merits of Watkins' argument that the Army's regulations must be subjected to strict scrutiny because homosexuals constitute a suspect class under equal protection jurisprudence. The Supreme Court has identified several factors that guide our suspect class inquiry. I now turn to each of these factors.

The first factor the Supreme Court generally considers is whether the group at issue has suffered a history of purposeful discrimination. *See, e.g., Cleburne,* 473 U.S. at 441, 105 S.Ct. at 3254–55; *Massachusetts Bd. of Retirement v. Murgia,* 427 U.S. 307, 313, 96 S.Ct. 2562, 2566–67, 49 L.Ed.2d 520 (1976); *Rodriguez,* 411 U.S. at 28, 93 S.Ct. at 1293–94; *Frontiero,* 411 U.S. at 684–85, 93 S.Ct. at 1769–70 (plurality). As the Army concedes,[28] it is indisputable that "homosexuals have historically been the object of perni-

cious and sustained hostility." *Rowland v. Mad River Local School Dist.,* 470 U.S. 1009, 1014, 105 S.Ct. 1373, 1376–77, 84 L.Ed.2d 392 (1985) (Brennan, J., dissenting from denial of cert.). Recently courts have echoed the same harsh truth: "Lesbians and gays have been the object of some of the deepest prejudice and hatred in American society." *High Tech Gays v. Defense Industrial Security Clearance Office,* 668 F.Supp. 1361, 1369 (1987) (invalidating Defense Department practice of subjecting gay security clearance applicants to more exacting scrutiny than heterosexual applicants); *see also BenShalom v. Secretary of the Army,* 703 F.Supp. 1372 (1989) (homosexuals historically subject to discrimination).

Discrimination against homosexuals has been pervasive in both the public and private sectors. Legislative bodies have excluded homosexuals from certain jobs and schools, and have prevented homosexuals marriage. In the private sphere, homosexuals continue to face discrimination in jobs, housing and churches. *See generally* Note, *An Argument for the Application of Equal Protection Heightened Scrutiny to Classifications Based on Homosexuality,* 57 S.Cal.L.Rev. 797, 824–25 (1984) (documenting the history of discrimination). Moreover, reports of violence against homosexuals have become commonplace in our society. In sum, the discrimination faced by homosexuals is plainly no less pernicious or intense than the discrimination faced by other groups already treated as suspect classes, such as aliens or people of a particular national origin. *See, e.g., Cleburne,* 473 U.S. at 440, 105 S.Ct. at 3254 (identifying suspect groups).

The second factor that the Supreme Court considers in suspect class analysis is difficult to capsulize and may in fact represent a cluster of factors grouped around a central idea—whether the discrimination embodies a gross unfairness that is sufficiently inconsistent with the ideals of equal protection to term it "invidious." Consideration of this additional factor makes sense. After all, discrimination exists against some groups because the animus is warranted—no one could seriously argue that burglars form a suspect class. *See* Tribe, *The Puzzling Persistence of Process—Based Constitutional Theories,* 89 Yale L.J. 1063, 1075 (1980); Note, *supra,* at 814–815 & nn. 115–116. In giving content to this concept of gross unfairness, the Court has considered (1) whether the disadvantaged class is defined by a trait that "frequently bears no relation to ability to perform or contribute to society," *Frontiero,* 411 U.S. at 686, 93 S.Ct. at 1770 (plurality); (2) whether the class has been saddled with unique disabilities because of prejudice or inaccurate stereotypes; and (3) whether the trait defining the class is immutable. *See Cleburne,* 473 U.S. at 440–44, 105

---

27. One district court has decided the question. *See supra* n. 10.

---

28. *See* Army's Second Supplemental Brief at 10.

S.Ct. at 3254–57; *Plyler*, 457 U.S. at 216 n. 14, 219 n. 19, 220, 223, 102 S.Ct. at 2394 n. 14, 2395–96 n. 19, 2396, 2397–98; *Murgia*, 427 U.S. at 313, 96 S.Ct. at 2566–67; *Frontiero*, 411 U.S. at 685–87, 93 S.Ct. at 1769–71 (plurality). I consider these questions in turn.

Sexual orientation plainly has no relevance to a person's "ability to perform or contribute to society." Sergeant Watkins' exemplary record of military service stands as a testament to quite the opposite. Moreover, as the Army itself concluded, there is not a scintilla of evidence that Watkins' avowed homosexuality "had either a degrading effect upon unit performance, morale or discipline, or upon his own job performance." ER at 26c.

This irrelevance of sexual orientation to the quality of a person's contribution to society also suggests that classifications based on sexual orientation reflect prejudice and inaccurate stereotypes—the second indicium of a classification's gross unfairness. *See Cleburne*, 473 U.S. at 440–441, 105 S.Ct. at 3254–55. I agree with Justice Brennan that "discrimination against homosexuals is 'likely . . . to reflect deep-seated prejudice rather than . . . rationality.'" *Rowland*, 470 U.S. at 1014, 105 S.Ct. at 1376–77 (Brennan, J., dissenting from denial of cert.) (quoting *Plyler*, 457 U.S. at 216 n. 14, 102 S.Ct. at 2394 n. 14).

The Army suggests that the opprobrium directed towards gays does not constitute prejudice in the pejorative sense of the word, but rather is simply appropriate public disapproval of persons who engage in immoral behavior. The Army equates homosexuals with sodomists and justifies its regulations as simply reflecting a rational bias against a class of persons who engage in criminal acts of sodomy. In essence, the Army argues that homosexuals, like burglars, cannot form a suspect class because they are criminals.

The Army's argument rests on two false premises. First, as I have noted throughout this opinion, the class burdened by the regulations at issue in this case is defined by the sexual *orientation* of its members, not by their sexual conduct. *See supra* at 712–716. To my knowledge, homosexual orientation itself has never been criminalized in this country. Moreover, any attempt to criminalize the status of an individual's sexual orientation would present grave constitutional problems. *See generally Robinson v. California*, 370 U.S. 660, 82 S.Ct. 1417, 8 L.Ed.2d 758 (1962).

Second, little of the homosexual *conduct* covered by the regulations is criminal. The regulations reach many forms of homosexual conduct other than sodomy such as kissing, hand-holding, caressing, and hand-genital contact. Yet, sodomy is the only consensual adult sexual conduct that Congress has criminalized, 10 U.S.C. § 925. Indeed, the Army points to no law, federal or state, which criminalizes any form of private consensual homosexual behavior other than sodomy. The Army's argument that its regulations merely ban a class of criminals might be relevant, although not necessarily persuasive, if the class at issue were limited to sodomists. But the class banned from Army service is not comprised of sodomists, or even of homosexual sodomists; the class is comprised of persons of homosexual orientation whether or not they have engaged in sodomy.

Finally, I turn to immutability as an indicator of gross unfairness. The Supreme Court has never held that only classes with immutable traits can be deemed suspect. *Cf., e.g., Cleburne*, 473 U.S. at 442 n. 10, 105 S.Ct. at 3255–56 n. 10 (casting doubt on immutability theory); *id.* at 440–441 (stating the defining characteristics of suspect classes without mentioning immutability); *Murgia*, 427 U.S. at 313, 96 S.Ct. at 2566–67 (same); *Rodriguez*, 411 U.S. at 28, 93 S.Ct. at 1293–94 (same). I nonetheless consider immutability because the Supreme Court has often focused on immutability, *see, e.g., Plyler*, 457 U.S. at 220, 102 S.Ct. at 2396; *Frontiero*, 411 U.S. at 686, 93 S.Ct. at 1770 (plurality), and has sometimes described the recognized suspect classes as having immutable traits, *see, e.g., Parham v. Hughes*, 441 U.S. 347, 351, 99 S.Ct. 1742, 1745, 60 L.Ed.2d 269 (1979) (plurality opinion) (describing race, national origin, alienage, illegitimacy, and gender as immutable).

It is clear that by "immutability" the Court has never meant strict immutability in the sense that members of the class must be physically unable to change or mask the trait defining their class. People can have operations to change their sex. Aliens can ordinarily become naturalized citizens. The status of illegitimate children can be changed. People can frequently hide their national origin by changing their customs, their names, or their associations. Lighter skinned blacks can sometimes "pass" for white, as can Latinos for Anglos, and some people can even change their racial appearance with pigment injections. *See* J. Griffin, Black Like Me (1977). At a minimum, then, the Supreme Court is willing to treat a trait as effectively immutable if changing it would involve great difficulty, such as requiring a major physical change or a traumatic change of identity. Reading the case law in a more capacious manner, "immutability" may describe those traits that are so central to a person's identity that it would be abhorrent for government to penalize a person for refusing to change them, regardless of how easy that change might be physically. Racial discrimination, for example, would not suddenly become constitutional if medical science developed an easy, cheap, and painless method of changing one's skin pigment. *See* Tribe, *supra*, at 1073–74 n. 52. *See generally* Note, *The Constitutional Status of Sexual Orientation: Homosexuality as a Suspect Classifica-*

Appendix A **319**

tion, 98 Harv.L.Rev. 1285, 1303 (arguing that the ability to change a trait is not as important as whether the trait is a "determinative feature of personality").

With these principles in mind, I have no trouble concluding that sexual orientation is immutable for the purposes of equal protection doctrine. Although the causes of homosexuality are not fully understood, scientific research indicates that we have little control over our sexual orientation and that, once acquired, our sexual orientation is largely impervious to change. *See* Note, *supra*, 57 S.Cal.L.Rev. at 817–821 (collecting sources); *see also* L. Tribe, *supra* note 23, at 945 n. 17. Scientific proof aside, it seems appropriate to ask whether heterosexuals feel capable of changing *their* sexual orientation. Would heterosexuals living in a city that passed an ordinance burdening those who engaged in or desired to engage in sex with persons of the *opposite* sex find it easy not only to abstain from heterosexual activity but also to shift the object of their sexual desires to persons of the same sex? It may be that some heterosexuals and homosexuals can change their sexual orientation through extensive therapy, neurosurgery or shock treatment. *See* L. Tribe, *supra* note 23, at 945 n. 17. *But see* Note, *supra*, 57 S.Cal.L.Rev. at 820–21 & nn. 147–149. But the possibility of such a difficult and traumatic change does not make sexual orientation "mutable" for equal protection purposes. To express the same idea under the alternative formulation, I conclude that allowing the government to penalize the failure to change such a central aspect of individual and group identity would be abhorrent to the values animating the constitutional ideal of equal protection of the laws.

The final factor the Supreme Court considers in suspect class analysis is whether the group burdened by official discrimination lacks the political power necessary to obtain redress from the political branches of government. *See, e.g., Cleburne,* 473 U.S. at 441, 105 S.Ct. at 3255; *Plyler,* 457 U.S. at 216 n. 14, 102 S.Ct. at 2394 n. 14; *Rodriguez,* 411 U.S. at 28, 93 S.Ct. at 1293–94. Courts are understandably reluctant to extend heightened protection under equal protection doctrine to groups fully capable of securing their rights through the political process. It cannot be seriously disputed, however, that homosexuals as a group cannot protect their right to be free from invidious discrimination by appealing to the political branches.

The very fact that homosexuals have historically been underrepresented in and victimized by political bodies is itself strong evidence that they lack the political power necessary to ensure fair treatment at the hands of government. In addition, homosexuals as a group are handicapped by structural barriers that operate to make effective political participation unlikely if not impossible. First, the social, economic, and political pressures to conceal one's homosexuality oper-

ate to discourage gays from openly protesting anti-homosexual governmental action. Ironically, by "coming out of the closet" to protest against discriminatory legislation and practices, homosexuals expose themselves to the very discrimination they seek to eliminate. As a result, the voices of many homosexuals are not even heard, let alone counted. *Cf.* J. Ely, *supra* note 21, at 163–64. "Because of the immediate and severe opprobrium often manifested against homosexuals once so identified publicly, members of this group are particularly powerless to pursue their rights openly in the political arena." *Rowland,* 470 U.S. at 1014, 105 S.Ct. at 1376–77 (Brennan, J., dissenting from denial of cert.).

Even when gays do come out of the closet to participate openly in politics, the general animus towards homosexuality may render this participation ineffective. Many heterosexuals, including elected officials, find it difficult to empathize with and take seriously the arguments advanced by homosexuals, in large part because of the lack of meaningful interaction between the heterosexual majority and the homosexual minority. Most people have little exposure to gays, both because they rarely encounter gays[29] and because—as I noted above—homosexuals are often pressured into concealing their sexual identity. Thus, elected officials sensitive to public prejudice and ignorance, and insensitive to the needs of the homosexual constituency, may refuse to even consider legislation that even appears to be pro-homosexual. *See* Note, *supra*, 98 Harv.L.Rev. at 1304 n. 96. Indeed, the Army itself argues that its regulations are justified by the need to "maintain the public acceptability of military service," AR 635–200, ¶ 15-2(a), because "toleration of homosexual conduct . . . might be understood as tacit approval" and "the existence of homosexual units might well be a source of ridicule and notoriety." Army's Opening Brief at 17, 19 n. 9, 30–31 n. 18. These barriers to the exercise of political power both reinforce and are reinforced by the underrepresentation of avowed homosexuals in the decisionmaking bodies of government and the inability of homosexuals to prevent legislation hostile to their group interests.[30] *See*

---

29. Because homosexuals are a minority and are frequently excluded from jobs, schools, churches, and heterosexual social circles, *see supra*, heterosexuals generally have relatively few opportunities to meet homosexuals and overcome their stereotypical thinking about homosexuality.

---

30. The Army claims that homosexuals cannot be politically powerless because two states, Wisconsin and California, have passed statutes prohibiting discrimination against homosexuals. Two state statutes do not overcome the long and extensive history of laws discriminating against homosexuals in all fifty states. *See, e.g.,* Note, *supra*, 57 Cal.L.Rev. at 803–07.

Frontiero, 411 U.S. at 686 & n. 17, 93 S.Ct. at 1770 & n. 17 (plurality) (underrepresentation of women in government caused in part by history of discrimination); *Cleburne*, 473 U.S. at 445, 105 S.Ct. at 3257 (reasoning that the existence of legislation responsive to the needs of the mentally disabled belied the claim that they were politically powerless).

In sum, all of the relevant factors drive me to the conclusion that homosexuals constitute a suspect class for equal protection purposes. Moreover, the principles that animate equal protection doctrine—the principles that gave rise to these factors in the first place—reinforce that conclusion. *See also* J. Ely, *supra* note 21, at 162–64 (classifications based on homosexuality merit heightened scrutiny); L. Tribe, *supra* note 23, at 944–45 n. 17 (same).

V

Having concluded that homosexuals constitute a suspect class, I now must subject the Army's regulations facially discriminating against homosexuals to strict scrutiny. Consequently, I may uphold the regulations only if they are " '*necessary* to promote a *compelling* governmental interest.' " *Dunn v. Blumstein*, 405 U.S. 330, 342, 92 S.Ct. 995, 1003, 31 L.Ed.2d 274 (1972) (quoting *Shapiro*, 394 U.S. at 634, 89 S.Ct. at 1331); *see also University of Calif. Regents v. Bakke*, 438 U.S. 265, 357, 98 S.Ct. 2733, 2782, 57 L.Ed.2d 750 (1978) (Opinion of Brennan, White, Marshall & Blackmun, JJ.). The requirement of necessity means that no less restrictive alternative is available to promote the compelling governmental interest. *See Dunn*, 405 U.S. at 343, 92 S.Ct. at 1003; *Bakke*, 438 U.S. at 357, 98 S.Ct. at 2782 (Opinion of four justices).

I recognize that even under strict scrutiny, my review of military regulations must be more deferential than comparable review of laws governing civilians. *See Goldman v. Weinberger*, 475 U.S. 503, 106 S.Ct. 1310, 1313, 89 L.Ed.2d 478 (1986). While the Supreme Court does not "purport to apply a different equal protection test because of the military context, [it does] stress the deference due congressional

choices among alternatives in exercising the congressional authority to raise and support armies and make rules for their governance." *Rostker v. Goldberg*, 453 U.S. 57, 71, 101 S.Ct. 2646, 2655, 69 L.Ed.2d 478 (1981) (citing *Schlesinger v. Ballard*, 419 U.S. 498, 95 S.Ct. 572, 42 L.Ed.2d 610 (1975)). I question whether this special deference is appropriate in Watkins' case given that Congress has chosen not to regulate homosexuality or any form of sexual conduct engaged in by military personnel save for one exception—Congress has chosen to criminalize sodomy by military personnel whether committed "with another person *of the same or opposite* sex." 10 U.S.C. § 925 (emphasis added). Hence, if anything, section 925 reflects an absence of congressional intent to discriminate on the basis of sexual orientation.

In any case, even granting special deference to the policy choices of the military, I must reject many of the Army's asserted justifications because they illegitimately cater to private biases. For example, the Army argues that it has a valid interest in maintaining morale and discipline by avoiding hostilities and " 'tensions between known homosexuals and other members [of the armed services] who despise/detest homosexuality.' " Army's Opening Brief at 17 (quoting and incorporating into their argument *Beller*, 632 F.2d at 811); *see also Id.* at 17–18, 19 n. 9, 30, 30–31 n. 18; Army's Second Supp.Brief at 30–31 & n. 17; AR 635–200, ¶ 15–1(a).[31] The Army also expresses its "

Moreover, at the national level—the relevant political level for seeking protection from military discrimination—homosexuals have been wholly unsuccessful in getting legislation passed that protects them from discrimination.

The Army also argues that the repeal of sodomy statutes by many states proves that homosexuals are not politically powerless. However, sodomy statues restrict the sexual freedom of heterosexuals as well as homosexuals. The repeal of sodomy statutes may thus reflect the liberalization of attitudes about heterosexual behavior more than it reflects the political power of homosexuals.

---

31. A somewhat different rationale conceivably could also underlie certain cryptic statements the Army makes about its concerns regarding "close conditions affording minimal privacy," " 'potential for difficulties arising out of possible close confinement,' " and "the intimacy of barrack's life." AR 635–200, ¶ 15–1(a); Army's Opening Brief at 15 (quoting *Beller*, 632 F.2d at 812); Army's Second Supp. Brief at 19 n. 9, 30. Conceivably, the Army could be concerned in part that the presence of gays in the ranks will create *sexual* tensions—as distinguished from tensions arising from prejudice—because of the practical necessity of housing gays with personnel of the same sex. The Army, however, never articulates this concern. Thus it gives no indication that it regards this concern as compelling or that it believes that weeding *all* homosexuals out of the military—even soldiers as exemplary as Sergeant Watkins—is necessary to advance a compelling military interest in reducing sexual tensions. Indeed, at points in its argument the Army implies that it is concerned about the close confinement of soldiers only insofar as such confinement might exacerbate hostilities and tensions assertedly created by the prejudice some heterosexuals have against homosexuals. *See* Army's Opening Brief at 17, 31 n. 18. Even if the Army had raised the argument that excluding homosexuals from barracks reduces sexual tension and had shown that reducing sexual tension serves a compelling interest, nothing in the record even suggests that a per se rule banning all homosexuals from the Army would be the least restrictive method of advancing this interest.

'doubts concerning a homosexual officer's ability to command the respect and trust of the personnel he or she commands' " because many lower-ranked heterosexual soldiers despise and detest homosexuality. *See* Army's Second Supp. Brief at 30–31 (quoting and incorporating *Beller*, 632 F.2d at 811); *see also Id.* at 31 n. 17; Army's Opening Brief at 17–18, 19 n. 9, 30; AR 635–200, ¶ 15–1(a). Finally, the Army argues that the presence of gays in its ranks "might well be a source of ridicule and notoriety, harmful to the Army's recruitment efforts" and to its public image. Army's Opening Brief at 31 n. 18; *see also Id.* at 15, 17, 19 n. 9, 30; AR 635–200, ¶ 15–1(a).

These concerns strike an all-too-familiar chord. For much of our history, the military's fear of racial tension kept black soldiers separated from whites. As recently as World War II both the Army chief of staff and the Secretary of the Navy justified racial segregation in the ranks as necessary to maintain efficiency, discipline, and morale. *See* G. Ware, William Hastie: Grace Under Pressure 99, 134 (1984).[32] Today, it is unthinkable that the judiciary would defer to the Army's prior "professional" judgment that black and white soldiers had to be segregated to avoid interracial tensions. Indeed, the Supreme Court has decisively rejected the notion that private prejudice against minorities can ever justify official discrimination, even when those private prejudices create real and legitimate problems. *See Palmore v. Sidoti*, 466 U.S. 429, 104 S.Ct. 1879, 80 L.Ed.2d 421 (1984).

In *Palmore*, a state granted custody of a child to her father because her white mother had remarried a black man. The state rested its decision on the best interests of the child, reasoning that, despite improvements in race relations, the social reality was that the child would likely suffer social stigmatization if she had parents of different races. A unanimous Court, in an opinion by Chief Justice Burger, conceded the importance of the state's interest in the welfare of the child, but nonetheless reversed with the following reasoning:

> It would ignore reality to suggest that racial and ethnic prejudices do not exist or that all manifestations of those prejudices have been eliminated.
> . . . The question, however, is whether the reality

of private biases and the possible injury they might inflict are permissible considerations for removal of an infant child from the custody of its natural mother. We have little difficulty concluding that they are not. The Constitution cannot control such prejudices but neither can it tolerate them. Private biases may be outside the reach of the law, but the law cannot, directly or indirectly, give them effect.

Id. at 433, 104 S.Ct. at 1882. Thus, *Palmore* forecloses the Army from justifying its ban on homosexuals on the ground that private prejudice against homosexuals would somehow undermine the strength of our armed forces if homosexuals were permitted to serve. *See also Cleburne*, 473 U.S. at 448, 105 S.Ct. at 3258–60 (even under rationality review of discrimination against group that is neither suspect nor quasi-suspect, catering to private prejudice is not a cognizable state interest).

The Army's defense of its regulations, however, goes beyond its professed fear of prejudice in the ranks. Apparently, the Army believes that its regulations rooting out persons with certain sexual tendencies are not merely a response to prejudice, but are also grounded in legitimate moral norms. In other words, the Army believes that its ban against homosexuals simply codifies society's moral consensus that homosexuality is evil. Yet, even accepting *arguendo* this proposition that anti-homosexual animus is grounded in morality (as opposed to prejudice masking as morality), and assuming further that the Army is an appropriate governmental body to articulate moral norms, equal protection doctrine does not permit notions of majoritarian morality to serve as compelling justification for laws that discriminate against suspect classes.

A similar principle animates *Loving v. Virginia*, 388 U.S. 1, 87 S.Ct. 1817, 18 L.Ed.2d 1010 (1967), in which the Supreme Court struck down a Virginia statute outlawing marriages between whites and blacks. Although the Virginia legislature may have adopted this law in the sincere belief that miscegenation—the mixing of racial blood lines—was evil,[33] this moral judgment could not justify the statute's discrimination on the basis of race. Like the Army's reg-

---

32. It took an Executive Order in 1945 by President Truman, issued against the advice of almost every admiral and general, to integrate our armed forces. M. Miller, Plain Speaking: An Oral Biography of Harry S Truman 79 (1983). It is also interesting to note that during World War II the Army deliberately minimized any publicity about the existence of black soldiers because it feared that such publicity would tarnish the Army's public image. *See* G. Ware, *supra*, at 100.

33. Indeed, the trial judge in *Loving* admonished Mildred and Richard Loving that interracial marriage was a violation of the Christian ethic of racial purity: "Almighty God created the races, white, black, yellow, malay and red, and he placed them on separate continents. And but for the interference with his arrangement there would be no cause for such marriages. The fact that he separated the races shows that he did not intend for the races to mix. *Loving*, 388 U.S. at 3, 87 S.Ct. at 1819.

ulations proscribing sexual acts only when committed by homosexual couples, the Virginia statute proscribed marriage when undertaken by mixed-race couples. In both cases, the government did not prohibit certain conduct, it prohibited certain conduct selectively— only when engaged in by certain classes of people. Although courts may sometimes have to accept society's moral condemnation as a justification even when the morally condemned activity causes no harm to interests outside notions of morality, *see Hardwick*, 478 U.S. at 196, 106 S.Ct. at 2847 (accepting moral condemnation as justification under rationality review), our deference to majoritarian notions of morality must be tempered by the equal protection principles which require that those notions be applied evenhandedly. Laws that limit the acceptable focus of one's sexual desires to members of the opposite sex, like laws that limit one's choice of spouse (or sexual partner) to members of the same race, cannot withstand constitutional scrutiny absent a compelling governmental justification. This requirement would be reduced to a nullity if the government's assertion of moral objections only to interracial couples or only to homosexual couples could itself serve as a tautological basis for the challenged classification.

The Army's remaining justifications for discriminating against homosexuals may not be illegitimate, but they bear little relation to the regulations at issue. For example, the Army argues that military discipline might be undermined if emotional relationships developed between homosexuals of different military rank. Army's Opening Brief at 17–18, 19 n. 9, 30; AR 635–200, ¶ 15–1(a). Although this concern might be a compelling and legitimate military interest, the Army's regulations are poorly tailored to advance that interest. No one would suggest that heterosexuals are any less likely to develop emotional attachments within military ranks than homosexuals. Yet the Army's regulations do not address the problem of emotional attachments between male and female personnel, which presumably subjects military discipline to similar stress. Surely, the Army's interest in preventing emotional relationships that could erode military discipline would be advanced much more directly by a ban on all sexual contact between members of the same unit, whether between persons of the same or opposite sex. *Cf. Cleburne*, 473 U.S. at 449–50, 105 S.Ct. at 3259–60 (rejecting certain asserted justifications under *rationality* review where the justification would extend to other groups but the challenged classification did not). Here the Army's regulations disqualify all homosexuals whether or not they have developed any emotional or sexual relationships with other soldiers.

Also bearing little relation to the regulations is the Army's professed concern with breaches of security. AR 635–200, ¶ 15–1(a). Certainly the Army has a compelling interest in excluding persons who may be susceptible to blackmail. It is evident, however, that homosexuality poses a special risk of blackmail only if a homosexual is secretive about his or her sexual orientation. The Army's regulations do nothing to lessen this problem. Quite the opposite, the regulations ban homosexuals only after they have declared their homosexuality or have engaged in known homosexual acts. The Army's concern about security risks among gays could be addressed in a more sensible and less restrictive manner by adopting a regulation banning only those gays who had lied about or failed to admit their sexual orientation.[34] In that way, the Army would *encourage*, rather than discourage, declarations of homosexuality, thereby reducing the number of closet homosexuals who might indeed pose a security risk. Moreover, even if banning homosexuals could lessen security risks, there appears to be no reason for treating homosexuality as a nonwaivable disqualification from military service while treating other more serious potential sources of blackmail as waivable disqualifications. *See* AR 635–200, ¶ 14–12(c) & (d) (making drug abuse and the commission of other serious military offenses waivable disqualifications).

CONCLUSION

The Army's regulations violate the constitutional guarantee of equal protection of the laws because they discriminate against persons of homosexual orientation, a suspect class, and because the regulations are not necessary to promote a legitimate compelling governmental interest. I would thus reverse the district court's rulings denying Watkins' motion for summary judgment in favor of the Army, and remand with instructions to enter a declaratory judgment that the Army Regulations A.R. 635-200, Chapter 15, and 601–280, ¶ 2–21(c), are constitutionally void on their face, and to enter an injunction requiring the Army to consider Watkins' reenlistment application without regard to his sexual orientation.

---

34. Watkins has forthrightly reported his homosexuality since his induction in 1967, and his homosexuality was always a matter of common knowledge. There is no suggestion in the record before us that Watkins ever feared public disclosure of his homosexuality.

Scott ISAACS, a minor, by his father and natural guardian, Howard Isaacs, Appellant,

v.

Lester M. POWELL and Arlyss R. Powell, doing business as Monkeytown, U.S.A., Appellees.

No. 71–683.

District Court of Appeal of Florida, Second District.

Oct. 4, 1972.

Rehearing Denied Nov. 13, 1972.

Father brought action on behalf of child against owner of monkey farm to recover for injuries sustained when chimpanzee grabbed child's arm. The Circuit Court, Pinellas County, C. Richard Leavengood, J., returned verdict for owner of chimpanzee, and father appealed. The District Court of Appeal, McNulty, J., held that owner or keeper of chimpanzee was liable under the strict liability doctrine for injuries inflicted on child by chimpanzee.

Reversed and remanded.

1. **Animals k69**   Owner or keeper of chimpanzee was liable under the strict liability doctrine for injuries inflicted on child by chimpanzee.

2. **Animals k69**   "Strict liability" does not mean the owner or keeper of a wild animal is an absolute insurer in the sense that he is liable regardless of any fault on the part of the victim.

> See publication Words and Phrases for other judicial constructions and definitions.

3. **Animals k71**   An owner or keeper of a wild animal is not relieved from liability by slight negligence or want of ordinary care on part of person injured but is relieved of liability only if victim's acts are such as would establish that, with knowledge of the danger, he voluntarily brought the calamity upon himself.

4. **Animals k69**   An owner or keeper of a wild animal is relieved from strict liability by the willful or intentional fault of a third party provided such fault is of itself an efficient cause and the sole cause of victim's injuries.

William F. Blews, of Chambers & Blews, St. Petersburg, for appellant.

John T. Allen, Jr., and Harrison, Greene, Mann, Davenport, Rowe & Stanton, St. Petersburg, for appellees.

McNULTY, Judge.

[1] This is a case of first impression in Florida. The question posed is whether Florida should adopt the general rule that the owner or keeper of a wild animal, in this case a chimpanzee, is liable to one injured by such animal under the strict liability doctrine, i.e., regardless of negligence on his part, or whether his liability should be predicated on his fault or negligence.[1]

Plaintiff-appellant Scott Isaacs was two years and seven months old at the times material herein. His father had taken him to defendants-appellees' monkey farm where, upon purchasing an admission ticket, and as was usual and encouraged by appellees, he also purchased some food to feed the animals. While Scott was feeding a chimpanzee named Valerie she grabbed his arm and inflicted serious injury.

The exact details of how Valerie was able to grab Scott's arm are in dispute. Appellees contend that Scott's father lifted the boy above reasonably sufficient protective barriers to within Valerie's reach, while appellants counter that the barriers and other protective measures were insufficient. But in any case, appellants do not now, nor did they below, rely on any fault of appellees. Rather, they rely solely on the aforesaid generally accepted strict or, as it is sometimes called, absolute liability doctrine under which negligence or fault on the part of the owner or keeper of an animal *ferae naturae* is irrelevant.[2] Appellees, on the other

---

1. Although the precise question has never been decided in Florida, our sister court in the third district recognized the general rule in dictum while deciding that the bees involved in that case were not wild animals and thus the rule of negligence applied regardless. *Ferreira v. D'Asaro* (Fla.App.1963), 152 So.2d 736.

---

2. *See, e.g.*, Anno., 21 A.L.R.3d pp. 608, 618; 4 Am.Jur.2d, Animals, § 80 et seq.; and Prosser, Law of Torts, § 75, Animals, p. 513.

hand, suggest that we should adopt the emerging, though yet minority, view that liability should depend upon negligence, i.e., a breach of the duty of care reasonably called for taking into account the nature and specie of the animal involved.[3] We will consider this aspect of the problem first and will hereinafter discuss available defenses under the theory we adopt.

The trial judge apparently agreed with the appellees that fault or negligence on the part of the owners of a wild animal must be shown. He charged the jury on causation as follows:

> "The issues for your determination are whether the proximate cause of Scott Isaacs' injuries was the improper protection for paying customers of the defendants in the condition of the cage, and whether the approximate cause of (sic) the placing of Scott by his father, Howard Isaacs, within the barrier placed by the defendants for the protection of customers of the defendant."

In other words the trial judge asked the jury to decide whether Scott was injured through the fault of defendants-appellees and/or through the fault of his father. The jury returned a verdict for the defendants; but obviously, it's impossible for us to determine whether, under the foregoing charge, the jury so found because they were unable to find fault on defendants' part, or whether they so found because they believed the cause of Scott's injury to be the fault of the father. If, of course, we adopt the negligence theory of liability there would be no error in submitting both issues to the jury. But we are of the view that the older and general rule of strict liability, which obviates the issue of the owner's negligence, is more suited to the fast growing, populous and activity-oriented society of Florida. Indeed, our society imposes even more than enough risks upon its members now, and we are reluctant to encourage the addition of one more particularly when that one more is increasingly contributed by those who, for profit, would exercise their "right" to harbor wild animals and increase exposure to the dangers thereof by luring advertising. Prosser puts it this way:[4]

> ". . . [Liability] has been thought to rest on the basis of negligence in keeping the animal at all; but this does not coincide with the modern analysis of negligence as conduct which is unreasonable in view of the risk, since it may not be an unreasonable thing to keep a tiger in a zoo. *It is rather an instance of the strict responsibility placed upon those who, even with proper care, expose the community to the risk of a very dangerous thing.* While one or two jurisdictions insist that there is no liability without some negligence in keeping the animal, by far the greater number impose strict liability." (Italics supplied)

Additionally, we observe that Florida has enacted § 767.04, F.S.A.,[5] relating to dogs, which abrogates the permissive "one bite" rule of the common law. That rule posited that an owner of a dog is liable to one bitten by such dog only if he is chargeable with "scienter," i.e., prior knowledge of the viciousness of the dog. Necessarily, of course, the cause of action therefor was predicated on the negligence of the owner in failing to take proper precautions with knowledge of the dog's vicious propensities.[6] Our statute, however, has in effect imposed strict liability on a dog owner (from which he can absolve himself only by complying with the warning proviso of the statute). It would result in a curious anomaly, then if we were to adopt the negligence concept as a basis for liability of an owner or keeper of a tiger, while § 767.04, *supra*, imposes potential strict liability upon him if he should trade the tiger for a dog. We are compelled to adopt, therefore, the strict liability rule in these cases.

[2] Concerning, now, available defenses under this rule we share the view, and emphasize, that "strict or absolute liability" does not mean the owner or keeper of a wild animal is an absolute insurer in the sense that he is liable regardless of any fault on the part of the victim. Moreover, we do not think it means he is liable notwithstanding an intervening, efficient independent fault which *solely* causes the result, as

---

3. *See, e.g., Hansen v. Brogan* (1965), 145 Mont. 224, 400 P.2d 265, 21 A.L.R.3d 595; and Anno., 21 A.L.R.3d, 618, 622.

---

4. See, Prosser, n. 2, at p. 513.

---

5. This section provides, in pertinent part: "The owners of any dog which shall bite any person, while such person is on or in a public place, or lawfully on or in a private place, including the property of the owner of such dogs, shall be liable for such damages as may be suffered by persons bitten, *regardless of the former viciousness of such dog or the owners' knowledge of such viciousness.* . . .; Provided, however, no owner of any dog shall be liable for any damages to any person or his property when such person shall mischievously or carelessly provoke or aggravate the dog inflicting such damage; nor shall any such owner be so liable if at the time of any such injury he had displayed in a prominent place on his premises a sign easily readable including the words 'Bad Dog.' " (Italics supplied.)

---

6. This indeed was also basis at common law of liability on the part of an owner of *any* animal *domitae naturae*. See, e.g., Prosser, n. 2, *supra*, pp. 514, 517.

was possibly the case here if fault on the part of Scott's father were the sole efficient cause.

[3] As to the fault of the victim himself, since the owner or keeper of a wild animal is held to a rigorous rule of liability on account of the danger inherent in harboring such animal, it has generally been held that the owner ought not be relieved from such liability by slight negligence or want of ordinary care on the part of the person injured. The latter's acts must be such as would establish that, with knowledge of the danger, he voluntarily brought the calamity upon himself.[7] This general rule supports the Restatement of Torts, § 515,[8] which we now adopt and set forth as follows:

> "(1) A plaintiff is not barred from recovery by his failure to exercise reasonable care to observe the propinquity of a wild animal or an abnormally

dangerous domestic animal or to avoid harm to his person, land or chattels threatened by it.
(2) A plaintiff is barred from recovery by *intentionally and unreasonably* subjecting himself to the risk that a wild animal or an abnormally dangerous domestic animal will do harm to his person, land or chattels." (Italics supplied)

[4] With regard to an intervening fault bringing about the result we have no hesitancy in expanding the foregoing rule to include as a defense the willful or intentional fault of a third party provided such fault is of itself an efficient cause and is the sole cause. If a jury were to decide in this case, therefore, that the *sole* efficient cause of Scott's injury was the intentional assumption of the apparent risks on the part of the boy's father and his placing of the boy within reach of the danger, it would be a defense available to appellees. Clearly, though, this defense would be related only to causation and is not dependent upon any theory of imputation of the father's fault to the son, which is now irrelevant in view of the extent of strict liability in these cases and the limited defenses available thereunder.

The judgment is reversed and the cause is remanded for a new trial on the theory of strict liability, and the defenses thereto, as enunciated above.

Reversed.

HOBSON, A. C. J., and MANN, J., concur.

---

7. *See, e.g.,* 21 A.L.R.3d, n. 2, *supra,* pp. 615, 618.

---

8. This rule is duplicated in § 484, Restatement, Torts 2d, which states that the plaintiff's contributory negligence is not a defense to the strict liability of the possessor of an animal, except where such contributory negligence consists in voluntarily and unreasonably subjecting himself to the risk of harm from the animal.

===

Jeff DONNER, Petitioner,

v.

ARKWRIGHT-BOSTON MANUFACTURERS MUTUAL INSURANCE COMPANY,
a Foreign Corporation authorized to do business in the State of Florida, B. R.
Styers and Edward F. Brown, Respondents.
No. 51996.
Supreme Court of Florida.
April 6, 1978.

Action was brought to recover for dog bite. Judgment was entered for dog owner at trial, and the District Court of Appeal, Third District, 346 So.2d 1210, affirmed, and writ of certiorari was granted. The Supreme Court, Sundberg, J., held that: (1) dog owner who is brought to trial pursuant to statutes concerning liability of dog owners for dog bites has available to him only defenses expressed in that statute, and (2) jury should not have been instructed separately on assumption of risk, but should have been charged solely on defenses expressed in statute governing liability of dog owners for dog bites, which provides that dog owners shall not be liable for damages to any person or his property when such person shall mischievously or carelessly provoke or aggravate dog inflicting such damage, and that dog owner is not liable if at time of dog bite he had displayed in prominent place on his premises easily readable sign including words "Bad Dog."

Petition granted, decision quashed, and cause remanded with instructions.

Overton, C. J., dissented.

1. **Animals k74(7)**   In action brought to recover for dog bite pursuant to statutes governing responsibility and liability of dog owners, jury should not have been instructed separately on assumption of risk but should have been charged solely on defenses expressed in statutes governing liability of dog owners, which provides that no dog owner shall be liable for any damages to any person or his property when such person shall mischievously or carelessly provoke or aggravate dog inflicting such damage. West's F.S.A. § 767.04.

2. **Animals k71**   Dog owner who is brought to trial pursuant to statute governing liability of dog owners has available to him only defenses expressed in statute, which provides that no dog owner shall be liable for any damages to any person or his property when such person shall mischievously or carelessly provoke or aggravate dog inflicting such damage, and that dog owner shall not be liable if he had displayed in prominent place on his premises easily readable sign including words "Bad Dog." West's F.S.A. § 767.04.

Edward A. Perse of Horton, Perse & Ginsberg, and Ratiner & Glinn, Miami, for petitioner.

Robert M. Klein, of Stephens, Schwartz, Lynn & Chernay & Brandy, P.A., Miami, for respondents.

SUNDBERG, Justice.

By petition for writ of certiorari, petitioner seeks review of a decision of the District Court of Appeal, Third District, reported at 346 So.2d 1210 (Fla.3d DCA 1977), which is alleged to be in conflict with our recent opinion in *Blackburn v. Dorta*, 384 So.2d 287 (Fla.1977). In *Blackburn*, this Court held that the defense of assumption of risk has become merged with the doctrine of comparative negligence and no longer constitutes a complete bar to a cause of action. We noted that assumption of risk was not a favored defense and that the "potpourri of labels, concepts, definitions, thoughts, and doctrines" which were indiscriminately applied to the doctrine produced an "enigma wrapped in a mystery." In the instant cause, in which petitioner sustained a dog bite injury, the trial judge instructed the jury on the doctrine of assumption of risk over petitioner's objection. The District Court of Appeal, Third District, affirmed per curiam notwithstanding

the principles enunciated in *Blackburn*, of which the district court was made aware prior to rendition of its decision. Accordingly, jurisdiction vests in this Court pursuant to Article V, Section 3(b)(3), Florida Constitution.

While visiting respondent Edward F. Brown at his home, petitioner sustained an injury when a dog owned by Brown bit him on the mouth. Respondent Arkwright-Boston Manufacturers Mutual Insurance Company was named as a co-defendant by virtue of the homeowners insurance agreement which it had with Brown.

The dog, a 60-pound female Doberman pinscher, had no prior history of vicious propensities but was in heat at the time the injury was inflicted. When petitioner first made a gesture to pet the animal, which was penned up in the kitchen of the Brown home, he was notified of her condition and also told that she was nervous because it was thundering outside. Consequently, he refrained from touching her. Shortly thereafter, petitioner returned to the location of the kitchen, began stroking the dog on the top of the head and scratching her under the chin, whereupon petitioner was bitten on the lip.

Pursuant to Sections 767.01 and 767.04, Florida Statutes (1975),[1] petitioner sought damages from respondents. At his jury trial, petitioner moved for a directed verdict on the liability question at the close of all the evidence, which motion was denied. A charge conference was then held at which point counsel for respondents requested charges on the statutory de-

---

1. § 767.01, Fla.Stat. (1975), reads as follows:

"*Owners responsible.*—Owners of dogs shall be liable for any damage done by their dogs to sheep or other domestic animals or livestock, or to persons."

§ 767.04, Fla.Stat. (1975), reads as follows:

"*Liability of owners.*—The owners of any dog which shall bite any person, while such person is on or in a public place, or lawfully on or in a private place, including the property of the owner of such dogs, shall be liable for such damages as may be suffered by persons bitten, regardless of the former viciousness of such dog or the owners' knowledge of such viciousness. A person is lawfully upon private property of such owner within the meaning of this act when he is on such property in the performance of any duty imposed upon him by the laws of this state or by the laws of postal regulations of the United States, or when he is on such property upon invitation, expressed or implied, of the owner thereof; Provided, however, no owner of any dog shall be liable for any damages to any person or his property when such person shall mischievously or carelessly provoke or aggravate the dog inflicting such damage; nor shall any such owner be so liable if at the time of any such injury he had displayed in a prominent place on his premises a sign easily readable including the words "Bad Dog."

fenses of mischievous or careless provocation or aggravation as well as assumption of risk defense. Petitioner's counsel objected to the giving of the assumption of risk charge, contending that the defense had been merged with the doctrine of comparative negligence in view of this Court's opinion in *Blackburn v. Dorta, supra.* However, as previously noted, the trial judge ultimately gave the standard jury charge on assumption of risk as well as the charge on the statutory defenses. The jury returned a verdict in favor of respondents and, in accordance therewith, a final judgment for respondents was entered. After his motion for a retrial was denied, petitioner appealed to the District Court of Appeal, Third District, which affirmed per curiam, without opinion, the final judgment.

[1] Petitioner now asks this Court to quash the decision of the District Court of Appeal, Third District, on the ground that the trial court erroneously instructed the jury on the defense of assumption of risk. He contends that the jury should have been charged exclusively on the language of the statutes, which language in no way articulates the assumption of risk doctrine, but which does create statutory defenses where the injured individual "mischievously or carelessly provokes or aggravates" the dog. While petitioner concedes that the statutory defenses would frequently be applied in much the same fashion as the doctrine of assumed risk, he suggests that to continue permitting trial courts to instruct on the common law doctrine will foster confusion. This is asserted because in *Blackburn v. Dorta, supra,* the doctrine of assumed risk was merged with that of contributory negligence. The latter doctrine it is argued is not applicable to dog bite cases where the action is not grounded in negligence; rather, the owner of a dog acts as a virtual insurer with regard to injuries caused by his dog. *Sand v. Gold,* 301 So.2d 828 (Fla. 3d DCA 1974); *cert. denied* 312 So.2d 752 (Fla.1975); *Vandercar v. David,* 96 So.2d 227 (Fla. 3d DCA 1957). We agree with petitioner that the jury should not have been instructed separately on assumption of risk but should have been charged solely on the defenses expressed in Section 767.04.

Prior to legislative enactment, the common law as adopted by Florida had become well settled regarding the liability of dog owners. In *Smith v. Pelah,* 2 Strange 1264, 93 Eng.Rep. 1171 (1747), the court proposed that it was a wrong to humanity to maintain a dog known to harbor vicious propensities. The gist of the action was the owner's knowledge of the dog's dangerous inclinations. Conversely, an owner who lacked knowledge of the vicious tendencies of his dog escaped liability. *Mason v. Keeling, See* 1 Ld.Raym. 606, 608, 91 Eng.Rep. 1305, 1307 (1700). However, it was often difficult and sometimes impossible to prove this

element of scienter.[2] Accordingly, the Florida Legislature enacted statutes designed to obviate the element of scienter,[3] and make the dog owner the insurer against damage done by his dog. In *Carroll v. Moxley,* 241 So.2d 681 (Fla.1970), which prior to the instant case was this Court's latest exposition on the subject statute,[4] we held that Section 767.04, Florida Statutes, superseded the common law in those situations covered by the statute. In that case, the plaintiff entered a store operated by her mother, the defendant. Defendant owned a German shepherd which she kept inside the store. Beside a counter inside was a gate with signs on it warning "Beware of Dog" and "Keep out." While plaintiff knew that the dog had previously bitten a customer, it had always been friendly to her. However, during this latest visit the dog bit her on the face. Plaintiff brought suit under Section 767.04, Florida Statutes, and also under the common law. The trial judge ruled that Section 767.04 superseded the common law and that liability did not lie under the statute since a "Bad Dog" sign was posted. He then entered summary final judgment in favor of defendant and plaintiff appealed to this Court. We stated:

> The contention that Plaintiffs have a cause of action both under Fla.Stat. § 767.04, F.S.A., and the common law is without merit. It has been previously held that the subject statute modified the common law, in that it makes the dog owner the insurer against damage by his dog with certain exceptions, departing from the common law doctrines grounded in negligence. *See Romfh v. Berman,* 56 So.2d 127 (Fla.1951); *Vandercar v. David,* 96 So.2d 227 (Fla.App. 3rd, 1957); *Knapp v. Ball,* 175 So.2d 808 (Fla.App. 3rd, 1965). It is concluded that Fla.Stat. § 767.04, F.S.A., supersedes the common law, only in those situations covered by the statute. 241 So.2d at 682.

---

2. See *Malafronte v. Miloni,* 35 R.I. 225, 86 A. 146, 147 (1913), wherein the court stated:

"One purpose, and possibly the main purpose of this statute was to relieve plaintiffs from the burden of proving knowledge, which was frequently difficult for them to do; their inability in that regard often resulting practically in a denial of justice."

---

3. Fla.Rev.Gen.Stat. § 2341 (1892) was included as Sec. 7044 of Compiled General Laws, 1927, and was reenacted in 1941 as § 767.01, Fla.Stat. (1941). § 767.04 was enacted in 1941 as S. 1, Chap. 25109, Laws of Florida (1949).

---

4. In *Seachord v. English,* 259 So.2d 136 (Fla.1972) (Ervin, J., dissenting), a case dealing with § 767.04, this Court discharged the writ of certiorari as being improvidently granted.

The Court then reversed in part the summary judgment finding that there existed a genuine issue of material fact as to whether the sign was posted in a prominent place. Thus, while we held that plaintiff did not have a cause of action under both the statute and the common law, it was unnecessary to expressly state at that time whether the corollary was also true, i.e., whether the common law defenses such as assumption of risk were superseded by those defenses specifically enunciated in the statute. Today we reach that question and find that these common law defenses were so superseded. Consistent with our reasoning in *Moxley, supra,* we can only conclude that in making the dog owner the insurer against damage done by his dog, thereby supplanting the common law negligence-type action, the legislature intended to shoulder him with the burden of his animal's acts except in the specific instances articulated in the enactment—where the dog is provoked or aggravated or the victim is specifically warned by a sign. With regard to those statutory defenses, the legislature apparently felt that good morals dictated that if a person kicks, teases, or in some other way provokes the dog into injuring him, he should not be compensated.

We recognize that our decision today appears to overrule a number of opinions issued by the District Courts of Appeal of this State stating that the doctrine of assumed risk is a valid defense under the statute. *See Allstate Insurance Co. v. Greenstein,* 308 So.2d 561 (Fla.3d DCA 1975); *Hall v. Ricardo,* 297 So.2d 849 (Fla.3d DCA 1974); *Issacs v. Powell,* 267 So.2d 864 (Fla.2d DCA 1972); *English v. Seachord,* 243 So.2d 193 (Fla. 4th DCA 1971); *Vandercar v. David, supra.* However, a careful reading of those cases will show that the defenses asserted, liberally labeled as assumption of risk, were in reality based upon provocation or aggravation of the animal.[5] It was precisely this indiscriminate and interchangeable use of the term assumption of risk which we condemned in *Blackburn v. Dorta, supra,* as creating an "enigma wrapped in a mystery."

The decision which seems to have initiated the proposition that assumption of risk constitutes a valid defense under the statute is *Vandercar v. David, supra.* In that case, appellee/plaintiff was injured from a fall

allegedly caused by appellant's dog. As stated by the District Court of Appeal, Third District:

> The case went to the jury on the issue of whether the defendant's dog caused the plaintiff's fall. The evidence on that issue included some facts of a kind which could have been relied on to establish *assumption of risk by the plaintiff, through inciting and provoking or inducing the dog's playful conduct which caused her to fall.* (Emphasis supplied) 96 So.2d at 228.

The court then went on to distinguish Section 767.01 from Section 767.04, noting that the latter by its express wording is concerned with a dog owner's liability for dog bites while the former applies to injuries to a person caused by a dog other than by biting. Appellant argued that Section 767.04 expressly allowing statutory defenses was applicable to an injury caused by an animal other than a dog bite injury. Appellee contended that Section 767.04 applied only to dog bite damage and that if Section 767.04 repealed and superseded Section 767.01 pursuant to this Court's holding in *Romfh v. Berman,* 56 So.2d 127 (Fla.1951), it did so only as to dog bite damage leaving Section 767.01 in effect for other injury by dogs. This Court then held that:

> We are not required to pass upon the conflicting contentions of the parties as to whether or not the 1949 act has superseded the earlier act for injuries by dogs other than by biting, because even under the latter, Section 767.01, the defense of assumption of risk can be raised.
> 96 So.2d at 229.

The following language from the California District Court of Appeal, Second District, was then cited, with approval by the District Court of Appeal, Third District, to substantiate its holding:

> While the Dog Bite Statute does not found the liability on negligence, good morals and sound reasoning dictate that if a person lawfully upon the portion of another's property where the biting occurred should kick, tease, or otherwise *provoke* the dog, the law should and would recognize the defense that the injured person by his conduct invited injury and therefore, *assumed the risk thereof.* (Emphasis supplied)
> *Smythe v. Schacht,* 93 Cal.App.2d 315, 321, 209 P.2d 114, 118 (1949).

Thus, the *Vandercar* court impliedly concluded that the provocation defense could be equated with the doctrine of assumed risk.

In *English v. Seachord, supra,* the District Court of Appeal, Fourth District, cited *Vandercar, supra,* in stating:

---

5. While petitioner concedes that the statutory defenses of "mischievously or carelessly provoking or aggravating the dog" would have to be applied in much the same fashion as the common law doctrine of assumed risk, we note that the statutory and common law defenses are not synonymous. One can knowingly and voluntarily expose himself to the danger of a vicious dog without necessarily provoking or aggravating him maliciously or carelessly.

Nor may an owner raise contributory negligence *as such* (emphasis theirs) as a defense to an action for injuries, although assumption of the risk, *usually based on provocation or aggravation* of the dog, is permissible as a defense. (Emphasis supplied)

243 So.2d at 194.

The court later found:

Plaintiff's conduct, then, may be considered in a dog injury case *only insofar as it amounts either to provocation* or to proximate causation. (Emphasis supplied)

243 So.2d at 195.[6]

---

6. Other cases, in citing *Vandercar*, blindly declare in dictum that assumption of risk is a valid defense under the statute. *Allstate Insurance Co. v. Greenstein, supra; Hall v. Ricardo, supra.* Yet, neither of the cases elucidate what constitutes assumption of risk within the context of § 767.04, Fla.Stat. (1975).

Thus, while these cases were conceptually accurate in finding that the defense to the statutory right of action was predicated upon provocation of the dog, as enunciated in the statute, they incorrectly classified this defense as assumption of risk.

[2] In sum, we find that a dog owner who is brought to trial pursuant to Section 767.04, Florida Statutes (1975), has available to him only the defenses expressed in the statute. To the extent that earlier decisions of the District Courts of Appeal express or imply the existence of a separate defense predicated upon assumption of risk, they are hereby overruled.

Accordingly, the petition for writ of certiorari is granted, the decision of the District Court of Appeal, Third District, is quashed, and this cause is remanded to that court, with instructions to remand to the trial court for further proceedings not inconsistent with the views expressed herein.

It is so ordered.

BOYD, ENGLAND and HATCHETT, JJ., concur.

OVERTON, C. J., dissents.

Mary J. TURNER, to her own Use and Benefit and to the Use of Employers Fire Insurance Company, Plaintiff,

v.

UNITED STATES of America et al., Defendants.
Civ. A. No. 77–0999.
United States District Court, District of Columbia.
July 25, 1979.

Employee of independent maintenance service sued the United States to recover for injuries which she sustained when assaulted while performing her duties in the South Building of the Department of Agriculture in Washington, D.C. The District Court, Gesell, J., held that: (1) absent a special relationship there is no implied guarantee of safety against violence in government buildings; (2) foreseeability of harm was not alone enough to impose tort liability; (3) a duty to protect those entering a government building from violent assault can exist, if at all, only where there is actual or constructive knowledge of an imminent probability of that particular type of harm; (4) Government was not liable absent showing of how assailant obtained entry or showing of any circumstances warranting special precautions against such incidents, there being no statute or regulation requiring such precautions; and (5) decision to maintain only two guards after hours and to lower lights to conserve energy were discretionary acts.

Judgment for defendant.

1. **United States k78(9)**   Absent special relationship such as employer-employee or landlord-tenant, there is no implied guarantee of safety against the occurrence of violence in a government building; it would be contrary to public interest to evolve a theory of liability which places on the government a continuing duty stringently to safeguard access to its various executive departments, at least in the absence of an imminent probability of harm to a visitor or employee of an independent contractor. 28 U.S.C.A. § 1346(b).

2. **United States k141(3)**   Maintenance service employee, seeking to recover from the government

for injuries sustained when she was beaten and robbed while performing her duties in Department of Agriculture building, bore burden of showing negligence. 28 U.S.C.A. § 1346(b).

3. **United States k78(9)**   United States was not liable for injuries sustained by an independent maintenance service employee in assault in government building, absent showing of circumstances under which assailant obtained entry or that the Government had actual or constructive knowledge of anyone in the building who presented an actual danger or existence of any statute or regulation requiring a particular standard of protection; in posting guards at designated entrances after business hours the Government adhered to a reasonable standard of care and, also, there was no showing that even if a higher standard of protection had been established and followed the incident would not have occurred. 28 U.S.C.A. § 1346(b); 40 U.S.C.A. §§ 318, 318a.

4. **United States k78(9)**   Although given prevalence of crime in District of Columbia it is "foreseeable" that harm can come to an occupant of a government building, foreseeability alone was not enough to impose tort liability on the Government for assault on independent maintenance contractor's employee. 28 U.S.C.A. § 1346(b).

5. **United States k78(9)**   A duty to protect those entering United States government buildings from violent assault can exist, if at all, only where there is actual or constructive knowledge of an imminent probability of that particular type of harm, and barring any such knowledge government is under no special duty to provide particular protection against violence. 28 U.S.C.A. § 1346(b).

6. **United States k78(12)**   Government's decision to maintain only two guards at South Building of Department of Agriculture after close of regular office hours and to lower the lights due to energy crisis were discretionary acts, for purpose of Tort Claims Act suit brought by employee of independent maintenance service to recover for injuries sustained in assault-robbery. 28 U.S.C.A. § 2680(a).

Edward S. Horowitz, College Park, Md., J. Edward Martin, Jr., Baltimore, Md., Thomas Hogan, Rockville, Md., for plaintiff.

Robert M. Werdig, Jr., Asst. U.S. Atty., Washington, D.C., for defendants.

MEMORANDUM OPINION

GESSELL, District Judge.

This matter came originally before the Court on defendants' motion for summary judgment. When the Court indicated a preference for having a full record before it, the parties agreed to submit the issue of liability to the Court on depositions, responses to interrogatories and stipulations. That entire record has now been thoroughly considered and the Court has had the benefit of the parties' briefs.

Plaintiff was beaten severely and robbed while performing her duties on the evening of September 30, 1975. Alleging negligence she sues for damages under the Federal Tort Claims Act, 28 U.S.C. §§ 1346(b), 2671–80. There are no material facts in dispute. Plaintiff was a regular employee in the South Building of the Department of Agriculture where she worked as a lithograph operator from 8:30 A.M. to 5:00 P.M.. At approximately 5:00 P.M. she assumed her duties as supervisor of a cleaning force working in the same building. She was employed as supervisor by the Springfield Building Maintenance Company, an independent contractor to the General Services Administration.

Plaintiff was injured about 6:00 P.M. while working on the second floor of the South Building. The circumstances of her injury are as follows. After reporting for work as an employee of Springfield and making certain preliminary assignments of the crew under her supervision, she proceeded to the second floor where she had agreed to assist one of the crew assigned to the cleaning maintenance operation on that floor. Plaintiff undertook these duties because several employees had failed to show up for work and the operation was shorthanded. She proceeded cautiously as she was about to enter a small unlighted office. There had been thefts from time to time in the building and on two prior occasions she had encountered unauthorized persons after hours. At approximately 6:00 P.M. she kicked the office door open as she was about to enter. She saw a man behind the desk in the room and screamed. The man followed her into the hall, dragged her back into the room, robbed her and beat her with a crowbar or chisel. Her assailant was subsequently identified, prosecuted and convicted. He has refused in spite of the earnest efforts of counsel on both sides to permit his deposition to be taken and persists in his testimony given at the criminal trial that he was not in the Agriculture building.* Thus there is no proof or available evidence to indicate how or when plaintiff's assailant entered the building.

The South Building is a large structure occupying the area between 12th and 14th Streets, S.W. and

---

*For the benefit of the parties, the Court delayed this case for a substantial period in the hope that, following his unsuccessful appeal, the assailant would be willing to testify. He has nonetheless refused to do so and remains incarcerated at Lorton for his crime.

Independence Avenue and C Street, S.W. It has a number of wings and many separate entrances. The General Services Administration ("GSA"), which is responsible for building operations, provides limited guard service. The building is open to the general public during regular office hours from 8:00 A.M. until 5:30 P.M. During this period individuals can come and go without identification of any kind and there are normally no special security arrangements in effect. From 6:00 P.M. to 10:00 P.M., the building is used for evening classes. Two Federal Protective Officers come on duty at 4:00 P.M., and after performing a general inspection of the building and other chores, they commence to secure the building at 5:30 P.M. The officers lower the flags and lock the various doors except for two, a process which takes about half an hour. At approximately 6:00 P.M. each officer is stationed at one of the two entrances that remain open, and access or departure is thereafter governed by a sign-in/sign-out procedure. The incident in question here occurred before the officers had completed their duties of securing the doors and initiating the evening sign-in/sign-out procedure.

Plaintiff's theory of negligence rests on the claim that the attack on her was foreseeable because a number of criminal incidents had previously occurred in the building; and that it was negligent to have left the evening entrances unguarded between 5:30 and 6:00, to have reduced by one the number of guards and to have lowered the lighting in the building for energy conservation reasons. The United States contends that it breached no duty toward the plaintiff; that its decisions with respect to the appropriate number of security guards, the procedures they would follow, and the extent of evening lighting were discretionary matters for which it cannot be sued under the Federal Tort Claims Act; and that in any event the attack could not have been predicted with reasonable probability based on the building's past experience, and therefore that no liability can be imposed.

[1] For purposes of tort liability, the degree of security which the Government must provide in its building with respect to non-structural dangers raises different considerations than were addressed by the Court of Appeals in *Kline v. 1500 Mass. Ave. Apt. Corp.*, 141 U.S.App.D.C. 370, 439 F.2d 477 (1970), where a landlord-tenant relationship created a variety of implied contract. *See Cook v. Safeway Stores, Inc.*, 354 A.2d 507, 510 (D.C.App.1976), or by the Supreme Court in *Lillie v. Thompson*, 332 U.S. 459, 68 S.Ct. 140, 92 L.Ed. 73 (1947), where an employer-employee relationship was involved. *See also Swanner v. United States*, 309 F.Supp. 1183, 1187–88 (M.D.Ala.1970). In the absence of any like relationship, there is no implied guarantee of safety against the occurrence of violence in a government building.

By their very nature, such buildings must, insofar as possible, remain accessible and open to the steady flow of dissimilar citizens who, occasionally under stress or in anger, seek information or assistance. This is a reality which courts must recognize. It would be contrary to the public interest to evolve a theory of liability which placed upon the Government a continuing duty stringently to safeguard access to its various executive departments, at least in the absence of an imminent probability of harm.

[2][3] Plaintiff bears the burden of showing negligence. Under the peculiar circumstances of this case, plaintiff could not show at trial the circumstances under which her assailant obtained entry. The attacker was apprehended and convicted, but he has steadfastly refused to give the parties any information as to how or when he obtained entrance to the building. It is entirely possible that he entered the building in normal fashion during public hours. Moreover, plaintiff cannot show that in this instance the Government had actual or constructive knowledge that there was any particular person in the building who presented an actual danger to its occupants. There had been no threat or forewarning of any kind.

[4][5] Given the prevalence of crime in the District of Columbia, it is, of course, always "foreseeable" that harm could come to an occupant of a government building. Foreseeability, however, cannot be enough to impose tort liability on the Government in this kind of case. *See Goldberg v. Housing Authority of Newark*, 38 N.J. 578, 186 A.2d 291, 293 (1962). A duty to protect those entering a government building from violent assault can exist, if at all, only where there is actual or constructive knowledge of an imminent probability of that particular type of harm. Circumstances can be imagined which would create such a duty with respect to those legitimately in the building after hours but circumstances of that sort did not exist here. Like all government buildings, this building had seen instances of petty theft, vandalism and occasional violence. During the several months immediately preceding the assault on plaintiff, however, most of these incidents had taken place during office hours, and when they were violent had involved disputes between employees. Nothing had occurred to warrant special precautions against the type of incident which caused injury to plaintiff. *See Cook v. Safeway Stores, Inc., supra*, 354 A.2d at 508–10; *Dwyer v. Erie Investment Co.*, 138 N.J.Super. 93, 350 A.2d 268 (1975); *Nigido v. First National Bank of Baltimore*, 264 Md. 702, 288 A.2d 127 (1972). Barring such an event or events, the United States was under no special duty to provide plaintiff any particular protection against violence.

No statute or regulation requires that such protection be given. 40 U.S.C. § 318 (1976). The responsibility for determining and providing protective service in a GSA-maintained building such as the Agriculture building is delegated to GSA, *See* 40 U.S.C. § 318a (1976), and defined in the Federal Property Management Regulations, 41 C.F.R. § 101–20.5. The regulations provide that "GSA will furnish as normal protection not less than the degree of protection provided by commercial building operators of similar space for normal risk occupants, as determined by GSA." 41 C.F.R. § 101–20.501. The regulations also set forth the criteria to be used by the agency in making the determination: Determination of the level of normal protective service will be made by GSA on a case-by-case basis and will consider the facility's location; size and configuration; history of criminal or disruptive incidents in the surrounding neighborhood not primarily directed toward the occupant agency's mission; extent of exterior lighting; presence of physical barriers; and such other factors as may be deemed pertinent. 41 C.F.R. § 101–20.502.

[6] There is no proof that this reasonable standard was violated in this instance. By establishing security at designated entrances after business hours, defendant was adhering to a reasonable standard of care consistent with community standards and there is no showing that a higher standard was required by any

facts known to defendant. There is, moreover, no proof that even if a higher standard of protective service had been established, the failure to follow a higher standard on the facts of this case could be said to be a proximate cause of the injury. Finally, the Government's decision to maintain only two guards and to lower the lights due to the energy crisis were clearly discretionary acts. *See Dalehite v. United States*, 346 U.S. 15, 73 S.Ct. 956, 97 L.Ed. 1427 (1953); *United States v. Faneca*, 332 F.2d 872, 874–75 (5th Cir.1964), *Cert. denied*, 380 U.S. 971, 85 S.Ct. 1327, 14 L.Ed.2d 268 (1965); *Monarch Insurance Co. v. District of Columbia*, 353 F.Supp. 1249, 1256–59 (D.D.C.1973), *Aff'd mem.*, 162 U.S.App.D.C. 96, 497 F.2d 684, *Cert. denied*, 419 U.S. 1021, 95 S.Ct. 497, 42 L.Ed.2d 295 (1974); *Taxay v. United States*, 345 F.Supp. 1284, 1285–86 (D.D.C.1972), *Aff'd mem.*, 159 U.S.App.D.C. 343, 487 F.2d 1214 (1973); 28 U.S.C. § 2680(a) (1976).

Plaintiff has failed to meet her burden of proof. No negligence on the part of defendants was established. The complaint must therefore be dismissed. The Clerk of Court shall enter judgment for defendants.

SO ORDERED.

RUFFINI et al.
v.
AVARA.
No. 16258.
Supreme Court of Colorado, in Department.
May 1, 1950.
Rehearing Denied June 19, 1950.

Action by John A. Burk, a mentally incompetent person, against Herman Ruffini, August Musso and Mike Petramala to cancel conveyances made by Burk to defendant Mike Petramala and another, of a ranch, to avoid transfers of personalty made to all defendants, and to secure cancellation of contract signed by Burk and defendant Mike Petramala. Since the trial of the case, Burk was formerly adjudicated a mental incompetent and thereafter appeared by his conservator, Oscar Avara. The District Court, Otero County, Harry Leddy, J., entered a judgment for the plaintiff, and the defendants brought error. The Supreme Court, Moore, J., held that evidence sustained the finding that at time of the agreement providing for the conveyances and transfers the conservator's ward was men-

tally incompetent and that the defendants entered into the agreement as part of a concerted plan to fraudulently procure the property.

Judgment affirmed.

1. **Deeds k211(1,3)**   In action to set aside conveyances and transfer of ranch, personalty and money, evidence sustained finding that at time of agreement providing for conveyances and transfers transferor was mentally incompetent and that defendants entered into the agreement as part of a concerted plan to fraudulently procure the property.

2. **Contracts k94(1)**   Even though a mental condition may not amount to legal insanity, it may be suf-

ficient to result in an inequality between the parties properly to be considered in connection with circumstances of unfair dealing and inadequacy of the consideration in determining whether a transaction was vitiated by fraud, either actual or constructive.

3. **Contracts k94(1)**   The principle on which a court of equity acts in relieving against transactions on the ground of inequality of footing between the parties is not confined to cases where a fiduciary relation is shown to exist, but extends to all the varieties of relations in which dominion may be exercised by one over another, and applies to every case where influence is acquired and abused, or where confidence is reposed and betrayed.

4. **Appeal and error k1011(1)**   If there is sufficient evidence to sustain the findings of the trial court, the judgment entered thereon will not be disturbed on review even though the evidence is conflicting.

A. T. Stewart, Pueblo, Lawrence Thulemeyer and John R. Stewart, La Junta, for plaintiffs in error.

A. L. Rotenberry, Carl M. Perricone, Denver, attorneys for plaintiffs in error on petition for rehearing.

Chas. E. Sabin and Robert R. Sabin, La Junta, for defendant in error.

MOORE, Justice.

We will herein refer to the parties as they appeared in the trial court, where defendant in error was plaintiff and plaintiffs in error were defendants.

The suit was instituted for the purpose of procuring the cancellation of conveyances made by Burk to defendant Mike Petramala, and Frances Petramala, of a ranch consisting of 2,160 acres of land in Otero county; to void transfers of personal property made to all the defendants; and to secure cancellation of a contract bearing the signatures of Burk and the defendant Mike Petramala. Since the trial of the case, Burk has been formally adjudicated a mental incompetent and appears here by his conservator Oscar Avara.

The complaint alleged as grounds for the relief sought, that "John A. Burk is now and at all times hereinafter mentioned has been mentally incompetent and incapable, unassisted, of properly managing and caring for his property," and that the transactions of which complaint is made were procured by defendants by "fraud, deceit, and the exercise of an undue influence," causing Burk to enter into a contract dated July 2, 1947, for the sale of real and personal property, without consideration, and as a part of a concerted plan to fraudulently procure the property of said John A. Burk. These allegations are denied by defendants.

Trial was to the court, resulting in findings and judgment for plaintiff. Defendants, seeking a reversal of the judgment, have sued out a writ of error. The points urged by them as grounds for reversal are stated in their brief as follows:

"1. There was no evidence to prove that John A. Burk is and has been mentally incompetent. (Specification of points: 5, 6, and 4.)

"2. The overwhelming preponderance of the evidence is against the findings of the trial court. (Specification of points: 2, 3, 4, and 6.)

"3. The trial court misconstrued the evidence and its findings that the sale price was inadequate is contrary to the evidence and the law. (Specification of points: 6, 1, and 4.)

"4. The evidence adduced proved the consideration was adequate and the transaction fair. (Specification of points: 7, 2, 1, and 3.)"

The points upon which defendants thus rely are directed solely to the sufficiency of the evidence to sustain the judgment.

The facts are fully set out in the findings of the trial court, as follows:

"The plaintiff, John A. Burk, is a man of about 42 years of age, and has spent most of his life on an isolated cattle ranch, the greater portion of which time he lived with his father and apparently their business dealings were carried on together. After the death of the father, plaintiff has continued to reside alone on said ranch and under somewhat squalid circumstances. The plaintiff and his father had apparently accumulated the ranch property and a considerable number of livestock and had money in the bank. The plaintiff had dealt with his neighbors, buying and selling livestock and also had made a few personal loans. The principal actor among the defendants is Mike Petramala, and the other two defendants appear principally as financial backers of Mike Petramala. Petramala operates a large beef farm and deals in livestock. He became acquainted with plaintiff some two years prior to the inception of this suit. His first dealings were the placing of cattle upon the ranch of the plaintiff for the purpose of pasturage, and further deals have also been made between the two in the exchange of livestock and buying and selling feed.

"On or about the second day of July, 1947, a contract was entered into by the plaintiff Burk, and the three defendants whereby plaintiff agreed to deed 2,160 acres of land, five horses, and some forty-seven head of cattle for $8,000; $2,000 to be paid upon the signing of the agreement and an additional sum of $6,000 to be paid when the abstracts were found satisfactory. The agreement specifically states that the real property has been leased for oil and that all rentals due under said lease should be paid to Burk, but any oil produced thereon should belong to the second parties. The defendants claim that other oral agreements were coupled with this written agreement to the effect that Burk should be permitted to live upon the property as long as he desired and that defendants would erect a suitable house within which the said Burk might live. That the defendant Petramala would also pay the said Burk $50.00 a month in consideration of his taking care of the cattle on said ranch as long as the price of cattle warranted such payment. These latter agreements were not incorporated in the written agreement. The defendants paid the $2,000 referred to in the agreement. Shortly thereafter, the defendant Petramala borrowed $2300 from the said John A. Burk, giving therefor his note without further security, and still later on, the sum of $1,000 was paid by the plaintiff to the defendant Petramala; the contention of the plaintiff being that it was a further loan, and the contention of the defendant being that the thousand dollars was given by Burk to Petramala for the purpose of buying furniture for the house in question. [This $1,000 was deposited with the clerk of the trial court by defendants.]

"Nine days after the execution of the agreement and prior to the time when the abstracts had been examined, the plaintiff Burk made a deed of conveyance to the defendants for the real property described in the complaint, which deed purported to receipt for the consideration and did not mention the oral agreements claimed by the defendants to have been contemporaneous with the original agreement; and shortly thereafter, the defendant Petramala started the erection, or reconstruction and addition to the dwelling house on the premises, and for two months, or such time as elapsed between the making of the agreement, and the bringing of the suit, paid the $50.00 per month alleged to have been within the oral agreement. At the time of the commencement of the lawsuit, the defendants, or some of them, had acquired title to all of the real estate of the plaintiff, practically all of his personal property, and $1300 in cash more than they had paid him."

The trial court found the value of the real estate to be $18,360.00, and the value of the cattle to be $3,758.00. The value of the improvements placed upon the land by defendant Petramala was fixed by the court at $1212.53. The findings and conclusions of the court, upon which judgment was entered, are in part as follows:

"The Court finds that plaintiff, John A. Burk, is now and at all times during the negotiations heretofore referred to was and has been mentally incompetent and incapable unassisted of properly managing and caring for his property. The Court finds that no consideration at the time of

the commencing of this lawsuit had passed to the plaintiff for the conveyance and transfers at that time made, and the Court further finds that the consideration mentioned in the said agreement was grossly inadequate even had it been paid.

* * * * * *

"The Court is of the opinion that at the time of the execution of the agreement, marked Exhibit 'A', and introduced in evidence as Plaintiff's Exhibit 'D', the plaintiff Burk had not the mental capacity to enter into such an agreement and the same was entered into by the defendants as a part of a concerted plan to fraudulently procure the property of the plaintiff. The Court is of the opinion that all of the property procured by the defendants from the plaintiff should be returned to him, together with $2300 in cash procured by the defendants since that time; that the promissory note given by the defendant Petramala to the plaintiff Burk should be surrendered and cancelled and that the agreement signed by the plaintiff, and the three defendants should be cancelled and held for naught and that the deed of conveyance by the plaintiff and to the defendant Petramala and his wife should be cancelled and held for naught.

"It further appears to the Court that the value of the improvements placed on said property should be charged to the plaintiff, and credit therefor be given the defendants in this judgment, and it appearing right and proper so to do, * * *."

[1] Dr. J. L. Rosenbloom, a psychiatrist at the Colorado State Hospital, testified that he had examined Burk and found that "he would probably fall into the actual group of mental defectives in the upper moron level," that he is without mental capacity to care for and manage his property; that his ideas were childish; and that he was a person who would be easily subjected to the influence and suggestions of others. Burk was called as a witness and testified at great length, both on direct and cross-examination, during the course of which the trial court had full opportunity to form an opinion concerning his mentality and his ability to manage and care for his property. We do not deem it necessary to detail the evidence which tends to support the findings of the trial court. It is sufficient to say that we have carefully considered the entire record, and are of the opinion that there is ample competent evidence to support the judgment.

The admitted facts, reduced to their essence, are that the defendants obtained all of Burk's property, real and personal, together with $1,300.00 more in cash than was paid to him by them, and that no deed of trust, mortgage, or security of any kind was given to secure the payment of the monies admittedly due Burk. These circumstances in themselves would seem to indicate a lack of capacity to manage property, and tend strongly to support the conclusions of Dr. Rosenbloom concerning Burk's mental condition.

[2] Defendants rely upon the case of *Hanks, Conservator v. McNeil Coal Corporation*, 114 Colo. 578, 168 P.2d 256, 260, in which we affirmed the judgment of the trial court sustaining the legality of a sale of property against the claim of incapacity of the vendor. In that case the facts were not comparable to those here present. We there recognized the rule which we consider applicable to the case at bar, and stated: "Even though a mental condition may not amount to legal insanity, it may be sufficient to result in an inequality between the parties properly to be considered in connection with circumstances of unfair dealing and inadequacy of the consideration in determining whether a transaction was vitiated by fraud, either actual or constructive."

[3] In *Dittbrenner v. Myerson*, 114 Colo. 448, 167 P.2d 15, 20, we held that fraud may be presumed from the circumstances and condition of the contracting parties to prevent advantage being taken of the weakness or necessities of one of them, and stated: "The essential condition precedent to the applicability of this doctrine is an 'inequality' between the parties; there must be weakness on the one side and advantage taken of that weakness on the other, and 'It must appear that the dominant party either brought about the unevenness in the conditions, or, finding it ready to his hand, utilized and traded on it to extract from the servient party a gift or contract which he would not otherwise have made.' Bower on Actionable Non-Disclosure, p. 390, § 428."

In the *Dittbrenner* case we quoted with approval from *Aylesford v. Morris*, 8 Ch.App. 484, the following: " '* * * when the relative position of the parties is such as prima facie to raise this presumption, the transaction cannot stand unless the person claiming the benefit of it is able to repel the presumption by contrary evidence, proving it to have been in point of fact fair, just, and reasonable.' "

We also in that case approved the following statement of the rule which is applicable to the case at bar: " 'The principle on which a court of equity acts in relieving against transactions on the ground of inequality of footing between the parties is not confined to cases where a fiduciary relation is shown to exist, but extends to all the varieties of relations in which dominion may be exercised by one over another, and applies to every case where influence is acquired and abused, or where confidence is reposed and betrayed.' *Sears v. Hicklin*, 13 Colo. 143, 148, 21 P. 1022, 1023, quoting from Kerr, Fraud & Mistake 183."

The foregoing principles are well established in the law (1 Story's Eq. Jur. [14th ed.] p. 339, § 355), and there is substantial evidence as appears in the record in the instant case, tending to prove all essential elements prerequisite to their application.

[4] Although conflicting, if there is sufficient evidence to sustain the findings of the trial court, the judgment entered thereon will not be disturbed on review.

The judgment is accordingly affirmed.

HILLIARD, C. J., and JACKSON, J., concur.

Irene M. PARRISELLA, Appellant,

v.

George FOTOPULOS and Chris Fotopulos, Appellees.

No. 11519–PR.

Supreme Court of Arizona, En Banc.

May 31, 1974.

Will contest. The Superior Court, Maricopa County, Cause No. P–82645, Ed W. Hughes, J., entered judgment for contestants following jury verdict in their favor, and proponents appealed. The Court of Appeals affirmed in a memorandum decision. The Supreme Court, Hays, C.J., held that evidence was not sufficient to support jury finding of undue influence on part of proponent at time will was made.

Decision of Court of Appeals vacated; judgment of Superior Court reversed with directions.

1. **Wills k166(2)** Evidence in will contest brought by testator's brothers who opposed probate of will leaving everything to proponent, who was testator's mistress, did not sustain jury's finding of undue influence on part of proponent at time of will's execution.

2. **Wills k155.1** "Undue influence" is conduct by which a person, through his power over mind of tes-

tator, makes the latter's desires conform to his own, thereby overmastering the volition of the testator.

See publication Words and Phrases for other judicial constructions and definitions.

3. **Wills k163(2)**   Presumption of undue influence which arises when person occupying confidential relationship to testator is active in procuring execution of a will and is also named as principal beneficiary did not arise where proponent of will who was named as principal beneficiary and was active in procuring will's execution was testator's mistress.

* * *

Kenneth P. Clancy, Phoenix, for appellees.

HAYS, Chief Justice.

This is a will contest case, tried to a jury in the Superior Court. After a verdict for the contestants, a judgment was entered in their favor and the proponents appealed. In a memorandum decision, the Court of Appeals affirmed and we granted review. The decision of the Court of Appeals is vacated, the judgment of the Superior Court is reversed, and the will is ordered admitted to probate.

The testator, who was called Gus, was a rollicking, roistering, heavy-drinking woman chaser. For a while he lived with his parents, but even then he was maintaining an apartment where he entertained girls, most of whom were considerably younger than he. He owned and operated a profitable bar.

He took up with an employee of his bar, Irene Parrisella, who thereafter lived with him. He gave her an engagement ring and publicly announced his intention to marry her. She was the sole beneficiary of his will. He had two brothers, Chris and George, the contestants of his will.

Gus had chronic asthma and an intestinal disorder, both of which he neglected until one day he was taken to the hospital with massive internal bleeding. While there he demanded that Irene call his lawyer to draw up his will, leaving everything to her. She did so, and her mother picked it up and delivered it to the hospital where it was executed. He died after surgery a few days later.

The only issue tried was whether Irene had used undue influence on Gus to make the will as it was made.

We have read the 900-page transcript. After the opening statements by the lawyers, the next fifty pages are devoted to testimony proving the will.

In this part of the transcript, one registered nurse testified that she witnessed the execution of the will;

that she considered Gus to be mentally alert and fully competent; that he refused all medication until the will had been drawn and executed; that Irene was present; that he said he disliked his brothers; that he showed genuine affection for Irene; that he read the will before signing it, and his only complaint was that he did not want to leave $1.00 to each of his brothers. At this point, the will was offered and received in evidence without objection.

A second attesting witness was also a registered nurse. She testified that she witnessed the will; that the testator was fully aware of the contents of the will; that he was not under any duress, but signed it and said it was just what he wanted; that he refused all medication until he had taken care of the execution of the will; that he said he did not want his brothers to have anything, referring to them as 'S.O.B.'s'; that Irene suggested he call one of his brothers, but he told her not to do so.

His physician and friend of many years testified that Gus was mentally sound and alert, even the day after he was admitted to the hospital; that he was a stubborn man who refused to go to the hospital many times before the day he was admitted; that he did not like to have his brothers visit him because they upset him and made his asthma worse; that he felt very affectionate towards Irene and wanted her present at all times.

[1] The next 300 pages of the transcript are devoted to evidence introduced by the contestants, and the rest of the transcript contains evidence rebutting that of the contestants. In this opinion, we disregard all of the rebuttal testimony because we have accepted all of the contestants' evidence as true, but we have concluded that there is not the slightest bit of evidence to prove undue influence exercised at the time the will was made. If there were any, it would be incumbent upon us to allow the verdict and judgment to stand. We cannot set aside a jury verdict simply because we would have decided the issues differently. *Schmerfeld v. Hendry*, 74 Ariz. 159, 163, 245 P.2d 420 (1952). So long as there is competent evidence to support the verdict, it must be allowed to stand. *Id.*

Five witnesses were used to bring out the facts from which the contestants asked the jury to find undue influence. The sum total of their testimony is as follows: The testator was divorced with no children, and he lived in Phoenix from 1941 until his death in May, 1970. Years before Gus's death, his brother Chris loaned him $3,000 to help him open the bar. By 1970 Gus's health was getting worse and he made considerable use of a room in the rear of his bar for resting and sleeping—sometimes with Irene who worked there. Irene did not want Chris to stay at Gus's house when he came to Phoenix for their mother's funeral, although he stayed there anyway. Irene claimed she did not know the contents of Gus's will, but this could hardly have been true because she telephoned the lawyer to give him Gus's instructions for drawing it. Irene said that if the brothers came to Gus's funeral she'd run them off. While Gus was in the hospital he asked Irene to try to find his brother Chris to 'help her run' the bar. The proponent's lawyer prepared the will the way Irene told him to do so over the phone, but Gus had previously discussed making a will with the same provisions some time before. The will, when dictated, was picked up by Irene's mother and taken to Gus at the hospital. Gus was engaged to Irene and she wore his engagement ring. Gus's brother George was told by a friend that Irene would not let him stay at Gus's house after the funeral, so he stayed in a motel, without checking this out with Irene. Gus's brother Chris helped paint and remodel the bar several times, but was never paid for it. Irene had told a witness that she would pay another witness to stay in Detroit. After the funeral of Gus's mother, Irene tried to get everyone to go to Las Vegas. Irene tried several times to get Gus to marry her, but he always said he was paying her to work at his bar and if she didn't like her arrangements, she could 'get her ass out.' After Gus's death, Irene said the brothers would not be allowed to stay in his house 'unless they did right' and that they might think they were going to take over, but weren't. Irene said she hated Chris and that he bothered both her and Gus when he was around.

[2] The above includes basically everything that was said from which the jury could have found undue influence. In Arizona, undue influence is defined as conduct by which a person unduly influences a testator in executing a will, when that person through his power over the mind of the testator makes the latter's desires conform to his own, thereby overmastering the volition of the testator. *In re Estate of McCauley*, 101 Ariz. 8, 415 P.2d 431 (1966). Nothing in the evidence of the contestants comes close to fitting this definition.

[3] It has been held that when a person occupying a confidential relation to the testator, is active in procuring the execution of a will and is also named as the principal beneficiary, there is a presumption of undue influence. *In re Estate of Vermeersch*, 109 Ariz. 125, 506 P.2d 256 (1973). This, however, is inapplicable to the facts of this case for several reasons.

First, the phrase 'confidential relationship' refers to the testator's doctor, guardian, religious advisor, partner, employer, landlord, business associate, etc. 94 C.J.S. Wills § 239, page 1093. In *Dees v. Mets*, 245 Ala. 370, 17 So.2d 137 (1944), the Court had before it a case where a testator left his estate to his mistress. The Court stated: 'It is the settled law of this state that illicit relationship is not sufficient *per se* to warrant a

conclusion of undue influence. And no presumption of undue influence arises merely from the fact that a man . . . makes a will in favor of his mistress.' 17 So.2d at 139.

In Arizona, we have clearly set out the applicable criteria in *In re Estate of Vermeersch, supra,* as follows: 'With regard to undue influence, again the law presumes that Mrs. Vermeersch was not acting under undue influence when she executed her will. . . . The presumption would switch to one of undue influence if the following facts were true: (1) that Jules Vermeersch occupied a confidential or fiduciary relationship to the decedent, (2) that he was active in the preparation of the will, and (3) that he was the sole beneficiary. . . . [T]he marital relationship is not one of the confidential relationships giving rise to the presumption of undue influence.' 506 P.2d at 259.

All three requirements must be present before this presumption can arise. *Vermeersch, supra.* However, there is no evidence that Irene occupied a confidential relationship with Gus; in fact, just the opposite appears. The record shows that as far as he was concerned, if she didn't like the treatment she was getting, she could leave. That is not the position of a man whose will has been overpowered by his mistress.

The Iowa Supreme Court, in a similar situation said: '. . . was a man of very definite ideas . . . and he managed his own affairs without interference or suggestions from other people. Were a jury to hold such a man was unduly influenced by Katherine so that his will was really the expression and will of Katherine, and not the free expression of his own will, under the record in this case, they would have to resort to strained and unreasonable conclusions and inferences. Frank . . . had the power to dispose of his property by his will. Our duty is not to criticize the conduct or morals of (Frank) or Katherine. . . .' The testator, if he chooses, may be actuated by base motives. The only essential is that the will which prompted him to make the bequest must be the will of the testator." *Glider v. Melinski*, 238 Iowa 140, 149, 25 N.W.2d 379, 384 (1947).

In *Sterling v. Dubin*, 6 Ill.2d 64, 126 N.E.2d 718 (1955), the facts are also nearly the same as in the instant case, and the Court's language included the following: 'It is argued a confidential relationship to Sterling was proved by the evidence of their illicit sexual relationship . . . that Sterling trusted her. . . . The evidence . . . does not show . . . that a fiduciary relationship existed. The mere facts that she had illicit sexual relations with Sterling and that she was his private secretary do not establish a fiduciary relationship.' 126 N.E.2d at 722–723.

In another similar situation, the court in *In re Lavelle's Estate*, 122 Utah 253, 248 P.2d 372 (1952), said: 'Their illicit relationship was undoubtedly one of the factors which induced the affection Mrs. Lavelle had for Hogg. . . . [S]he spoke of their plans for marriage . . . She gave him sums of money . . . and items of personal property during her lifetime. Respondents urge that this supports their contention of undue influence; but to the contrary, the fact that they were given, and over a considerable period of time, is strong indication of the constancy of her affection and regard for him and corroborates the idea that she wanted to make provision for him in her will. Where the affection and desire of a testatrix is genuine, it matters not that the illicit relationship may have played a part in inducing it.' 248 P.2d at 376.

In order to prove undue influence of the kind required to invalidate a will, such influence must not only be shown to have been exercised by one in a confidential relationship, but also must be shown to have been present at the time of the execution of the will. *See Vermeersch, supra,* which refers to testamentary capacity rather than to undue influence, but is very clear that attention must be directed to the situation at the time the will is executed in preference to some previous time. In the instant case, not even an attempt was made to show this last requirement. It is uncontested that Gus was in the intensive care unit of the hospital, under the watchful eyes of registered nurses. He was refusing medication in order to prevent any later charge that he was under sedation, and he was making demands for his lawyer to draw his will and for a notary public to witness a power of attorney which he also signed.

* * *

The decision of the Court of Appeals is vacated. The judgment of the Superior Court is reversed with directions to admit the will to probate.

CAMERON, V.C.J., and STRUCKMEYER, LOCKWOOD and HOLOHAN, JJ., concur.

ARIZONA, Petitioner
v.
James Thomas HICKS.
No. 85–1027.
Argued Dec. 8, 1986.
Decided March 3, 1987.

Defendant's motion to suppress evidence seized from apartment was granted by the Arizona Superior Court, Maricopa County, Cause No. CR–140258, Elizabeth Stover, J., and state appealed. The Arizona Court of Appeals, Livermore, J., 146 Ariz. 533, 707 P.2d 331, affirmed. After the Arizona Supreme Court denied review, the state petitioned for certiorari. The Supreme Court, Justice Scalia, held that: (1) no "seizure" occurred, for purposes of Fourth Amendment, when officer merely recorded serial numbers of stereo equipment he observed in plain view, but (2) officer's actions in moving equipment to locate serial numbers constituted "search," which had to be supported by probable cause, notwithstanding that officer was lawfully present in apartment where equipment was located.

Affirmed.

Justice White concurred and filed opinion.

Justice Powell dissented and filed opinion, in which Chief Justice Rehnquist and Justice O'Connor joined.

Justice O'Connor dissented and filed opinion, in which Chief Justice Rehnquist and Justice Powell joined.

1. **Searches and Seizures k16**   No "seizure" occurred, for purposes of Fourth Amendment, where officer merely recorded serial numbers of stereo system he observed in plain view. U.S.C.A. Const. Amend. 4.

See publication Words and Phrases for other judicial constructions and definitions.

2. **Searches and Seizures k16**   Truly cursory inspection, which involves merely looking at object that is already exposed to view, is not "search" for purposes of Fourth Amendment. U.S.C.A. Const.Amend. 4.

See publication Words and Phrases for other judicial constructions and definitions.

3. **Searches and Seizures k16**   Officer's actions, in moving stereo equipment in order to locate serial numbers and determine if equipment was stolen, constituted "search," notwithstanding that officer was lawfully present within apartment where equipment was located in plain view. U.S.C.A. Const.Amend. 4.

4. **Searches and Seizures k47**   "Plain view" doctrine may legitimate actions beyond scope of original exigencies that justified warrantless search; clarifying *Mincey v. Arizona*, 437 U.S. 385, 98 S.Ct. 2408, 57 L.Ed.2d 290. U.S.C.A. Const.Amend. 4.

5. **Searches and Seizures k42, 47**   Absent special operational necessities, any seizure that is unrelated to original exigencies that justified officers' warrantless entry onto premises must itself be supported by probable cause, even though object seized is located in plain view on premises. U.S.C.A. Const. Amend. 4.

6. **Searches and Seizures k47**   Officer's actions, in moving stereo equipment in order to locate serial numbers and determine if equipment was stolen, had to be supported by probable cause, notwithstanding that officer was lawfully present in apartment where equipment was located in plain view. U.S.C.A. Const.Amend. 4.

*Syllabus**

A bullet fired through the floor of respondent's apartment injured a man on the floor below. Police entered the apartment to search for the shooter, for other victims, and for weapons, and there seized three weapons and discovered a stockingcap mask. While there, one of the policemen noticed two sets of expensive stereo components and, suspecting that they were stolen, read and recorded their serial numbers—moving some of them, including a turntable, to do so—and phoned in the numbers to headquarters. Upon learning that the turntable had been taken in an armed robbery, he seized it immediately. Respondent was subsequently indicted for the robbery, but the state trial court granted his motion to suppress the evidence that had been seized, and the Arizona Court of Appeals affirmed. Relying upon a statement in *Mincey v. Arizona*, 437 U.S. 385, 98 S.Ct. 2408, 57 L.Ed.2d 290, that a warrantless search must be "strictly circumscribed by the exigencies which justify its initiation," the Court of Appeals held that ·the police-

man's obtaining the serial numbers violated the Fourth Amendment because it was unrelated to the shooting, the exigent circumstance that justified the initial entry and search. Both state courts rejected the contention that the policeman's actions were justified under the "plain view" doctrine.

Held:

1. The policeman's actions come within the purview of the Fourth Amendment. The mere recording of the serial numbers did not constitute a "seizure" since it did not meaningfully interfere with respondent's possessory interest in either the numbers or the stereo equipment. However, the moving of the equipment was a "search" separate and apart from the search that was the lawful objective of entering the apartment. The fact that the search uncovered nothing of great personal value to respondent is irrelevant. Pp. 1152–1153.

2. The "plain view" doctrine does not render the search "reasonable" under the Fourth Amendment. Pp. 1153–1155. ·
(a) The policeman's action directed to the stereo equipment was not *ipso facto* unreasonable simply because it was unrelated to the justification for entering the apartment. That lack of relationship always exists when the "plain view" doctrine applies. In saying that a warrantless search must be "strictly circumscribed by the exigencies which justify its initiation," *Mincey* was simply addressing the scope of the primary search itself, and was not overruling the "plain view" doctrine by implication. Pp. 1152–1153.
(b) However, the search was invalid because, as the State concedes, the policeman had only a "reasonable suspicion"—*i.e.*, less than probable cause to believe—that the stereo equipment was stolen. Probable cause is required to invoke the "plain view" doctrine as it applies to seizures. It would be illogical to hold that an object is seizable on lesser grounds, during an unrelated search and seizure, than would have been needed to obtain a warrant if it had been known to be on the premises. Probable cause to believe the equipment was stolen was also necessary to support the search here, whether legal authority to move the equipment could be found only as the inevitable concomitant of the authority to seize it, or also as a consequence of some independent power to search objects in plain view. Pp. 1153–1154.

3. The policeman's action cannot be upheld on the ground that it was not a "full-blown search" but was only a "cursory inspection" that could be justified by reasonable suspicion instead of probable cause. A

---

*The syllabus constitutes no part of the opinion of the Court but has been prepared by the Reporter of Decisions for the convenience of the reader. *See United States v. Detroit Lumber Co.*, 200 U.S. 321, 337, 26 S.Ct. 282, 287, 50 L.Ed. 499.

truly cursory inspection—one that involves merely looking at what is already exposed to view, without disturbing it—is not a "search" for Fourth Amendment purposes, and therefore does not even require reasonable suspicion. This Court is unwilling to create a subcategory of "cursory" searches under the Fourth Amendment. Pp. 1154–1155.

146 Ariz. 533, 707 P.2d 331, affirmed.

SCALIA, J., delivered the opinion of the Court, in which BRENNAN, WHITE, MARSHALL, BLACKMUN, and STEVENS, JJ., joined. WHITE, J., filed a concurring opinion, *post*, p. 1155. POWELL, J., filed a dissenting opinion, in which REHNQUIST, C.J., and O'CONNOR, J., joined, *post*, p. 1155. O'CONNOR, J., filed a dissenting opinion, in which REHNQUIST, C.J., and POWELL, J., joined, *post*, p. 1157.

Linda Ann Akers, Phoenix, Ariz., for petitioner.

John William Rood, Phoenix, Ariz., for respondent.

Justice SCALIA delivered the opinion of the Court.

In *Coolidge v. New Hampshire*, 403 U.S. 443, 91 S.Ct. 2022, 29 L.Ed.2d 564 (1971), we said that in certain circumstances a warrantless seizure by police of an item that comes within plain view during their lawful search of a private area may be reasonable under the Fourth Amendment. *See Id.*, at 465–471, 91 S.Ct., at 2037–2041 (plurality opinion); *Id.*, at 505–506, 91 S.Ct., at 2057–2058 (Black, J., concurring and dissenting); *Id.*, at 521–522, 91 S.Ct. at 2065–2066 (WHITE, J., concurring and dissenting). We granted certiorari, 475 U.S. 1107, 106 S.Ct. 1512, 89 L.Ed.2d 912 (1986), in the present case to decide whether this "plain view" doctrine may be invoked when the police have less than probable cause to believe that the item in question is evidence of a crime or is contraband.

I

On April 18, 1984, a bullet was fired through the floor of respondent's apartment, striking and injuring a man in the apartment below. Police officers arrived and entered respondent's apartment to search for the shooter, for other victims, and for weapons. They found and seized three weapons, including a sawed-off rifle, and in the course of their search also discovered a stocking-cap mask.

One of the policemen, Officer Nelson, noticed two sets of expensive stereo components, which seemed out of place in the squalid and otherwise ill-appointed four-room apartment. Suspecting that they were stolen, he read and recorded their serial numbers—moving some of the components, including a

Bang and Olufsen turntable, in order to do so—which he then reported by phone to his headquarters. On being advised that the turntable had been taken in an armed robbery, he seized it immediately. It was later determined that some of the other serial numbers matched those on other stereo equipment taken in the same armed robbery, and a warrant was obtained and executed to seize that equipment as well. Respondent was subsequently indicted for the robbery.

The state trial court granted respondent's motion to suppress the evidence that had been seized. The Court of Appeals of Arizona affirmed. It was conceded that the initial entry and search, although warrantless, were justified by the exigent circumstance of the shooting. The Court of Appeals viewed the obtaining of the serial numbers, however, as an additional search, unrelated to that exigency. Relying upon a statement in *Mincey v. Arizona*, 437 U.S. 385, 98 S.Ct. 2408, 57 L.Ed.2d 290 (1978), that a "warrantless search must be 'strictly circumscribed by the exigencies which justify its initiation,' " *Id.*, at 393, 98 S.Ct., at 2413 (citation omitted), the Court of Appeals held that the police conduct violated the Fourth Amendment, requiring the evidence derived from that conduct to be excluded. 146 Ariz. 533, 534–535, 707 P.2d 331, 332–333 (1985). Both courts—the trial court explicitly and the Court of Appeals by necessary implication—rejected the State's contention that Officer Nelson's actions were justified under the "plain view" doctrine of *Coolidge v. New Hampshire, supra*. The Arizona Supreme Court denied review, and the State filed this petition.

II

[1] As an initial matter, the State argues that Officer Nelson's action constituted neither a "search" nor a "seizure" within the meaning of the Fourth Amendment. We agree that the mere recording of the serial numbers did not constitute a seizure. To be sure, that was the first step in a process by which respondent was eventually deprived of the stereo equipment. In and of itself, however, it did not "meaningfully interfere" with respondent's possessory interest in either the serial numbers or the equipment, and therefore did not amount to a seizure. *See Maryland v. Macon*, 472 U.S. 463, 469, 105 S.Ct. 2778, 2782, 86 L.Ed.2d 370 (1985).

[2,3] Officer Nelson's moving of the equipment, however, did constitute a "search" separate and apart from the search for the shooter, victims, and weapons that was the lawful objective of his entry into the apartment. Merely inspecting those parts of the turntable that came into view during the latter search would not have constituted an independent search, because it would have produced no additional invasion of res-

pondent's privacy interest. *See Illinois v. Andreas*, 463 U.S. 765, 771, 103 S.Ct. 3319, 3324, 77 L.Ed.2d 1003 (1983). But taking action, unrelated to the objectives of the authorized intrusion, which exposed to view concealed portions of the apartment or its contents, did produce a new invasion of respondent's privacy unjustified by the exigent circumstance that validated the entry. This is why, contrary to Justice POWELL's suggestion, *post*, at 1157, the "distinction between 'looking' at a suspicious object in plain view and 'moving' it even a few inches" is much more than trivial for purposes of the Fourth Amendment. It matters not that the search uncovered nothing of any great personal value to respondent—serial numbers rather than (what might conceivably have been hidden behind or under the equipment) letters or photographs. A search is a search, even if it happens to disclose nothing but the bottom of a turntable.

III

The remaining question is whether the search was "reasonable" under the Fourth Amendment.

[4] On this aspect of the case we reject, at the outset, the apparent position of the Arizona Court of Appeals that because the officers' action directed to the stereo equipment was unrelated to the justification for their entry into respondent's apartment, it was *ipso facto* unreasonable. That lack of relationship *always* exists with regard to action validated under the "plain view" doctrine; where action is taken for the purpose justifying the entry, invocation of the doctrine is superfluous. *Mincey v. Arizona, supra*, in saying that a warrantless search must be "strictly circumscribed by the exigencies which justify its initiation," 437 U.S., at 393, 98 S.Ct., at 2413 (citation omitted), was addressing only the scope of the primary search itself, and was not overruling by implication the many cases acknowledging that the "plain view" doctrine can legitimate action beyond that scope.

We turn, then, to application of the doctrine to the facts of this case. "It is well established that under certain circumstances the police may *seize* evidence in plain view without a warrant," *Coolidge v. New Hampshire*, 403 U.S., at 465, 91 S.Ct. at 2037 (plurality opinion) (emphasis added). Those circumstances include situations "[w]here the initial intrusion that brings the police within plain view of such [evidence] is supported . . . by one of the recognized exceptions to the warrant requirement," *Ibid.*, such as the exigent-circumstances intrusion here. It would be absurd to say that an object could lawfully be seized and taken from the premises, but could not be moved for closer examination. It is clear, therefore, that the search here was valid if the "plain view" doctrine would have sustained a seizure of the equipment.

There is no doubt it would have done so if Officer Nelson had probable cause to believe that the equipment was stolen. The State has conceded, however, that he had only a "reasonable suspicion," by which it means something less than probable cause. *See* Brief for Petitioner 18–19.* We have not ruled on the question whether probable cause is required in order to invoke the "plain view" doctrine. Dicta in *Payton v. New York*, 445 U.S. 573, 587, 100 S.Ct. 1371, 1380, 63 L.Ed.2d 639 (1980), suggested that the standard of probable cause must be met, but our later opinions in *Texas v. Brown*, 460 U.S. 730, 103 S.Ct. 1535, 75 L.Ed.2d 502 (1983), explicitly regarded the issue as unresolved, *see Id.*, at 742, n. 7, 103 S.Ct. at 1543 n. 7 (plurality opinion); *Id.*, at 746, 103 S.Ct. at 1545 (STEVENS, J., concurring in judgment).

[5] We now hold that probable cause is required. To say otherwise would be to cut the "plain view" doctrine loose from its theoretical and practical moorings. The theory of that doctrine consists of extending to nonpublic places such as the home, where searches and seizures without a warrant are presumptively unreasonable, the police's longstanding authority to make warrantless seizures in public places of such objects as weapons and contraband. *See Payton v. New York, supra*, at 586–587, 100 S.Ct. at 1380. And the practical justification for that extention is the desirability of sparing police, whose viewing of the object in the course of a lawful search is as legitimate as it would have been in a public place, the inconvenience and the risk—to themselves or to preservation of the evidence—of going to obtain a warrant. *See Coolidge v. New Hampshire, supra*, at 468, 91 S.Ct. at 2039 (plurality opinion). Dispensing with the need for a warrant is worlds apart from permitting a lesser standard of *cause* for the seizure than a warrant would require, *i.e.*, the standard of probable cause. No reason is apparent why an object should routinely be seizable on lesser grounds, during an unrelated search and seizure, than would have been needed to obtain a warrant for that same object if it had been known to be on the premises.

We do not say, of course, that a seizure can never be justified on less than probable cause. We have held that it can—where, for example, the seizure is minimally intrusive and operational necessities render it the only practicable means of detecting certain types of crime. *See, e.g., United States v. Cortez*, 449 U.S. 411, 101 S.Ct. 690, 66 L.Ed.2d 621 (1981) (investigative detention of vehicle suspected to be transport-

---

*Contrary to the suggestion in Justice O'CONNOR's dissent, *post*, at 1160, this concession precludes our considering whether the probable-cause standard was satisfied in this case.

ing illegal aliens); *United States v. Brignoni-Ponce,* 422 U.S. 873, 95 S.Ct. 2574, 45 L.Ed.2d 607 (1975) (same); *United States v. Place,* 462 U.S. 696, 709, and n. 9, 103 S.Ct. 2637, 2645 and n. 9, 77 L.Ed.2d 110 (1983) (dictum) (seizure of suspected drug dealer's luggage at airport to permit exposure to specially trained dog). No special operational necessities are relied on here, however—but rather the mere fact that the items in question came lawfully within the officer's plain view. That alone cannot supplant the requirement of probable cause.

[6] The same considerations preclude us from holding that, even though probable cause would have been necessary for a *seizure,* the *search* of objects in plain view that occurred here could be sustained on lesser grounds. A dwelling-place search, no less than a dwelling-place seizure, requires probable cause, and there is no reason in theory or practicality why application of the "plain view" doctrine would supplant that requirement. Although the interest protected by the Fourth Amendment injunction against unreasonable searches is quite different from that protected by its injunction against unreasonable seizures, *see Texas v. Brown, supra,* 460 U.S., at 747–748, 103 S.Ct., at 1546 (STEVENS, J., concurring in judgment), neither the one nor the other is of inferior worth or necessarily requires only lesser protection. We have not elsewhere drawn a categorical distinction between the two insofar as concerns the degree of justification needed to establish the reasonableness of police action, and we see no reason for a distinction in the particular circumstances before us here. Indeed, to treat searches more liberally would especially erode the plurality's warning in *Coolidge* that "the 'plain view' doctrine may not be used to extend a general exploratory search from one object to another until something incriminating at last emerges." 403 U.S., at 466, 91 S.Ct. at 2038. In short, whether legal authority to move the equipment could be found only as an inevitable concomitant of the authority to seize it, or also as a consequence of some independent power to search certain objects in plain view, probable cause to believe the equipment was stolen was required.

Justice O'CONNOR's dissent suggests that we uphold the action here on the ground that it was a "cursory inspection" rather than a "full-blown search," and could therefore be justified by reasonable suspicion instead of probable cause. As already noted, a truly cursory inspection—one that involves merely looking at what is already exposed to view, without disturbing it—is not a "search" for Fourth Amendment purposes, and therefore does not even require reasonable suspicion. We are unwilling to send police and judges into a new thicket of Fourth Amendment law, to seek a creature of uncertain description that is neither a "plain view" inspection nor yet a "full-blown search." Nothing in the prior opinions of this Court supports such a distinction, not even the dictum from Justice Stewart's concurrence in *Stanley v. Georgia,* 394 U.S. 557, 571, 89 S.Ct. 1243, 1251, 22 L.Ed.2d 542 (1969), whose reference to a "mere inspection" describes, in our view, close observation of what lies in plain sight.

Justice POWELL's dissent reasonably asks what it is we would have had Officer Nelson do in these circumstances. *Post,* at 1156. The answer depends, of course, upon whether he had probable cause to conduct a search, a question that was not preserved in this case. If he had, then he should have done precisely what he did. If not, then he should have followed up his suspicions, if possible, by means other than a search—just as he would have had to do if, while walking along the street, he had noticed the same suspicious stereo equipment sitting inside a house a few feet away from him, beneath an open window. It may well be that, in such circumstances, no effective means short of a search exist. But there is nothing new in the realization that the Constitution sometimes insulates the criminality of a few in order to protect the privacy of us all. Our disagreement with the dissenters pertains to where the proper balance should be struck; we choose to adhere to the textual and traditional standard of probable cause.

The State contends that, even if Officer Nelson's search violated the Fourth Amendment, the court below should have admitted the evidence thus obtained under the "good faith" exception to the exclusionary rule. That was not the question on which certiorari was granted, and we decline to consider it.

For the reasons stated, the judgment of the Court of Appeals of Arizona is
Affirmed.

Justice WHITE, concurring.

I write only to emphasize that this case does not present, and we have no occasion to address, the so-called "inadvertent discovery" prong of the plain-view exception to the Warrant Clause. *See Coolidge v. New Hampshire,* 403 U.S. 443, 469–471, 91 S.Ct. 2022, 2040–2041, 29 L.Ed.2d 564 (1971) (plurality opinion). This "requirement" of the plain-view doctrine has never been accepted by a judgment supported by a majority of this Court, and I therefore do not accept Justice O'CONNOR's dissent's assertion that evidence seized in plain view must have been inadvertently discovered in order to satisfy the dictates of the Fourth Amendment. *See post,* at 1157. I join the majority opinion today without regard to the inadvertence of the officers' discovery of the stereo components' serial numbers. The police officers conducted a search of respondent's stereo equipment absent probable cause that the equipment was stolen. It is for this reason that the judgment of the Court of Appeals of Arizona must be affirmed.

Justice POWELL, with whom THE CHIEF JUSTICE and Justice O'CONNOR join, dissenting.

I join Justice O'CONNOR's dissenting opinion, and write briefly to highlight what seem to me the unfortunate consequences of the Court's decision.

Today the Court holds for the first time that the requirement of probable cause operates as a separate limitation on the application of the plain-view doctrine.[1] The plurality opinion in *Coolidge v. New Hampshire*, 403 U.S. 443, 91 S.Ct. 2022, 29 L.Ed.2d 564 (1971) required only that it be "immediately apparent to the police that they have evidence before them; the 'plain view' doctrine may not be used to extend a general exploratory search from one object to another until something incriminating at last emerges." *Id.*, at 466, 91 S.Ct. at 2038 (citation omitted). There was no general exploratory search in this case, and I would not approve such a search. All the pertinent objects were in plain view and could be identified as objects frequently stolen. There was no looking into closets, opening of drawers or trunks, or other "rummaging around." Justice O'CONNOR properly emphasizes that the moving of a suspicious object in plain view results in a minimal invasion of privacy. *Post*, at 1159. The Court nevertheless holds that "merely looking at" an object in plain view is lawful, *ante*, at 1154, but "moving" or "disturbing" the object to investigate a reasonable suspicion is not, *ante*, at 1152, 1154. The facts of this case well illustrate the unreasonableness of this distinction.

---

1. In *Texas v. Brown*, 460 U.S. 730, 103 S.Ct. 1535, 75 L.Ed.2d 502 (1983), the plurality opinion expressly declined to "address whether, in some circumstances, a degree of suspicion lower than probable cause would be sufficient basis for a seizure. . . ." *Id.*, at 742, n. 7, 103 S.Ct. at 1543 n. 7. Even the probable-cause standard, in the plurality's view, requires only facts sufficient to " 'warrant a man of reasonable caution in the belief' . . . that certain items may be contraband or stolen property or useful as evidence of a crime; it does not demand any showing that such a belief be correct or more likely true than false." *Id.*, at 742, 103 S.Ct. at 1543 (quoting *Carroll v. United States*, 267 U.S. 132, 162, 45 S.Ct. 280, 288, 69 L.Ed. 543 (1925)). *See also Texas v. Brown*, *supra*, at 746, 103 S.Ct. at 1545 (POWELL, J., concurring in judgment) (leaving open the question whether probable cause is required to inspect objects in plain view). As the Court recognizes, *ante*, at 1153, the statements in *Payton v. New York*, 445 U.S. 573, 587, 100 S.Ct. 1371, 1380, 63 L.Ed.2d 639 (1980), are dicta.

The officers' suspicion that the stereo components at issue were stolen was both reasonable and based on specific, articulable facts. Indeed, the State was unwise to concede the absence of probable cause. The police lawfully entered respondent's apartment under exigent circumstances that arose when a bullet fired through the floor of the apartment struck a man in the apartment below. What they saw in the apartment hardly suggested that it was occupied by law-abiding citizens. A .25-caliber automatic pistol lay in plain view on the living room floor. During a concededly lawful search, the officers found a .45-caliber automatic, a .22-caliber, sawed-off rifle, and a stocking-cap mask. The apartment was littered with drug paraphernalia. App. 29. The officers also observed two sets of expensive stereo components of a type that frequently was stolen.[2]

It is fair to ask what Officer Nelson should have done in these circumstances. Accepting the State's concession that he lacked probable cause, he could not have obtained a warrant to seize the stereo components. Neither could he have remained on the premises and forcibly prevented their removal. Officer Nelson's testimony indicates that he was able to read some of the serial numbers without moving the components.[3] To read the serial number on a Bang and Olufsen turntable, however, he had to "turn it around or turn it upside down." *Id.*, at 19. Officer Nelson noted the serial numbers on the stereo components and telephoned the National Crime Information Center to check them against the Center's computerized listing of stolen property. The computer confirmed his suspicion that at least the Bang and Olufsen turntable had been stolen. On the basis of this information, the officers obtained a warrant to seize the turntable and other stereo components that also proved to be stolen.

The Court holds that there was an unlawful search of the turntable. It agrees that the "mere recording of the serial numbers did not constitute a seizure." *Ante*, at 1152. Thus, if the computer had identified as stolen property a component with a visi-

---

2. Responding to a question on cross-examination, Officer Nelson explained that his suspicion was "based on 12 years' worth of police experience. I have worked in different burglary crimes throughout that period of time and . . . I'm just very familiar with people converting stolen stereos and TVs into their own use." App. 28–29.

---

3. Officer Nelson testified that there was an opening of about a foot between the back of one set of stereo equipment and the wall. *Id.*, at 20. Presumably this opening was large enough to permit Officer Nelson to view serial numbers on the backs of the components without moving them.

ble serial number, the evidence would have been admissible. But the Court further holds that "Officer Nelson's moving of the equipment . . . did constitute a 'search'. . . ." *Ibid.* It perceives a constitutional distinction between reading a serial number on an object and moving or picking up an identical object to see its serial number. To make its position unmistakably clear, the Court concludes that a "search is a search, even if it happens to disclose nothing but the bottom of a turntable." *Ante*, at 1153. With all respect, this distinction between "looking" at a suspicious object in plain view and "moving" it even a few inches trivializes the Fourth Amendment.[4] The Court's new rule will cause uncertainty, and could deter conscientious police officers from lawfully obtaining evidence necessary to convict guilty persons. Apart from the importance of rationality in the interpretation of the Fourth Amendment, today's decision may handicap law enforcement without enhancing privacy interests. Accordingly, I dissent.

Justice O'CONNOR, with whom THE CHIEF JUSTICE and Justice Powell join, dissenting.

The Court today gives the right answer to the wrong question. The Court asks whether the police must have probable cause before either seizing an object in plain view or conducting a full-blown search of that object, and concludes that they must. I agree. In my view, however, this case presents a different question: whether police must have probable cause before conducting a cursory inspection of an item in plain view. Because I conclude that such an inspection is reasonable if the police are aware of facts or circumstances that justify a reasonable suspicion that the item is evidence of a crime, I would reverse the judgment of the Arizona Court of Appeals, and therefore dissent.

In *Coolidge v. New Hampshire*, 403 U.S. 443, 91 S.Ct. 2022, 29 L.Ed.2d 564 (1971), Justice Stewart summarized three requirements that the plurality

thought must be satisfied for a plain-view search or seizure. First, the police must lawfully make an initial intrusion or otherwise be in a position from which they can view a particular area. Second, the officer must discover incriminating evidence "inadvertently." Third, it must be "immediately apparent" to the police that the items they observe may be evidence of a crime, contraband, or otherwise subject to seizure. As another plurality observed in *Texas v. Brown*, 460 U.S. 730, 737, 103 S.Ct. 1535, 1540–1541, 75 L.Ed.2d 502 (1983), these three requirements have never been expressly adopted by a majority of this Court, but "as the considered opinion of four Members of this Court [the *Coolidge* plurality] should obviously be the point of reference for further discussion of the issue." There is no dispute in this case that the first two requirements have been satisfied. The officers were lawfully in the apartment pursuant to exigent circumstances, and the discovery of the stereo was inadvertent—the officers did not " 'know in advance the location of [certain] evidence and intend to seize it,' relying on the plain-view doctrine only as a pretext." *Ibid.* (quoting *Coolidge v. New Hampshire, supra,* at 470, 91 S.Ct. at 2040). Instead, the dispute in this case focuses on the application of the "immediately apparent" requirement; at issue is whether a police officer's reasonable suspicion is adequate to justify a cursory examination of an item in plain view.

The purpose of the "immediately apparent" requirement is to prevent "general, exploratory rummaging in a person's belongings." *Coolidge v. New Hampshire*, 403 U.S., at 467, 91 S.Ct. at 2038. If an officer could indiscriminately search every item in plain view, a search justified by a limited purpose—such as exigent circumstances—could be used to eviscerate the protections of the Fourth Amendment. In order to prevent such a general search, therefore, we require that the relevance of the item be "immediately apparent." As Justice Stewart explained:

> "Of course, the extension of the original justification [for being present] is legitimate only where it is immediately apparent to the police that they have evidence before them; the 'plain view' doctrine may not be used to extend a general exploratory search from one object to another until something incriminating at last emerges. Cf. *Stanley v. Georgia*, [394 U.S. 557], 571–572 [89 S.Ct. 1243, 1251–1252, 22 L.Ed.2d 542] [(1969)] (Stewart, J., concurring in result)." *Id.*, at 466–467, 91 S.Ct. at 2038–2039.

Thus, I agree with the Court that even under the plain-view doctrine, probable cause is required before the police seize an item, or conduct a full-blown search of evidence in plain view. *Ante*, at 1153–1154. Such a requirement of probable cause will prevent the

---

4. Numerous articles that frequently are stolen have identifying numbers, including expensive watches and cameras, and also credit cards. Assume for example that an officer reasonably suspects that two identical watches, both in plain view, have been stolen. Under the Court's decision, if one watch is lying face up and the other lying face down, reading the serial number on one of the watches would not be a search. But turning over the other watch to read its serial number would be a search. Moreover, the officer's ability to read a serial number may depend on its location in a room and light conditions at a particular time. Would there be a constitutional difference if an officer, on the basis of a reasonable suspicion, used a pocket flashlight or turned on a light to read a number rather than moving the object to a point where a serial number was clearly visible?

plain-view doctrine from authorizing general searches. This is not to say, however, that even a mere inspection of a suspicious item must be supported by probable cause. When a police officer makes a cursory inspection of a suspicious item in plain view in order to determine whether it is indeed evidence of a crime, there is no "exploratory rummaging." Only those items that the police officer "reasonably suspects" as evidence of a crime may be inspected, and perhaps more importantly, the scope of such an inspection is quite limited. In short, if police officers have a reasonable, articulable suspicion that an object they come across during the course of a lawful search is evidence of crime, in my view they may make a cursory examination of the object to verify their suspicion. If the officers wish to go beyond such a cursory examination of the object, however, they must have probable cause.

This distinction between a full-blown search and seizure of an item and a mere inspection of the item was first suggested by Justice Stewart. In his concurrence in *Stanley v. Georgia*, 394 U.S. 557, 89 S.Ct. 1243, 22 L.Ed.2d 542 (1969), which is cited in *Coolidge*, Justice Stewart observed that the federal agents there had acted within the scope of a lawful warrant in opening the drawers of the defendant's desk. When they found in one of the drawers not the gambling material described in the warrant but movie films, they proceeded to exhibit the films on the defendant's projector, and thereafter arrested the defendant for possession of obscene matter. Justice Stewart agreed with the majority that the film had to be suppressed, but in doing so he suggested that a less intrusive inspection of evidence in plain view would present a different case: "This is not a case where agents in the course of a lawful search came upon contraband, criminal activity, or criminal evidence in plain view. For the record makes clear that the contents of the films could not be determined by *mere inspection*." *Id.*, at 571, 89 S.Ct. at 1251 (emphasis added) (footnote omitted).

Following Justice Stewart's suggestion, the overwhelming majority of both state and federal courts have held that probable cause is not required for a minimal inspection of an item in plain view. As Professor LaFave summarizes the view of these courts, "the minimal additional intrusion which results from an inspection or examination of an object in plain view is reasonable if the officer was first aware of some facts and circumstances which justify a reasonable suspicion (not probable cause, in the traditional sense) that the object is or contains a fruit, instrumentality, or evidence of crime." 2 W. LaFave, Search and Seizure § 6.7(b), p. 717 (2d ed. 1987); *see also Id.*, at 345 ("It is generally assumed that there is nothing improper in merely picking up an unnamed article for the purpose of noting its brand name or serial number or other identifying characteristics to be found on the surface"). Thus, while courts require probable cause for more extensive examination, cursory inspections—including picking up or moving objects for a better view—require only a reasonable suspicion. *See, e.g., United States v. Marbury*, 732 F.2d 390, 399 (CA5 1984) (police may inspect an item found in plain view to determine whether it is evidence of crime if they have a reasonable suspicion to believe that the item is evidence); *United States v. Hillyard*, 677 F.2d 1336, 1342 (CA9 1982) (police may give suspicious documents brief perusal if they have a "reasonable suspicion"); *United States v. Wright*, 667 F.2d 793, 798 (CA9 1982) ("[A]n officer may conduct such an examination if he at least has a 'reasonable suspicion' to believe that the discovered item is evidence"); *United States v. Roberts*, 619 F.2d 379, 381 (CA5 1980) ("Police officers are not required to ignore the significance of items in plain view when the full import of the objects cannot be positively ascertained without some examination"); *United States v. Ochs*, 595 F.2d 1247, 1257–1258, and n. 8 (CA2 1979) (Friendly, J.) (same).

Indeed, several state courts have applied a reasonable-suspicion standard in factual circumstances almost identical to this case. *See, e.g., State v. Noll*, 116 Wis.2d 443, 343 N.W.2d 391 (1984) (officer, upon seeing television, could check serial numbers); *State v. Riedinger*, 374 N.W.2d 866 (ND 1985) (police, in executing warrant for drugs, could check serial number of microwave oven); *People v. Dorris*, 110 Ill.App.3d 660, 66 Ill.Dec.390, 442 N.E.2d 951 (1982) (police may note account number of deposit slip because, when the police have a reasonable suspicion that an item in plain view is stolen property, the minimal additional intrusion of checking external identification numbers is proper); *State v. Proctor*, 12 Wash.App. 274, 529 P.2d 472 (1974) (upholding police notation of serial numbers on calculators); *People v. Eddington*, 23 Mich.App. 210, 178 N.W.2d 686 (1970) (upholding examination of the heels of shoes), *rev'd on other grounds*, 387 Mich. 551, 198 N.W.2d 297 (1972).

This distinction between searches based on their relative intrusiveness—and its subsequent adoption by a consensus of American courts—is entirely consistent with our Fourth Amendment jurisprudence. We have long recognized that searches can vary in intrusiveness, and that some brief searches "may be so minimally intrusive of Fourth Amendment interests that strong countervailing governmental interests will justify a [search] based only on specific articulable facts" that the item in question is contraband or evidence of a crime. *United States v. Place*, 462 U.S. 696, 706, 103 S.Ct. 2637, 2644, 77 L.Ed.2d 110 (1983). In *Delaware v. Prouse*, 440 U.S. 648, 654, 99 S.Ct. 1391, 1396, 59 L.Ed.2d 660 (1979), we held that the permissibility of a particular law enforcement practice should be judged by balancing its intrusion on the individual's Fourth Amendment interests against its promotion of legitimate governmental interests. Thus, "[w]here a careful balancing of governmental and private interests suggests that the public interest is best served by a Fourth Amendment standard of reasonableness that stops short of probable cause, we have not hesitated to adopt such a standard." *New Jersey v. T.L.O.*, 469 U.S. 325, 341, 105 S.Ct. 733, 743, 83 L.Ed.2d 720 (1985). The governmental interests considered include crime prevention and detection. *Terry v. Ohio*, 392 U.S. 1, 22, 88 S.Ct. 1868, 1880, 20 L.Ed.2d 889 (1968). The test is whether these law enforcement interests are sufficiently "substantial," not, as the Court would have it, whether "operational necessities render [a standard less than probable cause] the only practicable means of detecting certain types of crimes." *Ante*, at 1154. *See United States v. Place, supra*, at 704, 103 S.Ct. at 2643.

In my view, the balance of the governmental and privacy interests strongly supports a reasonable-suspicion standard for the cursory examination of items in plain view. The additional intrusion caused by an inspection of an item in plain view for its serial number is miniscule. Indeed, the intrusion in this case was even more transitory and less intrusive than the seizure of luggage from a suspected drug dealer in *United States v. Place, supra*, and the "severe, though brief, intrusion upon cherished personal security" in *Terry v. Ohio, supra*, at 24–25, 88 S.Ct. at 1881–1882.

Weighed against this minimal additional invasion of privacy are rather major gains in law enforcement. The use of identification numbers in tracing stolen property is a powerful law enforcement tool. Serial numbers are far more helpful and accurate in detecting stolen property than simple police recollection of the evidence. *Cf. New York v. Class*, 475 U.S. 106, 111, 106 S.Ct. 960, 964, 89 L.Ed.2d 81 (1986) (observing importance of vehicle identification numbers).

Given the prevalence of mass produced goods in our national economy, a serial number is often the only sure method of detecting stolen property. The balance of governmental and private interests strongly supports the view accepted by a majority of courts that a standard of reasonable suspicion meets the requirements of the Fourth Amendment.

Unfortunately, in its desire to establish a "bright-line" test, the Court has taken a step that ignores a substantial body of precedent and that places serious roadblocks to reasonable law enforcement practices. Indeed, in this case no warrant to search the stereo equipment for its serial number could have been obtained by the officers based on reasonable suspicion alone, and in the Court's view the officers may not even move the stereo turntable to examine its serial number. The theoretical advantages of the "search is a search" approach adopted by the Court today are simply too remote to justify the tangible and severe damage it inflicts on legitimate and effective law enforcement.

Even if probable cause were the appropriate standard, I have little doubt that it was satisfied here. When police officers, during the course of a search inquiring into grievously unlawful activity, discover the tools of a thief (a sawed-off rifle and a stocking mask) and observe in a small apartment *two* sets of stereo equipment that are both inordinately expensive in relation to their surroundings and known to be favored targets of larcenous activity, the "flexible, common-sense standard" of probable cause has been satisfied. *Texas v. Brown*, 460 U.S., at 742, 103 S.Ct. at 1543 (plurality opinion).

Because the Court today ignores the existence of probable cause, and in doing so upsets a widely accepted body of precedent on the standard of reasonableness for the cursory examination of evidence in plain view, I respectfully dissent.

Hugh FERGUSON, Plaintiff-Appellant,
v.
ARIZONA DEPARTMENT OF ECONOMIC SECURITY, John L. Huerta, Director, Arizona Department of Economic Security, and the Tanner Companies (United Metro), Defendants-Appellees.

No. 2 CA-CIV 3060.
Court of Appeals of Arizona, Division 2.
March 30, 1979.

The Department of Economic Security found that claimant voluntarily quit his job without good cause and was therefore ineligible for benefits. The Superior Court, Pinal County, Cause No. 30624, Barry De-

Rose, J., affirmed, and claimant appealed. The Court of Appeals, Howard, J., held that Department of Economic Security could not be faulted for its decision that there is no good cause for an employee's leaving prior to effective date of discharge unless he can show that he would suffer substantial detriment by remaining at work until date of discharge or if he quits to accept a definite offer of work with another employer.

Affirmed.

1. **Social Security and Public Welfare k251**   Purpose of Employment Security Act is to allow compensation for limited period to those who are capable of working and available for work and are involuntarily unemployed through no fault of their own. A.R.S. §§ 23–601 to 23–799.

2. **Administrative Law and Procedure k390**   Rules of administrative body are valid if reasonably related to purposes of enabling legislation.

3. **Administrative Law and Procedure k386**   Rule or regulation of administrative agency should not be inconsistent with or contrary to provisions of statute, particularly statute it seeks to effectuate.

4. **Social Security and Public Welfare k401**   Department of Economic Security's rule that there is no good cause for an employee's leaving prior to effective date of discharge unless he can show that he would suffer substantial detriment by remaining at work or if he quits to accept a definite offer of work with another employer does not conflict with purpose and intent of Employment Security Act, which requires that, in case of employee who leaves work voluntarily, leaving be with good cause in order to entitle employee to benefits, and thus, claimant, who submitted his resignation after being discharged instead of working until termination date, stating that to do so would have been "demeaning" and "untenable," was not entitled to unemployment benefits. A.R.S. § 23–775[1].

Wildermuth & Wildermuth by John R. Wildermuth, Coolidge, for plaintiff-appellant.

Robert K. Corbin, Atty. Gen. by James A. Tucker, Asst. Atty. Gen., Phoenix, for defendant-appellee Arizona Department of Economic Security.

Snell & Wilmer by Peter J. Rathwell, Phoenix, for defendant-appellee The Tanner Companies.

OPINION

HOWARD, Judge.

The issue here is whether an appeal tribunal of the Department of Economic Security was arbitrary and capricious when it found that appellant voluntarily quit his job without good cause.

The tribunal's findings of fact show that on April 28, 1977 appellant told his supervisor that he was looking for other employment. On May 5, 1977, his employer told him that a replacement had been found and his employment would be terminated on May 11. Instead of working until the termination date, on May 6 appellant submitted his resignation. He did not continue working until the discharge date because to do so would have been "demeaning" and "untenable". In his testimony before the tribunal, appellant stated that it would have been embarrassing for him to continue working after he had been fired.

The appellate tribunal found that appellant left work in violation of Regulation No. R6–3–50135, Arizona Compilation of Rules and Regulations, and was therefore ineligible for benefits from May 1, 1977 until he becomes re-employed and earns $425. The trial court affirmed.

[1] The purpose of the Employment Security Act, A.R.S. Secs. 23–601–799, is to allow compensation for a limited period to those who are capable of working and available for work and are involuntarily unemployed through no fault of their own. *Vickers v. Western Electric Co.*, 86 Ariz. 7, 339 P.2d 1033 (1959); *Beaman v. Safeway Stores*, 78 Ariz. 195, 277 P.2d 1010 (1954); *Sisk v. Arizona Ice & Cold Storage Co.*, 60 Ariz. 496, 141 P.2d 395 (1943).

A.R.S. Sec. 23–775 deals with an employee's disqualification from benefits. It states:

"An individual shall be disqualified for benefits:
1. For the week in which he has left work voluntarily without good cause in connection with his employment, if so found by the department, and in addition to the waiting week, for the duration of his unemployment and until he has earned wages in an amount equivalent to five times his weekly benefit amount otherwise payable."

Regulation No. R6–3–50135, cited by the appeals tribunal as the basis for its decision, states:

"D. Leaving prior to effective date of discharge (V L 135.25)
1. Generally a worker would leave without good cause in connection with his work if he quits before the effective date of discharge even though he has been told that the duration of his employment is limited.
2. He would leave with good cause connected with the work if:
a. He can show that he would suffer substantial detriment by remaining at work until the date of discharge, or
b. He quits to accept a definite offer of work with another employer."

Appellant contends that the above regulation conflicts with the purpose and intent of the Employment Security Act because it disqualifies him from receiving benefits for the entire statutory period when he would have been entitled to benefits if he had merely remained on the job instead of resigning. We do not agree.

A.R.S. Sec. 23–775(1) makes it clear that if an employee leaves work voluntarily and does so without good cause in connection with his employment, he is disqualified from benefits.

[2–4] Rules of an administrative body are valid if reasonably related to the purposes of the enabling legislation. *Serritella v. Engelman,* 462 F.2d 601 (3rd Cir. 1972). Furthermore a rule or regulation of an administrative agency should not be inconsistent with or contrary to the provisions of a statute, particularly the statute it seeks to effectuate. *McCarrell v. Lane,* 76 Ariz. 67, 258 P.2d 988 (1953). Since A.R.S. Sec. 23–775 requires, in the case of an employee leaving work voluntarily, that such leaving be with good cause in order to entitle the employee to benefits, we do not believe that the rule is unreasonable or inconsistent with the purposes of the Employment Security Act. While it may have been arguably wiser to have a rule which merely would disqualify appellant in a situation such as this from receiving unemployment compensation for the period of time between his resignation and when he would have been discharged, it is clear that A.R.S. Sec. 23–775(1) does not prohibit the department from adopting such a rule. Under the statute there are only two choices. Departure of the employee was either with or without good cause. We cannot fault the department for its decision that there is no good cause for an employee leaving prior to the effective date of discharge unless he can show that he would suffer substantial detriment by remaining at work until the date of discharge or if he quits to accept a definite offer of work with another employer.

Affirmed.

RICHMOND, C. J., and HATHAWAY, J., concur.

ST. JOSEPH's HOSPITAL AND MEDICAL CENTER, an Arizona corporation, Plaintiff-Appellee,
vs.
MARICOPA COUNTY, Arizona, a body politic, Defendant-Appellant
No. 17556
SUPREME COURT OF ARIZONA
688 P.2d 986, 142 Ariz. 94
September 26, 1984
Reconsideration Denied October 23, 1984.

Hospital filed action seeking reimbursement from county for care rendered to three resident indigent patients who had been admitted for emergency medical care. The Superior Court, Maricopa County, No. C-452325, Robert Pickrell, J., entered partial summary judgment for the hospital, and county appealed. The Supreme Court, Feldman, J., held that: (1) a hospital initially receiving an indigent emergency medical patient is obligated to continue to provide needed emergency care so long as it is "medically indicated"; (2) county is liable for the entire cost of the indigent patient's medical care, even after the emergent condition has been treated, when, after proper notice, it has failed to transfer the patient; (3) the fact that patients moved from the county after being released from the hospital was not relevant to their intention to stay in or leave the country before the accident so as to affect their status as residents of the county; (4) county was obligated to reimburse the hospital because illegal entry into nation does not disqualify an alien from becoming a "resident" of a county for the purposes of statutes governing emergency medical care; and (5) county regulation which attempted to limit eligibility for county payment of medical expenses for indigent residents admitted for emergency medical care to "legal" residents was invalid.

Affirmed.

Holohan, C. J. dissented.

1. **Hospitals k5**   Hospital initially receiving indigent emergency medical patient is obligated to con-

tinue to provide needed emergency care so long as it is "medically indicated."

2. Hospitals k5   If transfer of indigent emergency medical patient cannot be effected because of county's refusal to accept patient, private hospital may not simply release seriously ill, indigent patient to perish on streets.

3. Social Security and Public Welfare k241
County may not avoid its obligation to reimburse private hospital for continuing care of indigent, who was initially admitted for emergency care, simply by refusing to transfer patient once county has been properly notified of condition and location of patient. A.R.S. ss 11-297.01 subd. B, 41-1831.

4. Social Security and Public Welfare k241
County is liable for entire cost of medical care for indigent patient admitted to private hospital for emergency care, even after emergent condition has been treated, when, after proper notice, it has failed to transfer patient to county facility. A.R.S. ss 11-297.01, subd. B, 41-1837, subd. A.

5. Social Security and Public Welfare k241   Fact that indigent patients who were residents of county when they were admitted to hospital for emergency care returned to Mexico after being released from hospital was not relevant to their intentions to stay in or leave county before injury producing accident, where patients had lived or worked in county for substantial periods of time, had homes or established places of residence, had not traveled back and forth to Mexico and had indicated no intention of leaving.

6. Social Security and Public Welfare k241
County was obligated to reimburse private hospital for medical care received by indigent patients admitted for emergency care even though such patients were illegal aliens; illegal entry into nation does not disqualify alien from being "resident" of county for purposes of statutes governing emergency medical care. A.R.S. ss 11-297.01, subd. B, 41-1837, subd. A.

7. Domicile k2   "Residence" and "domicile" are not synonymous terms at common law.

8. Domicile k2   Generally, statutory usage of term "resident" carries same connotations as term "domicile."—Id.

9. Domicile k1   "Domicile" is primarily state of mind combined with actual physical presence in state or county. See publication Words and Phrases for other judicial constructions and definitions.

10. Domicile k1   "Domicile" involves basically subjective material.

11. Domicile k1   Under test which bases determination of domicile on state of mind combined with actually physical presence, three indigent patients admitted to private hospital for emergency medical care were residents of county at time they suffered their accidental injuries resulting in emergency treatment at hospital where they had lived and worked in county for substantial periods of time, had homes or established places of residence, had not traveled back and forth to Mexico and had indicated no intention of leaving.

12. Domicile k1   Impediments to finding of residence may follow from person's legal status, as where one's insanity makes it impossible for him to form requisite subjective intent.

13. Domicile k4(2)   Marital relationship may affect determination of one's "intent" to establish residency.

14. Domicile k5   Minor takes domicile of his parents or legal guardian.

15. Aliens k53   Deportation proceeding is purely civil action; it looks prospectively to respondent's right to remain in this country in the future, and past conduct is relevant only insofar as it may shed light on respondent's right to remain.

16. Domicile k4(1)   Illegal entry into country does not bar person from obtaining domicile within state.

17. Aliens k39   There is no federal impediment to undocumented alien becoming resident of county.

18. Social Security and Public Welfare k241
County regulation providing that undocumented alien was ineligible for county subsidized health care was invalid because it sought to amend statute enacted by legislature which extended eligibility to "residents" by impermissibly limiting statutory definition of eligibility to legal residents. A.R.S. s 11-297.

COUNSEL

Gammage & Burnham by Richard B. Burnham, Grady Gammage, Jr., Phoenix, for plaintiff-appellee.

   Thomas E. Collins, Maricopa County Atty. by Gordon J. Goodnow, Jr., Phoenix, for defendant-appellant.

JUDGES

En Banc. Feldman, Justice. Gordon, V.C.J., and Hays and Cameron, JJ., concur. Holohan, C.J., dissenting.

AUTHOR: FELDMAN

* * *

OPINION

Maricopa County appeals from an adverse partial summary judgment in which the trial court held that the County was obligated by statute to reimburse St. Joseph's Hospital (St. Joseph's) for emergency care rendered to three undocumented Mexican nationals living in Maricopa County. We have jurisdiction, Ariz. Const. art. 6 U 5(3) and transferred the case to this court pursuant to Ariz.R.Civ.App.P., Rule 19, 17A A.R.S.

FACTS

The case involves three patients treated at St. Joseph's for emergencies resulting from three different accidents. Following an automobile accident in which he received injuries resulting in quadriplegia, Pedro Alvarado was admitted as an emergency patient at St. Joseph's on February 21, 1981. Two days later Maricopa County was notified that Mr. Alvarado was being treated at St. Joseph's. The hospital determined that Mr. Alvarado was indigent, and was living and working in Maricopa County at the time of the accident. Therefore, it billed Maricopa County for the services rendered to Mr. Alvarado. Alvarado remained at St. Joseph's until October, 1982. Emergency care was completed long before Alvarado's release, and for the majority of his stay he received only skilled nursing care at St. Joseph's. Although the County had been notified of Mr. Alvarado's condition, it did not seek to transfer him to a county facility capable of providing appropriate treatment. Claiming that because Mr. Alvarado entered the United States illegally he could not be considered a resident of Maricopa County, the County refused to reimburse St. Joseph's. Even under Medicare/Medicaid rates Mr. Alvarado's bill exceeded $130,000. The bills for the other patients were much smaller.

St. Joseph's filed an action in January, 1982, seeking reimbursement from the County for the care rendered to the three patients. In defending, the County argued that "illegal" status made it impossible, as a matter of law, for the three men to be considered "residents" of Maricopa County. Following discovery, St. Joseph's and the County filed cross-motions for summary judgment. The trial court granted St. Joseph's motions and formal judgment was entered on December 29, 1982. Maricopa County filed a notice of appeal. We transferred the case because of the need for a final resolution of the important and recurring legal problem. Rule 19, *supra*.

C

The County draws attention to the Maricopa County Department of Health Services Eligibility Manual which sets forth certain regulations regarding residency. Specifically, Regulation 4.05–3 states that an undocumented alien is ineligible for County subsidized health care. The County contends that this regulation reflects the intent of the state eligibility statutes. We reject this contention. The County regulation is invalid because it seeks to amend a statute enacted by the legislature and impermissibly limits the reach of the statutory language. *Duncan v. Krull*, 57 Ariz. 472, 476, 114 P.2d 888, 889 (1941) ("[r]ules and regulations by an administrative or executive officer or body are always subordinate to the terms of the statute and in aid of the enforcement of its provisions"); *Cabral v. State Board of Control*, 112 Cal.App.3d 1012, 1015–16, 169 Cal.Rptr. 604, 606 (1980).

As initially enacted A.R.S. § 11–297 contained a single qualification on residency—an indigent had to have been a resident of the county for 12 months before the county was responsible for his medical care. This qualification of the residency requirement was struck down by the United States Supreme Court 10 years ago in *Memorial Hospital v. Maricopa County*, 415 U.S. 250, 94 S.Ct. 1076, 39 L.Ed.2d 306 (1974). Since that date the legislature has not sought to qualify the term "resident" as used in the statute in any way. The public policy, animated by statute, "that a general hospital may not deny emergency care to any person without valid cause" (*Thompson v. Sun City Community Hospital*, 141 Ariz. at 601, 688 P.2d at 609) is reinforced by the obligation of counties to reimburse private hospitals for rendering such care to indigent county residents. A.R.S. § 11–297.01(B). A county's attempt to limit the statutory definition of eligibility by administrative regulation, modifying the word "resident" by adding the adjective "legal," restricts the county's duty of reimbursement. Instead of reimbursing private hospitals for emergency medical care rendered to indigent "residents," the county, by its own regulation, seeks to limit its duty to reimbursing only for such care to "legal residents." The legislature is obviously aware of the considerable number of undocumented aliens in our state. Had it wished to limit emergency care to legal residents, or attempt to impose on private hospitals a duty to provide such care to "illegals" without reimbursement, it could have supplied the missing adjective itself. We believe the regulation is inconsistent with the legislature's choice not to limit the statutory language. *Duncan v. Krull*, *supra*.

Thus, we hold that undocumented aliens may qualify as county residents under the statutes mandating that the county reimburse a private hospital for providing emergency medical care. The trial court was correct in granting summary judgment to St. Joseph's. The judgment is affirmed.

* * *

CHAPTER TWO

PUTTING IT INTO PRACTICE
Captions: *Weirum v. RKO General, Inc.*, 539 P.2d 36 (Cal. 1975). (Italicized)

Procedural History:
Prior Proceedings: Plaintiff brought wrongful death action against defendant. Jury returned verdict against defendant. Defendant filed motion for judgment notwithstanding verdict, and court denied motion.

Current Proceedings: Defendant is appealing jury verdict and court's denial of motion.

moving around in a car

COGNITIVE CALISTHENICS
2(a) *Linthicum v. Nationwide Life Ins. Co.*, 150 Ariz. 326 (1986).
Procedural History:
Prior Proceedings: The Court of Appeals affirmed a jury award of compensatory damages on a bad faith and breach of contract claim but reversed a $2,000,000 award of punitive damages.

Current Proceedings: Arizona Supreme Court is reviewing punitive damage award.

2(b) *White v. Mitchell*, 157 Ariz. 523 (App. 1988).
Procedural History:
Prior Proceedings: A jury awarded plaintiffs compensatory and punitive damages for injuries incurred in a motor vehicle accident. Defendant employer and employee moved for a remittitur and a new trial.

Current Proceedings: Both defendants are appealing the verdict and the denial of their motion for a new trial.

2(c) *Olson v. Walker*, 162 Ariz. 174 (App. 1989).
Procedural History:
Prior Proceedings: Plaintiff sued defendant for damages resulting from injuries in a motor vehicle accident. The jury awarded $133,000 in compensatory damages and $100,000 in punitive damages. The trial judge denied defendant's motion for a new trial and request for remittitur.

Current Proceedings: Defendant is appealing jury verdict and denial of motion.

CHAPTER THREE

PUTTING IT INTO PRACTICE
Essential Facts: The essential facts in *Weirum v. RKO Industries, Inc.*, are that a rock radio station with an extensive teenage audience sponsored a contest to locate a well-known disc jockey and that two contestants racing to secure the prize killed another driver.

Significant Facts: Several facts are significant but not essential in *Weirum v. RKO Industries, Inc.* The radio station offered a monetary prize in the contest it conducted in the Los Angeles area during the summer. The purpose of the contest was to make the station appear "more exciting." The disc jockey who was the target of the search moved from one location to another, announcing his presence as he went. Two teenagers following the disc jockey drove up to 80 mph and, in their attempts to follow him, forced another driver off the road, causing the driver's vehicle to overturn, killing the driver.

COGNITIVE CALISTHENICS
1(a) This is arguably an essential fact since the court referred to it in its reasoning and its conclusion. In arguing that defendant's intoxication was beyond being "borderline," the court specifically pointed to defendant's reckless conduct and the fact that he had consumed Valium in addition to alcohol. Since the court relied on these two factors to support its contention that defendant's conduct went beyond merely being intoxicated to being outrageous, I think this fact should be included in the issue statement.

1(b) The exact speed defendant was driving is not essential to the outcome of the case. I believe that for purposes of a statement of facts, it suffices to indicate that defendant was driving recklessly prior to the accident without specifying exactly how fast he drove.

1(c) Since plaintiff's conduct was not an issue in this case, what he was doing at the time of the accident is not essential. You may want to include this fact in a statement of facts to get a clear picture of how the accident occurred, but since this fact had no bearing on the case whatsoever, I would not consider it a significant fact.

1(d) This fact is not essential to the case since the court relied on defendant's consumption of Valium before the accident rather than his predisposition toward using Valium to reach its conclusion. Since any driver could reasonably be expected to be agitated after an accident, this fact shows only that defendant had apparently relied on the calming effects of Valium in the past, a fact which would have little or no bearing on a punitive damage award. Although you would not be wrong in including this fact in a statement of facts in an effort to paint a vivid picture of defendant's demeanor after the accident, it would not be necessary to do so.

1(e) Unless you are aware of the relationship between blood alcohol level and number of drinks consumed, this fact would more vividly depict the extent of defendant's intoxication than a mere blood alcohol level. Remember that the question in this case is whether defendant's conduct is so outrageous that punitive damages are justified. Therefore, the extreme nature of defendant's conduct must be understood. This translation of blood alcohol level into drinks consumed is most certainly a significant fact and may be helpful to include in the issue statement, making it an essential fact.

1(f) The size of the punitive damage award in relationship to defendant's economic status is key to this case and so is an essential fact.

1(g) Defendant's salary is discussed in the dissent but not in the majority opinion. Since the majority does not even discuss defendant's salary in relationship to the award, one might conclude that this factor is not relevant. However, the dissent's reasoning suggests that other courts and litigants will look at the relationship between a punitive damage award and a defendant's income in deciding whether an award is excessive. For that reason, I would consider this an essential fact to be included in an issue statement.

1(h) Same answer as given in (g).

2(a) *Linthicum v. Nationwide Life Ins. Co.*
In September, 1979, Jerry Linthicum had a tumor removed from his parathyroid glands; his doctors concluded that the tumor was benign. In April, 1980, his wife, Sandra, obtained medical insurance from Na-

tionwide through her employer, Arizona Optical Company. The policy contained a ninety-day exclusionary period pertaining to preexisting illnesses. In June, 1980, Jerry became ill, and in July he was operated on; his doctors determined that the tumor thought to be benign in 1979 was actually malignant.

When Jerry's medical bills were submitted to Nationwide, the claims examiner concluded that the claim was excludable as a preexisting illness. Although all the doctors who had treated Jerry confirmed that the tumor had erroneously been believed to be benign in 1979, the claims examiner based her decision to deny Jerry's claim on her conclusion that he had been receiving treatment for cancer during the exclusionary period even though it had been undiagnosed at the time.

In October, 1980, a denial letter was sent to Arizona Optical (the policyholder), even though Nationwide was aware that Sandra no longer worked there. Sandra did not learn of the denial until Jerry was hospitalized in October, 1980, when she was informed that his previous hospital bills had not been paid. When she contacted Nationwide, she was informed of the denial for the first time. Jerry was transferred to another hospital as a charity patient as a result of the denial of insurance benefits. After an inquiry by a Phoenix newspaper, Nationwide reviewed the Linthicum file and reaffirmed its denial.

TIME LINE

DATE	EVENT
Sept., 1979	Jerry's tumor removed (tumor determined benign).
April 1, 1980	Sandra gets policy (ninety-day exclusionary period begins).
June, 1980	Jerry becomes ill.
July 1, 1980	End of exclusionary period.
July 11, 1980	Jerry operated on (tumor determined malignant).
Oct. 20, 1980	Denial letter sent.
Oct. 28, 1980	Jerry hospitalized; Sandra informed of denial.

2(b) *White v. Mitchell*
Defendant employee hit plaintiff's vehicle as he was attempting to make a left-hand turn. Defendant employee owned the tractor, and defendant employer owned the van-trailer portion. A diesel mechanic testified that the condition of the tractor brakes indicated total neglect and that given the brakes' condition the stopping distance of the tractor was one-third more than if the brakes had been in good condition. He also testified that the brakes could easily have been inspected and that an experienced driver would have known that

the brakes were not in reasonable condition. An accident reconstructionist testified that defendant employee was traveling 45 to 50 mph when he began to skid, that a reasonable speed with good brakes would have been about 40 mph, and that a reasonable speed given the actual condition of the brakes was 0 mph since the tractor should not have been on the road. He also indicated that the accident could have been avoided if the brakes had not been worn out.

Defendant employer became aware after hiring defendant employee that his license had been suspended. After discovering the suspension, defendant employer ordered defendant employee to return to the home office but did not instruct him to return immediately as it could have. Defendant employer had not inspected defendant employee's tractor for seven months, even though company policy required an inspection every ninety days. If defendant employee's vehicle had been inspected, the truck would have been "deadlined."

2(c) *Nienstedt v. Wetzel*
Facts: After the Wetzels unsuccessfully sued the Nienstedts for breach of contract, the Nienstedts sued the Wetzels for abuse of process based on the following misconduct in the contract dispute: (1) the Wetzels had inappropriately sought punitive damages; (2) Wetzel had filed a motion to continue because he falsely alleged that he was the attorney of record in another action; (3) Wetzel had entered default on an improper pleading and then scheduled a second default hearing when he knew that an identical default had already been set aside; and (4) Wetzel had engaged in improper tactics during discovery. The Nienstedts recovered both punitive ($50,000) and compensatory ($7350) damages but never introduced evidence at trial of the Wetzels' financial resources.

CHAPTER FOUR

PUTTING IT INTO PRACTICE
Issue: Does a ~~rock~~ radio station with an ~~extensive~~ teenage audience (owe a duty) to a driver who is killed as a result of having her car overturned ~~by teenagers who~~ were driving recklessly an~~d speeding up to 80 mph~~ in order to locate a well-known disc jockey and secure a monetary reward offered in a contest sponsored by the radio station?
Holding: Yes. (The issue as written above can be answered with a simple yes.)
Dictum: The court's discussion of analogous situations, such as an "ardent sports fan injured while hastening to purchase one of a limited number of tickets" or "injuries incurred in response to a 'while-they-last' sale" is arguably dictum, since these situations are not issues before the court. Even though the court's

response to the defendant's slippery slope argument is relevant, it would still not be binding on another court.

COGNITIVE CALISTHENICS
1(a) *Nienstedt v. Wetzel*
Issue: Is an award of $50,000 in punitive damages excessive as a matter of law when the compensatory damages are only $7,350 and the plaintiff fails to provide evidence of the defendants' financial status if the defendants in prior litigation made false allegations, pursued a default on improper grounds, used improper procedures, and engaged in questionable discovery tactics?
Holding: No.
1(b) *Linthicum v. Nationwide Life Ins. Co.*
Issue 1: May punitive damages be awarded in a bad faith claim if there is clear and convincing evidence that the defendant acted with an "evil mind" and demonstrated aggravated and outrageous conduct?
Issue 2: Does an insurer's denial of an insured's claim for medical costs arising from his cancer treatment on the basis that the insured was being treated for cancer during an exclusionary period even though the cancer was undiagnosed at the time justify an award of punitive damages?
Holding 1: Yes.
Holding 2: No.
1(c) *Olson v. Walker*
Issue 1: Is causing injury to another driver as a result of reckless driving after having consumed Valium and at least ten twelve-ounce beers an hour prior to the accident sufficient evidence of the "evil mind" required to award punitive damages?
Issue 2: Is a punitive damage award of $100,000 excessive for a defendant who earns $38,000 annually and who will require seventeen years to pay off such an award?
Holding 1: Yes.
Holding 2: No.

CHAPTER FIVE

PUTTING IT INTO PRACTICE
Inductive Reasoning: If you have seen previous movies starring the same actor and you did not enjoy this actor, you might use inductive reasoning to conclude that this movie will be like (analogous to) the previous movies and that all movies made by this actor are poorly done. Of course, if this is a different kind of movie, or if the actor's ability to act has improved tremendously, your reasoning would be flawed and you might miss seeing a good movie.

Inductive Reasoning in a Case: The court argues that the relationship between innkeepers and guests is analogous to the relationship between landlords and tenants in that in both cases the ability of the people submitting to the control of the other to protect themselves is limited. The court reasons that the person in control should take precautions to protect the one who has relinquished control. The court considers other relationships that it finds analogous to the landlord-tenant relationship for the same reason. The court then reasons that if innkeepers owe a duty of care to their guests, landlords should (by analogy) owe a duty of care to their tenants.

Deductive Reasoning: This reasoning is flawed because it is based on the major premise that all juveniles who commit crimes should be jailed. For some crimes, jail is an inappropriate punishment. We do not know the nature of Gerald's crime, and jail may be inappropriate in his case.

The reasoning regarding Mrs. Brown is flawed for two reasons. First, the major premise appears to be that taking a class from a teacher who gives hard exams will result in the student receiving a poor grade, and this is not necessarily true. Second, Mrs. Brown may in fact not give difficult exams, in which case the student who decides not to take her class may be avoiding her unnecessarily.

Deductive Reasoning in a Case: The court's premise is its definition of a burglary tool: "a tool, instrument or other article adapted, designed or commonly used for committing or facilitating offenses involving larceny by physical taking." Its minor premise is that a girdle is an article of clothing and does not fit the definition of burglary tool (i.e., it is not a tool, instrument or other article adapted, designed or commonly used for committing or facilitating offenses involving larceny by physical taking.") The court's logical conclusion is that a girdle is not a burglary tool.

Weirum v. RKO General, Inc.: The court relies on deductive reasoning. Its major premise is that duty is based on foreseeability, and its minor premise is that foreseeability is present in this case. The court concludes, therefore, that the defendant owed a duty of care to the plaintiff.

Defining Ambiguous Terms:

1. "[A]ccording to the fair meaning of their terms to promote justice and effect the object of the law ..." and they must "give fair warning of the nature of the conduct proscribed."

2. In favor of the defendant.

3. Only those persons "born alive" could be subject to homicide.

4. No.

5. One part of the manslaughter statute prohibits "recklessly causing the death of another person," while another prohibits "knowingly or recklessly causing the death of an unborn child at any stage of its development ..." The statute treats fetuses and persons separately.

6. By separating the crimes of abortion of a fetus and murder of a person, the legislature intended to maintain a distinction between the two.

7. Title 36 of Arizona law.

8. Because the legislature has sole authority to create new crimes, it is more attuned to the will of the people on public policy than are the courts, and the legislature conducts public hearings to explore all aspects of potential situations rather than being confined to ruling on a single case as courts are.

9. Its decision was in accord with the decision of courts in other jurisdictions.

10. Since Arizona is a "code state," the court is precluded from creating new crimes by expanding the common law. The court can interpret the law, not expand it (as a common law state can).

11. (a) The *Summerfield* court rejected any analogy between civil tort liability and criminal liability for causing death;
(b) The wrongful death statute is remedial in nature and must be interpreted to "advance the remedy," while the criminal statutes must be interpreted to give "fair warning";
(c) Recovery for tortious damage to a fetus has evolved through the common law, whereas common law principles have been abolished in reference to the criminal law;
(d) The Arizona legislature has not defined "person" under A.R.S. Sec. 12–611 (tort law), while it has defined "person" under the homicide statutes; and
(e) The word "person" can mean different things in different contexts.

Conflicts in the Law: The conflict being resolved is between a provision in the County Health Services Eligibility Manual and a statute. The County regulation requires that individuals be "legal residents" before they are eligible for subsidized health care; the statute requires only that they be "residents." The principle the court must invoke is that administrative regulations must defer to statutes.

Fitting the Facts: The question is whether a girdle fits the definition of burglar's tool.

Public Policy: The court resorts to a slippery slope argument in the last paragraphs of its decision in *In the Matter of Charlotte K.*: "The Court must also wonder whether such a contrary decision would not create a spate of unreasonable bulges that would let loose the floodgates of stop-and-frisk cases, with the result of putting the squeeze on the court resources already overextended in this era of trim governmental budgets."

The *Kline* court is struggling with the best entity to hold responsible for foreseeable criminal attacks. It reasons that the one most able to prevent attacks in apartment complexes is the landlord and concludes that this responsibility is not unfair in light of the responsibility that other members of society are being asked to shoulder to prevent crime. In other words, the court is attempting to formulate a policy that is fair for all parties and for future litigants.

Weirum v. RKO General, Inc.: The court's rationale is organized around a "fit the facts" pattern. The question is whether the record (the facts) supports a finding of foreseeability, in other words, whether the facts fulfill the elements of foreseeability. The court also uses a public policy argument in the next-to-last paragraph when it concludes that "the imposition of a duty here will [not] lead to unwarranted extensions of liability."

COGNITIVE CALISTHENICS

1(a) The court uses deductive reasoning to argue from the general principle that evidence of the defendant's wealth is unnecessary to award punitive damages to its conclusion that no such evidence was required in the case at hand. The court again uses deductive reasoning to reach its conclusion that the punitive damage award was not so excessive as to indicate passion or prejudice on the part of the jury. The court reasons that the record reflected evidence from which a jury could reasonably infer that the defendant acted with reckless indifference toward the plaintiffs, thereby conforming to the case law requirements that must be met to justify the award of punitive damages.

1(b) The court carefully lays out the foundation for its decision by reviewing the case law established in *Linthicum, Rawlings v. Apodaca,* and *Gurule v. Illinois Mutual Life and Casualty Co.* The court then applies the standards set forth in those decisions and concludes by deductive reasoning that defendant Mitchell's conduct created a "substantial risk of causing serious personal injury or death to pedestrians or other motorists. . ." Mitchell's conduct "fits" the criteria established in the previously discussed cases to justify punitive damages. The court reaches the opposite conclusion in reference to defendant Sitton, reasoning that "gross negligence or mere reckless disregard of the circumstances" does not justify punitive damages as established in previous Arizona decisions. In short, Sitton's conduct does not "fit" the punitive damage criteria.

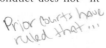
Prior courts have ruled that . . .

1(c) The court reviews previous decisions laying out the standard for the award of punitive damages and indicates that although in previous cases punitive damages had been awarded upon a showing of "gross or wanton negligence," current case law requires proof of "outrageous or egregious" conduct. Citing previous case law that held that such conduct can be inferred from the defendant's conduct, the court goes on to demonstrate how the defendant's conduct in this case fulfilled the requirements of an "evil mind," indicating that he should have recognized that his conduct "created a substantial risk of harm to others." The court then points out the fallacy in the defendant's attempts to apply case law from other jurisdictions. In each instance, the court shows that his reasoning by analogy fails because of significant factual differences between his facts and the facts of the cited cases.

In evaluating the size of the punitive damage award, the court turns to the public policy concerns supporting punitive damage awards, namely to punish the tortfeasor and to deter future misconduct of others. The court concludes that such purposes are met by the award in this case and, noting that the size of an award alone is not indicative of passion or prejudice on the part of the jury, finds the award justified. In reaching its conclusion, the court also looks at similar cases in which large punitive damages were awarded and concludes by analogy (to *Rustin v. Cook*) that the award is not excessive.

The dissent adds an additional criterion to evaluate the size of the award and considers the impact such an award will have on the defendant. Citing *Hawkins,* in which the court noted that punitive damages should not destroy an individual, the dissent balances the deterrent value of the award against the "long term effects upon society at large" and concludes that the award is excessive. This is a good example of how public policy arguments can lead to contradictory conclusions.

CHAPTER SIX

PUTTING IT INTO PRACTICE

Case Identification: *Isaacs v. Powell* (Fla.Dist. Ct.App. 1972)

Donner v. Arkwright-Boston Manufacturers Mutual Ins. Co. (Fla. S. Ct. 1978)

Procedural History:

Isaacs v. Powell

Prior Proceedings: Plaintiff sued on basis of strict liability; jury verdict rendered for defendants.

Current Proceedings: Plaintiff is appealing jury verdict.

Donner v. Arkwright-Boston Manufacturers Mutual Ins. Co.

Prior Proceedings: Plaintiff sued defendant homeowner and homeowner's insurance company under Florida statute for injuries as a result of being bitten by defendant's dog. Plaintiff's motion for directed verdict was denied. At charge conference, defendants requested charges on statutory defenses of mischievous or careless provocation or aggravation as well as assumption of risk defense, and the judge complied. After jury returned a verdict in favor of defendants and plaintiffs's motion for a retrial was denied, plaintiff appealed to District Court of Appeal, Third District, which affirmed, per curiam, the final judgment.

Current Proceedings: Plaintiff is appealing District Court's decision.

Facts:

Isaacs v. Powell Plaintiff, who was two years and seven months old at the time of the incident, was taken by his father to defendants' monkey farm. Plaintiff and his father were encouraged by defendant to feed the animals. While plaintiff was feeding a chimpanzee, the chimpanzee grabbed his arm and inflicted serious physical injury. The parties are in disagreement as to exactly how the chimpanzee was able to grab plaintiff's arm, i.e., whether plaintiff's father put plaintiff in danger or whether defendants created a dangerous situation.

Donner v. Arkwright-Boston Manufacturers Mutual Ins. Co. Defendant homeowner's Doberman pinscher, who had no previous history of viciousness, was in heat at the time plaintiff visited defendant's home, and defendant told plaintiff about her condition and the fact that she was nervous because of thunder. Plaintiff did not touch her at that time but later returned to pet the dog, stroking the top of her head and scratching her chin. The dog bit plaintiff on the lip.

Issues and Holdings:

Isaacs v. Powell

Issue (1): Should the owner of a chimpanzee be held strictly liable to a child injured by the chimpanzee or should liability be based on negligence?

Holding (1): The owner of a chimpanzee is strictly liable for injuries caused by the animal.

Issue (2): Should the owner of a chimpanzee be held strictly liable for injuries caused by the animal regardless of any fault on the part of the victim?

Holding (2): No.

Donner v. Arkwright-Boston Manufacturers Mutual Ins. Co.

Issue: Can a dog owner who is sued pursuant to Florida Statute 767.04 (strict liability for dog bites) assert the common law defense of assumption of risk?

Holding: No.

Rationale:

Isaacs v. Powell

Rationale (1): The risk for injury caused by wild animals should be borne by those who harbor them and not by society at large. Those who expose the community to the risk of a dangerous thing should be held strictly liable even though they use proper care. Furthermore, logic dictates that owners of wild animals should be strictly liable since Florida statute mandates that dog owners are strictly liable for injuries inflicted by their animals.

Rationale (2): A plaintiff who intentionally and unreasonably subjects himself to the risk posed by a wild animal should be barred from recovery since he voluntarily brought his injuries upon himself. On the other hand, owners should not be relieved from liability due to the plaintiff's failure to exercise reasonable care in dealing with wild animals.

Donner v. Arkwright-Boston Manufacturers Mutual Ins. Co.

Florida law modifies the common law of negligence in regard to liability of dog owners by making them the insurer against damages done by their dogs. Florida statutes do provide a defense, however, where the dog is provoked or aggravated or where the owner posts a warning sign, including the words "Bad Dog." According to the Florida Supreme Court, previous decisions permitting the use of assumption of risk as a defense were an inaccurate labeling of the defense. Although the courts correctly concluded that the plaintiff had either aggravated or provoked the dog, they had incorrectly classified this defense as assumption of risk. The Supreme Court clarified the confusion by clearly enunciating that a defendant could assert the statutory defenses of provocation and aggravation but could not assert the defense of assumption of risk.

Synthesis:

Owners of wild animals and dogs are strictly liable for injuries caused by their animals. Pursuant to Florida statute, however, a dog owner can raise as a defense evidence that the plaintiff aggravated or provoked the animal or that the dog owner posted a warning including the words "Bad Dog." Under the common law, owners of wild animals can raise the defense of assumption of risk.

COGNITIVE CALISTHENICS

2(a) *Nienstedt v. Wetzel* (Ariz. Ct. App. 1982)

Procedural History:

Prior Proceedings: Wetzels sued Nienstedts for alleged breach of contract. The trial court dismissed the Wetzels' complaint as a sanction pursuant to Rule 37 of the Arizona Rules of Civil Procedure. The Nienstedts then filed suit alleging abuse of process in the prior litigation. A jury awarded them $7,350 in compensatory damages and $50,000 in punitive damages.

Current Proceedings: The Wetzels are appealing the judgment entered on the jury verdict.

Facts: After the Wetzels unsuccessfully sued the Nienstedts for breach of contract, the Nienstedts sued the Wetzels for abuse of process based on the following misconduct in the contract dispute: (1) the Wetzels had inappropriately sought punitive damages; (2) Wetzel had filed a motion to continue because he falsely alleged that he was the attorney of record in another action; (3) Wetzel had entered default on an improper pleading and then scheduled a second default hearing when he knew that an identical default had already been set aside; and (4) Wetzel had engaged in improper tactics during discovery. The Nienstedts recovered both punitive ($50,000) and compensatory ($7350) damages but never introduced evidence at trial of the Wetzels' financial resources.

Issue: Is an award of $50,000 in punitive damages excessive as a matter of law when the compensatory damages are only $7,350 and the plaintiff fails to provide evidence of the defendants' financial status if the defendants in prior litigation made false allegations, pursued a default on improper grounds, used improper procedures, and engaged in questionable discovery tactics?

Holding: No.

Rationale: An award of punitive damages will not be disturbed unless there is evidence of passion or prejudice on the part of the jury. A defendant's conduct that demonstrates ill will or spite or that is wanton or reckless justifies an award of punitive damages. The record in this case supports a conclusion that the defendants acted with ill will, spite, or reckless indifference toward the plaintiffs. Defendants argue that the award of punitive damages was due to passion or prejudice because the plaintiffs failed to introduce evidence of defendants' financial resources so the jury could not connect the punitive damage award to the defendants' economic status. This argument fails because a plaintiff is not required under Arizona law to introduce evidence relating to the wealth of the defendant. Defendants' alternative argument that the punitive damage was excessive in comparison to the compensatory damage award also fails because no compensatory-punitive damage ratio exists under Arizona law. The size of a punitive damage award alone does not indicate passion or prejudice.

2(b) *Linthicum v. Nationwide Life Ins. Co.* (Ariz. 1986).

Procedural History:

Prior Proceedings: The Court of Appeals affirmed a jury award of compensatory damages on a bad faith and breach of contract claim but reversed a $2,000,000 award of punitive damages.

Current Proceedings: Arizona Supreme Court is reviewing punitive damage award.

Facts: In September, 1979, Jerry Linthicum had a tumor removed from his parathyroid glands; his doctors concluded that the tumor was benign. In April, 1980, his wife, Sandra, obtained medical insurance from Nationwide through her employer, Arizona Optical Company. The policy contained a ninety-day exclusionary period pertaining to preexisting illnesses. In June, 1980, Jerry became ill, and in July he was operated on; his doctors determined that the tumor thought to be benign in 1979 was actually malignant.

When Jerry's medical bills were submitted to Nationwide, the claims examiner concluded that the claim was excludable as a preexisting illness. Although all the doctors who had treated Jerry confirmed that the tumor had erroneously been believed to be benign in 1979, the claims examiner based her decision to deny Jerry's claim on her conclusion that he had been receiving treatment for cancer during the exclusionary period even though it had been undiagnosed at the time.

In October, 1980, a denial letter was sent to Arizona Optical (the policyholder), even though Nationwide was aware that Sandra no longer worked there. Sandra did not learn of the denial until Jerry was hospitalized in October, 1980, when she was informed that his previous hospital bills had not been paid. When she contacted Nationwide, she was informed of the denial for the first time. Jerry was transferred to another hospital as a charity patient as a result of the denial of insurance benefits. After an inquiry by a Phoenix newspaper, Nationwide reviewed the Linthicum file and reaffirmed its denial.

TIME LINE

DATE	EVENT
Sept., 1979	Jerry's tumor removed (tumor determined benign).
April 1, 1980	Sandra gets policy (ninety-day exclusionary period begins).
June, 1980	Jerry becomes ill.
July 1, 1980	End of exclusionary period.
July 11, 1980	Jerry operated on (tumor determined malignant).
Oct. 20, 1980	Denial letter sent.
Oct. 28, 1980	Jerry hospitalized; Sandra informed of denial.

Issue:

(1) May punitive damages be awarded in a bad faith claim if there is clear and convincing evidence that the defendant acted with an "evil mind" and demonstrated aggravated and outrageous conduct?

(2) Does an insurer's denial of an insured's claim for medical costs arising from his cancer treatment on the basis that the insured was being treated for cancer during an exclusionary period even though the cancer was undiagnosed at that time justify an award of punitive damages?

Holding:

(1) Yes.

(2) No.

Rationale:

(1) If punitive damages are to be the effective deterrent they were intended to be, they should be limited to those situations in which the defendant demonstrates outrageous or malicious misconduct. The "evil mind" that justifies punitive damages must be demonstrated by a deliberate intent to injure the plaintiff or by deliberate interference with the rights of others. Because punitive damages should be awarded in only the most egregious cases, the more stringent standard of proof (clear and convincing evidence) is required.

(2) Although Nationwide's failure to act in the best interests of its insureds and its attempts to construe its policy strictly in its own favor support a bad faith claim, such acts do not provide the basis for punitive damages. A tough claims policy is not indicative of an "evil mind" in that such a policy is not an "outrageous or oppressive" attempt to deny valid claims.

2(c) *White v. Mitchell* (Ariz. Ct. App. 1988)

Procedural History:

Prior Proceedings: A jury awarded plaintiffs compensatory and punitive damages for injuries incurred in a motor vehicle accident. Defendant employer and employee moved for a remittitur and a new trial.

Current Proceedings: Both defendants are appealing the verdict and the denial of their motion for a new trial.

Facts: Defendant employee hit plaintiff's vehicle as he was attempting to make a left-hand turn. Defendant employee owned the tractor, and defendant employer owned the van-trailer portion. A diesel mechanic testified that the condition of the tractor brakes indicated total neglect and that given the brakes' condition the stopping distance of the tractor was one-third more than if the brakes had been in good condition. He also testified that the brakes could easily have been inspected and that an experienced driver would have known that the brakes were not in reasonable condition. An accident reconstructionist testified that defendant employee was traveling 45 to 50 mph when he began to skid, that a reasonable speed with good brakes would have been about 40 mph, and that a reasonable speed given the actual condition of the brakes was 0 mph since the tractor should not have been on the road. He also indicated that the accident could have been avoided if the brakes had not been worn out.

Defendant employer became aware after hiring defendant employee that his license had been suspended. After discovering the suspension, defendant employer ordered defendant employee to return to the home office but did not instruct him to return immediately as it could have. Defendant employer had not inspected defendant employee's tractor for seven months, even though company policy required an inspection every ninety days. If defendant employee's vehicle had been inspected, the truck would have been "deadlined."

Issues:

(1) Is an employee's awareness that he is driving a vehicle with defective brakes that create a substantial risk of causing injury to others sufficient evidence of the "evil mind" required to award punitive damages?

(2) Is an employer's retention of an employee with a suspended license and its failure to prevent him from driving a vehicle with defective brakes sufficient evidence of the "evil mind" required to award punitive damages?

(3) Must a jury be provided with evidence of a defendant's wealth in order to award punitive damages?

Holdings:

(1) Yes.

(2) No.

(3) No.

Rationale:

(1) Punitive damages are justified when someone exhibits wrongful conduct with conscious disregard for the very real possibility that they may injure or violate the rights/interests of others. Continual operation of a vehicle whose brakes are so worn that the vehicle is no longer safe to operate and ultimately results in injury to another constitutes just such wrongful conduct.

(2) On the other hand, a defendant must be aware of and consciously disregard a risk in order for punitive damages to be justified. Although defendant employer's actions demonstrated gross negligence, they did not indicate conscious awareness and disregard of a risk. Any evidence supporting a punitive damage award against defendant employer was slight and inconclusive.

(3) A jury that is considering a punitive damage award need only be provided with sufficient evidence to enable it to calculate a reasonable award. Although the financial status of the defendant may be among that evidence provided to a jury, its provision is not required.

2(d) *Olson v. Walker* (Ariz. Ct. App. 1989)
Procedural History:
Prior Proceedings: Plaintiff sued defendant for damages resulting from injuries in a motor vehicle accident. The jury awarded $133,000 in compensatory damages, and $100,000 in punitive damages. The trial judge denied defendant's motion for a new trial and request for remittitur.

Current Proceedings: Defendant is appealing jury verdict and denial of motion.

Facts: Defendant rear-ended plaintiff's motorcycle and after attempting to leave the scene was restrained by two bystanders. Prior to coming into contact with plaintiff's vehicle, defendant was driving recklessly and was speeding. Defendant's estimated blood alcohol level at the time of the accident was 0.155 percent, and he demonstrated several indicia of intoxication. Defendant had been drinking approximately an hour before the accident, and an expert witness testified that defendant must have consumed ten or more twelve-ounce beers during that time period. Disputed testimony indicated that one-half hour prior to the accident, defendant took 20 mg of Valium, which would have intensified the effects of the alcohol.

Plaintiff was awarded $133,000 in compensatory damages and $100,000 in punitive damages. Defendant's annual salary was $38,000. After paying his bills, he had $500 left over each month. Even if he used all of that $500 each month to pay the punitive damage award, he would need seventeen years to pay the $100,000.

Issues:
(1) Is causing injury to another driver as a result of reckless driving after having consumed Valium and at least ten twelve-ounce beers an hour prior to the accident sufficient evidence of the "evil mind" required to award punitive damages?

(2) Is a punitive damage award of $100,000 excessive for a defendant who earns $38,000 annually and who will require seventeen years to pay off such an award?

Holdings:
(1) Yes.
(2) No.
Rationale:
(1) Punitive damages are justified when a defendant acts with an "evil mind" in that he consciously pursues a course of action that he knows creates a "substantial risk of significant harm to others." An evil mind can be inferred from outrageous conduct. Even if a defendant alleges that he was unaware that he was creating a substantial risk to others, punitive damages may be awarded if the defendant should have known he was creating such a risk. In this case, the defendant's relatively high blood alcohol level in conjunction with his consumption of Valium and his reckless driving are sufficient evidence of an "evil mind."

(2) The amount of an award alone is insufficient grounds to "shock the conscience" of a court. Both the defendant's wealth and the nature of the defendant's conduct can be taken into consideration when awarding punitive damages. Although the award in this case was high (two and one-half times the defendant's gross annual income), it was not necessarily the product of jury passion or prejudice since the jury could have concluded that the defendant's egregious conduct justified such an award and that it also served to deter others from engaging in similar conduct.

Synthesis: In order to recover punitive damages, a plaintiff must prove by clear and convincing evidence that the defendant acted with an "evil mind." Negligent conduct alone does not warrant punitive damages even if the defendant is grossly negligent. Since the purpose of punitive damages is to punish the defendant and deter future misconduct of others, punitive damages should be limited to only those most egregious circumstances in which the defendant's conduct reflects a knowing creation of substantial risk of significant harm to others or a deliberate intent to injure another. Although a defendant's conduct must indicate an awareness that he is creating such a risk, such awareness will be inferred if his conduct is so outrageous that he should have known he was creating a substantial risk.

A jury award of punitive damages will not be disturbed unless there is evidence of passion or prejudice. Although a defendant's wealth and the nature of his conduct may be taken into consideration by a jury when calculating the amount of punitive damages to be awarded, a plaintiff is not obligated to produce evidence of the defendant's economic status.

CHAPTER SEVEN

PUTTING IT INTO PRACTICE
STARE DECISIS: You should try to distinguish *Weirum*, because in *Weirum* the court found the defendant radio station to be liable for the injuries to the plaintiff. As a representative of the defendant, you will want to argue for nonliability.

Comparing Facts: In *Weirum*, the radio station actively encouraged its listeners to speed to win a prize. In the case at hand, the record company did not encourage or advocate suicide. The recording had been produced earlier, so the company was not interacting with the plaintiff at the time he listened to the recording. While the rock radio station in *Weirum* actively promoted a dangerous activity and continued to exhort listeners to follow the movements of a disc jockey, the record company had no such dynamic interaction. Furthermore, the plaintiff in the instant case was troubled and was the actual cause of his demise. His actions were irrational and unforeseeable, whereas the reactions of the teenagers in *Weirum* were not only predictable but were encouraged by the radio station.

Comparing Reasoning: The primary question is one of foreseeability. In *Weirum*, the court concluded that it was foreseeable that the teenage contestants would speed in their efforts to secure the prize and the momentary fame and would thereby create a danger to other motorists. By contrast, our client did nothing to prompt a particular response in their audience. Suicide was an irrational, unforeseeable consequence of the defendant's artistic endeavors.

The *Weirum* court also noted that "[l]iability is imposed only if the risk of harm resulting from the act is deemed unreasonable—i.e., if the gravity and likelihood of the danger outweigh the utility of the conduct involved." The likelihood of danger resulting from listening to music is minimal, whereas the value of artistic freedom is immeasurable. Strong First Amendment considerations must be weighed against a highly improbable act whose cause is infinitely more complex than the simple act of listening to lyrics. The "avalanche of obligations" envisioned by the defendant in *Weirum* and summarily dismissed by the court are very real concerns in a case involving artistic expression. Protecting the most fragile and troubled members of our society by restricting all but the most banal of compositions is too high a price to exact from the creative community.

COGNITIVE CALISTHENICS

1(a) In *Nienstedt v. Wetzel*, the court notes that the defendant "may not complain of the absence of evidence of his wealth when he has made no effort to introduce such evidence." Arguably, then, if the defendant did introduce evidence of his wealth, the court would be willing to consider that evidence, especially if the punitive damages were so excessive in comparison to the defendant's economic status as to indicate "passion or prejudice" on the part of the jury.

1(b) In *Linthicum*, all the people reviewing the claim concluded that the illness was preexisting. The court concluded that Nationwide followed a "tough claims policy" but that it was not "aggravated, outrageous, oppressive or fraudulent" and that there was no evidence that there was a "deliberate ignoring of the Linthicums' rights and needs." If two people reviewing the file, however, were to conclude that a valid claim existed and they were overruled by the senior claims examiner, a clearer case might be made that the insurance company was denying a valid claim. At least the plaintiff would have support from an agent of the defendant to back up his allegation that the illness was not preexisting.

1(c) In *White v. Mitchell*, the court concluded that no evidence was introduced to suggest that the trucking company was "aware of and consciously disregarded a substantial and unjustifiable risk that significant harm would occur." In this case, the trucking company inadvertently failed to inspect the driver's truck, a failure that the court concluded constituted gross negligence but not evidence of an "evil mind." If, however, the trucking company had inspected the brakes and found them to be defective but then failed to notify the driver's supervisor, its conduct might have fulfilled the requirements of an "evil mind." Its awareness of the problem and its failure to resolve that problem arguably would constitute a "conscious disregard of a substantial and unjustifiable risk" and would warrant an award of punitive damages.

1(d) The *Olson* court relied on several factors, only one of which was the defendant's blood alcohol content, in arriving at its conclusion that punitive damages were justified. In considering blood alcohol level, however, the court reasoned that the large amount the defendant would have had to drink (ten beers) to reach a blood alcohol level of 0.155 percent indicated that he "intended to become intoxicated or at least knew that would be the result." If his blood alcohol level had been lower (and possibly below the presumptive level, which is often 0.10 percent), the court would have probably found it more difficult to conclude that he intended to get drunk. If he could have legally driven at that blood alcohol level, he would have been less likely to have "consciously disregarded a substantial risk" by driving and, therefore, would have been lacking the "evil mind" required to award punitive damages.

3 Factual Similarities: Drinks at a bar prior to driving; consumes at least ten beers; combines alcohol with another drug before driving; rear-ends the plaintiff's vehicle; is cited for driving while intoxicated; a toxicologist testifies that defendant's blood alcohol level at the time of the accident was over the presumptive level; a jury awards the plaintiff compensatory damages and $100,000 in punitive damages; request for remittitur is denied and defendant appeals.

Factual Dissimilarities

OLSON	OUR CASE
Drinking with friends to relax.	Drinking after fight.
Leaves bar voluntarily.	Asked to leave bar.
Takes Valium.	Smokes marijuana.
Speeds.	Drives under speed limit.
Drives recklessly.	Gets involved in dispute with another driver.
Tries to leave accident scene.	Sits on hood of car.
Blood alcohol level at scene is 0.155 percent.	Blood alcohol level at scene is 0.12 percent.
$133,000 in compensatory damages is awarded.	$100,000 in compensatory damages is awarded.

Factual Unknowns: Length of time George was drinking; how much marijuana George consumed and whether he was under its influence when he was involved in the accident; whether George drove recklessly in addition to driving slowly; George's appearance at the accident scene (staggering, slurred speech, etc.); whether George was convicted of driving while intoxicated; whether marijuana intensifies the effects of alcohol.

Arguments Regarding the Award of Punitive Damages: George's conduct is sufficiently similar to Walker's conduct to justify the awarding of punitive damages. George, for example, was driving under the influence of alcohol and marijuana when he became involved in an accident just as Walker was driving under the influence of Valium and alcohol. The effects of combining alcohol with marijuana may differ from the effects of combining alcohol with Valium. Nevertheless, consuming alcohol over the legal limit in addition to taking another drug that also impairs driving ability is evidence of someone who is "consciously pursu[ing] a course of conduct knowing that it create[s] a substantial risk of significant harm to others."

On the other hand, marijuana may counteract some of the depressant qualities of alcohol and may actually enhance a person's ability to drive. Furthermore, George smoked marijuana for the specific purpose of "steadying his nerves." Therefore, he had no intent of causing injury to others but was actually trying to improve his driving ability. Rather than demonstrating evidence of a "conscious disregard for the safety of others," as Walker did by consuming Valium and alcohol, George was actually attempting to avoid driving in an unduly distraught state of mind by using a drug that would calm him.

CHAPTER EIGHT

PUTTING IT INTO PRACTICE

Burglary Statute: First, consult the definitions portion of the statute to determine if the legislature defined "dwelling." If it has not been defined in this portion of the statute, consider similar statutes (theft or arson, for example) where the term may have been defined. If no definitions are offered, research the case law in that jurisdiction to find cases in which the courts have defined the term. The legislative history of the statute should also be explored, since it may provide some insights as to how broad the legislature intended the statute to be. The canons of construction would, of course, have to be adhered to in interpreting the statute.

Interpretation of Drunk Driving Statute: The question is whether the defendant is in "actual physical control" of a vehicle when he is physically incapable of driving because of injuries and intoxication. In *Zavala*, being in "actual physical control" means having the "apparent ability to start and move the vehicle." Since medical testimony indicates that the defendant was physically incapable of driving, the court would likely conclude that he was not in "actual physical control." Moreover, this case is more analogous to *Zavala* than to *McDougall* because the motor was not running.

Hernandez (Court of Appeals)

1. Statutes are to be liberally construed "to effect their objects and to promote justice."
Statutes are to be construed "in the context of related provisions and in light of [their] place in the statutory scheme."
Apparently conflicting statutes must be harmonized if possible "in the absence of a manifest legislative intent to the contrary."
Legislative intent is to be found by examining "the words, context, subject matter, effects and consequences, reason, and spirit of the law."
When two statutes are "in irreconcilable conflict, the general rule is that the more recent one prevails."

2. The legislature acted in response to case law that established liability for tavern owners who served intoxicated patrons or minors. The legislature was attempting to prevent the spread of such liability to social hosts.

3. Because it would render the words "person, firm, [and] corporation" meaningless.

4. Sec. 4–312(B) implicitly repealed Sec. 4–301 by making it essentially redundant. Sec. 301 was en-

acted on an emergency basis in response to the case law emanating from the court; Sec. 312 was a non-emergency measure and was more comprehensive in scope.

Hernandez (Supreme Court)

1. Defendants argue that they are immunized under Sec. 4–312(B), which, they say, immunizes all persons, firms, or corporations not liable under Sec. 4–311.

2. The court believes that this argument stretches Sec. 4–312(B) too far because it overlooks Sec. 4–301 (which does not immunize nonlicensees who serve minors) and because common sense dictates that when the legislature granted immunity to those who serve liquor to those of legal drinking age, it did not intend to include those who serve liquor to those under the drinking age.

3. The law does not favor construing a statute as being implicitly repealed. In this instance, the two statutes can be rationally harmonized.

4. The plain meaning that the defendant gives the words in Sec.4–312(B) is incongruent with Sec. 4–301 and the section headings.

5. It reviews historical notes in the statutes, examines the legislative record, and considers a publicity pamphlet published by citizen groups attempting to put the legislation on the general election ballot.

6. The overall legislative scheme shows evidence of an attempt to curb the carnage created by underaged drinking. Numerous sections impose criminal sanctions on those who furnish alcohol to minors. Therefore, it is unreasonable to presume that the legislature intended to provide civil immunity to those who illegally serve liquor to minors.

7. The word "person" refers to a licensee's agent or employee.

8. The term "person, firm or corporation" in Sec. 4–312(B) immunizes licensees and their associates who conduct a transaction permitted under a license for the "sale, furnishing or serving" of alcohol. Sec. 4–312(B) has no effect on nonlicensee liability under Sec. 4–301, and Sec. 4–301 nonliability applies only when a nonlicensee furnishes alcohol to a "person of legal drinking age."

Interpretation of Regulations: Denying eligibility to convicted feons is similar to denying eligibility to undocumented aliens. Both limit the concept of residency and thereby limit the county's duty of reimbursement. As with undocumented aliens, the legislature could easily have restricted care to non-felons if it had desired to do so.

COGNITIVE CALISTHENICS

1. The question of being in "actual physical control" of a vehicle hinges on whether the defendant has the "apparent ability to move or start the vehicle." In *Zavala*, the court established a two-pronged test to prove lack of physical control—the vehicle must be removed from the roadway and the engine must be turned off. The facts of our case comply with this test in that the defendant removed his vehicle from the roadway by parking on a side street. Our facts are more consistent with *Del Vermuele* (in which the court found the defendant to be in "actual physical control), however, in that the defendant's engine was off but the key was in the ignition and the switch was in the "on" position. Unlike the defendant in *Del Vermuele*, our defendant was asleep when the police arrived. Because he was asleep, he was not capable of driving and, therefore, was not in "actual physical control." Although the defendant's subjective intent not to drive is irrelevant, the fact that he could not drive while asleep is relevant. The public policy of encouraging drunk drivers to refrain from driving until they are sober is served in this instance by a finding of not being in "actual physical control." The defendant did not drive (he remained parked next to the bar), he turned his engine on only in an attempt to contact his wife, and his falling asleep rendered him incapable of moving or starting the vehicle. He posed no threat to others and demonstrated no intent to do so.

The state will argue, on the other hand, that the defendant had the potential capacity to drive and that probably only good fortune prevented him from doing so. Like the defendant in *Del Vermuele*, he did not remove himself from the flow of traffic when he was impaired but actually got behind the steering wheel. When he turned on the engine switch, he increased the risk of danger to the public. Since he did not comply with the requirements of *Zavala*, he was in "actual physical control." The purpose of *Zavala* is to encourage drivers to pull off the road and turn off their engine without fear of being arrested. That purpose is not met when a driver takes affirmative steps to control his vehicle and then, fortuitously, is incapable of doing so because of his intoxicated state.

3. To resolve the conflict between subsections A and C of this statute, you need to determine the legislative intent underlying each section. To do this, you must find out whether subsections A and C were drafted simultaneously or whether C was added to ad-

dress a particular legislative concern. You should also compare this statute with similar statutes in the same jurisdiction to see if it conflicts with the other statutes or can be harmonized with them. The legislative history in this case will be very important. Since this statute addresses a controversial area of the law, legislative debate records and committee reports should contain comments and speeches that indicate the concerns and intentions of the legislature. The comments of the commission that drafted the statutes should also be consulted. Any political action that occurred subsequent to the passage of this statute would also clue you in as to the intent of the legislature. If this statute is based on the Model Penal Code, the drafter's comments as well as the interpretations of this statute by courts in other jurisdictions could be considered.

The defendant would probably argue that subsection C explains subsection A by defining what it means to be acting reasonably. Subsection A requires that the defendant "reasonably believe" that physical force or deadly physical force is immediately necessary to prevent one of the enumerated crimes. Subsection C then establishes a presumption that the defendant acted reasonably by virtue of attempting to prevent the commission of a particular crime. The legislative history may support such an interpretation if it shows that the legislature created this statute for the express purpose of empowering citizens with the right to use deadly force to protect themselves from crime.

The state would rebut this argument by pointing out that such interpretation allows the defendant to subjectively determine whether deadly force is justified. In other words, if the defendant uses deadly force to prevent one of the listed crimes, she is presumed to have acted reasonably. Since the law does not generally favor the use of a subjective standard in reference to justification, the state would probably counterargue that a more reasonable interpretation requires subsection C to be read in the context of subsection A. The latter requires that the defendant "reasonably believe that physical force or deadly physical force is immediately necessary" to prevent the commission of a specific crime. Such an interpretation demands that the defendant's conduct conform to an objective standard of "reasonable belief" and does not permit the use of deadly force simply because the defendant claims it to be necessary.

CHAPTER NINE

PUTTING IT INTO PRACTICE

Issue: Is the suicide of a person who listens repeatedly, and who is listening when he commits suicide, to a recording that encourages suicide reasonably foresee-able, resulting in a duty of care being owed by the studio that produced such recording to its listeners?

Rules:

"[A]ll persons are required to use ordinary care to prevent others from being injured as the result of their conduct."

"[F]oreseeability of the risk is a primary consideration in establishing the element of duty."

"The fortuitous absence of prior injury does not justify relieving defendant from responsibility for the foreseeable consequences of its acts."

"Liability is imposed only if the risk of harm resulting from the act is deemed unreasonable—i.e., if the gravity and likelihood of the danger outweigh the utility of the conduct involved."

"In such situations [sports fans buying limited number of tickets or department store staging 'while-they-last' sale] there is no attempt, as here, to generate a competitive pursuit on public streets, accelerated by repeated importuning by radio to be the very first to arrive at a particular destination. Manifestly, the 'spectacular' bears little resemblance to daily commercial activities."

Application: In *Weirum*, the rock radio station incited its listeners to speed after a disc jockey whose location was constantly changing in order to win a monetary reward. By contrast, the recording studio in our case in no way encouraged or promoted the commission of suicide and in fact could not have anticipated such an irrational response to their product. Although the studio engaged in a commercial enterprise, it did not attempt to "generate a competitive pursuit" as the defendant did in *Weirum*. Therefore, the risk of harm resulting from the production of such a recording was not unreasonable because the likelihood of suicide was extremely low. The element of foreseeability simply cannot be met when the harm caused can be traced solely to the plaintiff's conduct. However unfortunate the plaintiff's actions were, they resulted from his imbalanced state and not from any improper conduct on behalf of the defendant.

Plaintiff will likely argue, however, that suicide is foreseeable among an unstable and suggestible minority of listeners who mindlessly follow the suggestions of their idols. They will argue that although the likelihood of harm may be slight, the gravity of harm (death) is of such a magnitude as to outweigh the utility of such conduct (producing recordings that encourage suicide). In fact, they will most surely argue that the social benefits of such creative expression are minimal while the social damages in terms of its destructiveness are very high. They are also likely to point out that the "fortuitous absence" of previous suicides in relation to this recording does not relieve the defendant of liability.

Conclusion: Despite the fact that it is conceivable that some unstable and impressionable individuals may be so influenced by the lyrics of their favorite music that they may be driven to take their own lives, public policy dictates against holding writers and performers of such music responsible for their deaths. To do otherwise would put an unacceptable damper on the creative expression of all artists and would exact too high a price on society as a whole for the protection of a few. Therefore, I think it is unlikely that the courts will find the suicide to be a foreseeable result of listening to Osbourne's recording.

COGNITIVE CALISTHENICS

1(a) The conclusion is unclear. Is the writer suggesting that the plaintiff in the case at hand is just as likely to be able to recover punitive damages as was the plaintiff in *Olson?* The writer offers no explanation as to how the conclusion was reached.

1(b) Two variables are being discussed—actions after the accident and driving behavior. The writer draws a conclusion based on driving behavior but begins the argument discussing the defendant's actions at the scene of the accident.

1(c) Although a conclusion may be inferred, it is not clearly stated. An explanation for the conclusion is not given either.

1(d) The writer has made the same argument twice. Additionally, the writer has failed to tie the argument to the legal issue at hand. The question is not which drug is worse but whether combining marijuana and alcohol while driving is as outrageous as combining Valium and alcohol.

2. Driving Behavior: Mere intoxication alone may not justify the award of punitive damages. *Olson v. Walker,* 162 Ariz. 174 (App. 1989). In *Olson,* the defendant manifested signs of recklessness in addition to being intoxicated. He drove 10 to 15 mph over the speed limit, swerved in and out of traffic, forcing other drivers to take evasive action, and lost control of his vehicle. By contrast, the driver in the instant case drove 20 mph under the speed limit and argued with another driver, causing him to run into the plaintiff's vehicle because he was not paying attention.

On the one hand, we might argue that the defendant in our case was less reckless than the defendant in *Olson.* He did not endanger others by speeding nor did he interfere with other drivers by cutting them off. His loss of attention did not rise to the same level of recklessness evidenced by Walker losing control of his vehicle.

On the other hand, driving under the speed limit (especially when one's speed is substantially below that of other drivers) is arguably just as likely to cause accidents as speeding. The frustration that other drivers experience often leads them to take chances and engage in reckless behavior that they might otherwise avoid. It is certainly conceivable that the dispute between the defendant and the other driver was initiated because of just such frustration. Furthermore, driving much slower than the speed limit is a factor that officers typically consider when they suspect someone of driving under the influence. Therefore, while our defendant may not have manifested the same type of manic behavior that Walker did, his driving was nevertheless consistent with someone who was severely intoxicated.

Is the defendant's conduct so egregious that it can be inferred that he "consciously disregarded the substantial risk of harm" to others? Although we do not know to what extent the defendant endangered others by his driving, we do know that he aggravated at least one other driver and that he caused injury to the plaintiff. While his conduct may not have been as overtly dangerous as Walker's, he in fact created as great a risk of harm to others and perhaps even more because of the tensions his inordinately slow driving created in others. Although my conclusion may be weakened or strengthened by additional information I receive pertaining to his driving behavior, I believe that the defendant's driving in our case is deserving of a punitive damage award.

Blood Alcohol Level: Was the defendant's blood alcohol level sufficiently high to merit an award of punitive damages? In *Olson,* defendant Walker's blood alcohol level of .155 percent (which was well beyond borderline) indicated that he drank at least ten beers in a one-hour period. He consumed this alcohol in a relaxed social environment. After the accident occurred, Walker staggered, smelled strongly of alcohol, and had trouble standing, all of which are obvious signs of severe intoxication. Consuming such a large amount of alcohol in a short period of time supports an inference that he intended to become intoxicated or at least knew that would be the result. Any reasonable person would have known it was unsafe to drive after drinking ten beers, yet the defendant drove and became involved in an accident that was a direct result of his intoxication. The defendant disregarded the fact that his impaired ability to drive created a substantial risk of significant harm to others.

By contrast, according to the toxicologist's testimony, the defendant in the case at hand consumed eight beers, resulting in a blood alcohol level of 0.12 percent, 20 percent lower than Walker's. When the police arrived at the scene, defendant George was sitting on the hood of his car and talking incoherently but was not staggering.

We might argue that the defendant in our case drank less, resulting in a lower blood alcohol level that might be considered "borderline" since it was barely over the legal limit. George did not exhibit the typical symptoms of severe intoxication that Walker did. Therefore, he may not have had reason to believe he was severely intoxicated. Although he appeared incoherent, that may have been due to the accident itself rather than intoxication. If the defendant did not knowingly drink to excess and then drive, he could not have known he was creating a risk of harm to others. From the facts, we cannot be sure that the accident was a result of intoxication rather than simple inattentiveness.

On the other hand, George's blood alcohol level was above the legal standard of .10 percent. Although he did not exhibit the typical signs of intoxication, those symptoms may have been diminished by other factors. The mere fact that blood alcohol levels differ by 20 percent is insufficient to show that our defendant was less intoxicated than Walker or less likely to have had reason to believe he was creating a risk of substantial harm to others.

Since blood alcohol levels taken out of context mean little, we will have to look at other factors, such as behavior, to determine the true degree of intoxication. One person with a blood alcohol level of .12 percent may appear falling down drunk, while another may seem perfectly normal. The fact that our defendant had a lower blood alcohol level although he admits to drinking the same number of beers as Walker may be the result of a larger body size, the amount of food eaten, and other factors of which I am unaware. I need additional information regarding the defendant's height, weight, and food intake before I can realistically assess the difference in blood alcohol levels, but without that information I believe that the defendant's blood alcohol level is less conclusive of his level of intoxication than his outward symptoms of intoxication. Since our defendant's overt conduct was not as outrageous as Walker's (George was not staggering, did not have bloodshot eyes, and did not attempt to leave the accident scene), I believe that punitive damages are not as clearly justified as they were in Walker's case.

Valium v. Marijuana: Does the use of marijuana in combination with alcohol constitute conduct as egregious as the use of Valium with alcohol? Valium and alcohol combined multiply the intensities of one another. In *Olson*, this factor was part of the court's reasoning that the defendant's conduct was outrageous. The effects of alcohol and marijuana, on the other hand, are additive rather than synergistic. Because we do not know how much marijuana George smoked or how potent the marijuana was, our discussion is, to some extent, speculative.

Looking at outward conduct only, Walker seems to have been more impaired than George. Walker took no precautions to make his driving safer, whereas George at least drove more slowly, presumably in an effort to be more cautious because of the drugs he had consumed. The mere fact that George became involved in a verbal dispute was not necessarily a result of his consumption of alcohol and marijuana, since drivers do not need drugs to be provoked into altercations. George's conduct, while negligent, is arguably not as outrageous as Walker's conduct and, therefore, not as deserving of punitive damages.

On the other hand, both Valium and marijuana alter an individual's behavior and when combined with alcohol intensify the effects on the body. Whether one drug is worse than the other is irrelevant. The simple fact that both George and Walker chose not only to drink but to ingest a drug is outrageous in so far as their disregard for the safety of others. Although their impairment was manifested in different forms (reckless driving and speeding as opposed to slow driving and arguing with others), they both demonstrated irresponsible and outrageous behavior. The consequences of their drug consumption rather than their choice of drugs is what is most important. Therefore, George, like Walker, should have punitive damages awarded against him.

Although Valium and marijuana interact differently with alcohol, they both adversely affect driving ability. It was the combination of alcohol and Valium that the *Olson* court considered in coming to its conclusion that Walker's conduct was outrageous. The degree to which one drug enhances the detrimental influence of alcohol seems irrelevant. Drinking and driving is irresponsible, but mixing drugs (when the resultant effect is by necessity unknown) and driving goes beyond the realm of negligence and falls within the purview of an "evil mind." George's choice of marijuana rather than Valium does not justify his being treated any differently than Walker. The plaintiff in our case is just as deserving of punitive damages as was Olson.

CHAPTER TEN

Suggested responses to Putting It Into Practice exercises and Cognitive Calisthenics are contained in the Instructor's Manual.

CHAPTER ELEVEN

PUTTING IT INTO PRACTICE
Thesis Sentence: To determine whether our client can successfully challenge the validity of the contract she entered into with defendant, we must compare our

facts with those in *Cundick v. Broadbent*, the only relevant case law in our jurisdiction.

Topic Sentences:

In contrast to Mr. Cundick's diagnosis of premature arteriosclerosis, our client has been diagnosed as suffering from Alzheimer's disease.

Unlike Mr. Cundick, who was able to present medical testimony indicating that he was a "confused and befuddled man with very poor judgment" at the time he entered into the contract, we will be unable to present any such expert testimony.

Unlike Mr. Cundick, our client was unrepresented by counsel at the time she entered into the contract.

Transitions:

Punitive damages are awarded to deter future misconduct of others and to punish wrongdoers. Therefore, a jury may consider a defendant's wealth and his conduct when awarding punitive damages. However, an award "must not financially kill the defendant" and cannot be the result of "passion or prejudice" or "shock the conscience of the court." To illustrate, in *Olson*, an identical punitive damage award was not found to be excessive when that defendant had almost the same income as our client. However, Judge Gerber in his dissenting opinion balanced the "long-term needs of society" against "destroying an individual" by poverty and debt. The defendant's family in that case played a significant role in Judge Gerber's decision that a punitive damage award of $50,000 would have been more appropriate.

On the one hand, we may argue that the punitive damage award "financially kills" our client because he cannot begin to pay it now or in the near future. If he has no income, he cannot pay any debt, no matter what its source. Furthermore, the punitive damage award should "shock the conscience of the court" because our client has no money. Therefore, the award is excessive.

On the other hand, the plaintiff may state that our client's conduct was found to be "outrageous" and in so being justifies any punitive damage award without "passion or prejudice." Even though his wealth is a factor the jury may consider, they are not required to do so. Additionally, the judgment against the defendant in *Olson* was upheld on appeal, and he was more sympathetic than our client in that he had three dependents. Consequently, the punitive damage award is not excessive.

I conclude that the punitive damage award against our client will not be altered on appeal. His current financial situation is parallel to but less sympathetic than the defendant's in *Olson*. Although Judge Gerber's dissent is more realistic than the majority opinion, since our client has no dependents, the dissent has little value for us. Therefore, proving "passion or prejudice" would be the only way to persuade a majority of the court to reverse the award. Because there is no evidence of "passion or prejudice," our client's chances of reversing the punitive damages award are slim.

Explain Your Thinking Process: Even though marijuana is not synergistic when it is combined with alcohol, it causes drivers to be impaired. Its unpredictability because of its variable potency makes it even more dangerous than Valium. In my opinion, a driver who consumes a drug that is known to impair driving but who cannot know the degree of impairment that that drug will cause acts in an outrageous manner.

Keep It Short: To establish "general acceptance," we must have the court review published and peer-reviewed scientific journals and law review articles. These journals and articles must be presented by experts from the relevant scientific communities named above. Additionally, the court will have to do its own research.

We must bear several things in mind when presenting evidence to the court. First, we must choose scientific communities that are relevant to DNA theories and procedural uses. Such communities are often self-selecting, because scientists that have no interest in novel scientific principles are unlikely to evaluate them. Second, no particular number of published and peer-reviewed scientific journals is needed to show "general acceptance." Third, "general acceptance" does not mean universal acceptance of the reliability of the scientific principles and procedures. Fourth, the procedures and principles need not be absolutely accurate or certain.

Keep It Simple:

1. Age is one problem that can arise in extracting DNA.

2. Before arguing that the heroin seized from our client during a pat-down search should be inadmissible, we must first determine whether the Arizona Supreme Court will follow the "plain feel" rule set forth in *Minnesota v. Dickerson*, U.S. , 113 S.Ct. 2130 (1993), or rely on its own no "plain feel" exception set forth in *State v. Collins*, 139 Ariz. 434, 679 P.2d 80 (App. 1983).

3. While we might once have argued that strict scrutiny was reserved for ethnic and racial groups, we must concede in light of cases such as *Watkins* that this same demanding level of review will soon be used to review other socially stigmatized groups.

4. The Supreme Court will undoubtedly refuse to overturn precedent in this area.

Say What Is Important First:

1. A major criticism of underinclusive statutes is lack of legislative accountability.

2. Because science is an ongoing search for truth and not a collection of facts, what is accepted at one time may be found to be completely wrong at a later time.

3. The officer had reason to believe the suspect had a weapon because the suspect reached inside his coat pocket.

4. A testing technique should be subjected to peer review and publication because of the likelihood that substantive flaws in methodology will be detected.

Avoiding the "In X v. Y" Construction: The Court rarely invalidates underinclusive laws. Laurence Tribe, *American Constitutional Law*, Sec. 1440 n. 4 (2d ed. 1988). The Court allowed an underinclusive classification to pass the rational basis test when an ordinance at issue demanded that vehicles displaying advertising be banned as traffic distractions but excluded vehicles advertising their own products. *Railway Express Agency v. New York*, 336 U.S. 106 (1949). The rationale of the majority was that equal protection does not demand that "all evil of the same genus be eradicated or none at all." *Id.* at 109. In other cases, such as *Minnesota v. Clover Leaf*, 449 U.S. at 446 (1976), and *Katzenbach v. Morgan*, 384 U.S. 641 (1966), the courts have allowed this step-by-step method of addressing legislative concerns. On the other hand, an underinclusive New Jersey statute,

which required unsuccessful appellants who were subsequently imprisoned to repay the cost of trial transcript preparation even though unsuccessful appellants sentenced to probation or fined were not required to reimburse the state's expenses, failed rational basis review. *Rinaldi v. Yeagar*, 384 U.S. 305 (1966). The Court concluded that despite the state's legitimate interest in reimbursement, the statute's underinclusiveness belied its assertion that its actual purpose was not invidious discrimination.

Proper Tense:

1. In *Olson v. Walker*, the defendant drove under the influence of alcohol in combination with Valium, causing an accident because of his reckless driving. Our client, on the other hand, drove under the influence of alcohol and marijuana. The *Olson* court reasoned that intoxication alone does not justify the award of punitive damages, but the plaintiff in our case argues that our client was not only intoxicated but drove in such an outrageous manner that he created a substantial risk of injury to others.

2. In *Dickerson*, the police continued their pat-down search of the defendant because they felt a small lump in the defendant's pocket. After manipulating, squeezing, and pushing the lump, they deduced that the lump was crack cocaine. The Court refused to allow the admission of the cocaine into evidence because it found that the search exceeded the bounds of *Terry*.

3. The Uniform Commercial Code precludes such an argument, but since the defendant raises this argument I think we must respond.

GLOSSARY OF PROCEDURAL TERMS

Ab initio: from the first act; commonly used in reference to statutes, estates, marriages, deeds, etc. The statute was void "ab initio."

Accrue: to come into fact or existence, as in a cause of action that "accrues."

Action ex delicto: cause of action that arises out of misconduct.

Ad damnum: amount of damages demanded.

Additur: increase by court in award made by jury.

Amicus curiae: friend of the court; one who calls the court's attention to a matter that might otherwise have escaped its attention.

Assignee: one to whom something is assigned.

Attachment: proceeding in which one's property is seized.

Bifurcation: separation into two parts, such as a bifurcated trial in which the culpability and sentencing issues are heard separately.

Case at bar: case being tried.

Cause of action: facts that give rise to the enforcement of a right.

Certiorari: writ used as a means of getting appellate review; with the U.S. Supreme Court, this writ is discretionary and will be issued if four out of nine justices vote to hear the case.

Cestui que **trust:** beneficiary of a trust.

Chancery court: court that applies equitable principles rather than the common law.

Collateral attack: special proceeding designed to challenge integrity of a judgment; habeas corpus is a type of collateral attack.

Collateral estoppel: requirement that those facts litigated in a proceeding are binding against those parties in all future proceedings.

Comity: one court's deference to the concomitant jurisdiction of another court (rule of courtesy rather than rule of law).

Complainant: person bringing a complaint.

Concurrent jurisdiction: jurisdiction shared with another court, thereby allowing plaintiff to bring suit in either court.

Conflict of law: area of law governing which laws apply when laws in two or more jurisdictions may be applicable.

Coram nobis: writ to obtain relief from errors which the court that entered judgment is alleged to have made.

Corpus delicti: "body" or elements of a crime.

Counterclaim: cause of action filed by defendant against plaintiff.

Court of equity: courts that are guided primarily by equitable principles; sometimes referred to as courts of conscience.

Cross-claim: claims filed by coplaintiffs or codefendants against each other.

Culpability: guilt or responsibility.

Cy pres: as near as possible.

Damnum absque injuria: damage without injury.

Declaratory judgment: judgment in which the rights of the parties are determined but nothing is ordered to be done.

De facto: in fact or reality.

Default judgment: judgment entered against defendant because of defendant's failure to respond to the plaintiff's action or to appear at trial.

De jure: by right or law; de jure indicates something accepted as a "matter of law," while de facto is accepted as a "matter of practice."

Demurrer: allegation that facts are not sufficient to constitute a cause of action; replaced in modern law by a motion to dismiss.

De novo: new or fresh, such as a trial de novo.

Derivative action: cause of action based upon injury to another; a survival action is a derivative action because it is brought by the decedent's estate based on injuries suffered by the deceased.

Dismissal with prejudice: cancellation of an action; such cancellation is considered a bar to future actions.

Dismissal without prejudice: cancellation of an action; such cancellation allows subsequent actions to be filed.

Ejusdem generis: of the same kind.

Equitable doctrine: law based on equity (fairness).

Ex parte: by or for one party; an ex parte proceeding is brought for the benefit of only one party.

Gravamen: essence of a complaint, charge, cause of action, etc.

Habeas corpus: writ demanding judicial determination of the legality of an individual's custody; in criminal cases, it is used to challenge the legality of a defendant's confinement.

Harmless error: error that is not so substantial as to prejudice defendant and thus require an overturning or modification of a lower court's decision.

Impleader: procedure by which a third party is joined in an action so that claims against the defendant as well as claims involving the third party can be resolved simultaneously.

In camera: judicial act performed while the court is not in session, that is, while the judge is "in chambers."

In delicto: in fault, although not in equal fault.

In forma pauperis: in the manner of a pauper; the right to proceed without having to pay costs or fulfill formal requirements.

Injunction: judicial dictate that a party refrain from doing something.

In loco parentis: in the place of a parent; often used to describe the relationship between school officials and their students.

In pari delicto: in equal fault.

In pari materia: on like subject matter; statues *in pari materia* relate to the same subject matter.

In personam jurisdiction: personal jurisdiction.

In propria persona: representing oneself (abbreviated pro per).

Interlocutory order: order made during the course of litigation; this order does not dispose of the case but assists the court in resolving the conflict.

Joinder: joining of several claims or parties in one suit; joinders can either be compulsory (mandated by law) or permissive (suggested as a matter of "judicial economy").

Judgment: final determination of the rights of parties by a court.

Judgment in rem: judgment concerning the status of property or of a thing rather than of a person.

Judgment notwithstanding the verdict: judgment on the merits; adjudication of factual issues rather than judgment resulting from a technical or procedural defect.

Jurisdiction: power to hear and determine a case.

Laches: such excessive delay in asserting a claim that a court denies the claim on equitable grounds.

Lex fori: law of the forum.

Lex loci: law of the place.

Lis pendens: a pending lawsuit; a notice of *lis pendens* warns buyers that title to property is in litigation.

Mandamus: writ issued by a court compelling performance of an act.

Mesne: intermediate.

Non obstante veredicto: notwithstanding the verdict (usually abbreviated n.o.v.).

Nunc pro tunc: order used by courts to correct the record; it supplements a prior order or judgment and means "now for then."

Original jurisdiction: first court that can hear a case (a trial court has original jurisdiction).

Per curiam opinion: relatively short opinion in which the author of the opinion is not given.

Ratio decidendi: rationale for a decision.

Remand: to send a matter back to the tribunal from which it was moved.

Remittitur: reduction by court in award made by jury.

Replevin: action to recover possession of goods.

Res: property that establishes the subject matter of *in rem* and *in personam* actions.

Res judicata: already adjudicated; principle by which a final judgment is binding on the parties in subsequent litigation.

Rule nisi: procedure by which one calls upon another to show why a ruling proposed in his or her order should not be made final by the court.

Sua sponte: without being prompted, as where a court declares a mistrial *sua sponte*.

Sub judice: before a court for consideration; a matter before the court is called a matter *sub judice*.

Sub nomine: under the name; used where the title of the case was changed at a later stage in the proceedings, as in *Smith v. Brown. aff'd sub. nom. Brown v. Webster.*

Subject matter jurisdiction: power of court to hear a particular kind of case.

Substantive issue: nonprocedural issue involving rights and obligations of parties.

Sui generis: unique.

Sui juris: having legal capacity and responsibility.

Summary judgment: judgment entered without trial because no issue regarding material facts is disputed.

Supersedeas: writ ordering a lower court not to take any steps toward enforcing a judgment.

Terminus a quo: the starting point.

Vel non: or not.

GLOSSARY OF KEY TERMS

Advocacy memorandum: a persuasive memorandum that advocates a particular position. Also referred to as a *points and authority memorandum* or a *trial memorandum.*

Analogous cases: cases in which the facts and legal issues are sufficiently similar to the facts and legal issues of your client's case so that the same principles of law can be applied.

Appellant: the party who initiates an appeal.

Appellee: the party responding to the appeal. In some states the appellee is also referred to as the *respondent.*

Binding authority: authority or law that the court is obligated to follow.

Black letter law: law that is standard and not subject to change, such as the basic elements of a contract or a tort.

Bluebook: another name for A *Uniform System of Citation.* The Bluebook provides instruction on the proper format for citing legal and nonlegal references.

Canons of construction: rules that guide courts in interpreting statutes.

Caption: the part of a printed opinion that provides the names of the parties and the nature of their relationship.

Case brief: condensed or summarized versions of case law that contain only the most pertinent information. A case brief contains the following elements: Procedural history, facts, issues, holdings, and rationale.

Case identification: the section of a case brief that identifies the name of the case, the year the case was decided, the level of the court hearing the case, and the jurisdiction of the court.

Case law: law created by the decisions of courts.

Case on point: (also known as *"on all fours"*) a case where the facts are virtually identical to your client's fact pattern.

Certiorari: a petition for certiorari seeks to convince the court that the issue the party wishes it to consider merits the court's attention.

Citation: the part of a printed opinion that provides information that identifies where a case can be found. This appears directly above the caption. Also known as a *cite.*

Conclusory writing: the type of writing where a conclusion is given with no explanation or discussion for how the conclusion was reached.

Conservative judge: a judge who generally believes that he or she is limited to a strict interpretation of statutes and constitutions.

Court reporter: a compilation of court opinions.

Deductive reasoning: reasoning that begins with a general principle that is then applied to a specific situation. The most common form of deductive reasoning used in the law is a *syllogism.*

Dictum: a remark made by a court that pertains to issues that were not raised by the parties and are not necessary to the court's decision.

Disposition: the disposition of a case is the practical effect of the court's decision. For instance, a case may be *remanded,* or reversed.

Distinguish (a case): to distinguish a case is to differentiate cases that are factually different.

Docket number: a number assigned by the court clerk to a case. The docket number usually appears directly beneath the caption.

En banc: the rendering of an opinion where all judges are involved, rather than individual judges or panels of judges.

Enabling statute: a statute that creates an administrative agency and establishes the parameters within which the agency must operate.

Essential fact: a fact whose modification or absence would alter the outcome of a case.

Finding: a court's resolution of a factual dispute.

Headnotes: short, numbered paragraphs that precede a court opinion in an unofficial reporter. The headnotes identify the point of law being discussed and summarize specific principles of law discussed by the court.

Holding: a court's resolution of a question of law.

Inductive reasoning: reasoning from a series of premises (or assumptions) to a general conclusion; or reaching a conclusion in a specific case using reasoning by analogy.

Insignificant fact: facts in an opinion that are neither essential nor significant to a full understanding of the case.

Interlocutory appeal: an appeal that takes place during a trial before a judgment has been entered.

Internal memorandum: a memorandum written for an attorney by a paralegal, law clerk, or associate. The purpose of an internal memorandum is to inform; therefore, both sides of every issue must be presented. Also referred to as an *office memorandum.*

IRAC: the process of legal analysis that includes four essential elements: Issue, Rule, Application, Conclusion.

Issue: the question of law the court is answering.

Judgment: the court's resolution of a dispute.

Key numbering system: numbering system developed by West Publishing Company, where legal issues are organized alphabetically by topic and numerically by subtopic. Each key contains a topic name (key name) and section (key number).

Legislative history: the history of a statute that includes the events that took place before the statute's passage and during its consideration that reflect on the bill's purpose.

Legislative intent: the intent, or purpose, of the legislature in creating legislation.

Liberal judge: a judge who perceives his or her role as going beyond literal interpretation of statutes and constitutions, and view themselves as protectors of minority groups and the politically disenfranchised.

Memorandum decision: a decision that identifies a court's decision or order but offers no opinion.

Model act: acts that are drafted for the purpose of standardizing statutory law across the United States. For example, the Uniform Commercial Code and the Model Penal Code. Also referred to as a *uniform act.*

Office memorandum: a memorandum written for an attorney by a paralegal, law clerk, or associate. The purpose of an internal memorandum is to inform; therefore, both sides of every issue must be presented. Also referred to as an *internal memorandum.*

Official reporter: case reporter that is published by governmental authorities.

Per curiam opinion: an opinion that has no author.

Persuasive authority: primary authority that the court has the option of either following or disregarding.

Petitioner: one who files a petition for review.

Plain meaning: the everyday meaning of a term.

Plurality opinions: decisions in which no majority exists because the judges come to the same conclusion but for different reasons. These opinions typically carry less weight than decisions commanding a clear majority.

Precedent: a court decision on a question of law that is binding authority on lower courts in the same court system for cases in which those courts must decide a similar question of law involving similar facts.

Primary authority: the law that is generated by the judiciary (in the form of cases), by legislatures (in the form of statutes), or by administrative agencies (in the form of administrative rules and regulations) or that emanates from a U.S. or state constitution.

Procedural history: the part of a case that discusses the nature and result of all proceedings that occurred previously in regard to the case currently being reviewed, as well as the nature of the current proceeding.

Public Policy: a guideline used by the courts when deciding a conflict where the legal principles are ambiguous or absent. Generally, the courts try to do what is most equitable for the parties and for future litigants.

Question of fact: a question at a trial or hearing that concerns facts or events, such as whether they occurred and how they occurred.

Question of law: a question that involves the application or interpretation of a law.

Rationale: the court's reasoning.

Remand: to return a case to the lower court for further proceedings.

Respondent: the party responding to the appeal. Also referred to as the *appellee.*

Secondary authority: authority that explains and discusses the law; includes treatises, dictionaries and legal periodicals. Secondary authority does not have the persuasive power of primary authority, and may be cited only when primary authority is not available.

Significant fact: a background or historical fact that allows the reader to understand the nature of the dispute between the parties.

Slippery slope: an argument where the court reasons that if it were to decide a case in a particularly beneficial way for one of the parties, the decision would open a floodgate of litigation that would overwhelm the court system.

Stare decisis: the principle that requires that appellate courts follow the precedents established by courts within the relevant jurisdiction.

Syllabus: a brief synopsis of the pertinent facts, issues and holdings in an opinion. In unofficial reporters, the syllabus is written by an editor; in official reporters, the syllabus is prepared by a designee of the court.

Syllogism: a type of deductive reasoning where a conclusion is derived from a major premise and a minor premise.

Synthesis: the section of a case brief that compares the outcomes of the applicable cases and harmonizes the outcomes into a set of logically consistent rules of law.

Thesis sentence: a memorandum's opening sentence which announces the subject of the memo.

Topic sentence: the sentence that opens each paragraph of a memorandum and describes the subject matter to be discussed in that paragraph.

Uniform act: acts that are drafted for the purpose of standardizing statutory law across the United States. For example, the Uniform Commercial Code and the Model Penal Code. Also referred to as a *model act*.

Unofficial reporter: case reporter that is published by a private company, such as West Publishing Company or Lawyers' Co-Operative Company.

INDEX